SPECIAL EDUCATION

POLICY AND PRACTICE

Accountability, Instruction, and Social Challenges

Edited by

Thomas M. Skrtic
University of Kansas

Karen R. Harris
University of Maryland

James G. Shriner
University of Illinois

LOVE PUBLISHING COMPANY®
Denver • London • Sydney

Published by Love Publishing Company
P.O. Box 22353
Denver, Colorado 80222
www.lovepublishing.com

Library of Congress Catalog Card Number 2004103472

Copyright © 2005 by Love Publishing Company
Printed in the United States of America
ISBN 0-89108-310-3

CONTENTS

4   To Ensure the Learning of Every Child with a Disability   83

5   Special Education Teacher Supply and Teacher Quality: The Problems, The Solutions   103

6   Access of Adolescents with Disabilities to General Education Curriculum: Myth or Reality?   129

7   Supporting Beginning Special Education Teachers   156

PART TWO
Prevention and Intervention Strategies   232

PREFACE

The essays in this volume were selected on the basis of their relevance to special education practitioners, graduate students, teacher educators, and researchers with respect to four themes that we believe encompass the issues, developments, and trends that are shaping special education policy and practice today.

The first theme is the unprecedented shift in special education policy from an accountability mechanism premised on procedural compliance with federal and state law to one based on the academic performance of students with disabilities. Introduced in the 1997 reauthorization of the Individuals with Disabilities Education Act (IDEA 97) and consolidated in the 2001 No Child Left Behind Act (NCLB), the policy shift reflects the aims and logic of the broader standards-based reform (SBR) movement in public education. As such, this theme is concerned with the nature and implications of the SBR framework of IDEA 97 and NCLB relative to the appropriate education of students with disabilities.

The second theme is concerned with the current conditions of special education practice under the SBR policy framework. Politically, the inclusion of students with disabilities in the outcomes-based accountability mechanism of NCLB is the most important advance in special education policy since enactment of the Education for All Handicapped Children Act of 1975.

The extent to which this policy move represents an actual advantage for students with disabilities, however, depends on the will, capacity, and working conditions of local educators. As such, this theme is concerned with the recognized need for, but current lack of, administrative and collegial support for special educators, adequate numbers of highly qualified special education teachers, and greater use of research-based instructional practices among general and special educators. It also is concerned with recommended strategies for improving these unacceptable conditions of practice, all of which are aimed at bringing the actual experiences of students with disabilities and their teachers more in line with the vision of reform put forth in IDEA 97 and NCLB.

The third theme centers on advances in school- and community-based prevention and intervention strategies for students with disabilities, as well as a number of associated issues and unresolved needs. Here we are concerned with advances related to the academic learning of students with disabilities, including effective research-based instructional approaches in reading, writing, and mathematics. This theme also addresses persistent and emerging issues and needs relative to postsecondary services for students with significant disabilities, development of self-determination among these and other students with disabilities, appropriate supports for students with health needs, and the implications of violence and disruption in schools for students with disabilities.

The fourth theme revolves around environmental risk factors associated with developmental and educational problems in children, as well as the nature and implications of the service integration reform movement as a means of addressing these risk factors. Whereas the first three themes are concerned almost exclusively with the impact of formal schooling on the development and achievement of children, this one relates more broadly to the impact of debilitating environmental conditions, including certain functional aspects of schooling itself. It also is concerned with the service integration reform movement — that is, with efforts under way to integrate separate categorical institutions and professions into a comprehensive system of care charged with addressing the welfare of children and families more contextually and interdependently.

As key components in the fragmented system of categorical institutions and professions that serve children and families, education and special education will, and should, be drawn more fully into the service integration reform movement in the immediate future. Although heated disagreements have arisen over special education policy and practice in the recent past, nearly everyone agrees that prevention of developmental and learning problems should be a central focus.

Thomas M. Skrtic
Karen R. Harris
James G. Shriner

ACKNOWLEDGMENTS

This book is the sixth collection of *Focus on Exceptional Children* essays published over the past 30 years. Like the earlier books, this one is composed of recently published essays that address issues, developments, and trends of particular relevance to special educators today. We commissioned most of the original essays that appear in this volume during our term as co-editors of *Focus on Exceptional Children* (2000–2002), and in four cases drew upon essays commissioned by the previous journal editors (Edward Meyen, Glen Vergason, and Richard Whelan, 1970–1999). We would like to thank the authors of all of the *Focus on Exceptional Children* essays that appeared during our editorship, and especially the authors whose essays appear in this volume. The work of these dedicated scholars informed our thinking on what we take to be the most important issues, developments, and trends in special education policy and practice today.

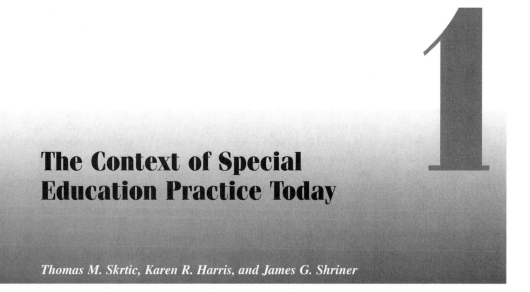

The Context of Special Education Practice Today

Thomas M. Skrtic, Karen R. Harris, and James G. Shriner

Public education has been in a constant state of reform for the past 20 years. Except for a brief period in the late 1980s and early 1990s, the direction of reform has been toward making school organizations more efficient. Historically, these reforms have resulted in *incremental* change—that is, in the elaboration of existing bureaucratic structures and processes in the interest of efficiency, which in most cases simply makes schools more bureaucratic (Tyack & Hansot, 1982). In rare cases, however, educational reforms have resulted in *fundamental* change—that is, in substantive modifications of the bureaucratic structures and processes of schools, in the interest of innovation (Cuban, 2000).

From the publication of *A Nation at Risk* (National Commission on Excellence in Education, 1983) until about 1988, a wave of state-level *effective schools* reforms sought to achieve educational excellence through what amounted to an incremental approach to change. Effective schools reformers did not question the bureaucratic structure of schools; "their passion was for making those structures more efficient" (Cuban, 1989, p. 784). As such, the effective schools reforms required more of existing school practices—more difficult courses, more homework, and more time in school—and instituted higher standards, more standardized testing, and greater standardization of teaching practices.

This had the effect of increasing "state control, with its emphasis on producing standardized results through regulating teaching" (Wise, 1988, p. 329), which turned "the goal of higher standards into more standardization" (Skrtic, 1995, p. 245; Wise, 1988). Ultimately, effective schools reforms intensified the problem of poor academic performance, especially for the most vulnerable students (Cuban, 1989; Stedman, 1987; Wise, 1988), including those with disabilities (Skrtic, 1988, 1991a, 1991b).

The failure of effective schools reforms gave rise to the *school restructuring* reform movement in the late 1980s (Elmore, 1987, Elmore & McLaughlin, 1988). School restructuring advocates criticized the homogeneous grouping practices of curricular tracking, in-class ability grouping, and compensatory pull-out programs as indications of "deep structural flaws in traditional school organization" (Skrtic, 1995, p. 246; cf. Goodlad, 1984; Sizer, 1984; Oakes, 1986a, 1986b). They proposed to achieve educational excellence and equity simultaneously through fundamental change. That is, they called for structural changes in school organization aimed at increasing "professional discretion and personalized instruction through collaborative problem solving among professionals and consumers at local school sites" (Skrtic, 1995, p. 245; cf. Boyer, 1983; Cuban, 1989; Elmore, 1987; McNeil, 1986; Oakes, 1985; Wise, 1988).

Advocates of inclusion embraced the school restructuring reform strategy because they saw it as advancing the type of fundamental change necessary for the implementation of inclusive education (Lipsky & Gartner, 1996; National Center on Educational Restructuring and Inclusion, 1994; Skrtic, 1991a, 1991b; Skrtic, Sailor & Gee, 1996). They saw this approach to change as potentially leading to the "unitary system" of collaborative problem solving and shared responsibility that is essential for meaningful inclusive practice in schools (see, e.g., Gartner & Lipsky, 1987; Pugach & Lilly, 1984; Reynolds & Wang, 1983; Sailor et al., 1989; Skrtic, 1988).

STANDARDS-BASED REFORM

Notwithstanding the controversy surrounding inclusive education in the field of special education, by the mid 1990s the stage appeared to be set for unprecedented reconciliation among advocates of excellence and equity in general education, compensatory education, and special education, premised on the reform logic of school restructuring. Beginning in 1994, however, a series of interrelated federal laws introduced and eventually mandated the current accountability-based reform logic of *standards-based reform* throughout public education, including special education.

In one form or another, accountability has been part of public education since the emergence of the common school in the 19th century. What is new with respect to standards-based reform (SBR), however, is the nature of the accountability mechanism. The central components of this mechanism are: (a) student outcomes as the measure of professional and system performance, (b) the school as the basic unit of accountability, (c) public reporting of student achievement, and (d) attachment of consequences to school performance levels (Elmore, Abelmann & Fuhrman, 1996).

Among the various types of accountability mechanisms, this one is representative of those that "take the school as the unit of analysis and seek to improve student learning by improving the functioning of the school organization" (O'Day, 2002, p. 293). As such, the SBR framework evident today in public education is an "outcomes-based bureaucratic model of school accountability . . . [which was] codified in extreme form in . . . the No Child Left Behind Act (NCLB) of 2001" (p. 294).

The first law leading to the eventual codification of this SBR framework was the 1994 enactment of the Goals 2000: Educate America Act (Goals 2000), which sought to achieve excellence and equity by aligning systems of standards, assessment, and accountability (Kleinhammer–Tramill & Gallagher, 2002, p. 26). Goals 2000 was significant for students with disabilities because it advanced the idea that all students, including those served in compensatory and special education, must achieve at higher levels through access to challenging curriculum and quality instruction (Riley, 1995).

The second law was the 1994 reauthorization of the Elementary and Secondary Education Act (ESEA) as the Improving America's Schools Act (IASA), the requirements of which were aligned with the SBR principles of Goals 2000. As such, the IASA was seen as an important vehicle for "promoting school improvement and infusion of resources to promote inclusive education and standards-based accountability for student progress" (Kleinhammer–Tramill & Gallagher, 2002, p. 27).

The next law, of course, was the 1997 reauthorization of the Individuals with Disabilities Education Act (PL 105-17, hereafter IDEA 97), which aligned special education systems, services, and accountability mechanisms with the emerging SBR framework of Goals 2000 and the IASA (McDonnell, McLaughlin, & Morison, 1997). Moreover, IDEA 97 embraced the fundamental goal of SBR, which by 1997 had become the unification of educational systems and services to support all students in achieving high standards. According to the SBR logic, this was to be achieved by aligning assessment and accountability systems to hold schools accountable for the academic progress of all students (Kleinhammer–Tramill & Gallagher, 2002).

Although IDEA 97 required the inclusion of students with disabilities in assessments of progress, it did not require that their assessment results be considered in programmatic decision making (Yell & Shriner, chapter 2; Thurlow, 2002). This consideration had to await the fourth law in the series, the 2001 reauthorization of the ESEA as the No Child Left Behind Act. Under NCLB, the assessment results of all students, including those with disabilities, must be part of a single accountability system premised on "adequate yearly progress," a requirement that put "teeth into the accountability intentions of IDEA 97" (Thurlow, 2002, p. 2).

With the enactment of IDEA 97 and NCLB, then, special education accountability, which had been based on procedural compliance with the IDEA, was merged with that of general education under the reform logic of outcomes-based accountability (McLaughlin & Tilstone, 2000; Salvia & Ysseldyke, 2004). As of this writing, the fifth law in the series, what we assume will be the 2004 reauthorization of the IDEA, is pending. Nevertheless, both the House and the Senate reauthorization bills currently under consideration retain and extend the SBR framework of IDEA 97 and NCLB (Council for Exceptional Children, 2003).

Politically, the inclusion of students with disabilities in the outcomes-based accountability mechanism of NCLB is the most important advance in special education policy since enactment of the Education for All Handicapped Children Act of 1975. Given its emphasis on standards, standardized testing, and what amounts to standardized teaching (given the NCLB requirement for fidelity to instructional practices validated through "scientifically based research"), however, the extreme bureaucratic nature of NCLB appears to be a return to the effective schools approach to change (Skrtic, 2003). Nevertheless, even staunch supporters of school restructuring and inclusive education have been willing to give the IDEA 97/NCLB outcomes-based accountability framework a chance, especially those who see in these laws and other SBR legislation provisions that promote school restructuring (e.g., Lipsky & Gartner, 1996; Sailor, 2002; Skrtic & Kleinhammer–Tramill, 2003).

These provisions include those in IDEA 97 and NCLB that emphasize the principles of personalization of services through collaborative problem solving, including especially those that promote "school unification," or the integration of general, compensatory, and special education systems and services through site-based management and budgeting practices. The provisions also include the related NCLB provisions that encourage integrated, schoolwide Title I services over traditional "pullout" programs, as well as the "incidental benefit" provision of IDEA 97, which permits schools under certain conditions to use special education funds to enrich the education of all children.

Finally, inclusive education advocates see IDEA 97, Goals 2000 [Sec. 306 (f)(2)], and IASA (Title XI) as creating a legislative basis for "service integration." That is, they see these laws as promoting collaboration among schools, other human service agencies, and families to address social and economic barriers to learning such as poverty, hunger, and inadequate health and child care (Sailor, 2002; Skrtic & Kleinhammer–Tramill, 2003). Moreover, advocates support these provisions because, by promoting the idea of collaborative problem solving and shared responsibility among professionals and citizens in schools, other human service agencies, and communities, they advance the possibility of strong or participatory democracy (Sailor, 2002; Skrtic, 1991a, 1995; Skrtic et al., 1996).

Whether the SBR framework of NCLB and IDEA 97 will advance the aims of educational excellence and equity, school unification, inclusive education, and service integration depends on whether the bureaucratic or (nonbureaucratic) school restructuring features of NCLB and IDEA 97 are emphasized. Ultimately, then, it depends on which model of SBR is used. William Spady, architect of outcomes-based education, cautioned SBR reformers at the start of the movement to avoid what he called the "traditional" model of SBR (Spady & Marshall, 1991). Spady and others raised this concern because, in effect, the traditional model is an incremental approach to change, in that it merely attempts to make existing school bureaucracies more efficient by aligning performance standards with existing curricula and conventional professional practices (Champlin, 1991; Spady & Marshall, 1991). Although this may increase individual student achievement at the classroom level, the gains are limited to those resulting from small, narrowly focused units of instruction that become ends in themselves (Spady & Marshall, 1991).

As an alternative to the traditional or bureaucratic approach, Spady recommended the "transformational" model of SBR, which he characterized as representing "the highest evolution of the [standards-based reform] concept" (Spady &

Marshall, 1991, p. 70). Premised on the belief that the purpose of schooling is to prepare students for successful community life, the transformational approach begins by having teams of school and community stakeholders agree upon broad school outcomes leading to desirable conditions of life for students as future citizens. At this point, "districts set their existing curriculum frameworks aside" (Spady & Marshall, 1991, p. 70), allowing their curriculum, instructional practices, and organizational structure to evolve in support of educational outcomes leading to the agreed-upon desirable future for students and communities.

What is troubling about Spady's warning, of course, is that NCLB (and thus IDEA 97) mandates an outcomes-based bureaucratic model of school accountability, an extreme form of the traditional model of SBR. Achieving the ultimate reform aims of educational excellence and equity, school restructuring, inclusive education, and service integration requires a transformational or nonbureaucratic approach to SBR leading to collaborative problem solving and shared responsibility among professionals and citizens in schools and communities. Whether this nonbureaucratic vision of fundamental change will be recognized and embraced is uncertain. What is clear, however, is that, even under the bureaucratic SBR framework of NCLB and IDEA 97, achieving the more modest goal of access to the general education curriculum for students with disabilities will require far more flexibility, adaptability, and collaboration than traditional school bureaucracies have been able to provide. Given these students' need for and right to individualized instruction, providing them with meaningful access to the general education curriculum will require considerable innovation through unprecedented levels of collaboration among instruction-oriented special educators and curriculum-oriented general educators.

CONDITIONS OF SPECIAL EDUCATION PRACTICE

The enactment of IDEA 97 was a watershed event in special education policy, a fundamental shift from an accountability mechanism premised on procedural compliance with administrative regulations to one based on student outcomes (McLaughlin & Tilstone, 2000; Salvia & Ysseldyke, 2004). The extent to which this represents an actual advantage for students with disabilities or simply a shift from one bureaucratic accountability mechanism to another depends on the will, capacity, and working conditions of local educators. To realize the policy advantage for students with disabilities requires meaningful collaboration among highly qualified teachers using innovative evidence-based instructional practices, as well as administrative leadership in creating and sustaining a supportive and collegial organizational context, a learning community premised on flexible, adaptive, and collaborative practice (Brownell & Skrtic, 2002).

Although there is broad agreement on the necessary conditions of practice, the evidence to date indicates that in most respects they do not exist in schools. For example, the Bright Futures study commissioned by the Council for Exceptional Children (Kozleski, Mainzer, Deshler, Coleman & Rodriguez–Walling, 2000) found that special educators are neither adequately prepared for their new roles and responsibilities under IDEA 97 nor adequately supported in carrying them out. More than three-fourths of the special educators who participated in the study said that the amount of paperwork they must complete hinders their teaching, and nearly one in five reported that their caseloads were unmanageable (Kozleski et al., 2000).

Moreover, they reported that the level of support they receive from district and building administrators is inadequate, and that, far from being meaningfully engaged in collaborative relationships, they are isolated from their general education colleagues and from other special educators (also see Chapter 6, by Schumaker Deshler, Bulgren, Davis, Lenz & Grossen). Special educators also reported being torn by ambiguous and competing responsibilities, as well as feeling fragmented and conflicted by ill-defined and contradictory expectations of parents, administrators, and society (Kozleski et al., 2000; Mastropieri, 2001). This finding is consistent with other research that points to an additional layer of political complexity that exacerbates the problems of special education practice today.

For example, McIntire (2001) reported that special educators "must, by the nature of their responsibilities (both legal and ethical), advocate for the resources and supports necessary to effectively teach individuals with disabilities within a society that does not always have the will or capacity to do so" (p. 49). In this regard, McIntire concluded that efforts to improve the working conditions of special educators must recognize the essentially political nature of the work they do, work that requires them to navigate complex, fractured social systems that often yield less than desirable results for students with special educational needs.

Regarding ways to improve their working conditions, participants in the *Bright Futures* study stressed the need for more qualified special educators, noting that many entering the field today are not prepared for the new complexities and increased demands of special education practice under the IDEA 97 (Kozleski et al., 2000). This latter observation of the participants reflects the fact that approximately 12,000 special education teaching positions were vacant or filled by unqualified personnel in 1999–2000 (Kozleski et al., 2000). Moreover, in 2000–01 this number increased threefold to more than 37,000 special education positions vacant or filled by unqualified personnel (10% of the special education workforce) and it increased to 40,000 positions in 2001–02 (Chapter 4, by Mainzer, Deshler, Coleman, Kozleski & Rodriguez–Walling; U.S. Department of Education, 2001). Assuming that all these positions were filled, in 2001–02 nearly 750,000 students with disabilities were served by unqualified personnel (Chapter 4, by Mainzer et al.).

One reason for the shortage of qualified special education personnel is that the attrition rate among special education personnel (14%) is significantly higher than the overall teacher attrition rate of 8% (U.S. Department of Education, 1999). A major contributing factor in this regard is that 40% of special educators leave the field during their first five years of teaching (Kozleski et al., 2000). This alarming statistic supports the idea of a link between the critical shortage of special educators and the increased and competing practical demands and political complexities of inclusive special education practice under the SBR framework of IDEA 97 and NCLB (Brownell & Skrtic, 2002; Kozleski et al., 2000; McIntire, 2001).

In addition to the current shortage of qualified special education teachers, the U.S. Department of Education estimates that by 2005 we will need more than 200,000 new special educators nationally. The problem here is that, given increasing numbers of students identified as having a disability and a critical shortage of special education faculty, colleges and universities have the capacity to prepare only about half the number of special education personnel that will be needed (Kozleski et al., 2000; Smith, Pion, Tyler, Sindelar & Rosenberg, 2001).

Although nearly all general educators (96%) currently have students with disabilities in their classrooms, only one-third say they are prepared to serve them adequately (Boyer & Mainzer, 2003). We should not be surprised by this finding, given that the only national effort to reform the preservice preparation of general educators relative to serving students with disabilities, the Deans' Grant Projects (1974–1984), failed to achieve meaningful or lasting reform. Research on implementation of the Deans' Grant Projects has shown that neither of the two primary reform strategies— infusion of special education content into general education courses, and development of separate special education courses for general education majors—produced sustainable and satisfying results (Fiore, Kleinhammer–Tramill & Peters, 2000; Grosenick & Reynolds, 1978). Infused content was largely eliminated when projects ended, while separate courses did little to promote the idea of shared responsibility and general/special education collaboration.

In terms of the professional development of general educators relative to serving students with disabilities, currently only one in four teachers participates in the kind of in-depth, focused professional development activities necessary for changing their practices (National Center for Education Statistics, 1998). Furthermore, although some states require teacher induction and professional development programs, many of these programs lack clear expectations and learning objectives with respect to teaching students with disabilities. Under such conditions, it is difficult to create systematic professional development learning experiences that support the inclusion of students with disabilities in the general education curriculum (Hirsch, Koppich, & Knapp, 2001).

Finally, research in high schools on the contextual variables that influence the adoption of research-based instructional practices has indicated that the necessary coordination, planning, and collaboration among secondary teachers and administrators is virtually nonexistent (Chapter 6, by Schumaker et al.). The most significant implementation barriers are insufficient time for teachers to learn to use the research-based practices, and inadequate administrative support relative to implementing the practices with fidelity. Similar implementation research on adoption of research-based instructional practices for students with disabilities in elementary schools reached the same conclusions relative to insufficient time for teachers to learn to use research-based practices and inadequate follow-up support (Klingner, Ahwee, Pilnieta & Menendez, 2003). Moreover, the tendency among elementary teachers who are attempting to implement research-based practices is to "alter or eliminate so many components of the practice that the original instructional method is rendered barely recognizable" (Klingner et al., 2003, p. 424).

ADVANCES AND ISSUES IN
PREVENTION AND INTERVENTION

Prior to enactment of the Education for All Handicapped Children Act of 1975, as many as one million of an estimated eight million children with disabilities in the United States were excluded from public education, and at least another three million were under-served (Smith, Dowdy, Polloway, & Blalock, 1997). In the ensuing years, legislation, litigation, research, and social change resulted in significant changes in the way children with disabilities are educated. Moreover, the current emphasis on SBR, new developments in instructional research, and identification of new and unresolved needs continue to impact how students with disabilities are educated in schools and communities. These shaping forces include the drive for broader use of research-based instructional practices under NCLB and IDEA 97, as well as advances in integrating diverse knowledge bases into balanced instructional approaches. They also include efforts to address nonacademic issues such as services for students with significant disabilities through the age of 21, the development of self-determination among students with disabilities, support for students with health needs, and the nature and implications of school violence.

A major goal of the SBR framework of IDEA 97 and NCLB is to improve the quality of education for all students. A key mechanism for addressing this goal is the NCLB requirement that teachers use evidence-based instructional practices—in the language of NCLB, practices that have been validated by "scientifically-based research" (Odom et al., 2003). Given the goal of the SBR framework to improve instruction and the NCLB requirement for how this is to be achieved, there has been a significant increase in efforts to synthesize instructional research to determine "best practices" and to make this information more readily available to educators, administrators, and parents.

Although this synthetic approach has value, determining the "best" practices for meeting the individual needs of heterogeneous populations of students is more complicated and challenging. To address the challenges inherent in meeting individual needs within an increasingly diverse community of students, including students with disabilities, many educators and educational researchers have begun to integrate research-based instructional methods.

In the 1970s and 1980s, a skills-based, "back-to-basics" instructional approach dominated public education. This and other direct or explicit approaches to instruction were, and continue to be, criticized as being devoid of meaning for students, lacking in authentic learning experiences, and thus resulting in little generalization of learning (Heshusius, 1995; Poplin, 1988). In response to such criticism, a strong movement toward constructivist approaches to teaching and learning emerged in the late 1980s and early 1990s, perhaps best exemplified by the whole language approach to reading instruction (Pressley & Harris, 1998). This and other constructivist approaches are premised on the idea that humans learn by making their own sense of the world rather than by acquiring fixed knowledge that already exists (Chapter 10, by Knight). Thus, these approaches typically postulated that children will come to learn all that they need to know in due developmental time through rich social interaction and immersion in authentic learning experiences (Harris & Graham, 1996a).

By the late 1990s, however, parents and educators were voicing concerns about the number of elementary students who were not learning to read, write, and spell naturally. At the same time, special educators were demonstrating that students with special educational needs, including those with disabilities, need more extensive, structured, and explicit instruction to develop skills, processes, strategies, and understandings that come more easily to their normally achieving peers (Harris & Graham, 1994, 1996b).

Given these developments, a movement emerged in the 1990s to empower educators and researchers to integrate what has been learned from research on teaching and learning regardless of differing underlying theoretical bases or belief systems, including those that may appear to be incompatible (Harris & Graham, 1994, 1996b). Reports from researchers and practitioners indicate that a balanced, integrated approach is more effective than explicit or constructivist approaches used alone or predominantly. Moreover, balanced, integrated approaches to reading and writing instruction have been shown to be effective for all students, including students with disabilities (Chapter 12, by Harris, Graham, & Mason; Chapter 11, by Pressley, Roehrig, Bogner, Raphael, & Dolezal). Although there has been far less research on balanced mathematics instruction, a rationale for such approaches in mathematics and calls for rigorous research on their effectiveness are beginning to appear in the literature (Chapter 13, by Jones & Southern).

Academic achievement has not been the only target for improvement. Other important nonacademic concerns also have received increased attention. These include concerns about education and transition services for students with significant disabilities through the age of 21, development of self-determination among these and other students with disabilities, support for students with health needs, and school violence and disruption relative to students with disabilities.

Over the past two decades, adolescents with significant disabilities have been provided with functional or community-based instruction during the high school years, then supported employment, independent living, or adult daycare services after leaving the public education system (Neubert & Moon, 1999). More recently, however, questions have been raised about the efficacy of this approach, including concerns about the timing and extent of community-based instruction during high school, the relatively exclusive nature of educational and transitional services, and the adequacy of resulting post-school outcomes (Quirk & Bartlinski, 2001). Even though research and development in this emerging but significant area of need are in early stages, recommendations of professionals, families, and advocates, and the new models that are emerging to address them, seek to achieve more appropriate post-school outcomes for students with significant disabilities. The key components of these models include more appropriate high school programming for these students, and continuation of their education in post-secondary settings, including participation in age-appropriate educational, transitional, and social activities on college campuses and in vocational-technical schools (Chapter 16, by Neubert, Moon & Grigal).

Developing self-determination, or the ability to act as the primary causal agent in one's life, has become an increasingly important area of research and development in the field of special education, especially for students with significant disabilities (Wehmeyer & Sands, 1998). The emphasis on self-determination predates the incorporation of SBR accountability in IDEA 97, stemming initially from the 1990 IDEA mandate regarding provision of transition services for adolescents with disabilities (Ward, 1996). Throughout the 1990s, moreover, researchers in this area have worked to assure that self-determination is recognized as a key educational outcome within the SBR accountability framework, especially in light of two potential conflicts between SBR and the needs of students with disability. The first concerns the extent to which the SBR accountability framework may overemphasize core academic content at the expense of the functionality of curriculum for students with disabilities (Wehmeyer, Lattin, Lapp-Rincker, & Agran, 2003). The second potential conflict is between the apparently competing mandates for access to the general education curriculum in IDEA 97 and NCLB, and individualization of instruction and treatment in IDEA 97 and previous federal legislation (Chapter 17, by Wehmeyer & Schalock).

Providing appropriate supports for students with health needs in school has emerged as a major concern, in part because of a significant increase in the number of students who require such support. In the 1999–2000 school year, the number of students classified as "other health impaired" topped 250,000, which represents an increase of more than 350% over the number of students so classified in 1990–91 (U.S. Department of Education, 2001).

Beyond the increase in number of students requiring health-related supports in school, a major concern is that these students are being placed at significant risk because special and general educators are inadequately prepared to serve them (Heller, Fredrick, Dykes, Best, & Cohen, 1999). Additional challenges and issues include planning appropriate health-care services and related accommodations, developing individual health-care plans, adequacy of procedures for administration of medication, emergency care, and universal precautions, and recognizing and accommodating individual differences among students with the same health conditions (Chapter 18, by DePaepe, Garrison–Kane, & Doelling).

School violence and disruption is another important area of concern, especially since the school shootings at Columbine High School in Colorado and similar incidents in several other states. Although these incidents affect all of us and the entire educational system, the topic of school violence and disruption has become an important area of research and development in special education, in part because questions have been raised about the role played by students with disabilities in violent and disruptive acts (Egnor, 2003). Some critics actually have pointed to special education rules and regulations as part of the problem, arguing that these rules prevent principals from disciplining students with disabilities (Hymowitz, 2000). This criticism is largely unfounded, given that IDEA 97 gives principals wide discretion in disciplining students with disabilities who are involved in weapons and drug offenses or who present a danger to themselves or others, including placing them in interim alternative programs (Chapter 2, by Yell & Shriner). However unfounded, the reality that views such as this continue to be expressed makes school violence and disruption an important area of special education research. Moreover, special education research in this and related areas is essential for addressing a range of issues associated with school violence, disruption, and discipline concerning students with disabilities. This includes issues such as the implementation of the IDEA 97 discipline provisions, the nature and interpretation of school suspension rates among students with disabilities, and school and community-based violence-prevention and intervention programs and models (Chapter 19, by Leone, Mayer, Malmgren, & Meisel).

SOCIAL CHALLENGES AND OPPORTUNITIES

The social and economic transformations associated with post-industrialization and globalization are producing new forms and increasing rates of poverty, hunger, disease, homelessness, and crime. The scope and significance of these interrelated problems is affecting virtually every area of social policy and professional practice, particularly those of education, health, and social welfare whose clients increasingly are being placed at risk by changing environmental conditions (Skrtic & Sailor, 1996). One positive development in this regard has been increased attention to the growing body of research on risk. Although the study of risk is common in a number of fields, including some concerned with children and families, the application of the risk concept in special education is new, especially in the expanded sense of environmental risk.

Special educators have long been concerned with in-child risk factors such as genetic and biological conditions and organic insults, but have been far less concerned with environmental risks such as those associated with poverty, crime, and violence. As such, special educators have not taken full advantage of "transactional" risk research, which considers risk from the standpoint of the child in context (see Lewis & Feiring, 1998), and thus has important implications for special education practice and policy (Keogh & Weisner, 1993).

Transactional risk research does not negate the importance of in-child factors; rather, it enriches our understanding of developmental and educational problems by helping us understand the ways in which children's characteristics and environments both contribute to associated risks (Chapter 20, by Keogh). Risk researchers working from this perspective define risk in terms of potentially negative conditions that impede or threaten normal development and learning, thereby turning risk into a probability statement in which early individual and environmental conditions are used to predict future outcomes. The advantage here is that this allows risk researchers to identify what they call "protective" or "promoting" factors that can minimize or mitigate the impact of in-child and environmental risk conditions. These factors can be in-child factors such as dispositional attributes or biological predispositions, environmental variables such as a stable family or safe neighborhood, or a variety of positive events such as gaining access to needed services (Chapter 20, by Keogh).

In terms of the present discussion of SBR and conditions of practice, perhaps the most important facet of this line of research is its analysis of the risk and protective factors associated with the functional environment of schooling, including instructional approaches, curriculum, and teacher perceptions and expectations. In such functional analyses, risk status is, in part, a function of "goodness of fit" between child attributes and schooling demands (Chapter 20, by Keogh). From this perspective, failure to learn is too often attributed to limitations of children and families when, in reality, the problem may be the result of a poor fit between child and instructional approach, curriculum, and/or teacher attitudes, beliefs, and expectations for children's behavior and achievement.

Moreover, these analyses raise serious questions about the SBR framework of NCLB and IDEA 97. Although it seems reasonable to hold teachers and schools responsible for children's learning problems, and to assume that their effectiveness can be measured through standardized testing, transactional risk researchers caution that, as complex social systems, schools themselves may be at risk (Chapter 20, by Keogh). In this regard, these researchers note that, although questions of risk and protective factors in schools require further research, other functional aspects of schools—large classrooms and caseloads, unqualified teachers, inappropriate instructional materials, and inadequate resources and administrative support—are risk conditions that require immediate action, not research (Chapter 20, by Keogh).

Another important development associated with the deteriorating social and economic conditions of children and families and the environmental risk factors noted above is the "service integration" reform movement. The concept of integrating human service systems emerged in the 1970s, but the contemporary service integration reform did not take shape until the late 1980s and 1990s, as educators and other human services professionals began to recognize that public education cannot prepare children for full participation in society if their basic human needs go unmet (Kagan & Neville, 1993; Kirst, 1989). In turn, this led many to question the adequacy of existing human service systems—education, public health, social and child welfare—to respond to the problems resulting from social and economic changes in society.

As such, the service-integration reform movement is the most ambitious policy agenda in response to this situation. It is premised on minimizing the effects of recognized environmental risk factors by integrating human service systems, promoting interprofessional collaboration within and across these systems, and ultimately connecting them and their professionals with schools and the children, families, and communities they serve (Sailor, 2002; Skrtic & Sailor, 1996). The goal is to integrate educational, social welfare, and health-care services into a single, coordinated delivery system in which educators, social workers, and health care workers collaborate among themselves and with consumers to provide a complete array of personalized human services to students and their families.

A good deal of confusion surrounds the service integration concept because of a proliferation of associated concepts and terms, and, more important, a rapid succession of alternative reform models. Some of these concepts, terms, and models include case management, wrap-around services, school-linked service integration, full-service schools, and, most recently, comprehensive systems of care. Nevertheless, to one degree or another, these concepts and models and the broader movement itself are premised on transforming the existing system of discrete professions, service organizations, and categorical government agencies into an integrated, coordinated human service delivery system (Chapter 21, by Lawson & Sailor). Moreover, the succession of alternative reform models progressively has brought public schools and their local patrons into the center of service integration reform efforts. The initial, largely incremental change models of service integration reform were largely ineffective and involved schools only tangentially, but the current and emerging models place schools and educational reform at the forefront of reform. For example, the "school-linked services" model currently operational in several states requires integrated services to be linked to schools, because it is concerned primarily with the effects of worsening environmental conditions on children's readiness to learn (Sailor, 2002).

Further, according to Lawson and Sailor (see Chapter 21), an emerging model of reform seeks to link the service-integration concept with educational reform by making school-linked services a key component of school improvement. Finally, Lawson and Sailor characterize the nascent "comprehensive systems-of-care" model as addressing poverty and its correlates by integrating school-linked and community-based integrated services, which is premised on both interprofessional and lay-professional collaboration.

Although the original school-linked services model has been criticized for simply adding services to schools without changing their deep structure, the emergent and nascent models are premised on the principles of school restructuring and transformational reform noted above. This is consistent with Keogh's (see Chapter 20) point about the deleterious effects of certain functional aspects of conventional schooling, as well as her argument that, as such, conventional schools themselves may be at risk. That is, the emergent and nascent models of service integration recognize that "schools have to be readied for the learning and healthy development of children, youth, and families" (Lawson & Sailor, Chapter 21, p. 567), including assuring that they provide optimal conditions "for professionals' work" (p. 567).

Finally, the emergent and nascent models of service integration are consistent with Keogh's position on the importance of social ecology, in that they take a social and ecological view of schools, families, and their community context. In this regard, the nascent comprehensive systems of care model stresses that meaningful school improvement is unlikely unless the family and community contexts of children's learning and development are addressed simultaneously through "family-centered collaboration, inter-organizational collaboration, and broad-based community collaboration" (Lawson & Sailor, Chapter 21, p. 568).

As noted above, inclusion advocates support the pro-restructuring provisions in SBR legislation because they promote the kind of fundamental change necessary for meaningful inclusive education, and also because they form a legislative basis for service integration (Lipsky & Gartner, 1996; Sailor, 2002; Skrtic & Kleinhammer–Tramill, 2003; Skrtic & Sailor, 1996). Service integration is important because, in addition to benefiting children, families, and schools and advancing inclusion, by revitalizing neighborhood communities and reviving civic engagement, comprehensive models of service integration reform also safeguard and strengthen democracy (Lawson & Sailor, chapter 21; Sailor, 2002; Skrtic & Kleinhammer–Tramill, 2003; Skrtic et al., 1996).

In terms of the student performance goals of IDEA 97 and NCLB, moreover, comprehensive, school- and community-based systems of care hold the promise of minimizing environmental risk factors and maximizing the protective factors associated with developmental and educational problems. Without such a means for addressing these environmental factors, children, families, communities, and schools will remain or be placed at risk for failure.

Again, however, whether the SBR framework of NCLB and IDEA 97 advances the concepts of educational excellence and equity, school unification, inclusive education, and service integration depends on whether the bureaucratic or restructuring features of NCLB and IDEA 97 are emphasized. It depends on whether the traditional or transformational model of SBR is used to reform public education and special education. Further, given the interdependence of human needs, achievement, and social conditions, it depends on whether transformational reform is extended beyond the school, on whether we address the welfare of children and families more contextually and interdependently, working across social contexts, institutions, and professions.

REFERENCES

Boyer, E. L. (1983). *High school.* New York: Harper & Row.

Boyer, L., & Mainzer, R. W. (2003). Who's teaching students with disabilities? A profile of characteristics, licensure, status, and feelings of preparedness. *Teaching Exceptional Children, 35*(6), 8–11.

Brownell, M. & Skrtic, T. M. (2002). *Assuring an adequate supply of well qualified teachers to improve the educational outcomes of students with disabilities.* Invited testimony presented to the President's Commission on Excellence in Special Education, Denver.

Champlin, J. (1991). Taking stock and moving on. *Journal of the National Center for Outcomes Based Education, 1*(1), 5–8.

Council for Exceptional Children (2003, June). *Summary of House passed Bill H.R. 1350.* Arlington, VA: Council for Exceptional Children.

Cuban, L. (1989). The "at-risk" label and the problem of urban school reform. *Phi Delta Kappan, 70,* 780–784, 799–801.

Cuban, L. (2000). Myths about changing schools and the case of special education. *Remedial and Special Education, 17*(2), 75–82.

Egnor, D. E. (2003). *IDEA reauthorization and the student discipline controversy.* Denver: Love Publishing.

Elmore, R. F. (1987). *Early experiences in restructuring schools: Voices from the field.* Washington, DC: National Governors Association.

Elmore, R. F., Abelmann, C. H., & Fuhrman, S. H. (1996). The new accountability in state education reform: From process to performance. In H. F. Ladd (Ed.), *Holding schools accountable: Performance-based reform in education* (pp. 65–98). Washington, DC: Brookings Institution.

Elmore, R. F., & McLaughlin, M. W. (1988). *Steady work: Policy, practice, and the reform of American education.* Santa Monica, CA: Rand Corp.

Fiore, T. L., Kleinhammer–Tramill, P. J., & Peters, J. (2000). The federal role in preparation of special education personnel: An historical perspective. *Policy Perspectives.* Washington, DC: American Association of Colleges of Teacher Education.

Gartner, A., & Lipsky, D. K. (1987). Beyond special education: Toward a quality system for all students. *Harvard Educational Review, 57*(4), 367–395.

Goodlad, J. I. (1984). *A place called school: Prospects for the future.* New York: McGraw-Hill.

Grosenick, J. K., & Reynolds, M. C. (1978). Promising practices in the implementation of Deans' Grant Projects. In J. K. Grosenick and M. C. Reynolds, (Eds.), *Teacher education: Renegotiating roles for mainstreaming* (p. 173). Reston, VA: Council for Exceptional Children.

Harris, K. R., & Graham, S. (1994). Constructivism: Principles, paradigms, and integration. *Journal of Special Education, 28,* 233–247.

Harris, K. R., & Graham, S. (1996a). Memo to constructivists: Skills count, too. *Educational Leadership, 53*(5), 26–29.

Harris, K. R., & Graham, S. (1996b). Constructivism and students with special needs: Issues in the classroom. *Learning Disabilities Research and Practice, 11*(3), 134–137.

Heller, K. W., Fredrick, L. D., Dykes, M. K., Best, S., & Cohen, E. T. (1999). A national perspective of competencies for teachers of individuals with physical and health disabilities. *Exceptional Children, 65*(2), 219–234.

Heshusius, L. (1995). Holism and special education: There is no substitute for real life purposes and processes. In T. M. Skrtic (Ed.), *Disability and democracy: Reconstructing (special) education for postmodernity* (pp. 166–189). New York: Teachers College Press.

Hirsch, E., Koppich, J., & Knapp, M. (2001). *Revisiting what states are doing to improve the quality of teaching: An update on patterns and trends.* Center for the Study of Teaching and Policy. Seattle: University of Washington.

Hymowitz, K. S. (2000). Who killed school discipline? *City Journal, 10*(2), 34–43.

Kagan, S. L., & Neville, P. R. (1993). *Integrating human services: Understanding the past to shape the future.* New Haven, CT: National Center for Service Integration, Yale University Press.

Keogh, B. K., & Weisner, T. (1993). An ecocultural perspective on risk and protective factors in children's development: Implications for learning disabilities. *Learning Disabilities Research & Practice, 8,* 3–10.

Kirst, M. W. (1989). *The progress of reform: An appraisal of state education initiatives.* New Brunswick, NJ: Center for Policy Research in Education.

Kleinhammer–Tramill, J. & Gallagher, K. (2002). The implications of Goals 2000 for inclusive education. In W. Sailor (Ed.), *Whole-school success and inclusive education: Building partnerships for learning, achievement, and accountability* (pp. 26–41). New York: Teachers College Press.

Klingner, J. K., Ahwee, S., Pilnieta, P., & Menendez, R. (2003). Barriers and facilitators in scaling up research-based practices. *Exceptional Children, 69,* 411–429.

Kozleski, E., Mainzer, R., & Deshler, D., Coleman, M., & Rodriguez–Walling, M. (2000). *Bright futures for exceptional learners: An agenda to achieve quality conditions for teaching and learning.* Reston, VA: Council for Exceptional Learners.

Lewis, M., & Feiring, C. (1998). *Families, risk, and competence.* Mahwah, NJ: Erlbaum.

Lipsky, D. K., & Gartner, A. (1996). Inclusion, school restructuring, and the remaking of American society. *Harvard Educational Review, 66*(4), 762–796.

Mastropieri, M. A. (2001). Introduction to the special issue: Is the glass half full or half empty? Challenges encountered by first-year special education teachers. *Journal of Special Education, 35,* 66–74.

McDonnell, L. M., McLaughlin, M. J., & Morison, P. (1997). *Reform for one and all: Standards-based reform and students with disabilities.* Washington, DC: National Academy of Sciences Press.

McIntire, J.C. (2001). Case in point: Bright futures? *Journal of Special Education Leadership, 13*(2), 48–51.

McLaughlin, M. J., & Tilstone, C. (2000). Standards and curriculum: The cornerstone of educational reform. In M. McLaughlin & M. Rouse (Eds.), *Special education and school reform in the United States and Britain* (pp. 38–65). London: Routledge.

McNeil, L. M. (1986). *Contradictions of control: School structure and school knowledge.* New York: Methuen/Routledge & Kegan Paul.

National Center of Educational Restructuring and Inclusion, (1994). *National study of inclusive education.* New York: City University of New York, NCERI.

National Center for Education Statistics. (1998). *Toward better teaching: Professional development in 1993–1994.* Washington, DC: U.S. Department of Education.

National Commission on Excellence in Education (1983). *A nation at risk: The imperative for educational reform.* Washington, DC: Government Printing Office.

Neubert, D. A., & Moon, M. S. (1999). Working together to facilitate the transition from school to work. In S. Graham & K. R. Harris (Eds.), *Teachers working together: Enhancing the performance of students with special needs* (pp. 186–213). Cambridge, MA: Brookline Books.

Oakes, J. (1985). *Keeping track: How schools structure inequality.* New Haven, CT: Yale University Press.

Oakes, J. (1986a). Keeping track: Part 1. The policy and practice of curriculum inequality. *Phi Delta Kappan, 68*(1), 12–17.

Oakes, J. (1986b). Keeping track: Part 2. Curriculum inequality and school reform. *Phi Delta Kappan, 68*(2), 148–154.

O'Day, J. A. (2002). Complexity, accountability, and school improvement. *Harvard Educational Review, 72*(3), 293–329.

Odom, S. L., Brantlinger, E., Gersten, R., Horner, R., Thompson, B., Harris, K. R. (2003). *Research in special education: Scientific methods and evidence-based practices.* Manuscript submitted for publication.

Pickett, A. L. & Gerlach, K. (1997). *Supervising paraeducators in school settings.* Austin, TX: Pro-Ed.

Poplin, M. S. (1988). Holistic/constructivist principles of the teaching/learning process: Implications for the field of learning disabilities. *Journal of Learning Disabilities, 21*(7), 401–416.

Pressley, M., & Harris, K. R. (1998). Constructivism and instruction. *Issues in Education: Contributions from Educational Psychology, 3*(2), 245–255.

Pugach, M., & Lilly, M.S. (1984). Reconceptualizing support services for classroom teachers: Implications for teacher education. *Journal of Teacher Education, 35*(5), 48–55.

Quirk, C., & Bartlinski, A. K. (2001, March). *No more community-based instruction?* Paper presented at Maryland Coalition on Inclusive Education Conference, Maryland State Department of Education, College Park.

Reynolds, M. D., & Wang, M. C. (1983). Restructuring "special" school programs: A position paper. *Policy Studies Review, 2*(1).

Riley, R. W. (1995). Reflections on Goals 2000. *Teachers College Record, 96*(3), 380–388.

Sailor, W. (2002). *Whole-school success and inclusive education: Building partnerships for learning, achievement, and accountability.* New York: Teachers College Press.

Sailor, W., Anderson, J. L., Halvorsen, A. T., Doering, K., Filler, J., & Goetz, L. (1989). *The comprehensive local school: Regular education for all students with disabilities.* Baltimore: Paul H. Brookes.

Salvia, J., & Ysseldyke, J. E. (2004). *Assessment in special and inclusive education* (9th ed.). Boston: Houghton Mifflin.

Sizer, T. R. (1984). *Horace's compromise: The dilemma of the American high school.* Boston: Houghton Mifflin.

Skrtic, T. M. (1988). The organizational context of special education. In E. L. Meyen & T. M. Skrtic (Eds.), *Exceptional children and youth: An introduction* (pp. 479–517). Denver: Love Publishing.

Skrtic, T. M. (1991a). *Behind special education: A critical analysis of professional culture and school organization.* Denver: Love Publishing.

Skrtic, T. M. (1991b). The special education paradox: Equity as the way to excellence. *Harvard Educational Review, 61,* 148–206.

Skrtic, T. M. (1995). Deconstructing/reconstructing public education: Social reconstruction in the postmodern era. In T. Skrtic (Ed.), *Disability and democracy: Reconstructing (special) education for postmodernity* (pp. 233–273). New York: Teachers College Press.

Skrtic, T. M. (2003). An organizational analysis of the overrepresentation problem in special education. *Multiple Voices, 6*(1), 41–57.

Skrtic, T. M. & Kleinhammer–Tramill, P. J. (2003). *Building-level administration of special education services.* Funded proposal, Preparation of Leadership Personnel, U.S. Department of Education, Office of Special Education Programs.

Skrtic, T. M., & Sailor, W. (1996). School-linked services integration: Crisis and opportunity in the transition to postmodern society. *Remedial and Special Education. 17*(5), 271–283.

Skrtic, T. M., Sailor, W., & Gee, K. (1996). Voice, collaboration and inclusion: Democratic themes in educational and social reform initiatives. *Remedial and Special Education, 17*(3), 142–157.

Smith, D.S., Pion, G., Tyler, N. C., Sindelar, P., & Rosenberg, M. (2001). *The study of special education leadership personnel: With particular attention to the professoriate.* Nashville, TN: Vanderbilt University; Gainesville: University of Florida; & Baltimore: Johns Hopkins University.

Smith, T., Dowdy, C., Polloway, E.A., & Blalock, G.E. (1997). *Children and adults with learning disabilities.* Boston: Allyn and Bacon.

Spady, W., & Marshall, K. (1991). Beyond traditional outcome-based education. *Educational Leadership, 49*(2), 67–72.

Stedman, L. C. (1987). It's time we changed the effective schools formula. *Phi Delta Kappan, 69,* 215–224.

Stoddart, T., & Floden, R. (1995). *Traditional and alternative routes to teacher certification: Issues, assumptions, and misperceptions.* East Lansing, MI: National Center for Research on Teacher Learning, (ERIC Document No. ED383697).

Thurlow, M. L. (2002, July). *Accountability: A national perspective.* Paper presented at OSEP Research Project Directors' Conference, U. S. Department of Education, Office of Special Education Programs, Washington, DC.

Tyack, D., & Hansot, E. (1982). *Managers of virtue: Public school leadership in America, 1820–1980.* New York: Basic Books.

U. S. Department of Education (1999, April). *Federal education legislation enacted in 1994: An evaluation of implementation and impact, executive summary.* Washington, DC: U.S. Department of Education, Planning and Evaluation Service, Office of the Under Secretary.

U. S. Department of Education (2001). *Twenty-third annual report to Congress on implementation of the Individuals with Disabilities Education Act.* Washington, DC: Author.

Ward, M. J. (1996). Coming of age in the age of self-determination: A historical and personal perspective. In D. J. Sands & M. L. Wehmeyer (Eds.), *Self-determination across the life span: Independence and choice for people with disabilities* (pp. 1–14). Baltimore: Paul H. Brookes.

Wehmeyer, M. L., Lattin, D., Lapp-Rincker, G., & Agran, M. (2003). Access to the general curriculum of middle-school students with mental retardation: An observational study. *Remedial and Special Education, 24,* 262–272.

Wehmeyer, M. L., & Sands, D. J. (1998). *Making it happen: Student involvement in education planning, decision making and implementation.* Baltimore: Paul H. Brookes.

Whitaker, S. D. (2003). Needs of beginning special education teachers: Implications for teacher education. *Teacher Education and Special Education, 26,* 106–117.

Wise, A. E. (1988). The two conflicting trends in school reform: Legislated learning revisited. *Phi Delta Kappan, 69*(5), 328–333.

Zemelman, S., Daniels, H., & Hyde, A. (1998). *Best practice: New standards for teaching and learning in America's schools* (2d ed.). Portsmouth, NH: Heinemann.

PART ONE

Standards-Based Reform and the Conditions of Practice

James G. Shriner and Thomas M. Skrtic

The chapters in this part of the book address two of our main themes: the nature and implications of the policy shift in special education from procedural compliance to standards-based accountability, and the deteriorating conditions of special education practice under the standards-based reform (SBR) policy framework. The first theme is addressed in the first two chapters, relative to the nature and history of SBR and the justification for adopting it as a policy framework in special education. Together, these chapters explain how, in the broader SBR environment of the 1990s, IDEA 97 was crafted to address the goal of improved outcomes for students with disabilities through access to the general education curriculum, participation in assessments of educational results, and inclusion in state, district, and school accountability systems. Chapter 2 gives readers a sense of the promise and optimism that accompanied passage of IDEA 97. Chapter 3 traces the evolution of the SBR framework in the 1990s and its disappointing effects on students with disabilities prior to enactment of the No Child Left Behind Act (NCLB) in 2001.

The remaining chapters in Part One address the "conditions of practice" theme from two different perspectives. First, the major problems associated with implementing the SBR logic of IDEA 97 and NCLB are considered in Chapters 4–6. These problems include the general lack of administrative and collegial support for special educators, an inadequate supply of qualified special education teachers, and inadequate conditions for the implementation of research-based instructional practices. Second, several promising practices and models to address these problems and thereby improve the conditions of special education practice under SBR are considered in Chapters 7–9. These chapters highlight research on the implementation of SBR in special education since enactment of IDEA 97 and NCLB, and recommend accommodation strategies for bringing the actual experiences of students with disabilities and their teachers more in line with the vision put forth in these laws.

The work of these and other authors since the enactment of IDEA 97, including those of the first two chapters, indicates that in many respects the SBR framework required changes in special education practice that outpaced the research base to support them (Rouse, Shriner, & Danielson, 2000). Moreover, given the implementation problems discussed throughout this Part of the book, it is apparent that the SBR vision of IDEA 97 overestimated the capacity of schools to provide the administrative and organizational support necessary to achieve it.

In Chapter 2, "The IDEA Amendments of 1997: Implications for Special and General Education Teachers, Administrators, and Teacher Trainers," Mitchell Yell and James Shriner consider the implications and promise of IDEA 97 relative to discipline, IEP planning, and participation in assessments of educational results. The law sought to move special education away from its longstanding reliance on procedural compliance, extensive monitoring of programs, and tacit acceptance of a separate system of accountability for students with disabilities and their parents.

Of particular note in this regard is the requirement that students with disabilities be afforded opportunities for participation and progress in the general education curriculum. This requirement was significant, the authors note, because it extended the principle of "least restrictive environment" beyond physical environment to the instructional environment as well. But prior to enactment of NCLB at least, the primary mechanism for achieving the accountability intent of the requirement was far less effective than anticipated.

The intent of IDEA 97 was to make the academic performance of students with disabilities an integrated component of general education accountability systems and decision making. The vehicle for this was the requirement that the performance of students with disabilities on state assessments be publicly reported. Most advocates of the policy shift to SBR, including Yell and Shriner, accepted the assumption of IDEA 97 framers that public reporting of assessment results would mean that the performance of students with disabilities as a group would be used in programmatic decision making. This was a reasonable expectation, given the assumption that "*what* gets reported about *whom* [determines what] gets taught or is addressed [by policymakers]" (p. 43).

As the authors note, however, the required participation in assessments and public reporting of results did not lead to the meaningful inclusion of these results in state, district, and school accountability systems and decision making. This is especially true because IDEA 97 did not specifically require consideration of the results in accountability-based decisions (see Chapter 3, by Thurlow). Not until the 2001 enactment of NCLB were states, districts, and schools required to include the assessment results of students with disabilities in accountability decisions.

Under NCLB, accountability decision frameworks must consider the performance of the school as a whole, and also the performance of all disaggregated student subgroups, including students with disabilities. Failure to produce performance gains for any subgroup eventually will trigger negative consequences for the school and possibly lead to externally imposed sanctions. Thus, NCLB codified the accountability intent of IDEA 97, in that accountability processes must ensure that *what* gets reported about *whom* actually gets used in programmatic decision making. By holding states, districts, and schools accountable for improving the academic performance of all students, the logic holds, districts and schools will provide teachers and students, including students with disabilities, with the supports necessary to reach the goal of 100% content-area proficiency.

At the outset of the SBR movement in the early 1990s, students with disabilities and the professionals who serve them were largely excluded from the undertaking. This led the U.S. Department of Education, Office of Special Education Programs (OSEP), to create the National Center on Educational Outcomes (NCEO) at the University of Minnesota. The NCEO's mission was to develop a "viable partnership between general education and special education in the national agenda to raise expectations for all students" (Bruininks, Deno, McGrew, Thurlow, & Ysseldyke, 1989, p. 2).

In Chapter 3, "Standards-Based Reform and Students with Disabilities: Reflections on a Decade of Change," Martha Thurlow, an original NCEO staff member and now its director, shares her perspectives on a decade of efforts to include students with disabilities in general education assessment and accountability systems. The chapter details critical events and specific reforms in the complex process of implementing the SBR accountability framework relative to students with disabilities. In doing so, the author also gives her insights on more technical issues such as appropriate and valid test accommodations, fair reporting of assessment results, and the controversial issue of including students with disabilities in student-level and systems-level accountability frameworks.

With regard to appropriate test and test-item accommodations, for example, she reports a host of conflicting views and research findings. Even commonly used accommodations such as "extra time" apparently have varying effects on student performance, and other recommended accommodations at times produce negative effects on the performance of some students with disabilities. In an era of increasing emphasis on accountability based on large-scale assessment results, Thurlow is concerned about the extent of disagreement surrounding the appropriateness of specific accommodation strategies. Such disagreements persist because of differing interpretations of data on the extent to which accommodations affect the validity of inferences based on scores so obtained (Thurlow, 2002).

The author concludes the chapter by arguing for the accountability provisions that eventually were included in NCLB—the provisions requiring that the performance of all students be included in evaluating and improving the performance of schools. Writing prior to the enactment of NCLB, she is wary of the politics and rhetoric surrounding SBR and associated assessment and accountability debates, particularly with regard to students with disabilities. Historically, she notes, general and special educators have held low academic expectations for students with disabilities, and teachers and administrators have eschewed data-driven decision making. If past behavior is indicative of future action, she warns, the promise of an accountability system in which the performance of all students carries equal weight may be beyond the reach of public education. "Until students with disabilities count in the same way as other students do," she cautions, "it is too easy to discount their performance, and in discounting [it], to ignore it and the instructional needs it identifies" (p. 76).

Even though she was writing before NCLB put "teeth into the accountability intentions of IDEA 97" (Thurlow, 2002, p. 2), the author makes a strong case throughout the chapter for ensuring that students with disabilities attain success in a standards-based system. The only way to ensure that these students are provided with adequate supports and opportunities to learn to their maximum potential, she maintains, is to provide them with the "best instructional procedures available" (p. 77–78). In arguing for the importance of providing the best instruction possible, the author also foreshadows two other provisions of NCLB that are critical to meaningful SBR accountability for students with disabilities: the availability of *highly qualified teachers* and broader use of *research-based instructional practices.*

The extent to which these and other critical components of SBR are in place in schools today is addressed in Chapters 4–6. Together, these chapters address the need for, but current lack of, administrative and collegial support for special educators, an adequate supply of highly qualified special educators, and appropriate conditions for implementing research-based instructional practices. In doing so, they are ultimately addressing the most important and alterable variable in the lives of children: the quality and effectiveness of teaching. The effort to improve the quality of teaching, including meaningful professional collaboration and broader use of research-based instructional practices, places the quality and effectiveness of teaching at the forefront of SBR implementation.

An important development in this regard, which directly or indirectly is a sub-theme in all three chapters, is the emerging debate over what makes a good teacher—content knowledge, pedagogical fluency, or some combination of both. Another related sub-theme that runs through the chapters is the importance of administrative support in assuring quality teaching, including support of inclusive and collaborative practices, support and development of beginning and veteran teachers, and support of teachers' adoption of research-based practices.

The first of these chapters, "To Ensure the Learning of Every Child with a Disability" (Chapter 4), by Richard Mainzer, Donald Deshler, Ruth Coleman, Elizabeth Kozleski, and Matty Rodriguez–Walling, is a post-NCLB update of a major national report on the conditions of special education practice. These authors review, extend, and update the findings of the report *Bright Futures for Exceptional Learners: An Agenda to Achieve Quality Conditions for Teaching and Learning* (Kozleski, Mainzer, Deshler, Coleman, & Rodriguez–Walling, 2000), expanding upon their implications for successful implementation of the SBR framework of IDEA 97 and NCLB. There is no doubt that the SBR framework represents a positive and necessary advance in the delivery of special education service. The *Bright Futures* study, however, raised serious questions about the extent to which special educators are adequately prepared and supported relative to their new roles and responsibilities, questions which, according to this chapter (and Chapters 5 and 6) have not been resolved in the ensuing years.

Of the many institutional barriers that hamper the delivery of inclusive special education services under the SBR framework, the original *Bright Futures* report highlighted those that affect the professional practice of special education teachers most negatively. For example, more than 75% of the special educators who participated in the study reported that the amount of paperwork for which they are responsible interferes with their teaching, and nearly 20% reported that their caseloads were unmanageable. Moreover, special educators reported being hampered by ambiguous and competing responsibilities, as well as feeling fragmented and conflicted by ill-defined and often contradictory expectations of parents and administrators. Perhaps most alarming in terms of quality inclusive services, however, are two especially disturbing findings:

1. Special educators reported that they are inadequately supported by district and building administrators relative to including students with disabilities in general education classrooms.
2. Special educators reported that, far from being engaged in collaborative relationships with their general education colleagues, they continue to be isolated from them and from other special educators.

Finally, when asked about ways to improve their working conditions, study participants stressed the need for more qualified special educators, noting that many of those entering the field today are not prepared for the new complexities and increased job demands of IDEA 97 (Kozleski et al., 2000).

The authors of Chapter 4 expand upon their earlier findings regarding lack of collaboration by explaining that special educators' training, job responsibilities, and opportunities for planning and professional development tend to diminish the importance of belonging to the school community as a whole. Rather, special educators are reinforced for remaining separate by the current expectations, structures, and conditions of schooling. In addition, the authors contend that conflicting definitions of quality teaching act to extend and perpetuate the separation of general and special educators. In this regard, they note that the current "content versus pedagogy" debate is mistakenly viewed in terms of an either/or distinction.

Their position is similar to that of others who have addressed the "nature of teaching" question (see Chapter 5, by Brownell et al.). They believe that special educators must have a working knowledge of a wide array of subject matter content in the general education curriculum, as well as extensive pedagogical knowledge and skills to accommodate the needs of students with disabilities.

Finally, the Chapter 4 authors emphasize the importance of active and informed administrative support and leadership. Specifically, they argue that administrators must understand the roles and responsibilities of special educators under the SBR framework and actively campaign for the supports that they need. These supports include a collaborative environment for service delivery, shared planning time, and an inclusive, collegial work atmosphere. Perhaps most important, they believe that exemplary administrative leadership should guide and support all teachers in the use of research-based instructional practices, as well as assure that these practices are implemented with fidelity and monitored to ensure their coordinated use.

Related to this and other aspects of professional development, exemplary administrative leadership provides ample opportunities for teachers to engage in a process of professional renewal within a context of schoolwide commitment to, and enthusiasm for, ongoing professional development. Such a context is essential, the authors note, to promote communication and collaboration across disciplines and to establish a culture of lifelong learning and self-improvement.

In Chapter 5, "Special Education Teacher Supply and Teacher Quality: The Problems, The Solutions," Mary Brownell, Paul Sindelar, Anne Bishop, Lisa Langley, and Seonjin Seo address the national shortage of qualified teachers to serve students with disabilities. Through their work at the Center on Personnel Studies in Special Education (COPSSE) at the University of Florida, another national center sponsored by OSEP, they have investigated a range of issues associated with teacher supply and demand, induction, and retention.

They begin the chapter by contrasting the approach to improving the supply and quality of teachers articulated in the 1996 policy report of the National Commission for Teaching and America's Future (NCTAF) with the approach mandated in NCLB. Whereas the NCTAF emphasizes the importance of improving the pedagogical qualities and skills of teachers, NCLB emphasizes the importance of subject-matter and content knowledge over skills in pedagogy, characterizing quality teaching in terms of expert content knowledge plus "good communication skills."

The implications of these conflicting definitions notwithstanding, the authors stress that we must address several major issues that negatively affect the recruitment, retention, and working conditions of special educators. These issues include a lack of sufficient training (and often full certification) for one's primary teaching assignment, the relatively low salaries of teachers compared to professions that require similar training, and the inordinate amount of paperwork for which special educators are responsible. With regard to insufficient training, the authors note that special educators who are not fully certified for their teaching assignment are the least likely to remain in the field, and that lack of full certification is associated with poor decision making in both management and instructional matters. Moreover, even when special educators are adequately trained and appropriately certified, their poor working conditions often discourage many of them from remaining in the field, which contributes to a national shortage of special education teachers rivaling that of mathematics and science teachers.

The Chapter 5 authors describe several strategies for alleviating the problem of special education teacher attrition, emphasizing those that address beginning teacher induction and mentoring. In this regard, they highlight the efforts of the state of Connecticut, where policy and practice emphasize supporting teachers' learning in the early stages of their careers. The Connecticut model is premised on the assumption that teacher behavior directly translates to student performance and, as such, it provides beginning teachers with two consecutive years of mentoring and external evaluation with corrective and supportive feedback. The authors characterize the model as a coherent induction and mentoring program that helps beginning teachers gain skills and confidence relative to their role within the school, both professionally and personally.

Although significant challenges remain, the authors conclude that efforts to ensure an adequate supply of qualified special educators should be premised on a commitment to meaningful induction and mentoring practices. In addition, they stress that these efforts must simultaneously improve the capacity of building administrators to support new teachers and to improve the climate and working conditions of schools so teachers will want to remain and grow in the profession.

In Chapter 6, "Access of Adolescents with Disabilities to General Education Curriculum: Myth or Reality," Jean Schumaker, Donald Deshler, and their co-authors describe the work of the University of Kansas Institute for Academic Access (IAA) relative to enabling students with disabilities to benefit from the general education curriculum. Like the NCEO and COPSSE, the IAA was established by OSEP to address a critical aspect of IDEA 97 and SBR accountability: meaningful access to the general education curriculum. Research and development activities of the IAA are directed to the needs of high school students with disabilities, for whom access to the general curriculum has been particularly problematic historically.

In this regard, the authors review the findings of IAA research conducted in nine high schools on instructional and contextual variables that influence the learning of adolescents with disabilities in the core academic curriculum. Among other results, the study found that most of the schools had no specific supports in place for students with disabilities attending general education classes, and that, far from meaningful collaboration, special education and general education teachers worked in isolation from one another. Moreover, they found that, in most cases, general education teachers lacked the pedagogical knowledge and skills to teach students with disabilities, and that coordination with regard to planning and collaboration among teachers and administrators was virtually nonexistent. The authors emphasize that such unacceptable conditions of practice virtually preclude the implementation of research-based instructional practices in schools, and thus that it is highly unlikely that students with disabilities will benefit from the results of the past quarter century of special education instructional research.

The authors conclude Chapter 6 by recommending two broad areas of research and development aimed at improving educational outcomes:

1. Research on scalability and sustainability of research-based instructional interventions as an essential component in efforts to provide teachers with the instructional interventions necessary to serve students with disabilities adequately.
2. Broader use of research-based instructional methods in initial teacher education and ongoing professional development programs as a way to encourage the creation of effective school contexts.

Finally, the authors remind us that meaningful access to the general education curriculum for adolescents with disabilities should not focus on academics alone;

successful programming for these students must address their needs in the areas of personal development and social competence as well.

The final three chapters in Part One, Chapters 7–9, address the necessary supports to facilitate quality teaching, including effective methods of teaching the general education curriculum relative to the unique needs of students with disabilities. More detailed attention is given to the conditions of practice for beginning and veteran teachers, and to the factors that contribute to teacher shortages, including the increased demands placed upon special educators and the organizational conditions that make it difficult for teachers to work together. Collaboration is at the forefront in these chapters—collaboration among beginning and veteran teachers, general and special education educators, educators and related services personnel and community agencies, professionals and families, and professionals and paraprofessionals. With regard to paraprofessionals, Chapter 9 addresses key issues related to the increasing reliance on paraprofessionals in the education of students with disabilities, which continues to offer promise and raise questions.

The first topic examined in these chapters is the professional lives of teachers at the beginning of their careers. In Chapter 7, "Supporting Beginning Special Education Teachers," Susan Whitaker addresses the high attrition rate among special education personnel. She details the challenges of being a novice teacher and addresses them with suggestions for increasing the likelihood of being successful initially. Not surprisingly, she devotes considerable attention to the need for support from veteran colleagues and administrators. New teachers need colleagues who they can turn to for advice and resource options when they have questions or concerns about instruction, management, or the nature of the system in which they are expected to function.

In the author's view, the presence of an effective mentoring system is essential if beginning teachers are to deal with personal and professional issues that arise in the early years of teaching. The chapter specifies desirable characteristics of mentors and also of the system in which effective mentors operate. Notably, the author stresses that the responsibilities of institutions of higher education must be extended to include providing tangible assistance beyond graduation to novice teachers. She also recommends that school-based mentors and administrators consider the unique transitional needs of new teachers as they move from the college or university to their own classrooms.

In Chapter 8, "Collaboration to Support Students' Success," Chriss Walther–Thomas, Lori Korinek, and Virginia McLaughlin present a model for establishing a network of collaborative relationships among professionals, families, service providers, and support personnel. The model addresses the needed resources for educators to become reflective practitioners in their ongoing efforts to improve student learning, and includes four types or sources of support:

1. *Frontline support* consists of the immediate help available to professionals such as the student's immediate family members, grade-level teams, peer coaches and mentors, administrators and supervisors, and professional associations.

2. *Special needs support* comes from those involved directly in the teaching process such as school-level assistance teams, co-teachers, and paraprofessionals.
3. *Special education support* is most appropriate for help with learners who experience significant school problems. This type of support comes from technical assistance providers (e.g., child study teams, multidisciplinary teams, IEP teams, technical assistance centers).
4. *Interagency/community support* comes form the various agencies that serve students across ages and/or grade levels (e.g., early intervention teams, transition teams).

The authors also describe potential start-up problems in implementing their model and present strategies and implementation tactics for improving a team's ability to garner support. Like most chapters in this Part of the book, the authors emphasize the importance of administrative support in any collaborative effort. In this regard, they argue that, in an era of increased inclusion, administrative support is foundational to the essential elements of collaboration, such as shared leadership, coherence of vision, planning, sustainability, and evaluation.

In Chapter 9, "Students with Disabilities and Paraprofessional Supports: Benefits, Balance, and Band-Aids," the final chapter of Part One, Michael Giangreco and Mary Beth Doyle share their insights on the role of paraprofessionals in the education of students with disabilities. Although paraprofessionals have been assisting in the education of students with disabilities since the inception of IDEA, the authors are concerned that too much direct responsibility for teaching students with disabilities has been relinquished to them. In some cases, they note, paraprofessionals have become the "primary or exclusive service delivery mechanism" (p. 218), a tendency that is likely to continue, given the NCLB provisions for the involvement of paraprofessionals and the critical shortage of qualified special education teachers. At the same time, other educators seldom hold paraprofessionals in high regard, and their efforts too often go unrecognized and unrewarded. In response to this set of circumstances, the authors offer guidance and an action plan to ensure that the extent of direct instruction carried out by paraprofessionals is appropriate, and that their contributions are valued by professional educators and benefit the students they serve.

The test for determining the appropriate level of paraprofessional involvement is the question: "Would the paraprofessional teaching that is occurring be okay if the student being taught did not have a disability?" In the authors' view, if the answer is "no," the level of paraprofessional involvement is most likely not acceptable, and may be serving to perpetuate a double standard regarding the quality of services being provided for students with disabilities. The authors conclude by offering a 10-step action plan for improving the paraprofessional-supported instruction and social integration of students with disabilities in inclusive settings. The plan seeks to establish and maintain a sense of balance between the support offered by paraprofessionals and that provided by general and special teachers and student peers. In their view, securing this balance will maximize the benefits of paraprofessional involvement in the education of students with disabilities, and thus the value that professionals assign to their involvement.

REFERENCES

Bruininks, R. H., Deno, S. L., McGrew, K. S., Thurlow, M. L., & Ysseldyke, J. (1989). *National Center on Assessment of Outcomes for Children and Youth with Disabilities.* (Proposal to U. S. Department of Education, Office of Special Education Programs). Minneapolis: University of Minnesota, Institute on Community Integration.

Kozleski, E., Mainzer, R., Deshler, D., Coleman, M., & Rodriguez–Walling, M. (2000). *Bright futures for exceptional learners: An agenda to achieve quality conditions for teaching and learning.* Arlington, VA: Council for Exceptional Children.

Rouse, M., Shriner, J., & Danielson, L. (2000). National assessment and special education in the United States and England and Wales. In M. McLaughlin & M. Rouse (Eds.), *Special education and school reform in the United States & Britain* (pp. 66–97). London: Routledge.

Thurlow, M. L. (2002, July). *Accountability: A national perspective* (Paper presented at OSEP Research Project Directors' conference). Washington, DC: U. S. Department of Education, Office of Special Education Programs.

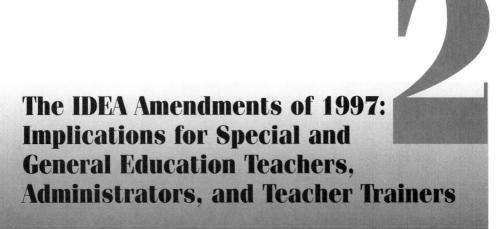

The IDEA Amendments of 1997: Implications for Special and General Education Teachers, Administrators, and Teacher Trainers

Mitchell L. Yell, and James G. Shriner

On June 4, 1997, President Clinton signed the Individuals with Disabilities Education Act Amendments of 1997, PL 105-17, into law. This law amended and reauthorized the Individuals with Disabilities Act (IDEA). The 1997 amendments added a number of major provisions to the IDEA that will result in substantial changes in the education of students in special education, as well as the roles of administrators, general educators, special educators, and teacher trainers.

In passing the amendments, Congress noted that the IDEA had been successful in ensuring access to a free appropriate public education and improving educational results for students with disabilities. Nevertheless, Congress indicated that the implementation of the IDEA had been impeded by low expectations for students, an insufficient focus on translating research to practice, and too much emphasis placed on procedural paperwork not tied to outcomes and legal requirements at the expense of teaching and learning.

To improve the IDEA, Congress passed the most significant amendments to the law since the original passage in 1975. These amendments were seen as the next step in providing special education and related services by ensuring that students with disabilities would receive a quality public education emphasizing the improvement of student performance.

Congress viewed the reauthorization process as an opportunity to strengthen and improve the IDEA by:

— strengthening the role of parents;
— ensuring access to the general education curriculum and reforms;
— focusing on teaching and learning while reducing unnecessary paperwork requirements;

— assisting education agencies in addressing the costs of improving special education and related services to children with disabilities;

— giving increased attention to racial, ethnic, and linguistic diversity to prevent inappropriate identification and mislabeling;

— ensuring that schools are safe and conducive to learning; and

— encouraging parents and educators to work out their differences using non-adversarial means. (Senate Report, p. 5)

We cannot cover all the detailed changes in this chapter, determine exactly how these changes will affect the daily lives of children and youth with disabilities, their parents, and the educators who serve them. Therefore, we will focus on areas of change to the IDEA that concern special educators most directly, including changes in the IEP process, discipline of students with disabilities, and procedural safeguards. We offer our interpretations of how these changes may affect the education of students with disabilities and set forth recommendations to teachers, administrators, and teacher trainers in meeting the requirements of the IDEA Amendments of 1997.

RESTRUCTURING OF THE IDEA

Originally, the IDEA was divided into nine parts or subchapters. In the IDEA amendments of 1997, the law was restructured into four parts. Subchapters one and two are referred to as Part A and Part B respectively.

■ Part A contains the general provisions of the law (e.g., definitions).

■ Part B details the grant program that requires states receiving federal assistance under the IDEA to ensure a free appropriate public education to all qualified children and youth with disabilities residing in the state. Part B also contains the procedural safeguards designed to protect the interests of children and youth with disabilities.

■ Part C extends part B protections to infants and toddlers with disabilities and strengthens incentives for states to provide services to infants and toddlers (birth to age 3). Part C (originally Part H) was added to the IDEA in 1986 with the passage of PL 99-457 (IDEA, 20 U.S.C. § 1471-1485).

■ Part D is composed of the discretionary or support programs. These programs have been enacted to address various concerns regarding the education of students with disabilities. Part D contains provisions regarding state improvement grants for educating students with disabilities, research, personnel preparation, technical assistance, and dissemination of information, parent training, and technology development.

The structure of the IDEA is depicted in Table 2.1.

EVALUATION

In a sense, special education "begins" with the referral and evaluation process that may lead to the provision of services. These activities have been the central concern

TABLE 2.1 ■ IDEA Amendments of 1997: Framework of the IDEA

Part	Title	Content
Part A	General Provisions	■ Definitions, findings, purposes
Part B	Assistance for education of all children with disabilities	■ SEA & LEA eligibility ■ Special education services: evaluations, eligibility, IEPs, placements, and procedural safeguards
Part C	Infants and toddlers with disabilities	■ Programs for infants and toddlers
Part D	National activities to improve education of children with disabilities	■ Discretionary or support programs: state improvement grants, research, personnel preparation, technical assistance, support, dissemination of information, technology

SEA = State Educastion Agency
LEA = Local Education Agency

for many people—educators and parents alike. As such, evaluation is a useful beginning point for our description of the changes found in IDEA. Table 2.2 contains the IDEA requirements regarding evaluations.

The formal assessment and evaluation procedures of IDEA are intended to ensure that: (a) special education services are provided to children and youth who demonstrate the need for such services, (b) decisions for service provision are fair and defensible, and (c) all requirements for evaluations are implemented consistently in all districts and states and monitored for appropriateness and compliance (Shriner & Spicuzza, 1995). Evaluation procedures of PL 105-17 essentially reflect current policy contained in the existing law and accompanying regulations. The new law will codify all requirements in one section (Sec 614).

A few important changes in evaluation procedures are attempts to clarify parents' rights to information. First in regard to the requirement of parents' consent for evaluation of their child, the new version puts consent in the legislative language and stresses that consent for evaluation is not consent for placement of a child. Furthermore, parental consent now is required for reevaluations unless the school can determine that the parents failed to respond to reasonable attempts to obtain their consent. A key addition to the procedures requires that all evaluations include information about the student's involvement and progress in the general curriculum or, for preschoolers, in appropriate activities. This information, in addition to existing rules that prior notice and explanations of all evaluation procedures, tests, records,

TABLE 2.2 ■ IDEA Requirements: Evaluations, Eligibility Determinations, Section 614	
Key Points	**Explanation**
Consent or Refusal	■ Informed consent required before evaluation ■ If parents refuse consent, the school may use mediation or due process procedures to secure permission to evaluate. ■ Consent is not required for reevaluation if parents fail to respond to reasonable attempts ■ Consent for evaluation is *not* consent for placement or related services
Eligibility for Special Education	■ Child can not be eligible because of a lack of instruction in reading or math or because of limited English proficiency
Reevaluations	■ At least every three years ■ Conducted if conditions warrant a reevaluation or if the parents or teacher requests ■ Additional data need not be collected, but parents must be informed of the reasons for this decision and their option to request assessments
Assessment Tools	■ The LEA is required to use a variety of assessment tools to gather relevant, functional, developmental information about the student ■ Existing data must be considered
Instruments & Tests	■ Technically sound instruments are required when assessing cognitive, behavioral, physical, or developmental factors. ■ LEAs must ensure that tests are not discriminatory (racially or culturally) and are provided in child's native language or mode of communication.

and reports be provided, assures parents of a more complete picture of what is happening for their child.

Great concern over the rising numbers of students classified as learning disabled led to the committee to include a key provision in Sec. 614 (b)(5). This special rule prohibits eligibility decisions to be made because the student has had a lack of instruction or because he or she has limited English proficiency. The provision is intended to force considerations of all factors that might be affecting a student's performance and reduce the number of students who are improperly placed in special education. The committee anticipates that this provision will cause schools to focus greater attention on mathematics and reading in the early grades (Senate Report, 1997).

The reevaluation process has been streamlined in PL 105-17. The 3-year reevaluation was a compliance and paperwork nightmare because it constituted a full assessment of the student. Sometimes students were put through a complete assessment battery for no reason other than to satisfy report requirements. Under the new law a 3-year evaluation may rely on existing information and assessments. If the

LEA believes that no additional data are needed and notifies the parent of this option, the reevaluation can be conducted without doing any new assessments. The parents must concur with this plan, or the school must demonstrate that the parents did not respond to notifications for consent to carry out a no-assessment evaluation. Alternatively, the parent or the school may believe it is best to conduct an assessment in any or all areas of development if such information would provide useful information about how to best teach the child. In this regard, the reevaluation process is more purposeful—seeking to assess only when there are valid reasons to do so.

THE INDIVIDUALIZED EDUCATION PROGRAM

Congress believed that the IDEA had been extremely successful in improving students' access to public schools, and that the critical issue in 1997 was to improve the performance and educational achievement of students with disabilities in both the special and the general education curriculum. To this end, Congress mandated a number of changes to the individualized education program (IEP). The major change is that the entire IEP process now is focused on student participation in the general education curriculum. Table 3.3 contains the new IDEA requirements regarding the IEP.

IEP Requirements

The IEP will remain the key to serving all children and youth with disabilities. All provisions related to the process and document are found in Sec. (614(d)). The accompanying committee report emphasizes the intent of Congress to ensure that the "IEP process . . . is devoted to determining the needs of the child and planning for the child's education with the parents and school personnel" (Senate Report, 1997, p. 28).

Participants

Included in Table 2.3 is a listing of the people to be involved as team participants (e.g., parents and special educators). The requirement that a general education teacher be involved if a student is participating or may participate in the general education environment reflects the emphasis on general curricular involvement found throughout IDEA. Most children with disabilities are in the mainstream for at least part of the day, so regular educators usually will be involved in the overall IEP process. The general education teacher, however, may not need to be involved in "all aspects of the IEP team's work" (Senate Report, 1997, p. 26). Some individual tasks (e.g., related services coordination) do not require the participation of general education.

Another person who must participate is a representative of the local school who has (a) authority to provide, or supervise the provision of, specially designed instruction to meet the needs of children with disabilities, (b) knowledge of the general curriculum, and (c) knowledge of the resources of the LEA. A psychologist is not specified as a required participant under the new law. Rather, a person who can interpret

TABLE 2.3 ▪ IDEA Requirements:
Individualized Educational Programs and Placement, Section 614

Key Points	Explanation
Required Participants Sec. 614 (d)(1)(B)	▪ Parent ▪ Regular education teacher ▪ Special education teacher ▪ LEA representative knowledgeable about general curriculum ▪ Person who can interpret the instructional implications of evaluation results (may be one of the above members)
Development Considerations Sec. 614 (d)(3)	▪ The team should consider: child's strengths, parents' concerns, most recent evaluation, language needs of LEP children, child's communication needs, and assistive technology; braille instruction when appropriate ▪ When behavior is an issue, strategies and supports to address that behavior ▪ Regular educators will participate in all above decisions
Placement Decisions	▪ The IEP team will make most decisions, but when they don't, LEAs must "ensure" parent participation
Content Sec. 614 (d)(1)(A)	▪ Present levels of performance (including how disability affects involvement and progress in general curriculum) ▪ Measurable annual goals including benchmarks or short-term objectives (related to meeting the child's needs to enable him or her to be involved in the general curriculum and other needs resulting from the disability) ▪ Special education and other services, supplementary aids, any program modifications or support for school personnel necessary for student to meet annual goals ▪ Explanation of the extent to which child will not participate in general education ▪ Individual modifications in administration of achievement tests, or explanation of why this is not appropriate and how child will be assessed ▪ Projected date for beginning services, anticipated service frequency, location, and duration ▪ Measures of progress toward annual goals and how parents will be kept informed of progress
Transition Services Sec. 614 (d)(1)(A)(vii)	▪ Beginning at age 14 and updated annually, statement of transition service needs that focus on student's existing program or courses ▪ Beginning at age 16, specific transition services including interagency responsibilities ▪ Beginning at least 1 year before the student reaches the age of majority, student informed has been of his or her rights
Review Schedules Sec. 614 (d)(4)	▪ At least once a year by IEP team, using the following criteria: any lack of progress toward annual goals and in the general curriculum, results of any reevaluation, information about child provided by parents, new information about child's anticipated needs.

instructional implications of evaluation results is needed. This could be a teacher or the LEA representative described above. Special services personnel, or persons with specific expertise, such as specialists in reading, may be involved when appropriate. School nurses are mentioned specifically in the committee report as likely IEP team members as schools assume greater responsibility for educationally related health-care costs.

Annual Goals and Benchmarks

Further changes to the IEP content require the development of measurable annual goals, including benchmarks or short-term objectives, that will enable parents and educators to accurately determine a student's progress. The IEP team determines annual goals and benchmarks or short-term objectives for students in special education. The goals are written to reflect students' needs to enable them to be involved in and progress in the general education curriculum and other educational needs related to the disability. As before, these goals focus on remediation of academic or nonacademic problems and are based on the student's current level of educational performance.

Goals and objectives, correctly written, enable the teachers and parents to monitor a student's progress in a special education program and make educational adjustments when necessary (Deno, 1992). The 1997 amendments emphasize accurate measuring and reporting a student's progress toward the annual goals. Annual goals are projections the team makes regarding the student's progress in one school year. Benchmarks or short-term objectives are written for each annual goal. Congress intended that short-term goals be, in effect, benchmarks. Congress viewed the requirement of "measurable" annual goals and benchmarks or short-term objectives as "crucial to the success of the IEP" (Senate Report, 1997, p. 25). If a student achieves the benchmarks or short-term objectives, therefore, he or she should achieve the annual goals also. The benchmarks or short-term objectives describe what a student is expected to accomplish in the given time period.

An accountability provision built into the annual goal-benchmark strategy reflects Congress' strong feelings about this issue. The new IDEA requires that the child's parents be informed of the child's progress toward annual goals (via benchmarks) as often as parents of nondisabled children are informed of their children's progress. For example, if a school normally sends home interim marking period reports at 4½ weeks and report cards at 9 weeks for each quarter of the school year, special educators might send home IEP progress reports at the same frequency.

The committee report goes so far as to suggest a possible method of providing feedback to parents about their child's progress: an IEP report card with "checkboxes or equivalent options that . . . enable the parents and the special educator to review and judge . . . performance on a . . . multipoint continuum." (Senate Report, 1997, p. 25). Students' progress and ratings on the benchmarks might be communicated on a scale ranging from "No Progress" to "Completed." In this way, the effects of the general education, special education and related services a student receives can be evaluated in concert so the student's total school experience is considered.

Development of the IEP

In developing the IEP, the law emphasizes again that the "purpose is to tailor the education to the child; not tailor the child to the education" (Senate Report, 1997, p. 27). Special education must be different from what the child typically would receive, and planning for this purpose must reflect this intent. Thus, sections (614)(d)(3)(A & B) list those "general" and "special" considerations that must be made (see Table 2). Categories of special considerations include: behavioral problems that impede learning, limited English proficiency (LEP), braille instruction, communication needs for children who are deaf or hard of hearing, and assistive technology.

The IDEA Amendments also specify that the IEP team is the proper forum for making placement decisions. Moreover, parents must take part in these decisions.

Transition

Transition services must be included in the IEP when the student reaches the age of 14. The transition plan will focus on a student's courses of study (e.g., student participation in a vocational education program). Also beginning one year before the student reaches the age of majority, the IEP must include a statement that the student be informed of his or her IDEA rights that will transfer to the student at the age of majority.

Curriculum

Consensus about the nature and content of the curriculum used in special education as reflected by the IEP has been lacking. Most teachers (55%) believe the IEP is the student's yearly curriculum with general curriculum considerations taking a backseat as source for students' IEPs (Schrag, 1996). Previously, IEPs had to include descriptions of special education and related services, including modifications needed for students in the mainstream. The total education of the student, including the appropriate curriculum of the mainstream, was not expected to be covered (IDEA Regulations, 1992). The concern about how the IEP connects with goals, outcomes, and standards established by the district or state for its students was raised by McLaughlin and Warren (1995). Those authors noted that the IEP process and curricular reform efforts resulted in a fragmented program for students with disabilities because they (a) operated independently at the system level, and (b) IEP team meetings included little or no discussion about how one should affect the other. Although the IEP actually contains many of the essential elements of standards (e.g., goals, performance levels, evaluation plans), special educators have tended to be passive observers of education reform (Shriner, Ysseldyke, & Thurlow, 1994). The tendency has been to avoid integrating the IEP process with a thorough examination of student needs related to reform-oriented instruction most often found in the mainstream. The IDEA now essentially makes such a position illegal.

Beginning with the development process for IEPs (Sec 614(d)(3)), active dialogue among special educators, general educators, and parents is necessary. The IEP team must include an individual who is knowledgeable about the general curriculum.

If the student is, or may be, in the general education environment, a general education teacher also must be involved throughout the process (Sec 614(d)(1)(B)). The requirements have been anticipated by groups such as the National Education Association (NEA) and the Council for Exceptional Children (CEC) and represent both an immediate opportunity and potential pitfall. On the one hand, teachers who spend the most time with the majority of students with disabilities will be involved in planning (Council for Exceptional Children, 1997). Others worry that these requirements promise only to produce excessive paperwork by adding descriptive sections to the IEP (Clymer, 1997).

Logic of the "LRE of the Curriculum"

The IEP will serve as documentation of the extent to which a student's educational program matches that provided to nondisabled students and addresses the goals and standards of the district and state. The concept of the LRE has applied mainly to the *location* of the student's education. The reauthorized IDEA and the supporting committee report affirm the intent of Congress to apply the logic of the LRE to the content of the education that would be provided to a student. Previously, only when the nature or severity of the disability was such that education in general education classes with the use of supplementary aids and services could not be achieved satisfactorily would removal of students with disabilities to a more restrictive setting be justified. Although this is still the case, both Sec. 612 and Sec. 614 emphasize that the general education curriculum is presumed to be the appropriate beginning point for planning an IEP for a student (Senate Report, 1997). Section 614(d)(1) uses the same logic for required components of the IEP by requiring:

> a statement of the special education and related services and supplementary aids and services to be provided to the child, or on behalf of the child, and a statement of the program modifications or supports for school personnel that will be provided for the child to be . . . involved and progress in the general curriculum. (Sec. 614(d)(i)(A)(iii))

Only when participation in the general curriculum with supplementary support and services can be demonstrated as not benefiting the student should "removal" to an alternative curriculum be considered. This provision includes the concept of partial participation to varying degrees in the general curriculum (Senate Report, 1997). Therefore, participants in the IEP meeting and process must begin with the general curriculum as the preferred course of study for all students. An important new activity will be to document the information that participants use and the decision-making process involved in justifications for divergent curricular goals. These curricular decisions will be the basis for determinations of how the child is included in accountability systems.

Participation in State- and District-wide Assessments

Sec. 614(d) outlines several new requirements concerning the participation of students with disabilities in state or district-wide assessments. Increased emphasis on involvement and progress in the general curriculum is of little use without information about students' progress. The committee report accompanying IDEA specifically cites a desire to reduce the unnecessary exclusion of students with disabilities from assessments because such exclusion places severe limits on students' opportunities for postsecondary education and employment (Senate Report, 1997).

As such, where participation decisions are part of the IEP already, as is the case in many school districts, the decision-making process must be examined and possibly refined. Participation in assessment decisions sometimes have confounded issues of existing characteristics, supports, and accommodations with inclusion eligibility. For example, time spent in general education classes has been an often-used criterion for participation (Erikson, Thurlow, Thor, & Seyfarth, 1996; Shriner, Gilman, Thurlow, & Ysseldyke, 1995), yet this consideration may be a misplaced marker. Accountability for results related to the performance goals and standards necessitates that the initial decision be one of whether the student should or should not take part or all of a general state or district-wide assessment.

The IEP team must document which portions of the curriculum, and therefore which goals and standards, are relevant to each student in special education. It may be that all curricular goals are pertinent regardless of where instruction is provided. In this case, the student should take part in the general state assessment even if accommodations are needed. If the student's instruction addresses only some of the curricular goals, partial participation is indicated. In this case, the student has a modified assessment plan. If the student is working on performance goals and standards unique to the student, participation in the general assessment probably is not indicated; an alternate assessment (Sec. 612(a)(17)) is the appropriate course and should be indicated properly on the IEP. In these cases, a plan for how the student will be assessed must be part of the IEP.

One final note regarding participation in assessments concerns students with disabilities in interim alternate educational settings and prisons. If a student is convicted as an adult and incarcerated in an adult prison, participation in general assessments is not applicable (Section 614 (d)(6)(A)(i)). If he or she is in an interim alternative educational setting, all requirements for access and participation remain in effect (Section 615 (k)(3)(B)).

Accommodations in Assessments

The IEP must include a statement of whatever modifications may be needed for participation in the assessments. In some districts and states many of these "new" requirements are part of the IEP process and document already. In South Carolina, several local education agencies (LEAs) are using state-prepared accommodation forms specific to each of the tests they use in the state-wide assessment, but the consistency with which these checklists are implemented and the detail with which they are documented is uncertain. In all likelihood, although the committee that worked on the IDEA did not intend the "size of the IEP [to increase] by dozens of pages" (Senate Report, 1997, p. 22), many districts must review their accommodation documentation procedures. Addenda to IEPs that document inclusion in curricular areas and assessments and that list appropriate modifications and accommodations will be new for many states. Examples of possible accommodations are included in Table 2.4.

ISSUES OF ASSESSMENT AS A MEANS OF ACCOUNTABILITY

The IDEA seeks to build upon the improving trends of inclusion of students with disabilities in accountability systems at both the district and the state levels. Over time, students with disabilities have been participating to a greater extent in state-wide assessments (Erikson et al., 1996; Shriner et al., 1995), yet tremendous variability remains in the extent of participation from state to state. The provisions Sec. 612 (a)(16) address this variability directly by requiring that students with disabilities be included in general state and district-wide assessments with appropriate accommodations when necessary. State education agencies (SEAs) and LEAs will be responsible for developing or revising participation guidelines not only for general assessments but for alternative assessments as well (Sec. 612(a)(17)). Also, states likely will be developing or revising their testing accommodation guidelines, as these also vary widely from state to state and district to district (Thurlow, Scott, & Ysseldyke, 1995).

The new requirement that is most likely to cause the biggest flurry of state- and district-level activity is that calling for an alternative assessment of progress for

TABLE 2.4 ■ Examples of Accommodations for Assessments

Flexible Time	Flexible Setting	Alternative Presentation Format	Alternate Response Format
Extended time	Test alone in test carrel or separate room	Braille or large-print edition	Pointing to response
Alternating lengths of test sections (e.g., shorter and longer)	Test in small-group setting	Signing of directions	Using template for responding
More frequent breaks	Test at home (with accountability)	Interpretation of directions	Giving response in sign language
Extended testing sessions over several days	Test in special education classroom	Taped directions	Using a computer
	Test in room with special lighting	Highlighted keywords	Allow answers in test book.

students who do not take part in the general state or district assessments (Sec 612(a)(16)). To date, accountability for special education students' programs has not emphasized the results of schooling. Rather, we as a nation have tracked the types of services provided, numbers of students by category, and the like—all inputs for the education of students with disabilities. The IDEA puts a rather abrupt "about face" on this orientation, and states' activities soon will change dramatically. Specifically, the law says that the State or the local education agency shall develop and conduct alternative assessments by July 1, 2000.

Alternate Assessment

Neither "general assessment" nor "alternate assessment" is defined in IDEA. Typically, general state assessments involve the use of criterion-referenced assessments or standardized norm-referenced tests. South Carolina, for example, uses a state-developed criterion-referenced test (Basic Skills Assessment Program, BSAP) and a norm-referenced test (Metropolitan Achievement Test-7th ed. MAT-7). Also, like many states, South Carolina is revising its criterion-referenced state assessment to better reflect the standards for coursework and achievement it has adopted for several content areas (e.g., language arts, mathematics, and science). Ysseldyke, Olsen, and Thurlow (1997) define *alternate assessment* as any "substitute way of gathering information on the performance and progress of students who do not participate in the typical state assessments used with the majority of students who attend schools" (p. 2).

Their definition is in response to the confusion surrounding the use of a similar term, *alternative assessment*. Alternative assessment is a generic term encompassing a variety of activities including authentic assessment, performance assessment, and portfolio (Taylor, 1997). Any or all of these could be part of what is intended by IDEA's alternate assessment requirements. Most important is the intention to ensure that all students have an opportunity to demonstrate what they have learned, whether that is by participation in the general assessment (which may, in fact, be an alternative assessment) or by some alternate process that the SEA or LEA will develop and implement. In this regard, alternate assessments are most appropriate for only a small percentage of students—most likely those with the most severe disabilities who are not working on any part of the general curriculum, and who will earn a differentiated diploma or certificate. Two states (Kentucky and Maryland) are cited often as having done the most work to develop and implement alternate assessments. Both states have used portfolios as the central means of gathering student information.

Kentucky uses an Alternate Portfolio to address a subset of the state's learner outcomes for students not working toward a regular diploma. Alternate portfolios contain at a minimum: (a) the students' schedule of school/work activities and routines, (b) a resume of job activities and experiences, and (c) examples of communication in the student's preferred mode (Kentucky Department of Education, 1992).

Maryland has pilot-tested the Independence Mastery Assessment Program (IMAP), for students with severe disabilities whose curriculum addresses learner outcomes different from those addressed by the state's general assessment. IMAP is portfolio-driven and measures student progress in four domains: (a) person management, (b) community functioning, (c) career vocational skills, and (d) leisure/recreation skills. IMAP portfolio entries include evidence of student communication, decision-making and academic and behavioral skills in these domains (Maryland State Department of Education, 1995).

Though a thorough discussion of alternate assessment is not the focus of this article, the IDEA has validated, the principles embraced by both states.

1. All students who are part of the educational community must be part of the assessment and accountability system used to judge the effectiveness and benefit of the schools.
2. Only a small percentage of the special education population is best served by assessment via an alternate system alone.
3. The alternate assessments are planned with a set of goals and standards for performances established ahead of time.

The purpose of such an assessment is to measure progress toward high expectations—exactly as is done for students in the general assessments that reflect the high standards adopted by the states.

DEVELOPMENT OF PERFORMANCE GOALS AND INDICATORS

In an effort to ensure that standard-based reforms benefit all the students, the IDEA requires that state education agencies (SEAs) establish goals for the performance of all students with disabilities. Nearly all states have developed or are developing standards for student knowledge and performance, and most use content areas (e.g., language arts, mathematics), as their organizational vehicle (American Federation of Teachers, 1996). The IDEA seeks to build upon these effects by requiring that developed goals and indicators are consistent, to the maximum extent appropriate, with other goals and standards the states have established for the students. In report language submitted in support of the IDEA, the emphasis on increased access to the general curriculum and expectations of high standards is reiterated:

> With regard to Section 612(a)(16), the committee wishes to make clear that its requirements are not intended to prevent the integration of performance goals and indicators for children with disabilities into [those] for nondisabled children, so that SEAs and LEAs can be held accountable for all children. (Senate Report, 1997, p. 16)

The National Center on Educational Outcomes (NCEO) has tracked the development of standards by states since 1994, with particular interest in the inclusion of students with disabilities. Although NCEO currently is evaluating all available standards from states, very few have separate standards for students with disabilities. Michigan is a notable exception, having developed categorically specific standards for students as early as 1990 (Frey & Lynch, 1992).

The IDEA does not specify exactly how the consistency of standards with those set for nondisabled students is to be evaluated. Shriner, Ysseldyke and Thurlow (1994) discussed alternative perspectives on standards and their use for students with disabilities. Among the possibilities presented were: (a) separate standards for special education students, (b) standards as expectations of progress across a range of performance, and (c) IEP's as standards. Each approach has advantages and disadvantages, and the IDEA language may be interpreted as seeking a combination of them all. First, the door seems to be left open to separate special education standards. The qualifier that newly developed performance goals be consistent "to the maximum extent possible" indicates the expectation that at least some of the goals and standards may be unique to special education students. Perhaps, students will be expected to meet standards in some core subjects and additional standards related to individual and unique student needs. It is not likely, however, that separate content standards will be established for all disability categories in all content and instructional areas.

In system-wide improvement standards an average performance standard is set and improvement for all students as a group is expected. This concept is similar to the average miles per gallon (mpg) standards once used in the automobile industry. Kentucky is one state that incorporates this idea in part of its standards and assessment system. All students' assessment results are included in school level averages that are used to measure progress of the system. Individual progress of students is not the focus of these activities—a position that Section 612 (a)(17) affirms in stating that assessments should not result in disclosure of performance results for individual students.

The IEP-as-standards approach reflects the overarching concept of "personal best" in which students are expected to achieve at progressively higher levels than they presently are achieving (Shriner, et al., 1994). The IEP is the cornerstone of existing accountability efforts and likely will maintain an important role. Much of the report language accompanying the IDEA refers to the IEP process and content as critical elements in addressing the unique needs of every student to progress in the general education curriculum. The report language strengthens the inclusive philosophy in so far as there appears to be a more direction to ensure that a student's total school program reflects a curriculum that is made to fit his or her needs, rather than allowing a student to be fit into a particular curriculum. Consider the following:

> Once a child [is] eligible for special education, the connection between special education and related services and the child's opportunity to experience and benefit from the general curriculum should be strengthened... [Section 614 (d)(IEP's)] is intended to ensure that a child's special education and related services are in addition to and are affected by the general curriculum, not separate from it. (Senate Report, 1997, p. 22)

REPORTING OF PERFORMANCE/ PROGRESS/ACCOUNTABILITY

New requirements for reporting progress for students with disabilities aimed at bringing the results of special education the same attention as is given to nondisabled students' progress and attainment. Although the term *accountability* is found only a few times in the IDEA, the committee members and policy makers clearly were thinking of accountability when the reporting requirements were written. These requirements move the status of students with disabilities one step further along what some have seen as an unwritten continuum of importance in education reform.

With reference to instructional time devoted to social results of schooling, Leone, McLaughlin, and Meisel (1992) warned that *"what* gets measured gets taught" (p. 12). In discussing the implications of inclusive decision making in testing programs, Yell and Shriner (1996) extended this logic to express that it also may be the case that *"who* gets measured gets taught" (p. 104). With increased emphasis on goals, standards, and indicators, access to the general curriculum, and inclusion in state and district assessments, the reporting requirements of IDEA validate that, in a very real sense, *"what* gets reported about *whom* gets taught or is addressed."

The IDEA addresses the issue of accountability by making data about the results of schooling for students with disabilities very public. Specifically, Sec. 612 requires that the SEA report to the public on the assessment performance of students with disabilities as often and in the same detail as it reports on the performance of nondisabled students. The new language is intended to be for students with disabilities *as a group*. The provision does not seek individual student results and, in fact, reports must protect the identity of individual students. Reports will include minimally:

- The number of children participating in general (regular) assessments
- The number of children participating in alternate assessments
- The performance of children with disabilities on general assessments (beginning not later than July 1, 1998) and on the alternate assessment (not later than July 1, 2000). (Sec. 612(a)(17)(B)).

There are several additional reporting requirements. Data from all reports related to students with disabilities must be disaggregated for assessments conducted after July 1, 1998. Also, every 2 years the SEA must submit a separate report to the U. S. Department of Education on the progress of students with disabilities toward meeting the performance goals and standards for all students. In addition, Sec. 653, State Improvement Plans, requires that all states include assessment data and comparisons of performance as part of their applications to the federal government for funds. Specifically, information concerning students with disabilities must include:

- Their performance on state assessments and other performance indicators established for all children, including drop-out and graduations rates and postsecondary education and employment.

■ How their performance on these indicators compared to that of nondisabled children. (Sec. 653(b))

The IDEA emphasizes that the vast amount of data collected on students with disabilities is to be used to focus change efforts toward attainment of better student results. Although not a specified part of new reports, states also must increase their evaluation of suspension and expulsion rates (Sec. 612(a)(22)). If students with disabilities are determined to represent a disproportionate number of long-term suspensions and expulsions (e.g., compared to students without disabilities), the state must review and, if appropriate, revise its policies and procedures for dealing with these issues. Again, accountability for appropriate outcomes—this time of a noncognitive nature—is the focus of the more prescriptive approach.

DISCIPLINE OF STUDENTS IN SPECIAL EDUCATION

Another significant addition of the 1997 amendments was a section affecting the discipline of students with disabilities. Congress heard testimony regarding the lack of parity school officials faced when making decisions about disciplining students with and without disabilities who violated the same school rules (Senate Report, 1997). To address these concerns, Congress added a section to the IDEA in an attempt to balance school officials' obligation to ensure that schools are safe and orderly environments conducive to learning and the school's obligation to ensure that students with disabilities receive a free appropriate public education. Figure 2.1 is a flowchart for disciplining students with disabilities.

Disciplinary Procedures

School officials may discipline a student with disabilities in the same manner as they discipline students without disabilities—with a few notable exceptions. If necessary, school officials may unilaterally change the placement of a student for disciplinary purposes to an appropriate interim alternative educational setting (IAES), another setting, or by suspending the student to the extent that these disciplinary methods are used with students without disabilities. The primary difference is that with students who have a disability, the suspension or placement change may not exceed 10 school days.

School officials may place a student with disabilities unilaterally in an appropriate IAES for up to 45 days if the student brings a weapon to school or a school function. For purposes of the IDEA, Congress defines a weapon as

> a weapon, device, instrument, material, or substance, animate or inanimate, that is used for, or is readily capable of, causing death or serious bodily injury, except that such term does not include a pocket knife with a blade of less than 2½ inches in length. (Senate Report, 1997)

Likewise, schools may remove a student to an IAES if the student knowingly possesses, uses, or sells illegal drugs or sells or solicits the sale of a controlled

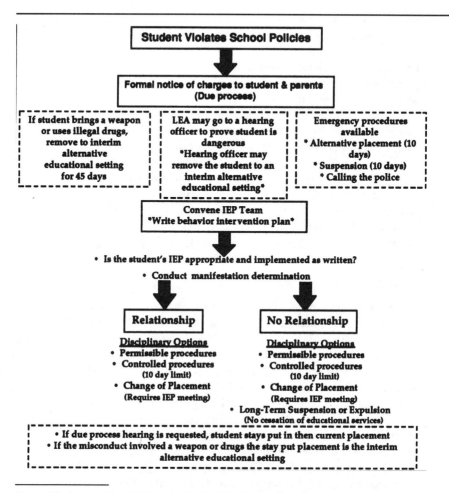

Source: *The Law and Special Education,* by M. L. Yell (Upper Saddle River, NJ: Prentice Hall/Merrill, in press). Reprinted with permission.

FIGURE 2.1 ■ Flowchart for Disciplining Students with Disabilities under IDEA Amendments of 1997

substances at school or a school function. Controlled substances are drugs, many of which have medicinal uses, that have a high potential for abuse. (For the list of controlled substances see the Controlled Substances Act, 21 U.S.C. § 812(c)). In addition, a hearing officer can order a 45-day change in placement when a student with disabilities presents a substantial risk to the safety of others. In such situations, school officials can request an expedited hearing to have a student removed from school. School officials must present evidence to the hearing officer that maintaining the student with disabilities in the current placement is substantially likely to result in injury to the student or others and that school officials have made reasonable efforts to minimize this risk of harm. Further, the school must have an appropriate IEP and placement and must place the student in an IAES that meets the requirements of the IDEA.

A hearing officer may order a change of placement to an IAES for not more than 45 days in situations in which a student with disabilities presents a danger to other students or staff. A hearing officer will order such a change in placement if he or she determines that the school has demonstrated by "substantial evidence" that (a) maintaining the current placement is substantially likely to result in injury to the student or others, (b) the IEP and placement are appropriate, (c) the school has made reasonable efforts to minimize the risk of harm, and (d) the IAES meets the criteria set forth in the IDEA Amendments. The IDEA Amendments define substantial evidence as being a "beyond a preponderance of evidence" (Sec. 615 (k)(10)(C)).

Behavior Intervention Plan

To deal with behavior problems proactively, the 1997 amendments require that if a student with disabilities has behavior problems (regardless of the student's disability category), the IEP team shall consider strategies, including positive behavioral interventions, strategies, and supports, to address these problems. In these situations, a proactive behavior intervention plan, based on functional behavioral assessment, should be included in the student's IEP. The behavior intervention plan for each student should delineate expected behaviors, inappropriate behaviors, and positive and negative consequences. The disciplinary process that will be followed, including intervention techniques, should be outlined in the plan. The plan also should include procedures for dealing with a behavioral crises. Some legal scholars believe that schools will have to include behavior intervention plans in the IEPs of all students with disabilities, and that school districts will have to hire full-time behavior specialists to write these plans (Discipline provisions, 1997).

If a school suspends or places a student with disabilities in an IAES for 10 days, or removes a student to an IAES for 45 days, and the school has not conducted a functional behavioral assessment and implemented a behavior intervention plan, the IEP team must develop a plan within 10 days. If such a plan is already included in the IEP, the team must meet to review the plan to review its appropriateness and modify it if necessary.

The Manifestation Determination

If school officials seek a change of placement, suspension, or expulsion for more than 10 school days, a review of the relationship between a student's disability and misconduct must be conducted within 10 days of the action. This review, called a *manifestation determination,* must be conducted by a student's IEP team and other qualified personnel. If a determination is made that no relationship exists between the misconduct and disability, the same disciplinary procedures as would be used with students who are not disabled may be imposed on a student with disabilities (i.e. long-term suspension or expulsion). Educational services, however, must be continued. If the team finds a relationship between a student's disability and misconduct, school officials still may seek a change of placement but cannot use long-term suspension or expulsion. The student's parents may request an expedited due process hearing if they disagree with the results of the manifestation determination. The student's placement during the hearing will be in an IAES.

Conducting the manifestation determination

In conducting the manifestation determination, the IEP team must consider all relevant information regarding the behavior in question. This includes evaluation and diagnostic results, information supplied by the parents, and direct observations of the student. Furthermore, the team must examine the student's current IEP and placement to determine if they are appropriate. The IEP team can determine that the misconduct was *not* a manifestation of a student's disability only when the following three criteria are met:

1. The student's IEP and placement were appropriate (including the behavior intervention plan) and the IEP was implemented as written;
2. The student's disability did not impair the ability of the student to understand the impact and consequences of the behavior subject to the disciplinary sanction;
3. The student's disability did not impair the student's ability to control the behavior at issue.

Interim Alternative Educational Setting

The IDEA amendments describe the standards that the interim alternative educational setting must meet. First, the setting must be determined by the IEP team. Although the IAES is not in the school environment, the student must be able to continue to participate in the general education curriculum and continue to receive the services and modifications listed in the IEP. Moreover, the students must continue to work toward the goals and objectives of the IEP, including goals that address the behavior problems that led to the placement.

The IDEA requirements regarding the IAES will not limit schools' ability to use homebound placements (Congressional Research Service, 1997). The crucial factor in using these placements is that the school must continue to provide special education services. Alternative placements also could include alternative schools or other settings.

Stay-Put Provision

The stay-put provision requires that "During the pendency of any proceedings . . . , unless the state or local education agency and the parents or guardians agree otherwise, the child shall remain in the then current educational placement (IDEA, 21 U.S.C. § 1415 (e)(3)). That is, if the parents and school personnel disagree on an aspect of a student's special education and either party requests a due process hearing, the child must stay where he or she was at the time the hearing was requested. In *Honig v. Doe* (1988), the U. S. Supreme Court ruled that the stay-put rule had no exceptions, even in cases in which a student posed a danger to others. Administrators argued that the stay-put rule placed schools in the untenable situation of having to keep potentially dangerous students with disabilities in classrooms (*Honig v. Doe*, 1988).

In the IDEA Amendments, Congress made some modifications to the stay-put provision in situations involving the discipline of students with disabilities. Administrators may unilaterally remove students who bring weapons or illegal drugs to school or a school function to an IAES for 45 days. If parents or guardians of a student placed in the IAES request a hearing regarding that placement or a manifestation determination, the then current placement is the IAES. Therefore, the student will remain in the IAES during the pendency of his or her hearing.

IDEA Protections for Students Not Yet Eligible for Special Education

Section 615 (k)(8)(A-C) addresses the issue of disciplining students not yet eligible under the IDEA. This issue became important as the result of a number of due process and judicial proceedings involving discipline in which attorneys for students who were not in special education asserted that the students they represented were protected under the IDEA and, therefore, the school district could not expel them without adhering to the procedural safeguards of the law.

According to the statutory language of PL 105-17, students who have engaged in misconduct or rule violation may assert protection under the IDEA only if school district personnel had knowledge that the student had a disability before the behavior that precipitated the disciplinary sanctions occurred. School district personnel will be determined to have prior knowledge of a student's disability if the parents of the student had expressed in writing (unless a parent is illiterate), to appropriate school personnel that the student needed special education, if a student's behavior or performance demonstrated the need for special education services, or if the parents or teacher had requested an evaluation or expressed concern to the appropriate personnel.

If school personnel, did not know, or could not reasonably have known, of the presence of a disability, prior to taking the disciplinary actions, the student will be subject to the same rules and sanctions applied to students without disabilities. If the parents request an evaluation during the period in which the student is being disciplined, the evaluation must be conducted expeditiously. If the school district determines that the student is indeed disabled under the IDEA, the school must provide special education and related services. While the evaluation is being conducted, the student shall remain in the educational placement determined by the school personnel.

Referral to Law Enforcement and Judicial Authorities

Schools may report crimes committed by a student in special education to the proper authorities. Furthermore, law enforcement agencies and judicial authorities may exercise their responsibilities with regard to enforcement of federal and state laws. According to Congress, nothing in the IDEA prevents either school officials or law enforcement authorities from discharging their duties in such matters (Senate Report, 1997). Moreover, the school district shall ensure that copies of the special education and disciplinary records of a student in special education be transmitted to the proper authorities when such situations occur.

Cautions in Interpreting the Discipline Requirements

Many questions have arisen regarding the discipline section of PL 105-17. The statutory language is somewhat ambiguous. This has led some to believe that the new law effectively precludes the discipline of students with disabilities; others have countered that the IDEA Amendments essentially codify case law and will allow schools greater discretion in discipline matters (Discipline provisions, 1997).

A memorandum issued by the Congressional Research Service has helped to clarify matters. The memo stated that the IDEA Amendments essentially codify existing laws developed in court cases and interpreted by the Department of Education. The memo points out that the intent of Congress in drafting the discipline section was to provide more disciplinary flexibility to schools and that the IDEA Amendments, when viewed in their entirety, codify this increased flexibility (Congressional Research Service, 1997). Until the regulations are promulgated and states rewrite their rules and guidelines, the issue will remain unclear; therefore, the opinion of the Congressional Research Service regarding the disciplinary section should be followed.

FURTHER PROCEDURAL SAFEGUARDS

In special education, procedural safeguards guide the method by which school officials make decisions regarding the education of students, and substantive due process rights identifies those personal rights that school officials may not abridge (Valente, 1994). In writing the IDEA, Congress created explicit procedural safeguards to be afforded students with disabilities and their parents. These safeguards were expanded in the IDEA Amendments of 1997. The changes in the procedural safeguards are depicted in Table 2.5.

Mediation

A much talked about addition to the procedural safeguards of IDEA is that of voluntary mediation of disputes between the school district and the parents of a child with a disability. Mediation is not new. Some states (e.g., Connecticut,

TABLE 2.5 ■ IDEA Requirements: Procedural Safeguards, Mediation, Section 615 (e)	

Key Points	Explanation
Availability	■ Mediation must be available whenever a hearing is requested.
Voluntary	■ Participation by both parties is voluntary.
Hearing delays	■ The State may not delay parental rights to a hearing under IDEA.
	■ Mediations must be conducted in a timely manner.
Mediators	■ The State must provide a list of qualified, trained, impartial mediators.
Explanations	■ A LEA or SEA may require parents who chose not to use mediation to meet with a disinterested third party who will explain the benefits of mediation and encourage its use.
Costs	■ The State will pay costs of mediation.
Agreements	■ Agreements will be in writing.
Confidentiality	■ Discussions will be confidential and may not be used as evidence in subsequent hearings.
	■ Parties may be asked to sign a confidentiality agreement.

Massachusetts) have used it for more than 20 years. Others, such as Delaware and South Carolina, have used it regularly for only a few years. Sec. 615 now requires all states to offer mediation as an initial avenue for conflict resolution while maintaining parents' rights to timely due process. Under Sec. 615 (e), schools and states must make information about mediation available to parents. If the parents refuse mediation, the LEA may, in fact, require them to meet with a disinterested third party to hear explanations of the benefits and usefulness of the process. These representatives likely would be from the Parent Training and Information Centers authorized by Sec. 682, or from other alternative dispute resolution groups.

States will be required to maintain a listing of trained mediators and will bear the cost of the mediation process. When mediation is used, attorneys may or may not be present. All discussions held in mediation will be treated as confidential and may not be used as evidence in any subsequent proceedings, including due process hearings and court proceedings. Parents and schools may be asked to sign an agreement of confidentiality *before* mediation begins.

If the mediation is successful the agreement reached must be put in writing. This requirement seeks to improve the follow-through of agreed-upon plans. The provisions for mediation seek three important outcomes.

First, mediation may enhance both the speed and the quality of decision making regarding programming for students. Even though everyone has the student's best interest in mind, wasted time and poor instruction do no good whatsoever.

Second, burdens on the due process system litigation activity should be reduced. The committee report emphasizes the hope that what is observed in states where mediation is often used will be observed in states where it is used less frequently.

Finally, mediation is a potential public relations boon. Amicable dispute resolutions through mediation may serve to increase the use of the process, making it the "normal" course of action while simultaneously reducing negative interactions that capture the news media's eye.

Attorneys' Fees

The new law retained provisions regarding attorneys' fees and added a few qualifications. Attorneys' fees may be reduced in situations where the attorney representing the parents failed to provide the local education agency with information regarding the specific nature of the parent's dispute. Attorneys have to notify school officials in a timely manner of the nature of the problem and any proposed solutions. In addition, because the IEP process should be devoted to students' needs and planning for their education, the IDEA amendments specifically exclude the payment of attorneys' fees for attorney participation in the IEP process. The only exception is when the IEP meeting is ordered in an administrative hearing or court proceeding.

The amendments also specifically adopted the *Hensley v. Eckerhart* (1983) standard for determining the amount of any attorneys' fees award. In that decision, the high court stated that the basis for determining attorneys' fees should be the extent of a plaintiff's success on the claims. That is, in determining awards, courts are required to assess the extent to which the plaintiffs prevailed on significant issues (Senate Report, 1997). When a plaintiff fails to prevail on significant issues, the hours the attorneys spent on the issue can be excluded from calculation of the fee. Of course, when the plaintiff fails to succeed on any issue brought, no attorneys' fees will be awarded.

SPECIAL EDUCATION IN THE CORRECTIONAL SYSTEM

The IDEA does not require states to provide special education services to persons aged 18 to 21 who are inmates in an adult prison if they were not receiving special education services prior to their incarceration. If they were receiving services, the obligation to provide services would continue. If a student was identified as eligible under the IDEA but left school prior to incarceration, that student must receive special education services. Essentially, inmates who had an IEP in their last educational placement must continue to receive special education services in the correctional institution. The obligation to provide special education services to youth in juvenile facilities remains unchanged.

PRIVATE SCHOOLS

A question that has vexed special educators, and has had no clear answer in the IDEA, concerns the extent of the public schools' responsibilities to students with disabilities whose parents enroll them in private schools. Do these students have the same right to special education and related services under IDEA as do students who are attending public school? The IDEA unquestionably extends some benefits to private school students with disabilities; however, the extent of these benefits is unclear.

The IDEA requires that local public school districts placing students with disabilities in private schools must provide special education and related services to these students. Further, case law clearly indicates that if a school district fails to provide an appropriate education to a student with a disability and the parent unilaterally places the child in a private school to receive an appropriate education, the school has to reimburse the parents for private school placement (*Burlington School Committee v. Department of Education,* 1985).

A more difficult issue arises when students for whom the school district normally would have been obligated to provide a special education are placed in a private school directly by their parents. That is, when parents choose a private school placement rather than the public school, including the special education services that the public school would have provided, does the public school still have an obligation to provide these services? In these situations, the public school will not be liable for the private school placement if the school's program is found inappropriate and the private school's program appropriate. The school, however, still retains some obligations to the privately placed student derived from its duty under IDEA to provide access to a free appropriate public education (FAPE) to students with disabilities residing within the school district.

The IDEA Amendments indicate that a school district's obligation to students placed in private schools ends once they make a FAPE available and the parents elect to place the student in a private school. That is, the school district does not have to pay for the private school placement. If, however, a hearing officer or court later determines that a FAPE was not made available to a student, the officer or judge may order reimbursement to the parents. In these situations, the crucial consideration is whether the special education the school district offered was appropriate to the student's needs and would have allowed the student to make meaningful educational progress.

To recover reimbursement for private school placements, the student must have been enrolled in the LEA, the parents must have notified the LEA of their intention to enroll the child in a private school, the LEA must not have consented to or referred the child to the private school, and the LEA must have failed to provide a FAPE in a timely manner. The amount of the reimbursement, which normally would be for the full cost of special education and related services, may be reduced if: (a) at the most recent IEP meeting the parents did not inform the LEA that they planned to enroll their child in a private school, (b) the parents did not give notice 10 days that they rejected the school's placement and intended to enroll their child in a private school, or (c) the parents acted unreasonably in removing their child from the public school and enrolling him or her in a private school.

FUNDING

Through the IDEA, the federal government provides funding to assist states with special education costs. To receive IDEA funds, states must submit a state special education plan to the U. S. Department of Education. This plan must show that a state is providing free appropriate special education services to all students with disabilities residing in the state between the ages of 3 and 21 in accordance with the procedures set forth in the IDEA. This includes students with disabilities who have been suspended or expelled from school. States that meet the IDEA requirements receive federal funding.

The IDEA funds are received by the state education agency (SEA) for distribution to the local education agencies (LEAs). The federal funds do not cover the entire cost of special education but, rather, are intended to provide financial assistance to the states. Congress originally intended to fund 40% of states' costs in providing special education services through the IDEA. The actual levels of funding to the states, however, have amounted to approximately 6% to 7% of total expenditures. The Omnibus Consolidated Appropriations Act Fiscal Year 1997, enacted in 1996, raised the federal contribution to close to 10%.

Federal expenditures are computed on a state-by-state basis in accordance to the number of students with disabilities served, which is referred to as the *child count formula*. No adjustments are made either for the category of disability or setting in which a student is served. This number is multiplied by 40% of the average per-student expenditure in public schools in the United States. The federal government caps the number of students in special education in each state that federal sources will fund. States cannot serve more than 12% of the total number of school-age students in the state.

A major change in funding was included in the 1997 amendments to the IDEA. The funding formula remains based on the child count until federal appropriations reach $4.9 billion. Federal appropriations above that level will be allocated according to a population-based formula with an adjustment for poverty rates. When the trigger of $4.9 billion is reached, the new formula, based on the state's population (85%) and poverty level (15%), will apply to all excess appropriations. Congress capped the total increases a state could receive under this formula as no more than 1.5% over the increase in federal funding from the previous year. Neither can states receive less than they did in fiscal 1997. The purpose of the caps and floors is to limit the increase in federal funding to states that gain from the formula change and prevent large decreases in states that receive less under the new formula.

The IDEA also requires that 75% of the federal funds the states receive be directed to the local schools and that 25% may be used at the state level. Most of the federal funding, therefore, flows from the federal to the state government and, in turn, to the local school districts. To receive state funds, local school districts must have programs that meet the state requirements. States are required to establish management and auditing procedures to ensure that federal funds will be expended in accordance with IDEA. States also must set up systems to allocate funds. The amount of flow-through funds given to a local education agency is in proportion to the district's contribution to the state total of students in special education.

The 25% of the federal funds that may be set aside for state agency activities may be used for administration and supervision, direct and supportive services for students with disabilities, and monitoring and complaint investigation (IDEA Regulations, 34 C.F.R. § 300.370 (a)). States may, however, use only 5% of the 25% of federal funds for administrative purposes. The states' administrative activities may include technical assistance to local education agencies administering the state plan, approval and supervision of local activities, and leadership activities and consultative services (IDEA Regulations, 34 C.F.R. § 300.621).

The IDEA Amendments of 1997 capped the actual dollar amount of the 5% that may be used for administrative purposes at the fiscal 1997 level. States also will be given increases equal to the inflation rate or the increase in federal expenditures, whichever is less. If inflation is lower than the percentage increase in federal appropriations, states are required to spend the difference on improvements in services to students with disabilities.

ADDITIONAL CHANGES TO THE IDEA

In this chapter we have explained some of the more significant changes to the IDEA. Other changes that will have a significant affect on special education have not been addressed here. Some of these changes are included in Table 2.6.

IMPLICATIONS FOR TEACHERS, ADMINISTRATORS, AND TEACHER TRAINERS

We wish to point out that many schools and professionals around the country are providing many of the "best practices" now part of the IDEA. Still, the Amendments will lead to changes in the manner in which students with disabilities are served in public education. The final form the changes will take have yet to be determined. Regulations implementing the IDEA Amendments of 1997 have to be written by the Department of Education, and many states will have to make changes to their laws to bring them into compliance with the IDEA. These regulations will clarify the role changes that will be necessary. In addition, court cases will help to clarify those areas of the law that remain unclear. Nevertheless, the roles of administrators and general and special educators in the education of students with disabilities will be expanded and altered as the amendments and regulations are enacted.

Teachers

The IDEA places a much greater emphasis on student participation in the general education curriculum. The IEP, thus, is reconceptualized as a broader document encompassing student goals and objectives for general education and special education. The

TABLE 2.6 ■ IDEA Requirements: Additional Changes

Key Points	Explanation
At-risk students	■ SEAs now may serve 3- to 9-year-olds at risk or developmentally delayed.
Infants and toddlers with disabilities	■ Part C emphasizes serving infants and toddlers in natural environments.
Related services	■ Orientation and mobility are added as a new category of related services.
Regulations	■ Limits the authority of the Secretary of Education to promulgate regulations and specifies new procedures for promulgating regulations.
Charter schools	■ When charter schools are within an LEA, the LEA must serve students with disabilities attending the charter school.
Terminology change	■ "Serious emotional disturbance" is referred to in the law as "emotional disturbance." The change is intended to eliminate the pejorative connotation of the term "serious" and is intended to have no substantive or legal significance.
Personnel standards	■ Paraprofessionals and assistants must be trained appropriately and supervised in accordance with state law. ■ SEAs may adopt a policy that includes the requirement that LEAs make an ongoing good-faith effort to recruit and hire appropriately trained personnel.
Methodology	■ While teaching methodologies are appropriate subjects for discussion and consideration by an IEP team, they are not expected to be written into the IEP.
Hearing rights	■ Parents may, at their option, require an electronic verbatim recording of a hearing.
Prior written notice	■ LEAs must include in notifications to parents sources they may contact to obtain assistance in understanding procedural safeguards.
Access to records	■ Parents can review *alll records.*

location of supplementary services to make the general curriculum accessible is a new requirement of Sec 614(d)(1)(A)(vi)). During IEP planning, participants will need to consider *when* and *where* instruction in the general curriculum will take place. We are used to the idea that special education services may be provided in the general education setting. It may be the case that the more appropriate location of instruction in the general curriculum is a special education setting. The extent to which the new IDEA has anticipated the impact of this contingency is not clear.

Regardless of where the education of a student occurs, the language of the IDEA consistently reinforces the intent of Congress to require the IEP to focus on how the student's needs resulting from his or her disability can be addressed so the student can participate, at the individually appropriate level and in the appropriate place in the general curriculum offered to all students (Senate Report, 1997). A more collaborative relationship between general educators and special educators is likely to be needed. Planning, implementing, and evaluating instructional programs will necessitate more frequent communication across disciplines than is sometimes found in today's schools.

Administrators

Administrators will have more discretion in disciplining students in special education. They may suspend a student with disabilities unilaterally for up to 10 school days. Further, in situations involving students with disabilities bringing weapons, using, possessing, or selling drugs, or selling a controlled substance at school or a school function, administrators may unilaterally remove the student in an IAES for up to 45 days. In writing a behavior intervention plan, in conducting a manifestation determination, or in situations involving long-term suspension or expulsion, however, administrators cannot act unilaterally. In these situations the IEP team must be involved.

Teacher Trainers

Special educators must receive more professional development and training activities so they can support and deliver instruction in the general curriculum. Few special education teachers are prepared adequately to teach content areas, yet they are not exempt from the responsibility to know the content of standards-oriented curricula (National Center on Educational Outcomes, 1996). Indeed, CEC foresees its professional development activities expanding in this and other areas to meet the demands of the reauthorization requirements (Council for Exceptional Children, 1997).

General education teachers will be more involved in the IEP process. Teacher preparation programs for general educators, therefore, should include preparations (i.e. special education courses) to help them assume their expanded roles.

Special educators will required in-depth training in writing legally correct goals and objectives. Further, the preparation should emphasize formative evaluation procedures for monitoring student progress toward these goals and objectives.

If a student has a history of behavior problems, the IEP must contain a behavioral intervention plan. Therefore, special education teachers and other professionals involved in the assessment process (e.g., school psychologists) must be trained in functional behavioral assessment and the principles and procedures of applied behavior analysis. Moreover, the IDEA's increased emphasis on assistive technology will necessitate teachers being prepared in the application of technologies such as augmentative communication and computer applications to education.

CONCLUSION

The IDEA Amendments of 1997 required changes in the way we educate students with disabilities. The majority of the changes we discussed in this chapter took effect when President Clinton signed the law on June 4, 1997 (e.g., discipline changes). The section of the IDEA that required modifications to the IEP, however, did not take effect until July 1, 1998. The regulations implementing the IDEA Amendments of 1997 became effective on May 11, 1999, further helping to clarify the law.

In addition, states will have to bring their rules and guidelines into conformity with the new law as well as the regulations. The meaning of the changes in the IDEA no doubt will be clarified further by the courts. Nevertheless, these changes portend significant alterations in the roles of special and general educators, administrators, and teacher trainers.

REFERENCES

American Federation of Teachers (1996). *Making standards matter: 1996.* Washington, DC: Author.

Burlington School Committee of the Town of Burlington v. Department of Education of Massachusetts, 471 U.S. 359 (1985).

Clymer, A. (1997, May 14). House passes bill for disabled that adds education resources. *New York Times,* pp. A1, A17.

Council for Exceptional Children. (1997, June). *IDEA sails through Congress! CEC Today, 3*(10), 1, 9, 15).

Deno, S. L. (1992). The nature and development of curriculum-measurement. *Preventing School Failure, 36,* 5-11.

Discipline provisions in new IDEA cause serious concerns. *Special Educator, 12,* (June 6, 1997), p. 1 & 4.

Erikson, R., Thurlow, M. L., Thor, K., & Seyfarth, A. (1996). *1995 state special education outcomes.* Minneapolis: University of Minnesota, Natural Center on Educational Outcomes.

Frey, W. D., & Lynch, L. (1992). *Using exit performance assessments to evaluate and improve programs for students with educable mental impairment and students with emotional impairments.* Lansing, MI: Disability Research Systems.

Hensley v. Eckerhart, 461 U.S. 424 (1983).

Honig v. Doe, 479 U.S. 1084 (1988).

Individuals with Disabilities Education Act Regulations, 34 C. F. R. Parts 300 and 301. (1992). Appendix C to Part 300: Notice of Interpretation. 57 Fed. Reg. 44839.

Individuals with Disabilities Education Act of 1990, 20 U.S.C. § 1401-1485.

Individuals with Disabilities Education Act Amendments of 1997, P.L. 105-17, 105th Congress, 1st session.

Johnson, Nancy. (May 30, 1997) Memorandum from the Virginia School Boards Association concerning the discipline provisions in H.R. 5 and S. 717, 105th Congress to Congressional Research Service. Unpublished document.

Kentucky Department of Education. (1992). KIRIS: *Kentucky alternate portfolio project— Teacher's guide.* Frankfort: Kentucky Systems Change Project, Author.

Leone, P. E., McLaughlin, M. J., & Meisel, S., M. (1992). School reform and adolescents with behavioral disorders. *Focus on Exceptional Children, 25*(1), 1-15.

Maryland State Department of Education. (1995). *Independence mastery assessment program: IMAP PILOT.* Baltimore: Author.

McLaughlin, M. J., & Warren, S. H. (1995). *Individual education programs: Issues and options for change.* College Park, MD: Center for Policy Options in Special Education, University of Maryland.

National Center on Educational Outcomes. (1996, February). *Focus group feedback on the National Science Standards to the National Committee on Science Education Standards and Assessments.* Minneapolis: University of Minnesota.

Omnibus Consolidated Appropriations Act, FY97, Senate Joint Resolution, N. 63, 104th Congress, 2nd session, Congressional Record, S12327 (1996).

Schrag, J. A. (1996). *The IEP: Benefits, challenges, and directions.* Alexandria, VA: Report of Project Forum, National Association of State directors of Special Education.

Senate Report of the Individuals with Disabilities Act Amendments of 1997, available at wais.access.gpo.gov.

Shriner, J. G. & Gilman, C. J., thurlow, M. L., & Ysseldyke, J. E. (1995). Trends in state assessment of educational reforms. *Diagnostique, 20,* 101–119.

Shriner, J. G. & Spicuzza, R. J. (1995). Procedural considerations in the assessment of students at risk for school failure. *Preventing School Failure, 39,* (2), 33-39.

Shriner, J. G., Ysseldyke, J. E., & Thurlow, M. L. (1994). Standards for all American students. *Focus on Exceptional Children 26*(5), 1-19.

Taylor, R. L. (1997). *Assessment of exceptional learners* (4th ed.). Boston: Allyn & Bacon.

Thurlow, M., Scott, D., & Ysseldyke, J. (1995). *A compilation of states' guidelines for accommodations in assessments for students with disabilities* (Synthesis Report 18). Minneapolis: University of Minnesota, National Center on Educational Outcomes.

Valente, R. (1994). *Law in the schools* (3d ed.). New York: Merrill.

Yell, M. L., & Shriner, J. G. (1996). Inclusive education: Legal and policy implications. *Preventing School Failure, 40*(3), 101-108.

Ysseldyke, J. E., Olsen, K., & Thurlow, M. L. (1997). *Issues and considerations in alternate assessments.* Minneapolis: University of Minnesota, National Center on Educational Outcomes.

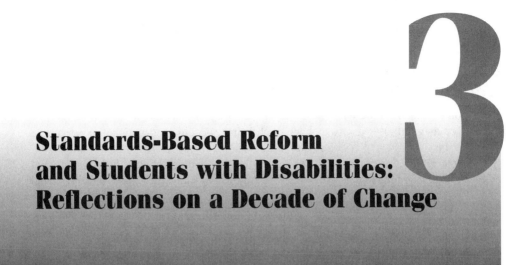

Standards-Based Reform and Students with Disabilities: Reflections on a Decade of Change

Martha L. Thurlow

Calls for higher and more rigorous standards for all students turned out to be the educational battle cry of the 1990s. State after state defined its content and performance standards, and a major push for change in education became known as "standards-based reform." Near the beginning of standards-based reform, special educators asked whether all students, in particular students with disabilities or the individuals who worked with them, were included in various aspects of the reform—setting standards, developing assessments, taking tests, getting data on test results, and so on.

Nearly a decade has now passed. What has happened? What has standards-based reform meant for students with disabilities? These questions are important to answer because the push for standards-based education continues to make the headlines and to be pushed forward by federal and state initiatives. I hope to answer the questions about where we are now in standards and standards-based reforms for students with disabilities.

First, I provide a brief history of standards and what standards-based reform has entailed. Then I describe what has occurred in including students with disabilities in all aspects of standards-based reform—setting standards, participating in assessments, making assessment accommodations, reporting results, developing accountability systems, and teaching/learning. Much of the information that I cite is based on investigations and analyses conducted by the National Center on Educational Outcomes (NCEO), a federally funded center that has followed these issues for 10 years. I conclude by highlighting what I believe to be some of the lessons we have learned about including students with disabilities in standards-based reform.

A BRIEF HISTORY OF STANDARDS
AND STANDARDS-BASED REFORM

Content standards define what students should know and be able to do (i.e., knowledge and skills) as a result of their schooling and other educational experiences. Performance standards define how well students must perform to demonstrate adequate knowledge and skills—"how good is good enough?" Together, content and performance standards have formed the kernal of standards-based reform in the United States in the past decade.

States started defining content standards in the early 1990s, often spurred by work on national standards (e.g., National Council of Teachers of Mathematics, 1989; National Research Council, 1993) or by the 1989 educational summit at which the national educational goals were first identified (see National Council on Education Standards and Testing, 1992). Various groups and news media began to rate standards (e.g., American Federation of Teachers, 1999; Fordham Foundation, 2000; State Policy Updates, 2000), further elevating their importance in the eyes of the public.

Federal laws also were written to promote the development and implementation of standards and educational reforms based on them. Table 3.1 summarizes three of the most important of these laws: Goals 2000, Title I of the Improving America's Schools Act, and the Individuals with Disabilities Education Act. These federal laws have helped to solidify the importance assigned to standards and the standards-based reform movement, as well as to highlight the notion that standards and reforms are meant for all students, including students with disabilities.

Standards-based reforms, however, have involved more than just setting standards. Hand-in-hand with them have come state and district assessments, reporting

Federal Law	**Year Enacted**	**Standards-Related Provisions**
TABLE 3.1 ■ Key Standards Provisions in Goals 2000, IASA (Title I), and IDEA		
Goals 2000: Educate America Act	1994	"It is the purpose of this part to establish a bipartisan mechanism for – . . . reviewing the voluntary national content standards, voluntary national student performance standards, and voluntary national opportunity to learn standards certified by the National Education Standards and Improvement Council. . ." [Sec. 201 (3)]
		"It is the purpose of this part to establish a mechanism to – (1) certify and periodically review voluntary national content standards and voluntary national student performance standards that define what all students should know and be able to do; (2) certify state content standards and State student performance

(continued)

TABLE 3.1 ■ *(cont.)*

Federal Law	Year Enacted	Standards-related Provisions
		standards submitted by States on a voluntary basis, if such standards are comparable or higher in rigor and quality to the voluntary national content standards and voluntary national student performance standards certified by the National Education Standards and Improvement Council." [Sec. 211. (1) (2)]
Improving America's Schools Act (Title I)	1994	"[Title I] programs need to become even more effective in improving schools in order to enable all children to achieve high standards; and in order for all students to master challenging standards in core academic subjects." [Sec. 1001 (b) (4) (5)]
		"If a state has not adopted State content standards and State student performance standards for all students, the State plan shall include a strategy and schedule for developing State content standards and State student performance standards for elementary and secondary school children served under this part in subjects as determined by the State, but including at least mathematics and reading or language arts by the end of the one-year period. . . ." [Sec. 1111 (b) (1) (C)]
		"State rules, regulations, and policies under this title shall support and facilitate local educational agency and school-level systemic reform designed to enable all children to meet the challenging State content standards and challenging State student performance standards." [Sec 1603 (a) (2)]
Individuals with Disabilities Education Act (IDEA)	1997	"All educational programs for children with disabilities in the State, including all such programs administered by any other State or local agency – . . . meet the educational standards of the State education agency. . . ." [Sec. 612 (a) (11) (A) (ii) II]
		"PERFORMANCE GOALS AND INDICATORS – . . . are consistent, to the maximum extent appropriate, with other goals and standards for children established by the State . . . ." [Sec. 612 (a) (16) (A) (ii)]
		"The Federal Government has an ongoing obligation to support programs, projects, and activities that contribute to positive results for children with disabilities, enabling them to meet their early intervention, educational, and transitional goals and, to the maximum extent possible, educational standards that have been established for all children." [Sec 671 (a) (1) (A)]

systems, and accountability mechanisms. Today, all except two states have state-level assessments. District-level assessments exist in the majority of districts spread throughout the states. High-stakes assessments that have significant consequences for districts, schools, administrators, educators, or the students themselves have mushroomed in an attempt to improve the performance of students (Education Commission of the States, 1999).

By the end of the century, 40 of the states had implemented (or were in the process of implementing) assessments that resulted in significant consequences (rewards or sanctions) for schools or the educators within them. More than 20 states had implemented (or were in the process of implementing) assessments that resulted in significant consequences for students (high school diplomas, promotion from one grade to the next). Assessment has become big business, a business that now is addressing how to include students with disabilities (and other formerly excluded students, such as students with limited English proficiency).

INCLUDING STUDENTS WITH DISABILITIES IN STANDARDS-BASED REFORM

The finding that students with disabilities were being excluded from national and state assessments (Ingels, 1993, 1996; Ingels & Scott, 1993; McGrew, Thurlow, Shriner, & Spiegel, 1992) was one of the first indicators that students with disabilities might not receive the benefits associated with standards-based reforms. Evidence of this exclusion came from parents and students themselves, who indicated that students were purposely being excluded (e.g., Why Johnny stayed home, 1997), as well as from surveys of states and attempts to collect data from national and state assessment data bases (McGrew, Algozzine, Ysseldyke, Thurlow, & Spiegel, 1995; McGrew, Vanderwood, Thurlow, & Ysseldyke, 1995), as well as from school districts (Zlatos, 1992). Inquiry into the exclusion of students with disabilities revealed that the problem existed at several points, each of which was a point of possible change.

Setting Standards

Probably the first point of exclusion occurred when standards were being developed. Initially, evidence of exclusion was found in the national standards under development by various national associations (Hofmeister, 1993; Shriner, Kim, Thurlow, & Ysseldyke, 1992; Ysseldyke, Thurlow, & Shriner, 1992). As states began to develop their own standards, analyses of them suggested that students with disabilities had not been considered (Thurlow, Ysseldyke, Gutman, & Geenen, 1998). This conclusion was supported by the findings that (a) only 17% of the states with standards (47 at the time of the analysis) had included individuals with disabilities (or those who were familiar with them) in developing their standards, and (b) 23.4% did not mention students with disabilities in any of their core subject area documents.

As part of the Improving America's School Act (IASA), Title I provisions, states must have standards in math and English/Language Arts, at minimum. And, when measuring adequate yearly progress, the performance of all students against these standards must be measured (U.S. Department of Education, 1999). Thus, standards (content and performance) must apply to all students (Thurlow & Ysseldyke, 2000) and, more important, these standards should be tied to effective assessments (Business Roundtable, 1996).

Participating in Assessments

Assessment is the mechanism by which states are measuring whether students are meeting standards. Yet, for nearly half of the past decade, students with disabilities were excluded from assessments not just during the time when assessments were administered but also when the items were developed and when results were tabulated and reported. In the early 1990s (Shriner & Thurlow, 1992), the rate of participation of students with disabilities in assessments ranged from 0% to 100%. Within a few years of this finding, it became evident that many states and districts did not really know how many students with disabilities had participated in assessments because their data management systems were not designed to address the participation of students with disabilities or they had not figured out how to keep track of whether these students had actually taken the test (Erickson, Thurlow, & Ysseldyke, 1996; Erickson, Ysseldyke, & Thurlow, 1997).

Excluding students with disabilities during administration of the test generally decreased over time, even as states began to have better estimates of participation rates. In the early 1990s, most states had 10% or fewer of their students with disabilities in assessments (Shriner & Thurlow, 1992). By the mid-1990s, this had changed somewhat. More states indicated that they knew how many students participated in assessments, and the number of states indicating that fewer than 10% of their students with disabilities were included in assessments decreased (Elliott, Erickson, Thurlow, & Shriner, 2000).

The reauthorization of IDEA in 1997 escalated these changes because it required that states include students with disabilities in their state and districtwide assessments and report on their findings by July 1, 1998 (see Table 3.2 for large-scale assessment requirements of Title I and IDEA). In 1999, estimates of participation rates by states were still variable, ranging from 15% to 100% (Thompson & Thurlow, 1999), but most states now had estimates of about 60%–65% of their students with disabilities participating in the statewide assessment.

Another indicator of participation that has changed over time is the written policies that states have about the participation of students with disabilities in the general state assessment. In the early 1990s, written-participation policies existed in fewer than half of the states (Thurlow, Ysseldyke, & Silverstein, 1993) and often indicated that students with disabilities need not take the general assessment. By the mid-1990s, 43 states had written participation policies, more of them indicating an intent to include students with disabilities in assessments (Thurlow, Scott, &

TABLE 3.2 ■ Key Assessment Provisions in IASA (Title I), and IDEA

Federal Law	Year Enacted	Assessment-Related Provisions
Improving America's Schools Act (Title I)	1994	". . . high-quality, yearly student assessments . . . that will be used as the primary means of determining the yearly performance of each local educational agency and school served under this part in enabling all children served under this part to meet the State's student performance standards. (A) Such assessments shall be the same assessments used to measure the performance of all children, if the State measures the performance of all children (F) . . . provide for the participation in such assessments of all students (i)." [Sec. 1111 (b) (3) (A) (F) (i)]

"A State educational agency shall – . . . publicize and disseminate to local educational agencies, teachers and other staff, parents, students, and the community the results of the State review, including statistically sound results, as required by section 1111 (b) (3) (1)." [Sec. 116 (d) (1) (B)]

". . . enable results to be disaggregated with each State, local educational agency, and school by . . . students with disabilities as compared to nondisabled students. . . ." [Sec. 1111 (b) (3) (I)] |
| Individuals with Disabilities Education Act (IDEA) | 1997 | "Children with disabilities are included in general State and district-wide assessment programs, with appropriate accommodations, where necessary." [Sec. 612 (a) (17) (A)]

"As appropriate, the State or local educational agency develops guidelines for the participation of children with disabilities in alternate assessments for those children who cannot participate in State and district-wide assessment programs." [Sec. 612 (a) (18) (A) (i)]

"The national assessments shall examine how well schools, local educational agencies, States and other recipients of assistance under this Act . . . including improving the performance of all children with disabilities in general scholastic activities and assessments as compared to nondisabled children; providing for the participation of children with disabilities in the general curriculum." [Sec. 673 (b) (3) (A) (B)]

"The State educational agency makes available to the public, and reports to the public with the same frequency and in the same detail as it reports on the assessment of nondisabled children, the following: the |

(continued)

TABLE 3.2 ■ (cont.)		
Federal Law	**Year Enacted**	**Standards-related Provisions**
		number of children with disabilities participating in regular assessments. The number of those children participating in alternate assessments. The performance of those children on regular assessments (beginning not later than July 1, 1998) and on alternate assessments (not later than July 1, 2000), if doing so would be statistically sound and would not result in the disclosure of performance results identifiable to individual children." [Sec. 612 (a) (17) (B) (i) (ii) (iii) (I) (II)]

Ysseldyke, 1995b). And, by the end of the century, all states with active assessment systems have written policies about participation in assessments (Thurlow, House, Boys, Scott, & Ysseldyke, 2000).

IDEA also required that states begin the development and implementation of alternate assessments, to be used with students unable to participate in the general state assessment. This would mean that every student with a disability would be included in some type of state or districtwide assessment. The first known alternate assessment was developed in Kentucky, in response to the Kentucky Educational Reform Act (KERA) (Ysseldyke, Thurlow, Erickson, Gabrys, et al., 1996). In Kentucky, the alternate assessment is a portfolio system, designed to be consistent with portfolio assessments used with other students.

As states neared the time when they were to have alternate assessments in place, most states had developed something (Thompson & Thurlow, 2000). As might be expected, however, states were at a variety of stages in their development process. Similarly, they had taken many different approaches in their alternate assessments (see Figure 1). This might be expected, since their general assessments were also quite varied in purpose and characteristics (Olson, Bond, & Andrews, 1999).

With the development of alternate assessments, it would be expected that all students with disabilities now will be included in each state's assessment system. The same should be true for district-wide assessments, although the extent to which this has happened is still unclear. The expectation that all students would be included in state and district assessments was made clear in an answer about alternate assessments given in a question-and-answer memo prepared for states by the Office of Special Education Programs (Heumann & Warlick, 2000):

> **12. Do the requirements to establish participation guidelines for alternate assessments and to develop alternate assessments apply to both SEAs and LEAs?**
>
> Yes. 34 CFR §300.138 specifically requires inclusion of children with disabilities in both State and district-wide assessment programs and requires

both the SEA and the LEA, as appropriate, to develop guidelines for the participation of children with disabilities in alternate assessments for those children who cannot participate in State and district-wide assessments, and develop alternate assessments.

Of course, if an LEA does not conduct district-wide assessments other than those that are part of the State assessment program, then the LEA would follow SEA guidelines and use the SEA alternate assessment(s). The requirements apply to district-wide assessments regardless of whether or not there is a State assessment. (Heumann & Warlick, 2000, p. 10)

Assessment Accommodations

Participation of students with disabilities in general state and district-wide assessments is intimately linked to the availability of accommodations for students with disabilities. Accommodations are "changes in testing materials or procedures that enable students with disabilities to participate in an assessment in a way that allows abilities to be assessed rather than disabilities" (Thurlow, Elliott, & Ysseldyke, 1998, pp. 28–29). More specifically, accommodations generally are considered to include changes in presentation, response, timing, scheduling, setting, and other aspects of the testing situation. A few examples of each of these are shown in Table 3.3.

For some time, researchers and others suspected that by allowing accommodations (or more accommodations than before), the participation rates of students with disabilities in assessments probably would increase (Thurlow, Elliott, & Ysseldyke, 1998; Ysseldyke, Thurlow, McGrew, & Shriner, 1994; Ysseldyke, Thurlow, McGrew, & Vanderwood, 1994). A study commissioned by the National Center for

---

TABLE 3.3 ■ Examples of Accommodations

Setting	Presentation
Study carrel	Repeat directions
Special lighting	Larger bubbles on multiple-choice questions
Separate room	Sign language presentation
Individualized or small group administration	Magnification device

Timing	Response
Extended time	Mark answers in test booklet
Frequent breaks	Use reference materials (e.g., dictionary)
Unlimited time	Word process writing sample

Scheduling	Other
Specific time of day	Special test preparation techniques
Subtests in different order	Out-of-level test

Education Statistics (Anderson, Jenkins, & Miller, 1996) showed empirically that this was true. A special study using the National Assessment of Educational Progress (NAEP), which is used as a report card for the country, evaluated whether participation rates would increase with the availability of accommodations. Reporting on the findings of that study, Mazzeo, Carlson, Voekl, and Lutkus (2000) noted that the participation rates did not increase as a result of changing inclusion criteria, but did increase when some accommodations were available during testing.

Although convincing evidence now exists that providing accommodations increases the participation of students with disabilities, accommodations remain controversial. This is a result, in part, of concerns that accommodations provide students who use them with an advantage that other students do not have. It also is related to some specific accommodations linked to the constructs being assessed (e.g., reading to the student a test of decoding skills), and therefore may produce invalid or noncomparable scores (e.g., Koretz, 1997).

Despite these concerns, state policies on accommodations have changed dramatically. In 1991, when NCEO first requested information from states about accommodations, fewer than half the states had written policies or guidelines (Shriner & Thurlow, 1992). In 1993, 21 states had written guidelines (Thurlow, Ysseldyke, & Silverstein, 1993), and by 1995, 38 states had them (Thurlow, Scott, & Ysseldyke, 1995a). By 1999, all states with state-level assessments had written policies or guidelines about the use of accommodations during state assessments (Thurlow, House, Boys, Scott, & Ysseldyke, 2000).

Although information about allowed accommodations existed (see also Olson et al., 1999), this information did not reflect the extent to which students with disabilities were using accommodations. NCEO had encouraged states to collect data on the use of accommodations, and by the end of the decade, several states had these data (Elliott, Bielinski, Thurlow, DeVito, & Hedlund, 1999; Thompson & Thurlow, 1999; Trimble, 1998). The data were very revealing (see Table 3.4) because variability in the use of accommodations was so great from state to state. In one state the use of accommodations at a particular grade level was less than 8% of the students; in another state the use of accommodations at a particular grade level was more than 80% of the students (Thompson & Thurlow, 1999). These data hint at the confusion surrounding the term "accommodation," the way in which accommodations are counted, and differences in beliefs about the appropriateness of using accommodations.

Confusion About What an "Accommodation" Is

Terminology has plagued our understanding of accommodations. *First,* different terms are sometimes used to mean the same thing. Thus, in some states acceptable testing changes are called accommodations, in others they are called modifications, and in others they are called adaptations. *Second,* the same term may be used to mean different things. For example, in some states and districts the term "modification" refers to an acceptable change in the test itself, such as a braille or large-print version. In other states and districts the term "modification" is used to mean a

TABLE 3.4 ■ State-Reported Levels of Use of Accommodations

State	Assessment/ Subject Area	Elementary Grades (K–5)	Middle School Grades (6–8)	High School Grades (9–12)
Florida	FL Writing Assessment	51%(Gr 4)	39% (Gr 8)	34% (Gr 10)
	FCAT (Reading)	47% (Gr 4)	38% (Gr 8)	40% (Gr 10)
	FCAT (Math)	50% (Gr 5)	38% (Gr 8)	39% (Gr 10)
Indiana	Statewide Assessment - Math	28% (Gr 3)	34% (Gr 6) 38% (Gr 8)	80% (Gr10)
	English/Language Arts	29% (Gr 3)	34% (Gr 6) 38% (Gr 8)	82% (Gr 10)
Kansas	KS Assessment Program – Math	21% (Gr 4)	14% (Gr 7)	08% (Gr 10)
	Reading	19% (Gr 3)	13% (Gr 7)	08% (Gr 10)
	Writing	23% (Gr 5)	17% (Gr 7)	09% (Gr 10)
Kentucky	Kentucky Core	82% (Gr 4)	72% (Gr 7)	50% (Gr 10)
	Content Test	82% (Gr 5)	70% (Gr 8)	57% (Gr 11)
				55% (Gr 12)
Massachusetts	Comprehensive Assessment System	61% (Gr 4)	38% (Gr 8)	25% (Gr 10)
Maryland	MSPAP—Reading	53% (Gr 3)	25% (Gr 8)	
		51% (Gr 5)	16% (Gr 8)	
	Language Usage	44% (Gr 3)		
		41% (Gr 5)		
	Math	20% (Gr 3)		
Nevada	Terra Nova Complete Battery	51% (Gr 4)	42% (Gr 8)	44% (Gr 10)
New York	PEP Test—Reading	50% (Gr 3)	50% (Gr 6)	
	Math	31% (Gr 3)	32% (Gr 6)	
	Writing	33% (Gr 5)		
Pennsylvania	Reading and Math Assessment	67% (Gr 5)	52% (Gr 8)	45% (Gr 11)
Rhode Island	Writing Performance Assessment	49% (Gr 3)	55% (Gr 7)	60% (Gr 10)
	Health Performance Assessment	39% (Gr 5)	61% (Gr 9)	
South Dakota	Stanford Achievement Test (Language, Math, Reading, Science, Social Science)	63% (Gr 2) 67% (Gr 4)	59% (Gr 8)	46% (Gr 11)
West Virginia	SAT 9—Language, Math, Reading, Science, Social Studies	64% (Gr 3–11)		

Source: From *1999 State Special Education Outcomes,* by S. J. Thompson & M. L. Thurlow (Minneapolis: University of Minnesota, 1999), Table 7: Percent of Students Receiving Special Education Services Who Used Testing Accommodations, reprinted by permission of the National Center on Educational Outcomes.

change that is not acceptable—a change that may compromise the construct being assessed (such as reading a test to a student that is designed to assess reading decoding skills).

Confusion About Which Accommodations To Count

Given the variability in terminology, it should be apparent that states and districts think about different accommodations in different ways. For example, if State A counts using a pencil holder or a slantboard on the desk as an accommodation, but State B does not, there will certainly be a difference in the number of students counted as using accommodations, and in the number of accommodations used during a test. This scenario reflects the current status of states that are tracking the use of accommodations. Some states are counting only those changes in testing about which they have concerns. Other states are counting all changes in the testing, regardless of whether they were considered to be perfectly acceptable or ones that challenged the meaningfulness of scores obtained when they were used.

Differences in Beliefs About the Appropriateness of Accommodations

Remaining at the core of confusion about how accommodations interact with the participation of students who have disabilities in assessments is an array of beliefs about the acceptability of either specific accommodations or accommodations in general. Clear evidence of these differences exists in the written policies and guidelines that states have developed. Although all states with assessments now have written information about which accommodations are allowed, the specific accommodations allowed and not allowed vary tremendously.

The variation extends beyond that expected from the different tests that states use. Even in states using the same test, accommodations on the allowed and not-allowed lists are different (Thurlow, House, Boys, Scott, & Ysseldyke, 2000). This indicates, in part, that the policies are not based on research findings about the appropriateness of specific accommodations.

In fact, test developers are just beginning to address accommodations issues (e.g., CTB McGraw-Hill, 2000). For many years, information on the accommodations that students could use when taking the major achievement tests used by districts and states (e.g., California Achievement Test, Iowa Test of Basic Skills, Metropolitan Achievement Test, Stanford Achievement Test) was either nonexistent or very limited (see summary in Thurlow, Elliott, & Ysseldyke, 1998). Today, a host of research efforts is underway to address the effects of specific accommodations on score comparability, as well as the decision-making process to identify specific accommodations needed by individual students. Many of these efforts are funded either by the Office of Special Education Programs (OSEP) or the Office of Educational Research and Improvement (OERI). In addition, several additional research efforts are emerging, often supported by states as they struggle with their own policies on accommodations.

Reporting of Assessment Results

Simply having students with disabilities take tests, with the accommodatons they need, is not enough to provide students with the benefits to be derived from standards-based reform. The importance of reporting the performance results of students with disabilities emerged as another critical aspect of including students with disabilities in standards-based reforms (Erickson, Ysseldyke, Thurlow, & Elliott, 1997). Although changes in individual programs may result from providing large-scale assessment information to teachers and parents, public reporting is what prompts programmatic improvements (Elmore & Rothman, 1999).

The first effort to determine the extent to which states reported on the performance of students with disabilities occurred just before the amendments to IDEA were enacted (Thurlow, Langenfeld, Nelson, Shin, & Coleman, 1998). The amendments required states to publicly report on the performance of students with disabilities in the same way and with the same frequency as they reported on the performance on other students.

This analysis, based on 1996 state reports, indicated that only 11 states provided test-based data on students with disabilities. Five of these states reported on the performance of students with disabilities in documents separate from those in which data on other students were presented.

Follow-up analyses, using state reports from 1998 (Ysseldyke, et al., 1998) and 1999 (Thurlow, Nelson, Teelucksingh, & Ysseldyke, 2000) showed meager increases—12 states in 1998 reports and 17 states in 1999 reports. The number of states publicly reporting will certainly increase in the next couple years, as data management, policy, and other issues are slowly resolved.

These data are important for a number of reasons, other than the importance of knowing how students with disabilities across the nation are performing. Besides confirming that, in general, students with disabilities are performing below their peers, the data open up avenues to exploring changes over time. Two such analyses have revealed important increases in the performance of students with disabilities over time in standards-based educational systems (Keller, 2000; Trimble, 1998). Other analyses have helped to identify how states can get better information when looking at trends in performance (Bielinski & Ysseldyke, 2000).

Accountability Systems

Accountability is one facet of standards-based reform that generates considerable emotion and controversy. Accountability systems can be focused either on the student (such as graduation exams and tests used to decide on promotion from one grade to another) or on the system (such as when schools are taken over, when staff members receive rewards, or when accreditation in based on student performance). State accountability systems vary in their approaches and in the consequences tied to them (Education Commission of the States, 1999).

Student Accountability

Holding the student responsible for his or her performance on state and district tests is increasing in popularity among governors and legislators. At the same time, concern about including students with disabilities in assessments is heightened because of these kinds of assessments (Thurlow, in press; Thurlow & Johnson, 2000). There is concern about large numbers of students with disabilities not passing these tests, and thereby being relegated to a pathway that is sure to lead to dropping out of school or eventually having poor prospects for employment and post-secondary training (Thurlow & Johnson, 2000). Despite numerous warnings that systems should be held accountable for student learning and have their systems in place for ensuring equal opportunity to learn to all students (Heubert & Hauser, 1999), this has not stopped the proliferation of these tests (see American Federation of Teachers, 1999; Guy, Shin, Lee, & Thurlow, 1999).

Guy et al. (1999) explored states' graduation requirements and found a confusing array of requirements designed specifically for students with disabilities, even in states using graduation exams. This confusion is exemplified not only in variations in course requirements and testing requirements for students with disabilities—in some states but not in others—but also in an array of diploma options, from IEP diplomas, special education diplomas, and modified diplomas to the same diploma but different documentation on transcripts.

In an NCEO report (Thurlow & Thompson, 2000), we highlighted these variations and related some thoughts about how all students can have access to the same array of diploma options (see Table 4). Unfortunately, this does not represent what is happening in most states.

High stakes exams that punish or reward students are going to continue to be a controversial topic until it is clear that all students have equal opportunity to learn. Court cases are addressing these issues now with increasing frequency (e.g., Olson, 2000), and the number of cases of this nature probably will continue to increase until some of the issues surrounding appropriate opportunity to learn for all students are adequately addressed.

Systems Accountability

When consequences are significant, complex formulas often are used to determine how accountability scores are calculated for schools and districts. Yet, these formula are not accessible to the public (Krentz, Thurlow, & Callender, 2000). Further, finding out how students with disabilities are included (or not) in these formula was nearly impossible. Some states do have clear information, often because their state legislatures have required it. The goal of the Improving America's School Act, of course, is that all students are to be included in the accountability system.

Because students with disabilities now are included in the assessments that form the basis of most accountability systems, we should expect to begin to see clear evidence of their inclusion in this component of standards-based reform. Through their inclusion in the accountability system, states and districts will begin to see the importance of ensuring that their instructional programs and placements are the best they can be.

Teaching and Learning

When the discussion turns to assessments and accountability systems, perhaps the most important elements of standards-based reform—teaching and learning—are often forgotten. It is important to remember that the impetus for standards-based reform was the desire to improve teaching and learning so all students could demonstrate the knowledge and skills needed in the global economy of today and the future.

With the emphasis given to assessments as the measures of whether students were achieving standards, several unintended consequences of standards-based reforms began to emerge. One was the tendency for the curriculum to narrow—to focus only on the knowledge and skills included in assessments (Heubert & Hauser, 1999; Linn, 2000; Linn & Herman, 1997; Shepard, 1991). Although some states argued that narrowing of the curriculum was appropriate if the test was measuring the appropriate standards, there continues to be concern about teaching to the test, and teaching students only how to take tests better—not to gain a broad knowledge base and set of skills that will be reflected in higher test performance (Heubert & Hauser, 1999; Kohn, 2000; Shepard, 1991).

Beyond this, when looking at state standards, it soon became apparent that not all standards were the same. Some states had relatively broad standards such as, "Students compare patterns of change and constancy in systems," whereas others had quite narrow standards such as, "Students describe the basic processes of photosynthesis and respiration and their importance to life" (examples from states cited in American Federation of Teachers, 1996). The extent to which standards are broad or narrow affects the nature of the curriculum for students with disabilities, particularly those who may be determined to be eligible to participate in the assessment system through the alternate assessment.

Discussions about how broad or narrow standards are is particularly relevant when considering the curriculum for students with disabilities. In the early 1990s the National Center on Education Outcomes devoted considerable time, and involved hundreds of stakeholders, in efforts to identify the important outcomes of education for students with disabilities (Ysseldyke, Thurlow, & Gilman, 1993a, 1993b, 1993c, 1993d; Ysseldyke, Thurlow, & Erickson, 1994a, 1994b). The outcome models that were developed were for all students, since the broad group of stakeholders kept all students in mind as the outcomes were developed. They reflected broad domains, including Presence & Participation, Accommodation and Adaptation, Physical Health, Social/Emotional Adjustment, Independence & Responsibility, Contribution & Citizenship, and Satisfaction, as well as Academic & Functional Literacy (see also Ysseldyke, Krentz, Elliott, Thurlow, Erickson, & Moore, 1998).

Regardless of what kinds of standards the states developed, however, state assessments tended to focus on material that was easy to test. The tendency not to use performance assessments, but instead to consider extended response items to be a proxy for performance assessments, turned around the discussion once again to concerns about the nature of the curriculum that might be directed only to doing well on a test.

Although this concern about narrowing of the curriculum permeated education, its effects might be most devastating for students with disabilities, particularly those who might not be headed for college. Would students who were not eligible for the alternate assessment be short-changed because their curriculum focused only on academics, with little concern about ensuring that they were learning broader skills or being prepared for transition into the world of work? These were legitimate concerns as the focus on standards-based education continued into the new century.

Elliott and Thurlow (2000) identified several characteristics of a standards-based classroom:

> "Students know the standards and level of proficiency required," (b) Students are provided multiple opportunities to learn," (c) Student assignments reflect an integration of facts, concepts, and strategies," and (d) "Each assignment is an assessment in itself." (pp. 42-43)

They suggest that IEPs must be linked to standards—a concept that aligns with access to the general education curriculum—and that standards must be backmapped to instruction. Nowhere is there the implication that the purpose is to narrow the curriculum or teach to the test. In fact, time and again, researchers have verified the importance of teaching broadly, using the best instructional procedures available.

The themes about the importance of the instructional process and an appropriate, standards-based curriculum were echoed by the National Research Council's report (Elmore & Rothman, 1999), *Testing, Teaching and Learning: A Guide for States and School Districts*. The importance of "authentic pedagogy" (see Newmann & Associates, 1996) for all students was highlighted. The instruction involves higher-order thinking, deep knowledge, substantive conversation, and connections to the world beyond the classroom. Classroom studies find that these qualities are rarely present (David, 1997; Spillane, 1997).

The National Research Council report presented five recommendations for ways to ensure that instruction is appropriate for standards-based learning (Elmore & Rothman, 1999):

■ Schools and districts should monitor the conditions of instruction—the curriculum and instructional practices of teachers—to determine if students are exposed to teaching that would enable them to achieve the standards they are expected to meet.

■ Districts and schools should use information on the conditions of instruction to require and support improvement of instruction and learning in every classroom.

- Teachers should use the information on conditions of instruction in their classroom, along with data on student performance, to improve the quality of instruction. Districts have a responsibility to assist schools in collecting and using such information.
- Schools should use the information on the conditions of instruction to organize the time and resources provided to teachers and demand support from the district.
- Districts should use the information on the conditions of instruction to improve the quality and effectiveness of the resources and support they provide to schools for instructional improvement. (p. 77)

With evidence that students who are lower-performing are least likely to get equal access to a standards-based curriculum, and are more likely to receive poorer instruction (Bradley, 2000; National Association of State Boards of Education, 1998; U.S. Department of Education, 1995), curriculum and instructional issues are likely to remain among the most important for students with disabilities as the move into standards-based education continues.

LESSONS LEARNED ABOUT INCLUDING STUDENTS WITH DISABILITIES IN STANDARDS-BASED REFORMS

Just prior to passage of the reauthorization of the Individuals with Disabilities Education Act in 1997, the National Research Council conducted a study of students with disabilities and standards-based reform (McDonnell, McLaughlin, & Morison, 1997). One product of this effort was the development of a set of recommendations as follows:

Recommendation 1. States and localities that decide to implement standards-based reforms should design their common content standards, performance standards, and assessments to maximize participation of students with disabilities.

Recommendation 2. The presumption should be that each student with a disability will participate in the state or local standards; however, participation for any given student may require alterations to the common standards and assessments. Decisions to make such alterations must have a compelling educational justification and must be made on an individual basis.

Recommendation 3. The committee recommends strengthening the IEP process as the formal mechanism for deciding how individual students with disabilities will participate in standards-based reform.

Although these recommendations address critical topics, they do not highlight some of the key lessons that have been learned about including students with disabilities in standards-based reform. I share some of the key lessons here.

Participation in assessments is only the first step— it is an important step, but not the most important goal of standards-based reform.

Low expectations and the belief that students with disabilities should be protected from harm continue to characterize too many special educators, creating a great disservice to students who will have to function in employment and postsecondary settings when they leave school. Standards-based reform, of course, focuses on much more than just assessments. Key elements include the following:

- Goals (content standards)
- Indicators of success (performance standards)
- Measures of progress
- Reporting
- Consequences

The measures of progress are the assessments, clearly just one piece of the picture. The most critical piece is the notion that we provide all students with the opportunity to learn. For students with disabilities, this often means access to the general education curriculum first, then the provision of accommodations during instruction to ensure equal access to the general curriculum.

One of the notions behind participation in assessments is that we cannot know how students are progressing unless we have data to show us that performance. A common argument is that state and district assessments are not the best way to measure student performance, and that for students with disabilities, it is better to continuously measure student progress toward achieving the goals noted on their IEPs. This argument has created difficulties for special education because it has resulted in the field having little meaningful data on the performance of students (McGrew, Vanderwood, Thurlow, & Ysseldyke, 1995). And it has created a situation in which it is easy to think that everything is okay and that any amount of progress is all right. This is not the case. Most students with disabilities should be meeting the same high standards as other students. We are unlikely to realize this goal unless instruction is significantly ratcheted up and directed toward the learning needs of students who are receiving special education services.

Accountability is the key to standards-based reform for all students. Anecdotal evidence has been accumulating for some time about the expectations held for students receiving special education services. This evidence suggests that special educators have low expectations for students with disabilities. Some special educators also hold the attitude that they are more devoted to their students and know better than anyone else how to protect them and care for them. This attitude is a disservice to students with disabilities.

One of the advantages of standards-based reform is that it points out the inappropriateness of too much protection. It also begins to challenge the low expectations that have been held for many students with disabilities by showing what they know and can do.

Views on accommodations reflect attitudes—accommodations are a key part of access to assessments, yet they are shrouded in conflicting attitudes.

Views about accommodations perhaps are one of the most telling indicators of individual views about including all students in standards-based reforms. For years we have respected assessments that have sterilized the information we collect on students: Everyone must perform under exactly the same conditions so we then can compare them to each other. A standards-based system looks at progress toward standards; it is not about comparing students to each other. Yet, we are unwilling to give up the old model of assessment, which, of course, then makes it more difficult to be accepting of accommodations.

To some extent, views on accommodations seem to reflect tolerance for differences. They also reflect, to some extent, views on how people work as adults. Today increasing numbers of accommodations are provided as natural supports for individuals to be successful in employment settings. These accommodations, furthermore, often are provided to all employees, not just those who have disabilities. Should our assessment system not reflect the conditions under which we expect individuals to work after they have left the educational system—that is, with the availability of lifelong accommodations?

The extent to which students are using accommodations during assessments also highlights some instructional problems. When NCEO began to talk about needed assessment accommodations, the link to instructional accommodations was apparent. If students are surprised by being provided an assessment accommodation to which they have never been exposed before, it likely will be of little help, and may actually be a hinderance to performance. Most state policies on accommodations now refer back to what happens during instruction (Thurlow, House, et al., 2000). Yet, we find that teachers' knowledge about how to identify and use instructional accommodations is limited (DeStefano, Shriner, & Lloyd, 2001; Fuchs, Fuchs, Eaton, Hamlett, & Karns, 2000; Scott, Vitale, & Master, 1998).

Consequences create complications—incentives to exclude students continue to exist and often are bolstered by high stakes accountability.

Accountability or, rather, counting all students equally is going to be the force that drives forward the benefits of standards-based reform for students with disabilities. Until students with disabilities count in the same way as other students do, it is too easy to discount their performance, and in discounting, to ignore it and the instructional need it identifies.

IDEA 97 required that students with disabilities be included in assessments, and that their performance be reported publicly in the same way and with the same frequency as performance is reported for other students. Even though states are having difficulty meeting the reporting requirement (Thurlow, Nelson, et al., 2000), that requirement is not really enough. Today's schools are driven by accountability systems that produce significant rewards or sanctions for the schools (Education Commission of the States, 1999)—teachers receive cash awards, schools lose their accreditation, and so on—all on the basis of student performance. These systems existed in 40 states in 1999, and the number is likely increasing.

Children who count in these high-stakes systems are the ones who most likely will be attended to first. For this reason, students with disabilities must not only participate in assessments and have their scores reported, but their scores must count just like those of other students. Is this happening? Analyses (Krentz, Thurlow, & Callender, 2000) suggest that finding out who exactly counts in state accountability formula is difficult—if you can even find the formulas being used for accountability. This is a huge gap in ensuring that all students have exposure to high standards and that they benefit from educational reforms. Unfortunately, as in the past, the students most likely to be left out are those with disabilities (along with those students of limited English proficiency).

Policy has outpaced the technology of standards-based education and assessment.

Policies surrounding the participation of students with disabilities in assessments, their access to the general education curriculum, and their inclusion in Title I services and evaluation systems have moved forward rapidly during the past decade. The policies have moved forward so rapidly that educators are still catching up. But not only educators are having to catch up. The test development industry is having to catch up as well. Test developers and publishers have not retooled their assessment instruments either to be accessible to all students or to be standardized appropriately with all students (along with their accommodation needs) included.

Technology is beginning to catch up to policy. For example, CTB-McGraw Hill's (2000) guidelines on accommodations are way ahead of the current thinking of most test publishers, at least in comparison to the information provided on accommodations in their test manuals.

There still is a need to go farther, however. At the time that items are developed, all students should be considered. I suspect that if items were developed to be more accessible to all students, the need for accommodations would be less. In addition, at the time of item reviews, a trained disability representative should participate on the bias review team to identify any nonaccessible items the item developers produced. This person has to be trained so inaccessibility can be identified for the entire range of disabilities. NCEO currently is in the process of putting together a manual that could be used to train individuals for participation on bias review teams and that item developers also could use.

The bottom line—instruction!

This lesson regarding the importance of instruction probably has come through already in the other lessons I have identified. It is an important lesson, however, and deserves repetition. As we have come to realize that students must be included in standards-based reform and as we have pushed students into assessments from which they were previously excluded, we have taken many side trails (including cheating), in an attempt to avoid the most important path of all: Students must receive appropriate instruction, characterized both by access to the general education curriculum and by appropriate accommodations. The instruction must reflect high expectations and data-based instructional corrections. Students with disabilities must have access to all the remedial and honors programs to which other students have access.

We have come a long way in the past decade. Although there are indications of changes in instruction as a result of the emphasis on standards and participation in state and district assessments, we still have a way to go. As we proceed through the next decade, the challenge remains to move beyond simply participation to full-blown success through comprehensive, inclusive, standards-based education for all students.

REFERENCES

American Federation of Teachers. (1996). *Making standards matter 1996: An annual fifty-state report on efforts to raise academic standards.* Washington, DC: Author.

American Federation of Teachers. (1999). *Making standards matter 1999.* Washington, DC: Author.

Anderson, N.E., Jenkins, F.F., & Miller, K.E. (1996). *NAEP inclusion criteria and testing accommodations: Findings from the NAEP 1995 field test in mathematics.* Princeton, NJ: Educational Testing Service.

Bielinski, J., & Ysseldyke, J. (2000). Interpreting trends in the performance of special education students. Minneapolis: National Center on Educational Outcomes.

Bradley, A. (2000, Jan 13). The gatekeeping challenge. *Quality counts 2000: Who should teach? (Education Week),* 19(18), pp. 20, 22–24, 26.

Business Roundtable. (1996). *A business leader's guide to setting academic standards.* Washington, DC: Author.

CTB/McGraw-Hill. (2000). *Guidelines for using the results of standardized tests administered under nonstandard conditions.* Monterey, CA: Author.

David, J.M. (1997). *The role of standards-based assessment in schoolwide instructional improvement: Necessary, perhaps, but not sufficient.* Paper presented for New Standards Evaluation Steering Committee (cited in Elmore & Rothman, 1999 *Testing, Teaching and Learning,* p. 76.

DeStefano, L., Shriner, J.G., & Lloyd, C.A. (2001). Teacher decision-making in participation of students with disabilities in large-scale assessment. *Exceptional Children, 68*(1), 7–22.

Education Commission of the States. (1999). *Education accountability in 50 states.* Denver: Author.

Elliott, J.L., Bielinski, J., Thurlow, M.L., DeVito, P., & Hedlund, E. (1999). *Accommodations and the performance of all students on Rhode Island's performance* (Rhode Island Report 1). Minneapolis: University of Minnesota, National Center on Educational Outcomes.

Elliott, J.L., Erickson, R.N., Thurlow, M.L., & Shriner, J. (2000). State-level accountability for the performance of students with disabilities: Five years of change? *Journal of Special Education, 34*(1), 39–47.

Elliott, J.L., & Thurlow, M.L. (2000). *Improving test performance of students with disabilities on district and state assessments.* Thousand Oaks, CA: Corwin Press.

Elmore, R.F., & Rothman, R. (1999). *Testing, teaching, and learning: A guide for states and school districts.* Washington, DC: National Academy of Sciences.

Erickson, R.N., Thurlow, M.L., & Ysseldyke, J.E. (1996). *Neglected numerators, drifting denominators, and fractured fractions* (Synthesis Report 23). Minneapolis: University of Minnesota, National Center on Educational Outcomes.

Erickson, R., Ysseldyke, J., & Thurlow, M. (1997). Neglected numerators, drifting denominators, and fractured fractions: Determining participation rates for students with disabilities. *Diagnostique, 23*(2), 105–115.

Erickson, R., Ysseldyke, J., Thurlow, M., & Elliott, J. (1997). *Reporting educational results for students with disabilities* (NCEO Policy Directions 8). Minneapolis: University of Minnesota, National Center on Educational Outcomes.

Fordham Foundation. (2000). *The state of state standards 2000.* Washington, DC: Thomas H. Fordham Foundation.

Fuchs, L.S., Funchs, D., Eaton, S.B., Hamlett, C.L., & Karns, K.M. (2000). Supplementing teacher judgments of mathematics test accommodations with objective data sources. *School Psychology Review, 29*(1), 65–85.

Guy, B., Shin, H., Lee, S.Y., & Thurlow, M.L. (1999). *State graduation requirements for students with and without disabilities* (Technical Report 24). Minneapolis: University of Minnesota, National Center on Educational Outcomes.

Heubert, J., & Hauser, R. (1999). *High stakes: Testing for tracking, promotion, and graduation.* Washington, DC: National Academy Press.

Heumann, J.E., & Warlick, K.R. (2000, Aug. 24). *Questions and answers about provisions in the Individuals with Disabilities Education Act Amendments of 1997 related to students with disabilities and state and district-wide assessments* (Memorandum to State Directors of Special Education, OSEP 00-24). Washington, DC: Office of Special Education Programs.

Hofmeister, A.M. (1993). Elitism and reform in school mathematics. *Remedial & Special Education, 14*(6), 8–13.

Ingels, S.J. (1993). *Strategies for including all students in national and state assessments: Lessons from a national longitudinal study.* Paper presented at National Conference on Large-Scale Assessment, Albuquerque, NM. (ERIC Reproduction Service No. ED 363-645)

Ingels, S.J. (1996). *Sample exclusion in NELS:88: Characteristics of base year ineligible students; changes in eligibility status after four years* (NCES Technical Report 96-723). Washington, DC: U.S. Department of Education, Office of Educational Research and Improvement.

Ingels, S.J., & Scott, L.A. (1993). *Exclusion of students with barriers to participation in NELS:88—Baseline excluded students two and four years later.* Paper presented at annual meeting of American Educational Research Association, Atlanta. (ERIC Document Reproduction Service No. ED 360-371)

Keller, B. (2000, April 12). More N.Y. special education students passing state tests. Education Week on the Web (http://www.edweek.org/ewstory.cfm?slug=31ny.h19&keywords=new%20york).

Kohn, A. (2000). Burnt at the high stakes. *Journal of Teacher Education, 51*(4), 315-327.

Koretz, D. (1997). *The assessment of students with disabilities in Kentucky* (CSE Technical Report 431). Los Angeles: National Center for Research on Evaluation, Standards, and Student Testing.

Krentz, J., Thurlow, M., & Callender, S. (2000). *Accountability systems and counting students with disabilities* (Technical Report). Minneapolis: University of Minnesota, National Center on Educational Outcomes.

Linn, R.L. (2000). Assessments and accountability. *Educational Researcher, 29* (2), 4–16.

Linn, R.L., & Herman, J.L. (1997). *Standards-led assessment: Technical and policy issues for meaningful school and student progress* (CSE Technical Report 426). Los Angeles: University of California, CRESST.

Mazzeo, J., Carlson, J.E., Voekl, K.E., & Lutkus, A.D. (2000). *Increasing the participation of special needs students in NAEP: A report on 1996 NAEP research activities* (NCES Statistical Analysis Report 2000-473). Washington, DC: U.S. Department of Education, Office of Educational Research and Improvement.

McDonnell, L., McLaughlin, M., & Morison, P. (1997). *Educating one & all: Students with disabilities and standards-based reform.* Washington, DC: National Academy Press.

McGrew, K. S., Algozzine, B., Ysseldyke, J. E., Thurlow, M. L., & Spiegel, A. N. (1995). The identification of individuals with disabilities in national databases: Creating a failure to communicate. *Journal of Special Education, 28* (4), 472–487.

McGrew, K.S., Thurlow, M.L., Shriner, J.G., & Spiegel, A.N. (1992). *Inclusion of students with disabilities in national and state data collection systems* (Technical Report 2). Minneapolis: University of Minnesota, National Center on Educational Outcomes.

McGrew, K.S., & Vanderwood, M. (1993). *The identification of people with disabilities in national data bases: A failure to communicate* (Technical Report 6). Minneapolis: University of Minnesota, National Center on Educational Outcomes.

McGrew, K.S., Vanderwood, M., Thurlow, M.L., & Ysseldyke, J.E. (1995). *Why we can't say much about the statutes of status of students with disabilities during educational reform* (Synthesis Report 21). Minneapolis: University of Minnesota, National Center on Educational Outcomes.

National Association of State Boards of Education. (1998). *The numbers game: Ensuring quantity and quality in the teaching workforce.* Alexandria, VA: Author.

National Council on Education Standards and Testing. (1992). *Raising standards for American education.* Washington, DC: U.S. Government Printing Office.

National Council of Teachers of Mathematics. (1989). *Curriculum and education standards for school mathematics.* Reston, VA: Author.

National Research Council. (1993). *National science education standards.* Washington, DC: National Committee on Science Education Standards and Assessment.

Newmann, F.M., & Associates. (1996). *Authentic achievement: Restructuring schools for intellectual quality.* San Francisco: Jossey-Bass.

Olson, J.F., Bond, L., & Andrews, C. (1999). *Data from the annual survey: State student assessment programs.* Washington, DC: Council of Chief State School Officers.

Olson, L. (2000, May 31). Indiana case focused on special ed. *Education Week on the Web (http://www.edweek.org/ewstory.cfm?slug=38stateshl98keywords=Indiana%20special%20education).*

Scott, B.J., Vitale, M.R., & Master, W.G. (1998). Implementing instructional adaptations for students with disabilities in inclusive classrooms: A literature review. *Remedial & Special Education, 19*(2), 106–119.

Shepard, L.A. (1991). *Will national tests improve student learning?* Los Angeles: University of California, CRESST.

Shriner, J.G., Kim, D., Thurlow, M.L., & Ysseldyke, J.E. (1992). *IEPs and standards: What they say for students with disabilities* (Technical Report No. 5). Minneapolis: University of Minnesota, National Center on Educational Outcomes.

Shriner, J.G., & Thurlow, M.L. (1992). Special education outcomes 1991. Minneapolis: University of Minnesota, National Center on Educational Outcomes.

Spillane, J.P. (1997). *External reform initiatives and teachers' efforts to reconstruct their practice: The mediating role of teachers' zones of enactment.* Paper presented at annual meeting of Association for Public Policy Analysis and Management (cited in National Research Council, 1999, pp. 75-76).

State policy updates (2000, Jan. 13). Quality counts 2000: Who should teach? (Education Week), 19 (18).

Thompson, S.J., & Thurlow, M.L. (1999). *1999 State special education outcomes.* Minneapolis: University of Minnesota, National Center on Educational Outcomes.

Thurlow, M.L. (in press). Focusing on state and local assessments. *ALERTS.*

Thurlow, M.L., Elliott, J.L., & Ysseldyke, J.E. (1998). *Testing students with disabilities: Practical strategies for complying with district and state requirements.* Thousand Oaks, CA: Corwin Press.

Thurlow, M.L., House, A., Boys, C., Scott, D., & Ysseldyke, J. (2000). *State assessment policies on participation and accommodations for students with disabilities: 1999 update* (Synthesis Report 33). Minneapolis: University of Minnesota, National Center on Educational Outcomes.

Thurlow, M.L., & Johnson, D.R. (2000). High stakes testing of students with disabilities. *Journal of Teacher Education, 51*(4), 305–314.

Thurlow, M., Langenfeld, K., Nelson, J.R., Shin, H., & Coleman, J. (1998). *State accountability reports: What are states saying about students with disabilities?* (Technical Report 20). Minneapolis: University of Minnesota, National Center on Educational Outcomes.

Thurlow, M.L., Nelson, J.R., Teelucksingh, E., & Ysseldyke, J.E. (2000). *Where's Waldo? A third search for students with disabilities in state accountability reports* (Technical Report 25). Minneapolis: University of Minnesota, National Center on Educational Outcomes.

Thurlow, M. L., Scott, D. L., & Ysseldyke, J. E. (1995a). *A compilation of states' guidelines for accommodations in assessments for students with disabilities* (Synthesis Report 18). Minneapolis: University of Minnesota, National Center on Educational Outcomes.

Thurlow, M. L., Scott, D. L., & Ysseldyke, J. E. (1995b). *A compilation of states' guidelines for including students with disabilities in assessments* (Synthesis Report 17). Minneapolis: University of Minnesota, National Center on Educational Outcomes.

Thurlow, M., & Thompson, S. (2000). *Diploma options and graduation policies for students with disabilities* (NCEO Policy Directions 10). Minneapolis, MN: University of Minnnesota, National Center on Educational Outcomes.

Thurlow, M.L., & Ysseldyke, J.E. (2000). Standard-setting challenges for special populations. In G. Cizek (Ed.), *Standard setting on peformance assessments* (Ch. 12). Mahwah, NJ: Lawrence Erlbaum Associates.

Thurlow, M., Ysseldyke, J., Gutman, S., & Geenen, K. (1998). *An analysis of inclusion of students with disabilities in state standards documents* (Technical Report 19). Minneapolis: University of Minnesota, National Center on Educational Outcomes.

Thurlow, M. L., Ysseldyke, J. E., & Silverstein, B. (1993). *Testing accommodations for students with disabilities: A review of the literature* (Synthesis Report 4). Minneapolis: University of Minnesota, National Center on Educational Outcomes.

Trimble, S. (1998). *Performance trends and use of accommodations on a statewide assessment* (NCEO Assessment Series, Maryland/Kentucky Report 3). Minneapolis: University of Minnesota, National Center on Educational Outcomes.

U.S. Department of Education. (1995). *Teacher supply, teacher qualifications, and teacher turnover, 1990–91.* Washington, DC: National Center for Education Statistics.

U.S. Department of Education. (1999). *Peer reviewer guidance for evaluating evidence of final assessments under Title I of the Elementary and Secondary Education Act.* Washington, DC: Author.

Why Johnny stayed home. (1997, Oct. 6). *Newsweek, 130* (34), 60.

Ysseldyke, J., Krentz, J., Elliott, J., Thurlow, M., Erickson, R., & Moore, M. (1998). *NCEO framework for educational accountability.* Minneapolis, MN: University of Minnesota, National Center on Educational Outcomes.

Ysseldyke, J., Thurlow, M., & Erickson, R. (1994a). *Educational outcomes and indicators for grade 4.* Minneapolis: University of Minnesota, National Center on Educational Outcomes.

Ysseldyke, J., Thurlow, M., & Erickson, R. (1994b). *Educational outcomes and indicators for grade 8.* Minneapolis: University of Minnesota, National Center on Educational Outcomes.

Ysseldyke, J., Thurlow, M., Erickson, R., Gabrys, R., Haigh, J., Trimble, S., & Gong, B. (1996). *A comparison of state assessment systems in Maryland and Kentucky with a focus on the participation of students with disabilities* (Maryland/Kentucky Report 1). Minneapolis: University of Minnesota, National Center on Educational Outcomes.

Ysseldyke, J., Thurlow, M., & Gilman, C. (1993a). *Educational outcomes and indicators for early childhood (age 3).* Minneapolis: University of Minnesota, National Center on Educational Outcomes.

Ysseldyke, J., Thurlow, M., & Gilman, C. (1993b). *Educational outcomes and indicators for early childhood (age 6).* Minneapolis: University of Minnesota, National Center on Educational Outcomes.

Ysseldyke, J., Thurlow, M., & Gilman, C. (1993c). *Educational outcomes and indicators for individuals at the post-school level.* Minneapolis: University of Minnesota, National Center on Educational Outcomes.

Ysseldyke, J., Thurlow, M., & Gilman, C. (1993d). *Educational outcomes and indicators for students completing school.* Minneapolis: University of Minnesota, National Center on Educational Outcomes.

Ysseldyke, J.E., Thurlow, M.L., Langenfeld, K.L., Nelson, J.R., Teelucksingh, E., & Seyfarth, A. (1998). *Educational results for students with disabilities: What do the data tell us?* (Technical Report 23).

Ysseldyke, J., Thurlow, M., McGrew, K. S., & Shriner, J. G. (1994). *Recommendations for making decisions about the participation of students with disabilities in statewide assessment programs* (Synthesis Report 15). Minneapolis: University of Minnesota, National Center on Educational Outcomes.

Ysseldyke, J., Thurlow, M., McGrew, K., & Vanderwood, M. (1994). *Making decisions about the inclusion of students with disabilities in large-scale assessments* (Synthesis Report 13). Minneapolis: University of Minnesota, National Center on Educational Outcomes.

Ysseldyke, J.E., Thurlow, M.L., & Shriner, J.G. (1992). Outcomes are for special educators too. *Teaching Exceptional Children, 25,* 36–50.

Zlatos, B. (1992). Don't test, don't tell: Is 'academic red-shirting' skewing the way we rank our schools? *The American School Board, 191* (11, 24–28.

To Ensure the Learning of Every Child with a Disability

Richard W. Mainzer, Donald Deshler, Mary Ruth Coleman,
Elizabeth Kozleski, and Matty Rodriguez-Walling

Today, students with disabilities are identified earlier, attend school, graduate and go on to post-secondary education and jobs in larger numbers, and learn in more inclusive settings than ever in history (American Youth Policy Forum & Center for Education Policy, 2001). Special education outcomes have never been more positive. Too many students with disabilities, however, still do not graduate from high school, too many are excluded from challenging learning outcomes, too many do not successfully make the transition to independence, and too many end up living lonely, unproductive lives. These quality-of-life indices are inextricably linked to the quality of education that people with disabilities experience. Even though access to a free and appropriate education has been achieved, the educational quality of that experience remains problematic.

The progress that special education has made in its three brief decades of existence is remarkable. Nevertheless, in the same spirit of social justice and advocacy in which special education was born and nurtured, special educators continue to advocate for improvements in the education of students with exceptionalities (Kode, 2002). Today, rather than advocating for inclusion in public education, special educators are working within the general education community to gain genuine access for students with disabilities to the challenging educational results that most individuals in our society take for granted. The push for research-based practice and results-driven accountability is being compromised by a crisis within the special education profession: Special educators labor under work conditions that contribute to attrition rates in special education that are twice as high as those of general educators (NCES, 2000).

Recognizing this burgeoning problem, the Council for Exceptional Children (CEC) established a CEC Presidential Commission on the Conditions of Teaching in

Special Education. The Commission (Kozleski, Mainzer, Deshler, Coleman, & Rodriquez–Walling, 2000) identified three outcomes fundamental to ensuring high and challenging learning results for every exceptional learner:

1. Every student with an exceptionality receives individualized services and supports of caring and competent professional educators.
2. Every special and general educator has the teaching and learning conditions to practice effectively.
3. Every instructional leader establishes strong expectations for the use of effective and research-validated instructional practices.

Three years have passed since CEC published *Bright Futures for Exceptional Learners* (Kozleski et al., 2000). In this article, we review progress on the three outcomes and update the recommendations made in that report.

CARING AND COMPETENT PROFESSIONAL EDUCATORS

In describing the importance of systematic preparation programs, Darling–Hammond (1997) concluded: "Teacher preparation . . . is by far the strongest correlate of student achievement in reading and mathematics." There is consensus that a quality teacher is the single most important factor in students' learning. In the No Child Left Behind Act (NCLB, 2002), both houses of Congress and the Administration committed the nation to ensuring that every student with disadvantages has a "highly qualified" teacher. Well prepared, beginning teachers have mastered the essential knowledge and skills nationally validated by practicing professionals and aligned with state licensing requirements, including mastery of subject matter.

Knowing content is critical, as the choice of pedagogy is informed by the nature of the information to be taught. Because students with disabilities rely on special educators' intervention across academic content areas, special educators must have a working knowledge of a wide array of subject-matter content across the general curriculum. When deep understanding of a subject matter is critical to designing new curriculum or helping students acquire new skills, special educators routinely collaborate with appropriate subject-matter specialists and general educators to adapt the content to the individualized needs of their students. For some individuals with disabilities, special educators provide rich individualized curricula to foster successful and fulfilling growth and independence in students. In a very central way, pedagogy is at the heart of practice in special education. Special educators are responsible for effectively altering instructional variables to optimize the learning of students with exceptionalities in whatever curriculum is most appropriate.

The *Bright Futures for Exceptional Learners* was designed to stem the tide of unqualified and underqualified instructors teaching students with exceptionalities. Yet, 3 years after its publication, even more unqualified individuals are teaching the students who need the most qualified and skilled special educators. Today, approximately 40,000 individuals teach approximately three quarters of a million students without having met even minimum state licensing requirements (USDOE, 2001). Approximately one in every 10 individuals practicing as special education teachers is not minimally qualified (Carlson & Billingsley, 2001). Of all new special education teachers, 32% are not fully certified (Boe, Cook, Bobbitt, & Terhanian, 1998). The strongest correlate of students' performance on national assessments is the percentage of fully qualified teachers (Darling–Hammond, 1998). Achieving educational parity for students with exceptionalities seems even more distant today.

If special education is to achieve high-quality results for all students in special education, the nation must recruit and prepare greater numbers of motivated and committed special education teacher candidates. Further, the nation's teaching force is overwhelmingly female (88%) and caucasian (92%) while the ethnic and linguistic diversity of our communities grows (NCES, 2000). Improved life chances of students of color demand that the field recruit and retain qualified teachers of color to our classrooms in general and special education. Given that the attrition rate in special education is twice that of general education, we must implement policies that effectively encourage the good teachers we have to make special education teaching a career. Finally, most states need to increase the capacity of their preparation programs. Whether this is accomplished through well designed and documented alternative preparation programs or through statewide coordinated systems of higher education, the state must accept its dual responsibilities of program accreditation and individual licensure as the best guarantee to the community that its teachers are prepared for professional practice.

The unprecedented demand for special educators can distract us from issues of teacher quality with shortsighted solutions focusing on quantity over quality. Moreover, the Study of Personnel Needs in Special Education (SPENSE, 2000a) documented that the use of unqualified individuals is felt most keenly in districts that have the highest levels of poverty. Teachers earn less than any other profession with a similar level of college preparation (National Center for Educational Statistics, 1992). Compensation does make a difference. Careers in teaching must be competitive with other equally preparation-intensive professional fields. In addition, respect given to them must parallel that for other professions, and career ladders that make continuing classroom practice a respected and viable career option must be implemented.

It is not encouraging when the U. S. Department of Education regulations regarding NCLB permit individuals who have never taught a class to be called "highly qualified" by simply being enrolled in a preparation program (NCLB Improving Teacher Quality State Grants, 2002). Some states are implementing "quick fix" programs to increase the number of teachers they produce. These quick-fix alternative preparation programs lower quality standards by assuming that special educators can be prepared for professional teaching responsibilities in a matter of weeks. No Child Left Behind has laid the groundwork to eliminate the use of unqualified individuals teaching disadvantaged students. The upcoming reauthorization of IDEA must require states to ensure that all special education teachers are fully prepared and qualified. There are no short-cuts to attracting, preparing, and retaining a sufficient cohort of caring and competent teachers. "Quick fixes" only exacerbate problems of both quantity and quality, and some data indicate that individuals prepared in these programs leave the profession at higher rates (Barry, 2003). Setting and holding rigorous expectations for quality is the only way to genuinely encourage individuals to select special education teaching as an initial or second career.

In other professions, practicing without a license is illegal. Teachers should be held to the same standard. Unprepared, and therefore unqualified, individuals should not be allowed to assume the mantle of professional teachers. Perhaps the most insidious deceit is that, in allowing unqualified people to practice as special educators, parents and community members are led to believe that children are receiving the educational supports and services they need to succeed. The special education profession must demand that all teachers demonstrate their competence to teach through robust teacher-preparation and rigorous licensure standards.

States also must assure that programs that prepare special educators meet rigorous national accreditation standards that require the programs to demonstrate what their teachers in training learn, not simply what they were taught or how many courses they took. In combination, program accreditation and individual licensing provide parents and the community the best assurance that the teacher possesses the nationally recognized knowledge and skill to practice safely and effectively.

Comprehensive Coordinated Workforce Planning

The severe and chronic shortage of special education teachers is well documented (ERIC, 2001, Carlson & Billingsley, 2001; USDOE, 2001); 98% of the nation's school districts are reporting shortages (AAEE, 1999). Many state agencies do not know how many new special educators are prepared within the state each year, or how many positions will become vacant each year. The answers to a myriad of important questions depend on the use of complex, comprehensive workforce planning models. If states are to assure a sufficient supply of well qualified educators, the stakeholder agencies, including school districts and preparation programs within states, must actively develop and implement coordinated comprehensive workforce-planning models in which the needs of all parties are considered.

Because states retain primary responsibility for education, the repair and transformation of the serious shortages of qualified teachers requires swift and effective policy implementation in each state. States must work with their local school systems to develop recruitment packages that will attract academically competent college students to careers in teaching. These packages must develop competitive salary scales that encourage well educated college graduates to choose teaching as well as law, medicine, and architecture as a respected and well compensated career. This means that states must develop and implement coordinated recruiting campaigns, unified job information banks, and streamlined application processes. Every state should establish a workforce-planning group made up of the stakeholders with the staff and resources to analyze, develop strategies, and disseminate their findings widely to the public regarding concerns such as:

- The extent to which the state infrastructure can provide the teachers and teacher educators needed over a forecast period
- Effective and ineffective strategies to retain teachers
- Effective and ineffective strategies to recruit a sufficient cohort of diverse teachers at both career entry, and mid-career points
- The extent to which special resources and strategies are needed to address specific situations (e.g., urban districts, preparation of teachers for low-incidence populations)
- Effective and ineffective models for career ladders in classroom teaching and the extent to which they are implemented across the state
- Effective and ineffective models for attracting paraeducators into special education and the extent to which they are implemented across the state
- Effective and ineffective models for induction and mentoring and the extent to which they are implemented across the state
- Effective and ineffective models for licensing entry level and advanced teachers and the extent to which they are implemented across the state.

If states are to begin to address the shortage of special education teachers, they must systematically collect the complex information to provide strategies to these and other complex questions. In addition, states must do all of this publicly, in ways that allow for separation of the data so it is usable by local school districts and for subpopulations, as well as statewide. Every school district should be required to collect information on the conditions in which special educators practice, including role ambiguity, paperwork, caseloads and class sizes, teacher credentials, administrative training, professional development, salaries and their competitiveness compared to other professionals. They must also be expected to use this information as the basis for strategic recommendations to improve the conditions.

Professional Development

The survey conducted for Bright Futures for Exceptional Learners (Kozleski, Mainzer, Deshler, Coleman, & Rodriguez-Walling, 2000) found that expectations for meeting the needs of students with exceptionalities have changed dramatically over the years. These changes include greater responsibilities for classroom teachers, the need for collaboration between general and special educators, and the increased emphasis on high standards of learning for all students. The general education teachers expressed feelings that they had not been adequately prepared to meet exceptional students' needs in their preservice programs and concern that they were not being given enough professional development support to compensate for this.

Special educators' concerns were centered on their lack of preparation for their roles in collaboration and content-related teaching. Overall, the administrators said they were very satisfied that their professional development was adequate and in place, whereas the teachers said that they do not have the knowledge and skills they need and that they were not being given professional development to acquire them.

TEACHING AND LEARNING CONDITIONS TO PRACTICE EFFECTIVELY

If all children with exceptionalities are to achieve high and challenging learning outcomes, special educators must have working conditions that allow the use of strong and effective instructional interventions. When job responsibilities are ambiguously defined and the work conditions offer little support, it is not surprising that those who hold these jobs have high levels of stress and leave in large numbers, and that few new individuals are attracted to careers in these jobs (SPENSE, 2001a; Mandlawitz, 2003).

Paperwork

Over the past two decades, the paperwork requirements of IDEA have increased to a point at which paperwork significantly reduces the amount of time that special educators can spend on instructional time. In a national study of special education, SPENSE (2001b) corroborated the Bright Futures for Exceptional Learners finding that special education teachers report spending twice as much time as general educators on what they perceive as compliance-focused paperwork that interferes with instructional time and positive communication with parents and colleagues. Special educators also reported a lack of clerical support for routine paperwork tasks and inadequate access to technology to facilitate paperwork tasks.

Yet, school districts continue to spend millions of dollars per year on triplicate forms and expect special educators to complete lengthy and complex forms. Teachers today are expected to operate in an information-based, technology-driven environment with tools from the industrial age. Virtually all professional fields except special education have specially designed software to manage and organize their tasks and records. In a time when even the UPS delivery driver uses a computer to plan deliveries and the recipient can check the delivery status virtually from anywhere at any time, it is time that special educators have appropriate technology to ease the paperwork burden.

In many school districts individuals largely untrained in information management systems developed the forms for documenting special education decisions. The result is the fragmented paperwork that we have today. These poorly designed forms accumulate into inadequately conceived and fragmented systems. It is time that states take a leadership role in developing well conceived, coordinated, and technologically based documentary systems with their school districts. It is also time for policymakers to seriously consider how to reduce the litigiously oriented paperwork burden that has been placed on the shoulders of special educators. As Bill East, the director of the

National Association for State Directors of Special Education, put it, "It is time for parents and educators to take back control of education from the attorneys (Tschantz & Markowitz, 2002, p. 25)."

With well designed technological solutions, timely reports and forecasts can be generated with the touch of a key. IEPs that address the unique needs of each child can be developed efficiently. Special education records can be confidentially transmitted instantaneously. With this type of software, teachers can lift their eyes from the pile of triplicate forms and make plans to address genuine educational needs with their colleagues, parents, and students. Moreover, there is simply no reason to use the most important and expensive resource, the teacher, to manage routine record-keeping tasks. Every special education program should have the support of a clerical assistant specifically trained in special education records.

Role Definition

Special educators assume a wide array of responsibilities depending on the specific context of the school and the needs of the individuals. But this cannot overshadow the importance of role clarity. The relationship of role ambiguity and job stress is strong and convincing (Billingsley, 1991; Singh & Billingsley, 1996). Moreover, Gersten, Keating, and Harniss (2001) found that poorly designed jobs affect teachers in negative ways, leading to withdrawal in the job to eventually leaving the position or the field.

School districts must clearly design job responsibilities of each of the special education positions within the agency and communicate them to parents, general educators, and the community. These roles may include responsibilities, such as direct, intensive, explicit instruction of students, ongoing collaboration and planning with professional colleagues, supervision of clerical and other assistants, administration and analysis of various special assessments, and communications and collaboration with parents and other individuals involved in the student's instruction.

The difference between how administrators and teachers perceive the need for and availability of communication and time for collaboration is striking (Kozleski et al., 2000). General and special education teachers alike indicated that they must have more time for collaboration and more ways to establish clear communication with each other if they are going to be able to meet the needs of their students with exceptionalities. They believe that, given the changing expectations and roles, the need for intense and ongoing collaboration is greater now than ever. Yet, the administrators indicated that they are satisfied that teachers have what they need to appropriately communicate and collaborate to meet the needs of their students with exceptionalities.

Caseloads

Closely related to role definition and paperwork are questions about how many students with disabilities a special educator can reasonably be expected to serve and implement the individualized instruction and close collaboration that is essential to students with disabilities. In a study of burnout and job dissatisfaction among nurses, Aiken, Clarke, Sloane, Sochalski, and Silber (2002) found that in hospitals with high nurse-to-patient ratios, surgical patients experienced higher risk-adjusted 30-day mortality and failure-to-rescue rates, along with increased rates of burnout and job dissatisfaction among the nurses. Clearly, class size and caseloads may have important implications for the achievement of students with disabilities and implications for reducing job stress and high attrition among special educators.

The relation between class size and achievement in general education classrooms has been studied and discussed extensively over the past several decades (Goldstein & Blatchford, 1998, Wested, 1999, Odden, 1990, Glass & Smith 1979, Slavin, 1986). More than half of the states currently have initiatives to reduce class size (Russ, Chiang, Rylance, & Bongers, 2001; Wexler et al., 2001). Yet, research on caseload, class size, and achievement in special education is relatively rare. In a review of the research, Russ et al. (2001) found that larger caseloads negatively impact students' math and reading achievement, individualization is more likely to occur in smaller groups, student engagement and achievement increase with smaller group sizes, and high teacher attrition and large caseloads seem to be related.

Unfortunately, caseloads and class sizes in special education remain highly inconsistent from state to state and even district-to-district (Ahearn, 1995). One troubling trend is that states seem to be abandoning statewide guidelines by allowing school districts to set whatever caseloads and class sizes they choose. During the research for Bright Futures for Exceptional Learners, special educators in forums around the United States reminded the CEC Presidential Commission that it is more complex than just the numbers of students in a class or caseload. Factors such as the range of grade levels and subject areas for which they are responsible, and the variations in their students' exceptionalities, also must be considered.

In addition, the time it takes special educators to provide consultation must be factored. Beginning this year, CEC will develop national benchmarks for caseloads and class sizes, collect relevant state law or guidelines, actual caseloads, and class sizes by state for use by policymakers.

Administrative and Collegial Support

In the survey of general and special administrators and teachers for Bright Futures for Exceptional Learners (Kozleski, Mainzer, Deshler, Coleman, & Rodriguez-Walling, 2000), administrators and teachers reported very different perceptions of the conditions that teachers faced in the classroom. Teachers reported more difficulties with the conditions they face than the administrators perceived. Another concern expressed by special education teachers in the same survey was a feeling of isolation from their school and special education colleagues. Special educators commented on the general education teachers' frustration in teaching students with exceptional learning needs. The special educators went on to say that this frustration was projected onto the special education teachers. As a result, special educators who work with students with the most intense needs are left feeling as if they receive the least amount of support.

One of the key elements of job satisfaction and retention is a sense that what we do is understood and appreciated by those for whom we work. In the case of teachers, this is the perception that administrators and colleagues understand and support the effort that goes into teaching. Gersten et al. (2001) found that building-level support from school administrators and other colleagues has a strong and direct effect on all critical aspects of teachers' working conditions. When administrative and collegial support is in place, teachers tend to feel positive about their work. When this understanding and support is perceived to be lacking, however, there is a profoundly negative impact (Gersten et al., 2001). The striking differences in perception between the administrators and teachers participating in the survey about the conditions of teaching children with exceptionalities is troubling and corroborates teachers' anecdotal reports that administrators do not understand what teachers are faced with in today's teaching world. Given these differences, it may not be surprising that the one area surveyed in which administrators were more positive than teachers was in "satisfaction with their work."

School principals and assistant principals are assuming more responsibility for the special education and related personnel and services. As the instructional leader of the school, the school administrator must understand and be able to clearly communicate, to parents, the community, and other colleagues, the scope and purpose of special education services. It is no longer sufficient to prepare administrators with broad platitudes such as "All means all" or "Leave no child behind." To use a metaphor, training with broad platitudes is like getting to know the United States by taking a supersonic jet from coast to coast. A more apt metaphor is the need for a bus ride from coast to coast. If special education services are to be genuinely included in the school culture, prospective school administrators must be explicitly and deeply prepared in the supervision, development, and evaluation of special education and related services within the schools and in how to effectively address their responsibilities for the individuals with exceptionalities in their schools.

In addition, like other preparation programs, programs preparing school administrators should be accountable to demonstrate that their graduates have mastered the knowledge and skills to explicitly develop, supervise, and improve school-based special education programs and services. Programs that prepare school administrators must evaluate the depth and breadth of special education knowledge and skill they require. Moreover, school districts must offer targeted professional development opportunities for their existing school administrators.

STRONG EXPECTATIONS FOR EFFECTIVE VALIDATED INSTRUCTIONAL PRACTICES

One of the major findings of the *Bright Futures for Exceptional Learners* study was the often insufficient focus on student outcomes. This finding is especially troubling in light of some highly significant policy shifts and emphases in recent years and months. First, the reauthorization of IDEA in 1997 marked a major shift in the law's intent. For the first time, schools were explicitly directed to measure the outcomes achieved by students and to include students with disabilities in accountability systems. Prior to 1997, IDEA had focused largely on the processes and procedures to ensure that all students with disabilities would receive a free and appropriate education. Second, with the NCLB, passed in 2001 (NCLB, 2002) and the publication of *A New Era: Revitalizing Special Education for Children and Their Families* (2002), the emphasis on achieving positive outcomes for students outlined in IDEA 1997 was strongly underscored; however, the bar was set even higher for educators by NCLB in calling for students to be taught with "scientifically based instructional practices."

Indeed, one of the cornerstones of the NCLB (2002) that was passed is its call for educational practices to be grounded in "scientifically based research." In that particular bill, the phrase "scientifically based research" appears 111 times. A belief shared by the U.S. Congress and the Administration alike is that improved outcomes for students must be linked to educational practices solidly grounded in research. Effective and validated practices based on scientifically based research are expected to be a central feature in the reauthorization of IDEA in the coming months.

Given the importance of ensuring that any investments on behalf of individuals with disabilities yield optimal outcomes, it is encouraging to have legislative initiatives that deal with individuals with disabilities tied so closely to instructional practices that have been shown to make a difference in the performance of individuals. As encouraging as it is to have legislation espousing and even requiring the use of scientifically based practices, there is no guarantee that results in our nation's classrooms will change unless we seriously confront the broad array of issues involved in effectively translating promising research findings into practice.

For years, educational practice has been plagued by the infamous research–practice gap (e.g., Carnine, 1997; Elmore, 1996; Gersten, Vaughn, Deshler, & Schiller, 1997; Greenwood & Abbott, 2001; Kauffman, 1996; Kennedy, 1997; Robinson, 1998). Too often, research in special education has been limited to small-scale fragmented research initiatives. Simply because a line of research has demonstrated promise in small-scale studies is no guarantee that the innovation will stand up in large-scale initiatives or whether it can be successfully integrated into the array of responsibilities expected of teachers. Although encouraging results continue to emerge in small-scale research studies, they rarely are brought to scale and sustained over a sufficiently extended period in a broad array of settings and under differing conditions. Only when a so-called scientifically based practice has been shown to get results in a scaled-up and sustained fashion can we say that it is scientifically based. If the practice ends up sitting on the shelf in classrooms because it is too cumbersome or burdensome, we must question the overall value of its contribution and the standards that lead to it being labeled as "scientifically based." Unless an innovation has been proven effective and usable in frontline settings, researchers cannot legitimately claim that an innovation is scientifically based. In short, if questions of external validity have not been answered satisfactorily in a broad array of contexts, the claim of "scientifically based" is premature.

Is it sufficient for educators and administrators to focus solely on the use of scientifically based instructional practices to improve student outcomes? If it isn't sufficient, what else must be in place to make a significant difference? During the past 25 years five important factors have emerged in the professional literature that, when applied collectively, have a high probability of improving student outcomes. These five factors might be conceptualized in terms of a "student success formula." That is, the probability of student success is significantly increased to the extent that *each* factor included in the student success formula is present. These factors, illustrated in Figure 4.1, are: validated interventions, fidelity of implementation, coordinated implementation, strong administrative leadership, and quality professional development.

Validated Interventions

Consistent with the expectations of NCLB 2001 and the report of the Presidential Commission on Excellence in Special Education (2002), validated interventions must be viewed as the core element in bringing about significant student gains. In the absence of effective and validated instructional practices, the likelihood of gains is greatly diminished. The field of special education is markedly different today than it was when PL 94–142 was originally passed. Several instructional materials and

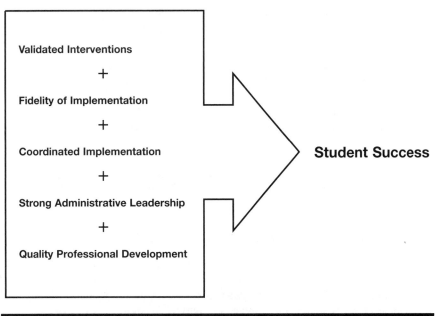

FIGURE 4.1 ■ Student Success Formula

practices have been validated. For example, through the support of the U.S. Department of Education, Office of Special Education Programs and the National Center for Learning Disabilities, several meta-analyses have synthesized the research in the following topics:

- Higher-order processing and problem solving (Swanson, 1999)
- Reading comprehension (Gersten, Williams, Fuchs, & Baker, 1998)
- Written expression (Gersten & Baker, in press)
- Grouping practices (Elbaum, Vaughn, Hughes, & Moody, 1999).

A review of these meta-analyses underscores the fact that special educators can call upon a significant array of validated instructional practices when designing programs for students with disabilities. Swanson (1999) found that the two most effective instructional programs for students with specific learning disabilities (LD) were *direct instruction* and *learning strategy instruction.* Although Swanson's meta-analysis of the intervention literature provides helpful direction to special educators, perhaps the most valuable part of this analysis is the types that Swanson found to operationally define each of these models. Specifically, teachers who used a direct instruction model were most frequently found to (a) break tasks into small steps, (b) administer probes, (c) supply feedback, (d) provide diagrams and pictures to enhance comprehension, and (e) provide ample independent practice. In contrast, teachers who implemented a learning strategies model were most frequently found to (a) provide elaborate explanations, (b) model learning processes, (c) provide prompts to use strategies, (d) engage in teacher-student dialogues, and (e) ask process-type questions. In short, the largest effect sizes in more than 270 intervention studies were produced when teachers incorporated instruction that was in alignment with these features.

In an article designed to summarize the prevailing messages in each of the meta-analyses cited above, Vaughn, Gersten, and Chard (2000) were able to draw several conclusions about existing validated instructional practice for students with disabilities. They found that the instructional practices that are visible and explicit, interactive between students and teacher and between students and students, controlled for task difficulty, and include strategies to guide student learning result in the greatest student achievement. The most pressing challenge, however, is to bring our level of implementation into alignment with what we know makes a difference for students with disabilities.

Fidelity of Implementation

The overall effectiveness of an intervention is tied closely to two factors: (a) how the intervention is designed and (b) how the intervention is taught. Fidelity of implementation is tied directly to the second factor. As defined in *Webster's,* fidelity means "strictness and thoroughness of performance, with exactness, with accuracy." Given the problems that many students with disabilities exhibit in information processing, teachers must carefully adhere to well established principles of learning and pedagogy, as well as strictly follow the instructional details outlined in intervention manuals or protocols.

When an intervention procedure is validated, it is taught according to a specified set of instructional guidelines. To reasonably expect similar results with a given intervention in "scaled-up" practice, the guidelines and principles of the intervention must be absolutely clear. An example of an instructional sequence that has been found to produce large effective sizes when teaching different learning strategies to students with disabilities to help them perform well in school has been validated by the University of Kansas Center for Research on Learning (CRL) (Deshler et al., 2001). This instructional sequence has been found to be sufficiently powerful to enable students with LD to learn strategies quickly and efficiently.

Eight stages comprise the instructional sequence (Ellis, Deshler, Lenz, Schumaker, & Clark, 1991):

1. Pretest and make acquisition commitments
2. Describe
3. Model
4. Verbal practice
5. Controlled practice and feedback
6. Advanced practice and feedback
7. Posttest and make generalization commitments
8. Generalization

Instruction within these eight stages is provided in the context of a learning apprenticeship (Hock, Schumaker, & Deshler, 1995) in which the teacher takes an active role in describing and modeling for students alternative ways to approach tasks in more potentially efficient and effective ways. As students begin to understand what being a strategic learner is all about, some of the scaffolding is removed and instruction shifts from an emphasis on teacher-mediation to an emphasis on student-mediation in the later stages of instruction (e.g., Deshler et al., 2001; Hock, Deshler, & Schumaker, 1993).

Validated interventions are generally successful because they are based on well established principles of learning and instruction. When implementation procedures for validated interventions are varied, they no longer follow validated procedure and the results on student performance are simply unknown. In short, implementation with fidelity is imperative to optimize student outcomes.

Coordinated Implementation

For students with disabilities to reduce the sizable deficits that characterize many of their profiles as learners, their instruction must be well coordinated in terms of the short- and long-term goals specified in their IEPs, as well as how the instruction is implemented and reinforced across teachers and settings alike. If the instruction is not clearly focused, carefully orchestrated, and precisely planned, the gains may be significantly reduced. First, an instructional plan must be conceptualized to systematically address the deficit areas targeted by the IEP. To do so, one skill or strategy has to be built upon another so students' overall competence in a deficit area is dramatically improved. As an example, if a student has significant deficits in written expression, the instructional plan specified by the IEP may call for intensive instruction in a validated scope and sequence of instruction in written-expression strategies including sentence writing, paragraph writing, theme writing, and error monitoring (Deshler, Ellis, & Lenz, 1996). If achieving these instructional goals takes more than one semester or academic year, alignment between instructional activities and IEP goals must be maintained to a high degree.

In addition, students with disabilities must receive instruction that is carefully coordinated across all of their teachers and different educational settings. This can be illustrated by considering a student with disabilities, Jason, who is in an elementary fifth-grade classroom. Jason has one teacher who is responsible for teaching all of his academic subjects and a special education resource services teacher who provides special education supports. Under this scenario, the fifth-grade teacher and special education teacher can readily collaborate and coordinate their instruction for Jason. The targeted skills or strategies that Jason is learning from the special education teacher should be ones that will help him respond successfully to the demands of the general education curriculum. In turn, the general education fifth-grade teacher can prompt and reinforce Jason's use of these targeted skills and strategies in each of the academic subjects and assignments throughout the school day.

When Jason moves from his elementary school to a middle school the following year, however, the challenge of collaboration among Jason's teachers around the coordination of his instruction across settings becomes much more challenging. The first step will be for Jason's fifth-grade teachers to collaboratively communicate with his sixth-grade special and general education teachers. More often than not, this communication link is not done well and the work with Jason in his new school is often unrelated to what occurred during the fifth-grade. Often the special educators, as case managers, have to take on the responsibility of forging strong communication links to ensure that the targeted skills and strategies in a student's IEP are continually stressed and practiced mastery will be a higher probability.

In the case of Jason, if his special education teacher were teaching him a vocabulary strategy to use in his classes, Jason optimally would master the strategy and see its relevance if *each* of his teachers would incorporate it into his or her classroom *and* set the expectation for Jason to apply the vocabulary strategy in all of his work in that class. When this type of collaboration and carefully coordinated instruction occurs across teachers and settings, it promotes learning, mastery and overall student success.

Strong Administrative Leadership

School administrators play a vital role in ensuring that each of the factors in the student success formula (see Figure 4.1) are in place. They can put the weight of their office behind the implementation of each factor in a variety of ways:

- They can advocate for funding from a variety of sources (e.g., the State, district, grants), set priorities, and restructure their budget allocations.
- They can ensure that research-based interventions are the focus of professional development activities.
- They can structure the professional development sequence to incorporate the four phases above.
- They can actively participate in all professional development activities.
- They can take an active role as instructional leaders by visiting classrooms, taking part in support team meetings, insisting that interventions be implemented, and ensuring that each staff member is accountable for student outcomes.

They also can ensure that the special educators have well defined roles that are clearly supported and communicated to parents and teachers. They can ensure that caseloads and other working conditions are in place so teachers can use validated and effective instruction, Finally, they can develop and implement schedules to optimize the communication and collaboration that is so critical to coordinating instruction.

Quality Professional Development

The vital role that quality professional development plays in improving students' outcomes has been repeatedly emphasized in the literature (e.g., Archer, 1999; Olson, 1997; Sanders, 1999). Professional development has to focus on changing instructional practice by ensuring that teachers use effective and validated practices. Further, equal attention must be directed to how professional development experiences should be conceptualized and delivered.

First, the content of staff development should emphasize instructional practices that are effective and validated. When a practice that does not have strong validation is recommended, it must be accompanied by clear and appropriate cautions. A research synthesis by Wang, Haertel, and Walberg (1993) provides direction regarding the kind of information around which professional development should be based. Their meta-analysis found that student learning was most affected when teachers focused instruction on key "proximal" variables such as students' self-regulation of their academic behavior, students' perseverance and enthusiasm for learning, the amount and quality of teacher–student interactions, and teacher modeling of appropriate academic behaviors.

Wang et al. (1993) found that proximal variables are more highly related to positive student outcomes than distal variables (i.e., variables not directly related to the student– teacher interactions, such as moving from a junior high school structure to a middle school structure). To achieve the greatest change in student performance, professional development programs should focus on proximal variables—those related to the instructional methods used with students with disabilities. The importance of focusing professional development on factors that lead to the largest student outcomes is especially important given Carnine's (1995) finding that the vast majority of interventions and materials that dominate current practice with students with disabilities are not validated.

Once the content of a professional development program has been chosen, the next issue is how to conceptualize and deliver the professional development program. To bridge the gap between research and practice—to make validated interventions available to teachers in a manner that will maximize their use over a sustained period and to impact student behavior in a positive way—professional development programs must be carefully structured. Several studies have identified ways to best provide professional development and enhance implementation rates. Most important, professional development must be viewed as a continuous process involving everyone in the school. Instead of participating in fragmented, one-shot sessions about a variety of topics, teachers have to participate in a planned sequence of learning sessions that they see as relevant to their role in the educational mission.

The professional development sequence must consist of at least four phases (Deshler & Schumaker, 1996; Ehren, 1999; Schumaker & Clark, 1990):

1. Initiation (to give basic information to potential implementers to help them determine the extent of appropriateness and alignment between the attributes of an innovation and existing instructional needs).
2. Learning and implementation (to give in-depth explanations, models, and practice and feedback).
3. Follow-up support (to back implementation efforts through coaching, troubleshooting, support-team meetings, and implementation refinement).
4. Maintenance (to establish the innovation within the system as routine).

CONCLUSION

Although the nation has made substantial progress over the last three decades in improving the education of students with disabilities, there is much left to do. The threefold focus laid out in Bright Futures for Exceptional Learners—that every child with exceptionalities receive individualized services and supports from competent and caring professionals; that special and general educators teach under conditions that support success; and that instructional leadership establish the expectation that effective and valid practices will be in place—provide the nation with the prerequisites to ensure that all children with exceptionalities achieve high and challenging learning outcomes.

The special education field will continue to lose its workforce without the active engagement of state and local policymakers who collaborate to ensure the following.

1. Robust teacher preparation programs must demonstrate that teacher education graduates develop content-area expertise, make professional judgments among research-validated practices to match student need to the appropriate

pedagogy, and use student performance data to continuously refine and improve their teaching practices.

2. Rigorous licensure standards have to be upheld even as states and local education agencies develop and refine alternative routes to licensure.

3. General and special educators alike are expected to modify, adapt, and accommodate their teaching practices to meet the educational needs of students with exceptionalities.

4. States and districts must develop information systems that relieve educators from the burden of excessive paperwork but maintain the original intent of the individualized educational program: accountability for results, effective and frequent communication with families, and clear expectations for what is to be learned.

5. States have to support local educational agencies by developing statewide recruitment and retention efforts designed to attract the most highly educated individuals to the teaching profession, emphasizing the importance of providing opportunities for children to learn from an ethnically, culturally, and linguistically diverse teaching force.

The issues and strategies presented here outline a blueprint for success. The responsibility to see that they happen is shared by educators, policymakers, families, and community members who all have a stake in the education of students with disabilities. Education is emancipation and therefore holds the greatest promise for enhancing the quality of life for each student, including those with the greatest need. During the next three decades the field can advance as much or more than it has in the past 30 years. It can be done if we have the collective will to do so.

REFERENCES

Ahearn, E. (1995). *Caseload/class size in special education: A brief analysis of state regulations.* Alexandria, VA: National Association of State Directors of Special Education.

Aiken, L., Clarke, S., Sloane, D., Sochalski, J., & Silber, J. (2002). Hospital nurse staffing and patient mortality, nurse burnout, and job dissatisfaction. *Journal of the American Medical Association, 288,* 1987– 1993.

American Association for Employment in Education. (1999). *Teacher supply and demand in the United States.* Evanston, IL: Author.

American Youth Policy Forum & Center for Education Policy (2001). *Twenty-five years of education children with disabilities: The good news and the work ahead.* Washington, DC: Author.

Barry, B., (2003). *Quality alternatives in teacher preparation: Dodging the "silver bullet" and doing what is right for students.* Chapel Hill, NC: Southeast Center for Teaching Quality. Retrieved on February 25, 2003 at http://www.teachingquality.org/resources/articles/silver bullet. htm

Billingsley, B. (1993). Teacher retention and attrition in special and general education: A critical review of the literature. *Journal of Special Education, 27,* 137–174.

Billingsley, B. (1991). Teachers' decisions to transfer from special to general education. *Journal of Special Education, 24,* 296–511.

Billingsley, B., & Tomchin, E. (1992). Four beginning LD teachers: What their experiences suggest for trainers and employers. *Learning Disabilities Research and Practice, 7,* 104–112.

Billingsley, B., Bodkins, D., & Hendricks, M. B. (1993). Why special educators leave teaching: Implications for administrators. *Case in Point, 7,* 23–38.

Boe, E. E., Cook, L. H., Bobbitt, S. A., & Terhanian, G. (1998). The shortage of fully certified teachers in special and general education. *Teacher Education and Special Education, 21,* 1–21.

Carlson, E., & Billingsley, B. (2001). *Working conditions in special education: Current research and implications for the field.* Paper presented at OSEP Project Directors' Conference, July 2001.

Carnine, D. (1995). The professional context for collaboration and collaborative research. *Remedial and Special Education, 16* (6), 368–371.

Carnine, D. (1997). Bridging the research-to-practice gap. *Exceptional Children, 63*(4), 513–521.

Darling–Hammond, L. (1992). Teaching and knowledge: Policy issues posed by alternative certification for teachers. *Peabody Journal of Education, 67,* 3, 123–154.

Darling–Hammond, L. (1997). *Doing what matters most: Investing in quality teaching.* New York: National Commission on Teaching and America's Future.

Darling–Hammond, L. (1998). Teachers and teaching: Testing policy hypotheses from a national commission report. *Educational Researcher, 27*(1), 5–15.

Darling–Hammond, L. (2000). "Teacher Quality and Student Achievement." *Educational Policy Analysis Archives, 2000.*

Deshler, D.D., Ellis, E. S., & Lenz, B. K. (Eds.) (1996). *Teaching Adolescents with Learning Disabilities: Strategies and Methods.* Denver: Love Publishing.

Deshler, D. D., & Schumaker, J. B. (1996). Getting research into the classroom. *Their World,* 16–18.

Deshler, D.D., Schumaker, J.B., Lenz, B.K., Bulgren, J.A., Hock, M.F., Knight, J., & Ehren, B.J. (2001). Ensuring content-area learning by secondary students with learning disabilities. *Learning Disabilities Research and Practice, 16,* 96.

Ehren, B. (1999). Language-sensitive SIM: Part 1. *Stratenotes, 7*(5), 1–8.

Elbaum, B., Vaughn, S., Hughes, M. T., & Moody, S. W., (1999). Grouping practices and reading outcomes for students with disabilities. *Exceptional Children,* 65, 399–415.

Ellis, E.S., Deshler, D.D., Lenz, B.K., Schumaker, J.B., & Clark, F.L. (1991). An instructional model for teaching learning strategies. *Focus on Exceptional Children, 24*(1), 1–14.

Elmore, R. F., (1996). Getting to scale with good educational practices. *Harvard Educational Review, 66*(1), 1–26.

ERIC Clearinghouse on Disabilities and Gifted Education (2001, April). *Educating exceptional children: A statistical profile.* Arlington, VA: Council for Exceptional Children.

Gersten, R., & Baker, S. (in press). Teaching expressive writing to students with learning disabilities: A meta-analysis. *Elementary School Journal.*

Gersten, R., Keating, T., & Harniss, M. (2001). Working in special education: Factors that enhance special educators' intent to stay. *Exceptional Children, 67,* 549–567.

Gersten, R., Vaughn, S., Deshler, D. D., & Schiller, E. (1997). What we know about using research findings: Implications for improving special education practice. *Journal of Learning Disabilities, 30*(5), 466–476.

Gersten, R., Williams, J., Fuchs, L., & Baker, S. (1998). *Improving reading comprehension for children with learning disabilities* (Final Report: Section 1, U.S. Department of Education Contract HS 921700). Washington, DC: U.S. Department of Education.

Glass, G. V., & Smith, M. L. (1979). Meta-analysis of research on class size and achievement. *Educational Evaluation and Policy Analysis, 1,* 2–16.

Goldstein, H. & Blatchford, P. (1998). Class size and educational achievement: A review of the methodology with a particular reference to study design. *British Educational Research Journal, 24,* 225–239.

Greenwood, C. R., & Abbot, M. (2001). The research to practice gap in special education. *Teacher Education and Special Education, 24*(4), 276–289.

Hock, M. F., Deshler, D. D. & Schumaker, J. B. (1993). Learning strategy instruction for at-risk and learning-disabled adults: The development of strategic learners through apprenticeship. *Preventing School Failure, 38*(1), 43–49.

Hock, M.F., Schumaker, J.B., & Deshler, D.D. (1995). Training strategic tutors to enhance learner independence. *Journal of Developmental Education, 19,* 18–26.

Improving Teacher Quality State Grants: Title II, Part A Non-Regulatory Draft Guidance, December 2002 (Question C-3). Retrieved on February 25, 2003 from http://www.ed.gov/offices/OESE/SIP/TitleIIguidance2002.doc

Kauffman, J. M. (1994). Places of change: Special education's power and identity in an era of educational reform. *Journal of Learning Disabilities,* 27(10), 610–618.

Kauffman, J. M. (1996). Research to practice issues. *Behavioral Disorders, 22*(1), 55–60.

Kauffman, J.M. (1999). Commentary: Today's special education and its message for tomorrow. *Journal of Special Education, 32*(4), 244–254.

Kennedy, M. M. (1997). The connection between research and practice. *Educational Researcher, 26* (7), 4–12.

Kode, K. (2002). *Elizabeth Farrell and the history of special education.* Arlington, VA: Council for Exceptional Children.

Kozleski, E., Mainzer, R., Deshler, D., Coleman, M., & Rodriguez– Walling, M. (2000). *Bright Futures for Exceptional Learners: An agenda to achieve quality conditions for teaching and learning.* Arlington, VA: Council for Exceptional Children.

Mandlawitz, M. (2003). *A tale of three cities: Urban perspectives on special education.* Washington, DC: Center on Education Policy.

McLeskey, J., Smith, D., Tyler, N., & Saunders, S. (2002). *The supply and demand of special education teachers: The nature of the chronic shortage of special education teachers.* Retrieved February 15, 2003 from http://www.coe.ufl.edu/copsse/PapersFiles/supplydemand.pdf

Miller, D., Brownell, M., & Smith, S. (1999). Factors that predict teachers staying in, leaving, or transferring from the special education classroom. *Exceptional Children, 65,* 210–218.

National Center for Educational Statistics, (1992). National adult literacy survey. In *The Condition of Education* 1995 (pp160). Washington, DC: Author.

National Commission on Teaching and America's Future. (1996). *What matters most: Teaching for America's future.* New York: Author.

No Child Left Behind Act of 2001 (2002). Retrieved on February 24, 2003 from http://www.ed.gov/legislation/ESEA02/107-110.pdf

Odden, A. (1990). Class size and student achievement: Research-based policy alternatives, *Educational Evaluation and Policy Analysis, 12,* 213–227.

Olson, L., "Keeping Tabs on Quality," *Quality Counts,* a supplement to *Education Week* (January 22, 1997).

Presidential Commission on Excellence in Special Education (2002). A New Era: Revitalizing Special Education for Children and Their Families. Washington, DC: Author.

Robinson, V. M. J. (1998). Methodology and the research-practice gap. *Educational Researcher, 27*(1), 17–26.

Rosenberg, M. S., & Sindelar, P. T. (2000). *The proliferation of alternative routes to certification in special education: A critical review of the literature.* Arlington, VA: Council for Exceptional Children National Clearinghouse for Professions in Special Education.

Russ, S., Chiang, B., Rylance, B., & Bongers, J. (2001). Caseload in special education: An integration of the research findings. *Exceptional Children, 67,* 161–172.

Schumaker, J. B., & Clark, F. L. (1990). Achieving implementation of strategy instruction through effective inservice education. *Teacher Education and Special Education, 13*(2), 105–116.

Singh, S., & Billingsley, B. (1996). Intent to stay in teaching: Teachers of students with emotional disturbance versus other special educators. *Remedial and Special Education, I 17,* 37–47.

Slavin, R. (1986). Best-evidence synthesis: An alternative to meta-analysis and traditional reviews. *Educational Researcher, 15,* 5–11.

Study of Personnel Needs in Special Education (2001a). Retrieved on February 25, 2003 from http://www.spense.org/scripts/tables/htdocs/ Table3_17.htm.

Study of Personnel Needs in Special Education (2001b). Retrieved on February 25, 2003 from *hours per week* http://www.spense.org/scripts/ tables/htdocs/Table1_79.htm.

Swanson, H. L. (1999). Instructional components that predict treatment outcomes for students with learning disabilities: Support for a combined strategy and direct instruction model. *Learning Disabilities Research and Practice, 14*(2), 129–140.

Tschantz, J., & Markowitz, J. (2002). *Policy forum: Special education paperwork*. Alexandria, VA: National Association of State Directors of Special Education.

United States Department of Education. (2001) *Twenty-third Annual Report to Congress on the Implementation of the Individuals with Disabilities Education Act*. Washington, DC: Author.

Vaughn, S. L., Gersten, R., & Chard, D. (2000). The underlying message in LD intervention research: Findings from research syntheses. *Exceptional Children, 67*, 99–114.

Wang, M. C., Haertel, G. D., and Walberg, H. J. (1993, Fall). Toward a knowledge base for school learning. *Review of Educational Research, 63*(3), 249–294.

Wested (1999, January). *Class size reduction: Great hopes Great challenges*. Retrieved on February 25, 2003 from http://www.wested.org/ cs/pol/view/rs/182

Wexler, E., Izu, J., Carlos, L., Fuller, B., Haywood, G. & Krist, M. (2001). *California's class size reduction: Implications for quality practice and implementation*. Retrieved August 23, 2001, from www.wested. org/policy/pubs/full-text/class-size/main.html

Special Education Teacher Supply and Teacher Quality: The Problems, The Solutions

Mary T. Brownell, Paul T. Sindelar, Anne G. Bishop,
Lisa K. Langley, and Seonjin Seo

Special education is facing the daunting challenge of increasing the supply of teachers while simultaneously upgrading its quality. Shortages of fully qualified teachers have plagued special education for two decades, and schools also have struggled to find qualified math, science, and ESL teachers. Shortages in all of these fields are likely to worsen as the teaching workforce ages and as statewide initiatives (such as reductions in class size) fuel increased demand. The quality of the teaching workforce also has come under scrutiny, as schools across the country are initiating standards-based reforms in which teacher competence is linked to student performance on high-stakes assessments.

In this chapter, we first consider two policy initiatives that address the dilemma of increasing numbers and improving quality simultaneously. We then consider the problem of attrition, which contributes in significant ways to both the quantity and quality issues. We explain why attrition is a particular problem for beginning teachers and describe programs that have proven effective in combating it.

In response to burgeoning demand and dissatisfaction with the quality of the existing workforce, the Bush Administration has promulgated policies to increase supply, notably through the No Child Left Behind (NCLB) Act, the most recent authorization of what had been known as the Elementary and Secondary Education Act. These initiatives are designed to promote easy entry to the profession via alternative training routes for specific populations of teacher candidates.

Previously, the National Commission for Teaching and America's Future (NCTAF) had issued a policy blueprint in 1996 that addressed shortages and quality in a different manner, emphasizing the professionalization of teaching and the enhancement of schools as workplaces. It was argued that fewer teachers would leave the field—and more candidates would be attracted to it—if they were to teach at schools that would support their work and foster their professional growth, and if they were to earn a professional wage.

NO CHILD LEFT BEHIND

No Child Left Behind (NCLB, 2001) is a policy package that focuses on statewide assessments, standards, and accountability. It also requires that all teachers be "highly qualified" by 2005–06, a challenge likely to necessitate dramatic change in state policy on teacher preparation and licensure. NCLB also lays the groundwork for such change. The act defines "highly qualified" teachers as individuals who hold full state licensure or who have a bachelor's degree and pass a state licensing examination. The emphasis in NCLB on alternative training routes is based upon the conviction that high-quality instruction places higher priority on content mastery than pedagogical training. Thus, teacher quality may be enhanced by attracting stronger candidates to the field. According to NCLB, stronger means better prepared in a subject area and having higher verbal ability.

The Administration has expressed its belief that formal teacher education programs have failed to produce the highly qualified teachers that NCLB demands and actually might discourage strong students from entering the field (U. S. Department of Education, 2002). Supply may be enhanced by facilitating entry to the profession. In NCLB, this is achieved by allowing states to develop alternative entry routes. The Administration has characterized traditional teacher education and licensure as imposing high barriers and tolerating low standards. By contrast, NCLB simultaneously eliminates barriers to entry and raises standards for teachers.

NATIONAL COMMISSION ON TEACHING AND AMERICA'S FUTURE

What teachers know also figures prominently in the National Commission on Teaching and America's Future (NCTAF) policy blueprint, but so does what teachers *do.* In this approach, teacher quality is fostered by program accreditation, initial licensure, and certification of accomplished practice. This approach recognizes the inadequacy of teacher education as it is commonly practiced today, but NCTAF advocates upgrading teacher education rather than fostering alternatives to it. In this plan, teacher quality is enhanced by improved professional preparation. In turn, improved professional preparation requires fundamental change in teacher education.

In "What Matters Most: Teaching for America's Future," NCTAF (1996) laid out a plan for teacher education reform. In it, teacher education is deferred until candidates receive bachelor's degrees. It emphasizes cognitive, social, and cultural foundations; a coherent program of mentoring and instruction, preferably at a professional development school; content pedagogy; and technology and teaming. Initial preparation is linked to high-quality professional development, and teacher practice in schools is organized to support their work.

It is thought that the quality of the work environment also figures into solving the problem of inadequate supply: By supporting teachers and fostering their professional growth, schools will lose fewer teachers to attrition. The plan includes additional initiatives designed to keep teachers in the field—among them, upgrading salaries and developing career ladders and other opportunities for advancement associated with advanced professional certification. NCTAF also argues for greater investment in quality teaching, an action that would reduce administration and increase the proportion of school professionals who work with children.

COMPARISON OF THE TWO APPROACHES

No Child Left Behind has much in common with "What Matters Most." Both plans support rigorous standards for students and teachers. Both stipulate that schools are responsible for the success of every student. Both seem motivated, at least in part, by a sincere concern about staffing high-poverty urban and rural schools. Both insist that schools hire only fully qualified teachers, and both recognize that teachers are underpaid. The two also differ in many ways, perhaps the most dramatic of which involves the role of teacher education. In "What Matters Most," upgrading teacher education is instrumental; in NCLB, alternatives are made readily available so that candidates may circumvent it.

To bolster supply, NCTAF advocates improving the job of teaching by (a) upgrading the profession, (b) improving the quality of the workplace, (c) supporting retention through mentoring and induction, and (d) basing teachers' salaries on knowledge and skills. NCLB provides more entry paths to teaching. Teacher education should be streamlined, and options to formal, campus-based training should be developed.

To improve teacher quality, NCTAF argues for better training. In this plan, all programs would be accredited, teachers would be held to rigorous standards, and teacher education would be more rigorous. The quality enhancement strategy implicit in NCLB is to recruit better trainees. Individuals with higher verbal ability and with stronger content preparation may be recruited into streamlined programs from which unnecessary and trivial requirements have been eliminated.

THE SPECIAL EDUCATION CONTEXT

The urgency of developing and sustaining an adequate special education teacher workforce is heightened by two factors:

1. The persistence of teacher shortages
2. The high level of attrition from the field.

Special education has had teacher shortages since the inception of the Education for All Handicapped Children's Act (1975), and there is little to suggest that this scenario might improve. The Bureau of Labor Statistics (1999) projected demand for more than 135,000 special additional education teachers between 1998 and 2008. Shortages also seem to be pervasive across states, with only a few states (e.g., Connecticut and Massachusetts) having no shortages and other states having rather dramatic shortages. In fact, according to the U.S. Department of Education (USDOE) (2001), more than half of Wyoming's special educators are uncertified. Shortages also vary by geographic location within states and by disability areas, with poor urban and rural schools and emotional and behavioral disorders experiencing the most severe shortages (American Association for Employment in Education, 1999; Ingersoll, 2001; National Center for Education Statistics, 1997; Riley, 1998).

Another aspect of the shortage issue is the underrepresentation of teachers from culturally and linguistically diverse (CLD) groups. In 1998, 14% of special education teachers were CLD, compared to 25% of the general population and 37.5% of all special education students (USDOE, 2001). Furthermore, the percentage of CLD teachers is predicted to drop to 12% by the year 2009 (Olson, 2000). Given the dramatic, chronic, and multifaceted nature of shortages in special education, it is not yet clear what impact NCLB's requirement for highly qualified teachers will have on our field, but policy makers (West, 2002) expect the new law to present a serious dilemma for schools as 2005–06 approaches.

An insufficient supply of new special education teachers, increasing student enrollments, a shrinking reserve pool (i.e., the number of teachers not currently employed), and high teacher attrition rates in special education contribute prominently to chronic shortages (McLeskey, Smith, Tyler, & Sanders, 2002). In 1998, 22,250 newly certified teachers graduated from teacher preparation programs to fill the 30,000 vacant special education positions that year (USDOE, 1998). Although the number of graduates had increased by nearly 4,000 since 1993, a shrinking supply from the reserve pool offset positive growth in graduation rates. An analysis of data from two Schools and Staffing Surveys (SASS) suggested that between 1990 and 1993 the percentage of new hires from the reserve pool dropped by 17%.

At the same time, growth in the population of students with disabilities and high teacher attrition rates in special education put considerable strain on states to provide an adequate supply of certified teachers. From 1992 to 1999, the nation's student population (aged 3 to 12) grew by 6.8%; at the same time, the number of special education students grew by 20.3%. The number of special education teachers who leave the field annually also outstrips the numbers of available new hires. In the most recent analysis of the SASS data, the number of special educators who left teaching more than doubled the number of new graduates from teacher education programs.

We can only speculate about the reasons for an inadequate supply of special education teachers. Some scholars assert that insufficient pay and poor working conditions undoubtedly affect teachers' decisions to enter and remain in the field. We do have some information about successful recruitment strategies and some research that documents why teachers—particularly beginning teachers—leave the field. In the sections to follow, we describe factors related to the attrition of general and special education teachers and consider why beginning teachers are most vulnerable. We also review strategies that states, districts, and schools have employed to recruit and retain teachers, and how some of these strategies simultaneously increase teacher quality. In doing so, we hope to provide school practitioners with information about what states, districts, and institutions of higher education might do to promote better recruitment and retention of qualified teachers.

MAJOR FACTORS CONTRIBUTING TO SPECIAL EDUCATION ATTRITION

An analysis of Schools and Staffing Survey data from 1987–88, 1990–91, and 1993–94, showed that the overall attrition rate for special educators was 6.1% compared to 5.7% for general educators. In addition, in 1990–91, special education lost teachers through transfer to general education. Although the net loss was only 5,264 teachers, the 14,559 special education teachers who transferred to general education represented more than 5% of the special education teaching force (Boe, Cook, Bobbit, & Weber, 1996).

Special education teachers abandon careers in the classroom for many reasons. Research over the past decade or so indicates that factors related to teacher attrition in special education seem to cluster into three major areas:

1. Teacher characteristics
2. Workplace conditions
3. Affective responses to teaching.

In the following sections we describe factors in these three areas that affect teachers' career decision making and highlight supporting research. For a more thorough review of these factors and others, we refer readers to major literature reviews by Billingsley (1993, 2002), and Brownell and Smith (1992).

Teacher Characteristics

Individual teacher attributes and their relationship to attrition have been studied extensively in the general education literature and to a somewhat lesser extent, in special education. In both general and special education, researchers have examined the relationship of age, experience, race, academic ability, and certification to teacher attrition. Although, in one or more studies, each of these variables has been related to teacher attrition, age, experience, and certification status have been the most consistent predictors of a teacher's decision to leave the classroom. More recent research in general education suggests that the preparation route a teacher takes also may influence retention; this research, combined with research on certification status, suggests that teachers' preparation for the classroom makes a difference in their decisions to remain.

Young, inexperienced teachers are the most vulnerable to attrition and most in need of extra support. National, state, and local studies have shown that young, inexperienced teachers are more likely to either leave the classroom or indicate an intention to leave than are their more experienced counterparts.

In a national study of special and general education teachers, Boe, Barkanic, and Leow (1999) found that early-year teachers were the most vulnerable to attrition and that risk for leaving dropped dramatically with experience. Both general and special education teachers in their first 2 years voluntarily left the classroom at a rate of about 8%. Voluntary attrition rates dropped to 5% for teachers with 7 to 13 years of experience and 2.5% for teachers with 14 to 22 years of experience.

Researchers collecting state and local data on special education teachers have consistently supported these findings (Cross & Billingsley, 1994; Miller, Brownell, & Smith, 1999; Morvant et al., 1995; Singer, 1993), suggesting that inexperienced teachers are a district's greatest risk for attrition. What is unclear in this research is how age and experience are interrelated in predicting attrition, as most inexperienced teachers also are young.

Not being fully certified for a main assignment puts general and special education teachers both at risk for attrition. Boe and his colleagues (1999) found that teachers who did not hold a certificate for their main assignment were twice as likely as those who were fully certified to leave the classroom or move to another classroom. Other studies at the national and state levels also have found that certification matters in decisions to remain in or leave the classroom. Carlson and Billingsley (2001) found in a national study of special education teachers that certification status was a significant indicator of intention to leave, and Miller et al. (1999), in their statewide study of Florida's special education teachers, found that certification status was one of the strongest predictors of a decision to leave the classroom or transfer to another school or district.

Research on traditional and alternative preparation routes has demonstrated that program duration affects retention of general education teachers. For instance, Andrew and Schwab (1995) reported that graduates of 5-year teacher education programs were more likely to remain in teaching than were graduates of 4-year programs. In a national study of college graduates, Henke, Chen, Geis, and Knepper (2000) found that teachers who entered the classroom without student teaching—a common route for untrained teachers and those entering via shortened routes—left the profession at nearly twice the rate of those who had completed training.

Darling–Hammond (1999) also found that graduates from 4- and 5-year programs were more likely to remain in the classroom than were graduates from short-duration alternative routes. She reported that attrition rates for individuals entering teaching through shortcut programs (e.g., bachelor's degree plus intensive summer training in a teaching field) were about 60%, compared to 30% for traditionally trained teachers and 10% to 15% for graduates of 5-year programs (Berry, 2001; Darling–Hammond, 1999). In contrast, longer duration alternative programs have demonstrated impressive retention rates (Southeast Center for Teaching Quality, 2002). These data combined with retention data for graduates of 4- and 5-year programs demonstrate that preparation contributes positively to teacher retention.

Working Conditions

Teachers are motivated or discouraged by the quality of their work environment. Salary, school climate, administrative support, and issues related to the role special education teachers play in schools have an impact on their decisions to stay or leave. When special educators believe they are adequately compensated for their efforts, in terms of both the intrinsic and the extrinsic rewards they receive, they are more likely to remain in the classroom.

Teacher Salary

How much money teachers make influences attrition and retention. Overall, teachers who earn more tend to remain in teaching and are less mobile than those who earn less. All other things being equal, attrition and mobility rates decline with increasing salary levels (Boe et al., 1999). Correlations between salary and attrition rates for districts are strongest at the top and bottom of the salary distribution. Hare and Heap (2001) found that Michigan, the state with the highest average salaries in the nation (after cost-of-living adjustments), had the lowest proportion of districts reporting difficulties in retaining teachers (21.9%), whereas, in Iowa, the state with the lowest average salaries adjusted for cost-of-living expenses, 44% of districts reported high rates of turnover.

Although the relationship between salary and attrition is strong, it is mediated by several factors, including opportunities to earn more in nearby districts, employment options outside of teaching, and working conditions. Teachers are more likely to quit teaching or transfer to another position when their salaries are low relative to salaries in nearby districts (Pogodzinski, 2000). Moreover, when salaries are comparatively low, other risk factors emerge. For example, the lowest paying districts lose teachers at a greater rate, and administrators in these districts are often left with few hiring options. In lower paying districts, administrators find themselves hiring more uncertified teachers than affluent districts, increasing the risk for attrition.

Even if districts could raise salaries, they may not be able to overcome attrition problems, particularly if higher paying job alternatives are available and working conditions are poor. When teachers have more opportunities to secure higher paying jobs outside of teaching, they are more likely to leave. The availability of higher paying job alternatives is the reason math and science have greater teaching shortages and urban districts have greater attrition than rural districts (Hanushek, Kain, & Rivkin, 2001). Undoubtedly, economic opportunities for teachers in urban areas are greater than those available in rural areas, where teaching may be the most attractive employment option.

Intrinsic Rewards of Teaching

The quality of a teacher's work life is often more important than a teacher's desire to earn more money. A study from the National Bureau of Economic Statistics showed that teachers would be willing to take a pay cut to transfer to schools where students would be more capable academically and where teachers would receive more resources to do their job (Hanushek et al., 2001). Similarly, Miller et al. (1999) found that school climate and perceived stress were much stronger predictors than salary of special education teacher attrition, even though teachers who earned less were more likely than their higher paid colleagues to leave.

From the special education teacher's viewpoint, workplace quality plays a crucial role in career decisions. Do special educators believe that their school is a good place to work? Is the environment safe for them and their students? Do they feel part of the mainstream? Answering no to these questions places special educators at risk for leaving the classroom. In fact, in statewide and national studies of special education teachers, school climate proved to be one of the strongest predictors of teacher attrition or movement to another school (Carlson & Billingsley, 2001; Miller et al., 1999).

Although we do not know all the factors that contribute to a positive school climate, support from an administrator undoubtedly is one of them. When teachers feel supported by their administrators, they are more likely to believe that their school is a good place to work and persist in the classroom. In special education, the amount of administrative support available at the building and district levels is a strong indicator of teachers' commitment to teaching and their decisions to remain in the field (Billingsley, 2002; Boe et al., 1999; Gersten, Keating, Yovanoff, & Harniss, 2001; Miller et al., 1999).

Having a clear sense of one's role in the school and a manageable workload also improves a special education teacher's commitment to teaching. Special education teachers may be burdened by unreasonable job responsibilities and contradictory expectations from parents, administrators, and their general education colleagues (Kozleski, Mainzer, & Deshler, 2000; Mastropieri, 2001). Over the past 4 years, special education teachers' workloads have increased by approximately 22% (Carlson, Schroll, & Klein, 2001; USDOE, 1998, 2000).

Moreover, changing student demographics and movement toward noncategorical services have resulted in more diverse caseloads for special educators. Special educators seem capable of handling more students, but increasing numbers combined with increasing diversity becomes less manageable. In a national study of special education teachers, Carlson and Billingsley (2001) found that teachers who served students with different disabilities felt the most overwhelmed by their job and expressed a strong intention to leave special education. Adding to their sense of burden is the excessive paperwork that many special education teachers must complete to meet federal and state regulations (Billingsley, Pyecha, Smith–Davis, Murray, & Hendricks, 1995; Schnorr, 1995; Westling & Whitten, 1996).

Increasing pressure to include students with disabilities adds to special educators' sense of role conflict and ambiguity. Some special educators are frustrated by general educators' resistance to inclusion (Billingsley & Tomchin, 1992; Boyer & Lee, 2001; Carter & Scruggs, 2001). Others experience conflict when placed in roles where their primary responsibility is to collaborate with general educators rather than to provide direct services to students (Embich, 2001; Morvant et al., 1995). In this case, special educators may feel deprived of the opportunity to do what they prepared themselves to do—teach. Moreover, special educators experience heightened anxiety and conflict when colleagues and principals do not make the education of students with disabilities an important focus in the school or do not provide sufficient professional growth opportunities (Gersten et al., 2001). Support and professional development undoubtedly help special educators feel better able to handle the challenges of their jobs.

Affective Responses to the Job

When special educators face undesirable working conditions day after day, their commitment to teaching, satisfaction with the job, and stress are likely to change for the worse, increasing the chances that they will leave the classroom (Billingsley & Cross, 1992; Cross & Billingsley, 1994; Gersten et al., 2001; Morvant et al., 1995; Singh & Billingsley, 1996). Conversely, when teachers feel that principals communicate openly, demonstrate their leadership, establish trust, and show appreciation for their efforts, teachers are more satisfied with their jobs (Cross & Billingsley, 1994; Singh & Billingsley, 1996). On the one hand, excessive paperwork, high caseloads, and frequent meetings cause many special educators to feel stressed and less committed to their workplace. On the other hand, the longer teachers work, the more able they are to handle the organizational demands of their job. Indeed, classroom experience is linked to higher levels of professional commitment (Cross & Billingsley, 1994).

WHY ARE BEGINNING SPECIAL EDUCATION TEACHERS MOST VULNERABLE TO ATTRITION?

Teaching is one of the few professions where novices are expected to meet the same demands as their more seasoned colleagues. "Similar to their more experienced colleagues, beginning teachers must plan lessons, teach content subjects, manage student behavior, collaborate with peers, communicate effectively with parents, and complete paperwork" (Brownell & Skrtic, 2002, p. 5). These challenges are enormous when one considers that beginning teachers have not yet developed basic classroom routines and are just starting to operationalize their knowledge of instruction.

Beginning special education teachers face the same challenges as all beginning teachers—and then some. Paperwork requirements, development of instructional and testing accommodations, IEP development and implementation, and collaboration all fall within the purview of special educators, novices and veterans alike (Billingsley & Tomchin, 1992; Boyer & Gillespie, 2000; Brownell & Skrtic, 2002; Kilgore & Griffin, 1998; MacDonald, 2001). Moreover, they are likely to have fewer colleagues at their schools and less chance for consistent mentoring. Beginning special educators also believe that they must face these demands with fewer curricular and technological resources than those available to their general education colleagues (Griffin, Winn, Otis–Wilburn, & Kilgore, 2002). Given the nature of their work and the supports they receive to do it, it is little wonder that beginning special educators question whether they can meet the demands of the job.

Some beginning special educators do not have the basic knowledge or skills to overcome the challenges they face. Inexperienced special educators are far less likely to be fully certified for their main position than are their more experienced counterparts. In a national study of beginning special education teachers, Billingsley (2001) found that only 63% of first-year teachers were fully certified for their job, compared to 91% of teachers in their fifth year. Although being uncertified places any teacher at risk for attrition, it is more problematic for beginners. High attrition rates among young, inexperienced special education teachers emphasize the vulnerability of this group and the need to consider strategies that will increase the likelihood of their remaining in the field.

STRATEGIES FOR RETAINING SPECIAL EDUCATION TEACHERS

We believe that policy and practice at the state and local levels may be designed to make teaching special education a more desirable career. We also believe that combating attrition would help to reduce chronic shortages. Most states and districts have paid less attention to retention than to recruitment, and, indeed, recruitment strategies may improve retention, particularly if they increase the numbers of fully certified teachers entering the classroom. Research suggests, however, that improving the preparation and induction of new teachers and the working conditions of all teachers may be more successful.

In this section, we describe state and district policies that hold potential for decreasing attrition. We provide information about the characteristics of alternative preparation and induction programs that also seem to be effective in improving retention rates. We then describe research studies that examine school environments with high retention rates for the purpose of identifying supports they provide to teachers.

State and District Strategies for Recruiting Certified Teachers

Long before No Child Left Behind, concern over dramatic shortages in the upcoming decade had produced a flurry of state- and district-level strategies for special education teacher recruitment. States and districts are instituting expensive, aggressive recruitment strategies, such as innovative internet recruitment sites, signing bonuses, compensatory pay for working in critical-shortage areas or hard-to-staff schools, loan forgiveness, and increases in teacher salaries.

In this section we provide some examples of the strategies districts and states are employing. Before we do, however, we must acknowledge that if we have fewer fully qualified special education teachers than special education jobs, no recruitment policy, however aggressive, will solve this problem nationally.

In this case, such policies may work only to shift the shortage burden from one school, district, or state to another. But if recruitment policy is designed to increase the number of individuals entering preparation programs, or to increase the number of general education teachers migrating to special education or of reserve pool members returning to teach, such policies would supplement total supply and not merely shift the burden of demand. Although this is an important distinction to bear in mind, we must recognize at the same time that states are obligated to provide a fully qualified teaching force and that state policy is designed to solve state and not national problems.

Aggressive recruitment strategies hold some promise for increasing the number of qualified special education teachers in a district or state. Web-based advertising seems to be an excellent tool for recruiting new teachers, particularly out-of-state teachers. In the Oregon Special Education Recruitment and Retention Project (2002), a survey of newly hired special education professionals revealed that more than half had found their current jobs over the internet and that more than 60% of out-of-state new hires were experienced special educators. Clark County School District in Las Vegas has developed an innovative recruitment website that sells the benefits of living in Las Vegas. In addition, 65 district representatives visit school districts nationwide to recruit teachers. In 1998, these recruitment strategies yielded an applicant pool of 4,500 qualified teacher candidates.

Other districts and states offer financial incentives to attract and retain teachers (Southeast Center for Teaching Quality, 2002). Pennsylvania recently instituted a $3.8 million recruitment program to pay signing bonuses—equal to 20% of a teacher's starting salary—to teachers willing to work in high-shortage areas (i.e., special education, math, science, and foreign language). New York, South Carolina, Mississippi, California, Louisiana, and Massachusetts all provide a variety of incentives to recruit teachers to hard-to-staff schools and critical-shortage areas. For example, New York provides an annual stipend of $3,400 to any certified teacher who takes a job in a critical-shortage area. Mississippi provides tuition scholarships to teachers who are willing to work toward a master's degree in a critical-shortage area and also assists with relocation costs.

Despite the enormous expense of these strategies, there is little evidence of their effectiveness in attracting or retaining teachers, and there is some indication that the strategies are not effective in attracting qualified teachers to hard-to-staff schools. New York's bonuses and aggressive recruitment strategies do seem to be increasing the overall supply of certified teachers, but South Carolina and Massachusetts have seen less success despite an enormous expenditure of recruitment funds. In South Carolina, an $18,000 signing bonus was effective in recruiting only 20% of the teachers needed to fill 500 positions. Teachers either were not sufficiently qualified or were unwilling to move to hard-to-staff schools.

In contrast, previous research on salary and teacher attrition has supported raising salaries to attract and retain qualified teachers. On average, teachers earn 20% less than professionals in other occupations requiring similar levels of education. Recognizing the problem, Louisiana, West Virginia, Iowa, Alabama, Arkansas,

North Carolina, and Connecticut have enacted legislation to increase salaries. Despite these efforts, Connecticut is the only state that has completely eradicated teacher shortages (Southeast Center for Teacher Quality, 2002). Thus, a closer examination of Connecticut's policy context may provide insights into how better to recruit and retain special education teachers.

Connecticut's Comprehensive Policy Initiative

Connecticut has enacted the best example of a comprehensive policy initiative to address teacher shortages, through careful attention to improving teacher quality much as NCTAF has proposed. After analyzing policies across the 50 states and conducting an indepth case study of Connecticut, Wilson, Darling–Hammond, and Berry (2001) found that the state's efforts to raise teacher quality represented the most notable, long-term, systemwide reform effort undertaken by any state to ensure quality teaching for all schools. Even though more than 25 states have passed legislation designed to improve teacher recruitment, education, certification, or professional development, only Connecticut has developed a policy approach to address them coherently.

Nearly 30 years ago, Connecticut's state department and legislature began to consider what might be done to address inequities in the learning outcomes of students from various socioeconomic backgrounds. They equalized school funding and created policies to ensure an adequate supply of qualified teachers for all schools. The state provided funds for increases in teacher salaries, incentives to attract high-ability teachers, and incentives for districts to hire certified teachers. It enacted a law prohibiting the hiring of uncertified teachers and began a strategic effort to educate the citizens about public education.

Along with these incentives, the state department of education worked collaboratively with colleges of education, district administrators, and teachers to develop high standards for teacher knowledge and performance aligned with state standards for student learning. A three-tiered teacher certification system (beginning, provisional, and professional certification) was established to ensure teachers' continuous progress toward these standards. To acquire a Beginning Certificate to practice in schools, potential teachers must pass a basic skills test and a test of knowledge in subject matter. To achieve Provisional Certification, teachers must successfully complete an induction program that includes rigorous evaluation and extensive mentoring. Professional Certification requires that all teachers with 2 or more years of successful teaching experience participate in 90 hours of professional development every 5 years for renewal.

To ensure that licensure standards were not just another hollow requirement, Connecticut implemented several strategies to support learning opportunities for teachers. The state designed and implemented one of the most impressive statewide teacher induction programs in the country, the Beginning Educator Support and Training Program (BEST). In BEST, beginning teachers are evaluated, according to state standards, over 2 years and receive considerable mentoring to meet those standards. To align standards for teaching and student learning, the state department provides data about student performance on indepth, low-stakes assessments of reading, writing, and mathematics. These data are made available to districts with the expectation that they will become the foundation for all professional development activities. In a study conducted by the National Education Goals Panel, Baron (1999) concluded that Connecticut's use of low-stakes, authentic assessment and its ability to make these data easily accessible to districts for further analysis are the keys to its impressive student achievement gains.

In addition to providing data, the state department provides supports to high-need districts, such as additional funds for professional development, preschool and all-day kindergarten, and smaller pupil–teacher ratios. More recently, Connecticut placed increasing emphasis on developing instructional leaders to support teachers' efforts in schools. The state is working with the Interstate School Leadership Licensure Consortium to create standards that emphasize the central role that teaching expertise plays in the development of instructional leaders who can foster teacher learning.

Connecticut's efforts to align teaching and administrator standards with standards for student learning combined with the ongoing provision of supports for teacher learning provide the foundation for one of the most coherent, continuous systems of teacher education in the country. Moreover, Connecticut has demonstrated that raising salaries, increasing teacher standards, and providing multiple learning supports can increase teacher quantity and quality. Compared to 43.7% nationally, more than 80% of all the state's teachers hold master's degrees (National Center for Educational Statistics, 1997), and in 1990 approximately 30% of new hires graduated from highly selective colleges or universities.

More important, rising student NAEP scores (at least for nondisabled students) over the past two decades indicates that this system of promoting teacher learning is successful. Although we do not know how these reforms specifically affected special education teachers, we do know that Connecticut reports no shortages in this area. Clearly, Connecticut's efforts to raise salaries, increase teacher standards, support beginning teachers, and improve teacher quality have "helped create a culture that value[s] teachers and teaching" (Wilson et al., 2001, p. 34). Moreover, the results of these efforts are so impressive in terms of student achievement that the public is willing to continue supporting them even during hard economic times.

High-Quality Alternative Routes

Alternative preparation routes also hold potential to increase the number of individuals particularly those from diverse backgrounds, entering the teaching profession (Zeichner & Schulte, 2001). Moreover, a small amount of existing research suggests that some of these programs produce competent graduates who are likely to remain in teaching. Clearly, alternative programs have been highly successful in recruiting culturally and linguistically diverse (CLD) students, and, because they do not compete with formal teacher education program for traditionally college-aged students, most programs contribute uniquely to the supply of new teachers.

In reviews of research on alternative programs in general and special education, Rosenberg and Sindelar (2001) and Zeichner and Shulte (2001) cited high proportions of CLD participants as a notable accomplishment. For example, in the Pathways to Teaching Careers program sponsored by the DeWitt Wallace–Reader's Digest Fund (*Focus: Pathways, 2002*), 79% of the participants in the paraprofessional program are minorities. Haberman (1999) found that 78% of the participants in the Milwaukee Metropolitan Teacher Education Program were minorities.

Programs for Paraprofessionals

One particularly promising approach for recruiting more diverse teacher candidates and improving retention rates involves training paraprofessionals. Districts typically offer these "step-up" programs in collaboration with campus-based teacher education programs (Epanchin & Wooley-Brown, 1993; Gaynor & Little, 1997). To date, programs of this sort described in the literature are "alternative" only in the sense of student demographics and the venues at which courses and field experiences are offered. Participants tend to be older than traditional college age and more experienced; they also are more likely to be first in their families to get college degrees.

Courses and field experiences are offered off campus, most often in schools in host districts. These programs do not offer shortcuts into teaching and often are as rigorous as traditional special education teacher preparation. Most participants in step-up programs enter with no college degree and complete a minimum of 2 years of preparation. They are likely to extensive experience with children and actually may be identified and selected on the basis of their classroom competence.

Graduates often go to work in districts (and sometimes schools) where they previously were employed as paraprofessionals. Those who do so come equipped with knowledge of the community, school routines, and district rules and regulations, and they can be counted on to hit the ground running. They tend to be stable members of their communities and are less likely to move than are younger teachers who have yet to put down roots.

Common sense suggests that retention may be less an issue for these individuals, and research bears this out. California has been offering paraprofessional step-up training for more than a decade. Between 1995 and 2001, 311 teachers graduated from such programs, and as of 2002, 99% had remained in the field (Southeast Center for Teaching Quality, 2002).

It is not surprising that "grow your own" programs such as these are becoming popular and widespread. For example, the Dewitt Wallace–Reader's Digest Fund has invested $45 million in its Pathways Program for paraprofessionals (and returning Peace Corps volunteers). The program has graduated more than 2,000 "scholars," as they are called, from 42 colleges and universities nationwide, and retention is estimated to be 90% (*Focus: Pathways, 2002*). Retention rates of both programs are considerably better than rates for both 4- and 5-year teacher preparation programs.

In special education we have similar examples funded through the Office of Special Education Programs (OSEP). Most of the graduates of the VCUF Program, an OSEP-supported collaborative program we conducted with the Volusia County

(Florida) schools, have remained in the field. At last count, 5 years after completing the program, 16 of 19 graduates were teaching, all in Volusia County (Rennells, Sindelar, & Austrich, 1997).

In addition to improving retention rates, step-up programs and other more intensive alternative preparation programs show promise of graduating competent teachers (*Focus: Pathways,* 2002; Sindelar, Rennells, Daunic, Austrich, & Eisele, 1999). In a comprehensive study of alternative and traditional programs (Sindelar et al., 1999), we used PRAXIS III to assess the competence of alternatively and traditionally trained graduates. PRAXIS III is a comprehensive assessment using observational and interview data to document how well beginning teachers plan and deliver instruction, organize their classrooms, and communicate with parents and other professionals. In a comparison of graduates of campus-based programs to two types of alternative programs—those offered through a university and district partnership and those offered by a district alone, special education graduates of step-up programs and campus-based programs were more skilled than graduates of programs offered exclusively by districts (Sindelar et al., 1999). Also, initial evaluations of the Pathways Program graduates demonstrated that graduates have achieved at least an average level of competence on all components on Praxis III (*Focus: Pathways,* 2002).

Programs for Career Changes

Other promising models of alternative preparation involve intensive, post-baccalaureate preparation to accommodate second-career professionals or non-education majors. These programs typically require students to participate in extensive coursework, provide mentoring by both university faculty and experienced classroom teachers, and involve collaboration between teacher education programs and school districts. Although little research has examined the effectiveness of these approaches, two studies in general and special education suggest that these programs produce competent teachers.

One such program is ALTCERT, offered collaboratively by the Johns Hopkins University and Baltimore County Schools (Rosenberg & Rock, 1994) and sponsored by OSEP. ALTCERT is a post-baccalaureate program for individuals with degrees and experience in other fields; it is based on Johns Hopkins's Master's-level teacher education program. Initial evaluations provided by special education supervisors and principals suggested that graduates of this program compared favorably to graduates of the campus-based program.

Miller, McKenna, and McKenna (1998) studied an alternative program for middle school teachers similar in structure to ALCERT. They compared graduates of this program to graduates of more traditional, campus-based programs and found them to be similar on an observational measure of classroom practice and in promoting student achievement.

Other alternative programs truly are abbreviated and expedite entry into the classroom. These shortcut programs differ dramatically from other alternative routes, as well as from traditional, campus-based programs, and the impact of these programs on retention and teacher quality is less clear. One well-known example is

Teach to America (TFA). Like ALTCERT, this program is geared to attract career changers.

TFA.   TFA offers recent college graduates—non-education majors—a 5-week summer institute and 1- or 2-week orientation before placing them in high poverty urban and rural schools, where they serve as teachers. Candidates obligate themselves to serve 2 years, during which time they receive formal support and additional training. Over the past 12 years, TFA has placed more than 8,000 teachers in 12 communities nationwide.

Despite the impressive number of teachers this program has placed, several research studies have called into question the effectiveness of the program. For one thing, TFA graduates have high attrition rates—more than 60%—and two studies questioned how adequately prepared TFA graduates are to teach. In a study comparing teachers from alternative routes to those from traditional routes, Darling–Hammond, Chung, and Frelow (2002) found that TFA graduates were less satisfied with their preparation programs and did not feel as well prepared on a variety of classroom practices. Laczko–Kerr and Berliner's (2002) study of alternative route and traditional route teachers demonstrated that TFA graduates and other undercertified teachers were less effective than graduates of traditional routes in promoting student achievement.

TTT.   Troops to Teachers (TTT) is a U. S. Department of Education program, authorized through 2006 by the No Child Left Behind Act. A support program more than a training program, TTT provides financial incentives to encourage retiring military personnel to enter teaching. Like TFA, TTT graduates agree to serve in high-need districts—in this case for 3 years. They also have 3 years to obtain a teaching license. A nationwide network of offices offers support in finding employment and training.

Since its inception in 1994, TTT has supported roughly 3,000 retirees who went on to teach. It is notable that the vast majority of them are men (90%), that minority representation is higher (29%), and that more TTT graduates pursue careers in special education than expected. The success of this program in providing a more diverse workforce, retaining teachers, and fostering effective classroom practice has received some support in initial evaluation studies (National Center for Education Information, 1998; Webber, Raffeld, & Kettler, n.d.). TTT graduates have retention rates equivalent to graduates of 5-year programs (e.g., 85% to 87% of these teachers remain in the field), and administrators tend to rate TTT graduates comparably to graduates of traditional programs (National Center for Education Information, 1998; Webber et al., n.d.).

Comparing TTT and traditionally trained teachers, however, should not be construed as a test of alternative route training. Indeed, many TTT teachers complete a post-baccalaureate or master's program to obtain their teaching license.

Given that the supply of graduates from formal teacher education programs is inadequate to meet the demand for new teachers and that burgeoning shortages loom on the horizon, alternative routes represent a viable strategy for increasing the supply. Although little can be said with certainty about alternative routes generally, some programs have been shown to produce competent teachers. They do bring into the field individuals for whom traditional, campus-based programs seem inappropriate—second career professionals and retired military personnel, for example—and they can help to diversify the teaching workforce. In our judgment, these are significant accomplishments.

The term "alternative route" encompasses a wide range of programs, and research to date has been limited to more extensive and rigorous ones. The verdict remains out on shortcut programs.

Induction Programs

High-quality induction has the potential to combat many of the challenges that confront beginning special education teachers as they enter the field. Although the primary purpose of induction is to help beginning teachers become more effective, good induction may contribute to teachers' decisions to remain in teaching. In fact, both general education and special education beginning teachers who participate in carefully designed programs, nested in a supportive working environment, are far more likely to become our veteran teachers of tomorrow.

Here, we identify the critical characteristics of high-quality induction programs for both general and special education teachers and highlight successful state and local efforts. We emphasize the importance of workplace conditions, recognizing that environments in which teacher learning is valued and supported also foster retention of both early career and veteran teachers.

Induction may be defined as a planned process of support (Griffin et al., 2002). Induction programs often are tailored to the specific needs of a jurisdiction or group and vary dramatically by design and definition. In their review of the induction literature, Griffin et al. (2002) drew from the earlier work of Moskowitz and Stephens (1996) and identified key characteristics of quality induction programs for both general and special education teachers. These characteristics were (a) a culture of shared responsibility and support, (b) interactions between new and experienced teachers, (c) a continuum of professional development, (d) de-emphasized evaluation, (e) clear goals and purposes, (f) rich instructional and pedagogical content, (g) mentoring, and (h) fiscal and political support. By addressing these key elements, interested states, districts, and collaborative partnerships have the ingredients for establishing effective induction programs.

Although the key characteristics identified by Griffin et al. (2002) are important components of induction programs for all teachers, some additional factors must be considered to address the specialized needs of special educators (Billingsley, 2001; Whitaker, 2000). Beyond the typical planning, management, and curricular issues, special education teachers also must wrestle with caseload management, collaboration, parental issues, accommodations, and paperwork. These burdens often are specific to a particular school culture (Griffin et al., 2001; Whitaker, 2000; White & Mason, 2001). Mentors offering individualized and contextual support must address the specialized challenges typically faced by early special educators (Rosenberg, Griffin, Kilgore, & Carpenter, 1997; White & Mason, 2001).

According to Griffin and her colleagues, effective features of mentoring programs in special education include (a) frequent contact between mentor and mentee, (b) nonevaluative support, (c) formal and informal support, (d) good mentor match, and (e) appropriate content of support. Special education teachers are different; they require mentors who focus on the their individual concerns and teaching context in a consistent, positive, nonevaluative manner. For a more thorough review of the guidelines for special educator mentorship, we refer readers to the Council for Exceptional Children website, http://www.cec.sped.org

Many states, districts, and collaborative partnerships have incorporated these key characteristics into induction and mentoring programs to support and retain beginning teachers. The National Association of State Directors of Teacher Education and Certification (NASDTEC) (NASDTEC, 2000, 2002) reports that 26 states and the District of Columbia provide some level of support for beginning teachers. Another report indicates support from as many as 28 states and the District of Columbia (Southeast Center for Teacher Quality, 2002). Although support from the state level seems to be increasing and some programs provide evidence of success, a review of beginning teacher induction programs for both general and special education indicates that programs vary dramatically according to level of funding, accessibility, and intensity of support (Southeast Center for Teacher Quality, 2002; Hirsch, Koppich, & Knapp, 1998; 2001).

When examining successful induction programs, two key elements clearly surface. The schools, districts, states, and collaborative partnerships highlighted in the induction literature exhibit a high level of *commitment* to teacher learning and provide adequate *fiscal support*. It is not surprising that schools that support teacher learning, foster collegiality, and promote professionalism also recognize the importance of nurturing early-career teachers. And fiscal commitment is vital in providing ongoing support for beginning teachers. A report from the Southeast Center for Teacher Quality (2002) indicated that the average cost for many of the most effective programs is $5,000 to $8,000 per teacher. It would be fair to assume that this price tag may be a bargain compared to the organizational costs that districts incur in replacing teachers.

Many local and state induction initiatives recognize the importance of funding initiatives to retain the teachers who already are on board. Connecticut, however, emerges as an exemplar in teacher retention, and its induction program is no exception (Wilson et al., 2001). The BEST Program represents Connecticut's commitment to teacher quality by serving as a change agent for new teachers and mentors alike. Beginning teachers are offered levels of support over 3 years and also are held to high subject-specific standards assessed by classroom observations and portfolios. For example, the portfolio for second-year teachers consists of lesson plans, videotapes, reflection, and student work samples. Trained state assessors who are familiar with the Connecticut Teaching Competencies and the Connecticut Competency Instrument Indicators evaluate this portfolio.

Further, mentors or cooperating teachers are trained and often involved in other levels of professional development such as training as the state assessor. Not surprisingly, mentors report improvements in their own teaching, which is consistent with other studies reporting this value-added effect (Gibb & Welch, 1998). Connecticut's induction program exemplifies its comprehensive commitment to improve teaching and learning.

We are beginning to gain evidence outside the state of Connecticut that induction is dramatically reducing the attrition rates among new teachers. For example, the California Beginning Teacher Support and Assessment program (BTSA) has reduced attrition rates among all new teachers by 66% (Berry, 2001). In a comparative analysis, attrition rates varied from 9% to 37%, based on availability of the BTSA induction program. Similarly, by providing comprehensive induction programs, districts in Ohio, including Cincinnati, Columbus, and Toledo, reduced attrition rates by more than two thirds (Darling-Hammond, 1997). Clearly, schools, districts, and states that exemplify the concept of learning communities and emphasize the development of early career teachers are better positioned to retain highly qualified professionals.

Whereas induction programs have the potential to support and retain new teachers in the field, high-quality mentoring alone obviously is subverted by an unhealthy workplace environment. In a 3-year evaluation of four mentoring programs in the Baltimore City Public School System (BCPSS), Silva and Silva (2001) concluded that school culture was the critical factor in determining whether a teacher remained with the BCPSS over the short- or long-term. Although three-fourths of the teachers interviewed in the study considered mentoring as useful, school culture dominated beginning teachers' decisions to leave or to remain in teaching. With this in mind, we now examine teachers' working conditions and highlight the elements of effective schools and healthy school cultures.

Fostering Supportive Working Conditions

Novices are not the only teachers struggling to survive. All special educators cope with extraordinary challenges. They often face isolation, lack of administrative support, role ambiguity, challenges with classroom management, a multifaceted curriculum, lack of planning time, parental concerns, and a multitude of rules and regulations (Billingsley, 2002; Brownell, Smith, McNellis, & Miller, 1997; Griffin et al, 2002). Thus, it is no surprise that many succumb to environments that lack adequate school and district support.

Nevertheless, a close examination of the major factors of attrition reveal that most of the issues can be addressed by systematically improving the organizational characteristics and working conditions in schools and districts (Ingersoll, 2001; Rosenholtz, 1991; Yee, 1990). By attending to a healthy school culture, all teachers—general education and special education, early career and veterans—find themselves in a collegial, stimulating environment that allows them to do what they entered the profession to do—teach.

The role of a competent administrative leadership at both the school and district levels is pivotal in retaining general and special education teachers. Effective leadership might ameliorate factors relating to attrition and also create a collaborative work environment in which students, teachers, and learning communities flourish (Brownell & Skrtic, 2002; Fullan & Hargreaves, 1991). Within these positive climates exists an "abundant spirit of continuous improvement" (Rosenholtz, 1991, p. 208), and school-level administrators hold the key to teacher retention.

Effective school principals are committed to creating and nurturing a quality teacher workforce. Earlier case studies of teacher commitment and retention suggest that exemplary principals establish a school climate of collegiality and collaboration by (a) fostering ongoing learning, (b) protecting beginning and veteran teachers from forces that inhibit their ability to teach, (c) promoting helping relationships, (d) engaging teachers in shared decision making, and (e) establishing common goals (Rosenholtz, 1991; Yee, 1990).

Principals who exhibit these characteristics also value induction and professional development programs, which in turn establish a sense of self-efficacy and competence and support instructional innovation (Joyce, Calhoun, & Hopkins, 1999; Yee, 1990). By addressing workload assignments, discipline, and unnecessary district and state edicts, principals allow special education teachers to focus on teaching.

The district and community context also contributes to a teacher's decision to remain in teaching (Ingersoll, 2001; Rosenholtz, 1991; Yee, 1990). In Rosenholtz's (1991) study of eight elementary school districts in Tennessee, she analyzed the effects of district-level practices by interviewing superintendents and high-ranking central office staff members. Profiles of "moving" and "stuck" districts emerged as quantitative and qualitative data were analyzed. The "moving" districts invested in quality induction programs, emphasized the importance of continuous learning, and provided shepherding for their beginning teachers. A high level of commitment for continued professional growth permeated the successful districts. In addition, higher overall retention rates of the teacher workforce occurred in "moving" districts.

CONCLUSIONS ABOUT POLICY AND PRACTICE IN REDUCING SPECIAL EDUCATION TEACHER SHORTAGES

The teacher-shortage issue is disconcerting, as it threatens the ability of public schools to provide an appropriate education to students with disabilities, particularly in our nation's poorest schools. But existing solutions have the potential to increase the retention of new hires and improve teacher quality. The Connecticut policy approach emphasizes improvement of teaching through standards and professional preparation—policy strategies recommended by NCTAF. It also holds great promise for reducing teacher shortages in special education. Clearly, creating state policies and district cultures that promote and reward high-quality teaching will improve the recruitment and retention of all teachers.

Unfortunately, many states have not created policy contexts that are as impressive as Connecticut's, nor do they have the political support in their state for doing so. Thus, many teachers, district and state administrators, and higher education faculty may be left wondering what role they can play in improving the supply of new teachers and increasing teacher retention, particularly when there seems to be little legislative will to increase resources to teaching and teacher education. Creating more high-quality alternative preparation programs seems to be one solution that many higher education faculty, sometimes in conjunction with district administrators, are already implementing to improve the supply and retention of teachers. Alternative programs offered to preservice students in remote, rural sites, such as the programs developed by the University of Utah and Utah State University, in collaboration with the state's Comprehensive System of Personnel Development, draw on a population of prospective teachers who are likely to remain in the rural communities in which they live. Other programs, such as one currently offered by Johns Hopkins University in conjunction with the Montgomery Public Schools and funded by OSEP, prepare paraprofessionals intending to become special education teachers. Many OSEP-funded programs, however, are expensive, and the institutional capacity for continuing them without ongoing federal support or additional state support seems unlikely.

State and district administrators can improve recruitment techniques, as the state of Oregon and the Clark County Public Schools have done. Advertising professional programs and benefits over the Internet seems to be a relatively easy, low-cost, and effective way to recruit new teachers. States and districts also should consider devoting funds to furthering the professional development of principals regarding special education and developing induction programs for all beginning teachers. In doing so, though, they must realize that successful mentoring requires training and time and that the needs of beginning special education teachers will be different and extensive.

In addition, states and districts have to collect better data on their efforts to recruit and retain teachers. These data may be used in collaborative efforts with teacher education researchers to identify the factors contributing to teacher shortages in special education and, more important, how to remedy them.

Administrators and teachers also may work together to provide supports at the school level that promote teacher retention and the induction of beginning teachers. Building administrators need to be aware of the barriers that special educators confront as they collaborate with general education teachers and complete procedural and paperwork requirements. As the instructional leaders in a building, principals may foster a vision that focuses on collaboration between special and general education to promote learning for all children. One way they can establish a vision is to create opportunities for special and general educators to work together on schoolwide initiatives, such as implementing a new literacy program or a schoolwide discipline program and determining the impact of these initiatives on student learning. Building administrators also may use resources creatively to assist special educators with paperwork and meetings, and to ensure that they have the same access as their general education counterparts to instructional materials.

Most important, principals and veteran special educators must be cognizant of beginning special education teachers' needs and must provide them the support they require to succeed. Principals and veteran teachers should be ready to provide advice and hands-on support to beginners who are struggling with behavioral and instructional problems. Principals may provide release time for veteran special educators to observe and coach their novice colleagues. Veteran special educators and principals must communicate frequently with new teachers about the issues they are confronting and help them find solutions. Only by promoting continuous teacher learning and collegiality in a supportive, healthy work environment can principals and teachers create schools that retain special education teachers.

Finally, state administrators, district administrators, teacher educators, and teachers need to collaborate in strategic efforts to educate the public about the teacher shortage and quality issues. Connecticut is a good example of how an educated public will support system-wide school reform.

REFERENCES

American Association for Employment in Education (AAEE) (1999). *Educator supply and demand.* Columbus, OH: AAEE.

Andrew, M. D., & Schwab, R. L. (1995). Has reform in teacher education influenced teacher performance? An outcome assessment of graduates of an eleven-university consortium. *Action in Teacher Education, 17,* 43–53.

Baron, J. B. (1999). *Exploring high and improving reading achievement in Connecticut.* Washington, DC: National Educational Goals Panel.

Berry, B. (2001). No shortcuts to preparing good teachers. *Educational Leadership, 58,* 32–36.

Billingsley, B. S. (1993). Teacher retention and attrition in special and general education: A critical review of the literature. *Journal of Special Education, 27*(2), 137–174.

Billingsley, B. S. (2001). *Beginning special educators: Characteristics, qualifications, and experiences: SPeNSE summary sheet.* Retrieved October, 2002, from http://www.SPeNCE.org

Billingsley, B. S. (2002). *Special education teacher retention and attrition: A critical analysis of the literature.* Gainesville, FL: University of Florida: Center on Personnel Studies in Special Education (COPSSE).

Billingsley, B., & Cross, L. (1992). Predictors of commitment, job satisfaction, and intent to stay in teaching: A comparison of general and special educators. *The Journal of Special Education, 25,* 453–471.

Billingsley, B. Pyecha, J., Smith–Davis, J., Murray, K., & Hendricks, M. (1995). *Improving the retention of special education teachers: Final report.* Research Triangle Institute (Prepared for Office of Special Education Programs, Office of Special Education and Rehabilitative Services, The U.S. Department of Education under Cooperative Agreement H023Q10001. (ERIC Document Reproduction Service No. ED 379 860)

Billingsley, B. S., & Tomchin, E. M. (1992). Four beginning LD teachers: What their experiences suggest for trainers and employers. *Learning Disabilities Research and Practice, 7*(2), 104–112.

Boe, E. E., Barkanic, G., & Leow, C. S. (1999). *Retention and attrition of teachers at the school level: National trends and predictors* (Data Analysis Rep. No. 1999–DAR1. Philadelphia: University of Pennsylvania. ERIC Document Reproduction Service No. ED436 485).

Boe, E. E., Cook, L. H., Bobbitt, S. A., & Weber, A. L. (1996). *Retention and attrition of teachers at the district level: National trends in special and general education.* Research Rep. No. 1996–TSD6 (ED410742). Philadelphia: Pennsylvania Univ. Philadelphia, Center for Research and Evaluation in Social Policy.

Boyer, L., & Gillespie, P. (2000). Keeping the committed: The importance of induction and support programs for new special educators. *Teaching Exceptional Children, 33,* 10–15.

Boyer, L., & Lee, C. (2001). Converting challenge to success: Supporting a new teacher of students with autism. *Journal of Special Education,* 35, 75–83.

Brownell, M. T., & Skrtic, T. (2002). *Assuring an adequate supply of well-qualified teachers to improve the educational outcomes of students with disabilities.* Testimony provided to President's Commission on Excellence in Special Education Professional Development Task Force.

Brownell, M. T., & Smith, S. W. (1992). Attrition/retention of special education teachers: Critique of current research and recommendations for retention efforts. *Teacher Education and Special Education, 15,* 229–248.

Brownell, M. T., Smith, S. W., McNellis, J. R., & Miller, M. D. (1997). Attrition in special education: Why teachers leave the classroom and where they go. *Exceptionality, 7,* 143–155.

Bureau of Labor Statistics (1999). *National industry–occupation employment matrix: Occupation report-teachers, special education.* Retrieved August 23, 2001 from http://www.bls.gov/ooq/2000/spring/contents.html

Carlson, E., & Billingsley, B. S. (2001, July). *Working conditions in special education: Current research and implications for the Field.* Paper presented at OSEP Project Directors' Conference, Washington, DC.

Carlson, E., Schroll, K., & Klein, S. (2001). *OSEP briefing on the study of personnel needs in special education (SPeNSE).* Retrieved August 24, 2001, from www.spense.org/results.html

Carter, K. B., & Scruggs, T. E. (2001). Thirty-one students: Reflections of a first-year teacher of students with mental retardation. *Journal of Special Education, 35,* 100–104.

Cross, L. H., & Billingsley, B. S. (1994). Testing a model of special educators' intent to stay in teaching. *Exceptional Children, 60,* 411–421.

Darling–Hammond, L. (1997). *Doing what matters most: Investing in quality teaching.* New York: National Commission on Teaching and America's Future.

Darling–Hammond, L. (1999). *Solving the dilemmas of teacher supply, demand, and standards.* New York: National Commission on Teaching and America's Future.

Darling–Hammond, L., Chung, R., & Frelow, F. (2002). Variation in teacher preparation: How well do different pathways prepare teachers to teach? *Journal of Teacher Education, 53,* 286–302.

Embich, J. L. (2001). The relationship of secondary special education teachers' roles and factors that lead to professional burnout. *Teacher Education and Special Education, 24,* 58–69.

Epanchin, B. C., & Wooley–Brown, C. (1993). A university-school district collaborative project for preparing paraprofessionals to become special educators. *Teacher Education and Special Education, 16,* 110–123.

Focus: Pathways. A periodic report on grantmaking programs of the DeWitt Wallace Reader's Digest Fund (n.d.) Retrieved on November 27, 2002 from http://www.wallacefunds.org/publications/pub_teach/

Fullan, M., & Hargreaves, A. (1991). *What's worth fighting for in your school?: Working together for improvement.* Buckingham, United Kingdom: Open University Press.

Gaynor, J. F., & Little, M. E. (1997). The expanding role of LEAs in special education teacher preparation: The view from a local school district. *Teacher Education and Special Education, 20,* 281–300.

Gersten, R., Keating, T., Yovanoff, P., & Harniss, M. K. (2001). Working in special education: Factors that enhance special educators' intent to stay. *Exceptional Children, 67,* 546–567.

Gibb, G. S., & Welch, M. (1998). The Utah Mentor Teacher Academy: Evaluation of a Statewide Mentor Program. *Teacher Education and Special Education, 21,* 22–33.

Griffin, C. C., Winn, J., Otis–Wilborn, A., & Kilgore, K. L. (2002). *New teacher induction in special education.* Center on Personnel Studies in Special Education. Retrieved October 1, 2002, from http://www.copsse.org/

Haberman, M. (1999). Increasing the number of high-quality African American teachers in urban schools. *Journal of Instructional Psychology, 26,* 208–212.

Hanushek, E., Kain, J. F., & Rivkin, S. G. (2001). *Why public schools lose teachers.* Cambridge, MA: National Bureau of Economic Research.

Hare, D., & Heap, J. L. (2001). *Effective teacher recruitment and retention strategies in the Midwest: Who is making use of them?* North Central Regional Education Laboratory. Retrieved October 16, 2002, from http://www.ncrel.org/policy/pubs/html/strategy/index.html

Henke, R. R., Chen, X., Geis, S., & Knepper, P. (2000). Progress through the Teacher Pipeline: 1992–93. College graduates and elementary/ secondary school teaching as of 1997. *Education Statistics Quarterly, 2,* 91–98.

Hirsch, E., Koppich, J. E., & Knapp, M. S. (1998). *State action to improve teaching* (Policy brief). Seattle: Center for the Study of Teaching and Policy.

Hirsch, E., Koppich, J. E., & Knapp, M. S. (2001). *Revisiting what states are doing to improve the quality of teaching: An update on patterns and trends.* Center for the Study of Teaching and Policy. Retrieved August 27, 2001, from University of Washington, Center for the Study of Teaching and Policy website: http://depts.washington.edu/ctpmail

Ingersoll, R. M. (2001). *Teacher turnover, teacher shortages, and the organization of schools* (ED445415). Paper presented, in part, at annual meeting of American Sociological Association, Center for the Study of Teaching and Policy, Seattle.

Joyce, B., Calhoun, E., & Hopkins, D. (1999). *The new structure of school improvement: Inquiring schools and achieving students.* Philadelphia: Open University Press.

Kilgore, K. L., & Griffin, C. C. (1998). Beginning special educators: Problems of practice and the influence of school context. *Teacher Education and Special Education, 21,* 155–173.

Kozleski, E., Mainzer, R., & Deshler, D. (2000). *Bright Futures for Exceptional Learners: An Agenda To Achieve Quality Conditions for Teaching & Learning.* Arlington VA: Council for Exceptional Children.

Laczko–Kerr, I., & Berliner, D. C. (2002, September 6). The effectiveness of "Teach for America" and other under-certified teacher on student academic achievement: A case of harmful public policy. *Education Policy Analysis Archives, 10*(37). Retrieved December 19, 2002, from http://epaa.asu.edu/epaa/v10n37/

MacDonald, V. (2001). *Making time: A teacher's report on her first year of teaching children with emotional disabilities.* Retrieved October 15, 2002 from http://www.findarticles.com/cf 0/m0HDF/2 35/77813333/ print.jhtml

Mastropieri, M. A. (2001). Is the glass half full or half empty? Challenges encountered by first-year special education teachers. *Journal of Special Education, 35,* 66–74.

McLeskey, J., Smith, D. D., Tyler, N., & Saunder, S. (2002). *The supply of and demand for special education teachers: A review of research regarding the nature of the chronic shortage of special education.* Gainesville, FL: COPSSE.

Miller, M. D., Brownell, M. T., & Smith, S. W. (1999). Factors that predict teachers staying in, leaving, or transferring from the special education classroom. *Exceptional Children, 65,* 201–218.

Miller, J. W., McKenna, M. C., & McKenna, B. A. (1998). A comparison of alternatively and traditionally prepared teachers. *Journal of Teacher Education, 49,* 165–176.

Morvant, M., Gersten, R., Gillman, J., Keating, T., & Blake, G. (1995). *Attrition/retention of urban special education teachers: Multi-faceted research and strategic action planning* (Final Performance Rep., Vol. 1). (ERIC Document Reproduction Service No. ED 338 154)

Moskowitz, J., & Stephens, M. (Eds.) (1996). *From students of teaching to teachers to students: Teacher induction around the Pacific Rim.* Washington, DC: U.S. Department of Education for Asia–Pacific Economic Cooperation.

National Association of State Directors of Teacher Education and Certification. (2000*). The NAS-DTEC manual on the preparation and certification of educational personnel* (5th ed.). Dubuque, IA: Kendall/ Hunt.

National Association of State Directors of Teacher Education and Certification. (2002*). The NAS-DTEC manual on the preparation and certification of educational personnel* (7th ed.). Dubuque, IA: Kendall/ Hunt.

National Center for Education Information (1998). *Profile of Troops to Teachers.* Retrieved on December 20, 2002 from http://www.dantes. doded.mil/Dantes_web/troopstoteachers/profile.htm

National Center for Educational Statistics (1997). *Digest of education statistics, 1997.* Washington, DC: U.S. Department of Education.

National Commission on Teaching and America's Future. (1996). *What matters most: Teaching for America's future.* New York: Author.

No Child Left Behind. Retrieved December 10, 2002, from http://www.ed.gov/legistration/ESEA02

Olson, L. (2000). Finding and keeping competent teachers. Quality counts: Who should teach. *Education Week Special Issue, 19,* 12–17.

Pogodzinski, J. M. (2000). *The teacher shortage: Cause and recommendations for change.* San Jose, CA: California Senate Office of Research.

Oregon Special Education Recruitment and Retention Project. (2002). *Detail findings related to recruiting special education personnel.* Teaching Research, Western Oregon University. Monmouth, OR. Retrieved October 9, 2002, from http://www.tr.wou.edu/rrp/surveyresults.htm

Rennells, M. S., Sindelar, P. T., & Austrich, C. (1997). *Volusia County/University of Florida collaborative training program case study.* Gainesville: University of Florida, Department of Special Education, Project SEART–C (Technical Rep. No. 8).

Riley, R. (1998). Our teachers should be excellent, and they should look like America. *Education and Urban Society, 31,* 18–29.

Rosenberg, M. S., Griffin, C. C., Kilgore, K. L., & Carpenter, S. L. (1997). Beginning Teachers in Special Education: A model for providing individualized support. *Teacher Education and Special Education, 20,* 301–321.

Rosenberg, M. S., & Rock, E. E. (1994). Alternative certification in special education: Efficacy of a collaborative, field-based teacher preparation program. *Teacher Education and Special Education, 17,* 141–153.

Rosenberg, M. S., & Sindelar, P. T. (2001). *The proliferation of alternative routes to certification in special education: A critical review of the literature.* Arlington, VA: Council for Exceptional Children, National Clearing for Professionals in Special Education.

Rosenholtz, S. J. (1991). *Teachers' workplace: The social organization of schools.* White Plains, New York: Longman.

Schnorr, J. (1995). Teacher retention: A CSPD analysis and planning model. *Teacher Education and Special Education, 18,* 22–38.

Silva, J. M., & Silva, D. (2001). *Year two: BCPSS mentor programs* (Status Report). Gainesville: University of Florida.

Sindelar, P. T., Rennells, M. S., Daunic, A. Austrich, C., & Eisele, M. (1999). *Systematic evaluation of alternative routes to teaching competence: Project SEART–C final report.* Gainesville, FL: Center for School Improvement (Technical Rep. No. 10).

Singer, J. D. (1993). Are special educators' career paths special? Results from a 13-year longitudinal study. *Exceptional Children, 59,* 262–279.

Singh, K., & Billingsley, B. S. (1996). Intent to stay in teaching: Teachers of students with emotional disorders versus other special educators. *Remedial and Special Education, 17,* 37–47.

Southeast Center for Teacher Quality. (January 2002). *Recruitment and retention strategies in a regional and national context* [Electronic Report]. Southeast Center for Teaching Quality Recruitment and Retention Strategies. Retrieved September 2, 2002, from http://www.teachingquality.org/resources/articles.htm

U.S. Department of Education (1998). Special education teachers: National trends and demand and shortage (Section III, pp. 1–23). In USDOE (Ed), *Twentieth annual report to Congress on the implementation of the Individuals with Disabilities Education Act.* Washington, DC: Author.

U.S. Department of Education (1998). *Twentieth annual report to Congress on the implementation of the Individuals with Disabilities Education Act.* Washington, DC: Author.

U.S. Department of Education (2000). *Twenty-second Annual Report to Congress on the Implementation of the Individuals with Disabilities Education Act.* Washington, DC: Author.

U.S. Department of Education (2001). *Annual report tables: IDEA Part B Personnel (1998–99), Table AC[1] and AC[2].* Retrieved August 23, 2001 from www.ideadata.org/arc_toc.html#partbCC

U.S. Department of Education (2002). *Meeting the Highly Qualified Teachers Challenge: The Secretary's Annual Report on Teacher Quality*: U.S. Department of Education, Office of Postsecondary Education.

Webber, J., Raffeld, P., & Kettler, M. (n.d.). *Troops as teachers in Texas are they effective?* Research report.

West, J. (2002, November). *Highly qualified special education teachers: The policy debate.* Paper presented at annual meeting of Teacher Education Division of Council for Exceptional Children, Savannah, GA.

Westling, D. L., & Whitten, T., M. (1996). Rural special education teachers' plans to continue or leave their teaching positions. *Exceptional Children, 62,* 319–335.

White, M., & Mason, C. (2001). *Mentoring induction principles and guidelines (draft).* Arlington, VA: Council for Exceptional Children.

Whitaker, S. D. (2000). Mentoring beginning special education teachers and the relationship to attrition. *Exceptional Children, 6,* 546–566.

Wilson, S. M., Darling–Hammond, L., & Berry, B. (2001). *A case of successful teaching policy: Connecticut's long-term efforts to improve teaching and learning.* Seattle: University of Washington.

Yee, S. M. (1990). *Careers in the classroom: When teaching is more than a job.* New York: Teachers College Press.

Zeichner, K. M., & Schulte, A. K. (2001). What we know and don't know from peer-reviewed research about alternative teacher certification programs. *Journal of Teacher Education, 52,* 266–282.

RESOURCES

Sites of Interest to Teachers

Beginning and Preservice Teachers, *www.sabine.k12.la.us/vrschool/newteachers.htm*
A website providing support and insight for new and beginning teachers.

LD Online, *www.ldonline.org*
A user-friendly website for parents, teachers and other professionals involved in the area of special education.

National Staff Development Council, *www.nsdc.org*
A robust site for information on staff development for educators: addresses issues of teacher quality, staff development, and school improvement.

New Teacher Center, *www.newteachercenter.org*
Website hosted by the University of California at Santa Cruz that is dedicated to teacher development and new teacher training.

Recruiting New Teachers, *www.rnt.org*
A website offering guidance and resources for prospective teachers, as well as information and research on current trends and issues in the field.

Special Education News, *www.specialednews.com*
A website that offers unique resources to special education professionals. Topics include educating students with disabilities as well as special education news and events across the country.

Teachers.Net *www.teachers.net*
A supportive site for beginning and experienced teachers.

Access of Adolescents with Disabilities to General Education Curriculum: Myth or Reality?

Jean B. Schumaker, Donald D. Deshler, Janis A Bulgren,
Betsy Davis, B. Keith Lenz, and Bonnie Grossen

As the United States begins to implement the historic No Child Left Behind (NCLB) legislation, one thing is clear: 6 million of this country's secondary-aged students are in serious danger of being left behind. These young people live in our cities, suburbs, and rural areas and reflect all income levels. Predictably, many of these at-risk students also have a disability. Adolescents with disabilities have found the demands and expectations of high school to be especially stringent, as reflected by the findings of the National Longitudinal Transition Study (Wagner, Blackorby, & Hebbeler, 1993). That study reported that a disproportionate number of students with disabilities (38%) drop out of school (compared to 25% of the general population). In addition, preceding their decision to drop out of school, students with disabilities generally demonstrate higher rates of absenteeism, lower grade-point averages, and higher course-failure rates than students in the general population (Wagner et al., 1993).

In spite of these striking problems presented by the adolescent population in our schools, the vast majority of attention and resources during the past decade have been devoted to increasing *early childhood* education opportunities and reaching the national goal of making sure that every child possesses basic literacy skills by the third grade. Although these goals are important and laudable, there is a potential danger in overemphasizing early intervention at the expense of interventions for older students—especially those who have reached high school.

Specifically, the calls for early intervention efforts may erroneously imply that by providing early intervention, most of the problems presented by students with disabilities will be ameliorated by the time they reach adolescence. Although this is certainly a desired outcome, research has shown that the disabilities of these students persist and continue to affect their learning at older ages as well (Warner,

Schumaker, Alley, & Deshler, 1980). Thus, as compelling as the case for early intervention can be, if that case is made at the expense of addressing the equally problematic and unique set of problems presented by older students, the long-term effects of that policy will be devastating for thousands of individuals with disabilities (Deshler, 2002).

Passage of the landmark NCLB legislation holds great promise for students. Nevertheless, the probability of realizing the vision set forth in NCLB must be as high for adolescents as it is for younger children, and it must hold the potential for impacting students with disabilities as much as it does for impacting students without disabilities. Regrettably, many educators report feeling overwhelmed with the task of implementing NCLB legislation across the entire age continuum (especially given the complex nature of secondary schools), and thus they have all but decided that the limited resources they have should be targeted to improving only the front end of the American educational system.

Indeed, the real tragedy is the quiet resignation that seems to pervade many education circles and the view that little, if anything, can be done for older students. In some quarters the promises inherent in NCLB do not extend to adolescents who continue to struggle to meet high standards or, worse, simply give up and leave school without a high school diploma (Alliance for Excellent Education, 2002).

ATTEMPTS TO INCREASE ACCESS FOR ADOLESCENTS WITH DISABILITIES

Although the number of federal and state-based initiatives targeted on adolescents has increased since passage of PL 94–142 in the mid 1970s, there is limited evidence prior to that time that adolescents with disabilities were considered capable of benefiting from traditional schooling, gaining competitive employment, or becoming valued citizens in the community (Sitlington, Clark, & Kolstoe, 2000). Fortunately, initiatives in the areas of career education of exceptional youth (e.g., Brolin & Kokaska, 1979; Kokaska & Brolin, 1985) have targeted the design of programs that would enable students to acquire an array of competencies in the areas of daily living skills, personal–social skills, and occupational guidance and preparation skills. In addition, in 1978, the Office of Special Education Programs funded five research institutes to study problems in the area of learning disabilities. One of these institutes (the Institute for Research in Learning Disabilities at the University of Kansas) had as its sole research focus the study of adolescents with learning disabilities. This was a significant investment (several million dollars), but the funding ended after 5 years.

In the mid–1980s, Madeline Will, director of the Office of Special Education and Rehabilitative Services, championed the transition movement that extended career education issues into the realm of transition programs and services and linkages with adult community services. The majority of state and federally supported initiatives that related to adolescents with disabilities were aimed at addressing issues and developing programs surrounding transition (e.g., transition assessment, transition to employment, job placement, transition to postsecondary education, transition to adult independent living); however, meager resources were directed to supporting efforts to design and validate academically based interventions to enable adolescents with disabilities to successfully respond to rigorous curricular demands leading to high school graduation.

Consequently, the country's relatively low priority for creating interventions that would enable adolescents with disabilities to gain access to and also succeed within an inclusive academic environment in high school settings has resulted in a largely unfavorable situation for these older students. As a result, American high schools, by and large, have failed to prepare adolescents with disabilities to obtain a standard diploma and also have fallen short in preparing them to face the demanding expectations of the globalization of commerce and industry, the dramatic growth of technology, and the dramatic transformation of the workplace and the very nature of work itself (Martin, 1999; Oliver, 1999; Rifkin, 1995).

As discouraging as the above state of circumstances may seem, a host of emerging trends may exacerbate the situation even further for adolescents with disabilities. Foremost among these trends are:

1. The increased expectation that *all* learners, including those with disabilities, meet the curriculum standards adopted by states and professional organizations (Thurlow, Elliot, & Ysseldyke, 2003; National Research Council, 1997);
2. The pressure to include adolescents with disabilities in the general education classroom for as much of the school day as possible (Wagner et al., 1993);
3. The explosion of knowledge and information and the growing expectation that all students not merely acquire but also integrate thinking skills with their content-area knowledge in authentic problem-solving activities (Kameenui & Carnine, 1998); and
4. The clear expectations set forth in PL 105–17 that programming for students with disabilities be outcome-based within the context of successfully mastering the general education curriculum (Turnbull, Rainbolt, & Buchele–Ash, 1997).

A RENEWED COMMITMENT TO MEANINGFUL ACADEMIC ACCESS

Under the leadership of Drs. Louis Danielson (Director of the Research to Practice Branch of the Office of Special Education Programs [OSEP]) and Bonnie Jones (Project Officer for Secondary and Transition Programs, OSEP), a growing set of federal investments have been made in initiatives designed to increase the array of research-based interventions available to practitioners who work with adolescents with disabilities for the purpose of enabling them to graduate from high school with a standard diploma. One of the major OSEP investments to this end was the creation of the Institute for Academic Access (IAA), a 5-year collaborative research project between researchers at the University of Kansas Center for Research on Learning (CRL) and the University of Oregon.

In the broadest sense, the purpose of the IAA is to determine ways to substantially improve educational outcomes for adolescents with disabilities who can be educated within the general education curriculum by conducting a high-impact program of research that takes into account the unique characteristics presented by these students *and* the complex dynamics that define the setting and circumstances unique to secondary curricula and schools. Together, special and general educators are seeking to redefine what they do in order to achieve results for students with disabilities that are consistent with the demands of standards-based reforms (National Research Council, 1997).

Three major goals guide the work of the IAA. First, investigators are *synthesizing current knowledge* in four areas:

1. Instructional planning for academically diverse classrooms;
2. Evidence-based instructional practices that can be used in challenging core classes;
3. Instructional technology, media, and materials; and
4. Contextual factors that influence learning in high schools.

Critical gaps in current knowledge are identified to guide IAA work.

Second, IAA partners conduct a rigorous program of *research* to:

1. Supply secondary educators with a menu of validated interventions from which they can build instructional programs that fit their courses and schools;
2. Make available high-quality teacher training programs to promote implementation of research-based practices and coordination of instruction; and
3. Provide educators with methods for working together, creating effective contexts for learning, and delivering combinations of interventions.

Third, Institute partners are designing, implementing, and evaluating a *dissemination approach* that will result in widespread use of the products of the IAA in high schools across the nation. In short, the IAA is attempting to generate timely and critical information on effective strategies for enabling adolescents with disabilities to benefit from the general education curriculum in high schools.

CONCEPTUAL FRAMEWORK FOR THE IAA

The conceptual framework for promoting the success of adolescents with disabilities in the core academic curriculum of secondary schools has been designed in conjunction with critical stakeholders (e.g., educators, parents, students). This framework represents a departure from instructional practices traditionally used in secondary schools. Typically, these programs are fragmented, consist mainly of tutoring activities (Mercer, Lane, Jordan, Allsop, & Eisele, 1996) and an occasional accommodation (Lancaster & Gildroy, 1999), and are oriented toward getting the student through assignments in basic required courses.

In contrast, the conceptual framework for this project represents an optimistic vision of what these students can accomplish and how they can accomplish it. The vision has grown out of a rich tradition of nearly 25 years of research conducted at the Universities of Kansas and Oregon in the area of disabilities (e.g., Bulgren, & Lenz, 1996; Grossen & Carnine, 1996; Kameenui & Carnine, 1998; Schumaker & Deshler, 1992). It embodies a different approach to instruction for the majority of adolescents with disabilities who are enrolled in the general education curriculum. Within this vision, students can meet academic standards in the core curriculum and become prepared for future education/training. The approach is founded on the contention that adolescents with disabilities have the greatest probability of being successful both in secondary school and beyond if they acquire critical knowledge that relates to their lives and can learn how to acquire additional knowledge through carefully structured practice opportunities.

The conceptual framework shown in Figure 6.1 specifies three major components being developed and validated, each of which contains several interventions. Collectively, these interventions eventually will provide educators with a *menu* of validated practices from which they can choose and through which they can build core academic courses and academic programs tailored specially to their students and schools.

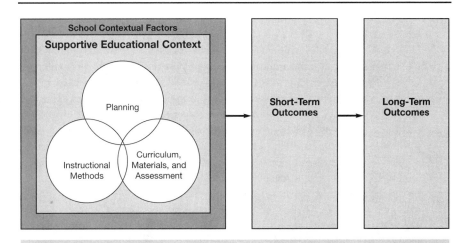

Short-Term: Attainment of standards, improved understanding, improved retention, average or above test grades, average or above course grades, improved short-term goals, improved hope, improved self-esteem

Long-Term: Completion of sequence of required courses, high school graduation lifelong learning skills, enrollment in postsecondary education

FIGURE 6.1 ■ Conceptual Framework for Creating Authentic Academic Access

Some of the interventions are being developed "from scratch" and validated through the IAA. Other interventions already have been validated as effective in improving the performance of middle school students with disabilities (e.g., Carnine, 1997; Engelmann & Carnine, 1988) and must be validated as effective for high school students. Still others to be included have already been validated in experimental studies as effective with high school students with disabilities in limited subject areas (e.g., Bulgren, Schumaker, & Deshler, 1994; Lenz, Alley, & Schumaker, 1987) but have yet to be validated in other subject areas and in combination with other interventions. The best ways of preparing teachers to use combinations of these interventions are being identified, and the structures and contexts within which they can be best combined and delivered are being developed.

The first intervention component in the conceptual framework illustrated in Figure 6.1 is *Planning*. Within this component are methods that teachers use to plan and structure core subject area courses so *all* students can succeed and attain required standards. Within the IAA, teachers and researchers are working together to create two types of planning methods:

1. Methods that enable them to match content to the standards their students are expected to meet, and to select or create materials, activities, assignments, and instructional methods that will help them instruct their students to meet these standards; and
2. Methods that enable IEP teams to work together to create IEPs for students with disabilities in relation to the required academic standards (e.g., state assessment standards).

The *Instructional Methods* component focuses on instructional methods that teachers can use in core required courses to ensure that students understand and retain the content. This component is founded on research-validated instructional principles (Carnine, 1995, 1997; Carnine, Engelmann, Hofmeister, & Kelly, 1987; Darch & Carnine, 1986; Darch, Carnine, & Kameenui, 1986; Kelly, Gersten, & Carnine, 1990), as well as extensive lines of programmatic research conducted through the auspices of both partner research sites.

This conceptual framework involves the general education teacher in the role of an expert learner who teaches, models, and guides students in acquiring the processes involved in learning content as well as the content itself through the use of teaching routines. Thus, interventions are being created for the Instructional Methods component that combine available teaching routines and other routines identified as needed by high school teachers and researchers with what is known about strategic instruction.

The third component of the framework is *Curriculum Materials and Assessment*. It is composed of learner-friendly materials (e.g., textbooks, videodisc programs, multimedia systems, graphic devices) that high school general education teachers can use, along with the instructional methods described above, to present content to their students. It also focuses on tools that can be practically and effectively used to assess students' progress toward attaining the standards and to report progress to students and parents.

Though many teachers focus on the nature of an instructional material (e.g., textbook versus computer discs), the critical dimension of quality in an instructional tool is not so much the delivery medium as the way instruction is designed. Thus, these materials are based on six design principles formulated by researchers at the University of Oregon, including elements such as big ideas, conspicuous strategies, mediated scaffolding, planned review, and so on.

The three instructional components illustrated in Figure 6.1 work together in a synergistic fashion to create a critical mass of interventions that are sufficiently powerful to impact the performance of students on rigorous academic tasks. In addition, they function within a supportive educational context, one in which teachers receive the necessary support from administrators, special educators, and other support staff to enable them to teach within the new instructional paradigm. This supportive educational context, in turn, functions within the larger context of a school reform structure in which the continuous learning and professional development of the teaching staff is valued and promoted through ongoing dialogue, planning, and activities in which parents, students and other members of the community are involved along with school staff.

UNDERSTANDING THE REALITIES OF THE HIGH SCHOOL CONTEXT

As depicted in Figure 6.1, interventions must be implemented within the realities and constraints of the high school setting. Hence, the first phase of IAA work has been to do a careful analysis of an array of high school settings to determine the nature of demands that adolescents with disabilities are expected to meet if they are to be successful within inclusive general education classrooms, as well as to understand the actual extent to which students with disabilities currently have access to and are succeeding in rigorous general education classes.

The purpose of this research was to study nine high schools representing geographic, demographic, and organizational diversity, to measure a broad array of instructional and contextual variables, and to identify contextual features that support or hinder the use of validated practices by teachers and the learning of adolescents with disabilities. The major findings and conclusions from this phase of IAA research are summarized here.

DETAILS OF THE DESCRIPTIVE STUDY

The School Settings

Nine public high schools serving grades 9 through 12 participated. Three types of high schools participated.

  1. Three represented schools, referred to as "urban high schools," located in high-density areas (i.e., urban/metropolitan areas populated by more than

150,000 people) and in which more than 50% of the student population consists of "students living in poverty," defined as students who had applied for and received free or reduced-price lunch benefits.

2. Three of the high schools, referred to as "rural high schools," were schools located in low-density population areas (i.e., towns of fewer than 10,000 people, and fewer than 150 people per square mile) and in which more than 10% of the student population consisted of students living in poverty.

3. Three of the high schools, referred to as "suburban high schools," were located in towns having a population of more than 45,000 people and fewer than 150,000 people and in which fewer than 10% of the student population was composed of students living in poverty.

Three of the high schools (one urban, one rural, and one suburban) were located in Kansas. Three of the high schools (one urban, one rural, and one suburban) were located in the state of Washington. Two schools (one rural, one urban) were located in California. One school (suburban) was located in Oregon. The student populations in the urban schools ranged in size from 1,031 to 3,508 students. In the rural schools, the populations ranged in size from 330 to 693 students. The student populations in the suburban schools ranged in size from 931 to 1,691 students.

The percentage of students with disabilities in the nine schools ranged from 3.9% in a suburban school to 14.8% in an urban school. Six of the schools had Caucasian majorities, ranging from 67% to 95% of the student population. One school had a Latino/Hispanic majority; one school had an African–American majority; and one had an Armenian majority.

Within these high schools, students were observed in three settings:

1. The *special education class setting,* defined as any classroom or space in which an adolescent with disabilities was receiving services to assist him or her to succeed in general education courses.

2. *General education classrooms,* in which rigorous ninth-grade general education courses were being taught. A rigorous general education course, defined as a math, English, social studies/history, science, or foreign language course that a student must pass to earn a standard high school diploma, that contributes credits toward a standard high school diploma (as in the case of a foreign language course), that has been designed for helping students meet state standards, and that was being taught by a teacher with credentials in the subject area. The specific rigorous courses targeted for this investigation were five courses typically taught to ninth graders: algebra I, ninth-grade English, biology, history, and Spanish I.

3. Some students also were observed in *settings before and after classes,* such as the hallways, lunch rooms, and school-entry areas. Teachers were observed both in special education classrooms and in general education classrooms.

The Participants

Students

The students with disabilities (SWDs) targeted in this project were students who had been formally classified as having a disability (e.g., a learning disability, emotional disorder/disturbance, behavioral disorder, physical disability, visual disability, hearing disability, or other health impairment) according to state guidelines. In addition, they were students who either had been enrolled in one or more rigorous general education course as defined above or were judged by their special education teachers as students who could have been enrolled in one or more rigorous general education courses successfully if they had had the appropriate instructional support.

These were students who were expected to earn standard high school diplomas by their special education teachers. Hereafter, this will be the only type of student with disabilities referred to in this report. In general education classes where no SWDs were enrolled, they were replaced in the study by "at-risk students." "At-risk (AR) students" were those who had each earned more than one failing grade in a required course in a previous semester or who already were failing at least one rigorous general education course as defined above at the time of the study. In addition, they were students who had not been formally classified as having a disability.

A third group of participating students were normally achieving (NA) students. These were students who were enrolled in the same ninth-grade English classes as participating students with disabilities and who were earning at least a "C" grade in the course. They were matched to the students with disabilities by gender and grade level.

Parents

Participating parents were those who had agreed to allow their sons or daughters to participate in the investigation.

Teachers

Participating general education teachers were those who were teaching the targeted general education courses (algebra I, English, history, biology, Spanish I) to heterogeneous classes of students, including students with disabilities and/or at-risk students. These teachers were certified to teach their subject area (e.g., certified to teach algebra). The special education teachers were teachers who were providing special education services to students with disabilities.

School Administrators

The principal of each school participated. An individual who had been designated as the person responsible for administering the special education program in the school and who had an office/classroom in the school participated as the special education administrator.

The Measurement Tools

A broad array of measurement tools and instruments was designed to help to gather the data needed to answer the major questions. Each instrument is described briefly in the following paragraphs. This description is intended to enhance an understanding of the findings from this comprehensive study of key contextual factors in high school settings and to provide a perspective on the breadth and depth of variables considered.

Student Instruments

Adolescents in the study were asked to complete three forms. On the first form, called the *Student Survey,* students indicated, using a 7-point Likert-type scale, how much they agreed or disagreed with each of 37 items. The items related to their attitudes about learning (e.g., "I don't want to do the hard work in a challenging class"); academic skills (e.g., "For the things that I am asked to do in my high school classes, I feel that I have good skills to be successful"); beliefs (e.g., "I believe I can get better as a learner"); and relationships with adults and students in the school (e.g., "I have a close relationship with at least one adult in this school").

On the second form, called the *Student Satisfaction Form,* students rated their satisfaction using a 7-point Likert-type scale for each item, with "1" indicating that they were "Completely Dissatisfied" and "7" indicating that they were "Completely Satisfied." Two forms of this questionnaire were used, one for SWDs and one for normally achieving students.

The items on the Student Satisfaction Form for SWDs related to their satisfaction with how their special education teachers help them succeed in general education classes, how their special education teachers and parents communicate, how their special education teachers are preparing them for life after high school graduation, how the teachers of their required academic courses help them learn, their comfort with and outcomes associated with those academic courses, and their overall high school experience. They also were asked to list three skills they have learned in high school that have been useful in their succeeding in required courses, and three skills they need to learn to get better grades in required courses.

The items on the Student Satisfaction Form for normally achieving students were the same as the items on the Satisfaction Form for SWDs except the wording was changed slightly. For example, the SWDs were asked to indicate how satisfied they were with how the *special education teacher* was helping them complete assignments for required courses, whereas the normally achieving students were asked to indicate how satisfied they were with how the *teachers of their required academic classes* were helping them complete assignments for required courses.

The third form, called the *Student Demographics Form,* was used to gather personal information about the participating students. This included items such as their age, race, sex, and whether they receive free or reduced-price lunches at school.

SWDs were administered two tests. The *Multilevel Academic Survey Test (MAST)* was given to provide a standard measure of student achievement across students in the different participating schools. This test yields achievement scores in reading and math. Percentile scores and grade-level achievement scores were utilized to describe the students.

In addition, the *vocabulary subtest of the WAIS–III* (or the WISC–R, as appropriate for age) was administered to obtain a measure of student ability across students in each school.

Further, the students were observed using three observation systems. First, SWDs were observed in their special education classes using the *Student Support Class Observation System,* a time-sample recording system consisting of a recording sheet and a behavioral code. The observer recorded the student's behavior and other factors associated with the ongoing instruction during 10-second intervals. Specifically, in the first column, the observer recorded the target student's behavior using a few words or a phrase. In the remaining columns, the observer placed tallies indicating whether a given behavior was instructional or noninstructional, whether the instruction during that interval was research-based, the type of academic response the student made, the instructional approach used with the student, the materials the student was using, the instructional grouping in which the student was included, and the sensory modalities the student was using. The observer also noted the number of students and teachers with whom the student was interacting during the interval.

Second, SWDs (or at-risk students, if no students with disabilities were enrolled in a given class) were observed in rigorous general education classes using the *Student General Education Class Observation System.* This system was similar to the observation system used in special education settings to observe students.

Third, SWDs and normally achieving students were observed throughout a whole school day using the *Case Study Observational System.* This system was composed of three observation forms. The *Class Observation Form* was used to record the student's behavior in relation to class activities, the number of contacts the student had with the teacher and other students, the number of minutes that elapsed before the student began work after the class period began, the student's mood/demeanor, the student's seat location, accommodations made for the student, and the homework assignment. This form was used in every class in which the student was enrolled and which the student attended during the day he or she was scheduled to be observed (some of the schools used block scheduling, so some of the students did not attend all the classes in which they were enrolled on the day they were observed).

The *Non-Class Observation Form* was used to observe the student before school, between classes, during lunch, and after school while on school grounds. Again, the student's demeanor and behavior, as well as the contacts made with teachers and students, were recorded.

In all the students' classes, the *Class Description Form,* which contained eight open-ended items, was used. The observer used this form to report, in sentence form, what had transpired during the class period. For example, the first item asked the observer to provide a general description of the lesson, the fourth item asked the observer to describe the relationship between the target student and other students, and the sixth item asked the observer to describe the general outcome of the class for the target student.

The students who were followed for a whole school day were also interviewed. The *Interview Protocol* included 13 open-ended questions that were asked orally of all the participating students individually. The students' oral responses were tape-recorded. In general, the questions focused on the student's reaction to the school day. For example, the students were asked to explain how the day had been typical or unusual, the best thing that had happened during the day, the discouraging things that had happened during the day, and what they planned to do after school.

In addition, the same students were asked to discuss, in small focus groups, their answers to oral questions. Participating students with disabilities in a school were grouped together, and participating normally achieving students in a school were grouped together for these discussions. The *Student Focus Group Protocols* contained 12 questions for the students with disabilities and 11 questions for the normally achieving students. The only difference between the two protocols was that the students with disabilities were asked the question, "In light of the fact that you have a disability, how difficult is it to be successful in this school?" and the normally achieving students were not. Other questions related to topics such as the workload they were carrying, their biggest worries about school, the helpfulness of the teachers, and barriers to their success in school.

Finally, information related to the participating students was gathered from school records using a form called the *Student Information Form*. Two versions of the form were created, one for the SWDs and one for the normally achieving students. The form was used to gather standardized test scores, the names of classes in which the student was enrolled, the semester grades the student earned, the number of days the student was absent, suspended, or expelled, the number of disciplinary actions incurred during each year of high school, and scores on state competency exams. The only difference between the version for the SWDs and the normally achieving students was that there was a place on the version for the SWDs to record the scores earned on individually administered achievement and aptitude tests and information about the student's disabilities.

Parent Instruments

Parents completed the *Parent Satisfaction Form*. Two forms of this questionnaire were used: one for parents of students with disabilities and one for parents of normally achieving students. The two forms were parallel, consisting of 56 items each. With the exception of a few differences in wording, the items on both were similar. Items were grouped in eight major sections relating to factors such as the parents' satisfaction with their relationship with school personnel, the ways teachers were helping their children succeed in high school, the ways teachers were helping their children prepare for life after high school, and their children's enrollment in required classes. For the large majority of the items, the parents were asked to rate their satisfaction on a 7-point Likert-type scale ranging from "1" (Completely Dissatisfied) to "7" (Completely Satisfied).

> Parents also participated in focus groups. The *Parent Focus Group Protocol* posed five open-ended questions to a small group of parents. The parents each were asked to respond to and discuss their answers to these five questions:
> What do you consider to be the greatest challenge that your son/daughter faces in being successful in high school?
> What do you expect your son/daughter to receive as a result of his/her high school education?
> What are your expectations for the nature of special education services provided to your son/daughter in high school?
> What skills and strategies does your son/daughter most need?
> What guidance would you give us as we design interventions?

The parents' responses were audiotape-recorded. After the session, their responses were written verbatim in sentence form.

Special Education Teacher Instruments

Special educators completed four forms. The purpose of the *Special Education Teacher Information Form* was to gather personal information about the teachers. The form contained 27 items that focused on information such as the teacher's age, race, sex, educational history, teaching certifications, and history as a teacher.

The *Special Education Teacher Questionnaire* gathered information about the teachers' perceptions of their roles as special educators, how they spend their time at school, how they make decisions about how students will be enrolled in courses, their beliefs about what the students need in order to succeed in rigorous courses, barriers to students' success, and the types of training they believed they need to help students succeed. Some of the questions asked the teachers to rank the items in a list of items indicating the most important. Other questions asked the teachers to specify the percentage of time or the number of hours per week they engaged in a certain activity.

The *Types of Classes Form* gathered information about the types of classes in which the students with disabilities were enrolled. The form consisted of five pages, each corresponding to a different type of class: (a) classes taken for general education credit that were taught by a special educator (Type A); (b) classes taken for general education credit in which only low-achieving students and students with disabilities were enrolled, which were taught by a general education teacher (Type B); (c) rigorous general education classes that were taught by a general education teacher and in which a heterogeneous population of students was enrolled (Type C); advanced placement classes (Type D); and other classes (e.g., electives such as physical education, art, band) (Type E). On each page were spaces for the teacher to specify the name of the course, name of the teacher teaching the course, and number of students with disabilities enrolled in the course.

The *Special Education Teacher Satisfaction Form,* the third form that special education teachers completed, gathered their satisfaction with the educational program for SWDs in their school, its outcomes, and their own performance as teachers. The questionnaire had 47 items formatted with a 7-point Likert-type scale ranging from "1" (Completely Dissatisfied) to "7" (Completely Satisfied). The items were organized into the following sections: those pertaining to how the general education teachers work with the special educator; those pertaining to the instruction provided to the SWDs by the general education teachers, those pertaining to progress reports created by general educators and shared with the special educator; those pertaining to student outcomes; those pertaining to professional development experiences in which the special educator had participated; and those pertaining to the special educator's own assessment of his or her performance with regard to ensuring SWDs' success (grades of "C" or above) in general education classes.

In addition to completing the three forms, the special education teachers were observed teaching in their classes, using the *Special Education Teacher Observation System.* This system was a time-sample recording system consisting of a recording sheet and a behavioral code. The recording sheet was used to record the teacher's behavior and other factors associated with the instruction taking place during 10-second intervals. The observer noted whether a given behavior was instructional or noninstructional, whether the instruction was research-based, the type of instructional methods used, the instructional approach used, the materials the students used, and the sensory modalities the students used. The observer also indicated the number of students and teachers with whom the special education teacher was interacting during the interval.

In addition, the observers completed four forms after observing the special education teacher. On the first, the *Technology Form,* the observer recorded any technology that the students used at the teacher's direction during the class period being observed. The observers also noted the name of the technology that was used (e.g., the name of software) and whether there was any evidence of a research base for the technology.

On the second form, the *Instructional Materials Form,* the observer recorded any instructional materials the students used at the teacher's direction during the class period being observed. The observers recorded the name of the material and whether there was any research base for the material.

The third form, the *Classroom Climate Checklist,* contained nine items representing the type of classroom climate the teacher had created. For example, the items included whether the classroom was neatly arranged, whether the room had any motivational posters, and whether the room had any instructional posters or aids.

The fourth form, the *Class Description Form,* contained nine items related to what had transpired during the class period. As examples, the first item asked the observer to provide a general description of the lesson, the second item asked the observer to describe the overall atmosphere the teacher had created, and the third item asked the observer to describe the students' attitude toward learning.

General Education Teacher Instruments

General education teachers completed three instruments. The first, the *General Education Teacher Information Form,* was identical in format and content to the Information Form designed for the special education teachers. The *General Education Teacher Satisfaction Form* was similar in format and content to the Special Education Teacher Satisfaction Form, but the words were changed slightly to fit the general education focus. For example, the general education teachers were asked to indicate how satisfied they were with the way the special education teachers worked with them, whereas the special educators were asked to indicate how satisfied they were with the way the general education teachers worked with them.

The purpose of the *General Education Teacher Questionnaire* was to gather information from the teachers about a particular course that they were teaching, including information about the instructional methods and assessments being used, the students enrolled in the course, demands associated with the course, teacher beliefs, and support received by the teacher from others in the school. The survey contained 90 items.

For instance, they were asked if they used a particular instructional method, type of assessment, or accommodation or the degree to which success in their course was dependent on students having a specific skill. For other items, the teachers were asked to indicate the percentage of work time they spent on a given activity. Still other items were open-ended, requesting the teachers to write an answer in either phrases or sentences (e.g., "Please list the five most common adaptations/accommodations you regularly use in this course"; "Please list the activities on which you collaborate with special education staff").

In addition to completing the three forms, the general education teachers were observed teaching one class, using the *General Education Teacher Observation System.* This system was similar to the observation system used with the special education teachers. In columns on the recording sheet, the observer recorded the teacher's behavior and other factors associated with the instruction, during 10-second intervals. The observer noted whether a given behavior was instructional or non-instructional, the type of motivational or instructional method being used, the materials the students were using, the way the students were grouped for instruction, and the sensory modalities the students were using. The observer also indicated the number of students and teachers with whom the general education teacher interacted during the interval.

As in the special education settings, the observers completed four forms after observing the general education teacher. These forms were identical to the ones used in the special education settings. On the *Technology Form,* the observer recorded any technology that the students used at the general education teacher's direction during the class period being observed. On the *Instructional Materials Form,* the observer recorded any instructional materials the students used at the teacher's direction during the class period being observed. On the *Classroom Climate Checklist,* the observer recorded whether nine items that might represent the type of classroom climate the teacher had created were present or absent. On the *Class Description*

Form, the observer recorded, in sentence form, descriptions of what had transpired during the lesson.

School Administrator Instruments

The *Principal Satisfaction Form* was designed to measure the principal's satisfaction with various aspects of the educational program for SWDs enrolled in general education classes. The questionnaire included 54 items, grouped into eight sets. Specifically, the principals were asked to indicate their satisfaction with how the special education teachers are working with the general education teachers, how the general education teachers who teach required courses are working with the special education teachers, how the special education teachers are helping students with disabilities succeed in required general education classes, the instruction provided by general education teachers for students with disabilities, the progress of students with disabilities in required general education classes, overall outcomes related to the education of students with disabilities, their own performance with regard to ensuring success for students with disabilities, and the professional development experiences that had been provided to teachers with regard to ensuring the success of students with disabilities in the general curriculum.

The *Principal Information Form* was a survey instrument containing 26 items. This form was designed to gather demographic and personal information about the principals, such as their age, race, sex, number of years in the education profession, and educational history.

The *Principal Interview Protocol* consisted of 68 questions grouped in seven sections. The purpose of the interview was to gather information from the principals about the ways their schools were serving students with disabilities, providing professional development experiences with regard to serving students with disabilities, and their attitudes about serving students with disabilities. The questions related to the school's organization and curriculum, programs that currently were serving students with disabilities, staff-development experiences, planning with regard to ensuring that students meet state standards, program-evaluation activities, instructional and adaptive technology available to the students with disabilities, and the school budget as it relates to serving students with disabilities and providing inservice programs for the staff.

Special Education Administrator Instruments

Three of the instruments (the *Special Education Administrator Satisfaction Form,* the *Special Education Administrator Information Form,* and the *Special Education Administrator Interview Protocol*) designed to gather information from the special education administrators were parallel in form and content to the instruments designed for the principals, except that the wording was changed slightly in some of the items to address the different job functions of the special education administrators. In addition, the special education administrators were asked to fill out the *Special Education Services Form,* designed to gather information about the special education services being offered in the school. Items related to the types of special education teachers and support staff working in the school, the numbers of each type of student with an exceptionality served in each general type of program (e.g., resource, self-contained), and names of the specific programs designed to support students with disabilities in rigorous general education classes.

School Instruments

Several forms were completed to collect data on the participating schools. The *School Climate Form* contained 16 items that an observer recorded as either present or not present in the school. Example questions included: "Are rules posted in the classrooms?" "Are there visual displays of student work?" and "Is there evidence of student academic goals posted?" The researcher filled out the form after taking a tour of the school.

The *School Data Form* contained places for the researchers to record information about the school, such as the number of different kinds of teachers in the school, the number of students receiving free lunches, the number of students representing different racial groups served by the school, and the number of students enrolled in the five target courses in each grade in the school. The *School District Data Form* contained places for researchers to record information about the school district associated with a participating school. Information included the number of schools in the district, the number of teachers employed by the district, the number of students served by the district, the staff development hours required for teachers each year, and the dropout percentage for the district.

The *Municipality Data Form* contained places for the researchers to record information about the town where the school was located. For example, the population of the municipality and the tax base for the municipality were collected on this form.

The *State Data Form* contained places for researchers to record information about the state where the participating school was located. This form was used to collect information such as the state requirements for high school graduation, total number of students enrolled in the state, and average per-pupil expenditure in the state.

THE MAJOR FINDINGS

Following is a brief synopsis of some of the findings from the descriptive study described above.*

Administrator Results

Although all of the administrators stated that they wanted to help SWDs be successful, eight of the nine high schools had no policy related to inclusion of SWDs

---

*Detailed research reports are available from the University of Kansas Center for Research on Learning, 518 J. R. Pearson Hall, 1122 West Campus Road, Lawrence, KS 66045; or these reports can be found online at: www.ku-crl.org

in general education courses. Further, the same schools had no methods for evaluating the outcomes of special education programs and no plan for improving these programs. Special education administrators were not familiar with the various academic tracks in which students could be enrolled within the general education curriculum.

In addition, according to the administrators, the general educators and special educators seemed to be quite isolated from each other in seven of the nine schools. Budgets for general and special education were separate, staff development activities were separate, planning time was not coordinated in such a way that general and special educators could consult with or collaborate with each other, their roles were separated, and responsibility for educating SWDs was not shared. Furthermore, for the most part, general educators had received no or very limited instruction on how to teach SWDs.

Urban principals were much more satisfied with their staffs and the way they instruct students with disabilities than were the suburban and rural principals. All of the urban principals' mean ratings were above 5.5 and several were above 6.3 on a 7-point scale. By contrast, many of the rural and suburban principals' ratings were in the 3- and 4-point range. When their ratings were averaged together, the principals were least satisfied with the way teachers report the progress of SWDs to them.

Overall, the ratings of the special education administrators were lower than the ratings of the principals. Although the suburban administrators were the most satisfied group, none of their mean ratings was above 5.6. Most of the mean ratings for the special education administrators fell within the 2-point, 3-point, and 4-point ranges. The administrators as a group were least satisfied with the professional development experiences that had been provided to teachers to help SWDs succeed in general education classes. The mean rating for items in this section was 2.9 on the 7-point scale.

Special Education Results

Seven of the nine schools had no designated services for providing support to SWDs enrolled in general education classes. In the two schools in which these services were available, one had a resource program in which SWDs received help with their homework and some remedial instruction in basic skills. In the other school, students received instruction in learning strategies, help with homework, and some instruction in career and life skills.

These were the only two schools in which the majority of SWDs were enrolled in rigorous general education courses taught by general education teachers in which a heterogeneous population of students were enrolled (Type C classes). The exception was a special algebra class in each of these two schools in which SWDs were enrolled. Otherwise, the students were enrolled in heterogeneous classes taught by general education teachers. One of these schools was the only participating school in which a written policy related to inclusion was in place.

In the other schools, SWDs either were enrolled in subject-area courses specially designed for special education students taught by a special education teacher (five of the schools) or were enrolled in subject-area courses specially designed for at-risk and special education students taught by a general education teacher or by a general educator teaming with a special educator. In courses taught solely by a special educator, students in several grades were often present in the classroom at the same time. Students worked independently on assignments and frequently were observed working on and asking the teacher for help on other assignments unrelated to the title of the course (e.g., working on math assignments when they were in English class). Thus, the roles of the special education teachers varied according to the types of classes they were teaching. In most of the schools, these teachers were teaching subject-area courses. The role of teaching the students skills and strategies was limited to only a few teachers in a few schools.

In response to questions on the survey, the special education teachers indicated that their most important roles with regard to supporting students in general education courses were teaching the students learning strategies and consulting with general education teachers. Before enrolling students in a general education course, they reported that they consider the general education teacher's attitude about teaching SWDs first, and the teacher's instructional methods second.

Results of the special education class observations showed that teachers and students were engaged in instruction for varying amounts of time in these classes across the schools. In one school, the teachers were engaged in instructing the students as much as 72% of the class time, but in most schools, they engaged in teaching the students about half of the time. In addition, they interacted with the students about half of the time. The percentage of time students spent in instruction ranged from 39% to 91%, depending on the school. Not surprisingly, the more time teachers spent in instruction, the more time students were engaged in instructional activities.

When they were instructing, special education teachers spent most of the time talking to students by either lecturing or giving directions. They also spent time monitoring students (watching students as they worked). They rarely used instructional methods that have been validated for teaching students with disabilities such as modeling, verbal rehearsal, and elaborated feedback. In only one school did teachers use research-based instructional programs, and those were the teachers who were teaching learning strategies. The teachers used few motivational behaviors during instruction, occasionally specifying expectations and giving brief feedback ("Good").

Overall, the special education teachers provided relatively low satisfaction ratings related to various aspects of their jobs, with many mean ratings falling in the "4" range on a 7-point scale. The teachers expressed the lowest satisfaction with the professional development experiences they had received in supporting SWDs in general education classes and the outcomes they were achieving in supporting these students in general education classes. Mean satisfaction ratings varied widely across the schools, with no clear pattern as to location of the school.

General Education Results

In filling out the General Education Teacher Survey, 70 high school teachers indicated that they frequently adapt curriculum and provide accommodations to improve the learning of SWDs. They also indicated that the teaching of strategies related to "how to learn" was of equal importance to teaching content. The teachers reported that smaller class sizes, more collaboration and communication with special education staff, and more competent staff are changes needed to help SWDs meet standards. On average, these teachers reported spending between 12 and 24 minutes per week in collaboration with special education teachers. Of interest is that general education teachers indicated that they believe SWDs are more likely to be successful in life than are students without disabilities who are low-achieving.

Relative to factors that general education teachers believe are contributors to academic failure for students with and without disabilities, teachers gave the highest rankings to youth goals/attitudes and youth skills/abilities. They indicated that they believe schoolwide structures and policies as well as instructional methods contribute least to academic failure. They also indicated that they believe student progress is satisfactory when about 50% of the students are mastering at least 50% of the content.

Through their written comments, the general education teachers indicated that they did not have an accurate idea of how many of their students have disabilities or which students have disabilities. Even when they did know, they indicated that they rarely knew the nature of the disability. They reported that sometimes they learned of the disability so late in the school year that they could do little to help the student succeed in the class at that point.

When general education teachers were observed, they engaged in instruction a mean of 59%–89% of the intervals observed, depending on the school. For the largest portion of these intervals, they were addressing the whole group of students. They were involved in interacting with students for a mean of 70% to 95% of the intervals, again depending on the school. Spanish teachers were the most involved in instruction, for a mean of 84% of the intervals, and they interacted the most with students, for a mean of 94% of the intervals. The teachers spent the largest portion of instructional time engaged in lecture or reading aloud to students—in some schools for an average of as many as 94% of the instructional intervals.

Other frequently observed teacher activities were giving directions, asking questions, and monitoring students as they worked. They engaged in few motivational behaviors. They also engaged in few, if any, research-based instructional methods. Math teachers used some modeling. They utilized few, if any, accommodations. None of the teachers used Content Enhancement Routines (Schumaker, Deshler, & McKnight, 2002), validated instructional methods for enhancing learning of all students (including those with disabilities) in subject-area classes. None of the teachers used technology-enhanced instruction.

When SWDs (or at-risk students, if no SWDs were enrolled) were observed, they engaged in instructional activities for a mean of 47%–72% of the intervals in general education classes. The amount of time they were engaged in instructional activities did not necessarily match the amount of time their teachers were engaged in the instruction. When the SWDs were engaged in an instructional activity (in most of the schools, more than 50% of the time), they spent the largest portion of time listening. They were expected to participate in whole-class activities for a mean of between 40% and 80% of the intervals. In addition, they were expected to be working independently some of the time in most of the classes (13%–25%). In some subject areas, small-group activities were in use for a mean of as many as 25% of the intervals.

Materials Results

The instructional materials used in ninth-grade general education courses in which SWDs were enrolled were examined. The courses included English/language arts, biology, history, algebra, and Spanish. The texts incorporated 50% to 60% of the features of considerate text. The readability of the texts ranged from five to seven grade levels higher than the reading levels of the students with disabilities taking the courses.

Across the schools, students were observed using the same types of materials in their courses, but the amount of time the students spent using the various materials varied widely across the schools. For example, the mean percentage of intervals during which students were referring to visual aids and textbooks ranged from a low of 2% to a high of 50%. The use of teacher-made materials (e.g., handouts, assignment sheets) ranged widely, from 0% in a couple of schools to 47% in another. In all of the schools, students were using basic materials such as pencils and paper at least 30% of the time. In none of the schools were students using computers or research-based materials.

In special education courses, the types of materials being used were somewhat similar across the schools, but as with the materials used in general education courses, the relative amount of time each type of material was used varied widely. In most of the schools, students were using basic materials, textbooks, and worksheets. In only two schools were the students using computers. In one of those schools, computers were used a mean of less than 1% of the intervals. In only one school were research-based materials in use for 5.7% of the intervals observed.

Student Results

The SWDs in this study were markedly different from students in the NA/AR group in terms of gender, ethnicity, and poverty. Surprisingly, they were relatively similar on measures of reading and math achievement. Specifically, 61% of the SWDs were males versus 47% males in the NA/AR group. For the SWD group, 22.12% were Hispanic/Latino and 13.3% were African–American. In the NA/AR group, only 9.5% were African–American and 1% were Hispanic/Latino. Reports on free and reduced lunch programs for SWDs indicated that 19% received free lunches (versus

3.5% for NA/ARs) and 6% received reduced lunch prices (versus 3.5% for NA/ARs).

On the Multilevel Academic Survey Test (MAST), the raw scores for reading were 29.3 for the SWDs versus 33.5 for the NA/ARs. Their mean math raw scores were nearly identical (12.2 for SWDs versus 13.2 for NA/ARs). On a measure of ability as indicated by the WISC III Vocabulary Subtest, the mean standard score for the SWD sample was 8.

Searches of records revealed that a very small percentage of the SWDs participate in rigorous general education classes taught by a general education teacher and in which a heterogeneous population of students is enrolled (Type C classes). Specifically, SWDs were enrolled in only about 5% of the potential core classes in which they could be enrolled. For example, for a sample of 153 SWDs in an urban high school (assuming that each student could be enrolled in four core courses), there would be a potential of 612 rigorous course enrollments [$153 \times 4 = 612$]). In this school, the actual number of rigorous general education enrollments was 8. In a suburban school, with 296 total possible enrollments for 74 students, only one actual enrollment was recorded. In short, SWDs are overwhelmingly enrolled classes taught by special education teachers or classes taken for credit in which only low-achieving students and students with disabilities are enrolled.

SWDs performed considerably poorer than their NA/AR counterparts in their coursework, as reflected by grade-point averages (GPAs). Specifically, in core courses, 56% of the SWDs achieved GPAs of D or F and 39% received GPAs of C. Thus, even though the majority of students are not enrolled in rigorous general education courses, they still are doing poorly in the courses in which they are enrolled. In contrast, only 18% of the NA/AR group received GPAs of D or F, and 49% received GPAs of C.

On state assessments or national tests (e.g., the MAT or the ITBS), SWDs performed more poorly than NA/AR students. For example, the percentage of SWDs receiving a score at or below the 20th percentile for reading achievement ranged from 86% to 100% across the schools. For math achievement, between 68% and 100% of SWDs scored at or below the 20th percentile, and for written expression, all of the SWDs scored at or below the 20th percentile. In contrast, the percentage of the NA/AR students scoring at or below the 20th percentile was less than half of the percentage of SWDs scoring at or below that level in each school.

Finally, on the Student Survey there were no discernable differences between the two groups on measures related to attitudes about learning, self-assessments about skills required to do well in school, and relationships with adults.

When SWDs were asked questions about how satisfied they were with their high school academic experiences and supports, most ratings were in the 4.5–5.5 range on a 7.0 scale (with 7.0 being completely satisfied). SWDs attending the suburban schools were generally more satisfied than students attending rural and urban schools. SWDs attending the suburban school where learning strategies were being taught were the most satisfied group. In fact, their mean ratings were above the 6.0 level (the "Satisfied" level) in all of the sections of the questionnaire except one. The level of satisfaction reported by the NA/AR students was comparable to the SWDs' ratings across the schools.

On this same survey, students were asked to report on the most useful skills they have learned in high school. Each group rated English/language arts as the most useful and mathematics concepts as the second most useful. The groups also were similar in the degree to which they endorsed the usefulness of typing and computer skills. Interestingly, however, the groups were quite different in their rating of the perceived usefulness of study skills, note taking, and life skills. In all cases, the NA/AR students rated these skills as more useful than did the SWDs. This finding may be related to what was found in the special education observation study, which indicated a lack of instructional emphasis in these areas.

Parent Results

In general, regarding communication and efficiency within the infrastructure of schools, parents reported that their students' school was not as responsive to the needs of SWDs as the parents would like. The parents cited little coordination or cooperation among special and general education teachers, exemplified by little awareness of students' Individualized Education Programs on the part of general education teachers. In addition, some parents noted lack of overall efficiency in assigning students to classes or correcting incorrect assignments to classes, frequent class-time interruptions, and interruptions in the flow of instruction caused by changes in the classroom such as the use of student teachers.

Regarding responses to students with disabilities in the general education classroom, parents reported that few adaptations or accommodations were made to help their students in general education classes, that they often were ignored or considered lazy, and that students were less likely to ask questions in general education classes than special education classes for fear of being embarrassed.

Regarding parental hopes and expectations for their students, parents mentioned that they wanted their students to leave school with social competence and the academic skills that would allow them to function in future educational or employment settings. In terms of social competence, parents specifically mentioned that they hoped their children would learn self-advocacy skills, become self-motivated, and have positive peer associations. Relative to their children's futures, parents wanted their students to get a diploma, to learn practical life skills including computer training, and ultimately to be employed in a good job.

Regarding responses that schools could make to enhance the educational results for their students, parent suggestions included the following:

- Special education teachers should provide more help for their students.
- Students should be taught how to learn through learning skills and strategies, with special emphasis on reading and notetaking.
- Instruction in these skills and strategies should be incorporated into general education classes.

■ Most important, these skills and strategies should be taught earlier than the high school years.

Two interesting items of feedback were that parents attached value to self-contained special education classes for difficult required subject-area courses, and they did not always appreciate that teachers expressed to students what the parents perceived to be unrealistic expectations that the students would and should go to college.

When parents were asked to indicate how satisfied they were with various facets of their children's educational program, many of the parents' ratings were low. In fact, only one mean rating for one section of the parent questionnaire reached the 6.0 ("Satisfied") level, and that was for parents of students enrolled in Suburban School #3 when they rated their relationship with school staff. Parents of students enrolled in that school were the most satisfied overall. Most of the other mean ratings by parents whose children were enrolled in the other suburban and the rural schools were in the 2-point, 3-point, and 4-point ranges. Overall, parents of students in the urban schools were the most satisfied group, with most of their mean ratings in the 5-point range.

SIGNIFICANCE OF THE FINDINGS

The results of this descriptive study indicate that the educational programs designed for SWDs in most of the participating high schools are not what they could be, given the research-based programs available today. First, none of the programs are comprehensive programs that include a number of components, such as intensive-strategy instruction, homework support, research-based instruction in general education courses, and career/vocational preparation. Although some of the programs had one or two components, only one program was utilizing a research-based component (learning strategy instruction), and that component was not in use for large proportions of students' time in class. This was the school that had the highest satisfaction ratings from general education teachers and the students with disabilities. It was one of the two schools in the study in which SWDs were enrolled in general education courses.

In the other seven schools, SWDs were either enrolled in subject-area courses taught by a special education teacher or in subject-area courses taught by a general education teacher (or team-taught by a general and special education teacher) that had been designed specifically for low-achieving students and students with disabilities. Observations of the classes being taught in the special education classroom indicated that they were more like study halls, in which students in several grades worked independently on assignments, than like actual subject-area courses.

These results are cause for concern because they indicate that, in most of the participating schools, SWDs are not receiving the benefits of the results of 25 years of research in the secondary special education field. Of course, the study summarized here focused on only nine high schools, and these schools cannot be considered to be representative of all high schools across the nation. Nevertheless, they are likely to be representative of some high schools across the nation, and IAA researchers, given their experience of observing schools in numerous districts throughout the country and working with staff members in many schools and state departments, believe that they do represent many high schools.

This relatively discouraging portrait of how SWDs are being served in high schools and minimal use of research-based practices raises some critical questions that must be addressed in future research.

■ Are the existing research-based interventions not sufficiently applicable given the conditions present within today's high schools?

■ Have teachers not been provided with quality professional development experiences that would enable them to effectively use these innovations?

■ Is there a lack of administrative leadership supporting the concentrated use of research-based practices?

■ Do teachers perceive a lack of alignment between the demands of statewide outcome assessments and research-based interventions?

These and other questions related to the scalability and sustainability of research-based interventions must be addressed to better understand how to increase the use of instructional practices that will improve student outcomes.

Clearly, much work remains to be done in high schools to set up comprehensive educational programs for SWDs. Schools must have visions of how SWDs are to be educated in such a way that they can succeed in rigorous general education courses, and they must have policies and procedures in place to match those visions. They also must have service-delivery mechanisms for delivering intensive strategy instruction and research-based homework assistance to SWDs so they can truly access the general education curriculum. Further, they have to restructure general education courses and their methods for assigning SWDs to general education courses so these courses become learner-friendly environments for these students and they can feel like valued and accepted members of the learning community.

Research is needed to address these whole-school issues. Ways of ensuring that school staff members create meaningful visions and policies for their schools have to be devised. Teachers need to be trained to use research-validated teaching methods and research-based instructional programs in such a way that they actually implement the programs. Administrators have to be trained to be instructional leaders such that they verbally support the new programs and also insist that the new programs be institutionalized and maintained. Ways for evaluating educational programs have to be devised and put into the hands of administrators. Until all these mechanisms are in place, SWDs likely will continue to flounder at the high school level, and they are not likely to have real access to the general education curriculum.

The magnitude of the challenges before the educational community has been intensified since passage of the NCLB Act. This legislation creates an even higher and more demanding set of expectations for adolescents with disabilities. Unless conditions are created that will enable SWDs to compete successfully with their normally achieving peers in high schools, the full potential of SWDs as learners in school, as future workers in the global economy, and as contributing community members will not be realized. These findings clearly underscore the notion that researchers must develop and schools must adopt and apply research-based interventions with fidelity in a coordinated, well-orchestrated fashion. In this way, adolescents with disabilities will receive genuine access to the general education curriculum.

REFERENCES

Alliance for Excellent Education (2002). *Every child a graduate: A framework for an excellent education for all middle and high school students.* http://www.all4ed.org/policymakers/Every/execsum.html

Brolin, D. E., & Kokaska, C. J. (1979). *Career education for handicapped children and youth.* Columbus, OH: Charles E. Merrill.

Bulgren, J. A., & Lenz, B. K. (1996). Strategic instruction in the content areas. In D. D. Deshler, E. S. Ellis, & B. K. Lenz (Eds.). *Teaching adolescents with learning disabilities: Strategies and methods* (2d ed., pp. 409–473). Denver: Love Publishing.

Bulgren, J. A., Schumaker, J. B., & Deshler, D. D. (1994). The effects of a recall enhancement routine on the test performance of secondary students with and without learning disabilities. *Learning Disabilities Research and Practice, 9*(1), 2–11.

Carnine, D. (1995). Trustworthiness, use ability, and accessibility of educational research. *Journal of Behavioral Education, 5*(3), 251–258.

Carnine, D. (1997). Instructional design in mathematics for students with learning disabilities. *Journal of Learning Disabilities, 30*(2), 130–141.

Carnine, D., Engelmann, S., Hofmeister, A., & Kelly, B. (1987). Videodisc instruction in fractions. *Focus on Learning Problems in Mathematics, 9*(1), 31–52.

Darch, C., & Carnine, D. (1986). Approaches to teaching learning-disabled students literal comprehension during content area instruction. *Exceptional Children, 53*(3), 240–246.

Darch, C., Carnine, D., & Kameenui, E. (1986). The role of graphic organizers and social structure in content-area instruction. *Journal of Reading Behavior, 18*(4), 275–295.

Deshler, D. D. (2002). Response to "Is learning disabilities just a fancy term for low achievement? A meta-analysis of reading differences between low achievers with and without the label." In R. Bradley, L. Danielson, & D. Hallahan (Eds.), *Identification of learning disabilities.* (763–771), Mahwah, NJ: Lawrence Erlbaum.

Englemann, S., & Carnine, D. (1988). *Earth science.* Washington, DC: Systems Impact, Inc.

Grossen, B., & Carnine, D. (1996). Considerate instruction helps students with disabilities achieve world class standards. *Teaching Exceptional Children, 28*(4), 77–81.

Kameenui, E. J., & Carnine, D.W. (Eds.). (1998). *Effective strategies for accommodating students with diverse learning and curricular needs.* Columbus, OH: Merrill.

Kelly, B., Gersten, R., & Carnine D. (1990). Student error patterns as a function of curriculum design: Teaching fractions to remedial high school students and high school students with learning disabilities. *Journal of Learning Disabilities, 23*, 23–29.

Kokaska, C. J., Brolin, D. E. (1985). *Career education for handicapped individuals* (2d ed.). Columbus, OH: Charles E. Merrill.

Lancaster, P. E., & Gildroy, P. (1999). Facilitating transitions: Learning in diverse schools and classrooms. In D. Deshler & J. Schumaker (Eds.), *Teaching every adolescent every day.* Cambridge, MA: Brookline Books.

Lenz, B. K., Alley, G. R., & Schumaker, J. B. (1987). Activating the inactive learner: Advance organizers in the secondary content classroom. *Learning Disability Quarterly, 10*(1), 53–67.

Martin, C. (1999). *Net future.* New York: McGraw–Hill.

Mercer, C.D., Lane, H.B., Jordan, L., Allsop, D. H., Eisele, M.R. (1996), Empowering teachers and students with instructional choices in inclusive settings. *Remedial and Special Education, 17*(4), 226–236.

National Research Council (NCR). (1997). *National science education standards.* Washington, DC: National Academy Press.

Oliver, R.W. (1999). *The shape of things to come.* New York: McGraw–Hill.

Rifkin, J. (1995). *The end of work: The decline of the global labor force and the dawn of the post–market era.* New York: Putnam.

Schumaker, J. B., & Deshler, D. D. (1992). Validation of learning strategy interventions for students with learning disabilities: Results of a programmatic research effort. In B. Y. L. Wong (Ed.), *Contemporary intervention research in learning disabilities: An international perspective* (pp. 22–46). New York: Springer–Verlag.

Schumaker, J. B., Deshler, D. D., & McKnight, P. (2002). Ensuring success in the secondary general education curriculum through the use of teaching routines. In G. Stover, M. R. Shinn, & H. M. Walker (Eds.), *Interventions for achievement and behavior problems.* Washington, DC: National Association of School Psychologists.

Sitlington, P. L., Clark, G. M., & Kolstoe, O. P. (2000). *Transition education and services for adolescents with disabilities.* Boston: Allyn & Bacon.

Thurlow, M. L., Elliot, J. L., & Ysseldyke, J. E. (2003). *Testing students with disabilities: Practical strategies for complying with district and state requirements.* (3d ed.). Thousand Oaks, CA: Corwin Press.

Turnbull, R., Rainbolt, K., & Buchele–Ash, A. (1997). *Individuals with disabilities education act: Digest of significance of 1997 amendments.* Lawrence, KS: Beach Center on Families and Disability.

Wagner, M., Blackorby, J., & Hebbeler, K. (1993). *Beyond the report card: The multiple dimensions of secondary school performance of students with disabilities. A report from the national longitudinal study of special education students.* Menlo Park, CA: SRI International.

Warner, M. M., Schumaker, J. B., Alley, G. R., & Deshler, D. D. (1980). Learning disabled adolescents in the public schools: Are they different from other low achievers? *Exceptional Education Quarterly, 1*(2), 27–35.

*This chapter is based on research supported by grant #PRH324S990001 from the Office of Special Education Programs. The information presented is the responsibility of the authors and does not necessarily represent the views of the U. S. Department of Education.

7

Supporting Beginning Special Education Teachers

Susan D. Whitaker

The first few years of teaching are indeed vital ones. During these years the novice emerges from the status of a student responsible for his or her own learning to that of a teacher responsible for promoting learning in others (Cooke & Pang, 1991). Tonnsen and Patterson (1992) described the first year this way:

> New teachers aren't always prepared for the challenges they'll find in the profession. They enter the field expecting–and often being expected–to do what the veteran teacher has been doing for years, with equal success. They face long days, filled with little time for reflection and planning. They face children with problems they can't understand. They face a bureaucracy that forces them to teach a prescribed curriculum in a prescribed manner . . . Just months earlier, most of these new teachers were carefree college students, idealistic to a fault. If they're thrown into a classroom and expected to succeed with little or no support, it's no wonder many of them quickly become disillusioned. (p. 29)

And it is no wonder that so many teachers leave the field early in their careers. Add to this description an ill-equipped classroom, limited materials and supplies, overwhelming amounts of paperwork, a myriad of legal and accountability issues, students of widely differing abilities, and students with serious emotional and behavioral problems, and you have the situation facing many beginning special education teachers. Thus the stage is set for a beginning year that will severely test the morale and dedication of even the most well prepared and enthusiastic new teacher.

An estimated 25% of beginning teachers do not teach more than 2 years and 40–50% leave the teaching profession within the first 5 years of teaching (Harris & Associates, 1992; Huling-Austin, 1986; Kirby & Grissmer, 1993; Schlechty & Vance, 1983). By the end of 5 years, 43% of the special educators newly hired in

Michigan and North Carolina were no longer teaching in those states (Singer, 1992). Although some of these teachers may have been teaching in other states and others may ultimately have returned to the profession, even the temporary loss of these teachers is significant. And far too many leave permanently. The Council for Exceptional Children's (2000) report "Bright Futures for Exceptional Learners" states that "four out of every ten special educators entering the field leave special education before their fifth year of teaching" (pg. 1).

Why does this happen to teachers who begin with such enthusiasm and so many high hopes? What are the needs and concerns of beginning special education teachers? What kinds of supports can we provide to these beginning teachers that will ease their transition into the classroom and reduce attrition early in their careers? To begin to answer these questions, I will review what we know about (a) the factors related to the difficulties teachers experience in their first year of teaching, (b) the needs and concerns of beginning teachers, (c) the needs and concerns of beginning special education teachers, and (d) induction and mentoring as supports for beginning teachers. I will conclude with recommendations for ways that various individuals can support beginning special education teachers.

FACTORS RELATED TO THE DIFFICULTIES EXPERIENCED IN THE FIRST YEAR

A review of the literature indicates that five factors are related to the difficulties many teachers face in their first year or years of teaching:

1. An inability to transfer learning from theory into practice
2. A lack of preparation for many of the difficulties and demands of teaching
3. Reluctance to ask questions or seek help
4. The difficulty of the teaching assignment and the inadequate resources provided
5. Unrealistic expectations and the associated loss of a sense of efficacy.

These factors significantly impact the needs and concerns of the novice teachers as they begin their teaching careers.

Inability to Transfer Learning From Theory into Practice

Many studies reveal that the novice teacher does not transfer what he or she knows on a theoretical basis from the preservice level to what is actually done on a practical daily basis in the public school classroom (Corcoran, 1981; Ryan, 1992). These teachers are confronted with unknown students and staff members, an unknown curriculum, unknown policies and procedures, and unfamiliar norms and rituals. This condition of "not knowing" results in data overload and can send beginning teachers into a state of shock in which they are unable to transfer the skills and concepts they mastered in the college setting into the public school classroom.

Lack of Preparation for the Demands of Teaching

This reality shock seems to stem, in part, from a lack of preparation for many of the difficulties and demands of teaching (Gaede, 1978; Gordon, 1991; Moran, 1990). In this regard, Gaede (1978) surveyed 272 teachers with a range of actual teaching experience. He measured self-assessed professional knowledge on a 5-point Likert scale. The results suggested a rise in self-assessed knowledge at every level except at the end of the first year of teaching, when the level actually drops. Gaede concluded, "Teachers discover during actual teaching that they were not as well prepared as they thought they were" (p. 407).

When difficulties arise for these teachers, it usually comes as a surprise (Ryan, 1992). Because they have spent 7 hours per day, 5 days per week, for 36 weeks a year since age 5 in a school setting, they tend to feel that they are on safe and familiar ground. But the reality is that even though the setting may be familiar, they have viewed it only from the perspective of the student. Now they must transfer to the teacher's perspective and into the teacher role. They must take the skills and knowledge they learned in a general way in the university setting and apply these in a specific context in their own classrooms.

Reluctance to Ask Questions or Seek Help

This problem is further complicated by the beginning teacher's need to appear both confident and competent (Corcoran, 1981). In his now classic study of beginning teachers, Lortie (1975) found that beginning teachers seek help infrequently. He also found that experienced teachers refrain from offering unsolicited advice. Glidewell, Tucker, Todt, and Cox (1983) confirmed these findings. In their study of 121 teachers, they found that 92% of novice teachers did not seek help from their colleagues except to swap stories about personal experiences. This lack of support leads to a profound sense of emotional, social, and professional isolation in which the beginning teacher is afraid to ask for help for fear of appearing incompetent, and the experienced teacher is afraid to offer help for fear of interfering.

Difficulty of the Initial Teaching Assignment And Inadequate Resources

Another challenge that novice teachers face is the difficulty of the initial teaching assignment and the inadequate resources they are often given (National Association of State Boards of Education, 2000). Rather than increasing the beginning teacher's responsibilities gradually over time, beginners are often given more responsibilities, the least desirable courses, the most time-consuming and least rewarding assignments, extracurricular duties the experienced teachers are unwilling to accept, and the most difficult students (Gordon, 1991).

The available jobs are often the ones that the experienced teachers do not want. "In most professions, the challenge of the job increases over time as one acquires experience and expertise. In teaching, we've had it reversed. Typically, the most challenging situation a teacher experienced was in his or her first year" (Glickman, 1990, p. vii).

Unrealistic Expectations and the Loss of the Sense of Efficacy

These challenges often leave the novice teacher believing by the end of the first year of teaching that he or she cannot teach effectively. At that time, the teacher either leaves the profession or becomes resigned to simply going through the motions (McLaughlin, Pfeifer, Swanson-Owens, & Yee, 1986). A teacher's sense of efficacy (the belief that teaching can influence student learning and that they themselves are competent teachers) is one of the few variables consistently found to be positively related to student achievement (Woolfolk, Rusoff, & Hoy, 1990). For this reason, the novice teacher's loss of the sense of efficacy is of serious concern for the personal well-being of the teacher and also for the academic achievement of the students.

Sadly, the Metropolitan Life Survey (Harris & Associates, 1991) reported that after one year of teaching, only 68% of the teachers strongly agreed that they can really make a difference in the lives of their students. This finding represents a significant decrease from the 83% who strongly agreed with the statement before beginning their first year of teaching.

Weinstein (1988) examined the expectations of 118 students enrolled in the elementary teacher education program at the University of Arizona. She developed a 33-item questionnaire based on Veenman's (1984) list of the most frequently perceived problems of first-year teachers. The prospective teachers were asked to rate how much of a problem they thought the average first-year teacher has with each item, and then how much of a problem they thought they would have with each item. The mean optimism values were all statistically significant (all but one beyond the .0001 level), indicating a significant tendency for the prospective teachers to expect the tasks of teaching to be less problematic for themselves than for most first-year teachers. Although this study used a restricted sample, Weinstein concluded, "The present results support the argument that unrealistic expectations contribute to the reality shock experienced by many beginning teachers" (p. 39).

Novice teachers enter teaching with a strong service ethic and dedication to helping students. When they no longer believe they can effectively accomplish these goals, they feel frustration and a sense of failure. This loss of a sense of efficacy results in severe disillusionment during the first year of teaching.

Needs and Concerns of Beginning Teachers

A number of studies have examined the needs and concerns of first-year teachers. In a comprehensive study, Veenman (1984) rank-ordered the problems identified in the research literature as the primary problems of beginning teachers at that time. Table 6.1 identifies the 24 most frequently perceived problems of beginning teachers from that study. Dollase (1992) surveyed beginning teachers regarding their perceptions of the severity of the problems on Veenman's list in today's classroom (rated on a 5-point Likert scale). Table 7.1 summarizes the results of this study as well.

Results of the two studies are quite similar in that eight of the top 12 problems are the same in both lists. Motivating students and dealing with individual differences were ranked second and third in Veenman's study and ranked third and second in Dollase's study. A striking difference, however, is that lack of spare time is ranked first in the Dollase study and 22nd in the Veenman study. Another notable difference is that in the Dollase study, problems related to individual students, such as dealing with problems of individual differences, dealing with slow learners, dealing with students of different cultures and backgrounds, and determining the learning level of students, are ranked higher than in the Veenman study.

TABLE 7.1 ■ Comparison of Most Frequently Perceived Problems of Beginning Teachers

Problem	Veenman's (1984) Rank Order	Dollase's (1992) Rank Order
Classroom discipline	1	6
Motivating students	2	3
Dealing with individual differences	3	2
Assessing students' work	4 (tie)	16
Relations with parents	4 (tie)	19
Organization of class work, time, and activities	6 (tie)	11
Insufficient materials and supplies	6 (tie)	9
Dealing with problems of individual students	8	5
Heavy teaching load resulting in insufficient preparation time	9	8
Relations with colleagues	10	23
Planning of lessons and school days	11	18
Effective use of different teaching methods	12	10
Awareness of school policies and rules	13	20
Determining learning level of students	14	7
Knowledge of subject matter	16 (tie)	16
Burden of clerical work	16 (tie)	12
Relations with principals/administrators	16 (tie)	24
Inadequate school equipment	18	21
Dealing with slow learners	19	4
Dealing with students of different cultures and deprived backgrounds	20	14
Effective use of textbooks and curriculum guides	21	13
Lack of spare time	22	1
Inadequate guidance and support	23	17
Large class size	24	22

Issues of management such as classroom discipline and organization of classwork, class time, and activities are ranked higher in the Veenman study. These differences may be attributable in part to the fact that the Dollase study is more current or that Veenman reported the *frequency* of occurrence of the problem in the literature and Dollase examined the perceived *severity* of the problem. Also, approximately one-third of the studies that Veenman examined were conducted outside of the United States and may not be representative of the needs and concerns of beginning teachers in the United States.

Huling-Austin and Murphy (1987) surveyed more than 150 beginning teachers in 10 school districts in eight states. The areas in which beginning teachers most frequently reported that they needed assistance were managing discipline, finding time to plan, grade papers, and keep records, motivating students, and dealing with individual differences. Odell's (1986) research identified the following needs (in rank order): (a) ideas about instruction, (b) personal and emotional support, (c) information on resources and materials, (d) information on district policies and procedures, and (e) suggestions regarding classroom management. These findings are similar to those of Veenman and Dollase.

Regardless of the date of the study, the sample used in the study, or the methodology employed in the study, the results have been remarkably consistent. The following 12 needs of first-year teachers consistently emerge, although the rankings vary across studies (Gordon, 1991, p. 5):

- managing the classroom
- acquiring information about the school system
- obtaining instructional materials and resources
- planning, organizing, and managing instruction and other professional responsibilities
- assessing students and evaluating student progress
- motivating students
- using effective teaching methods
- dealing with individual students' needs, interests, abilities, and problems
- communicating with colleagues, including administrators, supervisors, and other teachers
- communicating with parents
- adjusting to the teaching environment and role
- receiving emotional support.

Needs and Concerns of Beginning Special Education Teachers

Although all beginning teachers seem to have some of the same needs and concerns, certain additional needs and concerns are specific to beginning special education teachers. Results from a series of focus groups and from a survey of beginning special education teachers in South Carolina indicated that beginning special education teachers needed assistance in the following areas (from greatest reported need to least reported need): system information related to special education, emotional support, system information related to the school, materials, curriculum, and instruction, discipline, interactions with others, and management (Whitaker, 2000b; Whitaker, in press). These teachers reported needing significantly more assistance in each area than they actually received. They reported receiving the most assistance in the area of emotional support. The area in which they reported the largest discrepancy between what they needed and what they received was system information related to special education. Table 7.2 summarizes the needs of beginning special education teachers.

The studies also examined the types of support that beginning special education teachers said they needed. The teachers reported needing both formal and informal meetings with support teachers to discuss areas of concern and to ask questions. They also reported needing opportunities to observe other teachers and to be observed themselves and to receive feedback from the observations.

Special education teachers reported receiving the most assistance from other special education teachers. They also reported receiving quite a bit of assistance from their assigned mentors and from building administrators. They reported

TABLE 7.2 ■ Comparison of Most Frequently Perceived Problems of Beginning Teachers

Category	Subcategories	Sample Statements From Beginning Teachers
Forms of Supports/ Assistance	**Scheduled meetings**: face-to-face contacts formally scheduled between mentor and IYT (induction-year teacher)	We need formal scheduled meetings with our mentors at least once or twice a month even if it's only for 30 minutes.
	Unscheduled meetings: face-to-face contacts not formally scheduled between mentor and IYT	The mentor needs to stop by and check on you periodically and not just wait until you have a question.
	Observations of First-Year Teacher: classroom observations of IYT by mentor	I would have been less nervous when I started ADEPT this year if I had been observed by my mentor and gotten feedback.
	Observations by First-Year Teacher: classroom observations of the mentor or of other teachers made by IYT	I would like to be able to observe my mentor also. . . . I would like to observe once a month at least.
	Telephone calls: telephone contacts between the mentor and the IYT	A lot of times you'll call and you can't get in touch with them [the mentors].
	Written communication: notes, letters, e-mail, and other forms of written communication between mentor and IYT	When you have to wait and write down a question and get back to someone, it can be tiresome.

(continued)

TABLE 7.2 ■ *(cont.)*

Category	Subcategories	Sample Statements From Beginning Teachers
Content of Supports/ Assistance	**System information related to the school**: giving information about policies, procedures, guidelines, expectations, evaluation procedures (ADEPT), and unwritten rules that pertain to the operation and culture of the school	What are the school's expectations? You may be doing something that is out of step with what the procedure is at that particular school. . . In college they don't teach you the unwritten rules.
	System information related to special education: giving information about policies, paperwork, procedures, guidelines, and expectations related to the district special education program	The most important thing we need help with is paperwork and IEPs. . . . When I did my first IEPs, she sat down with me for the first few I did.
	Resources/Materials: locating, collecting, disseminating, or selecting materials, equipment, or other resources for use by the teacher	My biggest problem now is materials—what to use. You just don't know enough about materials in your first year.
	Curriculum/Instruction: providing information about assessment of needs, teaching methods and strategies, curriculum, and evaluation of student progress	I need help with my curriculum. Curriculum is very hard because you have to build it yourself.
	Management: giving assistance related to scheduling, planning, organizing, daily routines, and managing the school day	To me, scheduling was the most difficult and foreign. Nothing prepares you for how to go about doing that.
	Discipline: providing guidance and ideas related to student behavior	Behavior management is critical. [Beginning teachers] need help with discipline.
	Emotional support: offering support by listening, sharing experiences, and encouraging	Special ed teachers feel more isolated in schools. We need that personal support.
	Interactions with others: assisting the induction-year teacher in working with parents, colleagues, and administrators	Mentors need to help us get to know faculty and staff like people in the office do—and how to work with them

Source: Audiotaped transcripts from beginning special education teachers, December 14, 1998, January 13, 1999, January 19, 1999, and November 22, 1999.

receiving less assistance from general education teachers and from special education administrators (Whitaker, in press). Given the specialized nature of the special education teacher's job and the high need for assistance in areas specific to special education such as system information related to special education and selecting and locating materials, it makes sense that beginning special education teachers would find other special education teachers most helpful. They found their mentors more helpful if the assigned mentors were also special education teachers (Whitaker, 2000a).

The relatively high level of support from school administrators that beginning special education teachers perceive is an encouraging finding given the research indicating the importance of building-level support in job satisfaction and in teacher retention (Billingsley, 1993; Billingsley & Cross, 1991; Cross & Billingsley, 1994; Karge & Freiberg, 1992; Miller, Brownell, & Smith, 1999). The lower level of support they perceive from special education administrators is unfortunate but is consistent with the research indicating that beginning teachers in general perceive less support from district-level administrators (Billingsley & Cross, 1991; McKnab, 1983).

Some evidence indicates that beginning special education teachers have somewhat different needs and concerns at different times during their early years of teaching. Cheney, Krajewski, and Combs (1992) studied 42 first-year teachers, nine of whom were special education teachers. Through this study they generated and analyzed microphases of development in the first year of teaching.

During the first microphase, called "order and time-filling," special education teachers' needs revolved around scheduling and organizing. "They consistently reported feeling overwhelmed by the demands of IEPs and other procedural matters and by the task of having to work around the schedules of regular classroom teachers and related service providers" (Cheney et al., 1992, p. 20).

During the "timing, planning, and management" microphase the needs of the special education teachers centered on individual students but only the ones who interfered with their ability to conduct lessons. The teachers' concerns still focused on their own self-adequacy. Requests for help from mentors were related to developing and implementing behavior management plans, assessing students using standardized instruments, and communicating with parents and other teachers.

"Experimentation," the next microphase, typically began several months into the school year. In this phase teachers began using more difficult techniques and needed ideas about how to implement these techniques as well as feedback on their effectiveness.

The next microphase typically occurred toward the end of the school year and related to "long-range planning." Here the special education teachers were able to look at and develop goals for an entire school year and begin to plan individually for students.

The last microphase typically reached in the first year was the "focus on students." Not all beginning teachers reached this phase, but when they did, they were able to identify and plan for individual student needs. Cheney et al. (1992) concluded, "It seemed that the teachers needed to gain confidence in their own abilities and adequacy as teachers before they were able to shift their focus more fully to students" (p. 23). This is consistent with other findings indicating that the needs of beginning special education teachers seem to be directed first to their own personal needs and then to the mechanics of the job. They reported needing and receiving less assistance in areas directly impacting students, such as curriculum and instruction and discipline (Whitaker, 2000a; Whitaker, in press). This may well be related to the fact that they were simply not ready as first year teachers to focus on those aspects of teaching yet.

The various descriptions of the first-year teaching experience remain remarkably consistent whether they are taken from retrospective accounts of experienced teachers (Lortie, 1975), from journals and interviews with beginning teachers (Ryan, 1992), from ethnographic case studies (Corcoran, 1981; Kuzmic, 1994), or from descriptions of teacher-induction programs (Odell, 1989a). Linda Darling-Hammond (1985) concluded:

> Teaching is the only profession in which there is so little concern for clients that we are willing to give new practitioners the most difficult and burdensome assignments, leave them without teaching materials, close the door, and tell them to sink or swim on their own. This is not only a disservice to new teachers (half of whom leave within a few years, in part because of this lack of support), but it is also, of course, a tremendous injustice to students. (p. 214)

And yet, in their national survey of 1,007 beginning teachers, Harris and Associates (1991) found that, when asked what would have been most beneficial in helping these teachers be more effective in their first year of teaching, 46% responded that an experienced teacher who was assigned to assist and advise them would have been most beneficial. Harris and Associates further found that both first-year and experienced teachers rank direct and immediate access to advice and assistance as being of the most help in their becoming effective teachers.

INDUCTION AND MENTORING AS SUPPORTS FOR BEGINNING TEACHERS

Teacher induction with a strong mentoring component is frequently suggested as a means of easing the entry of beginning teachers into the field (Huling-Austin, 1986; Odell & Ferraro, 1992; Recruiting New Teachers, 1999). Teacher induction may be defined as "a planned program intended to provide some systematic and sustained assistance, specifically to beginning teachers for at least one school year" (Zeichner as cited in Huling-Austin, 1990b). Huling-Austin (1990b) points out that a beginning teacher program, to be considered an induction program, must provide systematic and sustained assistance and not just a series of orientation meetings or an evaluation process used with the beginning teachers. High-quality induction programs include (a) mentoring relationships between new and experienced teachers, (b) targeted professional development, (c) a focus on at least the first year of teaching, and (d) an evaluation component with planned remediation of weaknesses (National Association of State Boards of Education, 2000).

As explained previously, the very nature of the teaching profession tends to inhibit the induction process. The isolation that most teachers experience and the

KAREN'S STORY

We have a shortage of teachers, especially in special education for many reasons. I, myself, quit early in my career, vowing never to teach again. A year later I found myself back in a classroom for what I thought would be a 1-year stint until I had enough money saved to continue with an alternative plan. But I am still here.

Something I have observed and believe I experienced myself is that the newest, greenest teachers are given the most difficult classes and students to work with. I remember my first teaching job. It was in a Junior High that had sixth through ninth-grade students. My classroom was an old, dilapidated book room with a hodge-podge of books that looked like the dregs or leftovers from previous decades. The paint was peeling off of the walls. I had a full caseload, and the only support I got was from the special education coordinator, who came by to see me sometimes. She was wonderful, but it would have been nice to have a mentor there.

I stayed the second year. The heat to my room had been cut off and an electric heater installed in its place, It sat in my teacher's chair because the electric cord would not stretch to the electric socket if the heater were to be on the floor. The principal decided that I could take over the homeroom and extra duties that his friend, the PE teacher, had been doing. I also had students for whom I was unprepared—such as the 17-year-old boy who came to my room to use my stapler before school to staple the fly on his pants. His mom was in jail for murder, and he was pretty much on his own. I was only a few years older than he was.

After that year I left. I had a great year off, ran out of money, and decided to teach another year to save up some money so I could do something else. I fell into a great position teaching in a resource room, loved it, and have been here ever since. I nearly fainted when I was handed my IEPs and I could hold them in my hands instead of needing a big a cardboard box. The IEP was printed on some paper that allowed us to write our IEP once and it would transfer to the other two copies. I thought I had gone to heaven! Even though that year my classroom was a windowless audiovisual room, I was fortunate to work with very supportive people. I am still overworked and underpaid, but I have learned not to take things too seriously. I do not really know what has made the difference. Maybe it was that year off. And maybe it is my situation.

The school is great. I now have a full-sized classroom. I have a computer that is hooked up to the Internet, and a tape player, an overhead projector, a language master, shelves, and a painted and carpeted room. My room has a color television and a VCR. I even get $400 each year to buy supplies for my classroom, and 1,000 sheets on the copier each month. I get to do my own scheduling. I can control the thermostat in my room. The room is air-conditioned and heated.

The room has a lovely view of the swamp and giant bamboo forest. Spanish moss drapes the crepe myrtle tree in front of my own private parking space. And my own two children are allowed to attend with me even though they are out of zone. I am within 5 minutes of my home. The teachers here are nice to work with. The principal has a special education background and is supportive. In other words, I like my environment. Where you work, I'm convinced, makes a big difference. Not everyone can make it in special education long enough or be lucky enough to find that right place. Thank goodness I did.

Source: A beginning teacher. Email communication June 21, 2001.

expectation that the beginning teacher will handle the same job responsibilities as do experienced teachers do not lend themselves to a natural induction process (Glickman, 1990). To be effective, induction must be systematic, planned, and sustained.

Lesley Huling-Austin (1986) identified five implicit and explicit goals of most induction programs:

1. To improve the teaching performance of novice teachers
2. To increase the retention of novice teachers during the induction years
3. To promote the personal and professional well-being of novice teachers
4. To satisfy mandated requirements related to induction and certification
5. To transmit the culture of the system and of the profession.

In addition to these goals of school districts, Hirsh (1990) suggested that it is important to consider the induction goals of the novice teachers. He identified these goals as

1. Deriving personal satisfaction from teaching
2. Developing professional competence
3. Acquiring a sense of community security.

These goals closely parallel the organizational goals identified by Huling-Austin.

The concerns of beginning teachers should be used to identify the types of support to be provided (Odell, 1990). Induction programs must work toward identified goals but remain flexible enough to provide the kinds of assistance that beginning teachers need at the time they need it (Huling-Austin, 1987). The primary strategy for induction has been to offer some form of structured assistance and support to first-year teachers to ease their transition from university student to effective teacher. Mentoring of the first-year teacher by an experienced, competent teacher has developed as a favored option for providing this support (Little, 1990). Theresa Bey (1990) listed three primary reasons for mentoring programs:

1. To help beginning teachers cope with "dissatisfactions, disappointments and difficulties" (p. 51) of the first year of teaching
2. To combat high turnover and to reduce attrition
3. To improve teacher performance.

Klug and Salzman (1991) also found that beginning teachers preferred structured programs as opposed to unstructured programs. Wildman, Magliaro, Niles, and Niles (1992) cautioned, however, that "mentoring programs should not attempt to rigidly specify mentoring roles" (p. 205). They suggested that mentoring programs will be beneficial when they do not seek to rigidly specify the roles and responsibilities of the mentor but, rather, tailor the assistance to the specific needs of the beginning teacher. Huling-Austin, Putman, and Galvez-Hjornevik (1986) have recommended a middle-of-the-road approach with enough flexible structure to accommodate the emerging needs of the participants. They added that

> a prepackaged, "canned" program determined in advance will not be flexible enough to meet the variety of needs that are likely to emerge. . . . It is important to closely monitor the specific emerging needs and concerns of participants and to select appropriate interventions accordingly. (pp. 52–53)

Thus, it seems that it is important to have clear goals for mentoring programs and a flexible structure that allows the mentor to tailor the assistance to the specific individual needs of the beginning teacher. Huling-Austin (1990a) concluded that there is no magic formula for mentoring. She referred to mentoring as "squishy business" (p. 48), in which the mentor must vary the role to meet the needs of beginning teachers. The benefits of mentoring identified in the research seem to focus on the support provided to first-year teachers, their perception that mentoring has helped them be better teachers, the increased satisfaction with the job that, it is hoped will lead to a lower rate of attrition, and greater willingness to ask for assistance and support.

RECOMMENDATIONS FOR SUPPORTING BEGINNING SPECIAL EDUCATION TEACHERS

Given what we know about the needs and concerns of beginning special education teachers and the importance of the early years of teaching, additional supports clearly should be provided to these young professionals. A successful first-year experience is a critical factor in retaining special education teachers (Billingsley, 1993; Bogenschild, Lauritzen, & Metzke, 1988; Harris and Associates, 1991; Smith-Davis & Cohen, 1989). To encourage more support for beginning special education teachers, the Council for Exceptional Children (CEC) adopted standards for special educators who are entering professional practice; these standards include a minimum of a 1-year mentorship beginning the first year of professional special education practice (Council for Exceptional Children, 1996). CEC (1998) identified five purposes of a mentorship program for special educators:

1. To facilitate the application of knowledge and skills
2. To convey advanced knowledge and skills
3. To assist timely acculturation to the school climate
4. To reduce stress and enhance job satisfaction
5. To support professional induction.

White and Mason (2000) further offer the following guidelines for a mentoring program for special educators.

> 1. The objectives of the Mentoring Program, its purposes, and options are clear and have been agreed upon by beginning teachers,

experienced mentors, and representatives from the district and building level administrators.

2. Information concerning roles, expectations, policies, provisions, and desired outcomes of the Mentoring Program is readily available and shared with beginning teachers, mentors, and administrators.

3. The Mentoring Program is planned and adequately funded.

4. All first year teachers are expected to participate in the mentoring program.

5. Mentoring for special education teachers may be coordinated with other, more general, mentoring programs within the school district, but must specifically address those issues unique to special education.

6. The Mentoring Program is designed to provide assistance and support only and is not related to any formal evaluations, certification requirements, or reemployment issues. (p. 6)

Effective mentoring has been found to be correlated with both job satisfaction and improved retention of beginning special education teachers (Whitaker, 2000a) and thus has emerged as a favorite form of support.

The Role of the Mentor and Other Special Education Teachers

I conducted a series of focus groups, two surveys, and a series of interviews with beginning special education teachers and their mentors to examine the needs and concerns of beginning special education teachers and the supports that seem to be needed. Beginning special education teachers identified other special education teachers and their assigned mentors as the individuals who provided the most support and assistance to them (Whitaker, in press).

Several studies have found that the mentor for a beginning special education teacher is perceived as more effective if the mentor is also a special education teacher (Whitaker, 2000a; White, 1995). To be effective, mentoring must be provided on a consistent basis with contact between the mentor and protégé occurring at least weekly (Whitaker, 2000a). Thus, mentors must be willing to dedicate a significant amount of time to the mentoring process.

The beginning special education teachers reported that the informal unscheduled meetings were the most frequently provided method of support and also were the most effective form of support. They did report needing longer scheduled meetings periodically to deal with more complex issues such as developing the first IEP or discussing specific students (Whitaker, 2000a). They reported that they needed opportunities to observe other teachers and to be observed. Many beginning special education teachers, however, were not given these opportunities. When they were, they found them very helpful (Whitaker, 2000a). Boyer and Gillespie (2000) stress that support at the classroom level is most important for new special education teachers and that what happens inside the classroom is a critical factor in supporting teachers and retaining them.

Given this information, mentors and other special education teachers can be most helpful to beginning special education teachers by:

1. *Stopping by to check on the beginning special education teacher at least weekly* (and preferably several times per week). These visits need not be long but should afford opportunities for the beginning teacher to ask questions and for the more experienced teacher to answer questions and reassure and encourage the beginning teacher.

2. *Scheduling longer meetings at least once a month to address issues of concern to the beginning teacher.* Concerns might be developing a behavior management plan, writing the first IEP, or planning an instructional unit. Some of the concerns require more time and more planning for the more experienced teacher to be of much assistance. These are issues that cannot be dealt with effectively "on the fly" and require uninterrupted time for both teachers. Finding the time is often a challenge when the teachers do not share the same planning period. Sometimes the meetings can be held before or after school, over lunch, or when another staff member can occasionally cover a class for one of the teachers.

3. *Introducing the new teacher to staff members and orienting him or her to the new school.* A tour of the school is helpful to the new teacher. Where are the staff restrooms, the library, the copy machines? Novice teachers also appreciate being introduced to key staff members—the principal, assistant principal, guidance counselor, psychologist, secretary, custodian, librarian, and other teachers and paraprofessionals. Including the new teacher at lunch and making sure that he or she is not sitting alone at faculty meetings are good ways of reducing the isolation that beginning special education teachers often feel.

4. *Arranging for the beginning special education teacher to observe other, more experienced teachers* and then sitting down and discussing what was observed and what the teacher learned from the observation. Observations are most effective if the teacher has time to discuss the observation afterward. Focused observations are often particularly helpful. For example, if the beginning teacher reports having difficulty with getting students into the room and started on their work, the opportunity to observe an experienced teacher handle this aspect of the school day may be appropriate and probably would require only a 15-minute observation.

5. *Observing the beginning special education teacher and providing feedback.* The teachers need to know what they are doing right as well as areas in which they could improve. Often the observations can concentrate on a specific area of concern identified by the beginning teacher. Also important are follow-up discussions, in which the more experienced teacher helps the beginning teacher analyze his or her own lessons and learn from the discussions.

6. *Providing assistance with special education policies, procedures, and paperwork.* This is the area in which the beginning special education teachers reported needing the most assistance and in which they reported the greatest discrepancy between the amount of assistance needed and the amount received. Certainly special education is replete with paperwork and procedural requirements. These aspects of the job often are overwhelming to the novice teacher. The more experienced special education teacher can be of great assistance by providing samples of completed forms, answering questions regarding the procedures and forms, assisting the novice in completing the paperwork, and modeling how to follow the required procedures. Too often the beginning special education teachers report being left to "sink or swim," and while some manage to swim, too many sink in the process.

Fellow special education teachers can share their organizational strategies for managing the paperwork burden and for making sure that procedures are followed. They can check up on the beginners periodically and reassure them that they are "doing it right." The beginning teachers feel a tremendous responsibility to follow all of the procedures and get the paperwork completed correctly but often are completely confused regarding how to accomplish this goal.

7. *Orienting the beginning special education teacher to the school and district and to the school policies and procedures.* Beginning special education teachers report being confused by the school's written and unwritten rules. Each school has its own policies and procedures—how to get supplies, how to refer a child for counseling, from whom to get textbooks, how many copies can be run on the copier, whether parents are allowed to observe in classes, how to schedule a field trip, which teachers work well with which types of students, and so on. Although most veteran teachers no longer worry about these issues, they remain critical for the beginning teacher.

8. *Introducing the teacher to available materials and other resources.* Beginning special education teachers report being overwhelmed by trying to find appropriate materials for the diverse population of students they serve. In some cases the teachers do not have much in terms of readily available materials. These teachers struggle to make everything that they use in the classroom. Other teachers report having closets and shelves full of materials but not knowing where to start to select the most appropriate materials for certain students.

The experienced teacher can be helpful in suggesting a limited number of good materials with which the novice teacher can become familiar and use initially with the students. Then, as the beginning teacher becomes comfortable with those materials and indicates a need for additional resources, the experienced teacher can refer the teacher to other materials or other sources for materials. Introducing materials over time avoids the potential problem of overwhelming the novice teacher with too much too soon.

9. *Consulting with the beginning special education teacher regarding discipline*—both in terms of overall classroom management and with individual students. The way the school year begins is crucial to the success of the novice teacher. Thus, a more experienced special education teacher can help by sitting down with the beginner and helping him or her develop a classroom discipline plan. The two can jointly develop classroom rules and consequences and have those posted for the first day or plan to have the teacher and students jointly develop the rules and consequences the first day. They also can plan procedures and routines for the students for entering the classroom, getting started on their work, asking for assistance, going to the restroom, and leaving the classroom at the end of the period or end of the day. The teacher then can proceed to teaching the rules, procedures, and routines during the first week. This helps the teacher know what to do with the students from the first day and helps to assure a smooth beginning of the school year.

As the school year progresses, the beginning teacher typically struggles with discipline, particularly with certain students. Often the novice teacher is afraid to admit that he or she cannot handle a certain student for fear of appearing incompetent. Colleagues need to watch for signs that the novice teacher is struggling with discipline and reassure the novice that this is normal and that all teachers are challenged by some students and their behaviors.

Once the teacher has been reassured, it is easier to sit down and begin to brainstorm strategies for intervening with the behavior. Beginning special education teachers report that the assistance they were given with discipline was not particularly helpful. This may reflect the difficulty in assisting someone else with behavior management or may reflect the lack of expertise of the teachers providing the assistance. At times the novice teacher may have to be referred to the psychologist, an administrator, or other professional who may be able to provide additional assistance with specific students.

10. *Assisting the beginning special education teacher with scheduling, planning, and organization and management systems.* Colleges rarely are able to fully prepare special education teachers for the challenge of developing a schedule, planning units and lessons, and managing the large amounts of paperwork that special education generates. Experienced teachers develop shortcuts and systems for getting these tasks done efficiently, but beginning special education teachers report spending long hours trying to get everything done. Several teachers might share their "secrets" with the new teacher so he or she can pick and choose from the various systems and develop one that will work best for him or her.

11. *Consulting with the novice teacher regarding curriculum and instruction.* Beginning special education teachers report feeling overwhelmed by the

task of developing their own curriculum and finding the appropriate instructional methods for so many different students with so many different learning styles who are working at so many different levels. In most special education programs the teachers cannot just plan to go to the next chapter in the textbook. Although this is not an area on which most first-year special education teachers are ready to focus, they did report needing quite a bit more assistance than they received.

Based on studies of teacher development, this is an area that beginning teachers are more ready to tackle during their second year. For this reason, support should not stop after the first year of teaching. Certainly, issues of curriculum and instruction are important and should be addressed. As the novice teacher moves through the first year, the mentor or more experienced special education teacher can begin to encourage more discussion of issues related to curriculum and specific instructional strategies. Initially these discussions may be directed more at whole-class concerns, but by the end of the first year or during the second year, they should shift to individual students.

12. *Providing encouragement and support.* There is no more critical role than just being there for the beginning teacher to provide a shoulder on which to cry, a partner with whom to share successes, and a sounding board on which to try out new ideas. The number one need identified by beginning special education teachers was emotional support. The job is difficult—especially for beginners. Most of these young teachers want to do a good job and need to hear that they are doing well and are making a difference with the students. They need that reassurance. They also need to hear that all lessons don't go perfectly even for the most experienced teacher, and that it is all right when a lesson doesn't go well. And they need to learn to celebrate their successes and to learn from their mistakes. Finally, they need to hear that eventually the job does get at least a little bit easier.

The Role of the Administrator

Although the mentor or other special education teachers play the most significant roles in providing support to beginning special education teachers, perceived lack of support from administrators is one of the reasons most frequently cited for special education teachers leaving the classroom (Billingsley & Cross, 1991; Karge & Freiberg, 1992; Westling & Whitten, 1996). Thus, the role of the administrators is critical in supporting beginning special education teachers. Administrators can be most helpful to beginning special education teachers by:

1. *Assigning a good experienced special education teacher as a mentor to the novice special education teacher.* Research has shown that the best mentor for a special education teacher is another special education teacher who teaches students with the same disabilities and who is perceived as

approachable, trustworthy, supportive, enthusiastic, and comfortable working with other teachers and who has good communication skills in addition to strong professional knowledge (Whitaker, 2000a). The mentors selected have to be willing to devote a significant amount of time to the mentoring— checking with the teacher at least once a week and meeting more formally at least once a month. One of the most important steps an administrator can take to support beginning special education teachers is to assign them good mentors.

2. *Arranging time for the mentors or other special education teachers to work with the beginning special education teacher.* Mentoring is perceived as significantly more effective if the mentor and protégé have the same planning period at least once a week (Whitaker, 2000a). Administrators can arrange for the two teachers to have the same planning period, or they can arrange for time to be made available periodically by providing substitutes or other teachers to periodically cover their classes. Administrators also can make sure that mentors and their protégés are not overburdened with additional duties such as bus duty or hall duty so they can meet briefly during those times as well.

3. *Providing staff development for the mentors.* Mentors are more likely to be effective if they know what is expected of them as mentors and what the first-year special education teachers are likely to need from them. Administrators might provide a workshop for the mentors that covers (a) the role of the mentor, (b) needs of beginning teachers in general and of beginning special education teachers specifically, (c) strategies for providing assistance, (d) techniques for observing and conferencing, and (e) a suggested schedule of mentoring activities. Many resources are available for mentors and beginning special education teachers. Some of these are listed at the end of this article.

4. *Arranging observations of other teachers.* Just as other special education teachers can assist in arranging observations, administrators can assist in selecting teachers to observe and making arrangements so the novice teacher is free to make the observations.

5. *Observing the beginning special education teacher and providing feedback.* Because the first year of teaching is stressful for most teachers, it may be best if other teachers make the first observations and provide feedback. These initial observations may assist the beginning teacher in becoming more comfortable with the observation process. By the end of the first month, the administrator(s) should begin doing walk-through observations to get a feel for how things are going for the teacher and to begin to identify areas in which assistance may be needed. These walk-through observations should be followed by more formal observations.

Feedback should be given after the observations, as the beginning teacher will want to know what the administrator thinks and recommends. The administrator should note positive aspects of the observation and then focus on one area for assistance, which ideally should be decided through joint discussions with the administrator, beginning teacher, and mentor. These observations should be positive, and the administrator should provide encouragement and assistance rather than be evaluative or punitive with the novice teacher, who is just beginning to learn the profession.

6. *Planning district level induction activities.* District-level administrators should plan district-wide induction activities for all beginning teachers— explaining the mission and philosophy of the district, presenting the expectations for the teachers, explaining policies and procedures, introducing district support staff, explaining payroll and benefits packages, and generally welcoming and orienting the new teachers to the school district. In addition, the special education administrator should present an orientation to special education, presenting the expectations for special education teachers; explaining special education policies, procedures, and paperwork; introducing special education support staff; explaining how to get needed supplies and materials; and again generally welcoming and orienting the teachers to the special education department.

Beginning teachers are so overwhelmed during the first few weeks of school that these orientation meetings should be held prior to the opening of the school year. Certainly, paying a stipend for attending is nice, but most beginning special education teachers indicate that they would be happy to attend without pay just to get the needed assistance.

7. *Providing a handbook of policies, procedures, and forms.* School districts should provide a general district employee handbook of policies and procedures and should review this with all beginning teachers. In addition, each school should have a teacher handbook that includes school policies and procedures. A school administrator should ensure that the beginning special education teacher has a copy of the school handbook and should review the contents with the teacher and answer any questions.

Finally, the special education department should have a handbook of policies and procedures and sample forms. Beginning special education teachers report that such a handbook is a lifesaver. With it, they should be able to refer to procedures as they are needed and to see samples of completed forms as they fill out those forms for their own students.

8. *Making the demands placed on the beginning special education teacher reasonable.* Too often, beginning teachers are placed in the most difficult teaching assignments: They often have the most difficult students, the largest caseloads, and the most preparations each day (Glickman, 1990; Gordon, 1991). In addition, 25–30% of beginning special education are placed in positions in which they find themselves teaching students they are not certified to teach (Boe, Cook, Bobbitt, & Terhanian, 1998; Whitaker, 2000a).

Clearly this situation is not in the best interest of the students or the teacher. Administrators can help by placing beginning special education teachers in positions for which they are prepared and in which they can be successful. Administrators should keep the caseloads reasonable and limit the number of extra duties these teachers have to manage during their first year.

9. *Making the needed resources available.* Administrators can assist beginning special education teachers by making sure that they have adequate classroom space, access to needed equipment, the necessary supplies in their classrooms, and an adequate supply of materials to use with their students. Administrators also need to be sure that beginning special education teachers know what resources are available in the district (audiovisual equipment, instructional materials resource centers, etc.) and how to order needed materials and supplies.

10. *Including the beginning special education teacher and making him or her feel a part of the school.* Beginning special education teachers talk a lot about feeling isolated (Whitaker, 2000b). Because they often are not part of a grade level or a department, they tend to be excluded. It is disheartening when teachers are given $200 for supplies but the special education teacher is not included . . . or when memos go out and the special education teacher is forgotten . . . or when materials are ordered for classroom teachers and the special education teacher is told that nothing was ordered for special education. Administrators can show their support by being more cognizant of including the beginning special education teacher (and, indeed, all special education teachers) in whatever transpires at the school.

11. *Supporting the beginning special education teacher in his or her dealings with other staff, parents, and students.* Beginning special education teachers may need assistance in negotiating their roles with other teachers, in gaining faculty support, and in securing the necessary supports for their students. Administrators can help by showing their faith in the skills of the beginning teacher and making clear the expectation that the school staff will work with the new teacher in the best interests of the students.

Beginning teachers sometimes are intimidated by parents and may want the administrator present for certain meetings in which conflict is expected. Administrators should make clear to the novice special education teacher that they are available as needed to assist with these meetings.

Finally, beginning special education teachers may need support and assistance with certain students. Administrators again should make clear that they are there to assist and will help the novice teacher in working with these difficult and challenging students—and then should make every effort to provide that assistance themselves or to access other support personnel to assist. Because beginning teachers are often hesitant to ask for help, the administrator must be observant and offer help when it seems to be needed.

12. *Providing encouragement and support.* All teachers need to hear occasional words of encouragement and support from their administration, and this is even more critical for novice special education teachers who are just beginning to define themselves as teachers. They need to hear that they are appreciated, that their efforts are noticed, and that the administration is aware of their hard work. They need to have their positive accomplishments recognized. Administrators can do much to help the beginning special education teacher retain his or her sense of efficacy, thereby promoting student achievement as well as increasing the likelihood that the novice teacher will remain in the field.

The Role of the College or University Professor

College and university professors also have a role in supporting beginning special education teachers (Boyer and Gillespie, 2000). Certainly the education they provide should be a support to the beginning teacher when he or she begins teaching. Traditionally, however, colleges and universities have viewed their role as complete when a student graduates. Perhaps it is time to reexamine that position. The novice special educators often have had fairly close relationships with professors and are accustomed to going to those professors for encouragement and advice. Must that relationship end with graduation? College and university professors can be most helpful to beginning special education teachers by:

1. *Adequately preparing them for their first year of teaching.* Beginning teachers who feel that they have been adequately prepared are more likely to remain in the field, particularly if their field-based experiences were perceived as positive (Brownell & Smith, 1992; Brownell, Smith, McNellis, & Lenk, 1994–95). Many beginning teachers report feeling inadequately prepared for the challenges they faced during their first year of teaching.

   Providing more practical experiences to preservice teachers and putting more emphasis on real-life problem-solving seem to promote transfer of learning from the college classroom to the first teaching assignment. In addition, special education faculty at the college and university level need to be aware of the areas in which beginning special education teachers require the most assistance so the faculty can revise the curriculum to provide additional preparation in those areas wherever possible.

2. *Helping the preservice teacher develop a more realistic view of the first year of teaching.* Many preservice teachers enter the profession with an unrealistic view of their own expertise and of the challenges they will face. Although we do not want to dampen their enthusiasm, they need to be better prepared for the "reality shock" of the classroom. Activities such as interviewing a first-year teacher or reading some of the accounts of the first year of teaching (see the Resources at the end of this article) would be helpful in preparing these teachers for the shock of that first year.

3. *Encouraging the preservice teachers to ask questions and seek assistance and support.* Beginning teachers tend to hesitate to ask for assistance for fear of appearing incompetent. College and university instructors can work to develop a supportive atmosphere in which students feel comfortable asking questions and asking for assistance. They then can encourage (and even require) the preservice teachers to ask questions and seek assistance from a variety of sources during their field experiences to establish the habit of consultation and collaboration.

4. *Continuing to be available to the first-year special education teachers.* At the beginning of the school year, first-year teachers have not yet gotten to know or feel comfortable with the district staff. If their professors can continue to be available through visits, telephone calls, on-line discussion groups, and e-mail, the beginning special educator has someone to whom to turn even in those early days and even if little support is provided at the school or district level. This aspect of support is particularly critical for beginning teachers who teach students with low-incidence disabilities and those who teach in small, rural school districts that may not have other, more experienced professionals to whom to turn for assistance.

5. *Following up with graduates during their first year* to learn how the graduates are doing and what they, as professors, could have done to better prepare the novice teachers. Asking beginning special education teachers what components of their preservice education were most beneficial and what components were insufficient will enable the college and university staff to make their programs even more effective in the future.

6. *Offering graduate courses that prepare experienced teachers to be mentors.* Many school districts are too small to have enough special education teachers to fill a graduate course. And few school districts have staff members who are qualified to teach a graduate level course on mentoring. And yet, mentoring is a new role for most teachers—a role that requires good professional development for the mentor to understand and perform adequately in the role.

FINAL THOUGHTS

The amount and perceived effectiveness of support provided to beginning special education teachers correlates with job satisfaction and with retention in the field (Whitaker, 2000a). And certainly any assistance and support provided to these novice teachers should improve their effectiveness as teachers (Council for Exceptional Children, 1998). Even though the mantra "It takes a village to raise a child" is frequently repeated and generally accepted, there is less acceptance of the need for the whole village to support the teacher, and especially the beginning special education teacher. With the current shortage of special education teachers, we all need to do whatever we can to support our beginning teachers, help them become the best teachers they can be, and increase the chances of retaining them in the field.

REFERENCES

Bey, T. M. (1990). A new knowledge base for an old practice. In T. M. Bey & C. T. Holmes, (Eds.), *Mentoring: Developing successful new teachers,* Reston, VA: Association of Teacher Educators. (ERIC Document Reproduction Service No. ED 322 118)

Billingsley, B. S. (1993). Teacher retention and attrition in special and general education: A critical review of the literature. *Journal of Special Education, 27,* 137–174.

Billingsley, B. S., & Cross, L. H. (1991). Teachers' decisions to transfer from special to general education. *Journal of Special Education, 24,* 496–511.

Boe, E. E., Cook, L. H., Bobbitt, S. A., & Terhanian, G. (1998). The shortage of fully certified teachers in special and general education. *Teacher Education & Special Education, 21,* 1–21.

Bogenschild, E. G., Lauritzen, P., & Metzke, L. (1988). *A study of teacher attrition. Information on personnel supply and demand.* (ERIC Document Reproduction Service No. ED 311 614)

Boyer, L. & Gillespie, P. (2000). Keeping the committed: The importance of induction and support programs for new special education teachers. *Teaching Exceptional Children, 33*(1), 10–15.

Brownell, M. T., & Smith, S. W. (1992). Attrition/retention of special education teachers: Critique of current research and recommendations for retention efforts. *Teacher Education & Special Education, 15,* 229–248.

Brownell, M. T., Smith, S. W., McNellis, J., & Lenk, L. (1994–95). Career decisions in special education: Current and former teachers' personal views. *Exceptionality, 5,* 83–102.

Cheney, C. O., Krajewski, J., & Combs, M. (1992). Understanding the first year teacher: Implications for induction programs. *Teacher Education & Special Education 15*(1), 18–24.

Cooke, B. L., & Pang, K. C. (1991). Recent research on beginning teachers: Studies of trained and untrained novices. *Teaching & Teacher Education, 7*(1), 93–110.

Corcoran, E. (1981). Transition Shock: The beginning teacher's paradox. *Journal of Teacher Education, 32*(3), 19–23.

Council for Exceptional Children (1996). *What every special educator must know: The international standards for the preparation and certification of special education teachers,* (2d ed.). Reston, VA: Council for Exceptional Children.

Council for Exceptional Children (1998). *What every special educator must know: The international standards for the preparation and licensure of special educators.* (3rd ed.). Reston, VA: The Council for Exceptional Children.

Council for Exceptional Children (2000). *Bright Futures for exceptional learners: An action agenda to achieve quality conditions for teaching and learning* [On-line]. Available: Http://www.cec.sped. org/spotlight/cond/bf_intro.html

Cross, L. H., & Billingsley, B. S. (1994). Testing a model of special educator's intent to stay in teaching. *Exceptional Children, 60,* 411–412.

Darling-Hammond, L. (1985). Valuing teachers: The making of a profession. *Teachers College Record, 87,* 205–218.

Dollase, R. H. (1992). *Voices of beginning teachers: Visions and realities.* New York: Teacher's College Press.

Gaede, O. F. (1978). Reality shock: A problem among first year teachers. *Clearing House, 51,* 405–409.

Glickman, C. D. (1990). Preface. In T. M. Bey & C. T. Holmes (Eds.), *Mentoring: Developing successful new teachers.* Reston, VA: Association of Teacher Educators.

Gordon, S. P. (1991). *How to help beginning teachers succeed.* Alexandria, VA: Association for Supervision & Curriculum Development.

Glidewell, J. C., Tucker, S, Todt, M., & Cox, S. (1983). Professional support systems: The teaching profession. In A. Nadler, J. Fisher, & B. DePaulo (Eds.), *New directions in helping: Vol. 3. Applied perspective on help-seeking and receiving* (pp. 182–212). New York: Academic Press.

Harris, L., & Associates, Inc. (1991). *The Metropolitan Life survey of the American teacher, 1991: The first year: New teacher's expectations and ideals.* New York: Metropolitan Life Insurance Company. (ERIC Document Reproduction Service No. ED 354 224)

Harris, L. & Associates, Inc. (1992). *The Metropolitan Life survey of the American teacher, 1991: The second year: New teacher's expectations and ideals.* New York: Metropolitan Life Insurance Company. (ERIC Document Reproduction Service No. ED 354 226)

Hirsh, S. A. (1990). Designing induction programs with the beginning teacher in mind. *Journal of Staff Development, 11*(4), 24–26.

Huling-Austin, L. (1986). What can and cannot reasonably be expected from teacher induction programs? *Journal of Teacher Education, 37*(1), 2–5.

Huling-Austin, L. (1987). Teacher induction. In D. M. Brooks (Ed.), *Teacher induction: A new beginning* (pp. 3–24). Reston, VA: Association of Teacher Educators.

Huling-Austin, L. (1990a). Mentoring is squishy business. In T. Bey & C. T. Holmes (Eds.), *Mentoring: Developing successful new teachers* (pp. 39–50). Reston, VA: Association of Teacher Educators.

Huling-Austin, L. (1990b). Teacher induction programs and internships. In W.R. Houston (Ed.), *Handbook of research on teacher education.* New York: Macmillan.

Huling-Austin, L., & Murphy, S. C. (1987, April). *Assessing the impact of teacher induction programs: Implications for program development.* Paper presented at annual meeting of American Educational Research Association, Washington, DC. (ERIC Document Reproduction Service No. ED 283 779)

Huling-Austin, L., Putman, S., & Galvez-Hjornevik, C. (1985). *Model teacher induction project study findings. Final report.* Austin: University of Texas Research and Development Center for Teacher Education. (ERIC Document Reproduction Service No. ED 270 442)

Karge, B. D., & Freiberg, M. R. (1992, April). *Beginning special education teachers: At risk for attrition.* Paper presented at annual meeting of American Educational Research Association, San Francisco. (ERIC Document Reproduction Service No. ED 353 235)

Kirby, S. & Grissmer, D. W. (1993). *Teacher attrition: Theory, evidence, and suggested policy options.* Santa Monica, CA: Rand Corporation. (ERIC Documentation Reproduction Service No. ED 364 533)

Klug, B. J. & Salzman, S. A. (1991). Formal induction vs. informal mentoring: Comparative effects and outcomes. *Teaching & Teacher Education, 7,* 241–251.

Kuzmic, J. (1994). A beginning teacher's search for meaning: Teacher socialization, organizational literacy, and empowerment. *Teaching & Teacher Education, 10*(1), 15–27.

Little, J. W. (1990). The mentor phenomenon and the social organization of teaching. In C. B. Cazden (Ed.), *Review of research in education* (Vol. 16, pp. 297–351). Washington, DC: American Educational Research Association.

Lortie, D. C. (1975). *Schoolteacher: A sociological study.* Chicago: University of Chicago Press.

McKnab, P. (1983). *Special education personnel attrition in Kansas, 1976 to 1982: A summary of attrition rates and an analysis of reasons for quitting.* Office of Special Education and Rehabilitative Services, Division of Personnel Preparation. Washington, DC. (ERIC Document Reproduction Service No. ED 238 231)

McLaughlin, M. W. Pfeifer, R. S., Swanson-Owens, D., & Yee, S. (1986). Why teachers won't teach. *Phi Delta Kappan, 67,* 420–426.

Miller, M. D., Brownell, M. T., & Smith, S. W. (1999). Factors that predict teachers staying in, leaving, or transferring from the special education classroom. *Exceptional Children, 65,* 201–218.

Moran, S. W. (1990). Schools and the beginning teacher. *Phi Delta Kappan, 72,* 210–213.

National Association of State Boards of Education. (2000, April). Teacher induction programs. *Policy Update, 8*(5).

Odell, S. J. (1986). Induction support of new teachers: A functional approach. *Journal of Teacher Education, 37*(1), 26–29.

Odell, S .J. (1989a). Characteristics of beginning teachers in an induction context. In J. Reinhartz (Ed.), *Teacher induction* (pp. 42–51). Washington, DC: National Education Association.

Odell, S. J. (1989b). *Developing support programs for beginning teachers: Assisting the beginning teacher* (pp. 19–38). Reston, VA: Association of Teacher Educators.

Odell, S. J. (1990). *Mentor teacher programs: What research says to the teacher.* Washington, DC: National Education Association. (ERIC Document Reproduction Service No. ED 323 185)

Odell, S. J., & Ferraro, D. P. (1992). Teacher mentoring and teacher retention. *Journal of Teacher Education, 43,* 200–204.

Recruiting New Teachers. (1999). *Learning the ropes: Urban teacher induction programs and practices in the United States.* Belmont, MA.

Ryan, K. (Ed.). (1992). *The roller coaster year.* New York: HarperCollins.

Schlechty, P. C. & Vance, V. S. (1983). Recruitment, selection, and retention: The shape of the teaching force. *Elementary School Journal, 83,* 469–487.

Singer, J. D. (1992). Are special educator's career paths special? Results from a 13-year longitudinal study. *Exceptional Children, 59,* 262–279.

Smith-Davis, J. & Cohen, M. (1989). *Preventing attrition through teacher induction and mentoring [and] entry-year induction programs and practices: A bibliography.* Information on supply and demand. (ERIC Document Reproduction Service No. ED 314 923)

Tonnsen, S., & Patterson, S. (1992). Fighting first-year jitters. *Executive Educator, 14*(1), 29–30.

Veenman, S. (1984). Perceived problems of beginning teachers. *Review of Educational Research, 54,* 143–178.

Weinstein, C. S. (1988). Preservice teachers' expectations about the first year of teaching. *Teaching & Teacher Education, 4,* 31–40.

Westling, D. L. & Whitten, T. M. (1996). Rural special education teachers' plans to continue or leave their teaching positions. *Exceptional Children, 62,* 319–335.

Whitaker, S. D. (1999). *Induction-year special education teachers: Perceptions of mentoring and its relationship to attrition.* Unpublished doctoral dissertation, University of South Carolina, Columbia.

Whitaker, S. D. (2000a). Mentoring beginning special education teachers and the relationship to attrition. *Exceptional Children, 66,* 546–566.

Whitaker, S. D. (2000b). What do first-year special education need? *Teaching Exceptional Children, 33*(1), 28–36.

Whitaker, S. D. (in press). Needs of beginning special education teachers: Implications for teacher education. *Teacher Education & Special Education.*

White, M. (1995). *Factors contributing to special education teacher attrition: How a one year internship affects the attrition rates of special education teachers in Kentucky.* Unpublished doctoral dissertation, Vanderbilt University, Nashville, TN.

White, M., & Mason, C. (2000, June 26). *Mentoring induction principles and guidelines* (draft). Reston, VA: Council for Exceptional Children.

Wildman, T. M., Magliaro, S. G., Niles, R. A., & Niles, J. A. (1992). Teacher mentoring: An analysis of roles, activities, and conditions. *Journal of Teacher Education, 43,* 205–213.

Woolfolk, A., Rusoff, B., & Hoy, W. (1990). Teachers' sense of efficacy and their beliefs about managing students. *Teaching & Teacher Education, 6,* 137–148.

Collaboration to Support Students' Success

Chriss Walther-Thomas, Lori Korinek,
and Virginia L. McLaughlin

As the new millennium approaches, students and professionals in public schools face complex challenges. Typical discussions in student cafeterias and faculty lounges range from concerns about school violence and personal safety to a mounting sense of pressure stemming from heightened academic expectations and more rigorous performance standards. Research on schools that are effective amid widespread challenges shows that no single factor guarantees both student achievement and professional satisfaction (Goertz, Floden, & O'Day, 1995; Fuhrman, 1993; National Commission on Teaching and America's Future [NCTAF], 1996; Rosenholz, 1989; Stoll, 1991). Instead, many influences combine to support students and professionals (Little, 1982; Little & McLaughlin, 1993; Louis, Marks, & Kruse, 1996; McGregor & Vogelsberg, 1998; Ravitch, 1995; Stoll, 1991).

Supportive features include shared leadership and family involvement, a cohesive school vision, comprehensive program planning, adequate resources, sustained implementation, and ongoing performance evaluation and improvement. Collaboration also is cited frequently as contributing significantly to well-being and productivity in schools (Darling-Hammond, 1997; Little, 1982; McDonnell, McLaughlin, & Morison, 1997; NCTAF, 1996; Slavin, 1995; Walther-Thomas, 1997; Walling, 1994; Walther-Thomas, Korinek, McLaughlin, & Williams, 2000). Indeed, many current reform initiatives designed to increase student achievement are based on the presumption that effective collaborators will work together to achieve the desired aims (Algozzine, Ysseldyke, & Campbell, 1994; Louis et al., 1996; NCTAF, 1996).

In programs for students with disabilities and others with significant problems in achievement, collaboration is particularly important (Cramer, 1998; Fishbaugh, 1997; Friend & Bursuck, 1999). As schools become more inclusive learning communities, effective collaboration is crucial for success (McDonnell et al., 1997; McGregor &

Vogelsberg, 1998; NCTAF, 1996; Walther-Thomas et al., 2000). Recognizing the importance of collaboration to facilitate students' achievement and the support of educators, many professional groups have recommendations for preparation and practice that emphasize the importance of well developed collaborative skills. These include, among others, the Council for Exceptional Children (1995, 1998); Council of Chief State School Officers (1996); National Association of State Boards of Education [NASBE] (1992); National Center on Educational Restructuring and Inclusion [NCERI] (1995); National Council on Disability (1995); National LEADership Network (1993); National Staff Development Council (1994, 1995).

Most education professionals agree that collaboration is a worthy goal. Collaborative relationships in schools, however, are difficult to develop and even more challenging to maintain because of many factors, such as competing priorities, limited resources, and lack of professional development. In this article, we explore some fundamental features that foster the development of collaborative relationships and, in a broader sense, collaborative communities. We also present effective mechanisms for accessing and improving collaborative support networks. Finally, we address some start-up problems that arise in many schools.

FUNDAMENTALS OF EFFECTIVE COLLABORATION

Collaboration is a nebulous concept. Friend and Cook (1996) refer to it as a style of direct interaction that characterizes many types of group processes and projects. Idol, West, and Lloyd (1988) define collaboration as

> an interactive process that enables teams of people with diverse expertise to generate creative solutions to problems. The outcome produces solutions that are different from those any individual team member would produce independently (p. 55).

Similarly, Skrtic, Sailor, and Gee (1996) suggest that effective collaboration is a

> multivocal discourse among participants who have different but equal status as they work together in an interdependent fashion (p. 144).

According to Walther-Thomas and colleagues (2000), effective collaboration emerges out of concerns by individuals who are like-minded in some ways and very different in others. Typically, effective collaborators care deeply about the same issues, but their perspectives and priorities are very different from one another. For example, when school teams work together to make their schools inclusive, the roles and responsibilities of team members affect their participation and priorities. Principals tend to focus on schoolwide issues such as achievement trends, financial implications, professional development, student placement, professional schedules, and community relations. Teachers and specialists typically are more interested in classroom issues such as individual and group performance, IEP planning, and new demands on their roles and responsibilities. Added to this complex mix of concerns are the priorities of families, who care most about the potential impact of new initiatives on their children. All of these constituents have to be assured that innovations will enhance their students' success in schools.

Ultimately, the unique, dynamic, and sometimes problematic differences between team members are what are likely to make collaborative undertakings more effective than efforts of individuals working alone. Sharing different vantage points, knowledge, and strategies facilitates development of more creative and comprehensive solutions to complex problems. Plans that are developed and implemented collaboratively also are more likely to succeed because they have a broader base of support and commitment.

When thinking about collaborative relationships, a few key points are as follows.

1. Collaboration is *not* synonymous with inclusion or with any of the specific formats (e.g., co-teaching, peer consultation) used to facilitate the process.
2. Friendship is *not* a prerequisite for effective collaboration. Although previous experience in working together can help new collaborators feel more comfortable initially and reduce some of the awkwardness of new collaborative relationships, effective and lasting collaboration grows out of mutual trust and respect, equity, expertise in one's domain, willingness to share, and valuing contributions of participants (Cramer, 1998; Friend & Cook, 1996; Walther-Thomas, 1997).
3. Effective collaboration is neither easily nor quickly achieved. Initially it is labor-intensive. Productive partnerships develop from time spent together exchanging ideas, opinions, and information, as well as solving problems together. Time and practice are necessary to build trust and to develop the informal and formal operating procedures that enable teams to work together effectively (Larson & LaFasto, 1989).
4. Participation in collaborative relationships should be voluntary, as it helps solidify each team member's commitment to the effort (Friend & Cook, 1996; Orelove & Sobsey; 1996, Walther-Thomas, 1997). This is not always possible or appropriate. Most schoolwide initiatives require full participation by faculty and staff to ensure successful and lasting implementation.
5. New collaborators might overwork the process unintentionally as they strive to involve each other in important decision making. Teams and individuals have to determine when collaboration is appropriate and when it is not. A genuine commitment to effective collaboration does not mean that every decision must be made in this manner. Clearly, shared decision making makes sense when partners or larger teams are addressing fundamental issues, but it may not be necessary or even desirable to address certain day-to-day professional responsibilities collaboratively.

   For example, most effective co-teachers work together to develop a mutually accepted system for grading student work. Together they establish grading rubrics, design appropriate modifications and accommodations for some class members, calculate semester grades, complete report cards, and confer with parents and students regarding progress. Most collaborators do not meet at the end of the day to correct daily assignments together. They are more likely to divide student work and trust the other's judgment to follow the policies and procedures they have established as a team.

CREATING COLLABORATIVE COMMUNITIES

Teaching and learning partnerships thrive in school communities where collaboration is the norm. These communities recognize the powerful potential of teamwork to help individuals and groups accomplish their goals (Friend & Cook, 1996; Walther-Thomas et al., 2000). These schools believe that all individuals are valuable to the community. Formal and informal support structures are developed to ensure that all participants are successful. In addition, these schools provide opportunities for all members to contribute to the well-being of the community, because every person has skills, talents, knowledge, and experiences to offer that will make the school a better place.

Characteristics of collaborative communities often are manifested through the distribution of professional responsibilities, as well as in accepted decision-making procedures, use of shared resources, and well-developed accountability measures (Little & McLaughlin, 1993; Louis et al., 1996). As Skrtic and colleagues (1996) note, these communities recognize the power of dialogue to foster more effective problem solving and solution finding. Through shared experiences, participants change, resulting in realigned and redefined power relationships (Little & McLaughlin, 1993). Typically these schools are more democratic and less hierarchical. Collaborative communities often reflect openness in discussions, teaching that is personal but not private, clear respect for others' opinions and beliefs, and a healthy sense of belonging to a group and working as a team.

Collaborative communities support ongoing teamwork in many ways. Multiple formats are used to foster knowledge sharing, skill development, and support. Some formats are based on ongoing two-person relationships such as co-teaching (Walther-Thomas, Korinek, McLaughlin, & Williams, 1996), peer collaboration (Pugach & Johnson, 1995), and peer coaching (Joyce & Showers, 1995). Others facilitate ongoing work by larger groups including teacher assistance teams (Chalfant & Pysh, 1989) and various types of school-improvement committees. Finally, some structures are designed to encourage teamwork between children and youth through ongoing peer tutoring (Utley, Mortweet, & Greenwood, 1997) and cooperative learning (Slavin, 1995). We will examine these structures in greater detail in the following sections.

PROVIDING COLLABORATIVE SUPPORT FOR PROFESSIONALS

The ultimate purpose of professional collaboration is to support the ongoing efforts of individual educators to improve student learning. Collaborative opportunities enhance the value of individual professional practice by introducing other perspectives and voices into the processes of reflective planning and problem solving. The basic reflective processes—planning, acting, and evaluating—are the same whether an individual, a dyad, or a small group applies them. Through collaboration with others, reflection becomes a true "conversation of practice" (Yinger, 1990). The goal for program development, therefore, should be to create a full network of collaborative options that teachers and other professionals can access as needed to support their individual reflective practice. Individuals should be able to access the specific type and amount of collaborative support they need at any point in time.

Figure 8.1 illustrates a professional collaborative network that incorporates frontline support, special needs support, special education support, and interagency support. In actual schools, certain features of these collaborative structures sometimes are blended or combined, and the names for teams and services often are unique to the individual setting. The intent of the discussion here is to provide an

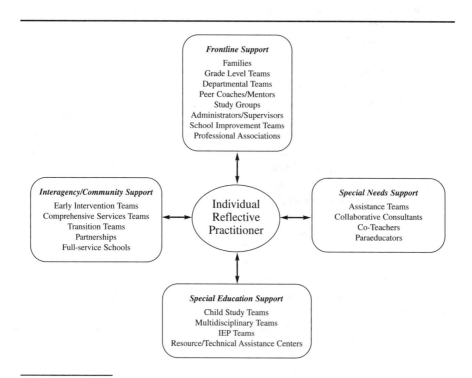

Source: Adapted from C. Walther-Thomas, L. Korinek, V. McLaughlin, and B. Williams (2000), *Collaboration for Inclusive Education: Developing Successful Programs,* p. 74 (Needham Heights, MA: Allyn & Bacon).

FIGURE 8.1 ■ Professional Collaborative Network

overview of the possibilities, not an exhaustive or prescriptive list of collaborative support structures. After each type of collaborative support is introduced, we offer specific suggestions for accessing it.

Frontline Support

Ongoing relationships provide the most immediate or frontline support for professional concerns, and most schools offer numerous opportunities for developing and nurturing these relationships. Frontline support is proactive and preventive, enabling educators to deal with issues before they become serious. Partnerships with students' families are recognized as especially critical. The importance of family-school collaboration has been so strongly and consistently supported by research that it is no longer considered an option but a professional obligation (Corrigan & Bishop, 1997).

Beyond collaboration with families, educators can turn to their colleagues for support. Most schools are organized into departmental or grade-level teams that enable professionals to share ideas, improve school programs, and problem solve issues of common concern (Dickinson & Erb, 1996; Pounder, 1998). As a special source of support for beginning teachers, many districts provide mentors who offer emotional support, information about school policies and procedures, and assistance with professional responsibilities such as curriculum, classroom management, and testing (Ganser, 1996; Halford, 1998; Stedman & Stroot, 1998).

Teachers and other school professionals also might have access to peer coaching opportunities. Peer coaches often are lead teachers with designated responsibilities for assisting their colleagues in improving instructional skills, strategies, and techniques (Joyce & Showers, 1995). In some settings, peer coaches are co-equals with reciprocal support expectations. One specific variation is peer collaboration (Pugach & Johnson, 1995), which involves pairs of general education teachers working together over time as voluntary problem-solving partners. School-level study

---

ACCESSING FRONTLINE SUPPORT

- Identify the various types of support available in the school.
- Participate actively in team meetings; keep the focus on teaching and learning.
- Confer with a supervisor on an instructional issue.
- Volunteer for mentoring or peer coaching programs.
- Join relevant professional associations and get involved in local or state activities.
- Join a study group to investigate issues of interest or common concern.
- Work with others to start a school- or district-based study and support group.

groups extend opportunities for peer support by providing a less formal forum for in-depth exploration of selected instructional topics (Crowther, 1998). For example, study groups sometimes engage in action research to test interventions in actual classroom settings (Murphy, 1999).

Educators in leadership positions, especially principals, supervisors, and department heads, are critical members of the support network (Fullan & Hargreaves, 1996; Goor, Schwenn, & Boyer, 1997; McDonnell et al., 1997). Dramatic changes in both teaching behavior and student learning are possible when school leaders communicate support and empowerment to their faculties (Felner et al., 1997). As renewal and accountability are recognized increasingly as community responsibilities, many schools have created school improvement teams to plan, coordinate, and evaluate local initiatives. Individuals might find meaningful support from fellow members of their school improvement teams who are committed to professional and organizational growth.

Affiliations with local, state, and national chapters of professional associations (e.g., American School Counselors' Association, Association for Supervision and Curriculum Development, Council for Exceptional Children, Council for Learning Disabilities) provide excellent opportunities for professionals to stay abreast of significant developments in their fields. Membership helps practitioners develop a better understanding of current issues in ways that are often difficult without connections to a broader professional network. Active involvement also facilitates ongoing knowledge and skill development through conferences, workshops, journals, newsletters, chapter meetings, and leadership opportunities. Many professional organizations provide electronic support through interactive web sites that are updated on an ongoing basis. A sampling of these web sites can be found in the Appendix.

Special Needs Support

The collaborative opportunities described thus far are routinely available to teachers and other school professionals to support them in their day-to-day work with students. When educators want additional assistance to deal with specific academic or behavioral concerns, they might request special support from assistance teams, consultants, co-teachers, or paraeducators. Assistance teams are school-based, problem-solving groups of peers who can help generate intervention strategies and develop an action plan to meet a specific need (Chalfant & Pysh, 1989; Whitten & Dieker, 1995). As an alternative, teachers might work with a single colleague or specialist to address their concerns about students' programs. Interactive problem solving that enables individuals with varied expertise to clarify and resolve classroom concerns is described as collaborative consultation (Friend & Cook, 1996; West & Idol, 1990). In general, most assistance from teams or consultants is considered "indirect" support in that professionals tend to work with each other rather than interact directly with students. Teachers maintain primary responsibility for implementing student interventions.

ACCESSING SPECIAL NEEDS SUPPORT

- Find out which types of support are available.
- Learn the procedure for requesting assistance from support providers.
- Talk with colleagues who have used available services.
- Become familiar with the areas of expertise of various teachers and specialists.
- Seek assistance for persistent instructional or behavioral problems.
- Keep detailed records on target behaviors, as well as interventions tried, to facilitate collaborative problem solving as needed.
- Observe experienced collaborators in action.
- Try co-teaching: plan, teach, and evaluate a unit of instruction with a willing colleague.

Other structures for addressing special needs extend beyond indirect support to engage collaborators in direct work with students. Cooperative teaching or co-teaching is one such option. Co-teaching typically involves a specialist and a classroom teacher jointly planning, instructing, and evaluating heterogeneous groups of students in general education classrooms (Bauwens & Hourcade, 1995; Walther-Thomas, 1997; Walther-Thomas et al., 2000). By intentionally varying their roles, the co-teachers more fully share responsibility for their classes.

True co-teaching is possible only when partners have comparable professional credentials. Paraeducators however, provide another source of direct support. By definition, paraeducators do not have the professional preparation and licensure to practice independently but, rather, work under the supervision of licensed teachers or specialists. Despite the role differential, paraeducators are important members of the team. With appropriate preparation, role expectations, and supervision, they can contribute significantly to planning and delivering educational programs and provide much needed collaborative support to teachers and other professionals (French, 1996; French & Gerlach, 1998; Pickett & Gerlach, 1997).

When professionals have access to these types of collaborative support, they can serve students with a broad range of abilities and skills in inclusive general education classrooms. More extensive support might be necessary when teachers and specialists encounter severe and persistent concerns about student performance, as discussed next.

Special Education Support

Although the Individuals with Disabilities Education Act (IDEA) does not explicitly mandate prereferral assistance prior to a comprehensive evaluation, all states either require or recommend some level of assistance prior to a full-scale evaluation for a suspected disability (Turnbull, Turnbull, Shank, & Leal, 1995). Many schools have resource or child study teams who oversee this process. Typically, these teams are composed of an administrator, a specialist, and one or more classroom teachers. Effective child study teams function much like assistance teams and provide support to teachers attempting classroom interventions (Hayek, 1987). When performance does not improve after reasonable modifications, the child study team might decide that a full multidisciplinary evaluation is warranted to determine whether the student has a disability.

Multidisciplinary teams plan and conduct comprehensive assessments of students' strengths and needs in all areas of concern. The teams must determine students' eligibility and need for special education services according to the criteria for recognized disabilities specified in federal and state regulations. Multidisciplinary evaluation team reports should provide detailed information to support the development of appropriate instructional programs for students. Like child study teams, these are composed of teachers, specialists, administrators, and parents.

When students are found to be eligible for special education, written individualized education programs (IEPs) must be developed specifying the special education and related services that students will receive. IEP teams include the parents or guardians of identified students, the students themselves, as appropriate, at least one general education teacher, one or more specialists from the multidisciplinary evaluation team, and a representative of the educational agency who will supervise the provision of services. Other participants can be included at the discretion of either the parents or the school. When students demonstrate significant behavioral challenges, IEP teams are involved in functional assessments and behavioral intervention planning as well. Active IEP teams provide invaluable guidance and support to the classroom teachers and specialists who work directly with identified students.

Beyond what is available within a school or district, additional support for teachers, specialists, and administrators is often provided by state or regional resource and technical assistance centers. Services include professional development, onsite and telephone consultations, information searches, lending libraries, newsletters, regional network information, and facilitation of communication among clients, schools, and

---

ACCESSING SPECIAL EDUCATION SUPPORT

- Know the procedures for making referrals to child study and multidisciplinary evaluation teams.
- Participate actively in the process when students are referred.
- Use special education support teams to plan, implement, and monitor student-specific interventions.
- Identify training and technical assistance centers in the area, services they provide, and ways to access assistance.
- Monitor student performance continuously, especially in areas of concern, and seek help before problems escalate.

sponsoring agencies (Ayers, 1991; Brinckerhoff, 1989; Haslam, 1992). Successful technical assistance providers also might work with administrators and decision-making teams to plan and support systems change (Janney & Meyer, 1990).

Interagency Support

The collaborative structures described so far are primarily school-based options. School personnel also might interact closely with professionals from other agencies to address more complex student and family needs. In both early childhood and secondary programs, interagency teams contribute perspectives that are essential for effective transition planning. Even though early childhood transitions involve entry into school programs and secondary education transitions involve exiting from school programs, the roles of these interagency teams are parallel in many respects (Repetto & Correa, 1996). Professionals from health care, employment, social services, recreation, and other fields can become members of the transition teams responsible for development of individualized plans, particularly the required transition components of Individualized Family Service Plans (IFSPs) for preschool children and IEPs for adolescents by age 14.

Interagency teams also are essential when student and family needs extend beyond the capabilities of the schools. Although each locality has its own array of agencies that provide services to youth and their families, most communities have public and private day care, public health, mental health, social services, parks and recreation, vocational rehabilitation, juvenile justice, and United Way information and referral services (Haley, VanDerwerker, & Power-deFur, 1997). Recently, many states have initiated comprehensive services teams that engage professionals from relevant agencies in the development and delivery of a wide array of community-based services tailored specifically to meet the needs of students with severe behavior and emotional disorders and their families (Hill, 1996).

ACCESSING INTERAGENCY SUPPORT

- Identify community programs and agencies most closely involved with students and families.
- Talk with guidance counselors or school social workers about available services and appropriate procedures for contacting service providers.
- Participate on teams that plan and coordinate interagency services for students.
- Visit a full-service school to observe the range of programs offered.
- Involve all students in peer tutoring or peer mentoring programs.
- Work with others to develop partnerships with businesses, churches, civic clubs, and universities to provide additional onsite support for students and professionals.

More and more communities are defining closer relationships among professionals in education, health, and human service agencies using a model of school-linked services to streamline the process of accessing support through a more "user-friendly" network (Skrtic & Sailor, 1996; Sullivan & Sugarman, 1996). Some communities are creating full-service schools that provide a broad array of services such as individual and family counseling, after-school tutoring and recreation, child care, health services, and job training and placement. Human-services professionals (e.g., school personnel, nurses, counselors, psychologists), as well as mentors from local businesses, work together to provide students and families with "one-stop" educational and community services (Dryfoos, 1994, 1998). Through extensive and intensive collaboration, professionals in these schools are addressing in a seamless manner a broad range of educational and noneducational issues that have an impact on students and their families.

In addition, educational partnerships that involve businesses, churches, civic organizations, federal agencies, and higher education institutions in support of schools have proliferated in recent years. Among the many services provided through community partnerships are tutor/mentorship programs and school-to-work transition programs often targeted at specific groups of students, such as dropouts, non-college-bound students, and students at risk (U.S. Department of Education, 1996). Teachers who work with more challenging students, therefore, often are able to access extra support from the community at large.

Although all of the structures depicted in Figure 1 are not likely to be available in any single school, every school system should offer a range of collaborative support options to help professionals address students' unique needs. The nature and extent of collaborative support that professionals may want at any given point will depend on numerous factors. Common considerations include the complexity and severity of a student's needs; the academic curriculum and setting demands; the teacher's skills, comfort level, and preferences; and the class configuration. School-improvement teams should strive continuously to improve and expand the array of support options available in their communities. In the next section, we will briefly review some frequently used support options designed exclusively for students.

PROVIDING COLLABORATIVE SUPPORT FOR STUDENTS

Although the focus of this article is professional collaboration, we point out that students, just as school professionals, need a broad array of support structures to be successful. Ideally, school communities provide students with supports that parallel adult support networks. Basic school supports should include positive discipline policies, diversity and disability awareness programs, and special-interest clubs and activities that are open to all students regardless of their academic standing.

In addition, weekly or monthly school themes should focus on topics such as cooperation, peer support, self-discipline, and respect for others. Developing and celebrating school community rituals, traditions, and anniversaries can raise school spirit and help students learn about others. When the development of positive and

> ### MAKING STUDENT SUPPORT SERVICES ACCESSIBLE
>
> * Make positive peer relationships a priority in planning at all levels—class-room, school, district, and community.
> * Work with colleagues, families, and community agencies to develop a comprehensive plan to facilitate the development of positive peer relationships.
> * Involve others (school counselors, school psychologists, community agency personnel, families, volunteers, older students) in ongoing classroom activities designed to build better peer relationships.
> * Embed ongoing social skills instruction into academic instruction whenever possible.
> * Offer students an array of peer support opportunities.

caring relationships with others is a high priority for student learning, school leaders provide opportunities that facilitate interaction, enrich individual strengths and interests, and help participants develop new skills or refine existing ones.

Some structures are designed to provide support for specific student academic or social needs. For example, cooperative learning groups (Johnson, Johnson, & Holubec, 1994; King-Sears, 1997) and peer tutoring (Fuchs & Fuchs, 1998; Greenwood & Delquadri, 1995; Utley et al., 1997) are powerful forms of student collaboration that facilitate academic learning. After-school clubs and homework hotlines provide extra help for students. Many schools prepare students to serve as peer mediators to facilitate problem solving and conflict resolution. Groups focused on specific topics can help students cope with challenging situations at home such as divorce, blended families, or the loss of a family member.

Effective student support networks extend beyond the school building to involve families and community members. Organized activities in the community related to scouting, church, and neighborhood recreation groups can provide support and opportunities for developing skills for both academic and interpersonal success. Relationships with adult volunteers from businesses, universities, and churches also are important. Many students volunteer for service projects in which they work in hospitals, retirement facilities, homeless shelters, and other service settings. Other students benefit from business partnerships that provide mentors, tutors, and other types of beneficial relationships with adult role models.

In collaborative cultures, all students consistently receive the message that school is a place where everyone belongs, is cared for, receives needed support, and has much to contribute. School or community service clubs, student representation on all school committees, and peer-tutoring programs are examples of activities that can simultaneously involve and support students. All students, even those with significant support needs, should be involved in providing some type of assistance to others as part of developing a sense of efficacy and responsibility (Downing, 1996).

Programs designed to change the behavior of individual students are most successful when peers also are learning to support one another in an atmosphere of acceptance and respect. The classroom social environment significantly affects student attitudes, engagement, and achievement (Johnson & Johnson, 1995; Walberg & Greenberg, 1997). If students feel unwelcome or unsafe in schools, they have more difficulty changing inappropriate behaviors or benefiting from academic instruction.

Recent school violence is a sobering reminder of the harm that can result when students feel disconnected and disenfranchised. Networks of student support that parallel structures available for adults help ensure that all students know they are important and valued members of the school community. Student support is an explicit goal in schools that are committed to collaboration. Ongoing modeling, instruction, practice, and feedback help students access available supports and facilitate their participation in assisting and supporting others.

CONSIDERATIONS FOR EFFECTIVE COLLABORATION

Establishing a collaborative culture to support more inclusive education represents a major shift in thinking for many school professionals. In addition, it means significant changes in team members' roles and in ways that support services are provided. To be successful, this complex endeavor requires six essential elements derived from research on successful organizational change: shared leadership, a coherent vision, comprehensive planning, adequate resources, sustained implementation, and continuous evaluation and improvement (Walther-Thomas et al., 2000). These elements of successful innovations provide collaborators with the structure and support needed to modify existing practices, create more collaborative approaches, and maintain them over time. These features are the building blocks of effective schools and form the foundation for collaborative service delivery and appropriate inclusive education. Schools are most successful when they build on existing strengths and systematically address weaker aspects of their programs. The six elements and accompanying questions presented in this section are intended to help school teams assess their current status and progress toward more collaborative programming.

Shared Leadership

Shared leadership means including everyone involved with students in meaningful decision making, either directly or through effective representation. Key participants have input and share information at all phases of planning, implementation, and ongoing evaluation. Leaders at every level (state, district, school) take an active role in mobilizing and motivating participants, establishing direction, supporting changes, and sharing decision making (Krug, 1992; Tindall, 1996). Planning teams address concerns (e.g., regarding resources, assignments, and schedules) in a proactive manner, offering ideas and solutions that are mutually beneficial given input from key participants. Inclusive programs are most effective when shared leadership prevails (Walther-Thomas, 1997).

ASSESSING SHARED LEADERSHIP

- Do school team members have opportunities for providing input and sharing information at all phases of program development and implementation?
- Are team members clear about their roles and responsibilities?
- Are team members involved actively in decision making?
- What effective collaborative planning and problem-solving dyads or teams already exist onsite?
- What are the logical next steps and next structures to enhance support for students and adults at this school?

Coherent Vision

A coherent vision refers to a clear, well-defined, and shared view among administrators, teachers, specialists, students, and families of what the school's future should be like—a collective sense of why the school is moving toward more collaborative and inclusive services and what team members are trying to accomplish. Such a vision enables teams to make more informed decisions and facilitates collaboration toward common goals. A well-articulated vision induces commitment among participants and enhances efforts in planning and project management (Miles, 1995; Senge, 1990). It helps team members understand how their individual and collective efforts fit together. But rather than adopting a complete vision at the very beginning, participants are open to the emergence of a shared vision resulting from their teamwork, actions, and outcomes that occur along the way (Larson & LaFasto, 1989). Visions for collaborative service delivery and inclusive education typically include a fundamental belief that all students can learn, have a right to be educated with their peers, and are better served when team members work together to support academic, social, and personal growth (McGregor & Vogelsberg, 1998; Van Dyke, Pitonyak, & Gilley, 1997).

ASSESSING THE VISION

- Do teams share the belief that all students can learn and have a right to be educated with their peers?
- Do team members share responsibility for all students in the school?
- Can team members articulate common values and goals to be accomplished?
- Can team members articulate the benefits of working collaboratively?
- Do team members see how their efforts contribute toward common goals, and do they value the contributions of others toward these ends?

Comprehensive Planning

Comprehensive planning requires careful consideration of all essential program components in relationship to the vision—goals, student characteristics, curriculum and instruction, program structures and systems, roles and responsibilities, stakeholder involvement, and evaluation. Planning teams, therefore, assesses strengths, target problem areas, coordinate initiatives, and determine logical "next steps" for program improvement. Comprehensive plans, in turn, guide resource allocation, professional development, personnel assignments, and student schedules. Plans facilitate information sharing and efficient, effective use of resources. They establish meaningful links between programs and initiatives. In the absence of comprehensive planning, daily implementation and evaluation problems are likely to continue without satisfactory resolution. Haphazard planning leads to duplication of effort, gaps in services, frustration, and cynicism toward change (Fullan, 1993).

ASSESSING COMPREHENSIVE PLANNING

- Are multi-year plans and timelines in place to ensure that collaboration remains a top priority over time?
- Do planning teams assess strengths, target problem areas or gaps in services, and coordinate initiatives?
- Do comprehensive plans guide resource allocation, professional development, personnel assignments, and student and staff schedules?
- Are districtwide and school-based planning teams available to facilitate and monitor collaborative service delivery?
- Do planning teams regularly provide opportunities offering input and sharing information with key participants affected by program changes?

Adequate Resources

Resources are the tools that implementers need to do the job successfully. Resources typically include administrative support, personnel, professional development opportunities, planning time, materials, and technology. Further, to develop and implement successful collaborative programs, student and teacher schedules, class sizes, and specialist caseloads must be reasonable. Even though programs seldom receive all the desired resources, support must be sufficient to make programs viable. Often this is accomplished by reallocating existing resources and personnel. Without adequate resources, even the most committed advocates become discouraged and enthusiasm for new initiatives quickly wanes.

ASSESSING RESOURCES

- Do multi-year plans ensure that collaborative initiates will continue to receive funding support over time?
- Does the district-level administration provide policies, materials, personnel, and other resources to support collaborative service delivery?
- Does the building-level administration provide policies, materials, personnel, and other resources to support collaborative service delivery?
- Are class sizes and specialists' caseloads reasonable to allow for effective collaboration?
- Is common planning time scheduled for professionals to work with colleagues daily or weekly?
- Are daily schedules of professionals and students designed to facilitate ongoing collaboration?

Sustained Implementation

Sustained implementation refers to the ability of program implementers and supporters to stay focused and committed while bringing others on board. Collaborative service delivery to support inclusive education must remain a priority for the long term at every level. All major changes take time and sustained effort (Fullan, 1993; Sarason, 1993; Senge, 1990). Therefore, district and school initiatives must be coordinated and ongoing instead of changing dramatically from year to year. Multi-year plans should guide systematic movement toward more collaborative services supported by professional development opportunities to keep implementers and newcomers on track.

ASSESSING IMPLEMENTATION

- Are multi-year plans designed to guide systematic movement toward greater collaboration implemented over time?
- Is ongoing professional development provided to keep experienced implementers on track and to give newcomers the skills they need to collaborate effectively?
- Do new district-level initiatives complement and support one another rather than pull personnel and resources in different directions from year to year?
- Do new school-level initiatives complement and support one another?

Continuous Evaluation and Improvement

Ongoing quantitative and qualitative evaluation provides collaborators the information they need to make well-reasoned, data-based decisions about continuing or

---

ASSESSING EVALUATION AND IMPROVEMENT EFFORTS

- Is student achievement the key feature in decision making?

- Are academic and behavioral outcomes for all students monitored on an ongoing basis?

- Do written program descriptions specify both individual and team behaviors related to collaboration in clear and measurable terms?

- Is ongoing program implementation monitored over time?

- Are program modifications documented to allow for more efficient replication?

- Do school- and district-level evaluation plans facilitate program review, systematic improvement, and replication as appropriate?

---

modifying programs to make them more effective (McLaughlin & McLaughlin, 1993). Evaluation includes detailed descriptions of program efforts to allow for replication and adjustment as well as measures of outcomes for students, families, and educators. It provides supportive evidence for the aspects of collaboration that are working well and those that require adjustment. Ongoing assessment helps stakeholders determine progress and answer questions about intended outcomes, such as the academic performance of students with and without disabilities in inclusive programs (McGregor & Vogelsberg, 1998). This information can help sustain the commitment and enthusiasm of program supporters and focus efforts toward continuous improvement.

In summary, collaboration is most productive when it takes place in the larger context of effective program development characterized by shared leadership, coherent vision, comprehensive planning, adequate resources, sustained implementation, and continuous evaluation for improvement. If some elements are lacking in a given setting, planning teams can identify strategies at district, school, and classroom levels for developing them and deliberately moving toward more inclusive and collaborative programs. Though it is no quick or easy task, cultivating the essential elements is the surest path toward successful programs for educators and students alike. In the final section, we will note some common start-up problems related to these features and strategies for addressing them.

COMMON START-UP PROBLEMS AND STRATEGIES FOR SUCCESS

Many school teams experience similar problems as they implement collaborative initiatives (Cramer, 1998; Fishbaugh, 1997; Walther-Thomas, 1997; Walther-Thomas et al., 2000). Commonly mentioned concerns addressed in this section include building administrative support, providing professional development, cultivating staff commitment, creating balanced classroom rosters and manageable specialist schedules, and finding common planning time. These problems often are linked. If one is present, others probably are, too. For example, a lack of administrative support often affects professionals' teaching schedules, caseloads, and availability of scheduled time for collaborative planning.

Some of the suggestions offered here might seem somewhat generic or overlapping. Just as problems are linked, so are solutions. As a result, solving one significant problem might provide relief in other areas as well. Some proposed problem-solving strategies serve only as quick fixes; they will provide temporary relief but not enough support to keep collaborators working together. The most effective long-term solutions require resources and administrative support related to the essential features presented previously. Finally, some readers might question the feasibility of certain suggestions that seem too costly or more "creative" than imaginable in some schools. Nevertheless, all of the suggestions offered here are used in real schools.

Building Administrative Support and Leadership

Clearly, administrative support is a basic factor in effective collaboration (Fullan & Hargreaves, 1996; Larson & LaFasto, 1989). District- and building-level leadership

---

PROVIDING ADMINISTRATIVE SUPPORT

- Make available an array of professional development opportunities such as tuition for courses, books, video/audiotapes, mentors, coaches, software, and onsite workshops.
- Participate actively with faculty in professional development programs.
- Write grants to secure additional funding sources for classroom and school-wide projects.
- Schedule collaborators' classes first to ensure common planning time for teams.
- Recognize professional efforts (e.g., handwritten notes, e-mail messages, verbal comments, classroom visits) on an ongoing basis.
- Write individual and team letters of support and commendations for personnel files.
- Compensate staff members for "start-up" work done outside school to support new initiatives with money, time, recertification points, journal subscriptions, or conference registrations.
- Hire faculty and staff members who share a collaborative vision.
- Communicate regularly with teams to discuss progress and address concerns.
- Use e-mail and voice mail to reduce faculty meeting time, and reallocate this time for professional development and collaborative planning.

ensures a stronger commitment for new program initiatives and greater support (Fullan, 1993). For example, fiscal resources generated at the district level help principals and teachers get the tools they need to implement new efforts successfully. Also, district leadership in planning reduces duplication of effort across schools, facilitates communication within the system and in the larger community, and fosters better cooperation and collaboration among schools (Walther-Thomas et al., 2000). Finally, leadership at this level helps ensure that potential consequences of proposed initiatives are considered in a comprehensive manner before implementation. For example, if one middle school decides to provide inclusive classroom support for all students with disabilities, district planners have to consider how this decision could affect students, families, teachers, and administrators at other schools in the community.

At the school level, principals play critical roles in the development of collaborative communities (Stoll, 1991). Their efforts to ensure the provision of needed resources—such as professional development, manageable class sizes and specialist caseloads, balanced classroom rosters, and scheduled common planning times—enable individuals and teams to work more effectively (Fullan & Hargreaves, 1996). Principals find capable teachers and specialists who also are willing to serve as leaders in new collaborative initiatives. Professionals who have worked successfully with others in the past are good candidates for these new efforts. To encourage participation and to recognize the extra time and effort involved, leaders find ways to compensate participants for their work.

Providing Adequate Professional Development

Typical complaints about collaborative initiatives can be traced back to a lack of adequate professional development prior to implementation. When school leaders implement new ideas before teams are prepared adequately for their new roles and responsibilities, problems often develop (Fullan, 1993; Fullan & Hargreaves, 1996; Walther-Thomas et al., 2000). Negative attitudes, poor communication skills, and inadequate team problem solving are just a few of the many difficulties that can be resolved through appropriate professional development.

Traditionally, school professionals are better prepared to work with children and youth than to work with professional colleagues and family members. Despite recent improvements, preservice programs still offer little preparation regarding skills for effective collaboration. Consequently, few beginning teachers and specialists have mastered the basic communication skills needed for effective teamwork—such as active listening, group problem solving, conflict resolution, and negotiation (Friend & Cook, 1996). In most traditional schools, few professional development opportunities focus specifically on communication and collaboration.

Without adequate skill development before implementation and ongoing encouragement and support during implementation, many fledgling teams give up on collaboration as a viable option for them and for their schools. Other teams continue to work together but never fully achieve the potential of their teaming efforts.

**PROFESSIONAL DEVELOPMENT OPTIONS
TO IMPROVE COLLABORATORS' SKILLS**

- Enroll with colleagues in university or district classes on interpersonal communication, collaboration, or inclusive education.
- Start or join a study group on collaboration in the school or in the district.
- Review case studies and role-play potential problem situations with colleagues.
- Watch and discuss videotapes of actual team meetings to improve personal skills and group behaviors.
- Visit model schools with teammates; observe effective collaborators in action.
- With teammates, attend conferences, workshops, or symposia on collaboration.
- Recruit more experienced collaborators to serve as mentors for new teams.
- Surf the Internet to find collaboration-based resources; share your findings with others.

Offering a variety of professional development choices allows professionals to select the activities that will be most valuable to them.

As new teams begin working together, regular use of a teaming checklist to assess individual and team behaviors can facilitate communication and target areas in which professional development is needed. In addition to encouraging individual team members to monitor their own behavior and make personal changes as needed, the process helps beginning teams focus on important communication skills as they work together.

Figure 8.2, the *Teamwork Checklist,* provides teams with a focus for their communication and collaboration. New team members might want to review the checklist items individually before meeting with team members. This allows them to assess their own teamwork behaviors and set individual goals for self-improvement. As teams work together over time, they can use the checklist periodically to monitor their progress in developing effective teaming skills.

Cultivating Staff Commitment

Willingness to make a commitment to work with others over time should be an important part of the selection criteria for participants in new initiatives. Time and commitment are necessary to become an effective collaborator. This enables teams to develop positive working relationships, effective roles and responsibilities, and genuine appreciation for each partner's contributions (Walther-Thomas, Korinek, McLaughlin, & Williams, 1996). Even thoroughly planned initiatives experience

Self-Assessment

	Needs Work—Satisfactory—Outstanding				
	1	2	3	4	5
1. Expression and body language are monitored.					
2. Comfortable eye contact is maintained.					
3. Sufficient rapport is established.					
4. Speaker is given undivided attention.					
5. Speaker's content is paraphrased correctly.					
6. Feelings are reflected when appropriate.					
7. "I messages" are used appropriately.					
8. Questions are asked effectively.					
9. Key ideas/themes are identified accurately.					
10. Checks for accuracy are made frequently.					

Strongest aspect(s) of my communication:

Specific target(s) for more effective communication:

Team Assessment

	Needs Work—Satisfactory—Outstanding				
	1	2	3	4	5
1. Members are clear about the task to be accomplished.					
2. Members are clear about their roles and responsibilities.					
3. All members participate actively.					
4. Members stay on-task and on-topic.					
5. Communication is clear and jargon-free.					
6. Members listen openly to diverse perspectives.					
7. Members make supportive comments.					
8. Student problems are clearly identified.					
9. Specific intervention goals are identified.					
10. Brainstorming results in a variety of alternatives.					
11. Specific interventions are selected.					
12. A progress measurement plan is developed.					
13. The team accomplishes the task effectively.					
14. Members follow a clear process for reaching consensus.					
15. Members leave knowing who does what by when.					

Strongest aspect(s) of team problem solving:

Specific target(s) for more effective teamwork:

FIGURE 8.2 ■ Teamwork Checklist

"rocky" times during start-up. Perseverance during this period is critical to long term success. Effective collaborators need time to change their old ways of thinking and behaving.

Individuals adjust to change at different rates. Some level of personal resistance is actually a healthy response to change (Friend & Cook, 1996; Fullan and Hargreaves, 1996). Resistance prevents individuals and groups from making hasty decisions that are not well thought out. Most of the resistance to collaborative efforts, such as teacher assistance teams and co-teaching, stems from limited understanding of the processes, lack of prior experience, participation in poorly implemented models, and fear of the unknown. If school leaders recognize that initial resistance is normal, they can use strategies such as phased-in implementation, personalized professional

> **STRATEGIES THAT STRENGTHEN COLLABORATIVE COMMITMENTS**
>
> - Start new initiatives with voluntary participation.
> - Respond to participants' concerns with personalized support.
> - Encourage language that emphasizes "our students" rather than "my students/your students."
> - Provide comparable material, supplies, and status for all partners.
> - Communicate with families and students as a team (e.g., on the first day of classes, at back-to-school-night presentations, in progress reports).

development, and modeling by volunteers to break down barriers effectively (Darling-Hammond, 1997).

Despite these efforts, some professionals choose not to participate in collaborative programs because of their strong philosophical beliefs. With sufficient time and support, most individuals will recognize the benefits of collaboration. A few might seek employment in settings where the vision is more compatible with their own.

Creating Balanced Classroom Rosters and Manageable Professional Schedules

Scheduling students appropriately is one of the most important tasks in planning successful collaboration and inclusion. A typical mistake of many well-intentioned teams is to schedule too many students with special needs into a single classroom. This usually is done because placing a significant number of identified students in one room helps to justify additional resources (e.g., consultant time, daily co-teaching, smaller class size) that will be provided for that classroom. Also, placing students with special needs in a limited number of rooms makes specialists' schedules more manageable and allows them to provide more intensive support services. Although these decisions make sense on one level, the result is often classrooms that present more academic and behavioral challenges than even the most skilled and committed collaborators can handle successfully.

In developing classroom rosters, the principle of natural proportions must be kept in mind (Brown et al., 1989). Inclusive classrooms are heterogeneously grouped environments (McGregor & Vogelsberg, 1998). Students with special needs should represent not more than about 20% of the total classroom. Ideally, in a class of 25 students, no more than four or five class members should have identified disabilities in the mild to moderate range or other related problems that make them at risk of school failure. If the identified disabilities are more severe and necessitate more support, fewer special education and at-risk students should be included in these classroom rolls. The underlying goal in developing classroom rosters is heterogeneity. Although computerized scheduling software can be a helpful tool, most inclusive classes still must be scheduled by hand to achieve appropriate classroom configurations. Planning teams cannot rely on the random results generated by most computer scheduling programs.

In schools with a high concentration of students with special needs, it is easy to overload classrooms with students who present challenging problems. Typically, it is easier to create balanced classrooms in elementary and middle schools, where mixed grouping is generally the norm. High schools present a greater challenge. Lower-level courses such as Algebra I and Basic English often are filled with students who have learning or behavior problems—most of whom do not qualify for special education services. School teams have to assess student needs and available resources carefully (e.g., co-teaching time, educator time, scheduled planning periods, class size, and specialist caseloads) when making student placement decisions and co-teaching assignments.

For example, in districts where Algebra I is a basic requirement for graduation, to offer co-teaching throughout the day in pre-Algebra and Algebra I courses makes sense. Many students who wait to take this course until high school lack the fundamental skills, ability, and confidence to perform well. By offering several co-taught sections, all students in the school can benefit from the additional support. Multiple sections also allow schedulers to distribute students with disabilities and others with documented math problems in classes across the full school day rather than trying to concentrate them into one or two periods.

In many schools, teams are redefining specialists' roles to facilitate more direct classroom support and make specialists' schedules more manageable. In school systems that use this approach, all specialists (e.g., special educators, gifted education teachers, counselors, psychologists, Title I teachers, English as Second Language and Limited English Proficiency teachers) are required to provide direct support for a designated number of classrooms. Most work cross-categorically and serve as the case managers for any students with special needs (e.g., special education, gifted, Title 1) who are included in the classrooms where they collaborate with general educators.

FINDING ADDITIONAL RESOURCES TO SUPPORT NEW COLLABORATIVE INITIATIVES

- Establish supportive partnerships with community businesses.
- Recruit tutors and classroom assistants through service groups and other community organizations.
- Establish a professional lending library and systematically share reading materials, instructional strategies, and management techniques with colleagues.
- Create professional development school partnerships with universities.
- Encourage involvement of college students in schools.
- Write grant proposals for classroom and schoolwide projects.
- Teach PTA leaders how to recruit and prepare skilled classroom volunteers.

The specialists meet regularly to discuss the progress of targeted students, problem-solve concerns, and exchange classroom strategies. This arrangement works well in schools that include many students with special needs and a large number of specialists. It also is effective in rural areas as an alternative to having specialists travel long distances to see students on their categorical caseloads.

Scheduling Common Planning Time

Collaborators need common planning time to work together (Bauwens & Hourcade, 1995; Friend & Cook, 1996; Walther-Thomas, 1997). Ideally, they should have a minimum of one hour of scheduled common planning time each week for activities such as instructional planning, problem solving, and progress monitoring. Establishing common planning times for collaborators is a challenging task for administrators and teachers. It necessitates thoughtful consideration of the many professional schedules and can be achieved only if it is an administrative priority.

SCHEDULED COMMON PLANNING TIME: SHORT- AND LONG-TERM SOLUTIONS

- Schedule daily or weekly planning periods.
- Schedule weekly or monthly early-release periods.
- Cover classes with "floating" substitute teachers during planning.
- Allow compensatory time for before-school or after-school planning.
- Replace meeting time with planning periods.
- Use e-mail for planning and communication.
- Plan during lunch time.
- Plan during walk-and-talk sessions before or after school.
- Plan in the classroom during videotapes and practice periods.
- Double-up classes for some activities (e.g., films, library time, speakers).
- Hire and prepare paraeducators to cover teachers' classes once a week for additional planning.
- Create a daily master schedule that uses a time "banking" system (e.g., school day plus 15 additional minutes a day) to create full or partial teacher workdays each month.
- Use "late start" mornings; early dismissal days; and block art, physical education, music, and keyboarding classes together to create longer planning periods.

CONCLUSION

Collaborative approaches are gaining popularity to help professionals address students' complex and diverse needs. Though collaboration should not be viewed as an end in itself, collaborative processes can be effective tools for facilitating student achievement. The network of support discussed in this article illustrates the broad range of collaborative possibilities available in many school communities. The focus of the model presented here is on the professional side of collaboration; it describes potential support structures available to assist professionals in their work with students.

Like other innovations, collaborative networks must be built on a firm foundation of shared leadership, coherent vision, comprehensive planning, adequate resources, sustained implementation, and continuous evaluation and improvement. Even with all of these elements in place, problems arise, especially among new collaborators who likely lack the necessary skills and experience needed to work effectively with others.

Typical start-up problems include lack of administrative support, inadequate professional development, resistance to change, imbalances in classroom rosters and specialist schedules, and limited planning time. Many common problems that teams encounter can be linked. Similarly, certain strategic actions may solve multiple problems. Educators have to recognize that collaborative relationships are complex, and they take time to mature into productive support mechanisms. Perseverance and ongoing problem solving will help teams collaborate effectively to promote students' success.

REFERENCES

Algozzine, B., Ysseldyke, J. E., & Campbell, P. (1994). Strategies and tactics for effective instruction. *Teaching Exceptional Children, 26*(3), 34–35.

Ayers, E. J. B. (1991). An alternative approach to staff development. *Journal of Visual Impairment & Blindness, 85*(7), 302–305.

Bauwens, J., & Hourcade, J. J. (1995*). Cooperative teaching: Rebuilding the schoolhouse for all students.* Austin: Pro-Ed.

Brown, L., Long, E., Udvari-Solner, A., Davis, L., VanDeventer, P., Ahlgren, C., Johnson, F., Grenewald, L., & Jorgenson, J. (1989). The home school. *Journal of the Association for Persons with Severe Handicaps, 19*(3), 223–232.

Brinckerhoff, R. F. (1989). Resource centers serve the needs of school science teachers. *School Science & Mathematics, 89*(1), 12–18.

Chalfant, J. C., & Pysh, M. V. (1989). Teacher assistance teams: Five descriptive studies on 96 teams. *Remedial & Special Education, 10*(6), 49–58.

Corrigan, D., & Bishop, K. K. (1997). Creating family-centered integrated service systems and interprofessional educational programs to implement them. *Social Work in Education, 19*(3), 149–163.

Council for Exceptional Children. (1995*). Creating schools for all our schools: What twelve schools have to say.* Reston, VA: Council for Exceptional Children.

Council for Exceptional Children. (1998). *Retention of special education professionals: A practical guide of strategies and activities for educators and administrators.* Reston, VA: National Clearinghouse for Professions in Special Education.

Council of Chief State School Officers. (1996). *Model standards for beginning teacher licensing and development: A resource for state dialogue.* Washington, DC: Council of Chief State School Officers.

Cramer, S. F. (1998). *Collaboration: A success strategy for special educators.* Boston: Allyn & Bacon.

Crowther, S. (1998). Secrets of staff development support. *Educational Leadership, 55*(5), 75–76.

Darling-Hammond, L. (1997). *Doing what matters most: Investing in quality teaching.* New York: National Commission on Teaching and America's Future.

Dickinson, T. S., & Erb, T. O. (Eds.). (1996*). We gain more than we give: Teaming in middle schools.* Columbus, OH: National Middle School Association.

Downing, J. E. (1996*). Including students with severe and multiple disabilities in typical classrooms.* Baltimore: Paul H. Brookes.

Dryfoos, J. (1994). *Full service schools: A revolution in health and social services for children, youth, and families.* San Francisco: Jossey-Bass.

Dryfoos, J. (1998). *A look at community schools in 1998.* New York: National Center for Schools and Communities, Fordham University.

Felner, R., Jackson, A., Kasak, D. T., Mulhall, P., Brand, S., & Flowers, N. (1997). The impact of school reform for the middle years: A longitudinal study of a network engaged in *Turning Points*-based comprehensive school transformation. *Phi Delta Kappan, 78*(7), 528–532.

Fishbaugh, M.S.E. (1997). *Models of collaboration.* Boston: Allyn and Bacon.

French, N. K. (1996*). Teacher as executive: Preparing special educators to supervise paraeducators.* Paper presented at 18th International Conference on Learning Disabilities, Nashville, TN.

French, N. K., & Gerlach, K. (1998, February). *What does it mean to be a professional educator? Role differentiation for paraprofessionals and professionals.* Paper presented at annual meeting of American Association of Colleges for Teacher Education, New Orleans.

Friend, M., & Bursuck, W. (1999). *Including students with special needs: A practical guide for classroom teachers* (2d ed.). Boston: Allyn & Bacon.

Friend, M., & Cook, L. (1996). *Interactions: Collaboration skills for school professionals* (2d ed.). White Plains, NY: Longman.

Fuchs, L., & Fuchs, D. (1998). General educators' instructional adaptation for students with learning disabilities. *Learning Disability Quarterly, 21,* 23–33.

Fuhrman, S. H. (1993). The politics of coherence. In S. H. Fuhrman (Ed.), Designing coherent education policy: Improving the system. San Francisco: Jossey-Bass.

Fullan, M. (1993). *Change forces: Probing the depths of educational reform.* Bristol, PA: Falmer Press.

Fullan, M., & Hargreaves, A. (1996). *What's worth fighting for in your school.* New York: Teachers College Press.

Ganser, T. (1996). What do mentors say about mentoring? *Journal of Staff Development, 17* (3), 36–39.

Greenwood, C. R., & Delquadri, J. (1995). Classwide peer tutoring and the prevention of school failure. *Preventing School Failure, 39*(4), 21–25.

Goertz, M.E., Floden, R.E., & O'Day, J. (1995). *Studies of education reform: Systematic reform: Vol. 1. Findings and conclusions.* New Brunswick, NJ: Rutgers University, Consortium for Policy Research in Education.

Goor, M. B., Schwenn, J. O., & Boyer, L. (1997). Preparing principals for leadership in special education. *Intervention in School & Clinic, 32,* 133–141.

Haley, P. H., VanDerwerker, W., & Power-deFur, L. A. (1997). Supporting inclusive education through interagency collaboration. In L. A. Power-deFur & F. P. Orelove (Eds.), *Inclusive education: Practical implementation of the least restrictive environment* (pp. 117–130). Gaithersburg, MD: Aspen.

Halford, J. M. (1998). Easing the way for new teachers. *Educational Leadership, 55*(5), 33–36.

Haslam, M. B. (1992). *Assisting educators to improve education: A review of the research* (Report Contract No. LC 89089001). Washington, DC: U.S. Department of Education.

Hayek, R. A. (1987). The teacher assistance team: A prereferral support system. *Focus on Exceptional Children, 20*(1), 1–7.

Hill, E. B. (1996). *Comprehensive services for students with serious emotional disturbance: An analysis of state legislation and policy.* Unpublished doctoral dissertation, College of William and Mary, Williamsburg, VA.

Idol, L., West, J. F., & Lloyd, S. R. (1988). Organizing and implementing specialized reading programs: A collaborative approach involving classroom, remedial, and special education teachers. *Remedial & Special Education, 9*(2),54–61.

Janney, R., & Meyer, L. H. (1990). A consultation model to support integrated educational services for students with severe disabilities and challenging behaviors. *Journal of the Association for Persons with Severe Handicaps, 15*(3), 186–199.

Johnson, D. W., & Johnson, R. T. (1995). *Reducing school violence through conflict resolution.* Alexandria, VA: Association for Supervision & Curriculum Development.

Johnson, D. W., Johnson, R. T., & Holubec, E. J. (1994). *The new circles of learning: Cooperation in the classroom and school.* Alexandria, VA: Association for Supervision & Curriculum Development.

Joyce, B. & Showers, B. (1995). *Student achievement through staff development: Fundamentals of school renewal* (2d ed.). White Plains, NY: Longmont.

King-Sears, M. E. (1997). Best academic practices for inclusive classrooms. *Focus on Exceptional Children, 29*(7), 1–22.

Krug, S. E. (1992). Instructional leadership: A constructivist perspective. *Educational Administration Quarterly, 28*(3), 430–433.

Larson, C. E., & LaFasto, F. M. J. (1989). *Teamwork: What must go right—What can go wrong.* Newbury Park, CA: Sage.

Little, J. W. (1982). Norms of collegiality and experimentation: Workplace conditions of school success. *American Educational Research Journal, 19*, 325–340.

Little, J. W., & McLaughlin, M., (Eds.). (1993). *Teachers' work: Individuals, colleagues, and contexts.* New York: Teachers College Press.

Louis, K. S., Marks, H. M., & Kruse, S. (1996). Teachers' professional community in restructured schools. *American Educational Research Journal, 33*(4), 757–798.

McDonnell, L. M., McLaughlin, M. J., & Morison (Eds.) (1997). *Educating one and all: Students with disabilities and standards-based reform.* Washington, DC: National Academy Press.

McGregor, G., & Vogelsberg, R. T. (1998). *Inclusive schooling practices: Pedagogical and research foundations.* Baltimore: Brookes.

McLaughlin, J. A., & McLaughlin, V. L. (1993). Program evaluation. In B. S. Billingsley (Ed.), *Program leadership for serving students with disabilities* (pp. 343–370). Blacksburg, VA: Virginia Tech.

Miles, M. B. (1995). Mapping basic beliefs about learner-centered schools. *Theory into practice, 34*(4), 279–287.

Murphy, C. U. (1999). Use time for faculty study. *Journal of Staff Development, 20*(2), 20–25.

National Association of State Boards of Education. (1992, October). *Winners all: A call for inclusive schools.* Alexandria, VA: Author.

National Center on Educational Restructuring and Inclusion. (1995). *National study of inclusive education.* New York: City University of New York, National Center on Educational Restructuring and Inclusion.

National Commission on Teaching and America's Future (NCTAF). (1996). *What matters most: Teaching for America's future.* New York: Author.

National Council on Disability. (1995). *Improving the implementation of the Individuals with Disabilities Education Act: Making schools work for all of America's children.* Washington, DC: National Council on Disability.

National LEADership Network. (1993). The National LEADership network study group on restructuring schools. *Total quality management: The leader's odyssey.* Washington, DC: U.S. Department of Education, Office of Research and Improvement.

National Staff Development Council. (1994). *Standards for staff development: Middle level edition.* Oxford, OH: Author.

National Staff Development Council. (1995). *Standards for staff development: Elementary school edition.* Oxford, OH: Author.

Orelove, F.P., & Sobsey, D. (1996). *Educating children with multiple disabilities: A transdisciplinary approach* (3d ed.). Baltimore: Brookes.

Pickett, A. L., & Gerlach, K. (1997). *Supervising paraeducators in school settings.* Reston, VA: Council for Exceptional Children.

Pounder, D. G. (1998). Teacher teams: Redesigning teachers' work for collaboration. In D. G. Pounder (Ed.), *Restructuring schools for collaboration* (pp. 65–88). Albany, NY: State University of New York Press.

Pugach, M., & Johnson, L. J. (1995). Unlocking expertise among classroom teachers through structured dialogue: Extending research on peer collaboration. *Exceptional Children, 62*(2), 101–110.

Ravitch, D. (1995). *National standards in American education: A citizen's guide.* Washington, DC: Brookings.

Repetto, J. B., & Correa, V. I. (1996). Expanding views on transition. *Exceptional Children, 62*(6), 551–563.

Rosenholz, S. (1989). *Teachers' workplace: The social organization of schools.* New York: Longman.

Sarason, S. (1993). *The case for change: Rethinking the preparation of educators.* San Francisco: Jossey-Bass.

Senge, P. (1990). *The fifth discipline: The art and practice of the learning organization.* New York: Doubleday.

Skrtic, T.M., & Sailor, W. (1996). School-linked services integration: Crisis and opportunity in the transition to postmodern society. *Remedial & Special Education, 17*(5), 271–283.

Skrtic, T.M., Sailor, W., & Gee, K. (1996). Voice, collaboration, and inclusion: Democratic themes in educational and social reform initiatives. *Remedial & Special Education, 17*(3), 142–157.

Slavin, R.E. (1995). *Cooperative learning: Theory, research, and practice* (2d ed.). Boston: Allyn & Bacon.

Stedman, P., & Stroot, S. A. (1998). Teachers helping teachers. *Educational Leadership, 55*(5), 37–39.

Stoll, L. (1991). School effectiveness in action: Supporting growth in schools and classrooms. In M. Ainsoow (Ed.), *Effective schools for all* (pp. 68–91). London: David Fulton Publishers.

Sullivan, C. J., & Sugarman, J. M. (1996). State policies affecting school-linked integrated services. *Remedial & Special Education, 17*(5), 284–292.

Tindall, E. (1996). *Principal's role in fostering teacher collaboration for students with special needs.* Unpublished doctoral dissertation. College of William and Mary, Williamsburg, VA.

Turnbull, A. P., Turnbull, H. R., Shank, M. & Leal, D. (1995). *Exceptional lives: Special education in today's schools.* Englewood Cliffs, NJ: Prentice Hall.

U. S. Department of Education. (1996). *A back to school special report: The baby boom echo.* Washington, DC: Author.

Utley, C. A., Mortweet, S. L., & Greenwood, C. R. (1997). Peer-mediated instruction and interventions. *Focus on Exceptional Children, 29*(5), 1–23.

Van Dyke, R. E., Pitonyak, C. R., & Gilley, C. T. (1997). Planning, implementing, and evaluating inclusive education within the school. In L. A. Power-deFur & F. P. Orlove (Eds.), *Inclusive education: Practical implementation of the least restrictive environment* (pp. 27–41). Gaithersburg, MD: Aspen.

Walberg, H.J., & Greenberg, R. C. (1997). Using the learning environment inventory. *Educational Leadership, 54*(8), 45–47.

Walling, D. R. (Ed.). (1994). *Teachers as leaders: Perspectives on the professional development of teachers.* Bloomington, IN: Phi Delta Kappa.

Walther-Thomas, C. S. (1997). Co-teaching: Benefits and problems that teachers and principals report over time. *Journal for Learning Disabilities, 30*(4), 395–407.

Walther-Thomas, C.S., Korinek, L., McLaughlin, V.L, & Williams, B.T. (2000). *Collaboration for inclusive education: Developing successful programs.* Boston: Allyn & Bacon.

Walther-Thomas, C.S., Korinek, L., McLaughlin, V. L., & Williams, B. T. (1996). Improving educational opportunities for students with disabilities who are homeless. *Journal of Children in Poverty, 2*(2), 57–75.

West, J. F., & Idol, L. (1990). Collaborative consultation in the education of mildly handicapped and at-risk students. *Remedial & Special Education, 11*(1), 22–31.

Whitten, E., & Dieker, L. (1995). *What are the characteristics of effective assistance teams?* Paper presented at annual meeting of Teacher Education Division of Council for Exceptional Children, Washington, DC.

Yinger, R. J. (1990). The conversation of practice. In R. T. Clift, W. R. Houston, & M. C. Pugach (Eds.), *Encouraging reflective practice in education* (pp. 73–94). New York: Teachers College Press.

APPENDIX

A Sampling of Web Sites for School Teams Interested in Collaboration, Professional Development, and Student Achievement

Association for Supervision and Curriculum Development
www.ascd.org:80

ERIC Clearinghouse on Teaching and Teacher Education
www.ericsp.org/

LD OnLine
www.ldonline.org/

League of Professional Schools
www.coe.uga.edu/lps

National Board of Professional Teaching Standards
www.nbpts.org.

National Center to Improve Practice
www.edc.org/FSC/NCIP

National Center to Improve the Tools of Educators
idea.uoregon.edu/~ncite/
National Council for Staff Development
www.nsdc.org

National Education Association
www.nea.org

National Partnership for Excellence and Accountability in Teaching
www.npeat.org

New American Schools
www.naschools.org

Pathways to School Improvement
www.ncrel.org/sdrs/pathwayg.htm

Professional Development Partnerships Project
aed.org/us/index.html

Students With Disabilities and Paraprofessional Supports: Benefits, Balance, and Band-Aids

Michael F. Giangreco and Mary Beth Doyle

If you have had any connection to special education during the past decade, you already know what a valuable asset paraprofessionals can be to support the education of students with, and without, disabilities. You do not need this chapter to tell you what the literature has been reporting for years—that too many paraprofessionals have been, and continue to be, inadequately appreciated, compensated, oriented, trained, and supervised (Doyle, 2002; Giangreco, Edelman, Broer & Doyle, 2001; Jones & Bender, 1993; Pickett & Gerlach, 1997).

You are already aware that a variety of approaches and materials are available to train paraprofessionals (CichoskiKelly, Backus, Giangreco, & Sherman–Tucker, 2000; Institute on Community Integration, 1999; Parsons & Reid, 1999; Salzberg, Morgan, Gassman, Pickett & Merrill, 1993; Steckelberg & Vasa, 1998). You probably already know that the numbers of paraprofessionals have increased dramatically in the last decade (French & Pickett, 1997).

TRENDS

The increasing numbers of paraprofessionals and corresponding issues likely are reflected in your local schools. Consider the example of one Vermont school district where the increasing use of paraprofessionals in special education was characterized as "an explosion" given an 83% increase in the hours of paraprofessional services per day between 1994 and 1999, without any significant change in child count (Giangreco, Broer, & Edelman, in press).

Definitive, data-based reasons for the increasing numbers of paraprofessionals are not available. Nevertheless, a small amount of data and reasoned speculation in the literature suggest that the increases have been fueled by a number of factors

(French, 1999; Giangreco, Broer & Edelman, 2002; Killoran, Templeman, Peters, & Udell, 2001; Passaro, Pickett, Latham, & HongoBo, 1994; Pickett, 1999; Pickett & Gerlach, 1997; Rogan & Held, 1999):

- Shortages of teachers and special educators
- Increases in early childhood special education services
- Increases in services for transition-aged students with disabilities
- Increasing numbers of students with high-intensity needs, such as those with the labels autism, emotional/behavioral disorders, and multiple disabilities
- Increasing responsibilities being assumed by general education teachers.

Most recently, the advancement of inclusive educational opportunities for students with increasingly severe disabilities has contributed to the increasing numbers of paraprofessionals (Giangreco, Broer, & Edelman, 1999). For many general education classroom teachers, having a paraprofessional accompany a student with a disability to class is considered an essential support (Downing, Ryndak, & Clark, 2000; French, 1999; Werts, Wolery, Snyder, Caldwell, & Salisbury, 1996; Wolery, Werts, Caldwell, Synder, & Liskowski, 1995). In many schools, assigning a paraprofessional to support students with disabilities has become the primary or exclusive service delivery mechanism to operationalize inclusive education.

CHANGING ROLES

Undoubtedly, assigning a paraprofessional to support the education of a student with a disability is intended to be a benevolent action. On the surface, it seems like an obvious support solution, is a relatively easy-to-implement response to advocacy for more support, and costs less than hiring professional staff members. When well conceived and implemented, paraprofessional support can be an appropriate service to offer. So what is the problem with continuing the trend of hiring more paraprofessionals? Wouldn't everything be okay if we just were to do a better job of orienting, training, supervising, compensating, and appreciating paraprofessionals?

Even though such actions are warranted and could be helpful toward the goal of having a more qualified and satisfied paraprofessional workforce, those important outcomes presume that the utilization of paraprofessionals as a primary mechanism to support the education of students with disabilities is an effective and desirable direction to maintain and advance. Although we have no doubt that paraprofessionals will continue to have vital and valued roles in special education, confusion about their changing roles has led to a situation in which some students with disabilities receive their special education services primarily or exclusively from paraprofessionals.

In a review of the paraprofessional literature, Giangreco, Edelman, Broer, and Doyle (2001) raised the following concerns that have yet to be addressed adequately in the professional literature:

> Are models of service provision that rely heavily on paraprofessionals to provide instruction to students with disabilities appropriate, ethical, conceptually sound, and effective? Does it make sense to have the least

qualified employee primarily responsible for students with the most complex challenges to learning? Is it acceptable for some students with disabilities to receive most of their education from a paraprofessional, regardless of training level, while students without disabilities receive the bulk of their instruction from certified teachers?

Do students with disabilities who receive a significant portion of their instruction from paraprofessionals have comparable outcomes as those who have more consistent interactions with qualified professionals? Is it fair to pay paraprofessionals less than a livable wage and expect them to perform duties that typically are expected of teachers, such as planning, adapting, and instructing? (p. 58)

We are concerned that in some cases the assignment of paraprofessionals as an expedient support solution might be both unfair to paraprofessionals and questionably effective for students with disabilities. Of course, whether paraprofessional supports are or are not effective depends on what they are intended to accomplish.

Consider that in a study by Marks, Schrader, and Levine (1999), paraprofessionals reported their perception that they bore the "primary burden of success" for the students with disabilities with whom they worked and the sense that they were responsible for inclusion of those students. These paraprofessionals reported perceptions that their roles included: (a) not being a "bother" to the classroom teacher, (b) being primarily responsible to provide "on the spot" curricular modifications, and (c) being expected to be the "expert" for the student. If this is what we intend paraprofessional supports to accomplish, it speaks volumes about the continuing devalued status of students with disabilities in our schools and the lack of real support for paraprofessional services.

What also is quite telling in the professional literature is what it *does not* say about the reasons for the increases in paraprofessional support to students with disabilities. Nowhere does the literature say that the expanded utilization and increasingly instructional roles of paraprofessionals have been based on efficacy data suggesting that students with disabilities do as well or better educationally with paraprofessionals than they do with special educators or general education teachers. Nowhere does the literature present a strong conceptual or theoretical rationale that explains the practice of assigning the least qualified staff members to make crucial decisions and provide primary instruction for students with the most complex needs.

In fact, the professional literature is nearly devoid of student outcome data as it pertains to the utilization of paraprofessionals. In response to these types of concerns, and while acknowledging the outstanding work accomplished by many paraprofessionals, Brown, Farrington, Ziegler, Knight, and Ross (1999) simultaneously stated that, because of their learning challenges, students with significant disabilities "are in dire need of continuous exposure to the most ingenious, creative, powerful, competent, interpersonally effective, and informed professionals" (p. 252).

Our existing dual system of general and special education continues to treat some students with disabilities like a hot potato that no one wants to hold on to. In these cases, paraprofessionals often are the ones who step in to fill the void and support the student as best they can with whatever skills, dedication, and energy the paraprofessionals bring to the job. At times when professionals did not provide sufficient direction and guidance, one paraprofessional described her concern this way: "It just got [to] the point that it was just easier to do it than to keep asking people to do it" (Marks et al., 1999, p. 320). One of the overall findings of Marks et al. (1999) was: "For the most part, paraeducators found themselves in situations in which waiting for teachers and other professionals to make curricular and teaching decisions was not feasible" (p. 312).

QUESTIONS REGARDING PARAPROFESSIONAL SUPPORTS

The remainder of this article addresses five contemporary questions within the sphere of control of school personnel, either individually or collectively, to improve paraprofessional supports for students with disabilities:

1. To what extent should paraprofessionals be teaching students with disabilities?
2. What impact does the proximity of paraprofessionals have on students with disabilities?
3. How does the utilization of paraprofessional support affect teacher engagement, and why should it matter?
4. How can authentic respect, appreciation, and acknowledgment of the important work of paraprofessionals be demonstrated?
5. What can be done to improve paraprofessional supports schoolwide?

For each question, we offer pertinent information from the literature and implications for practice. In an interrelated fashion, these five questions address the *benefits* associated with well conceived paraprofessional supports and the *balance* of paraprofessional supports with supports provided by others (e.g., classroom teachers, special educators, related services providers, peers). This is set within a context that challenges us to consider whether our existing or proposed actions to improve paraprofessional supports offer viable solutions that truly accomplish what we intend for students with disabilities or whether they are merely band-aids.

Question 1: To what extent should paraprofessionals be teaching students with disabilities?

What the Literature Says About Question 1

Reauthorization of the Individuals with Disabilities Education Act Amendments of 1997 (IDEA) (20 U.S.C. § 1400 *et seq.*) allows for

> paraprofessionals and assistants who are appropriately trained and supervised . . . to be used to assist in the provision of special education and related services to children with disabilities (20 U.S.C. §1412(a)(15)(B)(iii).

The IDEA does not expound upon that provision. How should paraprofessionals assist? What does "appropriately trained and supervised" really mean? This is up to states and local schools to determine within the boundaries of the IDEA requirement to ensure that *all* children and youth with disabilities receive a free, appropriate, public education.

Confusion about these and related issues have led, over the last decade, to a steady stream of due process hearings, Office of Civil Rights complaints, and court rulings regarding the legal parameters of paraprofessional services in special education (Katsiyannis, Hodge, & Lanford, 2000).

The literature is filled with statements suggesting that paraprofessionals should work under the direction and supervision of qualified professional educators, special educators, or related services providers (Demchak & Morgan, 1998; Doyle, 2002; French, 1999; Gerlach, 2001; Pickett & Gerlach, 1997, Salzberg & Morgan, 1995; Wallace, Shin, Bartholomay & Stahl, 2001). As suggested by Pickett (1999), paraprofessionals "work alongside their teacher/ provider colleagues and carry out tasks that support the different teacher/provider functions" (p. 14).

It has been suggested that the increasingly instructional role of paraprofessionals has led to the shifting of teachers' roles. In such models (French, 1999), teachers assume the roles of *"delegator, planner, director, monitor, coach, and program manager"* (p. 70). Although engaging in roles such as these has always been part of the teacher's job when working with others in the classroom (e.g., assistants, parent volunteers, student teachers, peer tutors), the connotation attached to these models seems to be that teachers will teach less and release more of their instructional role to paraprofessionals. This undoubtedly is happening in some locations across the country. But is it a trend that should continue?

The National Joint Committee on Learning Disabilities (1999), recently clarified its position on the utilization of paraprofessionals by noting, "The intent of using paraprofessionals is to supplement, not supplant, the work of the teacher/service provider" (p. 38). Yet, an emerging descriptive database provides information suggesting that paraprofessionals often operate in isolation and are given relative autonomy to make critical curricular and instructional decisions without the benefit of a qualified professional's designing the plans or being substantively involved in ongoing implementation (Downing et al., 2000; Giangreco, Broer, & Edelman, 2001b; 2002; Giangreco, Edelman, Luiselli, & MacFarland, 1997; Marks et al., 1999).

Some teachers have suggested that paraprofessionals should not be responsible for teaching new skills. As one general education teacher stated, (Giangreco, Broer, & Edelman, 2001b), "Paraprofessionals are not supposed to be teaching new skills. I do that. [A paraprofessional] is used to reinforce them and provide practice." (p. 80). Yet, this statement is merely the opinion of one teacher and does not necessarily reflect a universally accepted standard for the involvement of paraprofessionals in instruction. The lack of any such standard cuts to the core of an age-old dilemma pertaining to paraprofessionals: What are their appropriate roles, especially as they relate to instruction? Correspondingly, what constitutes professional accountability by teachers and special educators?

There is no doubt that the involvement of paraprofessionals in instruction has increased over the past few decades and now constitutes one of their dominant roles (Downing et al., 2000; French, 1999; Gerlach, 2001; Pickett & Gerlach, 1997; Giangreco, Broer, & Edelman, 2001b). Yet, the data presented in the literature establishing instruction as a key role for paraprofessionals is based almost exclusively on descriptive questionnaire or interview data that document the opinions and perceptions of professionals, paraprofessionals, and parents about what their role should be (Downing et al., 2000; French, 1998; French & Chopra, 1999; Giangreco et al., 2002; Hadadian & Yssel, 1998; Lamont & Hill, 1991; Minondo, Meyer & Xin, 2001).

It could be argued that much of these data merely reflect what currently exists rather than represent an ideal of service provision toward which we should strive. As suggested earlier, the basis for this more extensive involvement of paraprofessionals engaging in instruction seems to have evolved in response to factors such as personnel shortages and increasing demands for services rather than a defensible conceptualization of how, or under what circumstances, it makes sense for students with or without disabilities to be instructed by paraprofessionals.

Given the absence of student outcome data to assist in making decisions about the role of paraprofessionals in instruction, one of the main challenges in establishing some parameters around this issue is the variation that is present in terms of individual student needs and individual paraprofessional skills, as well as the match between their roles, compensation, training, and supervision. The incredible variability of factors influencing decisions about the type and level of paraprofessional involvement in instruction precludes any highly specific or one-size-fits-all standard for their involvement in instruction.

Sometimes schools are fortunate enough to find or train highly skilled paraprofessionals who can reasonably assume some instructional responsibilities based on professionally designed plans, given corresponding training and supervision. At other times, the paraprofessionals who are hired struggle with academic skills themselves and find it challenging to offer academic support to students. The literature describes teachers' concerns about the academic skillfulness and assignments of some paraprofessionals (Giangreco et al., 2001b).

These concerns relate to paraprofessionals who have less than acceptable skills in spelling and grammar and those who, for example, "don't do algebra." In other cases, academically capable paraprofessionals are inappropriately assigned to subjects in which they have insufficient background or skills. This is especially problematic in high schools where paraprofessionals may be asked to support students in subjects that require specialized content knowledge in areas such as math, science, and foreign language.

To retain special education's emphasis on individualization and specialized instruction, any standard for the potential involvement of paraprofessionals in instructional roles must be broadly conceptualized. Any such standard must consider relevant factors such as the student's characteristics and needs, potential impact on the student, support needs of the teacher, paraprofessional's skills and training, as well as the match between the paraprofessional's proposed role/assignment, compensation, training, and supervision.

Implications for Practice Pertaining to Question 1

When considering the extent to which paraprofessionals should be instructing students with disabilities, we suggest a simple but important rule-of-thumb to help guide individualized decision-making. Consider the following scenarios that happen to some students with disabilities in our schools, and then ask: Would it be okay if the student didn't have a disability?

■ An elementary grade student receives his primary reading instruction from a paraprofessional who is not a trained teacher or reading instructor? *Would it be okay if the student didn't have a disability?*

■ A team assigns a paraprofessional, rather than a certified teacher, to provide 75% to 100% of the daily instruction to a student. *Would it be okay if the student didn't have a disability?*

■ When a student is having difficulty in algebra, she is assigned a paraprofessional as her tutor. The paraprofessional is unskilled in algebra and is uncomfortable with the subject matter. *Would it be okay if the student didn't have a disability?*

■ Throughout the school day a student's workspace is separated from the rest of the class so he can work on separate tasks with a paraprofessional. *Would it be okay if the student didn't have a disability?*

■ During a large-group lesson by the teacher, a paraprofessional decides that something different should be happening for a particular student, so the paraprofessional removes her from the lesson without consulting the teacher. *Would it be okay if the student didn't have a disability?*

These are just a few of the situations encountered by some students with disabilities that, though done with good intentions, would likely be unacceptable if they were suggested to support the education of students without disabilities. These scenarios point out the double standards that exist between education for students with and without disabilities. It is imperative that paraprofessional supports, particularly pertaining to instruction, be offered in ways that do not perpetuate that double standard.

Therefore, the team should explicitly discuss how the classroom teacher and the special educator will interact with students who have disabilities and participate in teaching them (Doyle & Gurney, 2000). If the team determines that the teacher needs assistance, it is important to explore paraprofessional roles that enable the teacher to maintain or improve his or her ability to be the teacher for all of the students in the classroom.

The role of paraprofessionals might include tasks that are both instructional and noninstructional. For example, sometimes having paraprofessionals engage in noninstructional roles—completing clerical tasks, preparing materials, providing personal supports to students, supervising on the playground—can create more opportunities for teachers to teach. These roles can be extremely valuable.

At other times it can be equally important to have paraprofessionals engage in instructional roles such as implementing a teacher-planned small-group lesson, assisting students during independent seatwork, providing individual tutoring as a follow-up to a teacher's lesson, or providing practice opportunities to reinforce previously learned skills. A careful analysis of how the teacher's time is spent can reveal tasks that can be carried out appropriately by paraprofessionals to enhance the work of teachers and special educators.

Question 2: What impact does the proximity of paraprofessionals have on students with disabilities?

What the Literature Says About Question 2

When a paraprofessional is assigned to support a student with a disability, it is not surprising that the paraprofessional would be in close proximity to the student. Sometimes that proximity is warranted and necessary to provide personal care, ensure safety, or provide instructional supports (e.g., verbal or physical prompting/ guidance, tutoring). Problems arise when the proximity is excessive or unnecessary.

Only two studies have reported specifically on the effects of proximity between paraprofessionals and students with disabilities. Young et al. (1997) collected observational data pertaining to the proximity between paraprofessionals and three elementary-aged students with autism in inclusive classrooms in the same school. They reported variation in the extent of proximity of paraprofessionals to these students and mixed results pertaining to the relationship between paraprofessional proximity and student behavior (e.g., on-task, in-seat, self-stimulation, inappropriate vocalizations), as well as initiation of interactions by classmates, teachers, and paraprofessionals. In this study, teacher initiations toward the students with autism were higher when the paraprofessional was more than 2 feet away from the students with autism.

The fact that student responses associated with paraprofessional proximity were varied highlights the importance of individualization when planning supports for students with disabilities. Young et al. (1997) emphasized the importance of further studying paraprofessional supports and expressed their strong concerns about certain models of inclusive education, "particularly when the inclusion is full time with a paraprofessional who has not been trained in the field and whose presence supplants a teacher's involvement" (p. 38).

Davern et al. (1997) suggest that such scenarios, in which students with disabilities are placed in general education classes without appropriately trained support personnel or the classroom teacher has minimal involvement, represent fragmented efforts that are labeled inaccurately as inclusive education. We concur.

In the other study dealing with paraprofessional proximity, Giangreco et al. (1997) reported findings based on 2 years of observational and interview data collected from 134 team members (paraprofessionals, teachers, special educators, related services providers, parents, administrators) who supported the general education placements of 11 students with multiple disabilities in 11 different schools. Based on qualitative analysis of these data, it was reported that paraprofessionals assigned to the students in this study were in close proximity to them much of the time. Sometimes that proximity was considered excessive and was associated with inadvertent detrimental effects.

The assignment of a paraprofessional presented both physical and symbolic barriers that interfered with the teachers getting directly involved with the students with disabilities who were placed in their classes. Further, excessive paraprofessional proximity was associated with creating unnecessary dependence on adults as well as interfering with competent instruction, peer relationships, gender identity, and appropriate personal control (Giangreco et al., 1997).

Shukla, Kennedy, and Cushing (1999) conducted a single-subject experimental study to explore a peer support strategy as an alternative to paraprofessional supports for three middle school students with profound disabilities in general education classes. Although this study did not address paraprofessional proximity directly, it reported favorable evidence for the use of a peer support strategy in comparison to direct assistance from paraprofessionals. Their intervention resulted in higher levels of social interaction between the students with disabilities and peers without disabilities, as well as increased social support behaviors from those peers.

Active engagement of students with disabilities showed no differences in certain activities (e.g., art, industrial crafts) and some improvements in others (e.g., math, social studies). Of the five peers without disabilities who provided supports, two showed no decrease in active classroom engagement and three (who were identified as having academic problems) increased their active classroom engagement as a result of participating in the peer support strategy. Considered together, these three studies highlight the importance and potential impact of paraprofessional proximity on students with disabilities and viable alternatives.

Implications for Practice Pertaining to Question 2

The implications of this initial research on paraprofessional proximity can be broadly categorized as the four *A's: awareness, assessment, actions,* and *alternatives.* First, it is vital to raise the *awareness* of all team members about paraprofessional proximity and the potential for inadvertent detrimental effects. This can be accomplished by taking simple steps such as sharing the professional literature among team members and devoting team meeting time to a discussion of these issues.

Next, it is important for the team to do an *assessment* of the extent of paraprofessional proximity. This should include both the times and activities where paraprofessional proximity is and is not occurring as well as collective judgments by the team about whether proximity is warranted and is helpful or not academically, socially, and personally. Any such assessment of paraprofessional proximity should include the student's perspective and involve the student directly whenever appropriate.

Based on the information and insights gained from assessment, *actions* can be taken to improve existing paraprofessional supports. Any actions should be rooted in ongoing role clarification, not only for paraprofessionals but for classroom teachers and special educators as well, so their efforts to support students with and without disabilities are collaborative and effective. These actions might include administrative changes in areas such as job descriptions, hiring policies, and staffing (e.g., assigning paraprofessionals to classrooms rather than individual students). Actions also might include specific training for paraprofessionals about how to reduce or fade prompts and supports and to recognize circumstances when it is appropriate to step back from students rather than provide too much proximity.

Finally, while simultaneously strengthening existing paraprofessional supports, teams are encouraged to consider *alternatives* to paraprofessional proximity. This may include more extensive use of natural supports (e.g., peers, parent volunteers), changes in instructional formats (e.g., cooperative learning groups), and increased involvement of teachers and special educators in providing instruction to students with disabilities within the classroom through co-teaching models.

Question 3: How does the utilization of paraprofessional support affect teacher engagement, and why should it matter?

What the Literature Says About Question 3

The term *teacher engagement* in this context refers to general education teachers having: (a) ongoing instructional contact with students with disabilities who are placed in their class, and (b) active involvement in planning and implementing their instruction along with other appropriate team members (e.g., special educator). Teacher engagement is a critical variable that can affect the appropriateness and quality of a general education placement (Hunt & Goetz, 1997; Villa & Thousand, 2000; York-Barr, Schultz, Doyle, Kronberg, & Crossett, 1996).

To date, only one study has reported a primary focus on the relationship between the utilization of paraprofessionals and teacher engagement. Giangreco, Broer, and Edelman (2001b) reported data based on 56 semistructured interviews and 51 hours of observation in four schools (grades K–12) across a full school year. They found that paraprofessionals were utilized in two primary ways: as one-on-one or program/classroom-based paraprofessionals.

The study's findings suggested that general education teachers were more engaged with their students with disabilities when the paraprofessionals supporting those students were program/classroom-based and that the general education teachers tended to be less engaged when the paraprofessionals were assigned one-on-one to a student with disabilities. The authors cautioned that the differences in teacher engagement were not necessarily the result of the paraprofessional service models alone.

The study described the characteristics when teachers were more and less engaged with students with disabilities as summarized in Table 9.1. The study further described phenomena associated with teacher disengagement, such as isolation

---

TABLE 9.1 ■ Variations in Teacher Engagement

When Teachers Are More Engaged with Students with Disabilities	When Teachers Are Less Engaged with Students with Disabilities
■ Expressed attitude of ownership and responsibility for the education of *all* students in the class, with and without disabilities	■ Expressed attitude of ownership and responsibility primarily for the education of students *without* disabilities in the class
■ Highly knowledgeable about the functioning levels and learning outcomes of their students with disabilities	■ Less knowledgeable about the functioning levels of their students with disabilities
■ Collaborated closely with paraprofessionals and special educators based on clear roles	■ Deferred communication with parents to paraprofessionals Limited collaboration with paraprofessionals and special educators, roles were unclear
■ Planned lessons and activities for paraprofessionals to implement	■ Did not plan lessons and activities for paraprofessionals to implement
■ Retained instructional decision-making authority for their students with disabilities	■ Relinquished instructional decision-making authority for their students with disabilities to paraprofessionals
■ Spent approximately as much time with students with disabilities as those without disabilities	■ Spent substantially less time with students with disabilities as those without disabilities
■ Had substantial instructional interactions with students with disabilities	■ Had limited instructional interactions with students with disabilities
■ Communicated directly with students with disabilities	■ Communicated indirectly with students with disabilities
■ Directed the work of paraprofessionals in class	■ Did not direct the work of paraprofessionals in class
■ Provided mentorship to paraprofessionals and maintained an instructional dialogue with them	■ Did not provide mentorship to paraprofessionals nor maintained an instructional dialogue with them
■ Pursued fading out paraprofessional supports or declined such services if perceived as not needed	■ Did not pursue fading out paraprofessional supports or declining such services; perceived as always needed

Source: M. F. Giangreco, S. M. Broer, and S. W. Edelman (2001), *Journal of the Association for Persons with Severe Handicaps, 26,* 75–86. Reprinted by permission.

of students with disabilities within the classroom, insular relationships between students with disabilities and one-on-one paraprofessionals, and stigma experienced by students with disabilities as a result of receiving one-on-one paraprofessional supports (Giangreco et al., 2001b).

Implications for Practice Pertaining to Question 3

The primary consideration of the aforementioned information for educational teams and administrators is whether the roles of paraprofessionals and existing models of service delivery are contributing to, hindering, or replacing teacher engagement. The characteristics of teacher engagement (see Table 1) can be utilized by educational team members as a form of self-assessment or as a set of reflective prompts to identify areas of concern to improve practices. It is vital to take actions that account for variations in the reasons that have contributed to teachers' lack of engagement.

For example, if a general education teacher thinks she is not supposed to be very involved in the instruction of a student with disabilities in her classroom, this might call for role clarification among the team members. If a teacher expresses a willingness to be instructionally engaged with his students with disabilities but does not know how to accomplish this, it might call for capacity building, such as more collaboration with special educators, consultation, training, or structural changes (e.g., class size, ratios of students with and without disabilities). Changes such as these can create conditions for teachers to become more instructionally engaged with their students who have disabilities.

In the rare occurrences in which teachers express unwillingness to be more instructionally engaged with students who have disabilities, administrators may have to provide supportive supervision and facilitate the development and ongoing clarification of expectations, often reflected in their mission statement, policies, and guidelines.

Question 4: How can authentic respect, appreciation, and acknowledgment of the important work of paraprofessionals be demonstrated?

What the Literature Says About Question 4

Respect, appreciation, and acknowledgement are important for establishing and maintaining a satisfied and productive paraprofessional workforce, as well as building and sustaining the capacity of a school to serve its students. Although the literature has a limited focus on this topic (Palma, 1994), it does suggest that, in part, shortages and attrition of paraprofessionals are related to lack of respect in the form of low wages, limited opportunities for advancement, and lack of administrative support (Passaro, Pickett, Latham & HongBo, 1994).

One of the more visible ways by which people have attempted to show more respect for paraprofessionals is to use different language to refer to them. Although the IDEA uses the term *paraprofessional,* some people consider the terms *teacher assistant* and *classroom assistant* more descriptive, and these labels often are perceived as more respectful than the term *aide*. Over the past decade the term *paraeducator* has been popularized as a respectful and descriptive term suggesting that the paraprofessional is *working alongside* an educator (Pickett & Gerlach, 1997).

Our only caution is that whatever term is used must be accurate in its definition and connotation. For example, some proponents of the *paraeducator* label equate it with the titles of *paramedic* and *paralegal*. An analysis of these three professions suggests that they are not equivalent. Unlike individuals hired and given the title paraeducator, both paramedics and paralegals are required to have extensive training and meet national or state standards *before* they are inducted into their respective professions. Virtually anyone with a high school diploma can be referred to as a *paraeducator*.

Ultimately, states or local school districts have to decide how they will refer to paraprofessionals. To be descriptive, respectful, and accurately reflect the job, we encourage the use of any terms that are synonymous with the IDEA term *paraprofessional*.

Only one study was identified that specifically addressed the issues of respect, appreciation, and acknowledgment of paraprofessionals (Giangreco, Edelman, & Broer, 2001). The themes of this study included: (a) nonmonetary signs and symbols of appreciation, (b) compensation, (c) being entrusted with important responsibilities, (d) noninstructional responsibilities, (e) wanting to be listened to, and (f) orientation and support.

Beyond the obvious finding that paraprofessionals felt disrespected and "taken advantage of" by low wages, this study highlights the complex and interrelated nature of how paraprofessionals perceived respect. While the paraprofessionals welcomed symbolic signs of appreciation and recognition, they accepted the signs differentially based on who was offering them. Signs of appreciation were most meaningful when they came from those who were in the best position to be authentically knowledgeable about the paraprofessional's work (e.g., student, parents, teachers, special educators).

Paraprofessionals took it as a sign of respect when professionals oriented and trained them, provided plans for their work, and supervised them. The respectful message embedded in these activities was that the paraprofessionals' work was important enough to warrant substantial time, energy, and resources from professionals.

Paraprofessionals also felt respected when they were considered an integral member of the classroom team and were given opportunities to provide input into important decisions about the classroom and students. Paraprofessionals indicated that they appreciated being entrusted with important responsibilities.

The challenge related to this finding was that some paraprofessionals considered instruction as their only important responsibility and sought to distance themselves from noninstructional responsibilities (e.g., clerical, personal care of students, classroom set-up and clean-up). As Giangreco, Edelman, and Broer, 2001 stated:

> One of our collective challenges is to communicate the value of all of the roles played by paraprofessionals, not just the instructional ones. Having paraprofessionals engage in clerical roles can create time for teacher

assessment, planning, or teamwork. We especially need to affirm the value of providing personal care supports (e.g., bathroom, dressing, positioning, mobility, eating supports) for students with the most severe and multiple disabilities as a valued role. Unless we establish and communicate the importance of engaging in such roles (e.g., access, health, personal dignity, readiness for learning), we risk the danger that the devaluing of the roles inadvertently may result in the devaluing of the students for whom those supports are provided. (p. 494)

Implications for Practice Pertaining to Question 4

In considering how we might express respect, appreciation, and acknowledgement to paraprofessionals, an important implication is that they each must be approached individually, as each has skills, strengths, support needs, and different motivations for doing the job. Although some paraprofessionals use the job as a stepping-stone to becoming a teacher or special educator, we should not assume that all paraprofessionals want to become professional educators or that they all aspire to engage in instructional roles. Therefore, part of respecting the work of paraprofessionals is to respect the nature of the job as it exists and to acknowledge that all the varied functions they serve have value.

Even as school boards, administrators, and unions wrestle with issues such as compensation, school personnel can demonstrate respect and positive regard for paraprofessionals in several ways: extending signs of welcome and thanks, clarifying roles and responsibilities, providing training and supervision that are aligned with their work, and involving the paraprofessionals as valued members of the team.

At the beginning of the year, the classroom teacher should welcome the paraprofessional by:

- Providing the paraprofessional a space of his or her own in the classroom (e.g., desk, table, mailbox, coffee cup).
- Putting the paraprofessional's name on the door alongside the classroom teacher's.
- Showing the paraprofessional where the classroom materials are located and communicating that he or she has access to all of them.
- Orienting the paraprofessional to the school, highlighting locations that the classroom teacher frequents and introducing the paraprofessional to other school personnel.
- Being certain that the paraprofessional understands important school policies and procedures by reviewing the school handbook and engaging in conversations around key topics (e.g., confidentiality, communication with families).

When the students arrive, the teacher should model that the teacher and the paraprofessional are a team and introduce the paraprofessional in the same way as other adults in the building. For example, if the teachers and others are referred as Ms., Mr., or Mrs., paraprofessionals should be referred to using this form of address.

The teacher should make sure that the paraprofessional interacts with all of the students in the class, not just those with disabilities, by encouraging the paraprofessional to greet all the students as they arrive each morning and by giving the paraprofessional morning responsibilities that are helpful in organizing the daily routine. These tasks might involve taking attendance, preparing a learning center, and preparing materials for the teacher, for example.

The teacher should clarify the paraprofessional's role on the classroom team, discuss the associated expectations, and clarify participation in team meetings. The paraprofessional should receive the team's meeting agenda in advance and know how to get items placed on the agenda. In preparing to be an active participant and have input in the meetings, the paraprofessional might formulate written questions to ask and bring student data collected since the last meeting, for instance. Given the paraprofessional's role and schedule, he or she may or may not participate in all team meetings or activities. In a healthy team the teacher and the special educator should know at least as much, and hopefully more, than the paraprofessional about the student's characteristics, needs, and progress. Therefore, if the paraprofessional is not in attendance for some reason, his or her input should be able to be represented at the team meeting by the teacher or special educator.

The teacher should explicitly discuss the paraprofessional's roles and responsibilities relative to (a) instructional and noninstructional tasks, and (b) students with and without disabilities. The licensed teacher or special educator should take the lead in planning the instruction, describing and demonstrating how to implement the planned instruction. Then the teacher and paraprofessional should establish a time when the two will meet to discuss ongoing responsibilities.

It is amazing how important it is to say *"thank you"* for a job well done. The thanks should be specific: "Thank you for implementing that small-group lesson today; it was a good review that the students really needed." "I really appreciate that you volunteered to do hall duty for me today; it gave me time to tutor James." Sometimes the thanks is especially meaningful when it is expressed in a written note. Gestures of appreciation go a long way in establishing a positive relationship among team members and they also model important social skills for the students in the classroom.

Providing initial and ongoing training, as well as supervision, is a powerful way to demonstrate respect and appreciation for the work of paraprofessionals. Designing training that is in alignment with their roles and responsibilities communicates an understanding of what paraprofessionals do daily. When designed well, paraprofessional training ensures that the range of work that paraprofessionals do is valued within the broader scope of the learning community.

For example, a paraprofessional who assists with instruction in a high school science class might need training related to specific topical areas. Another paraprofessional, who supports a student with severe disabilities, might need training related to individualized mealtime procedures or ways to support the student in initiating interactions with peers. Regardless of the specific tasks, communicating the importance and value of each task is vital.

When paraprofessionals feel valued and respected, the foundation is laid for a productive working relationship. Together, the classroom team can create a positive classroom community in which all students are making progress toward their individualized learning goals.

Question 5: What can be done to improve paraprofessional supports schoolwide?

What the Literature Says About Question 5

Two contemporary resources address paraprofessional supports schoolwide. The National Education Association (Gerlach, 2001) published *Let's Team Up: A Checklist for Paraeducators, Teachers, and Principals*. This booklet offers three interrelated sets of practice statements representing actions that can be taken by paraprofessionals, teachers, and principals, respectively. The checklist statements cover the full range of topics (e.g., roles, orientation, hiring, assigning, training, supervision). Although no data are available on the use of the checklist in schools, it reflects much of the current literature on paraprofessional issues and can serve as a useful reference to assist in schoolwide planning.

A Guide to Schoolwide Planning for Paraeducator Supports (Giangreco, Broer, & Edelman, 2001a) is a 10-step action-planning process designed to assist school-based teams in assessing their own status in terms of paraprofessional supports. The process guides a team through a self-assessment of 28 key indicators of paraprofessional support. It proceeds by helping the team identify priorities pertaining to paraprofessional supports, develop a corresponding plan of action, implement the plan, and evaluate its impact.

The guide booklet provides more explicit instructions for each step and worksheets to guide the process. The process has been field-tested in four schools (Giangreco, Broer & Edelman, in press) and currently is being field-tested in 47 schools across 16 states. The guide, a list of the field-test sites, and related information are available online at: http://www.uvm.edu/~cdci/parasupport/

Implications for Practice Pertaining to Question 5

The implications pertaining to Question 5 are brief and straightforward. No matter how much you do as an individual, it never will be as powerful, effective, strategic, or sustainable as it could be if you join forces with colleagues, parents, and community members to take positive steps schoolwide.

If you are concerned about the status of paraprofessional supports in your school, we strongly encourage you to review either or both of the documents referred to in Question 5. They might help you determine if they are applicable in your situation or how they might be adapted to your school's needs.

10-STEP ACTION-PLANNING PROCESS

1. Inform your local school board of your intention to establish a team, or use an existing team, to address paraeducator issues.

2. Ensure that the team includes the appropriate members of the school and local community.

3. Have the team assess its own status and fact-find in relation to the six paraeducator topics:

   (a) Acknowledging paraeducators
   (b) Orienting and training paraeducators
   (c) Hiring and assigning paraeducators
   (d) Paraeducator interactions with students and staff
   (e) Roles and responsibilities of paraeducators
   (f) Supervision and evaluation of paraeducator services.

4. Prioritize and select topics and specific issues that reflect areas of need within the school that the team will work on first.

5. Update your local school board regarding the team's ranked priorities.

6. Design a plan to address the team's ranked priorities.

7. Identify local, regional, and statewide resources to assist in achieving team plans.

8. Implement the team's plans.

9. Evaluate the plan's impact and plan next steps.

10. Report impact and needs to your local school community.

Source: *A Guide to Schoolwide Planning for Paraeducator Supports*, by M. F. Giangreco, S. M. Broer, & S. W. Edelman (Burlington: University of Vermont, Center on Disability and Community Inclusion, 2001).

CONCLUSIONS AND FUTURE DIRECTIONS

In conclusion, we suggest a three-pronged approach to improving paraprofessional supports for students with disabilities. First and most obviously, we need to do a better job with paraprofessional supports that are already in place at the local level by pursuing role clarification, role alignment with paraprofessional skills, orientation, training, and supervision.

Second, we need to do a better job in determining when paraprofessional supports are warranted and appropriate. Only recently have articles begun to emerge that offer guidelines (Giangreco, Broer & Edelman, 1999) or processes (Mueller & Murphy, 2001) for determining situations that call for paraprofessional supports. More development efforts in this area are desperately needed, accompanied by data-based evaluation of these decision-models to fill the existing void.

Third, we need to explore alternatives to our heavy reliance on paraprofessional supports, especially in inclusive classrooms. Although paraprofessionals undoubtedly will continue to play important roles in supporting the education of students with disabilities, any models that rely too heavily on paraprofessionals to provide instruction present a conundrum. When paraprofessionals remain inadequately supported in terms of training, planning, and supervision, the model is flawed. When paraprofessional roles are not in alignment with their skills, training, or work expectations, the model is flawed. When paraprofessionals are appropriately trained at a level that would allow them to engage in teacher-level activities (e.g., instruction, adaptations) yet continue to be paid a nonlivable wage, the model is flawed.

The conundrum is that if we train paraprofessionals sufficiently to engage in teacher-level activities, align their roles with those teacher skills, and pay them accordingly, why hire them instead of teachers? Even though there will likely be some overlap between what teachers, special educators, and paraprofessionals do, effective models have to clarify the distinctions that allow schools to use resources most effectively to meet student needs.

In closing, we emphasize that substantial *benefits* can accrue for students and teachers when well conceived paraprofessional supports are implemented. These benefits require a *balance* between supports offered by paraprofessionals and those offered by teachers, special educators, peers, and others. When paraprofessional supports are implemented in fragmented or haphazard ways, they may work for a while, but ultimately they are only band-aids.

REFERENCES

Brown, L., Farrington, K., Ziegler, M., Knight, T., & Ross, C. (1999). Fewer paraprofessionals and more teachers and therapists in educational programs for students with significant disabilities. *Journal of the Association for Persons with Severe Handicaps, 24,* 249–252.

CichoskiKelly, E., Backus, L., Giangreco, M. F., Sherman-Tucker (2000). *Paraeducator entry-level training for supporting students with disabilities* (Instructor and participant manuals). Stillwater, OK: National Clearinghouse of Rehabilitation Training Materials.

Davern, L., Sapon-Shevin, M., D'Aquanni, M., Fisher, M., Larson, M., Black, J., & Minondo, S. (1997). Drawing the distinction between coherent and fragmented efforts at building inclusive schools. *Equity and Excellence in Education, 30*(3), 31–39.

Demchak, M. A., & Morgan, C. R. (1998). Effective collaboration between professionals and paraprofessionals. *Rural Special Education Quarterly, 17*(2), 10–15.

Downing, J., Ryndak, D., & Clark, D. (2000). Paraeducators in inclusive classrooms: Their own perspective. *Remedial & Special Education, 21,* 171–181.

Doyle, M. B. (2002). *The paraprofessional's guide to the inclusive classroom: Working as a team (2nd ed.).* Baltimore: Paul H. Brookes.

Doyle, M. B., & Gurney, D. (2000). Guiding paraeducators. In M.S. Fishbaugh (Ed.), *The collaboration guide for early career educators* (pp. 57–78). Baltimore: Paul H. Brookes.

French, N. K. (1998). Working together: Resource teachers and paraeducators. *Remedial & Special Education, 19,* 357–368.

French, N. K. (1999). Topic #2 Paraeducators and teachers: Shifting roles. *Teaching Exceptional Children, 32*(2), 69–73.

French, N., & Pickett, A. L. (1997). Paraprofessionals in special education: Issues for teacher educators. *Teacher Education & Special Education, 20*(1), 61–73.

Freschi, D. F. (1999). Guidelines for working with one-to-one aides. *Teaching Exceptional Children, 31*(4), 42–47.

Gerlach, K. (2001). *Let's team up! A checklist for paraeducators, teachers, and principals.* Washington, DC: National Education Association.

Giangreco, M. F., Broer, S. M., & Edelman, S. W. (1999). The tip of the iceberg: Determining whether paraprofessional support is needed for students with disabilities in general education settings. *Journal of the Association for Persons with Severe Handicaps, 24,* 280–290.

Giangreco, M. F., Broer, S. M., & Edelman, S. W. (2001a). *A Guide to schoolwide planning for paraeducator supports.* Burlington: University of Vermont, Center on Disability and Community Inclusion. Online: http://www.uvm.edu/~cdci/parasupport/guide.html

Giangreco, M. F., Broer, S. M., & Edelman, S. W. (2001b). Teacher engagement with students with disabilities: Differences between paraprofessional service delivery models. *Journal of the Association for Persons with Severe Handicaps, 26,* 75–86.

Giangreco, M. F., Broer, S. M., & Edelman, S. W. (2002). "That was then, this is now!" Paraprofessional supports for students with disabilities in general education classrooms. *Exceptionality, 10,* 47–64.

Giangreco, M. F., Broer, S. M., & Edelman, S. W. (in press). Schoolwide planning to improve paraprofessional supports: A pilot study. *Rural Special Education Quarterly.*

Giangreco, M. F., Edelman, S. W., & Broer, S. M. (2001). Respect, appreciation, and acknowledgement of paraprofessionals who support students with disabilities. *Exceptional Children, 67,* 485–498.

Giangreco, M. F., Edelman, S. W., Broer, S. M., & Doyle, M. B. (2001). Paraprofessional support of students with disabilities: Literature from the past decade. *Exceptional Children, 68,* 45–64.

Giangreco, M. F., Edelman, S., Luiselli, T. E., & MacFarland, S. Z. C. (1997). Helping or hovering? Effects of instructional assistant proximity on students with disabilities. *Exceptional Children, 64,* 7–18.

Hadadian, A., & Yssel, N. (1998). Changing roles of paraeducators in early childhood special education. *Infant-Toddler Intervention, 8,* 1–9.

Hunt, P., & Goetz, L. (1997). Research on inclusive education programs, practices, and outcomes for students with severe disabilities. *Journal of Special Education, 31,* 3–29.

Institute on Community Integration. (1999). *Strategies for paraprofessionals who support individuals with disabilities* (5 module series). Minneapolis: University of Minnesota, Institute on Community Integration.

Jones, K. H., & Bender, W. N. (1993). Utilization of paraprofessionals in special education: A review of the literature. *Remedial & Special Education, 14,* 7–14.

Katsiyannis, A., Hodge, J., & Lanford, A. (2000). Paraeducators: legal and practice considerations. *Remedial & Special Education, 21*(5), 297–304.

Killoran, J., Templeman, T. P., Peters, J., & Udell, J. (2001). Identifying paraprofessional competencies for early intervention and early childhood special education. *Teaching Exceptional Children, 34*(1), 68–73.

Lamont, L. L., & Hill, J. L. (1991). Roles and responsibilities of paraprofessionals in the regular elementary classroom. *British Columbia Journal of Special Education, 15*(1), 1–24.

Marks, S. U., Schrader, C., & Levine, M. (1999). Paraeducator experiences in inclusive settings: Helping, hovering, or holding their own? *Exceptional Children, 65,* 315–328.

Minondo, S., Meyer, L., & Xin, J. (2001). The roles and responsibilities of teaching assistants in inclusive education: What's appropriate? *Journal of the Association for Persons With Severe Handicaps, 26,* 114–119.

Mueller, P. H., & Murphy, F. V. (2001). Determining when a student requires paraeducator support. *Teaching Exceptional Children, 33*(6), 22–27.

National Joint Committee on Learning Disabilities. (1999, March). Learning disabilities: Use of paraprofessionals. *ASHA, 41* (Suppl. 19), 37–46.

Parsons, M. B., & Reid, D. H. (1999). Training basic teaching skills to paraprofessionals of students with severe disabilities: A one-day program. *Teaching Exceptional Children, 31*(4), 48–55.

Passaro, P. D., Pickett, A. L., Latham, G., HongBo, W. (1994). The training and support needs of paraprofessionals in rural and special education. *Rural Special Education Quarterly, 13*(4), 3–9.

Pickett, A. L. (1999). *Strengthening and supporting teacher/provider-paraeducator teams: Guidelines for paraeducator roles, supervision, and preparation.* New York: City University of New York, Graduate Center, National Resource Center for Paraprofessionals in Education and Related Services.

Pickett, A. L., & Gerlach, K. (1997). *Supervising paraeducators in school settings: A team approach.* Austin, TX: Pro-Ed.

Rogan, P., & Held, M. (1999). Paraprofessionals in job coach roles. *Journal of the Association for Persons with Severe Handicaps, 24,* 272–279.

Salzberg, C. L., & Morgan, J. (1995). Preparing teachers to work with paraeducators. *Teacher Education & Special Education, 18,* 49–55.

Salzberg, C. L., Morgan, J., Gassman, G., Pickett, A. L., & Merrill, Z. (1993). *Enhancing skills of paraeducators: A video-assisted training program.* Logan: Utah State University, Department of Special Education and Rehabilitation.

Shukla, S., Kennedy, C. H., & Cushing, L. S. (1999). Intermediate school students with severe disabilities: Supporting their education in general education classrooms. *Journal of Positive Behavior Interventions, 1,* 130–140.

Steckelberg, A. L., & Vasa, S. F. (1998). How paraeducators learn on the web. *Teaching Exceptional Children, 30*(5), 54–59. (http://para.unl.edu/)

Villa, R. A., & Thousand, J. S. (2000). *Restructuring for caring and effective education: Piecing the puzzle together (2d ed.).* Baltimore: Paul H. Brookes.

Wallace, T., Shin, J., Bartholomay, T., & Stahl, B.J. (2001). Knowledge and skills for teachers supervising the work of paraprofessionals. *Exceptional Children, 67,* 520–533.

Werts, M. G., Wolery, M., Snyder, E. D., Caldwell, N. K., & Salisbury, C. L. (1996). Supports and resources associated with inclusive schooling: Perceptions of elementary school teachers about need and availability. *Journal of Special Education, 30,* 187–203.

Wolery, M., Werts, M., Caldwell, N. K., Snyder, E., & Liskowski, L. (1995). Experienced teachers' perceptions of resources and supports for inclusion. *Education & Training in Mental Retardation & Developmental Disabilities, 30,* 15–26.

York-Barr, J., Schultz, T., Doyle, M. B., Kronberg, R., & Crossett, S. (1996). Inclusive schooling in St. Cloud. *Remedial & Special Education, 17,* 92–105.

Young, B., Simpson, R., Myles, B.S., & Kamps, D.M. (1997). An examination of paraprofessional involvement in supporting students with autism. *Focus on Autism & Other Developmental Disabilities, 12*(1), 31–38, 48.

PART TWO

Prevention and Intervention Strategies

Karen R. Harris

This Part consists of 10 chapters that address the book's third theme: advances in prevention and intervention strategies for students with disabilities. The first six chapters address the academic learning of students with disabilities. Topics include effective research-based approaches for teaching students with disabilities; specific reading, writing, and mathematics instructional techniques based on these approaches; and literacy instruction for Latino students. The next two chapters address students with disabilities through 21 years of age—including one on post-secondary education and transition services for students with significant disabilities ages 18 through 21, and one on the development of self-determination among students with disabilities and its effect on their quality of life. The final two chapters in Part two are concerned with supporting students with health needs, and with violence and disruption in schools relative to students with disabilities.

Notwithstanding the diversity of topics covered, five sub-themes are evident across the chapters, and each chapter addresses several, if not all, of the sub-themes. The first two sub-themes relate to key components of the standards-based reform (SBR) framework relative to students with disabilities: the need for standards-based accountability, and access to and success in the general education curriculum. The third sub-theme is one that has resonated throughout the history of special education: the need to understand and work with individual differences. The fourth sub-theme is a call for using integrative, balanced instructional approaches in the education of students with disabilities—approaches that allow us to use all of what we have learned from research and practice regardless of different underlying theoretical bases or belief systems, including theories or beliefs that seem at first to be incompatible. Based on the current and evolving knowledge base on such balanced approaches, educators, parents, administrators, and community members are important collaborators in their effective implementation.

The fifth sub-theme is the need for special educators to continue to be innovative and open to new ideas and approaches, and the need for decisions to implement practices based on these ideas and approaches to be supported by research evidence that establishes their effectiveness.

In Chapter 10, "Crossing Boundaries: What Constructivists Can Teach Intensive-Explicit Instructors and Vice Versa," Jim Knight addresses all five sub-themes, with particular emphasis on the fourth theme: integrated, balanced instructional approaches. This chapter sets the stage for the four chapters that follow. Even though many researchers and practitioners have long considered constructivist and intensive-explicit instruction to be mutually exclusive pedagogies, a great deal of current research and practice indicates that the two can be integrated in meaningful ways that are more effective than either approach alone. The author begins by defining the terms "constructivist" and "intensive-explicit" and tracing the history of instruction in these pedagogies.

As Knight notes, constructivist instruction is based on the central thesis that people learn by making their own sense of the world rather than by acquiring fixed knowledge that already exists. Thus, teachers who work primarily from a radical constructivist paradigm spend more time creating learning opportunities, engaging in dialogue, and mediating conversations than they do directly explaining or teaching. Whole-language reading is one example of a constructivist approach, yet it is important to remember that there is no one definition or operationalization of whole-language reading instruction, which is true of constructivism itself. This chapter provides examples of constructivist teaching approaches, along with a discussion of the importance of constructivism in understanding social constructs that stereotype or oppress some individuals or groups.

Intensive-explicit instruction, as defined by the author, has no single ontology or epistemology; further, the boundary between constructivist and intensive-explicit instruction has become more difficult to establish as researchers and practitioners have integrated the two. In this chapter, intensive-explicit instruction is defined as a "set of instructional procedures that together efficiently and effectively enable teachers to convey content clearly to students in a manner that leads to students mastering information" (p. 246). It is intensive because it requires students to be engaged in learning and actively mastering content. It is explicit because it requires teachers to clearly model overt and covert behavior and thinking, as well as to provide detailed feedback to students as they progress toward mastery. The author identifies critical instructional components common to intensive-explicit approaches, and points out that, while intensive-explicit instruction also can take place in rich, meaningful contexts, an important goal is for students to understand, remember, and generalize content taught by the teacher.

The author compares and contrasts the two approaches to instruction across the dimensions of the teacher's role, conversations, questions, errors and activities, motivation, and truth and reality. How the two views tend to complement each other follows, detailing points of convergence across the two views. The author notes that a major purpose of the chapter is to offer "additional conversation starters and points to ponder" (p. 262) in the debate regarding the relative merit of these two approaches, saying that perhaps the strengths of each approach can accommodate the limitations of the other. The chapter ends with a discussion of potential ways of envisioning the integration of constructivist and intensive-explicit approaches to instruction.

In Chapter 11, "Balanced Literacy Instruction," Michael Pressley, Alyssia Roehrig, Kristen Bogner, Lisa Raphael, and Sara Dolezal extend to the area of literacy the discussion of integrated, balanced instructional approaches and the need for continued innovation. The authors contend that the "reading wars" have emphasized a false dichotomy between skills instruction and authentic, holistic literacy approaches such as whole language. Research, they say, favors the use of neither approach alone or predominantly, and they suggest that the idea of "balance" has definitely caught on in the field of reading, given the recognition that outstanding, effective teachers have been integrating the strengths of both approaches for some time.

As such, the authors' use of the term "balanced instruction" refers to "a lot of skills instruction in the context of massive holistic teaching" (p. 268). They review research indicating that outstanding primary teachers provide frequent skills instruction, in the context of actual reading and writing, as well as during intensive-explicit skills instruction in decontextualized lessons. Moreover, this pattern held true for instruction of students with reading difficulties. Skills instruction was more extensive and intensive for these students than for normally achieving students, but immersion in meaningful literature and writing experiences also was critical.

The authors provide detailed discussions of observations in classrooms of outstanding literacy teachers, including classrooms in school districts where whole-language models were predominant. The pattern of integration was evident in these classrooms as well, as was the finding that the teachers held high expectations that students could learn and that they would become readers and writers. The authors carefully detail the components of balanced literacy instruction, including phonemic awareness and the alphabetic principle, word-recognition instruction, vocabulary instruction, comprehension strategies, self-monitoring, extensive reading, teaching students to relate prior knowledge while they read, process-writing instruction, and motivating reading and writing.

Another important sub-theme of this chapter is the importance of accommodating individual differences and matching instructional approaches to students' strengths and needs. The authors conclude the chapter by emphasizing that a great many individual educational interventions have been validated and deserve a place in balanced literacy instruction, while reminding us of yet another sub-theme by summarizing the many questions and innovations that remain to be addressed by research.

Chapter 12, "Self-Regulated Strategy Development in the Classroom: Part of a Balanced Approach to Writing Instruction for Students with Disabilities," by Karen Harris, Steve Graham, and Linda Mason, presents a balanced, integrated approach to instruction in composition. Their approach is based on a careful and purposeful integration of constructivist and explicit approaches to instruction. Referring to more than 25 research studies conducted over 20 years, the authors demonstrate that this approach is highly effective in improving what and how students write, including normally achieving students and students with disabilities at all grade levels. Moreover, these studies show that the approach is effective in assisting students to meet standards for writing performance, and that it is effective with students with disabilities in inclusive classrooms.

The approach, which the authors refer to as *Self-Regulated Strategy Development* (SRSD), is designed to help students develop knowledge about writing and important skills and strategies involved in the writing process. These skills and strategies include planning, writing, revising, and editing; supporting students in the ongoing development of the self-regulation abilities needed to manage their own writing; and promoting students' development of positive attitudes about writing and themselves as writers.

Understanding individual differences and individualizing the SRSD approach to accommodate them is crucial. The authors contend that students who face significant and often debilitating difficulties benefit from an integrated approach that directly addresses their affective, behavioral, and cognitive characteristics, strengths, and needs. They also believe that these students often require more extensive, structured, and explicit instruction in skills, strategies, and concepts than their normally achiev-ing peers. In this regard, however, the authors emphasize that the level of explicit-ness, the choice of academic and self-regulation strategies, and specific SRSD instructional components should be adjusted to students' individual needs and strengths. They also provide a detailed description of the characteristics, stages, and evaluation of SRSD instruction, an in-depth classroom example of the approach involving writing persuasive essays, and tips for teachers. The authors conclude the chapter by delineating areas for further research and innovation, noting that SRSD is not a panacea but, rather, an important contribution to teachers' instructional repertoires.

In Chapter 13, "Balancing Perspectives on Mathematics Instruction," Eric Jones and Thomas Southern addresses three sub-themes: the need to address individual differences, use of integrated, balanced instructional approaches with students with disabilities, and the need for special educators to continue to be innovative and open to new ideas and approaches and to implement practices based on research evidence for their effectiveness. They offer a careful look at how the debate regarding a con-structivist approach to mathematics versus a behavioral approach has affected the field. The views and beliefs of both constructivists and behaviorists, particularly advocates of Direct Instruction, are carefully presented. After describing the devel-opment and hardening of ideologies within the history of mathematics reform and considering explanations for the continuation of ideological controversies, they con-clude that such ideological hardening is unproductive and counter to the needs of students with disabilities.

After describing "traditional" or "current" approaches to mathematics instruc-tion, Jones and Southern review the principles of learning and instruction that have been empirically validated and that we should be able to use without controversy, particularly in the instruction of students with special needs. Across these principles, they describe where both constructivist and behavioral theory and research have supported the same or similar principles, albeit using different terminology and conceptualizations. They also describe teacher education in mathematics, noting that many teachers lack sophisticated knowledge in this area of instruction.

Jones and Southern then review the history and role of research in mathematics education. They explain that research by mathematicians has tended to deal more with the content than the process of mathematics instruction at the secondary and college level, while psychologists have been more concerned with how mathematics is taught and learned at the elementary level. The authors contend that there is a lack of rigorous research in mathematics teaching and learning, and that the combined contributions of research by mathematicians and psychologists have not produced major improvements in elementary and secondary mathematics instruction and learning. More experimental intervention research and longitudinal studies are needed in this area. In addition, little research exists that integrates what we know about effective mathematics teaching and learning from the constructivist and behavioral approaches, and a great deal remains to be done here.

Jones and Southern conclude their paper with consideration of the "implications that developing (or failing to develop) more balanced conceptualizations of instruction can have on teacher education and practice" (pp. 341). Becoming ensnared in ideological perspectives is unproductive, they say, as it obscures the importance of using what we do know works in mathematics instruction, and limits the horizons for future research. They suggest that while there is an insufficient amount of empirical research in mathematics education, what research indicates does work from both ideological perspectives should be integrated, with attention to both skills and higher-order abilities. Research on thoughtful and purposeful integration of approaches is badly needed in this area.

In Chapter 14, "Searching for the Best Model for Instructing Students with Learning Disabilities," Lee Swanson offers a detailed look at what research has shown in terms of effective instruction for students with learning disabilities. Although students with learning disabilities comprise a heterogeneous group, the author presents a research synthesis that helps to identify the principles that underwrite effective instruction for these students. In doing so, he emphasizes the practical aspects of the findings. Technical reports of the research synthesis procedures and results are referenced and available to the interested reader.

Swanson begins with a brief presentation of previous syntheses of instructional research for students with learning disabilities, noting both the contributions and the limitations of these works, and then explains how the present synthesis expands upon previous syntheses and addresses their limitations. The author and his colleagues identified 913 data-based articles involving instructional research with students with learning disabilities published between 1963 and 1997. Each of thee studies was carefully evaluated, and 180 met the criteria that were established to ensure quality of research methodology. The 180 studies then were sorted by the intervention or treatment components of the instruction provided to students in experimental and control conditions.

Based on the characteristics of the instruction evident in the 180 studies, which were analyzed exhaustively, the studies were first sorted into two groups: those reflecting direct instruction and those reflecting strategy instruction. The author provides a detailed operationalization of both instructional models, noting that the boundaries and distinctions between the two can be difficult to discern in some aspects of instruction. The two models of instruction overlap, in that they share certain similarities in the sequencing of instructional events, and both assume that effective instruction includes daily reviews, statements of instructional objectives, teacher presentation of new material, guided practice, independent practice, and formative evaluations. The author, however, identifies 12 unique criteria for direct instruction (at least four had to be present for a study to be coded as such), and seven unique criteria for strategy instruction (at least three had to be present for a study to be coded as such). Based on these operational criteria, studies were identified as using direct instruction, using strategy instruction, combining both strategy instruction and direct instruction, or using neither type of instruction.

One important finding is that effective instruction seldom represents a single component, but rather, an interaction of multiple components. Further, the combined strategy-instruction and direct-instruction model was the most effective in remediating learning disabilities and was significantly more effective than either of the models alone. The author concludes that, in isolation, neither a bottom-up (direct instruction) nor a top-down (strategies instruction) approach leads to effective instruction. Rather, lower-order and higher-order skills interact to influence instructional outcomes. Further, performance at complex levels, including tasks such as reading comprehension and composition, cannot occur without some critical threshold of skills. This synthesis demonstrates that effective instruction draws from approaches that integrate high- and low-order instruction.

Finally, while strategy-instruction interventions were found to be more effective than direct-instruction interventions, the author stresses that because both direct instruction and strategy instruction are complex combinations of components that have many commonalties, we should not conclude that strategy instruction has better research support than direct instruction. Of the multiple components studied, explicit strategy instruction and small-group instruction were most important in improving outcomes for students with learning disabilities. Many research issues remain, so additional research on other instructional approaches not represented in these studies is needed.

Robert T. Jimenez, author of Chapter 15, "Fostering the Literacy Development of Latino Students," addresses all five sub-themes in exploring the enhancement of literacy development among Latino students. Citing evidence of the persistent, pervasive, and disproportionate academic failure of Latino students, he notes that the literacy achievement gap between White and Latino students has remained relatively static, as has progress in literacy for Latino students. Examining the roles played by educators, students, community members, and society at large, the author identifies several critical issues in the education of Latino students. These include school-based issues such as the professional development of educators, the optimal mix of language-sensitive instructional practices, the relationship of alternative literacies of the Latino community to school-based literacy, and the value in finding optimal ways of facilitating the transfer of information from first language and life experience to school-based tasks. The issues also include broader social issues such as the effects of the current sociopolitical environment; and questions raised by minority researchers concerning the academic performance of Latino students.

The author argues persuasively that educators need to develop a perspective that treats diversity as the norm and appreciates the possibilities created by diversity, which would benefit all students, including students from mainstream, monolingual, middle-class backgrounds. The linguistic and cultural knowledge that Latino students bring to the classroom is unknown by many educators, unexplored by mainstream researchers, and unacknowledged in prevailing instructional methods and curriculum materials. Because inclusive education cannot be effective unless this situation changes, the author calls for educators and others to recognize that the goal is "to acknowledge and respect students as capable and potentially successful, to recognize the linguistic and cultural knowledge that learners bring into the classroom" (p. 373). He argues that educators and schools that are effective with Latino students actively recognize and promote students' first-language strengths, accept and celebrate their cultures, and implement visible efforts to combat racism and social injustice.

Jimenez carefully explains the long-term nature of second-language acquisition, particularly in terms of literacy development. Full grade-level proficiency may occur within as few as 2 years, but typically takes at least 4 to 5 years and, in some cases, as many as 8 years. The age at which students enter U.S. schools and their previous backgrounds are both important factors in understanding this process. Further, the schools they attend in the United States are often poorly funded and located in urban settings. Two of the most critical features of instruction for English language learners, particularly immigrant students, are the provision of services and the quality of these services.

Given these issues and considerations, the author evaluates different models of instruction for Latino students and concludes that dual-language immersion seems to be the most effective and the most inclusive in terms of students, languages, and integration of multiple literacies. Finally, he identifies numerous issues and questions that require further research, attention, and innovation from the educational community relative to the education of Latino students.

In Chapter 16, "Post-Secondary Education and Transition Services for Students Ages 18–21 with Significant Disabilities," authors Debra Neubert, Sherril Moon, and Meg Grigal address the issue of appropriate services for students with significant disabilities who remain in public school programs until the age of 21. Traditionally, these students have participated in functional or community-based instructional programs during their high school years, but professionals, advocates, and families have begun to question when and how often participation in these programs is appropriate. Given the questions that are being raised, the authors contend that it is critically important to reconsider how older students with significant disabilities can be served in different ways in high school, with the aim of preparing more of them for participation in appropriate post-secondary activities.

After differentiating educational versus transitional services for secondary students with significant disabilities, the authors focus on the benefits of providing age-appropriate transition services for students with significant disabilities during their final years of school. These benefits include increased social interaction with same-age peers, age-appropriate courses and job opportunities, access to new environments, and greater opportunities for support from college and community personnel. Next, the authors provide detailed descriptions of two alternative approaches for older students with significant disabilities: programs in post-secondary settings, and individual supports in post-secondary settings. They provide examples of each approach and discuss them in terms of key features, opportunities for inclusion, funding and interagency linkages, logistics, and replicating and evaluating programs.

The authors do not endorse one approach over the other but, instead, offer their descriptions as a means of providing school personnel, families, and community members with information for considering alternative post-secondary options for students with significant disabilities. They also offer additional resources to help these individuals learn more about how some school systems are providing educational and transitional services to students with significant disabilities outside of the traditional high school approach. While the authors praise and encourage the development of innovative approaches for these students, they also note that research and documentation are lacking in terms of what educational experiences are most effective before or after 18 years of age, which presents the field with numerous challenges and opportunities for research.

Chapter 17, "Self-Determination and Quality of Life: Implications for Special Education Services and Supports," by Michael Wehmeyer and Robert Schalock, begins by linking self-determination with several major contemporary issues, including the efficacy of public education, standards-based reform, and individualization as a hallmark of special education legislation and practice. In this regard, they characterize self-determination as critically important to implementing the SBR policy framework within the context of individualization. Here they emphasize the place of self-determination in the process of accommodating the curricular and instructional needs of students with disabilities within the general education curriculum, especially in terms of transition services and delivery of a functional or occupational curriculum.

They further contend that a focus on promoting self-determination to achieve a higher quality of life is critical to the goal of educational excellence for all students. In terms of the SBR framework itself, moreover, they argue that in principle it emphasizes goal setting, problem solving, decision making, and other self-determination-related behaviors—illustrating the universal need for instruction in self-determination for all students.

The authors define self-determination as "acting as the primary causal agent in one's life and making choices and decisions regarding one's quality of life free from undue external influence or interference" (p. 405). Thus, for them self-determined behavior refers to situations in which the person acts autonomously, in a self-regulated, psychologically empowered, self-realizing manner. They consider each of these four characteristics in detail and identify 12 interrelated component elements of self-determined behavior. They describe these elements and suggest assessment and interventions relevant to each, emphasizing the importance of accommodating individual differences. In addition, the authors provide an in-depth discussion of the quality-of-life construct and its use in the field of special education. Although they base their arguments on existing theory and research, they clearly recognize the nascent nature of this area of study and the need for more innovation and research.

In Chapter 18, "Supporting Students with Health Needs in Schools: An Overview of Selected Health Conditions," Paris DePaepe, Linda Garrison-Kane, and Jane Doelling report that 254,110 students were identified as "other health impaired" in 1999–2000. This number represents a 351% increase since 1990–91, the greatest increase in any eligibility category since 1990. The overwhelming increase in students with health impairments has resulted in concerns that both initial teacher preparation and ongoing professional development are inadequate in this regard and that, as such, these students are at significant risk because educators are not adequately prepared to meet their specialized health care needs. The authors review standards developed by the Council for Exceptional Children regarding knowledge and skills critical to teaching students with health impairments, and describe how students with various health conditions may become eligible for special education services under either IDEA 97 or Section 504 of the Vocational Rehabilitation Act.

Next, the authors identify and detail major challenges and issues in planning appropriate health-care services and related accommodations, including: identifying school health services, developing individual health-care plans, administering medications, providing emergency care, and taking universal precautions. They also stress the need for written policies and procedures in each of these areas, as well as the need to recognize and understand individual differences among students with the same health conditions. The authors then detail medical management and school health care and related accommodations for food allergies, asthma, cystic fibrosis, HIV and AIDS, diabetes, epilepsy, and sickle cell disease. They conclude by presenting a four-step approach for determining related services and health care needs, which results in the necessary documentation and data to assist in providing students with health impairments with appropriate educational services.

The last chapter in Part Two is Chapter 19, "School Violence and Disruption: Rhetoric, Reality, and Reasonable Balance." Authors Peter Leone, Matthew Mayer, Kimber Malmgren, and Sheri Meisel present a well-argued discussion of factors related to prevention and intervention in the area of school violence and disruption. The authors begin by characterizing the specter of school violence as something that affects us all. As they note, school violence and disruption are not acceptable, and physical injury and disruptions that interfere with learning and create a climate of fear are legitimate and critical concerns. Nevertheless, recent dramatic acts of violence in schools have led many people to believe that school violence is on the increase when it actually has been steadily declining since 1993. Although addressing school violence remains vitally important, the authors contend that there is reason for optimism for the future. Research indicates that schools are safer than individual homes and neighborhoods; students are about three times safer in school than away from school. Moreover, the majority of school crime consists of non-violent theft, and there is less than a one-in-a-million chance that a student will suffer a school-related violent death.

To organize and support their presentation of issues related to school violence and disruption, the authors draw upon a vast body of research and evaluation in the fields of education, mental health, social services, and juvenile justice. Key issues for them include understanding the contexts of school violence, including family structure and poverty and other social and cultural issues, as well as basing our understanding of, and response to, school violence on existing data while recognizing the need for additional research to answer the many remaining questions. The authors stress the need to balance educational rights with an orderly school environment, which for them means considering numerous factors in addition to legislation and litigation. They also emphasize the importance of understanding how schools have responded to problems of school violence, including violence-prevention efforts. In this regard, they discuss principles of prevention and effective planning for school violence prevention, which involves assessment, support from parents and community, leadership, professional development, and evaluation.

The chapter concludes with the summary that effective interventions are multifaceted, targeted to specific risk factors, developmentally appropriate, and culturally sensitive. Further, the authors stress that it is critical that interventions involve parents, community members, and interagency collaboration, address multiple levels of students' lives, and include an evaluation component. Given that many research and practice challenges remain, and that the role of students with disabilities in school violence and disruption is not well understood, the authors call for a balanced, thoughtful approach to addressing the complex needs of students with behavioral difficulties.

10

Crossing Boundaries: What Constructivists Can Teach Intensive-Explicit Instructors and Vice Versa

Jim Knight

> The next ten years will require people to think and work across boundaries into new zones that are totally different from their areas of expertise. They will not only have to cross these boundaries, but they will also have to identify opportunities and make connections between them. (Mok, 2003)

> The one language we all share is a child's smile. It has the power to cross all boundaries.—Dr. William Magee, Jr., & Kathleen Magee, Operation Smile

Alex's parents had a lot of questions. Just recently, they had been asked to attend an IEP meeting at Alex's elementary school, and they were told that their third-grader was below an appropriate achievement level for his grade. Alex was a bright kid, everyone agreed, but he didn't seem to learn as effectively as others. The team at the school suggested that Alex be tested, and the subsequent assessment determined that Alex had a learning disability. Even though Alex's intelligence was above average, the educational professionals agreed that he would require special help to reach his potential in life.

Like many other children that Christmas, Alex received a sophisticated video game as a gift. He soon was plugged in and playing happily. Over the next few days, Alex played his game for hours each day, and he kept getting better at it. Four days after Christmas, Alex's older cousins, who were in high school, came to visit. They had received the same game for Christmas, but they had not yet learned nearly as much about it as Alex had. For two hours, Alex proceeded to tutor his older cousins in how to play the game, "Jump up and down here," he said, "and you'll find some coins." "Go through that door, and you'll turn invisible." The high schoolers were impressed—Alex had learned the entire language of the game in only 4 days, and he was only in third grade.

"How is it," Alex's parents asked, "that our son has learned so much about this game, and yet he's 'learning disabled' in school?" "Why does he love learning the game and hate learning in school?" "Are his teachers really seeing how smart he is?" "Are they building on his strengths?" "Are they teaching him in ways that will be best for him?" "Does he really have a learning disability?"

The questions that Alex's parents asked are precisely the questions that educational researchers ask. No doubt many researchers would add other, general questions: "What are the most motivating instructional methods?" "How can teachers enable students to 'internalize' or 'generalize' knowledge?" "What is the teacher's role?" "What should students do?" "How does learning occur?" These general questions, fleshed out in hundreds of more specific research questions, constitute much of the academic conversation on instruction for students with disabilities.

This chapter provides some notes for understanding aspects of this academic conversation. Specifically, I consider one central conversation: the sometimes opposing thoughts and statements of researchers and theorists embracing either a *constructivist* or an *intensive–explicit* (IE) approach to instruction. I chose as a topic this professional debate, though controversial and unsettling for some, because it is multiparadigmatic and therefore holds the potential to be fruitful. We can learn a lot when we listen to someone who views our world from the outside (Bernstein, 1991).

To consider how *intensive–explicit* and *constructivist* instruction can impact instruction for students with disabilities, this chapter: (a) reviews the *constructivist* and *intensive–explicit* approaches to instruction, (b) identifies points of contrast between the two approaches, and (c) identifies points of convergence between the two approaches. By seeing the world from within both paradigms, perhaps we may uncover new and useful ways of seeing instruction regardless of our paradigmatic orientation.

WHERE DID THE TERMS "CONSTRUCTIVIST" AND "INTENSIVE–EXPLICIT" COME FROM?

I have chosen to use the terms *constructivist* and *intensive–explicit*. Unfortunately, I cannot give precise, limited definitions of these terms because they are used so differently by so many in the literature. I will consider the terms in the manner proposed by Schwandt (who references Blumer, 1954):

> As general descriptors for a loosely coupled family of methodological and philosophical persuasions, these terms . . . steer the interested reader in the general direction . . . [and] merely suggest "directions along which to look" rather than "provide descriptions of what to see. (Schwandt, 1994, p. 221)

The terms *constructivist* and *intensive-explicit* refer to many different pedagogies, some of which are complementary, some of which are mutually exclusive. The term *constructivist* has been used liberally in the education literature to refer to an ontology, epistemology, pedagogy, and critical perspective and has been linked with such concepts as radical constructivism (Glasersfeld, 1995), social constructivism and psychological constructivism (Phillips, 2000). I use the term *intensive-explicit* instruction to stand for an amalgam of individually unique approaches that have been described variously as strategic (Ellis, Deshler, Lenz, Schumaker, & Clark, 1991), direct explanation (Roehler & Duffy, 1984), and cognitive (Meichebaum, 1977) instruction.

The difficulty in pinning down these definitions is further complicated as many researchers and authors (Englert et al., 1995; Harris & Graham, 1996; Pressley, Harris, & Marks, 1992) support practices that share attributes of *intensive–explicit* and *constructivist* approaches. Before proceeding to the heart of this discussion, I will provide descriptions of both terms.

WHAT IS CONSTRUCTIVIST INSTRUCTION?

A central theme in the literature on *constructivist* instruction is the suggestion that "each of us makes sense of the world by synthesizing new experiences into what we have previously come to understand" (Brooks & Brooks, 1993). Many constructivists contend that this deceptively straightforward idea has radical implications for how we live, think, learn, and teach, and even calls into question our notions of truth and reality. To understand *constructivist* instruction, then, we need to understand it as an approach that involves its own ontology, epistemology, and pedagogy.

Constructivist Ontology

If each of us constructs our own unique understanding of the world, it follows that each of us experiences (or constructs) our own unique world: Everyone's reality is different. As Glasersfeld (1995) has observed, radical constructivism

> . . . starts from the assumption that knowledge, no matter how it be defined, is in the heads of persons, and that the thinking subject has no alternative but to construct what he or she knows on the basis of his or her own experience. What we make of the world constitutes the only world we live in. It can be sorted into many kinds, such as things, self, others, and so on. But all kinds of experience are essentially subjective, and though I may find reasons that my experience may not be unlike yours, I have no way of knowing that it is the same. (p. 1)

Constructivists extend this discussion by agreeing with Kuhn's (1970) assertion that scientific knowledge can be understood as true only within a given paradigm and not in reference to an immutable standard in objective reality. Our notions of truth and objectivity, therefore, are open to question.

Furthermore, because some socially constructed terms limit, stereotype, or oppress individuals (especially women, people with disabilities, people in poverty, and racial minorities), issues of gender and power take on special significance.

Words can tell us who we are, and because words are created by humans, thinking people should reflect on whether the words they live by are authentic for them and others (Reid, Robinson, & Bunsen, 1995).

Constructivist Epistemology

Constructivist epistemology is the view that learning occurs because each of us uniquely creates or builds our own knowledge. In essence, we construct knowledge based on what we already know, and each idea we learn facilitates our ongoing intellectual development. Phillips (2000) summarizes this view as follows.

> [The] *constructivist* view is that learners actively construct their own ("internal" some would say) sets of meanings or understandings; knowledge is not a mere copy of the external world, nor is knowledge acquired by passive absorption or by simple transference from one person (a teacher) to another (a learner or knower). In sum, knowledge is *made,* not *acquired.* (p. 7)

Constructivist theory is derived in great measure from Piaget (Piaget, 1954; Poplin, 1988a), who suggested that we construct new knowledge when we experience new information that is incongruent with our prior knowledge. Learning and development take place when we try to reconcile new knowledge with what we already know. A central concept for Piaget is the process of assimilation:

> No behavior, even if it is new to the individual, constitutes an absolute beginning. It is always grafted onto previous schemes and therefore amounts to assimilating new elements to already constructed structures (innate, as reflexes are, or previously acquired). (Glasersfeld, 1995, p. 62)

Piaget's theory was extended by Vygotsky's "zone of proximal development," in which intelligence is seen as dynamic rather than fixed. For Vygotsky, the construction of knowledge is a process: "Learning and development do not coincide" (Vygotsky, 1978, p. 84). The zone of proximal development can be understood as the gap between a person's current intellectual level and a person's potential level. That is, the zone defines "those functions that have not yet matured but are in the process of maturing" (p. 86).

Thus, the zone is "the distance between the actual developmental level as determined by independent problem solving and the level of potential development as determined through problem solving under adult guidance or in collaboration with more capable peers" (p. 86). Vygotsky also suggests that each child's development within his or her zone of proximal development is enabled through frequent, social interaction.

Constructivist Pedagogy

Constructivist pedagogy is more general than specific, thereby allowing teachers the freedom to construct their own individual pedagogy based on constructivist principles. Nevertheless, Brooks and Brooks (1993) offer a list of constructivist traits, suggesting that constructivist teachers

(a) encourage and accept student autonomy and initiative (p. 103);
(b) use cognitive terminology . . . when framing tasks (p. 104);
(c) allow student responses to drive lessons, shift instructional strategies and alter content (p. 105);
(d) inquire about students' understandings of concepts before sharing their own understanding of those concepts (p. 107);
(e) encourage students to engage in dialogue (p. 108);
(f) provide time for students to construct relationships and create metaphors (p. 115); and
(g) nurture students' natural curiosity through frequent use of the learning cycle model. (p. 116)

Vygotsky's work is especially influential in the literature on constructivist instruction for students with disabilities (Englert et al., 1995; Mariage, 2000). Belief in the zone of proximal development repositions the teacher as a facilitator (rather than an expert), and thus a teacher strives to provide scaffolding (Wood, Bruner, & Ross, 1976) that enables students to develop their full potential. In addition, the teacher facilitates discourse and dialogue within the classroom, which enables students to internalize learning that takes place in school (Mariage, 2000). Although Moshman (1982) has described constructivism as occurring along a continuum of service, depending on the extent of teacher direction, most teachers using constructivist pedagogy spend more time mediating conversations and learning opportunities than they do directly explaining content.

Constructivist instruction, then, is an educational approach that involves an interwoven pedagogy, epistemology, and ontology, all based on the central thesis that people learn by making their own sense of the world rather than by acquiring fixed knowledge that already exists.

WHAT IS INTENSIVE-EXPLICIT INSTRUCTION?

The loosely coupled group of instructional practices that I refer to as intensive–explicit instruction has no single ontology or epistemology, although intensive–explicit instruction is often characterized as empiricist (Heshusius, 1995). In truth, the border between intensive–explicit and constructivist instruction is less and less obvious because, increasingly, authors consider themselves constructivists and still propose an intensive–explicit instruction pedagogy (Harris & Graham, 1999; Mercer, Jordan, & Miller, 1996).

Intensive–explicit instruction, at least for the purposes of this article, refers to a set of instructional procedures that together efficiently and effectively enable teachers to convey content clearly to students in a manner that leads to students' mastering information. IE is intensive because it involves teaching practices that ensure that students are engaged in learning and actively mastering content (Ellis et al., 1991). IE is explicit because it involves teachers' clearly modeling covert thinking (Mercer,

Lane, Jordan, Allsop, & Eisele, 1996; Roehler & Duffy, 1984) and providing detailed feedback as students move toward mastery of content (Kline, Schumaker, & Deshler, 1991).

Although IE instruction can take place in many rich, meaningful contexts (Deshler et al., 2001; Graham, Harris, & Larsen, 2001), a primary goal of intensive–explicit instruction is for students to understand, remember, and generalize content taught by a teacher. Simply put, instructors use intensive–explicit instruction so that students will have a picture of knowledge in their head that is similar to the picture teachers have in their head. Intensive–explicit instruction utilizes most of the following instructional stages to achieve this goal: describe, model, vocabulary memorization, practice and feedback, and generalization.

Describe

During the Describe stage of instruction, the teacher explains the content or procedural knowledge the students are going to master (Ellis et al., 1991; Harris & Graham, 1999). For example, a teacher teaching students the *Paraphrasing strategy* (Schumaker, Denton, & Deshler, 1984—Read a paragraph, ask yourself what the main idea and details are, put the main idea and details into your own words) would explain the strategy in detail during the Describe stage of instruction. The kind of discourse that takes place during this stage is highly interactive, much more interactive than some constructivists advise (Poplin, 1988b).

During the Describe stage, an IE teacher uses questioning techniques to maintain student engagement and to clarify whether students do or do not understand the material being presented.

IE teachers who employ the *strategic instruction model* (Ellis et al., 1991)—for example, follow a 3-to-1 rule; that is, they do not make more than three statements without having students respond in some way (for example, answering a question, turning to a neighboring student to paraphrase content, writing notes, responding to questions).

IE is designed to compensate for the learning difficulties many students have. Thus, content to be covered is enhanced to make it more easily understood through the used of acronyms, visual images, and graphic organizers (Deshler et al., 2001). In addition, IE provides explicit cues for note taking, and essential content is displayed visually, described verbally, and recorded physically by students.

Model

A central proposition with the IE paradigm is that people learn a great deal by watching what and how others do what they do (Bandura, 1971). Thus, once students have heard, seen, and recorded content, they benefit from explicit modeling of the thinking embedded in the content being learned (Ellis et al., 1991; Roehler & Duffy, 1984).

For example, a teacher teaching the Paraphrasing strategy demonstrates how to use the strategy on a reading passage. Modeling is highly structured, beginning with an advance organizer in which the students and teacher review content that was explained during the Describe stage of instruction. Following this, teachers deliberately demonstrate the thinking they want students to learn. Thus, rather than simply "thinking aloud," teachers using IE are deliberate about clearly demonstrating the essential thinking they want students to learn (Gildroy, 2001).

Once students have seen a complete model, teachers involve them in the task at hand—in this example, using the Paraphrasing strategy. The teacher calls on students to help them complete the task, and the teachers and students discuss the kind of thinking patterns that will lead to effective use of the strategy. This stage concludes with a teacher-led review.

Vocabulary Memorization

During the stage of Vocabulary Memorization, the teacher leads the students through activities that enable them to memorize the critical components of the content being learned (Ellis et al., 1991). Students learning the Paraphrasing strategy, for example, memorize the steps of the strategy and the criteria for successful performance of the strategy.

Activities may include rapid-fire verbal rehearsal, in which the teacher calls on students to speak back key terms quickly; peer practice, in which two students question each other about the terms and definitions; games that involve groups of students in friendly competition; sustained, silent review, and so on. During this stage the teacher's goal is for students to understand and remember all the essential vocabulary.

Practice and Feedback

"The essence of strategy instruction," Borkowski comments, "lies in explanation followed by challenging and extensive practice" (Borkowski & Muthukrishna, 1992). Consistent with this tenet, teachers using IE ensure that students master content by providing practice activities. These practice activities are organized so students develop their skills progressively; that is, they learn strategies, skills, and content by mastering increasingly difficult tasks. For example, a student learning Paraphrasing might start by paraphrasing words, then phrases, then whole sentences. Subsequently, the student might practice on short, easy-to-read materials before progressing to more difficult longer passages.

During the Practice and Feedback stage, the teacher provides extensive feedback to students on their progress, and students often chart their progress. Specifically, during each feedback session for Paraphrasing, the teacher (a) authentically praises each student for what he or she has done well, (b) notes a category of error in the students' work, (c) models for the student a way to avoid that error, (d) and ensures that the student understands what to do differently by asking the student to demonstrate how to perform the practice attempt correctly (Kline et al., 1991).

Feedback of this kind enables students to overcome learned helpless (Seligman, 1992) about major academic tasks by constantly demonstrating to students that they are developing. As students apply feedback in subsequent practice attempts, they become more and more skillful until they have mastered the content to be learned.

Generalization

A central goal of IE is that students' use of strategies, skills, or content becomes habitual in a variety of settings. As Deshler and Schumaker have observed about strategic instruction, "Over time, the focus of instruction should shift from teaching students to use a task-specific strategy to focus on how to meet the demands associated with a specific problem or to a focus on how strategies can be used to address similar problems in the same or other domains" (Deshler & Schumaker, 1993, p. 163). For that reason, teachers using IE instruction explicitly guide students to generalize their use of the information being learned. The teachers describe, when, where and why students should use knowledge such as Strategies in a variety of settings, both in school and in their lives.

Teachers using IE instruction often have students turn in assignments in which they demonstrate use of strategies in settings outside of their classroom, provide feedback on students' attempts at generalization, and encourage other teachers to cue students to use strategies taught in their classes. For example, a teacher teaching the Paraphrasing strategy might discuss with students how paraphrasing could be used as a listening strategy during conversation, a note-taking strategy during lessons, a reading comprehension strategy while doing research or reading textbooks, and so on. In addition, the teacher might have students actively practice use of the strategy on a variety of academic and less formal reading materials.

Intensive–explicit instruction is an amalgam of teaching strategies used in concert to ensure that students master content. Students experiencing intensive–explicit instruction receive explicit, interactive explanations of content, watch teachers model thinking, memorize key vocabulary, practice and receive feedback until they master content, and ultimately receive explicit instruction, prompts, and feedback to help them generalize their learning to other settings inside and outside school.

POINTS OF CONTRAST

One way to better understand the intensive–explicit and the constructivist approaches to instruction is to look at how they differ with respect to specific aspects of practice in the classroom and in schools. Each approach includes many practices that may be contrasted. For example, both approaches see the teacher's goal as enabling students to become independent, self-regulated learners (Deshler & Schumaker, 1988; Reid et al., 1995), and both approaches propose that teachers need to provide "scaffolds" to accommodate students' lack of prerequisite knowledge (Ellis et al., 1991; Mariage, 2000; Pressley, Hogan, Wharton-McDonald, Mistretta, & Ettenberger, 1996). However, the way teachers go about enabling self-regulation or providing scaffolds differs greatly between the two approaches.

The intent here is not to contrast specific constructivist and intensive–explicit teaching practice (though that certainly would be a profitable, if complicated, task). Rather, the focus will be on contrasting components of educational practice in the classroom: (a) the teacher's role, (b) conversations, (c) questions, (d) errors, (e) activities, (f) motivation, and (g) truth and reality.

Teacher's Role

Intensive–Explicit

The primary goal of teachers using the IE instruction approach is to teach so effectively that every student masters and generalizes the content being covered. The IE teacher uses teaching practices that accommodate students' learning challenges; the teachers are explicit about thinking processes, feedback, generalization, and so on because they want students to learn and generalize content in pretty much the same form as it is presented.

IE teachers alternate between assessing students and providing instruction (sometimes almost simultaneously). They assess whether students are comprehending instruction, or mastering application of knowledge, while teaching utilizing content enhancements that render content more accessible to students (Deshler, Schumaker, Bulgren et al., 2001; Deshler, Schumaker, Lenz et al., 2001).

Constructivist

Skrtic, Sailor, and Gee (1996) comment that, "In constructivist classrooms, teachers are viewed as agents who encourage students to be thinkers and who involve students in the whole problem-solving enterprise" (p. 147). A constructivist teacher plays a less central role in the classroom than does an IE teacher, but his or her challenge is no less complex.

A constructivist teacher is interested primarily in enabling all students to construct and internalize their own unique knowledge. Toward that end, constructivist teachers are mediators; they mediate the community of the classroom so the dialogue enables students to develop intellectually, and the teachers put in place scaffolds that enable students to develop within their zone of proximal development (Moll, 1990). Poplin's (1988b) comments clearly illustrate this new understanding of the teacher's role: "The more control educators have over the content, the less likely students will be to maintain and generalize skills and/or strategies."

Conversations

Intensive–Explicit

When using IE instruction, the teacher structures the conversation to ensure that students master content, although a good deal of conversation is interactive. During IE instruction, conversation serves two purposes:

1. The teacher explicitly explains the thinking embedded in the strategies, skills, or content (Pressley et al., 1990; Roehler & Duffy, 1984).

2. The teacher guides students to write appropriate information during note-taking, models thinking processes, and so on.

IE instruction is not a lecture, however. Teachers using IE use their entire repertoire of teaching skills to ensure that students are engaged and understand whatever is being discussed (Harris & Graham, 1999). Once students have mastered content, the teacher shifts the conversation to discuss how students can use what they have learned in a variety of settings in school and real life. Strategy mastery serves "as a good point of departure for stimulating dialogue between the teacher and student about 'learning how to learn'" (Deshler & Schumaker, 1993, p. 155).

A flowchart depicting the direction of conversation in an IE classroom would show conversation taking place between students (when they practice learning in teams or groups) and from students to teachers (when students ask for clarification of content, or when they extend the conversation based on teacher prompts). Nevertheless, the majority of conversations during IE instruction start with the teacher and end with the student.

Constructivist

Dialogue is the mode of discourse in constructivist classrooms. Dialogue is seen as a way for students to share their knowledge and thereby facilitate each other's construction of knowledge (Vygotsky, 1978). Bohm (1996) sheds light on the meaning of dialogue by uncovering the etymology of the term:

> Dialogue comes from the Greek word *dialogos. Logos* means "the word" or in our case we would think of the "meaning" of the word. And *dia* means 'through'… A dialogue can be among any number of people … the picture or image that this derivation suggests is of a *streaming of meaning* flowing among and through us and between. (p. 6)

For constructivists, dialogue is a necessary means to develop further thinking. In this sense, the contructivist understanding of dialogue is Frierean (Friere, 1997). That is, by providing us with a variety of perspectives on ideas, dialogue creates the freedom for us to re-create knowledge. For Friere, reflection that occurs through dialogue—the opportunity to recreate our own knowledge—is an essentially humanizing activity. Poplin (1995) builds upon other aspects of Friere's "revolutionary pedagogy" by suggesting that authentic education should empower students to reflect on and transcend their situation in the world.

By contrast to intensive–explicit instruction, a flowchart of the direction of conversation in a constructivist classroom would look quite chaotic, with multiple conversations between students working on authentic tasks, and between students and teachers. Unlike intensive–explicit instruction, more conversations would start with students and end with the teacher, or start with students and end with other students.

Questions

Intensive–Explicit

Teachers using IE pose questions primarily to gauge whether students understand or are mastering content. In addition, teachers pose question to help students clarify their own understandings and misunderstandings. Students ask questions when they are unclear about the content or the components of an assignment. This is not to say that IE teachers refrain from offering provocative, challenging questions. This sort of questioning is a characteristic of most exciting learning situations. During IE instruction, however, questions help the student and the teacher better understand whether a student has acquired the knowledge being taught. Also, because questions are used to assess student comprehension and development, they usually have right and wrong answers.

Constructivist

In constructivist classrooms questions are posed to inspire authentic problem solving. That is, questions bring to the surface incongruities that students have to address, and students frequently work in groups to construct new knowledge. Questions help students develop higher forms of knowledge by pointing out the limitations of their current thinking. Furthermore, because each individual makes her or his own sense of knowledge, questions often do not have "right" answers. Questions are points of departure for each individual's development and construction of knowledge.

Errors

Intensive–Explicit

Within IE instruction, errors are viewed within the larger context of students' developing, mastering, and fluently using knowledge. That is, the IE instructional process is seen as a methodology for students to gain confidence and develop skills by pointing out errors and explaining how they can be eliminated. Teachers address errors in a routine that begins with authentic acknowledgement of students' achievement on practice attempts. Following this, one or two categories of error are identified, and the teacher explains and models for students how to overcome the error.

By progressively overcoming errors, and building fluency, students overcome learned helplessness and become independent learners. Therefore, learning how to overcome errors is an important way in which students develop during IE instruction. Pressley (in Pressley et al., 1992) comments that during "good strategy instruction . . . errors are used not to penalize students, but rather as diagnostic tools, permitting the strategy teacher insights into the student processes" (p. 19–20).

Constructivist

Poplin comments that "probably the most significant and obvious difference between constructivist notions of learning and reductionist theories is the way in which error is perceived in the classroom" (Poplin, 1988a). In a constructivist classroom, errors are seen as the natural outgrowth of risk taking and meaningful learning. Mistakes are an essential component of the construction of knowledge; they are indicators that learning is taking place. "Constructivists . . . seek to create environments where 'penalty-free' errors can emerge and be realized" (Poplin, 1988a). In this sense, errors are to be celebrated, and teachers should not attempt to correct students when they are trying to learn.

As Brooks and Brooks (1993) state, " 'No' hurts, and makes students feel invalidated and foolish. 'No' communicates to students that their idiosyncratic thinking about issues is not particularly valued. It erodes their desire to think about and explore issues" (p. 86). In addition, constructivists suggest that it is often naïve to assume that there is a "right answer." Heshusius (1995) states, "The wrong answer can be perfectly right where it is the result of a personal and often complex process the child goes through" (p. 182).

Activities

Intensive–Explicit

During IE instruction, learning activities are set up so that students can become independent, empowered learners through activities that lead to mastery and fluent use of content. Students engage in a variety of activities. For example, they may watch or interact during teacher modeling of content, respond to questions, practice developing skills and strategies, listen to instructions or feedback, or apply new knowledge as they build their abilities. Assignments are structured so students can build their understanding of complex content through practice on increasingly difficult materials.

Students might work together or work independently. However they learn, the overriding goal is to learn the material that the teacher has presented. Students in an effective IE class are highly engaged, motivated by the progress they experience and by mastering knowledge.

Constructivist

Constructivist instruction involves students in activities that enable them to construct and reconstruct knowledge. Constructivist learning experiences may take many different forms. The Early Literacy Project (Englert et al., 1995) provides one example of how Vygotsky's social constructivism can be embodied in student activities. Students participating in the Early Literacy Project are engaged in "meaningful, purposeful, and integrated activities," and they take part in classroom dialogues that involve them "in social interactions within a cognitive apprenticeship model" (p. 254). Students experience "scaffolded instruction (word banks, partner reading) that . . . [allows] . . . them "to engage in reading and writing in advance of independent performance" (p. 261).

Students in a learning experience that is truly constructivist should find themselves swept up in activities that they find meaningful. In addition, they should progress and develop at the pace that is uniquely appropriate for them. Their learning experiences are interdisciplinary and not restricted by subject area. Thus, students may tackle complex problems that require knowledge from several disciplines.

Motivation

Intensive–Explicit

Student motivation in the intensive-explicit approach arises from a variety of factors. To begin with, in some approaches involvement is cast as a choice, with students being asked to make a personal commitment before instruction begins (Ellis et al., 1991). Teachers using IE are also explicit about the rationales for learning content and guide students to see the value in the learning they are experiencing through direct explanation in classroom conversation.

In addition, IE instruction is structured specifically to encourage student motivation, sharing many of the structural components of what others have identified as motivating or optimal experience (Csikszentmihalyi, 1991). That is, learning is set up so there is an ideal balance between the challenges of the activity and the skills of the student. Learning starts at an appropriate skill level for each student and then gets progressively more challenging as the children master content.

Also, while they are learning, students set goals and receive feedback on their progress toward their goals (Kline et al., 1991). Pressley (1992) comments, "Throughout instruction, teachers attempt to keep motivation high, largely by highlighting the empowerment that accompanies acquisition of powerful procedures that accomplish important academic tasks" (p. 11).

Constructivist

Students are motivated to learn during constructivist instruction because the learning they experience provokes their interest, inspires their curiosity, or is pleasurable. Students are motivated because they are curious to learn more about whatever problem they are considering. Students work on, explore, and play with material that is personally meaningful for them because "learners learn best from experiences about which they are passionately interested and involved" (Poplin, 1988a, p. 405).

Assignments also are "holistic activities" (Englert & Marriage, 1996) that provide students with the context for understanding why they learn what they learn. Thus, students who are learning about literacy experience it in the broader context of communication to create a community of learners. Students may write in journals, share their writing with others, engage in dialogues about writing, have their writing displayed in the classroom, write for multiple audiences, write with partners and in groups, and so on (Graham et al., 2001).

During constructivist instruction, teachers pay particular attention to creating an environment that frees students to experience the inherent joy of learning. Constructivist instruction emphasizes the important role that community plays for students' developing knowledge. In addition, constructivists try to create a setting in which students feel free to learn, by reducing disincentives in the classroom. Thus, as noted, teachers using constructivist instruction deemphasize students' errors so students will trust their teachers and be willing to take risks (Poplin, 1988a).

Truth and Reality

Intensive–Explicit

As noted, the intensive–explicit approach to instruction is not the product of one ontology, and it is possible to support both constructivist and IE instructional practices (Harris & Graham, 1996; Mercer, Jordan et al., 1996; Pressley et al., 1992). Nevertheless, a pedagogy intent on ensuring that students master the content chosen by teachers would seem to be most appealing to a teacher who believes there is an objective reality that everyone can reference and understand.

Perhaps IE teachers take a practical approach, choosing to assume, for the moment at least, that we can know laws and facts and act on them with certainty. To be sure, when we are riding a commercial jet, it is more reassuring to assume that the pilot believes in an objective reality than to believe that the pilot has constructed his or her own unique understanding of piloting and now will fly the plane accordingly.

Some IE instructors are impatient with constructivist theorizing. As one teacher and graduate student commented, "You have to stay in school a long time and read a lot of philosophy before you can start to wonder if reality is real or not." An instructor taking the IE approach may be inclined to put brackets around theorizing, and focus instead on enabling students to master essential skills and strategies (such as the ability to read and communicate orally and in writing).

Intensive–explicit instruction takes the perspective that there are rules, laws, concepts, and terms that competent people know, and that one important task for a teacher is to ensure that students have acquired that knowledge. Thus, IE instruction positions the teacher as an expert teaching students who have varying degrees of expertise.

Because it assumes the existence of objective reality, intensive-explicit instruction also places particular emphasis on how the environment affects student behavior. Consequently, intensive-explicit instruction is more behaviorist in orientation, often employing progress charts, goal-directed behavior, and the use of extrinsic rewards to shape behavior (Deshler & Schumaker, 1988).

Constructivist

From the constructivist perspective, the individual nature of constructivist epistemology renders objective reality a myth (Segal, 2001). "There is nothing 'out there' that is separate from our own construction of it. Reality is mind-dependent. In other words, *we* construct what we know. Who we are, with all our values, interests, and various needs, is part and parcel of what we come to construct as knowledge" (Heshusius, 1995, p. 175).

A constructivist epistemology leads to a different understanding of what a teacher's job is. Constructivists reject the idea that the teacher is the source of most knowledge in the classroom, and, indeed, they hold open to question all knowledge. Thus, the constructivist teacher's task is "to help students to search rather than follow" (Brooks & Brooks, 1993, p. 102).

Constructivist and intensive–explicit approaches to instruction differ in many ways, including the teacher's role, the type of conversations and questions, the way errors are perceived, what students do, how they are motivated, and even how reality and truth are perceived are all points of contrast between these two approaches. Despite these differences, however, I believe that constructivist and intensive–explicit instruction can be used together to accommodate the weaknesses in each approach. For that reason, we will next consider points of convergence between intensive–explicit and constructivist instruction.

POINTS OF CONVERGENCE

Contrasting intensive–explicit and constructivist approaches has brought to light the significant differences between these two approaches. I believe that classrooms integrating both approaches might serve students better than classrooms adhering to one or the other of these approaches dogmatically. Each approach has limitations that are accommodated by each other's strengths. For that reason, we can better understand how constructivist and intensive–explicit instruction might be integrated more effectively by first reviewing the criticisms of each approach.

Looking at each instructional approach from the outside, so to speak, brings out possible limitations in both approaches, thereby suggesting points at which the two approaches might come together. Once we have considered the critiques of both approaches, we will offer some ways by which the two approaches might work together.

Constructivist Critique of Intensive–Explicit Instruction

From the unique perspective afforded by their paradigm, constructivists, have criticized IE instruction as being "reductionist." According to Poplin (1988b), "Reductionism is the natural process by which we break ideas, concepts, and skills into parts in an attempt to understand and deal better with the whole" (p. 394). Constructivists contend that this "bits and pieces" approach to education (Heshusius, 1995, p. 178) removes the real meaning and pleasure from learning. Life is much more complex, ambiguous, and messy than learning that can be summarized on a learning sheet, and effective pedagogy should, therefore, recognize and privilege that ambiguity.

Another criticism leveled at intensive–explicit instruction is that it involves students in learning experiences divorced from real, meaningful life. For example,

Heshusius rejects the teaching practices of "mastery of components . . . the idea of additive and linear progress, and the view of the students as reactive (meaning active only in reaction to the teacher's curriculum . . . [as being based] on outdated beliefs inherent in the mechanistic paradigm" (p. 171).

IE instruction is criticized as a model that leads teachers to spend the bulk of their time preparing students, leaving little time for meaningful learning experiences. To illustrate, Heshusius cites a student's comment, "When are we going to stop readin' reading and start reading something?" (p. 178).

Constructivists cite Friere's notion of banking education, that teachers do not enable students to experience meaningful dialogue, as a critique of IE instruction. Although IE is interactive, and although during IE instruction there can be meaningful dialogue about how, where, and why to generalize learning, there is little dialogue in the sense Friere proposes. Dialogue during IE instruction, then, is not a form of praxis—that is, an activity that involves authentic reflection and reconstruction of knowledge (Friere, 1997).

A final critique, offered most forcefully by Poplin (1988b), is that IE fails to properly enable students to generalize learning. Although IE often involves practice and feedback, as well as the teaching of prerequisite skills and strategies, constructivists contend that because this is learning in preparation for real tasks, as opposed to real experiences themselves, students fail to generalize IE learning.

> Learning a skill one day and forgetting it the next is often implied as a characteristic of the learning disabled student. I propose, however, that this characteristic is more a result of reductionistic methods we employ than a characteristic of the students we serve. (Poplin, 1988b, pp. 393–394)

Intensive–Explicit Critique of Constructivism

When viewed from the perspective afforded by the IE paradigm, or at least from vantage points that are not entirely *constructivist,* the constructivist approach to instruction is also seen as having limitations. The constructivist predilection to deemphasize the limitations of students with learning disabilities (Poplin, 1988b), for example, has been criticized for putting students into learning situations from which they are unable to benefit fully.

Researchers who adopt an IE perspective believe that students with learning disabilities are students who come to learning with challenges that make it difficult for them to complete certain tasks (for example, decoding or comprehending texts, writing, social discourse, or reasoning). A learning disability, by definition, denies learners access to learning experiences that other children experience fully. Rather than deemphasizing limitations, the IE perspective holds that a central goal of special education is to ensure that students with disabilities develop the strategies and skills they need to ultimately have barrier-free access to curriculum (Deshler et al., 2001).

A second criticism of constructivism is that by ignoring mistakes and celebrating risk taking, teachers may not adequately attend to the important goal of ensuring that students acquire foundational knowledge essential for independent performance (Cromer, 1997). Teachers who adopt a constructivist approach to teaching reading may provide students with stimulating learning activities that enable students to piece together their own understanding of reading, but from the IE perspective such an approach might leave students dangerously at-risk because it does not systematically teach students essential components such as phonemic awareness. For example, Stanovich (1994) comments:

> The idea that self-discovery is the most efficacious mode of learning, that most learning can be characterized as "natural," and that cognitive components should never be isolated or fractioned during the learning process have been useful as tenets for comprehension instruction, but are markedly at variance with what is now known about the best ways to develop word recognition skill. Research has indicated that explicit instruction and teacher-directed strategy training are more efficacious, and that this is especially true for at-risk children, children with learning disabilities, and for children with special needs. (p. 259)

First Point of Convergence: Mechanical versus Metaphorical Knowledge

Both IE and constructivist instruction may address some of the limitations of each other. For example, as noted, IE instruction has been criticized for reducing rich learning experiences, whereas constructivism has been criticized for not ensuring that students master essential skills. Allowing students to discover how to read texts without IE instruction in some essential decoding skills might leave students unprepared for some academic tasks. At the same time, a step-by-step strategy to teach students how to determine the correct meaning of a story might significantly interfere with a student's meaningful appreciation of the story.

Appreciating a story seems to be an especially appropriate kind of activity for constructivist pedagogy. Wolfgang Iser has suggested that the act of reading a story is inherently constructivist, with readers identifying "gaps" in the text and constructing their own reading by filling in the gaps. In addition, readers create their own pictures of the setting, connect the narrative with their personal experiences, interpret the message of the story, if one exists, through the lens of their own morality, and so on.

In a very real sense, we all read our own story. Poplin comments that, for this reason, "Two adults reading the same novel often see the novel's message very differently because each person brings to the novel different experiences that interact in the text with significantly different ways" (Poplin, 1988a).

I refer to knowledge, such as that derived from reading a story, as *metaphorical knowledge*. It is by definition ambiguous, and functions indirectly. Metaphorical knowledge has no clearly right or wrong outcome. For example, each person determines and develops his or her own understanding of intellectual attributes such as aesthetic response, personal attributes such as compassion or heroism, and many creative acts such as higher-order writing activities. Metaphorical knowledge is complex, so ambiguous, and so uniquely individual that we damage it if we reduce it. For that reason, constructivist instruction may be more appropriate for metaphorical knowledge.

Not all knowledge to be learned is as complicated as our aesthetic response to narrative. When the content to be learned in a class is not ambiguous, and when the outcomes are unmistakable, perhaps an IE approach is more appropriate. For example, learning how to identify subjects and verbs in sentences (a skill that is necessary for meaningful conversation about many editorial concerns, such as run-on sentences, sentence fragments, subject–verb agreement, and verb tense) is fairly straightforward. Whether someone has or has not correctly identified the subject of a sentence is easily determined without ambiguity.

Knowledge that is unambiguous, when a right and wrong answer can be clearly identified, I have come to refer to as *mechanical knowledge*. Examples of mechanical knowledge are phonological awareness, some learning strategies, memorization of essential concepts terminology, and grammatical terms and concepts.

On the surface, IE instruction seems to be a superior pedagogy for enabling students to acquire mechanical knowledge because mechanical knowledge is unambiguous. When teachers can clearly identify a correct answer, they might find it more efficient to teach in a way that ensures that students share the same knowledge they do. IE instruction is a method for ensuring mastery of content, and for that reason it seems to be the most efficient and effective way to teach mechanical knowledge.

By the same token, constructivist instruction could be a superior pedagogy for metaphorical knowledge. If knowledge is so complicated and ambiguous that it cannot be reduced to a simple and clear explanation, perhaps the best way for students to make sense of it is through exploration, and dialogue, social construction in the classroom. When knowledge seems uniquely personal, such as how to define empathy or respect, perhaps a constructivist approach is more effective.

If students are failed by the education they receive today, perhaps that is because they experience the wrong pedagogy for the kind of knowledge they are learning. Perhaps, when students are taught five steps to understanding a poem, or are compelled to memorize the names of famous authors during literature classes, they lose sight of the emotional power and beauty of poetic expression.

In addition, when they are left on their own to discover how to construct a correct sentence, and not given *intensive–explicit* instruction on grammatically correct forms of expression, perhaps they are frustrated by what they do not know. By reducing the experience of literature, teachers can take the heart and soul out of it. Similarly, by leaving students free to construct their own sentences, without ensuring that they master some basic rules, teachers can frustrate students who are tentative and unsure of their abilities.

Mechanical knowledge is like the rules of a game that everyone must know before the game begins. Once the rules are mastered, however, the artistry of the game begins, and that is when metaphorical knowledge becomes more important.

Second Point of Convergence: Tacit Knowledge

Michael Polanyi's work represents an alternative way of considering constructivism that also represents a point of convergence between constructivist and IE instruction. Polanyi (1966) distinguished between the "tacit" and "explicit" aspects of knowledge. The tacit dimensions are those aspects of knowing that are so well internalized that we are unconscious of them. According to Polanyi, "We can know more than we can tell" (p. 4).

We can better understand tacit knowledge by considering an example. Imagine an outstanding hockey player. If we watch him or her play the game, we'll notice that the player performs with a level of expertise that is superior to others. Maybe the player seems to know just the right time to shoot the puck to score, the most efficient way to avoid opposing checkers, the best time to pass the puck to teammates, or the most appropriate place to skate to intercept a pass. An outstanding player seems to have an almost innate ability to see, act, and anticipate that enables outstanding performance. As the greatest hockey player of all time, Wayne Gretzky, has said, "I skate to where the puck is going to be."

If we were to interview such an outstanding player and ask him or her to explain how we could become similarly expert, chances are the player would not be able to tell us what he or she does to attain it. Expert performance is often something that is constructed and internalized over time. Polanyi called this process "indwelling." Once tacit knowledge becomes internalized, it can shape the way we think, move, and perceive, and often it is invisible to us. I would argue that there is a significant tacit dimension to the expertise of any skillful actor, whether we are talking about a hockey player, an airplane mechanic, a teacher, or a reader.

According to Polanyi, explicit knowledge stands in contrast to tacit knowledge. Explicit knowledge refers to knowledge that can be articulated in language and shared. Explicit knowledge, for example, is represented by grammar, mathematical formulas, and the specifications written in manuals. Explicit knowledge, because it has been encoded in language, can be shared. Explicit knowledge is the principal form of knowledge in schools today.

If we return to our hockey player, we will see that explicit knowledge also plays an important role in the player's development. Not all learning occurs on the fly, in the midst of the game, and most skillful players learn a great deal from various forms of IE instruction that teach them explicit knowledge. For example, masterful players might have attended power skating sessions to develop speed and agility on skates, or learned a step-by-step procedure for how to pass or shoot in a variety of effective ways.

No doubt, if they received effective instruction from coaches, they heard explicit instructions, watched multiple models of expert performance, developed their skills through progressively more difficult practices, received constructive feedback that enabled them to master their skills, and then generalized their developing skills in real-game situations. Tacit knowledge may be the dimension of knowledge that is most important, but much tacit knowledge is constructed, in part, as a result of explicit instruction.

Our example suggests another way in which the interplay between *constructivist* and intensive–explicit instruction might be structured. Perhaps IE instruction is necessary for some forms of explicit knowledge, whereas constructivist pedagogy is necessary to enable the "indwelling" of knowledge. IE instruction, then, can be used to teach students the knowledge that is codified in language and easily communicated, but constructivist instruction can be used to help students transform explicit knowledge into the tacit dimension.

Third Point of Convergence: Competence and Connoisseurship

The potential for interplay between constructivist and intensive–explicit instruction is broadened by work in linguistics, literary criticism (Culler, 1975) and aesthetic response (Eisner, 1991). All of these writers posit ways in which tacit knowledge enables us to masterfully interact with the world.

Eisner (1991) agrees with Polanyi that tacit knowledge plays a significant role in how we experience and appreciate the world. "Perception," he says, "is a function of the transactions between the qualities of the environment and what we bring to those qualities" (p. 63). Eisner explores this phenomenon by discussing connoisseurship. According to Eisner, a person develops the abilities of a connoisseur by internalizing knowledge that enables the masterful perception of some object.

To illustrate his idea, Eisner uses the example of a wine connoisseur. A wine connoisseur's expertise has to enable him or her to perceive and differentiate taste, color, and scent. The connoisseur has to place wine in its appropriate class, understand the science of winemaking, and bring other components of "antecedent knowledge" into play so as to fully appreciate a wine. Eisner extends the concept of connoisseurship to life in general:

> To some degree all people have some degree of connoisseurship in some area of life. In virtually all cases, however, the level of their connoisseurship can be raised through tuition. Teachers of literature can help people learn how to read a novel. . . . Coaches help players learn how to read a field of play in motion. . . . Critics of film and painting help others learn to see what they might otherwise not notice. . . . In the process, people's consciousness is raised, and they become more able to notice and respond to such material. (p. 69)

Culler (1975) makes similar claims about the role of knowledge in appreciating experience in his description of "literary competence." Drawing on Noam Chomsky's notion of linguistic competence, like Eisner, Culler sees our experience of the world as a being shaped by what we bring to experience. He summarizes Chomsky's notion of linguistic competence, an explanation of how our understanding of language is predicated upon a complex web of tacit and explicit knowledge, as follows:

> Whenever a speaker of a language hears a phonetic sequence, he is able to give it meaning because he brings to the act of communication an amazing

repertoire of conscious and unconscious knowledge. Mastery of the phonological, syntactic and semantic systems of his language enables him to convert the sounds into discrete units, to recognize words, and to assign a structural description and interpretation to the resulting sentence, even though it be quite new to him. Without this implicit knowledge, this internalized grammar, the sequence of sounds does not speak to him. (p. 113)

Culler extends the idea of competence to include the appreciation of literature and, like Eisner, concludes that the ability to sense a work in all of its richness requires extensive tacit knowledge. Just as we need linguistic competence to understand a speaker of a language, so we need "literary competence" to appreciate literary works.

To read a text as literature is not to make one's mind a tabula rasa and approach it without preconceptions; one must bring to it an implicit understanding of the operations of literary discourse which tells one what to look for. . . . Anyone lacking this knowledge . . . would be unable to read it as literature . . . because he lacks the complex 'literary competence' which enables others to proceed. He has not internalized the 'grammar' of literature, which would permit him to convert linguistic sequences into literary structures and meanings. (p. 114–115)

By describing how tacit knowledge enables learning, Culler and Eisner provide a final point for considering how constructivist and IE instruction can be integrated. Perhaps IE instruction is necessary for clear and efficient teaching of skills, strategies, conceptual knowledge, and so on, which are necessary components of being a connoisseur or of being competent in a discipline in the way Culler defines competence. Our rich construction of experience can be enhanced through intensive–explicit instruction.

CONCLUSION

In recent years, several authors have reconsidered the contention that constructivist and intensive-explicit instruction are mutually exclusive pedagogies (Harris & Graham, 1994; Pressley et al., 1992). I believe we will all benefit if this integrative exploration continues to be an important part of the conversation taking place in the research literature and in schools.

I have offered additional conversation starters and points to ponder by comparing and contrasting constructivist and intensive–explicit instruction and suggesting ways in which the two approaches may be integrated. Perhaps the strengths of each approach can accommodate the limitations of each. For example, if intensive–explicit learning takes place within the authentic, holistic learning experiences proposed by constructivist instruction, students will be more likely to generalize and internalize their learning. In the same light, if IE instruction is used to teach essential communication, literacy, computational, and social skills and strategies to students who are experiencing constructivist instruction, perhaps students will be better prepared to participate in activities that call for social construction of knowledge.

More research can help educators better understand how the two approaches can be integrated. My conception of mechanical and metaphorical knowledge may be one starting point. Although both mechanical and metaphorical knowledge exist along a continuum, the suggestion that intensive–explicit instruction is more appropriate for mechanical knowledge and that constructivist instruction is more appropriate for metaphorical knowledge appears to have face validity.

Polanyi's work provides another way of thinking about how to bring together the two approaches. Specifically, the distinction Polanyi makes between explicit and tacit knowledge provides a framework for better understanding how constructivist and intensive–explicit instruction can be integrated. The goal of internalization or generalization, central to both instructional approaches, may be better understood as the transformation of explicit knowledge into tacit knowledge, the act Polanyi refers to as "indwelling."

Finally, Culler's "competence" is a possible model for bridging the gap between constructivist and intensive-explicit instruction, as is Eisner's "connoisseurship." Chomsky's linguistic competence can be extended, as Culler suggests, to include literary competence and, I submit, scientific competence, mathematical competence, historical competence, as well as competence in many other disciplines. Therefore, if our experience of a phenomenon is dependent upon the development of "competence" through internalization of extensive tacit and explicit knowledge, educators need to consider carefully what kind of knowledge enables competence in each discipline. We need to better understand when IE instruction and constructivist instruction are most appropriate for teaching prior knowledge for these competencies, competencies that will enable people to construct richer, more meaningful experiences in life.

FINAL THOUGHTS

This chapter began with the story of Alex, who was diagnosed as having a learning disability but who learned a complicated video game so quickly that he mastered it in 4 days. The two instructional approaches considered here suggest different reasons that Alex learned his video game so well.

A constructivist might suggest that Alex was successful because he was working on an authentic task that was meaningful to him, that he felt free to make errors, that the game provided him a chance to internalize learning in a real-world, (if a video game can be considered real world) experience. Alex was not learning prerequisite skills for video games; he was learning while playing the game.

A teacher using intensive–explicit instruction might see Alex's success from a different perspective. Perhaps Alex learned the game quickly because his learning was goal-oriented, and his practice attempts were structured with increasing difficulty so he was able to master skills and keep moving forward to more complicated levels of the game. Maybe Alex was successful because he received immediate feedback on his correct and incorrect moves, and thus learned to eliminate errors and play the game with mastery.

Looking at Alex's learning from these different vantage points provides us with a much broader picture of the boy's learning experience. In brief, we have the potential to see more because we see from two different perspectives.

I hope that this discussion illustrates how better understanding constructivist and intensive–explicit instruction holds the potential to help us see more. By continuing to look at *constructivist* and *intensive–explicit* instruction from each other's vantage point, and by looking for innovative and powerful ways to integrate these two approaches, I hope we will learn how to render education more effective, authentic, and enjoyable for all children. Perhaps by learning how to better blend constructivist and intensive–explicit instruction, we can learn how to better create learning experiences that children find as captivating as Alex did his video game.

REFERENCES

Bandura, A. (1971). *Social learning theory*. New York: General Learning Press.

Bernstein, R. J. (1991). *Beyond objectivism and relativism*. Philadelphia: University or Pennsylvania Press.

Bohm, D. (1996). *On dialogue*. New York: Routledge.

Borkowski, J., & Muthukrishna, N. (1992). Moving metacognition into the classroom: "Working models" and effective strategy teaching. In E. McIntyre & M. Pressley (Eds.), *Balanced instruction: Strategies and skills in whole language*. Norwood, MA: Christopher–Gordon.

Brooks, J. G., & Brooks, M. G. (1993). *In search of understanding: The case for constructivist classrooms*. Alexandria, VA: Association for Supervision and Curriculum Development.

Cromer, A. (1997). *Connected knowledge: Science, philosophy, and education*. New York: Oxford University Press.

Csikszentmihalyi, M. (1991). *Flow: The psychology of optimal experience*. New York: HarperCollins.

Culler, J. (1975). *Structuralist poetics: Structuralism, linguistics and the study of literature*. London: Routledge & Kegan Paul.

Deshler, D., & Schumaker, J. B. (1988). An instructional model for teaching students how to learn. In J. L. Graden, J. E. Zins & M. J. Curtis (Eds.), *Alternative educational delivery systems: Enhancing instructional options for all students*. (pp. 391–411). Washington, DC: National Association of School Psychologists.

Deshler, D. D., & Schumaker, J. B. (1993). Strategy mastery by at-risk students is not a simple matter. *The Elementary School Journal, 94,* 153–167.

Deshler, D., Shumaker, J., Bulgren, J., Lenz, K., Jantzen, J.–E., & Adams, G., et al. (2001). Making learning easier: Connecting new knowledge to things students already know. *Teaching Exceptional Children, 33*(4), 82–85.

Deshler, D. D., Schumaker, J. B., Lenz, B. K., Bulgren, J. A., Hock, M. F., Knight, J., et al. (2001). Ensuring content-area learning by secondary students with learning disabilities. *Learning Disabilities Research and Practice, 16*(2), 96–108.

Eisner, E. W. (1991). *The enlightened eye: Qualitative inquiry and the enhancement of educational practice*. New York: Macmillan.

Ellis, E., Deshler, D. D., Lenz, B. K., Schumaker, J. B., & Clark, F. L. (1991). An instructional model for teaching learning strategies. *Focus on Exceptional Children, 23*(6), 1–24.

Englert, C. S., Garmon, A., Mariage, T., Rozendal, M., Tarrant, K., & Urba, J. (1995). The early literacy project: Connecting across the literacy curriculum. *Learning Disability Quarterly, 18*(4), 253–275.

Englert, C. S., & Marriage, T. V. (1996). A sociocultural perspective: Teaching ways-of-thinking and ways-of-talking in a literary community. *Learning Disabilities Research and Practice, 11*(3), 157–167.

Friere, P. (1997). *Pedagogy of the oppressed* (M. B. Ramos, Trans. 20th–Anniversary ed.). New York: Continuum.

Gildroy, P. (2001). *The development and evaluation of an instructional modeling routine for students with learning disabilities.* Unpublished doctoral dissertation, University of Kansas: Kansas.

Glasersfeld, E. V. (1995). *Radical constructivism.* Washington, DC: Falmer Press.

Graham, S., Harris, K., & Larsen, L. (2001). Prevention and intervention of writing difficulties for students with learning disabilities. *Learning Disabilities Research and Practice, 16*(2), 74–84.

Harris, K., & Graham, S. R. (1994). Constructivism: Principles, paradigms, and integration. *Journal of Special Education, 28*(3), 233–247.

Harris, K., & Graham, S. (1996). Constructivism and students with special needs: Issues in the classroom. *Learning Disabilities Research and Practice, 11*(3), 134–137.

Harris, K., & Graham, S. (1999). Programmatic intervention research: Illustrations from the evolution of self-regulated strategy development. *Learning Disability Quarterly, 22*(Fall, 1999), 251–262.

Heshusius, L. (1995). Holism and special education: There is no substitute for real life purposes and processes. In T. M. Skrtic (Ed.), *Disability and democracy: Reconstructing (special) education for postmodernity* (pp. 166–189). New York: Columbia University, Teachers College.

Iser, W. (1978). *The act of reading: A theory of aesthetic response.* Baltimore: The Johns Hopkins University Press.

Kline, F. M., Schumaker, J. B., & Deshler, D. D. (1991). The development and validation of feedback routines for instructing students with learning disabilities. *LD Forum, 14*, 191–207.

Kuhn, T. (1970). *The structure of scientific revolutions* (2d ed.). Chicago: University of Chicago Press.

Mariage, T. V. (2000). Constructing educational possibilities: A sociolinguistic examination of meaning-making in "sharing chair." *Learning Disability Quarterly, 23*(Spring 2000), 79–103.

Meichebaum, D. M. (1977). *Cognitive behavior modification.* New York: Plenum.

Mercer, C. D., Jordan, L., & Miller, S. P. (1996). Constructivistic math instruction for diverse learners. *Learning Disabilities Research and Practice, 11*(3), 147–156.

Mercer, C. D., Lane, H. B., Jordan, L., Allsop, D. H., & Eisele, M. R. (1996). Empowering teachers and students with instructional choices in inclusive settings. *Remedial and Special Education, 17*(4), 226–236.

Mok, C. (2003, January). Idea fest. *Fast Company,* p. 103.

Moll, L. C. (1990). Introduction. In L. C. Moll (Ed.), *Vygotsky and education: Instructional implications and applications of sociohistorical psychology.* Cambridge, UK: Cambridge University Press.

Moshman, D. (1982). Exogenous, endogenous, and dialectical constructivism. *Developmental Review, 2*, 371–384.

Phillips, D. C. (2000). An opinionated account of the constructivist landscape. In D. C. Phillips (Ed.), *Constructivism in education* (pp. 1–16). Chicago: National Society for the Study of Education/University of Chicago Press.

Piaget, J. (1954). *The construction of reality in the child.* New York: Ballantine Books, Inc.

Polanyi, M. (1966). *The tacit dimension.* London: Routledge & Kegan Paul.

Poplin, M. S. (1988a). Holistic/constructivist principles of the teaching/ learning process: Implications for the field of learning disabilities. *Journal of Learning Disabilities, 21*(7), 401–416.

Poplin, M. S. (1988b). The reductionist fallacy in learning disabilities: Replicating the past by reducing the present. *Journal of Learning Disabilities, 21*(7), 389–400.

Poplin, M. S. (1995). Looking through other lenses and listening to other voices: Stretching the boundaries of learning disabilities. *Journal of Learning Disabilities, 28*, 392–398.

Pressley, M., Burkell, J., Cariglia–Bull, T., Lysynchuk, L., McGoldrick, J. A., Schneider, B., et al. (1990). *Cognitive strategy instruction that really improves children's academic performance.* Cambridge, MA: Brookline Books.

Pressley, M., Harris, K., & Marks, M. B. (1992). But good strategy instructors are constructivists! *Educational Psychology Review, 4*, 3–31.

Pressley, M., Hogan, K., Wharton–McDonald, R., Mistretta, J., & Ettenberger, S. (1996). The challenges of instructional scaffolding: The challenges of instruction that support student thinking. *Learning Disabilities Research and Practice, 11*(3), 138–146.

Reid, D. K., Robinson, S. J., & Bunsen, T. D. (1995). Empiricism and beyond: Expanding the boundaries of special education. *Remedial and Special Education, 16*(3), 131–141.

Roehler, L. R., & Duffy, G. G. (1984). Direct explanation of comprehension processes. In G. G. Duffy, L. R. Roehler, & J. Mason (Eds.), *Comprehension instruction: Perspectives and suggestions* (pp. 265–280). New York: Longman.

Schumaker, J. B., Denton, P. H., & Deshler, D. D. (1984). *The paraphrasing strategy*. Lawrence: University of Kansas.

Schwandt, T. A. (1994). Constructivist, interpretive approaches to human inquiry. In Denzin & Lincoln, 1994, pp. 118–137.

Segal, L. (2001). *The dream of reality: Heinz von Foerster's constructivism* (2d ed.). New York: Springer.

Seligman, M. E. P. (1992). *Helplessness: On development, depression, and death*. New York: W. H. Freeman and Co.

Skrtic, T. M., Sailor, W., & Gee, K. (1996). Voice, collaboration and inclusion: Democratic themes in educational and social reform initiatives. *Remedial and Special Education, 17*(3), 142–157.

Stanovich, K. E. (1994). Constructivism in reading. *Journal of Special Education, 28*(3), 259–274.

Vygotsky, L. S. (1978). *Mind in society* (M. Cole, V. John-Steiner, S. Scribner & E. Souberman, Trans.). Cambridge, MA: Harvard University Press.

Wood, D., Bruner, J., & Ross, G. (1976). The role of tutoring in problem solving. *Journal of Child Psychology and Psychiatry, 17*, 89–100.

Balanced Literacy Instruction

Michael Pressley, Alysia Roehrig, Kristen Bogner,
Lisa M. Raphael, and Sara Dolezal

A few years ago, Pressley (1998) wrote a book about elementary-level literacy instruction, *Reading Instruction That Works: The Case for Balanced Teaching.* A main message in that book is that excellent elementary literacy instruction balances skills instruction (e.g., phonics, comprehension strategies teaching) and holistic literacy opportunities (reading of authentic literature, composing in response to text). In making that case, Pressley reviewed substantial evidence validating the positive impacts on literacy achievement of many elements of elementary literacy instruction. He also reviewed evidence that beginning literacy classrooms in which achievement is high are typified by balanced teaching.

The message was strong and clear that the two warring camps in elementary literacy were both wrong. The available evidence favors neither those promoting predominantly skills-focused literacy teaching nor those favoring environments filled with holistic experiences to the exclusion of skills instruction (e.g., whole language).

The term "balance" has definitely caught on. As is often the case, however, many began to wrap themselves in the term without regard to whether their position was consistent with Pressley's (1998) intention in *Reading Instruction That Works*. Thus, in the past several years, many other books have used the phrase "balanced instruction" or some variation of this phrase. Some of these recent books suggest heavy doses of skills, with many pages devoted to conceptualizing, describing, and defending skills instruction while mentioning holistic opportunities only in passing. Others devote many pages to conceptualizing, describing, and defending holistic teaching, and recommend skills instruction as something that can be done in the context of holistic reading and writing and only when the need arises.

We should have anticipated imbalanced conceptions of balanced teaching. Before Pressley wrote the book on balanced literacy instruction, he edited one with

Ellen McIntyre (McIntyre & Pressley, 1996). That text offered a variety of conceptions of balance, from conceptions more heavily favoring skills teaching to those clearly in the whole language camp. That somewhat confusing mishmash of conceptions, in fact, motivated the emphasis in Pressley's subsequent book that balanced instruction really means a lot of skills instruction in the context of massive holistic teaching!

Since his 1998 book, nothing has happened to persuade Pressley that he erred in favoring balanced instruction as conceived in that volume, despite the dual perspectives—those of some skills enthusiasts who believe that balanced instruction is simply whole language in thin disguise and some whole language theorists who view balanced instruction as skills instruction warmed over. As critics took aim, Pressley and his colleagues just kept studying effective and ineffective elementary instruction. Whenever they have found an elementary classroom in which literacy engagement was high, they found balanced teaching as conceived in the 1998 book, as well as evidence that literacy development was on course.

In this chapter, we review the evidence for balanced literacy instruction in the elementary years, focusing especially on recent developments that increase confidence in the 1998 conception. In doing so, we specifically make the case that the balanced instructional model is particularly appropriate and beneficial for students who have initial difficulties in learning to read and write. What will become apparent by the end of the article is that balanced instruction requires knowledge of how to carry out effective skills instruction as well as high awareness of how to teach holistic reading and writing. Balanced classrooms reveal both forms of instruction, teaching that is both complicated and coherent, as well as tailored to the needs of individual students.

BALANCING MANY ELEMENTS OF INSTRUCTION

A central claim made here is that excellent literacy instruction is balanced with respect to skills and holistic components. The following discussion explains how we know this to be the case.

Survey of Nominated-Effective Primary Teachers

Pressley, Rankin, and Yokoi (1996) surveyed well-respected primary-grade teachers about their literacy instruction practices. The first challenge was to identify a sample of teachers. To do so, Pressley et al. wrote to 50 reading supervisors across the nation and asked each of them to nominate one kindergarten, one grade-1, and one grade-2 teacher in their district as effective in educating their students to become readers and writers. In general, the supervisors nominated teachers whom they had observed directly and who had excellent reputations with administrators, other teachers, and/or parents as being effective in stimulating literacy development.

In the first phase of the investigation, each nominated teacher was asked to list 10 instructional practices essential to his or her literacy instruction. Teachers who responded in the first phase mentioned more than 300 different practices. In the second phase of the study, the teachers responded to a more focused questionnaire, which posed one question for each of the 300 practices cited in the first phase of the study, to determine the prevalence of the various practices.

The overarching finding in the study was that these primary-grade teachers did many different things to support and encourage the literacy development of their students. The teachers in this study reported being extremely eclectic in their literacy instruction. Yes, this group favored whole-language principles, with 97% reporting that their instruction reflects at least somewhat the tenets of whole-language instruction. Yet they also reported offering frequent skills instruction, both in the context of actual reading and writing and in lessons in which the skills were isolated and presented in a decontextualized situation.

Their responses did not seem to be consistent with any of the more extreme perspectives that have been offered in the literacy debates of the 20th century. They certainly did not advocate skills-first instruction, nor did their responses reveal anything consistent with a whole-word approach. Their version of whole language was tempered by much attention to skills instruction, although the more committed the teacher was to whole language, the less skills instruction he or she reported.

These teachers were committed to balancing a number of components, some more consistent with whole language and some more consistent with skills instruction. Although a number of primary-level researchers (e.g., Adams, 1990; Cazden, 1992; Delpit, 1986; Duffy, 1991; Fisher & Hiebert, 1990; McCaslin, 1989; Pressley, 1994; Stahl, McKenna, & Pagnucco, 1994) had advocated such balancing before this study appeared, Pressley, Rankin, and Yokoi (1996) fleshed out the balancing model. Their teacher reports raised the possibility that the balance model was extremely complicated. Based on Pressley, Rankin, and Yokoi (1996), effective curricular balancing is analogous to juggling hundreds of balls in the air. To further complicate this intricate juggling act, the precise balance of balls varies from child to child and situation to situation during the school day.

Followup on Literacy Development

One of the most interesting and surprising findings of the survey of nominated-effective primary-grades teachers was the teachers' reports about teaching struggling beginning readers. Basically, they said that instruction for struggling readers did not differ qualitatively from instruction for their other students. Yes, skills instruction was more extensive and intensive than with normally achieving students, but struggling readers also were immersed in literature and writing experiences.

This finding was intriguing enough to prompt Rankin-Erickson and Pressley (2000) to follow it up. Specifically, the follow-up research surveyed primary-level teachers who are especially concerned with struggling readers—that is, primary-level special education teachers whom their administrators considered to be highly effective in stimulating literacy development. The methodology in the study was similar to the methodology in the Pressley et al. (1996) investigation, with an open-ended question (What are the essential elements in your literacy instruction?) followed by a detailed questionnaire asking teachers about each of the instructional practices they mentioned in their open-ended responses.

Just as was the case with the survey of nominated-effective primary-level teachers, the nominated-effective, primary-level special educators mentioned hundreds of specific elements of instruction in their responses to the open-ended question. The second questionnaire tapped 436 instructional practices, as had been the case in the Pressley, Rankin, and Yokoi (1996) study.

The most interesting, overarching conclusion of the study was that the instruction reported by the nominated-effective, primary-level special educators was not much different from the instruction reported by the nominated-effective first-grade teachers. They described a great deal of skills instruction in their lessons, but they also reported extensive literature and writing experiences. In general, the explicitness and completeness of skills instruction was reported as increasing with the severity of the students' difficulties in learning to read.

Although some skills instruction was portrayed as decontextualized, most skills instruction was reported to occur in the context of real reading and writing. These teachers were emphatic in stating that whole language and skills instruction are not contradictory but, rather, complementary approaches in their instruction of struggling beginning readers. The teachers reported providing education to students in special education that was not much different from the instruction they provided to other students. The special education students did receive more intensive sound-, letter-, and word-level skills instruction, but they also received the rich mix of literacy experiences that excellent primary-grades general education teachers reported providing to average and above-average students.

Observations of Outstanding Teachers

Pressley and his associates followed up the surveys with observational studies of some outstanding primary-level teachers—in particular, outstanding grade-1 teachers. The observations of classrooms were complemented by interviews. The data were analyzed using a method known as *constant comparison* (Strauss & Corbin, 1990). The initial result was a detailed summary of the elements of instruction for each classroom in the study and how those elements were related to one another. Then the results for individual classroom were analyzed to generate more general conclusions across classrooms.

Upstate New York Study

In the first such study (Wharton-McDonald, Pressley, & Hampston, 1998), administrators and reading specialists in a number of upstate New York school districts were asked to nominate a first-grade teacher in their district whose teaching was considered exemplary in promoting literacy, and another teacher in the district who was considered more typical of the district's grade-1 teachers. When the study began, the sample consisted of 10 teachers, 5 of whom were nominated as outstanding in promoting their students' literacy and 5 of whom were nominated as more typical.

Several observers made multiple visits to the 10 first-grade classrooms. The visits to a classroom continued until the observers were confident that they were coming to no new insights about what was going on in the classroom. The teacher interviews were driven by the observations. That is, questions were designed to clarify what the observers had seen during the classroom visits, and each interview was tailored to what they had seen in each teacher's own classroom.

As part of the observations, the researchers explicitly looked for indicators of literacy achievement in classrooms, because the researchers did not want to accept the school district's appraisals of teachers as exemplary or more typical without any corroboration. Three indications of achievement characterized classrooms with high literacy achievement compared to those with less achievement:

1. By the end of the study, reading achievement clearly was better in some classrooms than others. That is, in some classrooms most students were reading books at or above grade level by the end of first grade, whereas in other classrooms many students were reading books well below grade level.

2. By the end of the year, writing was more advanced in some classrooms than in other classrooms. In some classrooms most students were writing longer than one-page stories that were reasonably coherent. In these same classrooms, the students' punctuation, capitalization, and spelling were often quite good. In contrast, in the classrooms taught by more typical teachers, the stories were much shorter on average (e.g., perhaps two or three lines long) with less evidence that students understood and correctly used punctuation, capitalization, and spelling conventions.

3. In some classrooms student engagement was much more consistent than in other classrooms (i.e., in some classrooms, more of the students engaged in productive reading, writing, or other academic activity more of the time than in other classrooms). Most striking, classrooms with high reading achievement also showed high writing achievement. Moreover, in the classes with high reading and writing achievement, most students seemed to be working productively on literacy tasks most of the time.

During the course of the study, one teacher dropped out because of personal reasons unrelated to the study, leaving a total of 9 teachers who were observed and interviewed over the course of the year. Of these nine, three stood out in promoting reading achievement, writing achievement, and engagement. (Two of these originally were nominated as outstanding teachers, and one was originally nominated as more typical of his district.) Three teachers stood out as not being as successful as the others in getting their children to read and write and be engaged in literacy activities. Three were in the middle with respect to success in promoting their students' literacy and engagement.

In addition to differences in achievement, some striking differences became apparent in the teaching in classrooms with high achievement on average, especially relative to the classrooms with low achievement on average. In the three classes in which reading and writing achievement seemed especially positive, the students seemed most motivated to achieve, with high engagement in these classes. Students in these classes were reading and writing all the time:

Put simply, literacy was part of virtually everything that went on in the top three classrooms. When we asked one teacher to estimate what percentage of her students' day was spent actively reading, she replied:

> I would say everything we do in here…is so integrated that, to do any activity in here, they need to read something. So I would say for everything we do in here, there is a reading portion. So most of the day…they are immersed in that text! So—well, you just find ways to incorporate it. It *can't* separate. You can't be driving along and say, "Oh, I've got to read that sign. So I'd better stop, read the sign, and then go on." It's just there. It's part of your day. And that's how it is in here, too. (Wharton-McDonald et al., 1998, p. 119)

In fact, in these classes, 90% of the time when observers looked around and estimated the percentage of students who were on task, 90% of the students were on task. The high-achieving classrooms were busy classrooms, abuzz with reading and writing activity.

Although all nine teachers combined skills instruction with reading literature and writing, the teachers with the highest achieving students seemed to integrate the skills instruction with the holistic activities better than did the teachers whose students had lower levels of achievement. During the interviews the teachers with high-achieving students were emphatic that neither an exclusive skills orientation nor an exclusive whole-language approach would fit their students well. According to one of the three teachers with the highest achievement, teaching beginning reading is

> a fine balance between immersing the child in whole language and teaching through…sounds, going back to using skills. . . . If you don't have a balance, it's kind of like trying to fit a square through a circle. It doesn't work. You don't connect with everyone if you don't use a variety of [teaching] strategies. (Wharton-McDonald et al., 1998, p. 114)

Given the predominance of the whole-language model in upstate New York, we were struck at how open these teachers were about their skills instruction, with two of the three even using basal materials to develop phonics skills in students. In contrast, a teacher in the low-achieving group explained the purpose of her reading groups in this way:

> Well, basically, when we read out of the basal books, it's pretty much reading the next story, whatever that may be, and then there are some. . . . workbook pages. . . . The workbook page itself is an assessment of what they read—and how they follow, even down the page. . . . But just orally listening to them read; watching them to see if they're paying attention, following along while others read. You know, you can tell so much just in that short time—how they're coming along." (Wharton-McDonald et al., 1998, p. 116)

What was also striking during every visit to the three most balanced classrooms was the number of skill-oriented mini-lessons. These teachers seemed to monitor their students carefully to detect which ones needed a mini-lesson and when they needed it (e.g., a mini-lesson on the sound "h" makes as a student struggled to spell the word "heart"). Despite the frequency of mini-lessons, these classes never seemed like skills-driven classrooms, because the students were immersed in reading excellent children's trade books and in writing real stories and essays.

In contrast to the teachers of students with the highest achievement, the other teachers who were observed did not integrate skills instruction and holistic experiences nearly as well. Rather, classrooms seemed to have times set aside for skills teaching and times set aside for reading and writing. For example, in observing classes with lower achievement, the spelling lessons had no later connection to spelling during writing (invented spellings in compositions were accepted, even for words covered in spelling lessons). The connection between skills learning and application in the highest achieving classrooms was not as apparent in the other classrooms observed in this investigation.

Classrooms with the highest achievement always had a great deal going on—in particular, a lot of instruction. Even mundane events, such as filling a stapler, were transformed into lessons in the classrooms with the highest achievement (e.g., the teacher asked students to name the color of the stapler—which was silver, a new vocabulary word for them). In the higher-achieving classrooms, classroom routines, such as dismissal, were transformed into instruction (e.g., by requiring students to spell words to get into the dismissal line). In contrast, instruction was not nearly as much an every-minute thing in first-grade classes with lower achievement. Many more lessons in the higher-achieving classes involved scaffolding; the teacher provided just enough support so the student could begin to make progress on a task but not so much as to be doing the task for the student.

Scaffolding required that the teacher monitor students carefully and consistently. It also required that the teacher thoroughly understood the tasks students were attempting (e.g., having a complete knowledge of phonics to be able to scaffold students' sounding out words). Scaffolding was everywhere in the-high achieving classrooms and much more prominent in the higher-achieving than the lower-achieving classes.

In the higher-achieving classrooms students were strongly encouraged to do things on their own as much as possible. As children were taught word attack, spelling, and comprehension strategies, they also were taught to use the strategies whenever they were appropriate. When students did self-regulate, teachers with high-achieving classes often noted the self-regulation and reinforced it. Thus, after a boy named Kevin self-corrected himself during reading, his teacher remarked, "When Kevin made a mistake, what did he do? . . . Yes, he went back over it. It's okay to make mistakes." Teachers with high-achieving students consistently encouraged students to self-monitor how well they were doing and to make corrections as necessary.

The higher-achieving classrooms revealed a thorough integration of reading and writing. Consistently, students were asked to respond to what they read by writing.

Also, students in the high-achieving classes did a great deal of reading of their own writing, especially their rough drafts, as part of revising. Often, writing assignments required research, so students had to find materials in the library and other places and then read them. Then the students wrote about the topic by incorporating ideas from the materials they found in the library. Projects such as this permitted an integration of reading, writing, and content learning. These crosscurricular connections were prominent in the high-achieving classrooms.

The teachers with high-achieving classes had high expectations that their students could learn and that they could be readers and writers. The effective teachers communicated a "can-do" attitude to their students. Discipline was not a problem in classrooms characterized by high achievement. These teachers had a set of routines for the tasks that were repeated every day, with morning meetings, movement to special classes, and dismissals all taking place efficiently. Clearly, in these classrooms much planning had occurred in advance of the school day, but at the same time these teachers seemed to be able to accommodate flexibly the moment-by-moment needs of their students, many of which were unpredictable (e.g., providing mini-lessons to small groups of students when a need became apparent).

In summary, the strong classrooms in the Wharton-McDonald et al. (1998) study evidenced a balancing of a number of instructional components. Of particular relevance, all the students in the very best classrooms were integrated well into the balanced instruction, with every student receiving both skills instruction and holistic experiences at his or her competency level.

National Study of Grade-1 Teachers

After Wharton-McDonald et al., Pressley et al. (2001; see also Pressley, Allington, Wharton-McDonald, Block, & Morrow, 2001) studied a national sample of grade-1 teachers. Again, some teachers were outstanding in promoting achievement of their students and others were less effective. As in Wharton-McDonald et al. (1998), the balancing of skills teaching and holistic instruction was more certain in the strong classrooms than the weaker classrooms.

Also consistent with the Wharton-McDonald et al. (1998) study, much instruction was going on—of letter- and sound-level skills, word recognition skills, vocabulary, comprehension strategies, and writing strategies. And the students were reading excellent literature, literature that expands children's knowledge and understanding of the world. Every child in these classrooms was immersed in this rich multicomponent instructional world, a world in which every child received a balance of skills instruction and holistic experiences appropriate for him or her.

Motivation Studies

Most recently, Pressley and his colleagues had noted that the effective teachers they studied engaged their students in literacy instruction. They did much to motivate students to read and write. Thus, Bogner, Raphael, and Pressley (in press) decided to focus a study of grade-1 literacy instruction on motivation. They observed 7 grade-1 classrooms for a year. Two of these classrooms were distinguished in that their students were much more engaged in reading and writing than in the other class-rooms. The engagement was not accidental, however, for the engaging teachers, compared to the other five teachers, did much to motivate their students. In fact, the two most engaging teachers each used more than 40 different mechanisms to moti-vate their students to do things literate (Raphael, Bogner, Pressley, Shell, & Masters, 2001), including the following:

encouraging cooperative learning
downplaying competition
holding students accountable for their performances
projecting high expectations
scaffolding student learning
making library and crosscurricular connections to content covered in class
encouraging autonomy and choice
having a gentle, caring manner
interacting with students positively, making home-school connections
providing opportunistic mini-lessons
reteaching when students failed to understand the first time
making personal connections with students
supporting appropriate risk-taking
making the classroom fun
encouraging creative and independent thinking by students.

The classrooms of the two really engaging teachers were distinguished by interest-ing content and tasks, appropriately challenging material, and depth of coverage. The really engaging teachers also presented abstract content personally and con-cretely, had clear learning objectives, used effective praise and feedback, modeled thinking and problem-solving skills, encouraged stick-with-it-ness, and explained the relevance of what was being taught. The engaging teachers encouraged their stu-dents to believe they could achieve their goals with effort. Their classroom manage-ment was superb, so good that disciplinary events rarely occurred and were hardly noticeable when they did. The engaging teachers always knew what every member of the class was doing and intervened when students seemed puzzled or were not making progress.

One of the exemplary teachers from the nationwide study of effective first-grade literacy instruction (Pressley, Wharton-McDonald, et al., 2001) came from a district that implemented the Reading Recovery program. Reading Recovery is an early intervention program used typically with first-grade students who are making slow progress in learning to read in the general classroom (Lyons, Pinnell, & DeFord, 1993). Students are taken out of the classroom for a half hour daily for the one-to-one tutoring that is Reading Recovery.

These sessions follow a structured format, balancing phonics with strategy instruction during scaffolded reading and writing. The tutoring can continue for as long as a semester. The exemplary teacher, who had been trained as a Reading

Recovery tutor, was incorporating into her classroom teaching many of the instructional practices and strategies of Reading Recovery.

That this one teacher incorporated so much of Reading Recovery into classroom instruction prompted Roehrig, Pressley, and Sloup (2001) to explore how other teachers in the same district were transferring into their classrooms what they had learned as Reading Recovery tutors. Ten primary-level teachers were observed over the course of two years. Again, the method of constant comparison was used (Strauss & Corbin, 1990) in the iterative process of data collection and analysis. Teachers with more training and experience in Reading Recovery were more likely to use the instructional practices and teach the strategies emphasized in Reading Recovery in their general classroom instruction, and their instruction seemed more like the instruction of exemplary teachers in the earlier studies (Roehrig et al., in press). In particular, the literacy instruction of these teachers was a complex balance of direct instruction, often in the form of mini-lessons and in the context of authentic reading and writing activities, with the teachers being particularly sensitive to the competencies of each student and the scaffolding necessary for development of self-regulation.

As this article is being published, Sara Dolezal, Lindsey Mohan, Melissa Vincent, and Michael Pressley are carrying out a similar analysis at the grade-3 level. The preliminary results are similar: The minority of grade-3 teachers are really engaging, and the engaging teachers are doing much to motivate their students relative to the less engaging teachers.

The Pressley group has generated a great deal of research establishing that excellent elementary instruction entails a complex balancing of a number of components including both skills-based and holistic tasks. Also, much goes on to encourage students' will to learn, to encourage their engagement in literacy-development tasks, especially real reading and writing.

WELL VALIDATED COMPONENTS OF BALANCED ELEMENTARY LITERACY INSTRUCTION

If the results described in the last section have not been received positively by those who are strongly committed to skills instruction or whole language, they have been received enthusiastically by many others who recognize that effective instruction must include multiple components. Even so, for the most part, literacy researchers have concerned themselves with particular elements of instruction as they have carried out research on effective practice. This is consistent with the true experiment being a high ideal for establishing a cause-and-effect relationship between an instructional practice and an educational outcome (National Reading Panel, 2000).

True experiments lend themselves well to evaluating individual components of instruction. In fact, the many true experiments and quasi-experiments focusing on reading instruction have provided a great deal of information about components that can be added to instruction with benefit. (Quasi-experiments involve comparisons between instructed and noninstructed students when assigning students randomly to the instructional condition was not possible; the hallmark of the true experiment is random assignment to conditions). Readers should note especially that every one of the well validated components detailed in this section was detected in the effective classrooms that were the focus of research summarized in the foregoing section.

Most of the work reviewed in this section also is particularly pertinent in the context of a discussion of students with learning difficulties, for many of the single-component interventions have been aimed at specific problems that some children experience as they learn to read. Struggling young readers certainly have been studied much more extensively with respect to single-component reading interventions than have average or above-average young readers.

Phonemic Awareness and the Alphabetic Principle

Phonemic awareness is a special type of metacognitive awareness. It is awareness that words are composed of separable sounds that are blended together. The *alphabetic principle* is the awareness that sounds are represented in words by the letters of the alphabet. These fundamental awarenesses are critical for the beginning reader. Without awareness that letters map sounds that can be blended together, there would be little incentive for paying attention to the individual letters of words, and lessons about individual letter sounds would make little sense.

Phonemic awareness, in particular, has received a great deal of attention, largely because of demonstrations that low phonemic awareness in the early grades predicts reading problems in the middle grades (e.g., Bowey, 1995; Juel, 1988; Näslund & Schneider, 1996; Stuart & Masterson, 1992). More positively, however, phonemic awareness can be developed through instruction, and when it is, subsequent reading difficulties are reduced (e.g., Bradley & Bryant, 1983, 1985, 1991; Byrne & Fielding-Barnsley, 1991, 1993, 1995; Lundberg, Frost, & Peterson, 1988; Lie, 1991; O'Connor, Jenkins, & Slocum, 1995; Vellutino & Scanlon, 1987; Williams, 1980; Wise & Olson, 1995). Instruction typically involves word games, such as detecting words that rhyme, pronouncing words when one sound is removed from another word (e.g., What does *mat* sound like if the *m* is removed? What does *mat* sound like if the *t* is removed?), and pronouncing words when a sound is added (e.g., What does *at* sound like if an *m* is added at the beginning? What does *ma* sound like if a *t* is added to the end?).

This instruction typically occurs over the course of months for a few minutes each day. It increases phonemic awareness in the short term and contributes to reading skill in the long term, which provides incentive for including such instruction in the early primary years (i.e., kindergarten and grade 1), especially to students who lack phonemic awareness upon entering kindergarten or grade 1.

In arguing for including phonemic awareness in literacy instruction, we are emphatic that phonemic awareness instruction is not a one-time quick fix. Development of phonemic awareness in kindergarten and grade 1 accounts for only a very small proportion of reading success in the middle elementary grades (Bus &

van IJzendoorn, 1999). This warning is necessary because some policymakers seem to believe that instruction in phonemic awareness is a cure for preventing reading difficulties. In fact, it is only one ingredient in the cure, with the best medicine being a balanced reading instructional program involving skills instruction and holistic opportunities.

Particularly relevant in a discussion of balanced reading instruction are demonstrations of the effectiveness of phonemic awareness in programs that are otherwise whole language in outlook. The best known—and a well-designed—study was offered by Castle, Riach, and Nicholson (1994). Participants in the study were all enrolled in a whole language kindergarten. Students receiving phonemic awareness instruction participated in two 20-minute sessions a week, whereas control participants received instruction of skills not related to phonemic awareness. After 10 weeks of instruction, the phonemic awareness instruction improved the students' spelling skills as well as their sounding out of pseudowords. In general, inserting phonemic awareness into ongoing beginning literacy instructional environments has yielded positive effects on early reading skills (e.g., Blachman, Ball, Black, & Tangel, 1994; Byrne & Fielding-Barnsley, 1991, 1993, 1995).

Word Recognition Instruction

"The great debate" (Chall, 1967/1983) in beginning reading largely has been about what type of word recognition instruction works best with beginning readers. Chall's answer, based on the research available up until the middle 1960s, was that synthetic phonics instruction produced better readers than the whole word approach predominant in schools in those days. *Synthetic phonics* involves teaching students to map letters in words to their sounds and to pronounce the word by blending the sounds (i.e., sounding out the word). In contrast, the whole word approach involves learning words as wholes. After a number of whole words were known to readers as sight words, readers could be taught to analyze the sight words into their component sounds.

The whole word approach was used most prominently in the Dick-and-Jane readers published by Scott, Foreman, and Company. An especially important finding in the Chall analyses was that synthetic phonics seemed to be especially beneficial for weaker students.

Since the time of Chall's findings, a number of demonstrations have concurred that intensive synthetic phonics-type instruction can improve the word recognition skills of children who have difficulties with beginning reading (e.g., Alexander, Anderson, Heilman, Voeller, & Torgesen, 1991; Foorman, Francis, Fletcher, Schatschneider, & Mehta, 1998; Foorman, Francis, Novy, & Liberman, 1991; Lovett, Ransby, Hardwick, Johns, & Donaldson, 1989; Lovett et al., 1994; Manis, Custodio, & Szeszulski, 1993; Torgesen et al., 1996; Torgesen et al., 1999; Vellutino et al., 1996). Most children who have difficulties in initial word recognition problems can be helped by being taught how to sound out words using synthetic phonics.

Even so, synthetic phonics is not the only approach in the marketplace of word recognition interventions that seems to work with struggling beginning readers. People also can recognize new words by analogy to words they know already. They recognize *bat* because they already know *at;* they recognize *bar* because they already know *car.*

The best developed decoding-by-analogy program that I have encountered—the "Word ID" program (Gaskins, Gaskins, Anderson, & Schommer, 1995; Gaskins, Gaskins, & Gaskins, 1991, 1992)—was developed by Irene Gaskins, Linnea Ehri, and Patricia Cunningham at Benchmark School, a school dedicated to the education of students who struggle to learn to read. At the heart of the program are 120 key words that capture the key spelling patterns associated with the six English-language vowels. In addition, there are key words for the two sounds of *g* (e.g., girl, giraffe) and the two sounds for *c* (e.g., can, city). Some word parts that always sound the same (e.g., -tion) are taught as wholes.

For example, to decode the word *dispatcher,* the word-ID user would learn to identify a keyword for each syllable of the word. For the first syllable, *dis-,* the keyword *this* could be used, as the vowel *i* is followed by a consonant. For the second syllable, *-patch-,* the keyword could be *cat,* as the *a* in *-patch-* is followed by a consonant. For the final syllable, *-er, her* would apply. Thus, the student would know the sequence of vowel sounds in the word. The student, who is also learning the simple consonant-sound associations of English plus the digraphs and consonant blends, would then be able to sound out the word, *dispatcher.*

The program extends over several years at Benchmark, with keyword learning and practice of the approach both requiring substantial instructional time. After several years of experience with the program, most Benchmark students can use the memorized key words with ease to decode multisyllable words they have not encountered previously.

The effects of word ID and synthetic phonics instruction are roughly comparable (DeWitz, 1993; Lovett et al., 1994) in developing the decoding skills of beginning readers. Lovett et al.'s study was especially notable because it involved teaching students who had a great deal of previous difficulties in learning to read—much like Benchmark students. In general, teaching children to decode by analogy to known words is effective in developing young readers who can decode words they have not seen before (e.g., Ehri & Robbins, 1992; Goswami, 2000; Peterson & Haines, 1992; van Daal, Reitsma, & van der Leu, 1994).

Word ID lessons do much more than teach children to decode. When key words are introduced, children also learn the meanings of the key words. The key words also are used as part of story writing. The lessons include reading of patterned books. Students hear and read good literature every day they are enrolled at Benchmark.

The Benchmark approach is anything but a decoding-only approach. Rather, word-ID is embedded in a full literacy development program and is used to empower children so they can participate fully in reading real literature and writing. It is part of a balanced literacy program.

Although it is fine for a beginning reader to sound out words consciously or to use an analogy approach deliberately to recognize words, older, skilled readers use neither of these tactics deliberately. Rather, good readers simply recognize words they have encountered previously without making synthetic-phonics or word-ID efforts. That they can do so almost effortlessly frees up their consciousness (working memory) to attend to other aspects of the reading tasks—to comprehend what they are reading. The human mind can do only so many things at once, and word recognition requires so much effort that little consciousness remains for comprehension of the words being read (Baron, 1977; LaBerge & Samuels, 1974), let alone their combined meanings in sentences, paragraphs, and whole texts.

Fortunately, with experience in recognizing words comes automatic, rapid, accurate, and less effortful reading of individual words (Horn & Manis, 1987). Balanced word recognition instruction teaches tactics for effortful decoding but also provides many opportunities for students to practice reading words until word recognition is automatic.

Vocabulary Teaching

Good readers have good vocabularies (Anderson & Freebody, 1991; Nagy, Anderson, & Herman, 1987). Moreover, reading comprehension improves when vocabulary words are taught explicitly. For example, Beck, Perfetti, and McKeown (1982) taught grade-4 children a corpus of 104 words over a 5-month period. The children who received the instruction outperformed non-instructed children on subsequent comprehension tests (see also Beck & McKeown, 1991; Durso & Coggins, 1991).

Children learn the meanings of many words by experiencing the words in the actual world and in text worlds (e.g. Dickinson & Smith, 1994; Elley, 1989; Morrow, Pressley, Smith, & Smith, 1997; Pelligrini, Galda, Perlmutter, & Jones, 1994; Robbins & Ehri, 1994; Rosenhouse, Feitelson, Kita, & Goldstein, 1997). That is, they encounter the vocabulary without any explicit instruction in the words and their meanings (Stanovich, 1986; Sternberg, 1987). Such incidental learning is filled with potential pitfalls, however. For example, often the vocabulary meanings that readers infer from context are wrong (Miller & Gildea, 1987). Explicit teaching of the meanings of important vocabulary makes sense, for, in its absence, young readers may have substantial misconceptions about what critical vocabulary mean.

Comprehension Strategies

Good readers are aware of why they are reading a text. They overview text before reading, make predictions about the upcoming text, read selectively based on overviewing, associate ideas in text to what they already know, note whether their predictions and expectations about text content are being met, sometimes revise their thinking based on ideas in text, figure out the meanings of unfamiliar vocabulary based on context clues, underline and reread, make notes and paraphrase, interpret, evaluate the quality of the text, review important points as they conclude reading, and think about how they might use ideas they encounter in the text (Pressley & Afflerbach, 1995).

Balanced reading instruction can develop these active reading skills in students. A main approach for doing so is through instruction in comprehension strategies. A number of individual strategies can be taught, including predicting, questioning during reading, seeking clarification when confused, constructing mental images representing ideas in text, and summarizing (Pearson & Dole, 1987; Pearson & Fielding, 1991; Pressley, Johnson, Symons, McGoldrick, & Kurita, 1989). Of course, good readers do not use strategies such as these one at a time. Hence, balanced reading instruction includes teaching students to articulate these various strategies as they read.

Effective comprehension strategies instruction begins with extensive teacher explanation and modeling of strategies, followed by teacher-scaffolded use of the strategies, culminating in student self-regulated use of the strategies (e.g., Anderson, 1992; Brown, Pressley, Van Meter, & Schuder, 1996; Duffy et al., 1987). When the instruction has been successful, it always has been long-term, occurring over a semester to a school year at a minimum. The benefits are consistent and striking (e.g., Collins, 1991), with several compelling demonstrations that such teaching dramatically improves the reading comprehension of weaker readers.

Thus, balanced reading instruction includes modeling and explaining of comprehension strategies and student practice of the strategies with teacher support. Excellent teachers of comprehension strategies let students know that they should continue to use strategies when reading on their own. The teaching takes place across every school day in a well-balanced elementary literacy program, continuing as long as required to get all readers to use the strategies independently. Typically, this means that excellent comprehension strategies instruction occurs over a few years.

Self-Monitoring

Balanced reading instruction teaches children to be aware when they are having difficulties with reading and to react constructively to problems during reading. That is, balanced reading instruction requires teaching students to self-monitor their reading. Good readers know when they need to exert more effort to make sense of a text. For example, they are aware when they have sounded out a word but the sounded-out word does not make sense in the context (Isakson & Miller, 1976). When good readers have that feeling, they try rereading the word in question. Teaching young readers to self-monitor their reading of words makes good sense because they often read the wrong word (e.g., "Little Miss Muffett sat on her tupperware," Baker & Brown, 1984).

Balanced approaches to word recognition instruction incorporate a self-monitoring approach, in which readers are taught to pay attention to whether their decoding of words makes sense. When a word they read is not in synchrony with other ideas in the text and pictures accompanying the text (e.g., Iversen & Tunmer, 1993), balanced reading instruction emphasizes that students should try to decode it again (e.g., attempt carefully to sound it out).

Good readers also are aware when they are confused as they read; they self-monitor their comprehension (Baker & Brown, 1984). Teaching young readers to self-monitor and change their reading tactics when they are confused makes sense. Thus, balanced reading teachers teach their students to ask themselves, "Is what I am reading making sense?" They also teach students that initially confusing text often can be rendered sensible (e.g., by slowing down and reading more carefully, rereading confusing sections of text).

Extensive Reading

Many elementary classrooms have the banner "Read, Read, Read." It is good advice. Reading increases word recognition skills and the likelihood that beginning readers eventually will become fluent readers. Their vocabulary knowledge expands through reading. Reading high-quality books increases their world knowledge in general, which is critical, as well developed knowledge of the world facilitates comprehension in the future (Anderson & Pearson, 1984). For example, a child who has read a lot about Egypt will better understand an article about construction of the pyramids than will a reader who lacks prior knowledge about Egypt. In short, a balanced reading program should include extensive reading of good books, stories, and articles (e.g., Stanovich & Cunningham, 1993).

Despite the benefits of extensive reading, reading a great deal does not guarantee that a student will become an excellent reader. Many students actually get to college lacking the active comprehension skills of sophisticated readers (see Cordón & Day, 1996). That is why balanced reading programs include explicit teaching of comprehension strategies and self-monitoring, for these higher-order skills do not develop automatically from extensive reading, even if extensive reading does improve many word-level skills and increase factual knowledge.

Teaching Students to Relate Prior Knowledge While They Read

That extensive prior knowledge can increase comprehension does not mean that it always does so. Readers do not always relate their world knowledge to the content of a text, even when they possess knowledge relevant to the information in the text. Often, they do not make inferences based on prior-knowledge unless the text demands the inferences to make sense of it (McKoon & Ratcliff, 1992).

That even good readers often fail to relate what they know to a reading, however, means that more is needed in many cases for readers to benefit from their prior knowledge. A large number of experiments conducted in the late 1980s into the 1990s demonstrated the power of "Why?" questions. Why-questions encourage readers to orient to their prior knowledge as they read, to relate what they know already to what is being read (Pressley, Wood, Woloshyn, Martin, King, & Menke, 1992).

In those studies, readers were encouraged to ask themselves "why" the facts being presented in text made sense. This encouragement consistently produced a huge effect on memory of the texts. The most compelling explanation that emerged from analytical experiments (see especially Martin & Pressley, 1991) was that the why-questioning oriented the readers to prior knowledge that could explain the facts being encountered in text. Thus, a Canadian person reading that baseball in Canada started in Ontario might not automatically infer that Ontario was close to New York, where baseball was first popular in America, even if the reader knew much about the early days of baseball in New York. If that same reader were to ask himself or herself why it would make sense that Ontarians were the first Canadians to play baseball, the early history of New York baseball might come to mind and permit the insight that geographical proximity was an important determinant.

Typically, when readers process text containing new factual information, they do not automatically relate the new information to their prior knowledge, even if they have a wealth of knowledge that could be related to the information. The lesson emerging from these studies is to encourage readers to relate what they know to information-rich texts they are reading, with a potent mechanism for doing this being why-questioning (referred to as *elaborative interrogation* by Pressley and his associates). In balanced reading programs, students are taught to relate to what they read, information they know already about a content area.

Process Writing Instruction

In balanced classrooms, students not only read, read, and read, but they also write, write, and write. One model of student writing is simply to let the kids write, and they will improve. The difficulty with this approach is that improvement is often slow, especially compared to approaches in which students are taught explicitly how to write using process writing instruction.

Process writing instruction fundamentally involves (a) teaching students to plan before they write, (b) construct drafts, and (c) revise drafts with respect to meaning and mechanics (e.g., Flower & Hayes, 1980). Students can be taught a variety of specific strategies for each of these three steps, and specific students can be taught procedures for different types of writing (e.g., narratives, expositories, book reports; Harris & Graham, 1996). Important in this context are the many validations of writing process instruction with students who otherwise experience difficulties expressing themselves in writing (see Harris & Graham, 1996).

Motivating Reading and Writing

Motivating students to read and write is important, especially for students who at first have difficulty in learning to read. These students often conclude that they lack the ability to become literate, and this attribution undermines their efforts to read and write (e.g., Jacobsen, Lowery, & DuCette, 1986; Pearl, 1982).

A huge educational motivational literature has accumulated in the past quarter of a century, with many mechanisms for encouraging student motivation identified by educational researchers interested in motivation. The relevant mechanisms include teaching students to believe they can be successful with effort (see Borkowski, Carr, Rellinger, & Pressley, 1990), providing many rich print and reading experiences (Gambrell, 1996; Morrow, 1992; Morrow & Sharkey, 1993; Palmer, Codling, & Gambrell, 1994), providing holistic literacy experiences (e.g., opportunities to compose stories; Turner, 1995), connecting literacy instruction with content-area learning (e.g. Guthrie, 1996; Guthrie et al., 1996), and encouraging cooperative learning rather than competition (Ames, 1984; Nicholls, 1989).

SUMMARY

Lots of individual educational interventions have been validated and deserve a place in a balanced literacy instruction program. Can we really fold into one classroom instruction in phonemic awareness, teaching of word recognition, vocabulary development, inculcation of comprehension strategies, prior knowledge development and instruction about how to use prior knowledge, and teaching of self-monitoring? Can extensive holistic reading and process writing occur in a classroom in which so many reading skills are being taught? As teachers mix skills instruction with holistic reading and writing, can they also employ the many motivational mechanisms that have been validated?

The answer comes from the research review in the first half of this article. Excellent literacy teachers do it all! They balance skills teaching and holistic experiences while flooding their classrooms with motivation. The case in favor of balanced literacy teaching is growing, a case that follows from balanced reflection on qualitative analyses of effective classrooms and quantitative studies of specific components of instruction.

Plenty of work is left to be done. The research on balanced literacy instruction has focused mostly on the primary years, so much more research is needed in the upper elementary grades and the secondary years. We think the greatest challenge in the years ahead, however, is to find out whether more teachers can be developed who balance their literacy instruction in effective classrooms such as those described in this article.

We look forward to true experiments in which achievement is measured both in classrooms where teachers who previously were less balanced and more incomplete in their teaching have been taught to balance literacy instruction and in control classrooms in which instruction continues to be imbalanced and incomplete. If teaching teachers to be more balanced in fact changes the teachers' teaching and their students' achievement, it will provide powerful additional evidence in favor of the balanced literacy instructional model specified in Pressley's (1998) book.

Alysia Roehrig and Michael Pressley have begun research to explore whether beginning teachers can be transformed into more balanced and more effective teachers. A preliminary hypothesis emerging from this work is that only some teachers may be so open to such reeducation and modification of their teaching (see also Pressley & El-Dinary, 1997). If that turns out to be the case, maybe an important research question will be how to identify individuals who can become balanced and effective literacy teachers. How can teacher education programs be more selective about who is admitted to assure teachers who can and will do all that needs to be done to promote literacy engagement and achievement? Although much has been learned about balanced literacy instruction, much remains to be learned.

REFERENCES

Adams, M. (1990). *Beginning reading.* Cambridge, MA: MIT Press.

Alexander, A., Anderson, H., Heilman, P. C., Voeller, K. S., & Torgesen, J. K. (1991). Phonological awareness training and remediation of analytic decoding deficits in a group of severe dyslexics. *Annals of Dyslexia, 41,* 193–206.

Ames, C. (1984). Competitive, cooperative, and individualistic goal structures: A motivational analysis. In R. Ames & C. Ames (Eds.), *Research on motivation in education* (Vol. 1, pp. 117–207). New York: Academic Press.

Anderson, R. C., & Freebody, P. (1981). Vocabulary knowledge. In J. T. Guthrie (Ed.), *Comprehension and teaching: Research reviews* (pp. 77–117). Newark, DE: International Reading Association.

Anderson, R. C., & Pearson, P. D. (1984). A schema-theoretic view of basic processes in reading. In P. D. Pearson (Ed.), *Handbook of reading research.* New York: Longman.

Anderson, V. (1992). A teacher development project in transactional strategy instruction for teachers of severely reading-disabled adolescents. *Teaching & Teacher Education, 8,* 391–403.

Baker, L., & Brown, A. L. (1984). Metacognitive skills and reading. In P. D. Pearson, R. Barr, M. Kamil, & P. Mosenthal (Eds.), *Handbook of reading research* (pp. 353–394). New York: Longmans.

Baron, J. (1977). Mechanisms for pronouncing printed words: Use and acquisition. In D. LaBerge & S. J. Samuels (Eds.), *Basic processes in reading: Perception and comprehension* (pp. 175–216). Hillsdale, NJ: Erlbaum & Associates.

Beck, I. L., & McKeown, M. (1991). Conditions of vocabulary acquisition. In R. Barr, M. L. Kamil, P. Mosenthal, & P. D. Pearson (Eds.), *Handbook of reading research, Vol. 2* (pp. 789–814). New York: Longman.

Beck, I. L., Perfetti, C. A., & McKeown, M. G. (1982). Effects of long term vocabulary instruction on lexical access and reading comprehension. *Journal of Educational Psychology, 74,* 506–521.

Blachman, B., Ball, E., Black, R., & Tangel, D. (1994). Kindergarten teachers develop phoneme awareness in low-income, inner-city classrooms: Does it make a difference? *Reading and Writing, 6,* 1–17.

Bogner, K., Raphael, L. M., & Pressley, M. (In press). How grade-1 teachers motivate literate activity by their students. *Scientific Studies of Reading, 5.*

Borkowski, J. G., Carr, M., Rellinger, E. A., & Pressley, M. (1990). Self-regulated strategy use: Interdependence of metacognition, attributions, and self-esteem. In B. F. Jones (Ed.), *Dimensions of thinking: Review of research* (pp. 53–92). Hillsdale NJ: Erlbaum & Associates.

Bowey, J. A. (1995). Socioeconomic status differences in preschool phonological sensitivity and first-grade reading achievement. *Journal of Educational Psychology, 87,* 476–487.

Bradley, L., & Bryant, P. E. (1983). Categorizing sounds and learning to read—a causal connection. *Nature, 301,* 419–421.

Bradley, L., & Bryant, P. (1985). *Rhyme and reason in reading and spelling.* (International Academy for Research in Learning Disabilities Series). Ann Arbor: University of Michigan Press.

Bradley, L., & Bryant, P. (1991). Phonological skills before and after learning to read. In S. A. Brady & D. P. Shankweiler (Eds.), *Phonological processes in literacy: A tribute to Isabelle Y. Liberman* (pp. 37–45). Hillsdale, NJ: Erlbaum & Associates.

Brown, R., Pressley, M., Van Meter, P., & Schuder, T. (1996). A quasi-experimental validation of transactional strategies instruction with low-achieving second grade readers. *Journal of Educational Psychology, 88,* 18–37.

Bus, A. G., & van IJzendoorn, M. H. (1999). Phonological awareness and early reading: A meta-analysis of experimental training studies. *Journal of Educational Psychology, 91,* 403–414.

Byrne, B., & Fielding-Barnsley, R. (1991). Evaluation of a program to teach phonemic awareness to young children. *Journal of Educational Psychology, 83,* 451–455.

Byrne, B., & Fielding-Barnsley, R. (1993). Evaluation of a program to teach phonemic awareness to young children: A 1-year followup *Journal of Educational Psychology, 85,* 104–111.

Byrne, B., & Fielding-Barnsley, R. (1995). Evaluation of a program to teach phonemic awareness to young children: A 2- and 3-year followup and a new preschool trial. *Journal of Educational Psychology, 87,* 488–503.

Castle, J. M., Riach, J., & Nicholson, T. (1994). Getting off to a better start in reading and spelling: The effects of phonemic awareness instruction within a whole language program. *Journal of Educational Psychology, 86,* 350–359.

Cazden, C. (1992). *Whole language plus: Essays on literacy in the United States and New Zealand.* New York: Teachers College Press.

Chall, J. S. (1967). *Learning to read: The great debate.* New York: McGraw-Hill.

Chall, J. S. (1983). *Learning to read: The great debate* (updated ed.). New York: McGraw-Hill.

Collins, C. (1991). Reading instruction that increases thinking abilities. *Journal of Reading, 34,* 510–516.

Cordón, L. A., & Day, J. D. (1996). Strategy use on standardized reading comprehension tests. *Journal of Educational Psychology, 88,* 288–295.

Delpit, L. D. (1986). Skills and other dilemmas of a progressive black educator. *Harvard Educational Review, 56,* 379–385.

Dewitz, P. (1993, May). *Comparing an analogy and phonics approach to word recognition.* Paper presented at Edmund Hardcastle Henderson Roundtable in Reading, Charlottesville, VA.

Dickinson, D. K., & Smith, M. W. (1994). Long-term effects of preschool teachers' book readings on low-income children's vocabulary and story comprehension. *Reading Research Quarterly, 29,* 104–122.

Duffy, G. G. (1991). What counts in teacher education? Dilemmas in educating empowered teachers. In J. Zutell & S. McCormick (Eds.), *Learner factors/teacher factors: Issues in literacy research and instruction* (pp. 1–18). Chicago: National Reading Conference.

Duffy, G. G., Roehler, L. R., Sivan, E., Rackliffe, G., Book, C., Meloth, M., Vavrus, L. G., Wesselman, R., Putnam, J., & Bassiri, D. (1987). Effects of explaining the reasoning associated with using reading strategies. *Reading Research Quarterly, 22,* 347–368.

Durso, F. T., & Coggins, K. A. (1991). Organized instruction for the improvement of word knowledge skills. *Journal of Educational Psychology, 83,* 109–112.

Ehri, L. C., & Robbins, C. (1992). Beginners need some decoding skill to read words by analogy. *Reading Research Quarterly, 27,* 12–27.

Elley, W. B. (1989). Vocabulary acquisition from listening to stories. *Reading Research Quarterly, 24,* 174–187.

Fisher, C. W., & Hiebert, E.H. (1990). Characteristics of tasks in two approaches to literacy instruction. *Elementary School Journal, 91,* 3–18.

Flower, L. & Hayes, J. (1980). The dynamics of composing: Making plans and juggling constraints. In L. Gregg & E. Steinberg (Eds.), *Cognitive processes in writing* (pp. 31–50). Hillsdale NJ: Erlbaum & Associates.

Foorman, B. R., Francis, D. J., Fletcher. J. M., Schatschneider, C., & Mehta, P. (1998). The role of instruction in learning to read: Preventing reading failure in at-risk children. *Journal of Educational Psychology, 90,* 37–55.

Foorman, B., Francis, D., Novy, D., & Liberman, D. (1991). How letter-sound instruction mediates progress in first-grade reading and spelling. *Journal of Educational Psychology, 83,* 456–469.

Gambrell, L. B. (1996). Creating classroom cultures that foster reading motivation. *Reading Teacher, 50,* 14–25.

Gaskins, R. W., Gaskins, I. W., Anderson, R. C., & Schommer, M. (1995). The reciprocal relationship between research and development: An example involving a decoding strand for poor readers. *Journal of Reading Behavior, 27,* 337–377.

Gaskins, R. W., Gaskins, J. C., & Gaskins, I. W. (1991). A decoding program for poor readers—and the rest of the class, too! *Language Arts, 68,* 213–225.

Gaskins, R. W., Gaskins, J. C., & Gaskins, I. W. (1992). Using what you know to figure out what you don't know: An analogy approach to decoding. *Reading & Writing Quarterly, 8,* 197–221.

Goswami, U. (2000). Phonological and lexical processes. In M. L. Kamil, P. B. Mosenthal, P. D. Pearson, & R. Barr (Eds.), *Handbook of reading research* (Vol. 3, pp. 251–267). Mahwah, NJ: Erlbaum & Associates.

Guthrie, J. T. (1996). Educational contexts for engagement in literacy. *Reading Teacher, 49,* 432–445.

Guthrie, J. T., Van Meter, P., McCann, A. D., Wigfield, A., Bennett, L., Poundstone, C. C., Rice, M. E., Faibisch, F. M., Hunt, B., & Mitchell, A. M. (1996). Growth of literacy engagement: Changes in motivations and strategies during concept-oriented reading instruction. *Reading Research Quarterly, 31,* 306–332.

Harris, K. R., & Graham, S. (1996). *Making the writing process work: Strategies for composition and self-regulation.* Cambridge, MA: Brookline Books.

Horn, C. C., & Manis, F. R. (1987). Development of automatic and speeded reading of printed words. *Journal of Experimental Child Psychology, 44,* 92–108.

Isakson, R. L., & Miller, J. W. (1976). Sensitivity to syntactic and semantic cues in good and poor comprehenders. *Journal of Educational Psychology, 68,* 787–792.

Iversen, S., & Tunmer, W. E. (1993). Phonological processing skills and the reading recovery program. *Journal of Educational Psychology, 85,* 112–120.

Jacobsen, B., Lowery, B., & DuCette, J. (1986). Attributions of learning disabled children. *Journal of Educational Psychology, 78,* 59–64.

Juel, C. (1988). Learning to read and write: A longitudinal study of 54 children from first through fourth grades. *Journal of Educational Psychology, 80,* 417–447.

LaBerge, D., & Samuels, S. J. (1974). Toward a theory of automatic information processing in reading. *Cognitive Psychology, 6,* 293–323.

Lie, A. (1991). Effects of a training program for stimulating skills in word analysis in first-grade children. *Reading Research Quarterly, 26,* 234–250.

Lovett, M. W., Borden, S. L., Deluca, T., Lacerenza, L., Benson, N. J., & Brackstone, D. (1994). Treating the core deficits of developmental dyslexia: Evidence of transfer of learning after phonologically and strategy-based reading training programs. *Developmental Psychology, 30,* 805–822.

Lovett, M. W., Ransby, M. J., Hardwick, N., Johns, M. S., & Donaldson, S. A. (1989). Can dyslexia be treated? Treatment-specific and generalized treatment effects in dyslexic children's response to remediation. *Brain & Language, 37,* 90–121.

Lundberg, I., Frost, J., & Peterson, O. (1988). Effects of an extensive program for stimulating phonological awareness in preschool children. *Reading Research Quarterly, 23,* 263–284.

Lyons, C. A., Pinnell, G. S., & DeFord, D. E. (1993). *Partners in learning: Teachers and children in Reading Recovery.* New York: Teachers College Press.

Manis, F. R., Custodio, R., & Szeszulski, P. A. (1993). Development of phonological and orthographic skill: A 2-year longitudinal study of dyslexic children. *Journal of Experimental Child Psychology, 56,* 64–86.

Martin, V. L., & Pressley, M. (1991). Elaborative-interrogation effects depend on the nature of the question. *Journal of Educational Psychology, 83,* 113–119.

McCaslin, M. M. (1989). Whole language: Theory, instruction, and future implementation. *Elementary School Journal, 90,* 223–229.

McIntyre, E., & Pressley, M. (Eds.) (1996). *Balanced instruction: Strategies and skills in whole language.* Norwood, MA: Christopher-Gordon.

McKoon, G., & Ratcliff, R. (1992). Inference during reading. *Psychological Review, 99,* 440–466.

Miller, G. A., & Gildea, P. (1987). How children learn words. *Scientific American, 257* (3), 94–99.

Morrow, L. M. (1992). The impact of a literature-based program on literacy achievement, use of literature, and attitudes of children from minority backgrounds. *Reading Research Quarterly, 27,* 250–275.

Morrow, L. M., Pressley, M., Smith, J. K., & Smith, M. (1997). The effect of a literature-based program integrated into literacy and science instruction with children from diverse backgrounds. *Reading Research Quarterly, 32,* 54–76.

Morrow, L. M., & Sharkey, E. A. (1993). Motivating independent reading and writing in the primary grades through social cooperative literacy experiences. *Reading Teacher, 47,* 162–164.

Nagy, W., Anderson, R., & Herman, P. (1987). Learning word meanings from context during normal reading. *American Educational Research Journal, 24,* 237–270.

Näslund, J. C., & Schneider, W. (1996). Kindergarten letter knowledge, phonological skills, and memory processes: Relative effects on early literacy. *Journal of Experimental Child Psychology, 62,* 30–59.

National Reading Panel (2000). *Final report of the National Reading Panel.* Washington, DC: National Institute of Child Health & Development.

Nicholls, J. G. (1989). *The competitive ethos and democratic education.* Cambridge, MA: Harvard University Press.

O'Connor, R. E., Jenkins, J. R., & Slocum, T. A. (1995). Transfer among phonological tasks in kindergarten: Essential instructional content. *Journal of Educational Psychology, 87,* 202–217.

Palmer, B. M., Codling, R. M., & Gambrell, L. B. (1994). In their own words: What elementary students have to say about motivation to read. *Reading Teacher, 48,* 176–178.

Pearl, R. (1982). LD children's attributions for success and failure: A replication with a labeled LD sample. *Learning Disability Quarterly, 5,* 173–176.

Pearson, P. D., & Dole, J. A. (1987). Explicit comprehension instruction: A review of research and a new conceptualization of instruction. *Elementary School Journal, 88,* 151–165.

Pearson, P. D., & Fielding, L. (1991). Comprehension instruction. In R. Barr, M. L. Kamil, P. B. Mosenthal, & P. D. Pearson (Eds.), *Handbook of reading research,* (Vol. 2, pp. 815-860). New York: Longman.

Pellegrini, A. D., Galda, L., Perlmutter, J., & Jones, I. (1994). *Joint reading between mothers and their Head Start children: Vocabulary development in two text formats* (Reading Research Report No. 13). Athens, GA, & College Park, MD: National Reading Research Center.

Peterson, M. E., & Haines, L. P. (1992). Orthographic analogy training with kindergarten children: Effects of analogy use, phonemic segmentation, and letter-sound knowledge. *Journal of Reading Behavior, 24,* 109–127.

Pressley, M. (1994). State-of-the-science primary-grades reading instruction or whole language? *Educational Psychologist, 29,* 211–216.

Pressley, M. (1998). *Reading instruction that works: The case for balanced teaching.* New York: Guilford.

Pressley, M., & Afflerbach, P. (1995). *Verbal protocols of reading: The nature of constructively responsive reading.* Hillsdale, NJ: Erlbaum.

Pressley, M., Allington, R., Wharton-McDonald, R., Block, C. C., & Morrow, L. M. (2001). *Learning to read: Lessons from exemplary first grades.* New York: Guilford.

Pressley, M., & El-Dinary, P. B. (1997). What we know about translating comprehension strategies instruction into practice. *Journal of Learning Disabilities Research, 30,* 486–488.

Pressley, M., Johnson, C. J., Symons, S., McGoldrick, J. A., & Kurita, J. A. (1989). Strategies that improve children's memory and comprehension of text. *Elementary School Journal, 90,* 3–32.

Pressley, M., Rankin, J., & Yokoi, L. (1996). A survey of instructional practices of primary teachers nominated as effective in promoting literacy. *Elementary School Journal, 96,* 363–384.

Pressley, M., Wharton-McDonald, R., Allington, R., Block, C. C., Morrow, L., Tracey, D., Baker, K., Brooks, G., Cronin, J., Nelson, E., & Woo, D. (2001). A study of effective grade-1 literacy instruction. *Scientific Studies of Reading, 5,* 35–58.

Pressley, M., Wood, E., Woloshyn, V. E., Martin, V., King, A., & Menke, D. (1992). Encouraging mindful use of prior knowledge: Attempting to construct explanatory answers facilitates learning. *Educational Psychologist, 27,* 91–110.

Rankin-Erickson, J. L., & Pressley, M. (2000). A survey of instructional practices of special education teachers nominated as effective teachers of literacy. *Learning Disabilities Research & Practice, 15,* 206–225.

Raphael, L. D., Bogner, K., Pressley, M., Shell, A. S., & Masters, N. (2001). *Case analyses of two very engaging grade-1 teachers.* Notre Dame, IN: Institute for Educational Initiatives.

Robbins, C., & Ehri, L. C. (1994). Reading storybooks to kindergartners helps them learn new vocabulary words. *Journal of Educational Psychology, 86,* 54–64.

Roehrig, A. D., Pressley, M., & Sloup, M. (in press). Reading strategy instruction in regular primary-level classrooms by teachers trained in Reading Recovery. *Reading & Writing Quarterly.*

Rosenhouse, J., Feitelson, D., Kita, B., & Goldstein, Z. (1997). Interactive reading aloud to Israeli first graders: Its contribution to literacy development. *Reading Research Quarterly, 32,* 168–183.

Stahl, S. A., McKenna, M. C., & Pagnucco, J. R. (1994). The effects of whole language instruction: An update and reappraisal. *Educational Psychologist, 29,* 175–186.

Stanovich, K. (1986). Matthew effects in reading: Some consequences of individual differences in the acquisition of literacy. *Reading Research Quarterly, 21,* 360–407.

Stanovich, K. E., & Cunningham, A. E. (1993). Where does knowledge come from? Specific associations between print exposure and information acquisition. *Journal of Educational Psychology, 85,* 211–229.

Sternberg, R. J. (1987). Most vocabulary is learned from context. In M. G. McKeown & M. E. Curtis (Eds.), *The nature of vocabulary acquisition.* Hillsdale, NJ: Lawrence Erlbaum and Associates.

Strauss, A., & Corbin, J. (1990). *Basics of qualitative research: Grounded theory procedures and techniques.* Newbury Park, CA: Sage.

Stuart, M., & Masterson, J. (1992). Patterns of reading and spelling in 10-year-old children related to prereading phonological abilities. *Journal of Experimental Child Psychology, 54,* 168–187.

Torgesen, J. K., Wagner, R. K., Rashotte, C. A., Alexander, A., Lindamood, P. C., Rose, E., & Conway, T. (1996). *Prevention and remediation of phonologically based reading disabilities.* Paper presented at the Spectrum of Developmental Disabilities 18: Dyslexia. Baltimore: Johns Hopkins Medical Institutions.

Torgesen, J. K., Wagner, R. K., Rose, E., Lindamood, P., Conway, T., & Garvan, C. (1999). Preventing reading failure in young children with phonological processing disabilities: Group and individual responses to instruction. *Journal of Educational Psychology, 91,* 579–593.

Turner, J. C. (1995). The influence of classroom contexts on young children's motivation for literacy. *Reading Research Quarterly, 30,* 410–441.

van Daal, V. H. P., Reitsma, P., & van der Leu, A. (1994). Processing units in word reading by disabled readers. *Journal of Experimental Child Psychology, 57,* 180–210.

Vellutino, F. R., & Scanlon, D. M. (1987). Phonological-coding, phonological awareness, and reading ability: Evidence from a longitudinal and experimental study. *Merrill-Palmer Quarterly, 33,* 321–363.

Vellutino, F. R., Scanlon, D. M., Sipay, E. R., Small, S. G., Pratt, A., Chen, R., & Denckla, M. B. (1996). Cognitive profiles of difficult-to-remediate and readily remediated poor readers: Early intervention as a vehicle for distinguishing between cognitive and experiential deficits as basic causes of specific reading disability. *Journal of Educational Psychology, 88,* 601–638.

Wharton-McDonald, R., Pressley, M., & Hampston, J. M. (1998). Outstanding literacy instruction in first grade: Teacher practices and student achievement. *Elementary School Journal, 99,* 101–128.

Williams, J. P. (1980). Teaching decoding with an emphasis on phoneme analysis and phoneme blending. *Journal of Educational Psychology, 72,* 1–15.

Wise, B. W., & Olson, R. K. (1995). Computer-based phonological awareness and reading instruction. *Annals of Dyslexia, 45,* 99–122.

Self-Regulated Strategy Development in the Classroom: A Balanced Approach to Writing Instruction for Students With Disabilities

Karen R. Harris, Steve Graham, and Linda H. Mason

Writing is a highly complex process; the writer not only must negotiate the rules and mechanics of writing, but also must maintain a focus on important aspects of writing such as organization, form and features, purposes and goals, audience needs and perspectives, and evaluation of the communication between author and reader (Bereiter & Scardamalia, 1982; Scheid, 1991). In addition, writing requires extensive self-regulation and attention control (Graham & Harris, 1994, 1996, 2000). For skilled writers, writing is a flexible, goal-directed activity that is scaffolded by a rich knowledge of cognitive processes and strategies for planning, text production, and revision. Skilled writers engage in purposeful and active self-direction of these processes and strategies (Harris, Schmidt, & Graham, 1998). In fact, monitoring and directing one's own composing processes are crucial to the development of writing ability (Flower & Hayes, 1980).

Learning to write is difficult and demanding. National and state writing assessments indicate that we are not yet highly effective at developing this critical competency among our students, as the majority of children in American schools demonstrates significant difficulties with narrative, expository, and persuasive writing (Applebee, Langer, Mullis, Latham, & Gentile, 1994; Applebee, Langer, Jenkins, Mullis, & Foertsch, 1990). In addition, children in our schools frequently demonstrate a deteriorating attitude toward writing, even though most children begin school with a positive attitude toward composing (Applebee, Langer, & Mullis, 1986). Scardamalia and Bereiter (1986) have identified five areas of writing competence that are particularly difficult for the general school population: (a) generating content, (b) creating an organized structure for compositions, (c) formulating goals and higher level plans, (d) quickly and efficiently executing the mechanical aspects of writing, and (e) revising text and reformulating goals.

Researchers have found that students with learning disabilities (LD) or other special needs frequently have greater difficulty with writing than their normally achieving peers (Graham, Harris, & Larsen, 2001; Harris & Graham, 1992, 1999). Generally, students with learning problems produce writing that is less polished, expansive, coherent, and effective than students without learning disabilities (for greater details on the research base, see Graham & Harris, 2002). Research indicates that students with learning disabilities lack critical knowledge of the writing process; have difficulty generating ideas and selecting topics; do little to no advance planning; engage in knowledge telling; lack important strategies for planning, producing, organizing, and revising text; have difficulties with mechanics that interferes with the writing process; emphasize mechanics over content when making revisions; and frequently overestimate their writing abilities.

For more than 20 years, Graham, Harris, and their colleagues have been involved in the development and evaluation of an instructional approach to developing writing and self-regulation strategies among students with significant writing problems. This approach is referred to as Self-Regulated Strategy Development (SRSD). SRSD has been used in several academic areas, including math and reading (see Wong, Harris, Graham, & Butler, 2003), but in the area of writing the major goals of SRSD are threefold (Harris, Schmidt, & Graham, 1998):

1. Assist students in developing knowledge about writing and powerful skills and strategies involved in the writing process, including planning, writing, revising, and editing.
2. Support students in the ongoing development of the abilities needed to monitor and manage their own writing.
3. Promote children's development of positive attitudes about writing and themselves as writers (p. 134).

In this chapter, we discuss why SRSD is a good match to the needs of students with LD and others who struggle with writing, how SRSD is done in the classroom, how teachers can plan for and evaluate SRSD, and tips for getting started with this approach in the classroom. We also offer an example of SRSD instruction in an elementary classroom in which we have been working, illustrated with the performance of two of our students.

SRSD AND STUDENTS WITH SEVERE LEARNING PROBLEMS

While students with learning and behavioral problems are a heterogeneous group, research indicates that one commonality among these students is that the significant difficulties they face often arise from multiple problems of an affective, behavioral, and cognitive nature (Harris, 1982; Harris & Graham, 1992, 1996a; Harris, Graham, & Deshler, 1998). Ecological variables, including the situational, educational, cultural, and community networks the student is part of, are also critical concerns (Harris, 1982). As researchers have noted for some time, the transactional relationships among affect, behavior, cognition, and social and ecological variables need to be carefully considered (Harris, 1982; Kendall & Braswell, 1982).

Many students with LD have difficulty with self-regulation, including the self-regulation of organized, strategic behaviors (Graham, Harris, & Reid, 1992; Harris, 1986). They might have difficulty comprehending task demands, producing effective task strategies, and using strategies to mediate performance (Harris & Graham, 1992). Some might lack or fail to make use of effective verbal mediation processes or might not have developed an effective linguistic control system, and thus experience difficulties using verbalizations (often referred to as self-speech) to guide behavior. Many of these students also experience reciprocal relationships among academic failure, self-doubts, learned helplessness, maladaptive attributions, unrealistic pretask expectancies, low self-efficacy, and low motivation. Impulsivity, difficulties with memory or other aspects of information processing, low task engagement and persistence, devaluation of learning, and low productivity are also among the problems these students and their teachers might need to deal with.

SRSD: UNDERLYING PREMISES

Harris and Graham began development of the SRSD approach to instruction with the underlying premise that students who face significant and often debilitating difficulties would benefit from an integrated approach to instruction that deliberately and directly addresses their affective, behavioral, and cognitive characteristics, strengths, and needs (Harris, 1982). Further, they asserted that these students often require more extensive, structured, and explicit instruction than their peers to develop skills, strategies (including academic, social, and self-regulation strategies), and understandings. The level of explicitness of instruction should be adjusted to meet student needs (Harris & Graham, 1996b). This perspective requires that the same academic and self-regulation strategies are not necessarily targeted for all students, and that instructional components and processes need to be individualized. SRSD research indicates that as students' learning and behavioral challenges become more significant, strategy and self-regulation development becomes more complex and explicit, involving multiple learning tasks, components, and stages (Sawyer, Graham, & Harris, 1992; Sexton, Harris, & Graham, 1998).

Another premise evident from the beginning of Harris and Graham's work on SRSD was the need to integrate multiple lines of research from multiple theoretical perspectives in order to develop powerful interventions for students who face significant academic challenges (Harris, 1982; Harris & Alexander, 1998: Harris & Graham, 1985). Thus, SRSD has been, and continues to be, informed by research in areas such as development and characteristics of written language, expertise in written language among both children and adults, emerging practices in writing instruction, self-regulation, learning characteristics of students with significant learning problems, and effective teaching and learning. A thoughtful, effective integration of diverse, validated approaches to learning, regardless of whether the disciplines from which they originated are viewed as discordant (such as affective, behavioral, and cognitive approaches to teaching and learning), has been key to the development of SRSD.

SRSD, Constructivism, and Whole Language

While the idea that more explicit instruction is needed for students with severe learning problems is not unique to SRSD, it has created controversy in the context of constructivist and whole language movements in schools (cf. Harris & Graham, 1994, 1996b, 1996c; Harris, Graham, & Deshler, 1998). Constructivism is a philosophy about teaching and learning, rather than a specific teaching method or approach (for a more detailed discussion of constructivism and whole language, see Harris & Graham, 1994; Harris & Graham, 1996c). Constructivists see children as inherently active, self-regulating learners who construct knowledge in developmentally appropriate ways within a social context. Views of the child as passively responding to the environment and learning through directly internalizing knowledge given by others are rejected (though it would be difficult to find any learning theory today that would make such an argument). According to constructivism, real understanding occurrs only when children participate fully in learning, which results in deeper and richer understanding and use of knowledge, thus promoting access to and application of what has been learned.

Constructivists reject teaching discrete skills in a linear sequence, and the belief that mastery of basic skills is a necessary prerequisite to more advanced learning and higher order thinking. Learning is socially situated and enhanced in meaningful and authentic contexts. Teachers are encouraged to facilitate and assist the construction of knowledge rather than to explicitly provide knowledge and information (Harris & Graham, 1996b, 1996c; Harris & Pressley, 1991; Pressley & Harris, 1998).

Difficulties arise in the translation of constructivist theory into practice, however, not only for students with severe learning problems, but for many of their peers as well. Some see the emphasis in constructivism on maintaining an authentic and meaningful learning environment as totally incompatible with providing the level of explicit instruction we argue is needed for some students to gain important skills, strategies, and knowledge that come more easily to others. Some constructivists have even argued that teaching is a dirty word; they believe that it is neither necessary nor desirable (and even harmful) to teach explicitly, provide direct explanation, or require practice (Harris & Graham, 1994, 1996c). This belief has serious ramifications for students with special needs.

Whole Language and the Process Approach to Writing

Perhaps one of the best known applications of constructivism is whole language. While definitions and practices within whole language vary widely, one commonly held viewpoint is the rejection of explicit instruction. Some whole language advocates believe that through rich immersion in authentic learning experiences, children will come to learn all they need to know, and develop all of the skills and abilities they need, in due developmental time. Directly addressing areas in which children have difficulties is seen by some as "flogging" a child's weaknesses and ignoring her or his strengths (cf. Edelsky, Altwerger, & Flores, 1991; Kronick, 1990; Manning & Manning, 1995; Poplin, 1988; Pressley & Harris, 1998). Learning to read and write is believed to occur "naturally" within such environments, much as learning to speak does in early childhood.

Little or no explicit, focused, or isolated instruction and practice in basic skills may occur, although skills are addressed within the context of meaningful learning activities (Edelsky et al., 1991). Parents and educators across the country, however, have voiced concerns about the number of children who have not learned to write effectively, whose handwriting is illegible and labored in the upper elementary grades, and whose spelling remains "inventive" long past the early grades (Smith, 1994; Willis, 1993).

Writers' Workshop and the Process Approach

For more than a decade we have worked to advance the process approach to writing, often referred to as Writers' Workshop, in our schools. In general, however, until the late 1980s a product-oriented model of writing instruction prevailed in American schools (Applebee et al., 1990; Harris & Graham, 1992). In the product-oriented model, mechanics and grammar tended to be emphasized over content and process. Further, writing was given limited time and attention, and few activities pursued in classrooms required sustained writing. Students were taught little about the processes and strategies involved in writing, and little was done to promote their development. A great deal of learning to write was expected to occur by reading the work of others and independently determining how to create similar compositions. First drafts were often final drafts, read only by the teacher—who primarily marked errors in mechanics and assigned grades. The important roles that writing plays in learning and communicating were often neglected.

In the process approach, teachers create an environment where students have time not only to write, but to think and reflect upon what they are writing about. Instruction takes place in a supportive environment where students are encouraged to choose their own topics, help each other, and take risks. Students write for real purposes and for real audiences and are given opportunities for extended writing. Students learn to see writing as a process, and a first draft as a draft. Writing conferences, peer collaboration, mini-lessons, modeling, sharing, and classroom dialogue are all essential components of this approach. Students see writing as a process that is difficult and frustrating at times, yet also a challenging and enjoyable vehicle for learning and self-expression (Atwell, 1987; Graves, 1985).

Although the process-writing approach is all the support that some students need to help them develop and come to own important writing skills, abilities, and strategies, many other students, including those with severe writing problems, need more (Graham & Harris, 1994). Because instruction in process-writing classrooms often involves capitalizing on "teachable moments" and mini-lessons, students might not learn all they need to know about writing strategies and processes. Important strategies might not be introduced because "teachable moments" are overlooked or do not occur, and mini-lessons might not offer the extensive, explicit, and supported instruction students need to master important strategies and abilities.

We believe, and have data to support this belief (cf. Danoff, Harris, & Graham, 1993; Graham & Harris, 2003, MacArthur, Schwartz, Graham, Molloy, & Harris, 1996), that SRSD fits well with the process approach to writing or Writers' Workshop, an approach often found in whole language programs and in schools and programs that have not adopted a whole language approach. Further, students in the upper elementary, middle, and secondary grades face increasing demands for strategic writing performance, both as a means of learning and as a way to express what has been learned. The number of writing genres in which students need expertise also increases. Integrating SRSD with the process approach to writing provides a proactive, effective, and more efficient means for addressing these issues.

An Integrated Approach

Although some have argued that the integration of SRSD and other instructional approaches that include explicit and supported instruction with whole language or writing-process approaches is impossible and misguided, many teachers, schools, and communities are demonstrating otherwise (Harris & Graham, 1996b, 1996c). As we have argued elsewhere (Harris & Graham, 1996b; Harris & Pressley, 1991), the challenges faced by students with special needs, and indeed by all of us today, are complex. When we treat competing viewpoints with thoughtfulness and respect, a powerful repertoire for teaching and learning can be developed. We are obviously not advocating for a return to a primarily skills-oriented, back-to-basics curriculum. Rather, we are arguing that explicit, focused, and at times isolated instruction needs to be provided to the extent needed by individual children. Explicitness and structure do not necessarily equate with isolated skills training, decontextualized learning of subskills, passive learning, or the gradual accruing of basic skills (Harris & Graham, 1994). We believe that explicit, focused instruction must, however, be integrated into the larger literacy context. We note that many other constructivism or writing-process advocates agree with this point. Students' perceptions of what they are doing and why they are doing it, and of their teachers's intentions, are critical in this integration (Harris & Graham, 1996b, 1996c).

Teachers and schools have coherently integrated meaningful forms of explicit, and sometimes isolated, instruction within a larger, constructivism-based approach (Smith, 1994; Willis, 1993). Ideally, such coherent, integrated instruction is based in learning communities that are educationally purposeful, open, just disciplined, caring, and celebrative. Teacher goals and actions in these learning communities are based on ongoing assessment that includes students' cognitive and metacognitive abilities, skills, knowledge, and prior experience, as well as their affective and behavioral strengths, needs and characteristics. Students are provided the level of support needed (from explicit instruction through guided discovery) to acquire skills, abilities, and strategies and to develop and enhance important affective and behavioral targets, such as motivation, adaptive attributions, and engagement. Teachers are responsive to and plan for individual needs and differences, and students are given the time they need to attain valued outcomes of education (Harris & Graham, 1996b). Having shared our perspective on SRSD and an integrated approach to teaching and learning, we turn now to the data base for SRSD, and how SRSD is conducted in the classroom.

SRSD: THE RESEARCH EVIDENCE

Since 1985, more than 30 studies using the SRSD model of instruction in the area of writing have been reported, involving students from the elementary grades through high school. In many of these studies, instruction has been conducted by the special and general education teachers in their own classrooms, often as a part of writers' workshop (cf. Danoff, Harris, & Graham, 1993; De La Paz, 1999, 2001; De La Paz & Graham, 2001; MacArthur, Graham, Schwartz, & Shafer, 1995; MacArthur, Schwartz, & Graham, 1991; MacArthur, Schwartz, Graham, Molloy, & Harris, 1996; Sexton, Harris, & Graham, 1998). Teachers have been able to implement SRSD and have found SRSD acceptable and beneficial in their classrooms. Studies have been undertaken to determine the contributions of various components of the SRSD approach and the stages of instruction (Danoff, Harris, & Graham, 1993; Graham & Harris, 1989; Sawyer, Graham, & Harris, 1992). Studies have also been conducted by researchers independent of Graham, Harris, and their colleagues (Albertson & Billingsley, 1997; Collins, 1992; Tanhouser, 1994). The majority of SRSD research has involved writing; studies have also been conducted, however, in reading and math, and one group of elementary through high school teachers has applied SRSD to homework completion and organization for classes and the school day (Bednarczyk, 1991; Case, Harris, & Graham, 1992; Harris, Bennof, 1992; Johnson, Graham, & Harris, 1997; Mason, 2002).

SRSD research has resulted in the development of writing strategies (typically with the assistance of teachers and their students) for a variety of genres; these include personal narratives, story writing, persuasive essays, report writing, expository essays, and state writing tests. SRSD has resulted in significant and meaningful improvements in children's development of planning and revising strategies, including brainstorming, self-monitoring, reading for information and semantic webbing, generating and organizing writing content, advanced planning and dictation, revising with peers, and revising for both substance and mechanics (Harris & Graham, 1996a).

SRSD has resulted in improvements in four main aspects of students' performance: quality of writing, knowledge of writing, approach to writing, and self-efficacy (Graham, Harris, MacArthur, & Schwartz, 1991; Harris & Graham, 1999). Across a variety of strategies and genres, the quality, length, and structure of students' compositions have improved. Depending on the strategy taught, improvements have been documented in planning, revising, content, and mechanics. These improvements have been consistently maintained for the majority of students over time, with some students needing booster sessions for long-term maintenance, and students have shown generalization across settings, persons, and writing media. Improvements have been found with normally achieving students as well as students with LD, making this approach a good fit for inclusive classrooms (cf. Danoff et al., 1993; De La Paz, 1999; De La Paz, Owen, Harris, & Graham, 2000; MacArthur et al., 1996). In some studies, improvements for students with LD have resulted in performance similar to that of their normally achieving peers (Danoff et al., 1993; De La Paz, 1999; Sawyer, Graham, & Harris, 1992).

SRSD: STAGES OF INSTRUCTION

Six basic stages of instruction are used to introduce and develop the writing and self-regulation strategies in the SRSD approach. SRSD has been used successfully with entire classes, small groups, and in tutoring settings (Graham & Harris, 2003). Throughout the stages, teachers and students collaborate on the acquisition, implementation, evaluation, and modification of these strategies. The stages are not meant to be followed in a cookbook fashion. Rather, they provide a general format and guidelines. The stages can be reordered, combined (in fact, most lessons include at least two stages), revisited, modified, or deleted to meet student and teacher needs. Further, the stages are meant to be recursive—if a concept or component is not mastered at a certain stage, students and teachers can revisit or continue that stage as they move on to others. Some stages may not be needed by all students. For example, some students might already have had the background knowledge needed to use the writing strategy and self-regulation processes, and may skip this stage or act as a resource for other students who need this stage.

Lessons typically run anywhere from 20 to 60 minutes (depending on grade level and class schedules) at least three times a week. In most of our work with teachers and students, instruction takes less time than teachers anticipate. In the elementary grades, 8 to 12, 30- to 40-minute lessons have typically been what students need to complete the stages (further detail by grade and genre can be found in Graham & Harris, 2003).

The stages of instruction represent merely the bare framework of instruction. Thus, we follow this description with discussion of critical characteristics of SRSD instruction and guidelines for evaluation of this process. Additional explanation and discussion of the self-regulation strategies, planning for SRSD instruction, these writing strategies, and other writing strategies, can be found in Harris and Graham (1996a). Detailed lesson plans for story writing and persuasive essay writing are offered on the Center for Accelerating Student Learning (CASL) Web site, under Outreach, at www.vanderbilt.edu/CASL. In addition, all of the stages of instruction can be seen in both elementary and middle school classrooms in the video, "Teaching students with learning disabilities: Using learning strategies" (ASCD, 2002).

Procedures for promoting maintenance and generalization are integrated throughout the stages of instruction in the SRSD model. These include: identifying opportunities to use the writing and/or self-regulation strategies in other classes or settings, discussing attempts to use the strategies at other times, reminding students to use the strategies at appropriate times, analyzing how these processes might need to be modified with other tasks and in new settings, and evaluating the success of these processes during and after instruction. It is helpful to involve others, including other teachers and parents, to prompt the use of the strategies at appropriate times in other settings. Booster sessions, where the strategies are reviewed and discussed and supported again if necessary, are very important for maintaining the strategies for most of the students we have worked with.

Stage 1: Develop and Activate Background Knowledge

During this stage, background knowledge and any preskills, such as vocabulary (terms like setting, character, and so on as appropriate), concepts, and so on, students need for learning and using the writing and self-regulation strategies are developed. Preskills and background knowledge should be developed enough to allow students to move into the next stages, and their development can continue into stages 2 and 3.

In addition, we frequently start the development of individualized self-statements here. Self-statements, also referred to as self-speech, are a powerful form of self-regulation (for greater detail on their development and role in self-regulation, see Harris & Graham, 1996a). The teacher collaborates with students to develop statements relevant to writing and to students' individual needs and characteristics. For example, a student who tends to become frustrated and quit easily might think, "I can do this if I use my strategy and take my time." The teacher discusses with the students how the things they say to themselves can help them or hurt them, and students might share some of the self-speech they currently engage in when asked to write, and how it helps them or needs to be changed. Negative or ineffective self-statements, such as, "I'm no good at this," or, "I hate writing," can be identified, and how they interfere with performance can be discussed.

Stage 2: Discuss It

During this stage, the teacher and students discuss the strategies to be learned, with the writing strategy being carefully explained. Each step in the writing strategy is explained, as are any mnemonics to be used. The significance and benefits of the writing and self-regulation strategies are established. The teacher and the students discuss how and when to use the strategies; laying the foundation for generalization can begin here, as this discussion should not be limited to the current classroom or task at hand. Opportunities to use the strategy in new situations or for different tasks should be identified. The importance of student effort in strategy mastery and use is strongly emphasized, in part to increase motivation and to help develop positive, adaptive attributions (I can do this because I know the "trick of it"—the strategy— and I am trying hard). The goals of the strategies instruction are discussed and determined. During this stage, students are asked to make a commitment to learn the writing and self-regulation strategies and to act as a collaborator in both learning and evaluating the strategies.

Often, the teacher and students will also examine each student's current level of performance on the targeted writing genre, by looking through the student's writing portfolio and evaluating works or focusing on one or two recent compositions (students can also be asked to write a type of composition, such as a persuasive essay, to provide such a baseline if necessary). Examining current levels of performance can help set the stage for strategies instruction, helping students see what they are doing now and what they can expect to do once they learn the strategies. Current performance should be examined in a positive, collaborative manner with the emphasis on the changes to come. Examining current performance does not have to be done if the teacher thinks it will have a negative effect.

If current performance is assessed, graphing of performance might also be introduced at this stage. Aspects of the strategies instruction or goals of the instruction can be graphed, for example, students might graph how many of the seven common parts of a story they had in their current work, and then graph later stories as they learn a story-writing strategy. Graphing is a powerful part of self-monitoring and helps set the stage for both further self-monitoring and goal setting. If desirable, more than one goal can be graphed; students might also graph the number of words written, or the number of "million dollar words" (good vocabulary words) in each composition.

Stage 3: Model It

The teacher or a peer models the composition strategy and selected types of self-instructions while writing an actual composition during this stage. Types of self-instructions that can be introduced here include problem definition (what is it I have to do here?), focusing attention and planning (I have to concentrate; first I need to . . . then . . .), strategy-step statements (I need to write down my strategy reminder), self-evaluation and error correcting (have I used all my parts—oops, I missed one, better add it in), coping and self-control (I can handle this; go slow and take my time), and self-reinforcement (I like this ending!). All of these forms should not be introduced at once; rather, teachers should select types of statements and model statements specific to the needs and characteristics of their students.

It is important that the modeling be natural and enthusiastic and that the self-instructions have appropriate phrasing and inflection. The self-instructions modeled should be matched to the students' verbal style and language; while they will develop their own statements later, the modeled statements are critical in helping them do so. If students initially use prompts (we typically do), such as a graphic or chart listing the strategy steps or detailing a mnemonic, and a graphic organizer for writing, the model should use those also (examples can be found in the lesson plans on the CASL Web site mentioned earlier). The teacher can also set a goal for his or her composition, such as including all seven story parts, and evaluate the composition to see if the goal was met. Students can also be involved in the writing process by helping the model.

After self-regulation of the writing strategy has been modeled, the teacher and students should discuss the importance of the self-statements the model used as well as the goal setting and self-assessment. At this point, we typically have students begin to develop their own preferred self-instructions, recording them on paper (and often on bulletin boards). These self-instructions will be used in later stages; modeling, re-explanation, and further development of self-instructions can occur in later stages as needed. At this point, the teacher and students can also discuss the strategy steps and instructional components and collaboratively decide if any changes are needed to make the strategy more effective and efficient. This can also be discussed again in later stages. Generalization of the strategy to other tasks and settings can be discussed further at this point.

Teachers with whom we have worked have either creatively augmented live modeling or come up with alternatives. One teacher who was uncomfortable with modeling from memory or from notes when she first began strategy instruction came up with an innovative approach that worked well for her and her students. She worked out her modeling script, making sure she had all of the components, steps, and self-instructions she wished to model. She then put her self-talk on audio tape, reading from the script but speaking naturally and appropriately. She played this tape with her writing group, using the overhead projector to simultaneously plan for a composition. When the modeling of planning (using the strategy prompt and graphic organizer) was over, she and her students collaboratively wrote the actual composition, using the notes generated while modeling. In addition, teachers have successfully incorporated videotapes of peers who have already learned the strategy modeling their use of the writing and self-regulation strategies.

Stage 4: Memorize It

During this stage, students are required to memorize the steps in the composing strategy and the meaning of any mnemonics used either to represent the strategy steps or some part of the steps. The stage is particularly important for students who experience memory difficulties—as one of our students told us, "You can't use it if you can't remember it!" Some students may not need this stage, and thus may skip it. Memorization of the strategy can continue into the next stage, or be combined with the next stage. Students can paraphrase the strategy as long as the meaning remains intact. Students might also be asked to memorize one or more self-instructions from the personal lists they have generated.

Stage 5: Support It

Much like scaffolding provides support as a building is built, teachers at this stage support, or "scaffold," students' strategy use. Additional self-regulation strategies, such as goal setting, self-monitoring, or self-reinforcement, can be discussed, determined, initiated, or expanded. These components help to support motivation, maintenance and generalization, and cognitive and affective change. During this stage, students employ the strategy, self-instructions, and other self-regulation procedures as they actually compose. For example, each story written with support can be added to the graph the student has started. Due to the support received, performance should be high. The teacher provides as much support and assistance as needed, and may write collaboratively for a time with any students who need this level of assistance. Challenging but doable initial goals are individually determined collaboratively by the teacher and student—all students do not have to have the same goals. Criterion levels can be gradually increased until final goals are met.

Prompts, interaction, and guidance are faded at a pace appropriate to individual students until effective strategies use is achieved; thus students will move through this stage at different rates. Throughout this stage, the students and teacher continue to plan for and initiate generalization and maintenance of the strategies. This stage typically is the longest of the six stages for students who have serious writing difficulties. Students need to be given adequate time and support to master the strategy.

Stage 6: Independent Performance

If students have not already made the transition to use of covert ("in your head") self-instructions, this is encouraged at this stage while students now use the strategy independently. Self-regulation procedures are continued, but some can be gradually faded as appropriate and as determined by the teacher and students. Plans for maintenance and generalization continue to be implemented, including booster sessions over time. The teacher and students collaboratively evaluate strategy effectiveness and performance.

SRSD IN THE SECOND GRADE

Observing primary elementary students with disabilities and others who struggle with writing learn and then generalize and maintain planning and writing strategies has been an exciting component of our research. The characteristics inherent in the stages of SRSD instruction permit flexibility in developing and implementing lessons for these writers. Following SRSD instruction, we have seen students' writing evolve from one-sentence responses to multisentence papers that include critical rhetorical elements. Two planning strategies, a story-writing strategy and a strategy for persuasive essays, were recently taught to second-grade students in one of the schools we work in. The effectiveness of SRSD instruction for young elementary students who are struggling with writing can be illustrated by examining instruction and writing performance of two of these students, Lakeisha and Malcolm. As will be seen, modifications in the order of the 6 stages presented were made with these students.

POW Gives Power

A three-step framework for planning and writing—POW: Pick my idea; Organize my notes; Write and Say more—was used to structure the writing process before, during, and after writing. The writing instructor started the first lesson by initiating a discussion with Lakeisha and Malcolm about the "power" of the POW strategy and how the "organize my notes" step in POW is used to write different types of papers. SRSD instruction began with story writing, a reading and writing genre familiar to young students.

Once Upon a Time . . .

The story planning strategy, W-W-W, What=2, How=2, was taught in lessons that incorporated six stages for strategy acquisition—discuss it, develop preskills and background knowledge, model it, memorize it, support it, and independent performance. Procedures for developing self-instructions, goal setting, self-monitoring, and self-reinforcement were imbedded in the lessons. Seven story parts are included in W-W-W, What=2, How=2 (see Figure 12.1):

Discuss It

Lakeisha's and Malcolm's love of stories and storytelling became evident in the first lesson when W-W-W, What=2, How=2 was introduced and discussed. The students

POW

Pick my Idea
Organize my notes
Write and Say more

W-W-W What=2 How=2

Who is the main character?
When does the story take place?
Where does the story take place?
What does the main character do or want to do; what do other characters do?
What happens then? What happens with other characters?
How does the story end?
How does the main character feel; how do other characters feel?

FIGURE 12.1 ■ POW and W-W-W, What=2, How=2

eagerly applied their prior knowledge of story parts and story development to the strategy. Lakeisha, Malcolm, and the writing instructor read stories together, found story parts, and discussed how the story parts could be improved. Story parts were recorded on a graphic organizer (see Figure 12.2). To create a baseline for establishing writing goals, Lakeisha and Malcolm each read a story that they had previously written and charted the number of parts, out of the seven possible, included in this story on their rocket graphing sheet (see Figure 12.3) .

The difficulties that Lakeisha and Malcolm had demonstrated in the classroom with varying aspects of the writing process were reflected in the stories written prior to strategy instruction. Lakeisha had difficulties regulating the writing process and her emotions during writing. Her classroom teacher warned that any attempt to help Lakeisha could be met with uncontrollable tears. Malcolm had difficulty with the mechanics of writing. Malcolm's spelling and handwriting made it difficult for

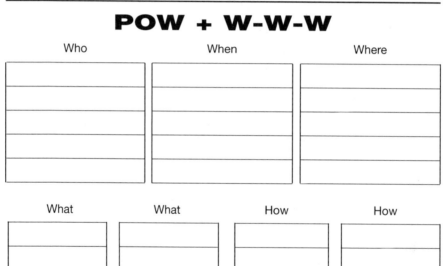

FIGURE 12.2 ■ Graphic Organizer for Story Parts

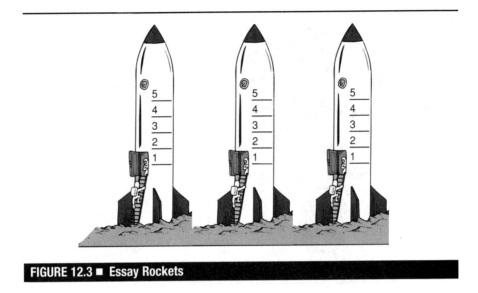

FIGURE 12.3 ■ Essay Rockets

anyone to read what he had written. During the discussion stage, the writing instructor stressed that Lakeisha and Malcolm's future stories would include all seven story parts because they were going to learn the "trick" or strategy for writing "fun" stories that had all the parts. A goal was established to write a fun story with all seven parts next time. Lakeisha and Malcolm were told that they would be writing partners and would help each other by providing reminders to use POW + W-W-W during the writing lessons and in the classroom. In fact, they would get to report to the writing instructor situations in which they helped each other and any strategy use at home or school. The following stories were written prior to instruction:

> The girl is looking at a egg. It have dots on it. It is hatching. She is looking down at the egg. (Lakeisha)
> They are trying to cook something for lunch or dinner. (Malcolm)

Develop Preskills and Background Knowledge

Often in the initial stages of instruction a teacher may notice that students with weaker skills and language difficulties require more support with the vocabulary and concepts. Mini skill lessons, adding picture cues to instructional material, and providing additional practice can serve as modifications for developing skills for effective implementation of the strategy.

Lakeisha and Malcolm initially had difficulty with correctly applying the concepts. They were encouraged to look at the picture cues provided on practice cue cards (see Figure 12.4). Both students were able to independently discriminate between the meanings by the guided practice lessons.

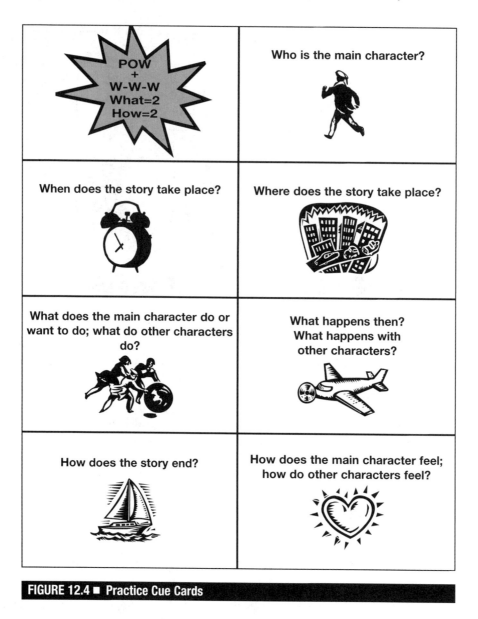

FIGURE 12.4 ■ Practice Cue Cards

Model It

During modeling, the instructor cognitively modeled (modeling out loud the steps and the thought processes of writing during all writing phases) using POW + W-W-W for story writing by including examples of how to set goals, self-monitor performance, and self-reinforce. During the modeling lesson, Lakeisha and Malcolm were allowed to give some ideas for the story, but the instructor was in charge of the writing process. Following the modeling lesson, the instructor, Lakeisha, and Malcolm discussed the things that were said while writing with POW + W-W-W. Lakeisha and Malcom developed and then recorded the things that they could say to themselves prior to, during, and after writing (see Figure 12.5). The instructor encouraged Lakeisha and Malcolm to develop statements, in their own words, which would help facilitate the writing process and success in using the strategies.

Lakeisha's self-statements directed her to remain positive and focused throughout the writing process—"I can do this; I will think about what I will do; Organize while I think; Do my best; I did my best." Malcolm's self-statements provided him with structure for the writing process and prompted him to be motivated during the process—"First, I need to pick an idea; I can think and write; I need to organize my notes; I can work my hardest; EXAMINE; I did a good job!"

Memorize It

Lakeisha and Malcolm began to memorize the W-W-W mnemonic and the meaning of the parts during the first lesson and continued to practice learning the strategy

---

W-W-W What=2 How=2

To think of good ideas:

_____

_____

_____

While I work:

_____

_____

_____

To check my work:

_____

_____

_____

FIGURE 12.5 ■ My Self Statements

parts until they achieved fluency in orally describing the strategy. After strengthening her vocabulary skills, Lakeisha had no difficulty with memorizing the strategy. Malcolm, however, struggled with the memorization step. Lakeisha helped her partner by playing a card game with the practice cards prior to the start of each lesson.

Support It

In order to scaffold instruction, the writing instructor, Lakeisha, and Malcolm collaboratively wrote a second story. This time the students were allowed to take more responsibility for story development. Two instructional segments followed collaborative writing. First, Lakeisha and Malcolm would plan and write their stories using the graphic organizer and self-statements. They were encouraged to write and say more by adding exciting or descriptive words to their stories—"million dollar words." After demonstrating success in writing stories with the seven parts of W-W-W, Lakeisha and Malcolm were taught to create their own organizers on a blank piece of paper. This step was especially hard for Malcolm who had difficulty with spelling the reminder parts. Malcolm and the instructor developed easily remembered abbreviations to help him with this process. Throughout guided practice, Lakeisha and Malcolm shared their stories, counted story parts, filled in the number of story parts they had included on the next rocket on their graph, and reinforced each other for a job well done.

Independent Performance

During independent practice, Lakeisha and Malcolm completed lessons that encouraged transfer of the POW + W-W-W strategy. These lessons included writing to a variety of story-prompt formats in diverse class settings. Lakeisha and Malcolm independently wrote the following seven-part stories following instruction:

> Once a boy named Cool J at 1:00 are at the home in New York. He scream loud because a bat was attacking him from behind. He was crying loud. His mother Aja was crying because she got attack too from behind too. The bat was still in the house flying. They both was sad not happy at all. They cry and cry all night long. Then the bat was kill one day and they was happy and happy the bat was kill. He was kill in the morning. The boy said to his mother, "Cool J and his mother Aja was not happy." So Aja, his sister, get a dog to guard them. (Lakeisha)

> Once upon a time a boy and a girl were walking. Then they found a dog lost so then they tried to put him in a wagon but he was too big so he bought a bigger wagon so the dog could fit and it worked but he was too heavy. Then the dog got out of the wagon. Then the dog pulled them through the town. And they was outside. It was at 9:00. He wanted to play with him. He was happy because he had a dog. (Malcolm)

That Is Why I Think . . .

Lakeisha and Malcolm were excited to learn the second strategy, POW + TREE, for planning persuasive essays (see Figure 12.6). By this time they had become more confident in their writing and more comfortable with the writing instructor. This was their first experience with persuasive writing, and they were eager to write papers that would tell the instructor their feelings about a topic. Lakeisha and Malcolm realized quickly that powerful persuasive essays could be written by using POW and by organizing notes using TREE. During *discuss it*, the instructor, Lakeisha, and Malcolm discussed POW + TREE while finding and recording the parts of TREE in persuasive essays.

Lakeisha recorded the number of parts of an essay (out of 5 possible: a topic sentence, three reasons, and an ending) she found in an essay that she had previously written. Malcolm, unfortunately, had responded to the essay prompt prior to instruction by simply recording the prompt sentence and was unable to use the graph. (We found that writing the prompt during pretest was not atypical for second-graders with disabilities.) The instructor again stressed that once the parts of TREE had been learned the rockets would be completed to the top, "busting" the rocket. Lakeisha wrote the following pretest essay:

> If you are about 9 and 10 you can pick out your own pet by yourself and a cat and a dog because they are big. (Lakeisha)

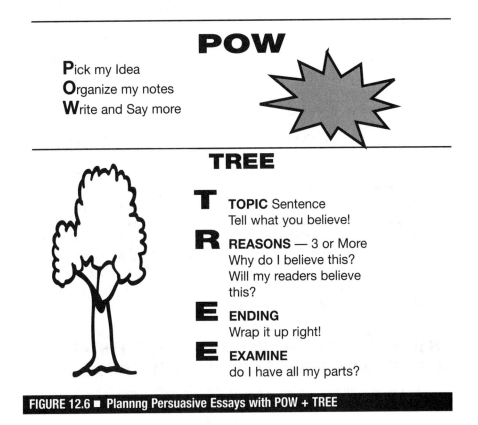

FIGURE 12.6 ■ Plannng Persuasive Essays with POW + TREE

Students who struggle with writing often have difficulties developing an organized thesis to present their arguments when writing persuasively. A list of transition words, therefore, was given to Lakeisha and Malcolm during the *develop preskills and background knowledge* stage. This list of simple transition words—first, second, third, fourth, next, then, also—helped Lakeisha and Malcolm focus attention on writing the parts in TREE in an organized manner when transferring ideas from the graphic organizer to the essay.

Following discussion and preskill development, the instructor cognitively modeled a persuasive essay using POW + TREE and a graphic organizer (see Figure 12.7). The instructor made a check mark at the end of the paper to indicate that she had "examined" the essay part. The instructor, Lakeisha, and Malcolm discussed the instructor's self-statements and updated their individual lists. Lakeisha and Malcolm *memorized* and learned to use the POW + TREE strategy within a few lessons. In fact, during *support it* less scaffolding was needed to support successful persuasive planning and writing. Transitioning from the organizer to writing their own notes was much easier because they had practiced this step before. As in the story writing lessons, *independent performance* was supported by transferring strategy use to a variety of writing prompts and instructional settings. Lakeisha and Malcolm wrote the following five-part persuasive essays following instruction:

> Yes I think kids should eat snack in the classroom. First, lunch is too short. Second, I get hungry in class. Third, I get thirsty in class. Fourth, I get hyper. Fifth, it helps kids to stay awake. This is why I think kids should eat snacks in the classroom. (Lakeisha)

> Teachers should ask children to write. First, they could have something to say. Second, you can have fun. Third, so you can listen. Fourth, so they can learn. That's why I think teachers ask children to write. (Malcolm)

Lakeisha and Malcolm were successful in improving the quality of their stories and persuasive essays as well as increasing the number of parts used and the number of words written. Following SRSD instruction, Lakeisha and Malcolm continued to support each other during classroom writing instruction. Their classroom teacher reported that their writing in the classroom had also improved and that she noticed a significant difference in the way that Lakeisha and Malcolm approached the writing process. Although Lakeisha and Malcolm have a lot to learn about the writing process, the strategies and self-regulation procedures they have cultivated will serve them well as they develop as writers.

CHARACTERISTICS OF EFFECTIVE SRSD INSTRUCTION: IT'S NOT JUST WHAT YOU DO BUT HOW YOU DO IT

Our work with teachers and students learning self-regulation and writing strategies has convinced us that *how* is every bit as important as *what* in strategy instruction.

POW + TREE

T **TOPIC** Sentence
Tell what you believe!

_____

_____

_____

R **REASONS** — 3 or More
Why do I believe this?
Will my readers believe this?

_____

_____

_____

_____

_____

E **ENDING**
Wrap it up right!

_____

_____

_____

E **EXAMINE**
Do I have all my parts?

 Yes?_____ No?_____

FIGURE 12.7 ■ POW + TREE Graphic Organizer

Teachers and students have helped us to identify several characteristics of the SRSD approach that are critical to effective implementation in schools and classrooms (Harris & Graham, 1996a).

First, SRSD *emphasizes collaborative learning* among teachers and students. While the teacher initially provides the necessary degree of scaffolding or support, the responsibility for recruiting, executing, monitoring, evaluating, and modifying strategies is gradually transferred to the student. For example, students can act as collaborators in determining the goals of instruction; completing the task; implementing, evaluating, and modifying the writing and self-regulation strategies; and planning for maintenance and generalization. Students also can collaborate with and provide support for each other.

Individualization of instruction based on each student's characteristics, strengths, and needs is a second important feature. Instruction does not need to be one-to-one, but teachers should strive to understand each child's current approach to writing as well as his or her affective and behavioral characteristics, and then work with the student to select and develop strategies and instructional components that fit his or her needs. Even when the writing and self-regulation strategies are appropriate for a group or entire class, the teacher can individualize aspects of instruction (the nature and content of self-instructions, goals for writing, affective goals, feedback and reinforcement, etc.).

The third important characteristic of SRSD is that *instruction is criterion based rather than time based.* Each student should be given the time he or she needs to meet appropriate affective, cognitive, and writing goals. Students progress through the stages at their own pace, moving on as they are ready to do so. Thus, teachers do not plan to teach a writing strategy within a set period of time, and when they are working with groups, they may frequently shift among entire-group, smaller-group, and individual lessons.

A fourth aspect teachers have found important is *anticipation and planning for glitches—areas of instruction that might be difficult or problems that might arise.* Teachers have found it helpful, before beginning instruction, to brainstorm things that could go wrong or prove difficult for some students, given what is known about the learners and the writing task. For example, some students (especially after third grade) may be resistant to using self-instructions out loud. Thus, the teacher might plan to describe it as "thinking out loud to yourself" and note that it can be done very quietly. If that doesn't work, teachers have allowed students to talk into a recorder as they work, or to read to themselves from their written statements. Students can collaborate in anticipating glitches as well. For example, maintenance and generalization can be challenging for some students. Together with the teacher, students can set a plan for booster sessions and prompts for generalizing.

Because teachers play such a critical role in helping students understand the meaning and efficacy of self-regulation and writing strategies, the fifth characteristic involves having *enthusiastic teachers working within a support network.* Enthusiastic, responsive teaching is an integral part of SRSD, as it is with all effective teaching. Given the complexity and demands of strategies instruction, a supportive network of teachers and administrators who can problem solve and share both successes and difficulties makes implementation considerably easier. Moreover, the impact of instruction on students is much greater, and maintenance and generalization of strategic performance across the curriculum and grades are more likely, when strategies instruction is embraced across a school or district.

The final characteristic we note here is *developmental enhancement*. To teach a strategy well, teachers need to help students see the meaning and the significance of the strategy, as well as its strengths and weaknesses. This requires an understanding of where the strategies to be taught fit in the larger scheme of things in terms of the students' development both as a writer and as a self-regulated learner. A skillful, effective writer employs strategies and conventions of the craft the way a jazz musician uses a melody. The mature writer is able to profit from the variations, the riffs, the twists, and ultimately the meaning of the strategies and conventions of writing. Thus, as students mature as writers, they continually refine, combine, and enhance the strategies they have mastered or created, using them in more sophisticated ways. Teachers can facilitate this process, particularly if they work together across the grades, by collaboratively planning for and supporting among their students the developmental enhancement of strategies and strategic performance (for examples, see Harris & Graham, 1996a).

EVALUATING SRSD INSTRUCTION

Students who are taught a strategy that does not improve their performance certainly will not be enthusiastic about learning a second strategy. Ongoing assessment, rather than assessment only at the end of instruction, allows teachers and students to determine what is working and what changes need to be made. SRSD facilitates meaningful, ongoing assessment. The interactive, collaborative nature of the SRSD learning process allows teachers to assess changes in affect, behavior, and cognition. The following is an explanation of some basic principles for assessing SRSD methods and procedures. The list is certainly not exhaustive, but it provides a good starting point for effective evaluation.

Involve Students as Coevaluators

Students should be included as partners in the strategy evaluation process. Coevaluation not only increases students' sense of ownership and reinforces the progress they are making, but also provides teachers with much greater insight into the effectiveness of the strategies and SRSD instruction. Students can participate in many ways, such as learning to evaluate their writing based on their goals (self-assessment), or discussing with the teacher which components of instruction are most helpful to them or where they would recommend changes. Helping students ask appropriate self-questions (e.g., "Am I ready to move on to the next step?"; "Is this working for me?"; "Do I need to do anything differently?") is another effective way to help students evaluate their own progress. By asking students to share their reflections, teachers also gain valuable insight into their progress and readiness for moving on. Collaborative peer evaluation, such as peer-revising strategies (see Harris & Graham, 1996a), is also a valuable component of the assessment process.

Consider the Level of Evaluation Needed

Strategies, methods, and procedures, such as W-W-W or TREE, that have been previously validated (both by research and by teachers in the classroom) typically need less scrutiny than a strategy being used for the first time. In other words, the amount of time and effort expended on assessing the usefulness of a strategy depends on the established validity of the strategy and a teacher's experience with it. However, it is important to remember that even well-validated strategies still need evaluation. At a minimum, teachers should know if (a) students are actually using the strategy, (b) usage of the strategy has a positive impact on performance and affective characteristics, and (c) students see the strategy as being valuable and manageable.

Assess Changes in Performance, Attitudes, and Cognition

Because the benefits of SRSD go beyond improving a student's performance, teachers should also look for changes in students' attitudes and cognitive processes. While teaching writing and self-regulation strategies, teachers might observe students for improvements in attitudes towards writing or confidence in their abilities. The teacher might also gather information about the amount and quality of writing the student does before and after SRSD instruction, or listen for spontaneous statements made about writing assignments. Open-ended questions—such as "What is good writing?" and "What do you most like to say to yourself while you write?"—can help provide insight. When evaluating performance, attitudes, and cognition, it is important to remember that some changes (e.g., reducing writing anxiety and improving attitudes) take more time than others to obtain.

Assess While Instruction Is in Progress

Often, classroom assessment occurs when teaching is "done." However, this is not a viable model for strategy instruction. Instead, assessment procedures need to reflect the developmental, dynamic, and ongoing process of learning to use a strategy.

Assess How Students Actually Use the Strategy

Over time, students will often modify a strategy or how they use it. As a result, it cannot be assumed that students are using the strategy as intended. Some modifications allow a strategy to meet a student's unique needs, but others (such as eliminating a necessary step) may not be useful or desirable. Teachers can monitor strategy usage directly by observing what students do as they write, asking questions, and discussing how things are working, or indirectly by looking for evidence of strategy usage in students' papers.

Assess Students' Use of the Strategy Over Time and in New Situations

We cannot assume that students will continue to use a particular strategy or successfully adapt a strategy to new situations. Therefore, it is beneficial to actively enhance maintenance and generalization of strategy usage from the very beginning of SRSD instruction. This might be done by periodically inviting students to explain the purpose of a strategy, or having students (and teachers) share ways they have used the strategy. A teacher might also ask students to keep a record of each time they use a strategy or how they modify it for other tasks. Ultimately, the goal is to determine if students need additional support to consistently apply the strategy in appropriate situations.

Collaborate With Colleagues During the Evaluation Process

If students are being taught a strategy that can be applied in different content areas or classrooms, it is important for teachers to involve colleagues in promoting this generalization and assessing whether the transition across subjects and settings is being made. It is also important to discuss with other teachers the strategy's effectiveness and whether it is appropriate in their classes, and, if not, how it could best be modified or what other strategies would be more useful. Working together in this way, teachers in different classes can provide reminders for students to use the strategy, help students with a particular aspect of the strategy as needed, or suggest modifications to make the strategy more effective for the present task.

Use Portfolio Assessment Procedures

Portfolio assessment is an ideal way to bring together many of the recommendations we have presented for SRSD evaluation. When students maintain portfolios, both teachers and students benefit. Students learn to engage in reflective self-evaluation, come to understand that development is as important as achievement (a major tenet of many process approaches to writing), and take greater responsibility for their own learning. Teachers gain new insights about assessment and teaching, and a greater understanding of their students' development and learning. Portfolio assessment does require that teachers establish the credibility of this approach with students and then become intimately involved in the maintenance and evaluation of student portfolios. Once teachers and students become comfortable with this form of assessment, positive results occur for both.

A FEW FINAL TIPS FOR SRSD

Take It Slow

For teachers just starting out with strategy instruction, we recommend starting slowly. It is tempting to try SRSD in the areas of instruction that present the greatest challenges or with students who are experiencing the most difficultly. However, despite good intentions, it is not fair to either party to take on too much too fast. Instead, begin with relatively simple strategies in an area where you are comfortable and anticipate success, and with students who are willing to learn the strategies. Although "nothing succeeds like success," initial failure can make persistence difficult for both teachers and students. Teachers can move on to greater challenges as they gain experience. We also recommend that strategies not be forced on students, but rather that they be offered to students.

Take Advantage of Strategies Already Developed

It is often easier to begin strategy instruction with an existing, already proven strategy, such as POW plus W-W-W or POW plus TREE strategy presented in this article. Rather than attempting to create an effective strategy and become comfortable with the process of helping students master the strategy at the same time, teachers can take advantage of a strategy that has already been developed and validated (cf. Harris & Graham, 1996a). Once the teacher and students are familiar with SRSD, then they can work together to create and evaluate new strategies, as they will often need to do to address their unique needs and situations.

Learn Together

If at all possible, teachers should collaborate with other teachers, as well as their students, while they learn to implement SRSD in the classroom. This professional collaboration allows teachers to share their personal triumphs and challenges with strategy instruction and serves to facilitate supportive feedback and problem solving.

CONCLUSION

Evaluations of SRSD by teachers and students have been positive, indicating sound social validity. One teacher, for example, commented how she could "see light bulbs going on" as her students learned to use writing strategies (Danoff et al., 1993, p. 315). One student proclaimed that SRSD should be "taught to all schools in the country" (Graham, Harris, & Troia, 1998, p. 30), and another noted that "the W-W-W strategy really builds up your resources." One student perhaps best described our goals for SRSD when he said, "*Now* this writing stuff makes sense!" When writing makes sense and children develop ownership of powerful self-regulation and writing strategies, every child can indeed write.

Harris and Graham have emphasized from the beginning, however, that SRSD should not be thought of as a panacea; promoting students' academic competence and literacy requires a complex integration of skills, strategies, processes, and attributes. However, by establishing affective, behavioral, and cognitive goals for instruction, SRSD represents an important contribution to teachers' instructional repertoires.

REFERENCES

Albertson, L., & Billingsley, F. (1997, March). *Improving young writers' planning and reviewing skills while story-writing.* Paper presented at the American Educational Research Association Conference, Chicago, IL.

Applebee, A., Langer, J., Jenkins, L., Mullis, I., & Foertsch, M. (1990). *Learning to write in our nations' schools.* Princeton, NJ: Educational Testing Service.

Applebee, A., Langer, J., & Mullis, I. (1986). *The writing report card: Writing achievement in American schools.* Princeton, NJ: Educational Testing Service.

Applebee, A., Langer, J., Mullis, I., Latham, A., & Gentile, C. (1994). *NAEP 1992: Writing report card.* Washington, DC: US Government Printing Office.

Association for Supervision and Curriculum Development (Producer). (2002). *Teaching students with learning disabilities: Using learning strategies* [Video]. (Available from ASCD, 1703 North Beauregard Street, Alexandria, VA 22311-1714).

Atwell, N. (1987). *In the middle: Reading, writing, and learning from adolescents.* Portsmouth, NH: Heinemann.

Bednarczyk, A. (1991). *The effectiveness of story grammar instruction with a self-instructional strategy development framework for students with learning disabilities.* Unpublished doctoral dissertation, University of Maryland, College Park.

Bereiter, C., & Scardamalia, M. (1982). From conversation to composition: The role of instruction in a developmental process. In R. Glaser (Ed.), *Advances in instructional psychology* (Vol. 2, pp. 1–64). Hillsdale, NJ: Erlbaum.

Case, L. P., Harris, K. R., & Graham, S. (1992). Improving the mathematical problem-solving skills of students with learning disabilities: Self-regulated strategy development. *Journal of Special Education, 26,* 1–19.

Collins, R. (1992). *Narrative writing of option II students: The effects of combining the whole-language techniques, writing process approach and strategy training.* Unpublished thesis, State University of New York, Buffalo.

Danoff, B., Harris, K. R., & Graham, S. (1993). Incorporating strategy instruction within the writing process in the regular classroom: Effects in the writing of students with and without learning disabilities. *Journal of Reading Behavior, 25,* 295–322.

De La Paz, S. (1999). Teaching writing strategies and self-regulation procedures to middle school students with learning disabilities. *Focus on Exceptional Children, 31,* 1–16.

De La Paz, S. (2001). Teaching writing to students with attention deficit disorders and specific language impairment. *Journal of Educational Research, 95,* 37–47.

De La Paz, S., & Graham, S. (2001). *Strategy instruction in planning: Enhancing the planning behavior and writing performance of middle school students.* Manuscript submitted for publication.

De La Paz, S., Owen, B., Harris, K. R., & Graham, S. (2000). Riding Elvis' motorcycle: Using self-regulated strategy development to PLAN and WRITE for a state exam. *Learning Disabilities Research and Practice, 15*(2), 101–109.

Edelsky, C., Altwerger, B., & Flores, B. (1991). *Whole language: What's the difference?* Portsmouth, NH: Heinemann.

Flower, L., & Hayes, J. (1980). The dynamics of composing: Making plans and juggling constraints. In L. Gregg & R. Steinberg (Eds.). *Cognitive processes in writing* (pp. 31–50). Hillsdale, NJ: Erlbaum.

Graham, S., & Harris, K. R. (1989). Improving learning disabled students' skills at composing essays: Self-instructional strategy training. *Exceptional Children, 56,* 201–216.

Graham, S., & Harris, K. R. (1994). The role and development of self-regulation in the writing process. In D. Schunk & B. Zimmerman (Eds.), *Self-regulation of learning and performance: Issues and educational applications* (pp. 203–228). New York: Lawrence Erlbaum.

Graham, S., & Harris, K. R. (1996). Self-regulation and strategy instruction for students with writing and learning difficulties. In S. Ransdell & M. Levy (Eds.), *Science of writing: Theories, methods, individual differences, and applications* (pp. 347–360). New York: Lawrence Erlbaum.

Graham, S., & Harris, K. R. (2000). The role of self-regulation and transcription skills in writing and writing development. *Educational Psychologist, 35*(1), 3–12.

Graham, S., & Harris, K. R. (2002). Prevention and intervention for struggling writers. In M. Shinn, G. Stoner, & H. Walker (Eds.), *Interventions for academic and behavior problems II: Preventive and remedial approaches* (pp. 589–610). Bethesda, MD: National Association of School Psychologists.

Graham, S., & Harris, K. R. (2003). Students with learning disabilities and the process of writing: A meta-analysis of SRSD studies. In H. L. Swanson, K. R. Harris, & S. Graham (Eds.), *Handbook of learning disabilities* (pp. 323–344). New York: Guilford Press.

Graham, S., Harris, K. R., & Larsen, L. (2001). Prevention and intervention of writing difficulties with students with learning disabilities. *Learning Disabilities Research and Practice, 16,* 74–84.

Graham, S., Harris, K. R., MacArthur, C. A., & Schwartz, S. (1991). Writing and writing instruction for students with learning disabilities: Review of a research program. *Learning Disability Quarterly, 14,* 89–114.

Graham, S., Harris, K. R., & Reid, R. (1992). Developing self-regulated learners. *Focus on Exceptional Children, 24*(6), 1–16.

Graham, S., Harris, K. R., & Troia, G. (1998). Writing and self-regulation: Cases from the self-regulated strategy development model. In D. Schunk & B. Zimmerman (Eds.), *Self-regulated learning: From teaching to self-reflective practices,* (pp. 30). New York: Guilford.

Graves, D. (1985). All children can write. *Learning Disability Focus, 1,* 36–43.

Harris, K. R. (1982). Cognitive-behavior modification: Application with exceptional students. *Focus on Exceptional Children, 15*(2), 1–16.

Harris, K. R. (1986). The effects of cognitive-behavior modification on private speech and task performance during problem solving among learning disabled and normally achieving children. *Journal of Abnormal Child Psychology, 14,* 63–76.

Harris, K. R., & Alexander, P. A. (1998). Integrated, constructivist education: Challenge and reality. *Educational Psychology Review, 10*(2), 115–127.

Harris, K. R., Bennof, A., Higdon, J., Liebow, H., Metheny, L., Nelson, V., Packman, S., & Strouse, C. (1992). The Charles County Academic Self-Management Consortium: SCOREing across the grades. *Learning Disabilities Forum, 17,* 37–42.

Harris, K. R., & Graham, S. (1985). Improving learning disabled students' composition skills: Self-control strategy training. *Learning Disability Quarterly, 8,* 27–36.

Harris, K. R., & Graham, S. (1992). Self-regulated strategy development: A part of the writing process. In M. Pressley, K. R. Harris, & J. T. Guthrie (Eds.), *Promoting academic competence and literacy in school* (pp. 277–309). New York: Academic Press.

Harris, K. R., & Graham, S. (1994). Constructivism: Principles, paradigms, and integration. *The Journal of Special Education, 28,* 233–247.

Harris, K. R., & Graham, S. (1996a). *Making the writing process work: Strategies for composition and self-regulation* (2d ed.). Cambridge: Brookline Books.

Harris, K. R., & Graham, S. (l996b). Memo to constructivists: Skills count, too. *Educational Leadership, 53*(5), 26–29.

Harris, K. R., & Graham, S. (1996c). Constructivism and students with special needs: Issues in the classroom. *Learning Disabilities Research and Practice, 11*(3), 134–137.

Harris, K. R., & Graham, S. (1999). Programmatic intervention research: Illustrations from the evolution of self-regulated strategy development. *Learning Disability Quarterly, 22,* 251–262.

Harris, K. R., Graham, S., & Deshler, D. (Eds.). (1998). *Advances in teaching and learning. Vol. 2: Teaching every child every day: Learning in diverse schools and classrooms.* Cambridge: Brookline Books.

Harris, K. R., & Pressley, M. (l99l). The nature of cognitive strategy instruction: Interactive strategy construction. *Exceptional Children, 57,* 392–405.

Harris, K. R., Schmidt, T., & Graham, S. (1998). Every child can write: Strategies for composition and self-regulation in the writing process. In K. R. Harris, S. Graham, & D. Deshler (Eds.), *Advances in teaching and learning. Vol. 2: Teaching every child every day: Learning in diverse schools and classrooms* (pp. 131–167). Cambridge: Brookline Books.

Johnson, L., Graham, S., & Harris, K. R. (1997). The effects of goal setting and self-instruction on learning a reading comprehension strategy among students with learning disabilities. *Journal of Learning Disabilities, 30*(1), 80–91.

Kendall, P., & Braswell, L. (1982). On cognitive-behavioral assessment: Model, measures, and madness. In C. Speilberger & J. Butcher (Eds.), *Advances in personality assessment,* (Vol. 1, pp. 35–82). Hillsdale, NJ: Erlbaum.

Kronick, D. (1990). Holism and empiricism as complementary paradigms. *Journal of Learning Disabilities, 23,* 5–8, 10.

MacArthur, C. A., Graham, S., Schwartz, S., & Shafer, W. (1995). Evaluation of a writing instruction model that integrated a process approach, strategy instruction, and word processing. *Learning Disability Quarterly, 18,* 278–291.

MacArthur, C. A., Schwartz, S., & Graham, S. (1991). Effects of a reciprocal peer revision strategy in special education classrooms. *Learning Disabilities Research and Practice, 6,* 201–210.

MacArthur, C., Schwartz, S., Graham, S., Molloy, D., & Harris, K. R. (1996). Integration of strategy instruction into a whole language classroom: A case study. *Learning Disabilities Research & Practice, 11,* 168–176.

Manning, M., & Manning, G. (1995). Whole language: They say, you say. *Teaching PreK–8, 25,* 50–55.

Mason, L. H. (2002). *Self-regulated strategy instruction: Effects on expository reading comprehension among students who struggle with reading.* Unpublished doctoral dissertation, University of Maryland, College Park.

Poplin, M. S. (1988). Holistic/constructivist principles of the teaching/ learning process: Implications for the field of learning disabilities. *Journal of Learning Disabilities, 21,* 389–400.

Pressley, M., & Harris, K. R. (l998). Constructivism and instruction. *Issues in Education: Contributions from Educational Psychology, 3*(2), 245–255.

Sawyer, R. J., Graham, S., & Harris, K. R. (l992). Direct teaching, strategy instruction, and strategy instruction with explicit self-regulation: Effects on learning disabled students' composition skills and self-efficacy. *Journal of Educational Psychology, 84,* 340–352.

Scardamalia, M., & Bereiter, C. (1986). Written composition. In M. Wittrock (Ed.), *Handbook of research on teaching* (3rd ed., pp. 778–803). New York: MacMillan.

Scheid, K. (1991). *Effective writing instruction for students with learning problems.* Columbus, OH: LINC Resources.

Sexton, M., Harris, K. R., & Graham, S. (l998). Self-regulated strategy development and the writing process: Effects on essay writing and attributions. *Exceptional Children, 64*(3), 295–311.

Smith, C. B. (Moderator). (1994). *Whole language: The debate.* Bloomington, IN: ERIC.

Tanhouser, S. (1994). *Function over form: The relative efficacy of self-instructional strategy training alone and with procedural facilitation for adolescents with learning disabilities.* Unpublished doctoral dissertation, Johns Hopkins University, Maryland.

Willis, S. (November, 1993), "Whole language in the io's." *ASCD Update, 35(9),* 1–8..

Wong, B., Harris, K. R., Graham, S., & Butler, D. L. (2003). Cognitive strategies instruction research in learning disabilities. In H. L. Swanson, K. R. Harris, & S. Graham (Eds.), *Handbook of learning disabilities* (pp. 383–402). New York: Guilford Press.

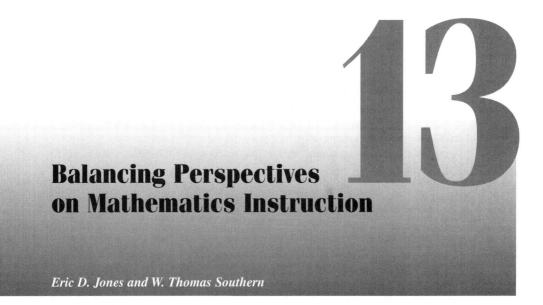

Balancing Perspectives on Mathematics Instruction

Eric D. Jones and W. Thomas Southern

Controversies in educational literature are often formed in the tones of a debate. Debate, however, has the effect of emphasizing contrasts in two bodies of literature and deemphasizing similarities, overlap, and the potential complementary use of different approaches. Pressley and his colleagues (Pressley, Roehrig, Bogner, Raphael, & Dolezal, 2002) published an article in *Focus on Exceptional Children* (volume 34, issue 5, January 2002), describing the balance that effective teachers provide between skills instruction and holistic opportunities for developing literacy. The thesis of their article is that productive efforts to develop literacy in children will require that teachers balance the efforts and the opportunities they provide for skills instruction (e.g, phonics, comprehension strategies), as well as opportunities to participate in authentic literary experiences (e.g., reading real literature, writing reports). In that article, effective teachers are reported as using a range of instructional procedures to promote the development of literacy.

Pressley et al. (2002) discuss the importance of teachers' making rational and balanced choices in selecting instructional procedures and experiences rather than merely responding to ideologies that supposedly are grounded in theoretical models for instruction. Pressley et al.'s discussion of teachers' practices echoes the suggestions by Dixon and Carnine (1994) that educators should focus their attention on the effectiveness and the efficiency of instructional practices rather than worrying a great deal about the apparent congruence of instructional procedures with specific ideologies.

The ideological debate in literacy education centers on the relative merit of so-called traditional skills instruction versus constructivist approaches to literacy development. A similar debate is being waged in mathematics education. Generally, the argument of constructivists has been that traditional teacher-led instruction does not lead to proficiency in mathematical reasoning and problem solving. They argue for more opportunities for students to engage in authentic problem-solving activities. Students will find mathematical experiences more meaningful and, thus, more motivating than if they are fed knowledge, directed through mathematical procedures, and led to the teacher's understandings.

In more extreme instances, the arguments for constructivism have veered off to discussions of personal freedom, social politics, and morality (cf. Brantlinger, 1977; Dixon & Carnine, 1992; Heshusius, 1991; Kauffman, 2002) In a less polemic vein, Mercer, Jordan, and Miller (1996) described the breadth of the constructivist conceptualizations of instruction and their compatibility with more behaviorally grounded theories of instruction.

We agree that becoming ensnared in ideological discussions about the merits of constructivism or its alternatives is generally unproductive. Those discussions tend to pit otherwise rational individuals against each other, and they are variously labeled with unflattering terms such as silly, flaky, and barbaric. Although one can sometimes achieve or maintain certain social and political cachets by labeling, the name-calling is unnecessary and unkind, and it also obfuscates the important issue of how pupils should be taught mathematical skills and strategies.

The arguments themselves have become important, we believe, because they have been going on for a long time and have not contributed constructively to practice in math education. The ideological arguments themselves are insufficient, sometimes misleading, and distracting. Generally, they have come to have limited value in providing direction to the reform of mathematics education.

In this chapter we discuss the debate over approaches to mathematics instruction. In other forums the debate has been generalized to mathematics education. Here we will also address issues that are more specific to teaching mathematics to students with special needs. We will begin with a brief discussion of the development and hardening of ideologies within the mathematics reform. After explaining the ideological controversies, we will discuss principles of learning and instruction that have been empirically validated and should be noncontroversial in their application to mathematics instruction, particularly in their application to the instruction of students with special education needs. Finally, we will consider the implications that developing (or failing to develop) more balanced conceptualizations of instruction can have on teacher education and practice.

This chapter will not provide a comprehensive analysis of the philosophical underpinnings of the debate. Our intent is to provide a discussion that will look at the history of the controversies, describe both approaches, and finally discuss the strengths of constructivism and of direct instruction, drawing conclusions as to how the two approaches might complement each other for the instruction of students with special education needs.

Following the publication of new standards for the reform of mathematics education (National Council of Teachers of Mathematics, 1989, 2000), published articles have been decrying the status of mathematics achievement in the United States, arguing for constructivist or behavioral models for instruction, and occasionally denouncing proponents of one model or the other. At the same time, relatively little effort has been given to documenting the effectiveness of instructional practices, whatever their roots. Thus, the ideological arguments seem to have generated far more heat than light.

The debates survive, without seeming to have had much influence on instructional practice, curriculum development, or teacher training. The current mathematics achievement crisis is at least as acute as it ever has been and may be even more desperate. The shortage of mathematics teachers across the nation continues and is projected to become more acute. In the next decade a large proportion of today's teachers, especially those in special education, math, and science, will be eligible for retirement (Ingersoll, 2001). Urban districts are finding it particularly difficult to hire mathematics teachers, and those they do hire generally do not stay long (Ingersoll, 2001; Merrow, 1999; National Education Association, 2002). Arguably, the standards for mathematics education reform proposed by the National Council of Teachers of Mathematics (1989, 2000) have not had documented effects on mathematics instruction, particularly in urban and rural communities, where the shortage of math teachers has been an increasingly acute, with a growing number of teachers teaching out of their licensure areas.

BALANCED INSTRUCTION: AN IMPLIED COMPARISON

A discussion of balanced instruction involves comparing the different models or approaches to instruction. In the case of mathematics, this is generally assumed to involve a comparison of behavioral and constructivist approaches. Proponents of both behavioral and constructivist approaches have made frequent and strong criticisms of traditional approaches to mathematics education. Proponents of each of these perspectives have been strong critics of the other as well. In their criticisms of each other's approaches, advocates of behavioral and constructivist approaches frequently have equated the opposing perspective to "traditional" approaches to mathematics instruction.

Before we compare the characteristics and the value of balancing behavioral and constructivist approaches, we will consider the nature of "traditional" approaches to mathematics instruction. Then we will discuss the relative merits of the different approaches to instruction and consider the value of balancing their use in practice. First, though, we will define these approaches.

Traditional or Current Approaches

Defining the features of so-called traditional or current approaches to mathematics instruction is an illusive task. Although we possibly can describe, through interviews and observational study, the precise nature of instruction in any given classroom, it would be difficult to discuss in detail the characteristics of mathematics instruction as it is delivered across a wide range of classrooms. Consequently, it is difficult to describe "typical" mathematics instruction precisely. The term *typical practices* must encompass the wide variations in organization, content, and delivery of instruction among teachers. The tradition of mathematics instruction in the United States provides for a great deal of autonomy and discretion by teachers. Despite the difficulties in defining what amounts to typical approaches to instruction, we can piece together some of the more general characteristics of mathematics instruction as it is practiced in the United States.

1. Math curricula vary but are dependent on commercially published programs (Carnine, 1992; Kameenui & Griffin, 1989; Tyson & Woodward, 1989).
2. Instruction tends to be teacher-led and didactic (Woodward & Montague, 2002), but
   a. teachers, especially at the elementary levels, do not have extensive knowledge of the content of mathematics (Porter, Floden, Freeman, Schmidt, & Schwille, 1988),
   b. the commercially available curricula rarely provide instructions for teachers that will assure consistent implementations of the curricular programs (Carnine, Jones, & Dixon, 1994; Maccini, & Gagnon, 2002; Stein, Silbert, & Carnine, 1997),
   c. teachers who provide instruction in basic mathematics knowledge and skills generally do not perceive themselves as having expertise in mathematics instruction (Porter et al., 1988), and
   d. their decisions on how to present curricula are heavily influenced by introspections, perceptions, and impressions of how they were taught the same mathematical skills and concepts (Porter et al., 1988).
3. Most commercial curricula in elementary or basic mathematics do not provide adequate sequences of instruction or adequate indications of the amounts and types of practice (Carnine, 1989; Stein, Silbert, & Carnine, 1997).
4. Commercial curricula do not provide adequate articulations of the scope and sequence of the domains of mathematical knowledge and skills (Carnine, 1992; Kameenui & Griffin, 1989; Stein, Silbert, & Carnine, 1997).
5. Math curricula tend to disproportionately emphasize computational skills at the expense of problem-solving skills (Woodward & Montague, 2002).
6. Math curricula tend to provide for instruction that involves a limited range of modes for presenting tasks and allowing for student responses (Cawley, Fitzmaurice, Lepore, Sedlak, & Althaus, 1979; Cawley, Fitzmaurice, Shaw, Kahn, & Bates, 1978).

Generally speaking, mathematics instruction is directed by teachers who do not perceive that they have sufficient expertise in mathematics content or instruction. They are apt to rely on commercially available curricula that have substantial inadequacies in organization, content, and direction for implementation. Teachers are inclined to teach mathematics knowledge and skills as they perceive what they were taught. In short, mathematics instruction, especially at the level of basic skills, seems to be neither well organized nor rationally delivered.

Although direct instruction and constructivism are based on quite different notions about teaching and learning, they are not discussed often in direct opposition to each other within professional literature. Instead, critics most often characterize each as exemplifying the faults of traditional mathematics instruction. The deficiencies of traditional mathematics are broad enough for proponents of direct instruction and constructivist instruction to use some aspect of traditional education as a basis for opposing the other. For example, proponents of direct instruction have criticized traditional or current state-of-the-art instruction for its lack of coherent teacher direction and explicit organization of curriculum content. Then, by extension, they have also criticized constructivist approaches because constructivists argue against explicit control of either presentation or content of instruction.

In a similar vein, constructivists have been critical of traditional practices as being excessively didactic and authoritarian, restricting opportunities for students to learn through concrete and authentic experiences, ignoring the social context of academic learning, avoiding communication and active engagement, and concentrating on lower levels of instruction to the detriment of problem solving. Their criticisms of typical instruction programs then are applied to direct instruction in its effort to exert explicit control over both the presentation and the content of instruction.

Some critiques of direct instruction (e.g., Palincsar, 1998; Woodward & Montague, 2002) are less circuitous. In her criticism of the efficacy of direct instruction, Palincsar (1998, p. 347) is substantially quoted by Woodward and Montague (2002, p. 91). She argues that:

> The research regarding direct instruction suggests that while it is an effective means of teaching factual content, there is less evidence that this instruction transfers to higher order cognitive skills such as reasoning and problem solving nor is there sufficient evidence that direct-instruction teaching results in the flexibility necessary for students to use the targeted strategies in novel contexts (Peterson & Walberg, 1979). In addition to these practical concerns with the limitations of direct instruction, there are significant theoretical limitations of the behavioral perspective, namely this perspective offers no satisfactory explanation to the mechanisms that account for learning. (p. 347)

Thus, direct instruction specifically, along with other approaches based on behavioral learning theory generally, is criticized because the efficacy of its applications to complex and difficult-to–teach-and-learn knowledge and skills is not as clearly demonstrated as with simpler instructional problems and contents. In translation, direct instruction is effective in teaching simple skills to difficult-to-teach students but seems to be less effective in teaching complex and difficult skills to hard-to-teach students. Palincsar (1998) does not offer a comparison with constructivist approaches and seems to ignore the obvious point that difficult skills and hard-to-teach students by definition challenge the effectiveness of any approach to instruction: They are hard to teach. These critiques amount to unsubstantial bits of red herring.

Criticisms that some elements of specific instructional approaches resemble general instructional practices are misleading and unhelpful for several reasons. *First*, the critics must establish that resemblances between the specific models and general practices are real similarities and not just matters of appearance or contrivance. Across the range of instructional practices that are referred to as *typical*, there are examples of practices that advocates of both behavioral and constructivist approaches both support and criticize. Therefore, it is hardly legitimate for either to try to criticize the other for what is going on in our schools.

Second, it must be determined that general instructional practices are characterized by the specific elements. *Third*, critics must provide clear evidence that those elements account for the shortcomings of the general curriculum. These second and third conditions are unlikely to be met because there have not been, and probably will never be, any studies that adequately characterize the diverse and sometimes idiosyncratic instructional behaviors that take place in mathematics instruction.

Fourth, comparisons between direct instruction and constructivism must be focused rather than relying on the current method of criticism-by-proxy. This condition can be addressed, but it requires that both direct instruction and constructivism be adequately characterized to avoid irresponsible constructions of straw-man arguments. It is difficult to arrive at definitions of constructivism and direct instruction that completely capture their essence. Although direct instruction and constructivism have some pronounced conceptual differences, other distinctions between the two are more apparent than real.

Direct Instruction

For more than 20 years direct instruction has been favored in special education. Support for direct instruction, however, has been more apparent within research and teacher-education programs than it has been in either general education or special education classrooms. Direct instruction also has been variously defined (Gersten, 1985). The term *direct instruction* has been used broadly to refer to behaviorally based instructional activities that are directly related to increasing achievement in basic academic skills. Accordingly, instructional procedures are considered to be "direct" if the explicit purpose of instructional activities is to increase academic achievement and if instruction emphasizes teacher behaviors and variables related to classroom structure, such as small-group instruction, teacher direction of learning, academic focus, high rates of accurate responding, controlled practice, use of higher cognitive-level questions, group responding, independent practice, and feedback to student responses (Rosenshine, 1978, 1979; Stevens & Rosenshine, 1981).

The earliest iteration of the model was evaluated and found to be the leading model of instruction in the national Follow Through Study (Stebbins, St. Pierre, Proper, Anderson, & Cerva, 1977). Unlike the more generic approaches to direct instruction (e.g., Good, Grouws, & Ebemeier, 1979; Rosenshine 1978, 1979; Stevens & Rosenshine, 1981), the University of Oregon Model of Direct Instruction places considerable emphasis on task demands and their presentation in the instructional sequence. Instructional sequences are based on the careful selection and sequencing of instructional examples.

Watkins and Slocum (2004) describe the University of Oregon Model and identify three characteristics that define and provide for its success: content analysis, curriculum design, and clear communication between the teacher and the student. Direct instruction involves extensive preparation before teacher/student interactions take place. It begins with analyses of the potential content of mathematics curricula to: (a) determine the scope and sequence of knowledge and skills that will be learned within and among the domains of mathematics, (b) identify the critical concepts and skills, and (c) identify important relationships between math concepts and skills. The curriculum then is designed based on the content analysis. Curriculum design has five elements:

1. The curriculum must be ordered around "big ideas" or mathematical concepts that have fundamental importance and facilitate the students' learning of generalizable problem-solving strategies.
2. Mathematical skills are sequenced according to detailed hierarchical levels of difficulty.
3. Directions to guide teachers' presentations must provide clear and economical language that pupils will interpret unambiguously.
4. Instructional formats or scripted lessons should be prepared to structure teachers' presentations and thereby assure reliable and efficient instruction.
5. Instructional programs are designed to provide for both continuous growth and cumulative review of learning across the numeration, computation, and problem-solving/applications domains.

The Oregon Model provides for efficient mastery of basic academic skills in the context of teacher-led instruction in which variations in the content and the presentation of lessons are rigorously controlled.

A sixth feature of the Oregon Model is that, since its development in the 1960s, it is continuously involved in a process of evaluation and refinement based on the results of empirical research. Empirical support for the principles and practices of direct instruction is drawn from several sources including the national Follow Through Study, research on components of the direct instruction model (see Carnine et al., 1994; Becker & Carnine, 1981; Vargas, 1984), and diverse researchers who have tested components of "effective instruction" (e.g., Archer et al., 1989, Ellis, Worthington, & Larkin, 1994; Lloyd & Keller, 1989). At its most developed level, direct instruction involves the explicit development and control of both the content and the process of instruction.

Content of Instruction

As Watkins and Slocum (2004) noted, the curriculum of direct instruction is designed around the concept of general case programming—which is a rigorous process of instructional design intended to increase the likelihood that students will efficiently learn new knowledge and skills, to transfer previously learned learning to novel and complex problems efficiently, and to retain learned skills over time. The first step is to examine the task and identify the range of problems of a given class for which training must be provided. The exemplars with the most generally occurring sets of critical attributes would be introduced earlier in training than more unusually occurring sets of attributes. The second step in developing a curriculum based on general case programming is to develop and maintain control over the range and characteristics of examples that will be used in instruction to increase the likelihood that students will efficiently learn, retain, and transfer new skills. The efficiency of general case programming is judged in terms of the extent to which mastery is accomplished (a) with the fewest number of trials, (b) with the fewest number of errors, and (c) with the greatest generalizability across tasks of a given classification.

Process of Instruction

Direct instruction is more readily identified with its explicit teacher-led instruction. Its highly structured didactic teacher/student interaction probably has been the source of greatest criticism. Instruction is delivered with a standard format in which the teacher secures the students' attention, prompts their overt responses during acquisition, requires overt and unassisted responses to demonstrate mastery, and follows acquisition with systematic practice. Figure 1 provides an outline of the teacher's instructional sequence.

The instructional sequence in Figure 13.1 is divided into three phases. In the first phase, the *opening of instruction*, the instructor begins by gaining the students' attention. The means of gaining attention may be subtle. The teacher might stand before the class and survey the students. Or the teacher might gain the students'

---

1. Opening of instruction
   - Gain all students' attention
   - Briefly review what has been previously learned
   - State the instructional objective for today's lesson

2. Body of Instruction
   - Model the learning
   - Prompt or lead the learning
   - Test what was learned

3. Conclusion of instruction
   - Briefly state what was learned
   - Tell the students the instructional objective for the next lesson
   - Provide practice activities

FIGURE 13.1 ■ Outline of the Direct Instruction Sequence

attention with more overt signals such as saying, "Class, we are going to begin. Please give me your attention."

Once the students are attending, the teacher briefly reviews what the students have learned already and introduces what they will be learning in the present session. For example, the teacher could say, "During the last several days we have been learning to solve story problems that can be solved using addition or subtraction. Today we are going to learn to solve story problems that require two steps." During the opening phase the teacher must gain the students' attention and provide a short statement of purpose for the day's lesson to facilitate their continued attention.

The second phase of instruction is the *body of instruction*. This phase is divided into three elements: (a) modeling the response or skill to be learned, (b) leading or assisting students in acquisition of the skill, and (c) testing the students' acquisition of learning. Both the teacher's and the students' responses are overt.

Behavioral assistance from the teachers during instruction has been termed *prompting* (e.g., Kameenui & Simmons, 1990; Wolery, Bailey, & Sugai, 1988). More recently, the metaphoric term *scaffolding* has been widely used to describe teacher assistance within discussions of direct instruction (e.g., Carnine et al., 1994; Kameenui & Simmons, 1990; Pressley, Hogan, Wharton–McDonald, Mistretta, & Ettenberger, 1996). Whether we use the term *prompting* or *scaffolding*, direct instruction is a process in which teachers actively assist students to efficiently acquire, maintain, and transfer new skills and knowledge. When students are confronted with new tasks, prompting will be most explicit.

For example, students with poorly developed skills in addition computation tend to solve problems by *counting up*. Thus, if they are presented with two quantities to be added, they count all objects in each group to find the total quantity. A more sophisticated step toward proficiency, and one that allows the students to better understand the relationships between numerations and computations, is the procedure of *counting on* from the larger quantity. Because the student probably will not be able to perform that operation without first being taught, the teacher provides explicit instructional prompting before requiring that the student attempt the strategy independently.

Generally, teachers first model the correct response for students who are in the initial phases of acquisition. Once teachers have shown students the correct response, they lead or prompt the students in the performance. As students' performances indicate that scaffolding is unnecessary, prompts are less explicit and eventually are withdrawn.

Finally, students are expected to respond independently. Teachers can use the student's performances during independent responding to test or to evaluate student learning and the effectiveness of instruction. When the tasks have been partially or previously learned, scaffolding may consist of fewer prompts and less precise prompts.

With the *conclusion of instruction*, the direct instruction model calls for opportunities for review and practice. A basic tenet is to provide much practice for acquisition, which is then distributed to maintain knowledge and skills (Englemann &

Carnine, 1991). Carnine et al. (1994) outlined a set of guidelines for providing effective practice and review. Practice activities, they state, should:

- Involve the practice of skills that the student has acquired already and can perform independently. If the student requires assistance, the skill will require additional teaching.
- Introduce information to review activities cumulatively.
- Distribute practice to build retention.
- Emphasize relationships to make learning more meaningful.
- Pre-teach components of strategies and algorithms.
- Require quicker response times.
- Use varied examples for review.

Although practice is deemed necessary for effective instruction, the efficiency of instruction is determined in part by the extent to which well designed instructional interactions can reduce the amount of practice necessary to acquire and maintain knowledge and skills. For example, Darch, Carnine, and Gersten (1984) demonstrated that well selected instructional content and well designed explicit instruction in generalizable strategy instruction resulted in more rapid acquisition of mathematical problem-solving strategies and required less practice than instruction that would be available from typical commercial mathematics curricula.

Constructivism

The constructivist perspective on appropriate approaches to instruction has been harder to define than direct instruction. Thus, the risk of misrepresenting it, or at least not representing it to the satisfaction of all concerned, is greater. The constructivist ideology emerged from the earlier discovery learning approach to instruction, which gained some popularity—as well as resounding criticism—in the 1960s. Advocates of constructivism (e.g., Cobb, 1994a, 1994b; Driver, Asoko, Leach, Mortimer, & Scott, 1994; Gadanidis, 1994; Palincsar, 1998; Poplin, 1988a, 1988b; Pressley, Harris, & Marks, 1992; Woodward & Montague, 2002) assert, as did the advocates of discovery learning (e.g., Bruner, 1961; Hawkins, 1966, Rogers, 1968) that students acquire the most meaningful understandings and appreciations of their learning and problem-solving experiences if they are engaged in learning activities that allow them to discover relationships and solutions for themselves.

A tenet of the constructivist ideology is that knowledge cannot be transmitted directly from the teacher to the student. Instead, the student constructs knowledge through active engagement in learning activities. In this process the student's previously existing understandings are adjusted to accommodate newly acquired information and understandings. In describing the process by which students construct expertise, constructivists emphasize that the content of education is not a body of knowledge and skills that exists as an independent entity outside their minds. Accordingly, the role of the constructivist teacher is to facilitate the learning of important mathematical principles by providing opportunities for students to learn to acquire new knowledge and to challenge their own understandings of previously acquired understandings. Constructivist teachers argue against exerting overt control over instruction and, rather, advocate teachers' "leading from behind."

The notion that teachers may frequently, reliably, and unobtrusively lead students to desired understandings is not unique to constructivism. Depending on whether new knowledge and skills are being learned for the first time or whether they are being reviewed or prepared for generalization, more behaviorally oriented teachers also may use relatively inconspicuous prompts.

In an effort to address some of the vagaries of the possible student–teacher roles in instruction, Moshman, (1982) identified three types of constructivist approaches: endogenous, exogenous, and dialectical. Harris and Graham (1994) brought his schema of constructivist approaches to the discussion within special education. Moshman's taxonomy has value because it sets out the range of possible perspectives on constructivism. It sets boundaries for extremely divergent understandings of constructivism and suggests realistic compromise.

Endogenous constructivism considers that knowledge is developed within the student. Accordingly, each student's understanding should be expected to be different in quality and to differ from the teacher's understandings. Knowledge cannot be transmitted precisely from the teacher to the student; therefore, varied understandings will be developed. Thus, according to the endogenous constructivist perspective, the appropriate role for the teacher is to facilitate learning by providing meaningfully structured experiences that provide active engagement in problem solving without overtly controlling the instructional interaction. Because the understandings of individual students will surely vary, teachers cannot expect to effectively transmit knowledge through didactic interactions with their students.

From the *exogenous constructivist* perspective, knowledge may be external to the individual learner and may be directly transmitted to the student by the teacher, provided that the process of instruction allows for unambiguous presentation. For the exogenous constructivist, the teacher's responsibility is to precisely define and organize the course of study and prepare unambiguous presentations of knowledge and skills so the knowledge may be transmitted directly from the teacher to the student. Exogenous constructivist teachers do not wait for desired understanding to develop. By attempting to control the details of instruction, they lead students' learning.

Between the two extremes of endogenous and exogenous constructivism is *dialectical constructivism*. Rather than taking a position that might indicate an extravagant disregard for the bodies of literature on cognitive development or learning, the dialectical constructivist perspective holds that students acquire knowledge through instructional experiences. In some cases the teacher assumes a highly didactic role, and in other cases the teacher provides less obvious support. For example, a teacher provides students with a formula for calculating the area of a surface and then explicitly models the procedure for them to follow. If the students have had prior experience in calculating the area of a surface and the task at hand is to determine the area of a room, the teacher would offer more subtle prompts for the students to recall and apply "the method you already learned for calculating the area of any surface." The teacher determines the extent to which explicit guidance or implicit support is needed to facilitate the desired learning, depending on the student's prior performances in instructional interactions (or the instructional dialogue).

RESEARCH IN MATHEMATICS EDUCATION

Given the history of research in mathematics education, we should not be surprised at how little the quality of mathematics instruction has improved despite continuing calls for the reform of math education. Kilpatrick's (1992) description of the historical development of research in mathematics education considers several issues that have had basic influences on the development of mathematics education and, likewise, on the development of debates about how mathematics should be taught.

Although mathematics has had a long history as a core subject in schools and universities, rigorous research about how to teach has been a relatively recent effort. In the beginning of the 19th century, university-level programs in teacher education began to emerge. By the end of the 19th century mathematics education began to develop as a field of study in several countries, including the United States, several European countries, and Japan. The emphasis of those programs was on the practical and rapid preparation of secondary-level mathematics teachers. Research did not flourish in those programs.

Increasingly, university programs began to assume that mathematics teachers should be rigorously prepared in the content and culture of specialized study in mathematics. Research in mathematics education increased as the status of teacher preparation and mathematics education became more elevated.

The effect that research can have on practice depends substantially on the questions researchers have been asking. Kilpatrick (1992) points out that two disciplines have had pronounced effects on the development of mathematics education: mathematics and psychology. The interests of mathematicians and psychologists have differed substantially. While interest in mathematics education has a long history among mathematicians, it also has been episodic. Mathematicians' flurries of interest in mathematics education have tended to be in response to personal curiosities, as well as concerns over issues. According to Kilpatrick (1992, "[I]nadequate preparations in lower schools, falling enrollments in advanced courses, the potential erosion of mathematics as a school subject, and threats to national status have from time to time prompted mathematicians to look into what schools are doing and how it might be improved" (p. 5).

A substantial portion of mathematicians' research has consisted of surveys and analyses of the content of school mathematics. How mathematics is, or should be, taught has been less frequently addressed. Mathematicians' research on the process of instruction and how education might be improved has frequently been drawn from introspective analyses of their own processes or from comparably impressionistic observational studies of their own children or grandchildren. Kilpatrick (1992) observed that, while the contributions from mathematicians were frequently not maintained, they were taken seriously in part because of the status of mathematicians in the academic community.

Perhaps one of the most widely cited examples of introspective heuristics from mathematicians has been George Polya's (1965a, 1965b) model for mathematical problem solving, an approach for strategic analysis for problem solving. Polya's writings describe the process at a level of abstraction that does not suggest that he was presenting a classroom-ready routine, but educators embraced it nevertheless. The problem has been that young children and children who have cognitive disabilities frequently do not use Polya's theoretical design, or at least they do not use it as their teachers intend that they use it.

The contributions to mathematics education by psychologists have offered some different characterizations to the field. Mathematicians' research in education has tended to deal more with the content than the process of mathematics instruction at the secondary and collegiate levels. Psychologists have been more concerned with how mathematics is taught and learned than with curriculum content. They also have been more interested in mathematics instruction of elementary than secondary or collegiate levels. Kilpatrick (1992, p. 5) stated:

> From the beginning of educational psychology, mathematics was a popular vehicle to use in investigating learning, probably because of perceptions regarding its important role in the school curriculum; its relative independence of non-school influences; its cumulative, hierarchical structure as a school subject; its abstraction and arbitrariness, and the range of complexity and difficulty in learning tasks it can provide.

Thus, psychologists used the examples of the content of mathematics as tasks and problems that would provide access to insights of intellectual ability, cognitive development, problem solving, and the effects of teaching. Although psychologists' research in mathematics has provided insight for math educators, the efforts of educational psychologists generally have not been directly concerned with how the content of mathematics should be arranged into curricula or how it should be taught.

The combined contributions of research by mathematicians and psychologists have not produced major improvements in achievement in elementary and secondary school mathematics. Historically, the relationship between the two disciplines can be more readily characterized as parallel-play than as collaboration, and while the previous efforts have resulted in important contributions, important issues clearly have been neglected and in some cases ignored or mishandled (Porter et al., 1988).

Although mathematicians have studied the complex hierarchies and relationships of the content of mathematics, their efforts have not been sufficiently extensive or sufficiently assessed by educators who study the teaching and learning of mathematics. As a result, inadequate attention has been directed to the importance of various hierarchical arrangements and conceptual maps for curriculum development (Porter et al., 1988). Clearly, one of the major challenges that teachers face in promoting mathematics achievement is choosing a limited set of instructional examples that will provide broad and accurate generalization of knowledge and skills to an infinite number of mathematical problems that cannot be included in instruction (cf. Ausubel, 1988; Bruner, 1961; Englemann & Carnine 1991; Gagne, 1965; Shulman & Keislar, 1966). As a result, professionals across a broad range of roles in mathematics education (including teachers, researchers, and policy makers) generally lack sophisticated understandings of the mathematical skill hierarchies.

Given that basic lack of knowledge, it is understandable that teachers have tended to continue to teach mathematics as they perceive that they have been taught (Porter et al., 1988), and it would be astounding if educators and curriculum developers were able to design instructional programs that would more effectively promote generalization of knowledge and skills. Likewise, it is understandable that many advocates of curriculum reform have proposed broad suggestions for curriculum reform with only slight attention to the content of mathematics (Carnine, 1992).

Even though the attention of mathematicians to mathematics education has been intermittent, the contributions from psychology and, more recently, from education have been fragmented in their focus and lacking in methodological rigor and, on occasion, irrational. Dixon, Carnine, Lee, Wallin, and Chard (1998) provide an example. In conducting an extensive review of rigorous experimental studies in mathematics education, they located 8,727 studies of elementary and secondary mathematics instruction published between 1971 and 1995. After further analysis of those studies, 956 studies satisfied the minimum criteria of experimental studies. Of those, only 110 passed a more rigorous analysis to identify high-quality studies. Those few studies were scattered across six broad areas of mathematics education: use of manipulatives; work among peers; design of instruction; computers and technology; grouping; reinforcement and motivational systems; and idiosyncratic or miscellaneous issues of instruction. None of the studies addressed the importance of the scope and sequence of instruction.

It is notable that of 8,727 published studies of mathematics, less than 2% had sufficient methodological rigor to be classified as high-quality experiments. Jacob (2001) has denounced the Dixon et al. (1998) report for limiting its analyses of mathematics research to experimental studies as "an unacceptable bias from the point of math educators" (p. 3). Though Jacobs may believe that Dixon et al. were too conservative in their selection of methodologically adequate studies, his complaint is unsupported by data. His presumed knowledge of the sentiments of mathematics educators is irrelevant, but unfortunate if it is true. Even if Dixon et al (1998) had been less conservative in their screening, clearly only a relatively small percentage of studies conducted in that 20-year period was sufficiently rigorous to provide generalizable information to educators.

It is unfortunate that so few longitudinal studies have been conducted in mathematics education. Although well-designed studies carried out over a few weeks or months are informative, studies that examine student achievement over a year or more could be much more informative. These studies would give a better perspective on the effects of different curricular content, sequences of curriculum, instructional procedures, and assessment.

Perhaps the most notable longitudinal study to consider mathematics education was the federally funded Project Follow Through, which ran from 1965 to 1995. The study sought to determine the relative efficacy of instruction based on different models of teaching in the areas of mathematics, as well as reading, spelling, math, language, self-esteem, and cognitive development. More than 75,000 low-income children from 170 communities participated. Project Follow Through remains the largest and most expensive (nearly $1 billion) longitudinal experimental study of instruction to have ever been conducted (Grossen, 1995–96).

Contrary to expectations and speculations in large portions of the education community, the results of the Project Follow Through study revealed that models with theoretical bases that were drawn from behavioral learning theory and provided for explicit direction by the teacher (the Applied Behavior Analysis Model and the Direct Instruction Model), produced substantially superior results compared to all other models (Grossen, 1995–96; Stebbins et al., 1977). Many subsequent studies have provided closer examinations and extensions of the principles of behaviorally based mathematics instruction for young children and for students with cognitive disabilities (for reviews, see Baker, Gersten, & Lee, 2002; Butler, Miller, Lee, & Pierce, 2001; Crawford & Snider, 2000; Gersten 1985; Harper, Mallette, Maheady, & Brennan, 1993; Kroesbergen & Van Luit, 2003; Mastroperi, Bakken, & Scruggs, 1991; Mastroperi, Scruggs, & Shiah, 1991; Swanson, Carson, & Saches–Lee, 1996; Watkins & Slocum, 2004).

Educators and educational psychologists whose interests lie primarily with more eclectic or with developmental approaches to education have largely ignored the results of the Follow Through study (Tashman, 1994). That is unfortunate but not really surprising, as researchers in mathematics education have been primarily interested in intellectual development, cognitive development, and problem solving, and they have not been as interested in or accepting of behavioral learning theory. Studies that deny the efficacy of eclectic and developmental approaches to instruction in favor of behavioral approaches are apt to be ignored by a substantial number of those individuals.

The paucity of longitudinal studies of mathematics instruction is unfortunate because they would allow for better examinations of the importance of content, organization, and presentation of content. They also would allow for more thorough examinations of the generalization and maintenance of learning—important knowledge, as skills in mathematics can take many months and years to develop and generalizations from instruction can take years to observe. Regrettably, policy makers probably will not fund another study of the scope of Follow Through. Additional longitudinal studies, however, would allow for better analyses and theory building, and theorists, researchers, and practitioners would not have to take such an anti-intellectual stance.

We should not be surprised at the current level of unproductive debate. Themes of the current debate have echoed over the past 40 years. The progress and the fallout from debates and efforts to reform mathematics for general education will influence mathematics instruction available to students with special education needs. As more students with special education needs receive more instruction in the general education classroom, educators will be challenged to provide them with access to general education and with appropriate instruction.

TEACHER EDUCATION AND PRACTICE

Many teachers, particularly in elementary grades and in special education, lack sophisticated knowledge in the area of mathematics. This condition has vexed efforts to improve mathematics education for many years (Kilpatrick, 1992; Porter et al., 1988). Most of these teachers are prepared as generalists and do not have great expertise in either the content or teaching of mathematics. Frequently, preservice elementary and special education teacher-trainees readily disclose that they do not feel adequate to teach mathematics because they have not done well in the subject themselves or because they do not feel prepared.

Clearly, teacher education is a major obstacle to improving mathematics instruction for students who have cognitive or learning disabilities. Typically, preservice teachers take a course or two in mathematics pedagogy. Later, as teachers, they are provided with a limited range of tools to support student learning. In many cases a teacher faced with students who are having difficulty in mastering concepts has to rely upon basal texts and supplemental resources, which often provide only additional drill and practice. The context in which great improvement in mathematics education will take place involves coping with the modest expertise of many teachers. Arguably, teachers who lack expertise in the content mathematics would have to support an approach that clearly articulates curricula and supports instruction. But explicitly designed curricula and instructional guidance probably will not be widely available.

Constructivism has become increasingly popular in the current mathematics education reform movement. Descriptions of the approach portray situations in which (a) teachers possess considerable knowledge of their subject matter, (b) teachers are able to draw on that knowledge to facilitate student achievement under conditions that require extemporaneous decision making, (c) students are highly motivated to persevere in difficult tasks for the purpose of developing greater understanding, and (d) during the course of instruction it becomes apparent that students are constructing increasingly sophisticated understandings of mathematics. Bereiter (1994) believes it would be truly exceptional if all of those conditions could be met. He identified three important obstacles to meeting the conditions:

1. Inadequate teacher education
2. The low tolerance of students who expect to fail, or who have difficulty in successfully completing tasks, for trial-and-error learning
3. Difficulty in observing progress during instruction.

Teachers who lack adequate preparation in the content and instruction of mathematics can hardly be expected to play the role of effectively facilitating students' active engagement in the direction and the progress of instruction. Students with cognitive and learning disabilities will not typically persevere through trial-and-error when they believe they will fail (Ausubel, 1968; Keislar & Shulman, 1966). Entry teachers and teachers involved in complex instructional dynamics have difficulty satisfying the expectation that both the teacher and the student will recognize progress as it occurs and respond appropriately.

Although the constructivist perspective envisions appealing scenarios of instruction, it is logically inadequate for the task of teaching students with cognitive and learning disabilities, and it is unsupported by empirical research. Constructivism, especially the less structured descriptions, rests on beliefs that will be difficult to implement (see Reid, Kurkjian, & Carruthers, 1994). Unfortunately, constructivism also is a set of beliefs that may fail to encourage the hard work of developing quality instructional programs for students who have difficulties in learning. Worse, its beliefs can obscure teachers' critical self-analysis and reflection on the quality of their teaching.

Constructivists and advocates of direct instruction agree that teachers should be trained in preservice and inservice in mathematical concepts. The realities of the situation, however, suggest that the task of developing preservice and inservice teachers' expertise to meet the assumptions of the constructivist approach is truly challenging. Hence, programs that provide detailed methodologies for teaching basic skills and knowledge, problem-solving strategies, critical thinking, curriculum design and adaptation, curriculum-based assessment, and peer-assisted instruction are strongly advised (Calhoon & Fuchs, 2003; Carnine et al, 1994; Cawley et al, 1978, 1979; Fuchs, Fuchs, & Karns, 2001; Fuchs, Fuchs, Yazdain, & Powell, 2002; Jones & Krouse, 1988; Jones, Wilson, & Bhojwani, 1997; Maccini & Hughes, 1997; Owen, & Fuchs, 2002). How the approach is labeled is not particularly important.

STRENGTHS OF BOTH APPROACHES

Both direct instruction and constructivism are more robust than their critics sometimes have characterized them, and both approaches have strengths to bring to the classroom. The comparisons between the approaches generally involve five issues:

- The teacher's role
- The apparent importance of curriculum and content
- The efficacy of instruction
- Levels of instruction (elementary versus secondary, and basic skills versus higher-level problem solving)
- Social interaction among students
- Language of the discourse

The Teacher's Role

In both approaches, the teacher plays an active role in engaging the students in learning. Constructivist approaches are concerned with actively engaging students in dialogues about the concepts being discussed. Typically, the teacher does not direct instruction overtly. Instead the teacher allows students to actively engage in carefully designed activities that draw them to meaningful understandings and applications of mathematical concepts. Instruction is problem- based, and teachers are to select instructional examples that will provide students with the greatest opportunity for learning and generalizing important mathematical concepts and relationships.

Student interest is also considered essential for engaging students in instruction. Student interests are emphasized when teachers select content and implement instruction. Direct instruction is an unambiguously teacher-led instructional model. Interactions between teacher and students are carefully crafted. The scripting of instruction makes it relatively easy to implement the model, to recognize the implementations of direct instruction, and to judge the fidelity of a teacher's effort to implement the model. The scripting of direct instruction also minimizes errors that might be introduced by a teacher's own faulty constructions of mathematical understandings. These programs tend to be economical in the presentation of material. Although issues of meaningfulness and student interest are included in the direct instruction model, they have received less discussion.

Advocates of direct instruction and constructivism both recognize that the content of mathematics can seem to be abstract and arbitrary to students. Further, both approaches seem to consider that teachers might have difficulty providing meaningful illustrations and applications that appeal to the interests of individual students. Advocates of direct instruction consider that students need to be provided opportunities to engage successfully in applications of knowledge and skills. Constructivists, by contrast, clearly recognize that some knowledge and skills will be learned most efficiently through teacher-led instruction.

The exogenous variation of constructivism (Harris & Graham, 1994; Moshman, 1992) clearly recognizes the importance of teacher control of the instructional process to increase the likelihood of students' successfully learning important skills. Both models hold that teachers are responsible for providing instruction that will minimize potential errors in the student's own constructions and will increase the efficiency of teaching and learning.

Importance of Content

The two perspectives seem to differ with regard to the importance of content, but the difference may be more apparent than real. Direct instruction calls for rigorous attempts to articulate the content of instruction into hierarchical sequences of knowledge and skills. Instructional examples are selected to maximize the probability that students will acquire knowledge and skills efficiently and later will generalize without errors in situations outside of instruction. According to the principles of direct instruction, explicit control of curriculum is vital to assure that students will learn critical skills rapidly.

Descriptions of constructivism seem to give more attention to the nature of teacher / student interactions than to articulating the content of mathematics. Some constructivist descriptions, through not adequately explicit about the importance of managing the content of instruction, clearly infer its importance. Frequently, constructivist conceptualizations of effective instruction argue that teachers should be able to respond to student achievement with appropriate selection of instructional activities. Contrary to critics, constructivists are aware of the importance of managing the structure and hierarchical sequences instruction. Constructivist approaches can be highly organized and tiered. Approaches such as *Connected Mathematics* (Lappan, Fey, Fitzgerald, Friel, & Phillips, 2002) provide detailed instructions to teachers about the underlying purposes of the activities and, thus, lessen the likelihood of errors induced by the teacher's faulty conceptual understanding.

The exogenous variation of constructivism (Harris & Graham, 1994; Mossman, 1992) clearly recognizes the importance of a well organized curriculum. The two models do seem to differ on this point, except that advocates of direct instruction do not expect teachers to substantially design curricula themselves (e.g., Carnine, 1992). Curriculum publishers should be responsible for providing well designed tools for teachers. Constructivists generally agree that most published math curricula are inadequate, but they seem to place more responsibility on teachers for organizing the content of instruction. In practice, teachers are keenly aware of the value of having well designed curriculum available to them (Maccini & Hughes, 2002).

Efficacy of Instruction

Proponents of both approaches recognize that the value of the instruction is ultimately judged by the *achievement* of students, not by its process. The importance of evaluating the effectiveness of daily instructional interactions is widely recognized and has been included as a basic criterion of the PATHWISE and PRAXIS models for teacher mentoring and evaluation (Educational Testing Service, 1995). Yet, neither of the approaches is explicit regarding what form of evaluation should be employed. Curriculum-based assessment has been coupled with direct instruction, but it is by no means incompatible with constructivism (e.g., Jones & Krouse, 1985; Jones, 1990; Jones et al., 1997). It is actually recognized for its contributions to student achievement independent of any specific approach to instruction (Jones, Southern, & Brigham, 1998).

If precise performance assessments are done frequently and student progress is graphed, teachers are readily able to engage in a productive cycle of judging students' mastery of content, considering the effectiveness of instruction, making rational decisions about how to adjust instruction, then further evaluating the effects of their instructional decisions. Curriculum-based assessment research has shown that this is an effective mechanism to enhance learning, especially for students who have difficulty in learning (Jones et al., 1998; Lloyd, Forness, & Kavale, 1998).

Levels of Instruction

Neither approach is necessarily limited in its value by the level of student achievement or the complexity of knowledge or skills being taught. Direct instruction was originally developed in application with disadvantaged and difficult-to-teach students (Becker & Carnine, 1981; Bereiter & Englemann, 1966; Stein, Silbert, & Carnine, 1997). Direct instruction, however, does not preclude higher-order learning. For example, problem-solving experiences are carefully tiered in difficulty to avoid frustration and practicing errors (Stein et al., 1997; Englemann & Carnine, 1991). The principles of direct instruction are effective for teaching complex problem solving or secondary-level content (Jones et al., 1997; Maccini & Gagnon, 2000; Miller, Butler, & Lee, 1998). For instruction at the higher levels of difficulty and complexity, teachers have great responsibility for understanding the content of mathematics and evaluating the effectiveness of their instruction.

Social Interactions Among Students

Constructivist and direct instruction programs both offer ample opportunities for students to engage each other in the learning process. Teams of students often work together gathering data and communicating results in mathematical formats. Discussions of direct instruction do not generally consider peer interactions, but neither do they suggest that peer interactions would conflict with student achievement. Actually, cooperative learning and other types of peer tutoring can facilitate proficiency and are compatible with direct instruction (Jones, 1990; Jones et al., 1997). Well organized peer tutoring is consistently associated with the achievement of students who have special education needs, because it is likely to increase the practice of recently acquired skills, provides incentives to demonstrate achievement, and reduces the likelihood that students will independently practice errors.

Although descriptions of constructivism tend to consider peer interactions as vital to the instructional process and critical to understanding what students achieve, they typically are not precise in describing how the processes are managed. Slavin (1983) argues that student groupings cannot be expected to reliably facilitate achievement unless teachers can account for individual achievement and provide group-oriented reinforcement. Peer groupings can be irrelevant to achievement and may even inhibit it.

Language of the Discourse

Elements of both approaches are not as mutually exclusive as the ideological debate might leave an observer to conclude. Finding the compatibilities, however, requires translating what is said by the proponents of each approach. It also requires some extrapolation of what they have said to what they possibly mean. Conjecture is perhaps useful in considering where there may be common ground, but it is not a reliable tool. Two problems arise from becoming too involved with translations of arguments.

    1. Translations can be a waste of time. By example, Skinner (1967) translated the psychodynamic theories of Freud into behavioral terms, but his efforts

did not, and should not, have been expected to resolve any differences between the two perspectives.

2. Translations and critiques to balance instruction do not address the problem that some interpreters of the debate will move from discussions of and about ideology to practice, or to the training of others who will practice instruction. In doing so, they will have bypassed empirical validation.

The value of considering the differences and congruence between descriptions is that the discussion identifies relationships between instruction and achievement in mathematics that can be illuminated by clearer description and validated by further research.

CONCLUSION

Balancing the ideologies of different approaches to instruction requires sorting out the combinations of meanings and contents that concern the proponents. Examining their arguments and evidence reveals some of the contributions and also the obstacles of differing perspectives. Determining balance or fair representation of the positions also requires consideration of the conditions and context of mathematics education. Consideration of the meanings, contributions, and contexts should result in suggestions for practical issues such as research, instructional practice, teacher education, and curriculum design.

Resolving some of the semantic issues involved in the debate might be easier if a common language were used. Constructivist arguments tend to use the representations of cognitive psychology, whereas advocates for direct instruction are apt to rely more on the language of behavioral psychology. Interpretation of meaning is also a critical issue. As arguments are heard and interpreted, their actual meaning can be changed, depending on what people think of what they heard and what they want to believe. In discussions of the relative merits of differing perspectives on mathematics education, it seems that incomplete understandings, misinterpretations, and wishful thinking have occurred. And it seems that a generous amount of sloppy thinking has been added to the mix. In some cases, the matter of understanding is a translation of terms, but in other instances, substituting terms may not capture what is meant.

For example, a major tenet of the constructivist approach is that frequently the teacher's role should be providing indirect guidance so students will construct their own understandings of multiple ways to understand and solve problems. According to the direct instruction model, that role is appropriate when the goal of instruction is to promote generalization. On the one hand, it can be interpreted in terms of Stokes and Baer's (1977) concept of *training loosely*. On the other hand, the concept of problem solving has long been understood to be a matter of solving simply written story problems. Generally, that concept of problem solving has been acceptable within the direction instruction model. Constructivists, however, have argued forcefully that this conceptualization is much too narrow.

In applied settings, quantitative problems usually do not emerge as simply stated choices of correct computational operations that result in a precise answer. That argument has had the value of prompting broader and more complex appreciations for what is involved with mathematical problem solving, which in turn have contributed to better curricula.

The problems of misunderstandings and wishful thinking have been important issues in the debate surrounding approaches to mathematics education. For example, constructivist arguments for the teacher to act as a facilitator for learning, and not as the director of the instructional interaction, can be interpreted as suggesting that the teacher is indirectly accountable for what students are taught and learn. By contrast, according to the principles of direct instruction, teacher/ student interactions are explicitly teacher-led. To some observers, that arrangement may seem unacceptable. Some critics might see the process as undemocratic, and others as a matter of too much rigor to teach relatively simple and perhaps unimportant skills.

Definitional issues are important to the debate and the balance between constructivist and direct instruction approaches. Constructivism has been so broadly described that it sometimes becomes frustrating to define its critical attributes and recognize examples in practice. Direct instruction has been described much more explicitly, and its application had been more clearly limited to teaching basic knowledge and skills in the lower elementary grades. Whereas constructivist approaches may be dismissed for being too vague, direct instruction is frequently regarded as being too didactic, overly structured, uninteresting, and too limited in application.

Proponents of both approaches share the responsibilities for the changes in interpretations that can occur as their descriptions move to practitioners, and proponents of both approaches should provide clear and fair representations of their own and opposing points of view. Misstating the position of critics has no value, and there is no justification for characterizing either approach as representing an unfortunate example of general practice in mathematics education.

The current context of an acute shortage of teachers who are adequately prepared to teach mathematical knowledge and skills, and to work effectively with students who have cognitive and learning disabilities, seems to influence the relative merits of constructivist and direct instruction approaches. Currently we are faced with the following conditions in mathematics education:

- An acute and increasing shortage of teachers in mathematics education and special education
- A persistent and continuing lack of expertise in the content of mathematics among practitioners, particularly at the elementary levels
- Clear expectations that schools and teachers show adequate achievement on standardized proficiency tests.

In this context, both short- and long-term responses are in order. Notwithstanding the sparse empirical research in mathematics education, there is sufficient research to suggest that teachers who are provided with well organized curricula and basic preparation in direct instruction, behavior management, and curriculum-based assessment can effectively teach basic mathematical skills. Higher-level mathematical skills are difficult to teach. Over the long term, significant efforts must be made to develop knowledge about most advantageous organizations of mathematical content in order to design instructionally adequate curricula. Therefore, at the very least, commitments must be made to:

- Produce significantly more research on the content of mathematics.
- Produce significantly more research on mathematics instruction, with emphasis on efficiency and effectiveness rather than ideology.
- Design defensible and rationally organized curricula.
- Provide ongoing preservice and inservice teachers with training and practice in the organization, design, adaptation, and presentation of curricula in mathematics.

In addressing those needs, ideological differences may provide the bases for productive debate. If those needs are not addressed, however, the ideological debates will be irrelevant. Teachers will continue to teach as they imagine they were taught or should have been taught. Empirical research provides the basis for rational and defensible curricula and instructional methodologies. Personal insight and conjecture are poor, and perhaps destructive, substitutes.

REFERENCES

Archer, A. L., Isaacson, S., Adams, A., Ellis, E. S., Morehead, M. K., & Shiller, E. P. (1989). *Design and delivery of academic lessons.* Reston, VA: Council for Exceptional Children.

Ausubel, D. P. (1968). *Educational psychology: A cognitive view.* New York: Holt, Reinhart, & Winston.

Baker, S., Gersten, R., & Lee, D. S. (2002). A synthesis of empirical research on teaching mathematics to low-achieving students. *Elementary School Journal, 103,* 51–73.

Becker, W. C., & Carnine, D. W. (1981). Direct instructions: A behavior theory model for comprehensive educational intervention with the disadvantaged. In S. W. Bijou & R. Ruiz (Eds.), *Behavior modification: Contributions to education* (pp. 145–210). Hillsdale, NJ: Erlbaum.

Bereiter, C. (1994). Constructivism, socioculturalism, and Popper's World 3. *Educational Researcher, 23(7),* 21-23.

Bereiter, C., & Engelmann (1966). *Teaching disadvantaged children in the preschool.* Englewood Cliffs, NJ: Prentice Hall.

Brantlinger, E. (1997). Using ideology: Cases of nonrecognition of the politics of research and practice in special education. *Review of Educational Research, 67,* 425–459.

Bruner, J. S. (1961). The act of discovery. *Harvard Educational Review, 31,* 21–32.

Butler, F. M., Miller, S. P., Lee, K., & Pierce, T. (2001). Teaching mathematics to students with mild to moderate mental retardation: A review of the literature. *Mental Retardation, 39,* 20–31.

Calhoon, M. B., & Fuchs, L. S. (2003). The effects of peer-assisted learning strategies and curriculum-based measurement on the mathematics performance of secondary students with disabilities. *Remedial and Special Education, 24,* 235–245.

Carnine, D. (1989). Designing practice activities. *Journal of Learning Disabilities, 22,* 603–607.

Carnine, D. (1992). Expanding the notion of teachers' rights: Access to tools that work. *Journal of Applied Behavior Analysis, 25,* 13–19.

Carnine, D., Jones, E. D., & Dixon, R. (1994). Mathematics: Educational tools for diverse learners. *School Psychology Review, 23,* 406–427.

Cawley, J. F., Fitzmaurice, A. M., Lepore, A. V., Sedlak, R., & Althaus, V. (1979). *Projects Math, Levels I, II, III, and IV.* Tulsa, OK: Educational Development Corp.

Cawley, J. F., Fitzmaurice, A. M., Shaw, R. A., Kahn, H., & Bates, H., III (1978). Mathematics and learning disabled youth: The upper grade levels. *Learning Disability Quarterly, 1*(4), 37–52.

Cobb, P. (1988). The tension between theories of learning and instruction in mathematics education. *Educational Psychologist, 23,* 87–103.

Cobb, P. (1994a). Constructivism in mathematics and science education. *Educational Researcher, 23*(7), 4.

Cobb, P. (1994b). Where is the mind? Constructivist and sociocultural perspectives on mathematical development. *Educational Researcher, 23*(7), 13–20.

Crawford, D. B., & Snider, V. E. (2000). Effective mathematics instruction: The importance of curriculum. *Education and Treatment of Children, 23,* 122–142.

Darch, C., Carnine, D., & Gersten, R. (1984). Explicit instruction in mathematics problem solving. *Journal of Educational Research, 77,* 351–359.

Dixon, R. C., & Carnine, D. W. (1992). A response to Heshusius' "Curriculum-based assessment and direct instruction: Critical reflections on fundamental assumptions." *Exceptional Children, 58,* 461–463.

Dixon, R. C., Carnine, D. W., Lee, S. L., Wallin, J., Chard, D. (1998). *Review of high quality experimental mathematics research.* Report to California State Board of Education. Retrieved February 21, 2004, from website of National Center to Improve the Tools of Educators. University of Oregon, Eugene, OR: http://idea.uoregon.edu/~ncite/documents/math/math.html

Driver, R., Asoko, H., Leach, J., Mortimer, E., & Scott, P. (1994). Constructing scientific knowledge in the classroom. *Educational Researcher, 23,* 5–12.

Educational Testing Service (1995). *PATHWISE: Classroom observation system orientation guide.* Princeton, NJ: Author.

Ellis, E. S., Worthington, L. A., & Larkin, M. J. (1994). *Executive summary of the research synthesis on effective teaching principles and the design of quality tools for educators.* Technical Report No. 6, produced for National Center to Improve the Tools for Educators, University of Oregon. National Center to Improve the Tools of Educators. Retrieved February 21, 2004 from the website of the National Center to Improve the Tools of Educators. University of Oregon, Eugene, OR: http://idea.uoregon.edu/~ncite/documents/techrep/tech06.html

Engelmann, S., & Carnine, D. (1991). *Theory of instruction: Principles and applications* (2d ed.). Eugene, OR: ADI Press.

Fuchs, L. S., Fuchs, D., & Karns, K. (2001). Enhancing kindergarteners' mathematical development: Effects of peer-assisted learning strategies. *Elementary School Journal, 101,* 495–510.

Fuchs, L. S., Fuchs, D., Yazdian, L., & Powell, S. R. (2002). Enhancing first-grade children's mathematical development with peer-assisted learning strategies. *School Psychology Review, 31,* 569–583.

Gadanidis, G. (1994). Deconstructing constructivism. *Mathematics Teacher, 87*(2), 91–97.

Gagne, R. M. (1965). *Conditions of learning.* New York: Holt, Rinehart and Winston.

Gersten, R. (1985). Direct instruction with special education students: A review of evaluation research. *Journal of Special Education, 19,* 41–58.

Good, T., Grouws, D., & Ebmeier, H. (1983). *Active mathematics teaching.* New York: Longman.

Grossen, B. (1995–1966). The Story Behind Project Follow Through. *Effective School Practices, 15*(1), Retrieved February 21, 2004 from website of *Effective School Practices*: http://darkwing.uoregon.edu/~adiep/ft/grossen.htm

Harper, G. F., Mallette, B., Maheady, L., & Brennan, G. (1993). Class-wide student tutoring teams and direct instruction as a combined instructional program to teach generalizable strategies for mathematics word problems. *Education and Treatment of Children, 16,* 115–134.

Harris, K. R., & Graham, S. (1994). Constructivism: Principles, paradigms, and integration. *Journal of Special Education, 28,* 233–247.

Hawkins, D. (1966). Learning the unteachable. In L. S. Shulman & E. R. Keislar (Eds.), *Learning by discovery: A critical appraisal.* Chicago: Rand McNally.

Heshusius, L. (1991). Curriculum-based assessment and direct instruction: Critical reflections on fundamental assumptions. *Exceptional Children, 57,* 315-328.

Ingersoll, R. M. (January, 2001) *Teacher turnover, teacher shortages, and the organization of schools.* Retrieved February 21, 2004 from website of Center for the Study of Teaching and Policy, University of Washington, Seattle. http://depts.washington.edu/ctpmail/PDFs/Turnover-Ing-01-2001.pdf

Jacob, B. (2001). Implementing standards: The California mathematics textbook debacle. *Phi Delta Kappan, 83,* 264–272.

Jones, E. D. (1990). Developing curricula for mathematical problem-solving. *LD forum, 16,* 42–48.

Jones, E. D. & Krouse, J. P. (1985, October). *Verbal math problem solving: What the research on instruction tells us.* Paper presented at National Conference of Council for Learning Disabilities, New Orleans. (ERIC Document Reproduction Service ED265719)

Jones, E. D., & Krouse, J. P. (1988). The effectiveness of data-based instruction by student teachers in classrooms for pupils with mild learning handicaps. *Teacher Education and Special Education, 11,* 9–19.

Jones, E. D., Southern, W. T., & Brigham, F. J. (1998). Curriculum based assessment: Testing what is taught and teaching what is tested. *Intervention in School and Clinic, 33,* 239–249.

Jones, E. D., Wilson, R., & Bhojwani, S. (1997). Mathematics instruction for elementary students with learning disabilities. *Journal of Learning Disabilities, 30,* 151–163.

Kauffman, J. M. (2002). *Educational reform,* Lanham, MD: Scarecrow Press.

Kameenui, E. J., & Griffin, C. C. (1989). A national crisis in verbal problem solving in elementary mathematics: A proposal for examining the role of basal mathematics programs. *Elementary School Journal, 5,* 575–594.

Kameenui, E. J., & Simmons, D. C. (1990). *Designing instructional strategies: Prevention of academic learning problems.* Columbus, OH: Merrill.

Kilpatrick, J. (1992). A history of research in mathematics education, (pp. 3–38). In D. Grouws (Ed.), *Handbook of research on mathematics: Teaching and learning.* New York: Macmillan.

Kroesbergen, E. N., & Van Luit, J. E. H. (2003). Mathematics interventions for children with special education needs: A meta-analysis. *Remedial and Special Education, 24,* 97–114.

Lappan, G., Fey, J. T., Fitzgerald, W. M., Friel, S. N., & Phillips, E. D. (2002). *Getting to know connected mathematics: An implementation guide.* Glenview IL: Prentice Hall.

Lloyd, J. W., Forness, S. R., & Kavale, K. A. (1998). Some methods are more effective than others. *Intervention in Schools and Clinic, 3,* 195–200.

Lloyd, J. W., & Keller, C. K. (1989). Effective mathematics instruction: Development, instruction, and programs. *Focus on Exceptional Children, 21*(7), 1–10.

Maccini, P., & Gagnon, J. C. (2000). Best practices for teaching mathematics to secondary students with special needs. *Focus on Exceptional Children, 32*(5), 1–22.

Maccini, P., & Gagnon, J. C., (2002). Perceptions and application of NCTM standards by special and general education teachers. *Exceptional Children, 68,* 325–344.

Maccini, P., & Hughes, C A. (1997). Mathematics interventions for adolescents with learning disabilities. *Learning Disabilities Research into Practice, 12,* 168–176.

Mastroperi, M. A., Bakken, J. P., & Scruggs, T. E. (1991). Mathematics instruction for individuals with mental retardation: A perspective and research synthesis. *Education and Training in Mental Retardation, 26,* 115–129.

Mastroperi, M. A., Scruggs, T. E., & Shiah, S. (1991). Mathematics instruction for learning disabled students: A review of research. *Learning Disabilities Research & Practice, 6,* 89–98

Mercer, C. D., Jordan, L., & Miller, S. P. (1996). Constructivistic math instruction for diverse learners. *Learning Disabilities: Research & Practice, 11,* 147–156.

Merrow, J. (September, 1999). *Teacher shortage: False alarm?* Retrieved February 21, 2004 from the website of Public Broadcasting Service: http://www.pbs.org/merrow/tv/tshortage/

Miller, S. P., Butler, F. M., & Lee, K. (1998). Validated practices for teaching mathematics to students with learning disabilities: A review of the literature. *Focus on Exceptional Children, 31,* 1–24.

Moshman, D. (1982). Exogenous, endogenous, and dialectical constructivism. *Developmental Review, 2,* 371–384.

National Council of Teachers of Mathematics. (1989). *Curriculum and Evaluation NCTM standards for school mathematics.* Reston, VA: Author.

National Council of Teachers of Mathematics. (2000). *Principles and NCTM standards for school mathematics.* Reston, VA: Author.

National Education Association (2002). *Attracting and keeping quality teachers.* Retrieved February 21, 2004 from the website of The National Education Association: http://dark wing.uoregon.edu/~adiep/ft/grossen.htm [http://www.nea.org/ teaching/shortage.html]

Owen, R. L., & Fuchs, L. S. (2002). Mathematical problem-solving strategy instruction for third-grade students with learning disabilities. *Remedial and Special Education, 23,* 268–278.

Palincsar, A. S. (1998). Social constructivist perspectives on teaching and learning. *Annual Review of Psychology, 49,* 345–375.

Peterson, P., & Walberg, H. J. (Eds.). (1979). Research in teaching, Berkeley, CA: McCutchan. Cited in A.S. Palincsar, A. S. (1998). Social constructivist perspectives on teaching and learning. *Annual Review of Psychology, 49,* 345–375.

Polya, G. (1965a). *Mathematical discovery: On understanding, learning, and teaching, problem solving* (Vol. 1). New York: Wiley.

Polya, G. (1965b). *Mathematical discovery: On understanding, learning, and teaching, problem solving* (Vol. 2). New York : Wiley.

Poplin, M. S. (1988a). Holistic/constructivist principles of the teaching/learning process: Implications for the field of learning disabilities. *Journal of Learning Disabilities, 21,* 401–416.

Poplin, M. S. (1988b). The reductionistic fallacy in learning disabilities: Replicating the past by reducing the present. *Journal of Learning Disabilities, 21,* 289–400.

Porter, A. Floden, R., Freeman, D., Schmidt, W., & Schwille., J. (1988). Current determinants of elementary school mathematics. In D. A. Grouws, T. J. Cooney, & D. Jones (Eds.), *Perspectives on research on effective mathematics teaching* (Vol. 1). Reston, VA: National Council of Teachers of Mathematics.

Pressley, M., Harris, K. R., & Marks, M. R. (1992). But good strategy instructors are constructivists! *Educational Psychology Review, 4,* 3–31.

Pressley, M., Hogan, K., Wharton–McDonald, R., Mistretta, J., & Ettenberger, S. (1996). The challenges of instructional scaffolding: The challenges of instruction that supports student thinking. *Learning Disabilities Research and Practice, 11,* 138–146.

Pressley, M., Roehrig, A., Bogner, K., Raphael, L. M., & Donlezal, S. (2002). Balanced literacy instruction. *Focus on Exceptional Children, 34*(5), 1–14.

Reid, D.K., Kurkjian, C, & Carruthers, S. S. (1994), Special education teachers interpret constructivist teaching. *Remedial and Special Education, 15,* 267–280.

Rogers, C. (1968). *The freedom to learn.* (2d ed.). Columbus, OH: Merrill.

Rosenshine, B. (1978). *Instructional principles in direct instruction.* Paper presented at annual meeting of American Educational Research Association, Toronto. ED 155 152.

Rosenshine, B. V. (1979). Content, time and direct instruction. In P. L. Peterson & H. J. Walberg (Eds.), *Research on teaching: Concepts, findings and implications.* Berkeley, CA:McCutchan.

Shulman, L. S., & Keislar, E. R. (1966). *Learning by discovery: A critical appraisal.* Chicago: Rand McNally.

Skinner, B. F. (1967). What is psychotic behavior? In T. Millon (Ed.), *Theories of psychopathology.* Philadelphia: Saunders.

Slavin, R. (1983). When does cooperative learning increase student achievement. *Psychological Bulletin, 94,* 429–445.

Stebbins, L. B., St. Pierre, R. G., Proper, E. C., Anderson, R. B., & Cerva, T. R. (1977). *Education as experimentation: A planned variation model*: Vol 4-A. *An evaluation of Follow Through.* Cambridge, MA: Abt Associates.

Stein, M., Silbert, J., & Carnine, D. (1997). *Designing effective mathematics instruction: A direct instruction approach* (3d ed.). Upper Saddle River, NJ: Prentice Hall.

Stevens, R., & Rosenshine, B. (1981). Advances in research on teaching. *Exceptional Education Quarterly, 2,* 1–9.

Stokes, T. F., & Baer, D. M. (1977). An implicit technology of generalization. *Journal of Applied Behavior Analysis, 10,* 349–367.

Swanson, H.L., Carson, C., & Saches–Lee, C. M. (1996). A selective synthesis of intervention research for students with learning disabilities. *School Psychology Review, 25,* 370–391.

Tashman, B., (November 15, 1994). Our failure to follow through. *New York Newsday.* Retrieved February 21, 2004 from the website of *Effective School Practices*: http://darkwing.uoregon.edu/~adiep/ft/grossen.htm

Tyson, H., & Woodward, A. (1989). Why students aren't learning very much from textbooks. *Educational Leadership, 47*(3), 14-17

Vargas, J. S. (1984). What are your exercises teaching? An analysis of stimulus control in instructional materials. In W. L. Heward, T. E. Heron, D. S. Hill, & J. Trap–Porter. *Focus on behavior analysis in education* (pp. 126–141). Columbus, OH: Charles E. Merrill.

Watkins, C. L., & Slocum, T. A. (2004). The components of direct instruction. In N. E. Marchand–Martella, T. A. Solcum, & R. C. Martella (Eds.), *Introduction to direct instruction.* Boston: Pearson Education.

Wolery, M., Bailey, D. B., & Sugai, G. M. (1988). *Effective teaching: Principles and procedures of applied behavior analysis with exceptional students.* Boston: Allyn & Bacon.

Woodward, J., & Montague, M. (2002). Meeting the challenge of mathematics reform for students with LD. *Journal of Special Education, 36,* 89–101.

Searching for the Best Model for Instructing Students With Learning Disabilities

H. Lee Swanson

tudents with learning disabilities (LD) comprise a heterogeneous group so no general instructional model can be recommended for all of them. Thus, the title of this article might seem to be somewhat of a misnomer. Nevertheless, some common general principles for teaching students with LD can be assumed to exist. Effective interventions include some instructional components that capitalize on these principles. Although these principles often operate in different ways with different students, in different content areas, and in different settings, they can be used in designing effective remediation programs for LD students.

In this chapter, findings are summarized related to a comprehensive educational intervention research synthesis for students with learning disabilities (Swanson, Hoskyn, & Lee, 1999) that attempts to identify the principles underlying effective instruction. Although there have been several technical reports related to this synthesis (e.g., Swanson, 1999; Swanson & Hoskyn, 1998; Swanson & Sachse-Lee, 2000), the purpose of this article is to consider more directly the practical aspects of the findings. More specifically, the focus will be on the question: What instructional components or activities characterize highly effective intervention programs for students with LD?

On the surface, identifying key instructional components that improve LD students' performance might seem to be a relatively simple, although time-consuming, task. One could simply take all the studies published in refereed journals that yield positive outcomes for students with LD and then summarize the instructional principles that make up those studies. In fact, most syntheses that attempt to translate research to practice rely on such procedures. Such an approach is problematic, however, because the published literature is biased toward reporting positive treatment outcomes (e.g., Begg, 1994).

A quick perusal of the published literature reveals a plethora of published treatments (i.e., bona fide instructional models) reflecting a diversity of approaches that yield positive outcomes for students with LD. Such a state of affairs has been called a "Dodo bird" effect (e.g., Lubrosky, Singer, & Luborsky, 1975). Taken from a conclusion of the Dodo bird in *Alice in Wonderland* (Carroll, 1965/1962), the bird stated, "Everybody has won, and all must have prizes" (p. 412). Unquestionably, this effect is disconcerting when attempting to search for some general principles of effective instruction.

In the case of children with LD, however, some treatments can be assumed to be less effective than others, and therefore not all treatments deserve prizes. How, then, can one determine the best approach to wade through all these studies that yield positive outcomes? One approach allowing comparison of the treatments that yield positive outcomes for students with LD is to place studies on the same level playing field. This is done by equating studies by their methodological sophistication (to be discussed later). If this is not done, the race as depicted in *Alice in Wonderland* becomes haphazard:

> [The competitors] were placed along the course, here and there. There was no "One, two, three and away," but they began running when they liked, and left off when they liked so that it was not easy to know when the race was over. (p. 45)

Thus, the assumption is made that if studies are put on an equal footing methodologically speaking with control for publication biases by including nonpublished studies in our synthesis, we can identify some common components that make for a generally effective instructional model. Before detailing attempts to sort through the literature to identify those components, however, we would do well to review what has been found in previous syntheses of the literature.

PREVIOUS SYNTHESES

Reviews of the instructional literature that have been influential in providing an understanding of treatment outcomes for students with LD use a procedure called *meta-analysis* (e.g., Kavale & Forness, 2000; Mastropieri, Scruggs, Bakken, & Whedon, 1996). Meta-analysis is a statistical reviewing technique that provides a quantitative summary of findings across an entire body of research (Cooper & Hedges, 1994). The results of individual studies are converted to a standardized metric or effect size. The scores then are aggregated across the sample of studies to yield an overall estimate of effect size. Particular attention is given to the magnitude of the effect size estimate. According to Cohen (1988), .80 is considered a large effect size estimate, .50 a moderate estimate, and .20 a small estimate.

There have been several excellent meta-analyses on instructional research in learning disabilities (e.g., Kavale & Forness, 2000, Mastropieri et al., 1996), but none to our knowledge has considered intervention research across a broad array of academic domains and/or controlled for variations in methodology. The only synthesis to my knowledge that provided an overall estimate of treatment effectiveness prior to the present synthesis was our own previous synthesis (Swanson, Carson & Lee, 1996). A collection was assembled of published group-designed studies (78) between 1967 and 1993, which focused on youth 6–18 years of age; and reported from a total of 324 effect sizes a mean effect size of .85 for treatment versus control conditions. Using Cohen's (1988) threshold of .80 for large effects, the earlier meta-analysis suggested that various instructional approaches have had a significant beneficial effect when used with children and adolescents who have learning disabilities.

Two important findings come out of this earlier synthesis. *First,* in contrast to the Dodo bird effect, our earlier synthesis suggested that not all forms of intervention work equally well. In this synthesis, studies were classified into one of four general instructional orientations: therapeutic (eclectic), remedial, direct instruction, or cognitive strategies. The classification was determined by the hypothesis of the study, as well as key words in the introduction, abstract, and title of each article related to the treatment of choice. Mean effect size scores were .59 for the eclectic approaches (approaches not directed specifically to academic skills), .91 for direct instruction, .68 for remedial instruction, and 1.07 for strategy instruction. Thus, a higher effect size emerged for direct and strategy instruction when compared to the other approaches.

Second, no particular academic or behavioral domain (e.g., reading, mathematics, spelling, language, social skills, memory, cognition) was resistant to change as a function of intervention. Although most of the research related to intervention was in the reading domain (reading comprehension, word recognition), no differences in effect sizes were found across targeted domains (processing, social skills, mathematics, spelling).

In summary, we must point out that, although this previous analysis found some advantages for direct and strategy instruction, other general models also produced high effect sizes. One reason for this may have been that the earlier synthesis relied on categorizing the intervention approaches by how the primary author labeled the experimental condition rather than by coding the actual procedures and components of instruction used in the study.

The former approach is problematic for several reasons, the most obvious being that treatments shared many of the same instructional activities (e.g., corrective feedback, active participation of the learner, teaching skill in a cumulative manner). Therefore, the distinction between various treatments was more artificial than real.

SEPARATING STUDIES INTO STRATEGY AND DIRECT-INSTRUCTION MODELS

To address this flaw in the earlier synthesis, studies in this new synthesis were sorted by components represented in the treatment studies. Thus, studies were divided along lines in terms of those that reflect strategies and those that emphasize direct instruction. Before discussing how the studies were sorted as reflecting either direct or strategy instruction in the current synthesis, we emphasize the distinctions and overlap between the two general instructional approaches. Readers have to keep in mind that the distinctions are sometimes subtle, which creates difficulties in clearly analyzing the two approaches.

Consider the following study in our synthesis that contrasts both approaches: Lovett et al. (1994) compare both strategy and direct instruction intervention models on word-recognition outcomes. Both approaches include a graduated sequence of steps with multiple opportunities for overlearning the content and skills in a reading program. Both instructional models include cumulative review routines, mass practice, and teaching of all component skills to mastery criterion.

For the strategy model, the students learn sound units with additional discussion given to metacognitive issues such as strategy implementation, strategy choice, and self-monitoring. Clear discussion is given to students about (a) *why* a strategy facilitates word recognition, (b) how to apply the strategy, and (c) how to check to see if the strategy is working. Students systematically practice these strategies with target words. A compare-and-contrast activity explicitly trains the students on what they need to know to help them decode a new word.

The direct instruction condition follows the same procedures as strategy instruction except for two variations:

1. Direct instruction focuses on subskills (sound units, such as letter sounds, or linguistic units, such as *mat-cat-hat*).
2. Discussion of processes and use of general rules is minimized.

Thus, what seems to separate the two instructional models is focus. The strategy program focuses on processes or global skills for a general approach to reading, whereas a direct instruction model focuses on word segmentation and "sound-getting skills." A further contrast between the two models is that the strategy model calls for teaching a few words to mastery, whereas the direct instruction model concentrates on a level of subanalysis or segmentation (phonological awareness).

Although direct and strategy instruction treatments may be distinguished by the unit of information (i.e., direct instruction focuses primarily on isolated skills, whereas strategy instruction focuses primarily on rules) and processing perspective (direct instruction is characterized as a bottom-up processing approach and strategy instruction as a top-down processing approach), other distinctions are less subtle. For example, components of direct instruction were reviewed by Engelmann and Carnine (1982), Kameenui, Jitendra, & Darch (1995), Rosenshine (1995), and Slavin, Karweit, and Madden (1989). These reviews show that direct instruction emphasizes fast-paced, well sequenced, and highly focused lessons. The lessons usually are taught in small groups of students who are given several opportunities to respond and receive feedback about accuracy and responses (See Kameenui et al., 1995, for a review of model variations).

Components related to effective strategy instructional programs also are reviewed elsewhere (see Borkowski & Turner, 1990; Levin, 1986; Pressley & Ghatala, 1990; Sternberg, 1998; Swanson, 1993). These components include:

- advanced organizers (providing students with a type of mental scaffolding on which to build new understanding)
- organization (directing students to stop from time to time to assess their understanding)
- elaboration (thinking about the material to be learned in a way that connects the material to information or ideas already in their mind)
- generative learning (making sense of what they are learning by summarizing the information)
- general study strategies (underlining, note taking, summarizing, having student generated questions, outlining, and working in pairs to summarize sections of materials)
- thinking about and controlling one's thinking process (metacognition)
- attributions (evaluating the effectiveness of a strategy).

Given the distinctions between the two models, how do they overlap? An answer to this question is important because it may account for some of the confusion in differentiating the two models. Strategy instruction and direct instruction models overlap in at least two ways. First, both models (in one form or another) assume that effective *methods* of instruction include (a) daily reviews, (b) statements of an instructional objective, (c) teacher presentation of new material, (d) guided practice, (e) independent practice, and (f) formative evaluations (see Rosenshine, 1995; Rosenshine & Stevens, 1986; Shuell, 1996; Slavin, Stevens, & Madden, 1988, for a review). *Second,* both direct instruction and strategy instruction follow a *sequence of events,* such as the following:

1. State the learning objectives and orient the students to what they will be learning and what performance will be expected of them.
2. Review the skills necessary to understand the concept.
3. Present the information, give examples, and demonstrate the concepts/materials.
4. Pose questions (probes) to students and assess their level of understanding and correct misconceptions.
5. Provide group instruction and independent practice. Give students an opportunity to demonstrate new skills and learn the new information on their own.
6. Assess performance and provide feedback. Review the independent work and give a quiz. Give feedback for correct answers and reteach skills if answers are incorrect.
7. Provide distributed practice and review.

No doubt the above sequence has variations within a strategy or direct instruction model (e.g., Graham & Harris, 1996; Lovett et al., 1994).

In summary, the instructional components that make up the two orientations have points of distinction as well as commonality. The present synthesis compares outcomes of studies that included these various components. Because of the tremendous overlap in components, however, we drew upon general literature reviews for comparative purposes to operationalize the models.

Specifically, treatments were coded as reflecting *direct instruction* if four of the following criteria were present:

1. Breaking down a task into small steps
2. Administering probes
3. Administering feedback repeatedly
4. Providing a pictorial or diagram presentation
5. Allowing for independent practice and individually paced instruction
6. Breaking the instruction down into simpler phases
7. Instructing in a small group
8. Teacher modeling a skill
9. Providing set materials at a rapid pace
10. Providing individual child instruction
11. Teacher asking questions
12. Teacher presenting the new (novel) materials.

Studies were categorized as *strategy instruction* if they included at least three of the following instructional components:

1. Elaborate explanations (systematic explanations, elaborations, and/or plan to direct task performance)
2. Modeling from teachers (verbal modeling, questioning, and demonstration from teachers)
3. Reminders to use certain strategies or procedures (cues to use taught strategies, tactics, or procedures)
4. Step-by-step prompts or multi-process instructions
5. Dialogue (teacher and student talk back and forth)
6. Teacher asks questions
7. Teacher provides only necessary assistance.

Based on the operational criteria, some studies could be expected to share *both* strategy instruction and direct instruction criteria. Therefore, studies were separated further into those that included only strategy components (SI-only model), those that included only direct-instruction components (DI-only), those that included both strategy and direct instruction components (combined model; i.e., includes a minimum of three strategy and four direct-instruction components), and studies that did not include the minimum number of components for either direct or strategy instruction (nondirect instruction and nonstrategy instruction model). Thus, the latter studies may have included some components of either model, but none of these studies met a critical threshold of strategy or direct instruction components.

[Note: To some, the classification of studies as direct or strategy instruction by meeting a minimum threshold of components may seem arbitrary. A comparison of studies, however, which listed more components than others (these were referred to as high-saturation studies), did not yield a difference in the pattern of results. Further, "minimum threshold" studies, because of page constraints, may have listed only the most important components and therefore were included to ensure that the findings were not biased by the studies that reported the treatment in greater detail.]

PROCEDURES IN SEARCHING AND CLASSIFYING THE LITERATURE

Consideration has been given to issues related to identifying effective instructional models before discussing the results of the most recent meta-analysis. At this point, we will review procedures used to assess the relevant literature, along with information related to three questions: (1) How were the studies selected for analysis?, (2) How were the instructional treatments categorized?, and (3) How were instructional components categorized?

How did we come up with the studies for analysis? The search procedures are described in detail in Swanson and Hoskyn (1998) and, therefore, are summarized here. The PsycINFO, MEDline, and ERIC on-line data bases were systematically scanned for studies from 1963 to 1997 that met the inclusion criteria described below. The computer search strategy used the following terms: "learning disabled (disabilities)," or "reading disabled (disabilities)," or "dyslexic," or "educationally handicapped," or "slow learners," paired with variations of "intervention" or "treatment" or "training" or "remediation" or "instruction." This search yielded approximately 2,900 abstracts including articles, technical reports, chapters, and dissertations. Because the computer search procedures excluded unpublished studies and the most recent literature, researchers (as identified by journal board affiliations with the *Learning Disability Quarterly, Journal of Learning Disabilities,* and *Learning Disabilities Research and Practice* and/or membership in the International Academy for Research in Learning Disabilities) were sent letters requesting copies of unpublished and/or ongoing intervention studies.

The pool of relevant literature was narrowed to studies that used an experimental design in which children or adults with LD received treatment to enhance their academic, social, and/or cognitive performance. This procedure narrowed the search to *913* data-based articles (or reports) that seemed to be potentially acceptable for including in the quantitative review. After a review of these studies, each data-based report was evaluated on five additional criteria for study inclusion.

1. The study had at least one between-instruction comparison (i.e., control condition) or within-design control condition (e.g., repeated measures design) that includes participants with LD.

2. The study provided sufficient quantitative information to permit the calculation of effect sizes.
3. Recipients of the intervention were children or adults with average intelligence who had problems in a specific academic, social, and/or related behavior domain.
4. The treatment group received instruction, assistance, or therapy over and above what they would have received during the course of their typical classroom experience. That is, the study focused on treatment rather than merely a description of the child's current placement followed by an evaluation.
5. The study had to be written in English.

Although design issues (e.g., no control condition) constituted the most frequent reason for excluding an article, other frequent reasons for excluding articles were the inability to calculate effect sizes, lack of clarity about whether students with LD were included, the inability to separate the performance of students with LD from other ability groups, no information on sample size, and/or faulty statistical applications (e.g., incorrect degrees of freedom).

How did we categorize the treatment variables? Based on the criteria provided in the introduction, studies to be classified fell into one of four models: strategy + direct instruction (referred to as the *combined model*), direct instruction (DI-alone), strategy instruction (SI-alone) and the nondirect + nonstrategy instruction model (nondirect instruction and nonstrategy instruction, i.e., studies that failed to reach a critical threshold of "reported" information). As a validity check on these classifications, classification of the treatment conditions was compared to that of the primary authors' general theoretical model and/or the label attached to the treatment condition. There was substantial overlap (approximately 70% of the studies) between the studies we classified ascombined, DI-alone, and SI-alone models with the primary authors' titles or description of the independent variables.

For example, frequent terms provided by the author were: "strategy," "cognitive intervention," "monitoring," "metacognition," "self-instruction," and "cognitive-behavior modification" for the strategy model. Those that were classified as DI by the present criteria used labels such as: "directed instruction," "advanced organizers," "adapting materials," or "corrective feedback" or "direct computation." Approaches that were below the component threshold (they did not include the minimum number of components required for being labeled as either direct instruction or strategy intervention) used, for example, labels such as "reinforcement-only," "modeling-only," or "social skills training."

How did we categorize instructional components? There were 45 instructional *activities* that were coded as present or not present in the study (see the Appendix to this article). Based on comprehensive reviews that have identified instructional components that influenced student outcomes (e.g., Brophy & Good, 1986; Leinhardt & Greeno, 1986; Pressley & Harris, 1994; Rosenshine, 1995; Shuell, 1996; Sternberg,

1998), we reclustered (or reconfigured) the 45 instructional activities shown in Appendix A into 18 clusters of components for later analysis.

We coded the occurrence of the following instructional components (also provided are the numbers related to the coding sheet provided in the Appendix):

1. *Sequencing.* Statements in the treatment description related to breaking down the task, and/or sequencing short activities (activity numbers 12 and 29).

2. *Explicit practice.* Statements in the treatment description related to distributed review and practice, repeated practice, sequenced reviews, daily feedback, and/or weekly reviews (activity numbers 23, 26, 27, 39, and 45).

3. *Novelty.* Statements in the treatment description about which a new curriculum was implemented, and/or emphasis on teacher presenting new material from the previous lesson (activity numbers 20 and 38).

4. *Attributions.* Statements in the treatment description about the teacher presenting the benefits of taught strategies (activity 41).

5. *Reinforcement.* Statements in the treatment description about intermittent or consistent use of rewards and reinforcers (activity 28).

6. *Peer modeling.* Statements in the treatment description about model peers presenting or modeling instruction (activity 18).

7. *Task reduction.* Statements in the treatment description about breaking down the targeted skill into smaller units, mastery criteria, and/or task analysis (activity nos. 1, 17, and 34)).

8. *Advanced organizers.* Statements in the treatment description about directing children to look over material prior to instruction, children directed to focus on particular information, providing prior information about task, and/or the teacher stating objectives of instruction (activities 2, 3, 11, and 40).

9. *Questioning.* Treatment description related to directing students to ask questions, the teacher and student or students engaging in dialogue, and/or the teacher asking questions (activities 33, 35, and 36).

10. *One-to-one instruction.* Statements in the treatment description about activities related to independent practice, tutoring, instruction that is individually paced, and/or instruction that is individually tailored (activities 9, 10, and 13).

11. *Control difficulty or processing demands of a task.* Treatment statements about probing learning, fading probes or prompts, short activities so the level of difficulty is controlled, and/or teacher providing necessary assistance (activities 4, 7, 16, and 42).

12. *Technology.* Statements in the treatment description about developing pictorial representations, using specific material or computers, and/or using media to facilitate presentation and feedback (activities 5, 31, and 44).

13. *Elaboration.* Statements in the treatment description about additional information or explanation provided about concepts, and/or redundant text or repetition within text (activities 6, 24, and 30).

14. *Skill modeling.* Statements or activities in the treatment descriptions that involve modeling from teacher in terms of skills (activity 19).

15. *Small-group Instruction.* Statements in the treatment description about instruction in a small group, and/or verbal interaction occurring in a small group with students and/or teacher (activity 14).

16. *A supplement to teacher involvement.* Statements in the treatment description about homework and/or parents helping reinforce instruction (activities 8, 21, and 22).

17. *Strategy cues.* Statements in the treatment description about reminders to use strategies or multi-steps, the teacher verbalizing steps or procedures to solve problems, and/or use of "think aloud models" (activities 25, 32, and 43).

18. *Large-group learning.* Statements in the treatment description about instruction in large groups and/or teacher-only demonstration (activities 15 and 37).

The components associated most often with strategy instruction programs are best reflected in component numbers 4, 8, 9, 11, 13, 15, and 17. For example, the *advanced organizer* component (no. 8) characterizes treatment approaches that activate prior knowledge or provide a precursor to the main instructional activity (e.g., Meichenbaum's [1977] cognitive-behavioral model). The component that reflected the *Control of difficulty or processing demands of a task* addressed the variations in teacher support of the student (e.g., the teacher provided necessary assistance, tasks sequenced from easy to difficult, i.e., help was provided to the student that covaries with the learner's ability) and reflected activities such as mediated scaffolding (e.g., Palincsar & Brown, 1984). Following an explicit set of steps and prompting the use of these steps *(strategy cue)* are considered to be important activities that underlie strategy instruction (Rosenshine, 1995).

Although all studies included in the present synthesis met all of selection criteria, this does not mean that the studies were of equal methodological sophistication. Just because a study has a control condition, it does not follow that methodological problems have been controlled. To address this issue, we coded each study on a number of methodological variables and created methodological composite scores related to both internal validity and methodological sophistication. Studies were assigned a positive score on the following methodological dimensions:

1. Instructional sessions greater than 10 (selection of this variable was based on the assumption that the intensity of instruction as reflected by the number of sessions yields more reliable and stable outcomes than shorter intervention sessions)

2. Random assignment to treatment

3. Multiple measures of treatment integrity (treatment was carried out as intended)

4. Use of standardized tests (higher reliability than experimental measures)

5. Internal validity scores of 11 [number reflects the best possible ratings on items—see above]
6. Score assigned to overlapping high control and treatment condition in terms of steps and procedures (at least three steps and/or procedures overlap).

The amount of standardized test information reported was included in the methodological composite score [if additional psychometric information beyond an IQ score was reported (e.g., reading scores)]. For each study, the composite score across the seven variables varied from 14 to 0, with 14 reflecting methodologically superior studies. The mean methodological composite score for the 180 studies was 7.25, suggesting that, on an average, studies fell in the middle of the present methodological continuum.

TYPICAL CHARACTERISTICS OF STUDIES IN THIS SYNTHESIS

The analyses yielded 180 group design studies, which encompassed approximately 1,600 effect sizes comparing students with LD in the experimental condition with students with LD in the control condition. The mean effect size, which takes into consideration the sample size across the 180 studies was .65. An average intervention study included 23 minutes of daily instruction, three times a week, over 36 days. The mean sample size for the study was 27. The mean treatment age was 11 years.

Materials for the experimental conditions were commercial (33% of the studies), novel (materials developed by the researcher, 54% of the studies), or a combination of commercial and novel (9% of the studies), or were not classifiable (4% of the studies). The most frequent commercial materials ($N = 54$) were related to direct instruction (e.g., Corrective Reading, Distar, SRA, 8%), Houghton Mifflin series (4%), Orton-Gillingham approach (4%), and Lindamood-Bell (4%). In terms of student activities during treatment, 30 of the studies had participants monitor or evaluate (via recording, counting, charting, checking, graphing, and/or verbalizing) their academic behavior.

A THREE-TIER STRATEGY FOR ANALYZING THE STUDIES

After the general characteristics of the studies had been analyzed, we analyzed the studies in terms of instructional approaches. We used a three-tier structure to investigate the various instructional approaches. For the first tier, four general intervention models were compared. As stated previously, the four general models were DI-alone (direct instruction components, but below a threshold of strategy components), SI-alone (strategy components, but below a threshold of DI components), direct instruction coupled with strategy instruction (*combined model,* which included both strategy and direct instruction components), and studies that did not meet the threshold for classification as either direct instruction or strategy instruction (referred to as the *nondirect instruction and nonstrategy instruction model*).

The four models yielded significantly different mean effect sizes when the methodological composite scores and the age of the sample were partialed from the analysis. The mean effect sizes and the total number of studies (N) were .84 (N = 55), .68 (N = 47) .72 (N = 28), and .62 (N = 43) for the combined, DI-alone, SI-alone, and nondirect instruction and nonstrategy instruction models, respectively. A follow-up test indicated that the combined model yielded significantly higher effect sizes than the other models (combined > DI alone = SI alone = nondirect instruction and nonstrategy instruction).

What do these findings suggest? Although the combined model superseded the other models, the magnitude of the effect sizes for all four general approaches is high. These high effects emerged even when the analysis took into account method-ological and age variations between studies. Thus, support is found for the afore-mentioned Dodo bird effect. This finding was a little disconcerting because it seems to suggest that no matter what the intervention, academic behavior always improves. Perhaps a more optimistic way of looking at these findings is to conclude that these studies are tapping some common components.

To address this question, Table 14.1 shows the percent of studies that included each of the 18 components. More than 40% of all the studies included instructional components related to sequencing, task reduction, one-to-one instruction, and tech-nology. Infrequently reported instructional components were related to attribution training, direct reinforcement, elaboration, and supplements to teacher instruction.

The analysis also determined whether studies that yielded high effect sizes as well as high methodological scores were more likely to use specific instructional components. Columns 2 and 3 in Table 14.1 show studies that achieved a high meth-ods composite score (> 7 with 14 as the highest) but yielded effect sizes at or above .60 and those below .60, respectively. These comparisons indicate that *no* one instructional component was reported in more than 40% of the studies.

The component in which 30% of the studies were represented was one-to-one instruction. For the high methods-high effect size studies, no instructional compo-nents except the one-to-one component was above 25%. For the high methods-low effect size studies, components that approached the 25% representation were sequencing (component no. 1) and task reduction (component no. 7).

The difficulty with the present analysis is that instruction seldom represents a single component but, instead, interacts with other components in treatment out-comes. That is, instructional components seldom act independently in the context of other components. For example, no teacher merely focuses on sequencing or strat-egy instruction without taking into consideration whether instruction should be one-to-one, small-group, or some combination of these settings. Thus, the next analysis identified those instructional components, when coupled with other components, that best predict effect size. Before this can occur, however, it is necessary to deter-mine components that seem to co-occur with other components in studies.

It was assumed that components that frequently co-occur reflect a common fac-tor. What are those factors? To determine the instructional components that shared a common factor (cluster together), an exploratory factor analysis was done.

TABLE 14.1 ■ Percent of Instructional Components Reported in Studies			
	Total	High Methods High Effect Sizes	High Methods Low Effect Sizes
1. Sequencing	46.7	21.84	25.29
2. Explicit practice	32.8	19.54	11.49
3. Novelty	39.4	18.39	19.54
4. Attributions	1.0	–	–
5. Reinforcement	6.1	1.15	2.30
6. Peer modeling	3.3	1.15	5.75
7. Task reduction	41.1	22.99	24.14
8. Advanced organizer	28.3	10.34	10.34
9. Questioning	15.0	4.60	17.02
10. One-to-one instruction	68.3	29.89	40.23
11. Control difficulty	38.9	21.84	19.54
12. Technology	50.0	21.84	22.89
13. Elaboration	5.0	1.15	0
14. Skill modeling	26.1	8.05	14.84
15. Small-group instruction	22.8	13.79	19.15
16. Supplemental instruction	6.1	4.60	1.15
17. Strategy cues	19.4	11.49	8.90
18. Large-group learning	38.3	16.09	21.84

As shown in Table 14.2, the analysis yielded an eight-factor solution. Complete details of this analysis are found in Swanson (in press). To simplify the table, an X is placed beside the component that loads (correlates) with a particular factor (i.e., a component with a factor loading greater than .39).

What do you think these eight factors represent? As shown in Table 14.2, the first factor loads highly on instructional components related sequencing, reducing task demands, advanced organizers, and the modeling of skills. Factor 1 clearly reflects the sequencing and segmentation of information. This factor was labeled as *explicit direct instruction* because such a model emphasizes that the steps of instruction are presented in an explicit sequential fashion (e.g., Lovett et al., 1994).

The second factor loads high on explicit practice, strategy cuing, and elaboration. The second factor was interpreted as reflecting direct and *explicit strategy* training. This factor is characteristic of some of the components found in models outlined by several authors (e.g., Borkowski, Weyhing, & Carr, 1988; Graham & Harris, 1989; Miller & Seier, 1994; Pressley, Brown, El-Dinary, & Allferbach, 1995). The steps include a description of the strategy, modeling its use, verbal rehearsal of steps, guided practice and feedback with material/or teacher instruction that elaborates information.

TABLE 14.2 ■ Factor Analysis of Components

	Factors							
Variable	1	2	3	4	5	6	7	8
1. Sequencing	XX							
2. Explicit practice		XX		XX				
3. Novelty			XX					
4. Attributions							XX	
5. Reinforcement				XX				
6. Peer modeling						XX		
7. Task reduction	XX							
8. Advanced organizer	XX		XX					
9. Questioning							XX	
10. One-to-one instruction				XX				
11. Control difficulty			XX	XX				
12. Technology								XX
13. Elaboration		XX						
14. Skill modeling	XX						XX	
15. Small-group instruction					XX			
16. Supplemental instruction		XX						
17. Strategy cues		XX						
18. Large-group learning					XX			

The third factor loads on components related to implementing new curriculum, advance organizers, and controlling the difficulty of item presentation. Because the components reflect the monitoring of new information, this component is referred to as instructional *monitoring*. Monitoring is emphasized in programs such as cognitive behavior modification (Meichenbaum, 1977).

The fourth factor loads highly on one-to-one instruction and reinforcement. Because these activities are associated with several skills-training programs (e.g., Lovett et al., 1994; Vellutino & Scanlon, 1991), this factor was labeled as *individualized remedial* instruction.

As with factor 4, factor 5 reflects a setting variable. Factor 5 contrasts the large-group setting with a small-group setting. This factor was referred to as *small interactive group* instruction.

Factor 6 loads highly on components related to peer modeling and ancillary activities (homework, parent help). This factor was referred to as a *teacher-indirect instruction,* and therefore we view this factor as ancillary or supplemental to direct or explicit instruction.

Factor 7 loads on the components related to attribution training as well as instruction that includes verbal questioning/dialogue and skill modeling. This factor includes components characteristic of several strategy models that rely on verbal mediation (e.g., Borkowski et al., 1988; Palincsar, 1986). This factor was referred to as *verbal questioning/ attribution* instruction.

Factor 8 loads highly on the medium of instruction. These mediums focus on computer presentations, strategy flow charts, and the like. This factor was referred to as *technology or media* moderated instruction. This is in contrast to factor 7, which focused directly on verbal dialogue as a mediation tool.

In sum, the instructional components can be boiled down to eight factors. Some of these seem to be clearly related to strategy components (e.g., factor 2, factor 7), whereas others are related to setting (factor 5) and still others to sequencing (factor 1).

Which factors contribute significantly to improving the magnitude of treatment outcomes? Although sorting the components that go together into factors made some empirical and practical sense, a question not addressed was which of the factors significantly improved the magnitude of the effect size. No doubt, an answer to this question is at the heart of this article. Thus, the next analysis summarized the results in more detail. The analysis used a special form of hierarchical regression analysis (see Hedge, 1994, for discussion). The eight factor scores, the methodological weighting of each study, and the age of the participants were used to predict the magnitude of treatment outcomes. The results are shown in Table 14.3.

The cumulative percentage of variance (R^2) associated with the addition of variables is presented in the first and third columns. An asterisk (*) is placed beside the R^2 if the factors significantly contributed to effect size. The increment in percentage associated with additional variables appears in the second and fourth columns.

Because the order of entry of these factors is known to influence the outcomes of regression analyses, several models were tested. To be precise, the amount of variance in effect size accounted for by (a) methods and age alone (model 1), and (b) methods and age after each factor score (model 2–9) was partialed out (controlled) was determined. Of interest was whether the contribution of methods and age to effect size was mediated by instructional components. As shown for the explicit strategy instruction (model 3), the factor score contributed significant variance to the magnitude of effect size. The results also indicated that small/ interactive instructional groups (model 6) contributed significant variance and reduced the contribution of the methods and age variables to effect size.

The largest contributor to effect size (7% of the variance) was explicit strategy instruction (model 3). Inspection of Table 3 also indicated that the total amount of variance related to the methods and age variable in predicting effect size was 6% (model 1). Following the addition of explicit strategy instruction (factor 2) in model 3, the contribution was reduced to 3%. The drop in variance seems to account for 50% of the methodological/age-related variance in effect size [i.e., (.06-.03)/.06].

Will predictions of effect size be enhanced if direct instruction, explicit strategy instruction, and small-group instruction (factors 1, 2 and 5) are included in the predictions of effect size? The question was answered by varying the order of entry to determine if the factor scores contributed unique variance. As shown in Model 10, the contribution of direct instruction (factor 1) was not significant.

TABLE 14.3 ■ Instructional Models for Predicting Effect Sizes

	R^2	Increment R^2		R^2	Increment R^2
Model 1			**Model 2**		
1. Methods	.06*	—	1. Direct Instruction	.01	—
2. Age	.06	—	2. Methods	.07*	.06
			3. Age	.07	—
Model 3			**Model 4**		
1. Strategy Instruction	.07*	—	1. Monitor	.00	—
2. Methods	.10*	.03	2. Methods	.06*	.06
3. Age	.10	—	3. Age	.06	—
Model 5			**Model 6**		
1. Individual Remediation	.00	—	1. Small-Group	.02*	—
2. Methods	.06*	.06	2. Methods	.07*	.05
3. Age	.06	—	3. Age	.07	—
Model 7			**Model 8**		
1. Indirect	.002	—	1. Attribution	.005	—
2. Methods	.06*	—	2. Methods	.06*	.05
3. Age	.06	—	3. Age	.06	—
Model 9			**Model 10**		
1. Technology	.0001	—	1. Direct Instruction	.01	—
2. Method	.06*	—	2. Small-Group	.03*	.02
3. Age	.06	—	3. Strategy Instruction	.08*	.06
			4. Methods	.12*	.04
			5. Age	.12	—
Model 11			**Model 12**		
1. Small-Group	.02*	—	1. Strategy Instruction	.07*	—
2. Direct Instruction	.03	.01	2. Small-Group	.08	.01
3. Strategy Instruction	.08*	.06	3. Direct Instruction	.08	—
4. Methods	.12*	.04	4. Methods	.12*	.04
5. Age	.12	—	5. Age	.12	—
Model 13			**Model 14**		
1. Strategy Instruction	.07*	—	1. Small-Group	.02*	—
2. Direct Instruction	.08	.01	2. Strategy Instruction	.08*	.06
3. Small-Group	.08	—	3. Methods	.12*	.04
4. Methods	.12*	.04	4. Age	.12	—
5. Age	.12	—			

Direct Instruction = explicit direct instruction model
Strategy Instruction = explicit strategy instruction model
Individual Remediation = individual remedial instruction model
Small-Group = small group interactive instruction model

In contrast, Models 11 and 14 showed that small-group interactions (factor 5) contributed significant variance to effect size when entered before explicit strategy instruction (factor 2). Models 12 and 13, however, showed that explicit strategy instruction (factor 2) partialed out (i.e., the effect is no longer significant) the influence small-group instruction (factor 5).

Thus, the results showed that Model 14 was the most parsimonious model because it removes the contribution of direct instruction (factor 1). The reduction in the methods/age variable in Model 14, however, was no better than that reported in Model 3.

In summary, Model 3, which included explicit strategy instruction (factor 2) provided the most parsimonious instructional model. This model also reduced the variance related to methods and age in predicting effect size. The multiple components model that yields the largest percentage of variance accounted for (largest R^2) included explicit strategy instruction (factor 2) and small-group instruction (factor 5). The reader has to remember that these factors reflect high loadings (see Table 2) for instructional components related to explicit practice, elaboration, strategy cues, and small-group instruction.

WHAT'S THE BIG PICTURE?

What can be concluded from this synthesis when we talk about a general model of instruction for students with LD? There are three important findings related to improving the academic performance of students with LD.

First, an effective general model of instruction combining the components of direct and strategy instruction supersedes other models for remediating learning disabilities. More specifically, the effects size (M = .84) of the combined strategy instruction and direct instruction model meets Cohen's (1988) criterion of .80 for a substantial finding. What are the instructional implications of this finding?

Over the years the literature has presented some lively debate about whether instruction should be top-down, via emphasizing the knowledge base, heuristics, and explicit strategies, or a bottom-up emphasis entailing hierarchical instruction at the skill level (e.g., Palincsar & Brown, 1984; Vellutino & Scanlon, 1991). In this synthesis, the combined model was contrasted with one approach (DI-only) considered as a bottom-up model and the other (SI-only) considered as a top-down model. The results show that combinations of specific components that reflect both of these orientations enhance yield higher outcomes. Based on the magnitude of the effect sizes for the DI and SI models (.68 for DI-only and .72 for SI-only) in isolation, both approaches seem viable for students with learning disabilities. Nevertheless, these approaches were smaller than the combined model in the magnitude of effect sizes.

Based on these findings, we conclude that effective instruction is neither a bottom-up nor a top-down approach in isolation. Lower-order and higher-order skills interact to influence treatment outcomes. Clearly, performance at complex levels (writing prose, inferring the meaning of text) cannot occur without some critical threshold of skills. Children with LD vary in these skills. What is clear from this synthesis, however, is that varying degrees of success across treatment domains draw from treatments that focus on both high- and low-order instruction (i.e., strategy and direct instruction).

Second, eight major instructional factors captured most intervention programs for students with LD. These factors were referred to as explicit direct instruction (sequencing and segmentation), explicit strategy training, monitoring, individualized remedial training, small interactive group instruction, teacher-indirect instruction, verbal questioning/ attribution instruction, and technology-mediated instruction.

As will be discussed below, however, not all of these factors predict (i.e., significantly improve) treatment outcomes. The coding of various components that loaded on the various factors was based on a thorough investigation of the literature. Several of these reviews have narrowed down effective instruction to the following: (a) daily reviews, (b) statements of an instructional objective, (c) teacher presentation of new material, (d) guided practice, (e) independent practice, and (f) formative evaluations (see Rosenshine, 1995; Rosenshine, & Stevens, 1986; Slavin et al. 1988, for a review). These categories have been considered as reflecting a basic effective instructional core (Rosenshine & Stevens, 1986; Slavin, Stevens, & Madden, 1988). The components in the present synthesis that matched these basic instructional core practices are: explicit practice (component 2), orientation to a task (component 8), presentation of new material (component 6), teacher modeling of steps (component 14), sequencing (component 1), and systematic probing (component 5).

What the factor analysis shows is that all these components, except one, reinforcement, load on the first two factors in the present analysis. These factors reflect explicit direct instruction and explicit strategy instruction. In addition, both models contribute significant variance to the magnitude of effect size. The results also show that an additional factor, small interactive group instruction, not mentioned in this basic instructional core, significantly improves treatment outcomes.

Finally, the explicit strategy instruction factor better predicts the magnitude of treatment outcomes than any of the other competing factor models. As discussed previously, explicit strategy instruction has three instructional components. One component is *explicit practice.* Studies that include this component in their treatment programs focus on activities that relate to distributed review and practice, repeated practice, sequenced reviews, daily feedback, and/or weekly reviews.

Another component of this factor is *strategy cues.* Studies that include this component have statements in the treatment description about reminders to use strategies or multi-steps, the teacher verbalizing steps or procedures to solve problems, and use of "think aloud models." The final component is *elaboration.* Studies that include this component have statements in their treatment description about additional information or explanation provided about concepts, and/or redundant text or repetition within text.

One interesting finding was that the factor score related to explicit strategy instruction was more important than a direct instruction model in predicting outcomes. That is, the explicit strategy instruction score partials out the influence of the direct instruction composite score in predicting the magnitude of treatment outcome.

Clearly, performance at complex levels (writing prose, inferring the meaning of text) cannot occur without some critical threshold of skills delivered by direct instruction techniques. Children with learning disabilities vary in these skills. What is clear from this synthesis, however, is that varying degrees of success across treatment domains draw from treatments that include strategy instruction.

Because direct instruction and strategy instruction are complex combinations of components, however, we would *not* argue from these results that strategy instruction has better support than direct instruction for treatment outcomes. This is because strategy instruction program and direct instruction have many commonalities. Both approaches involve the active presentation of information, clear organization, step-by-step progression from subtopic to subtopic, use of many examples, demonstrations, and visual prompts. All emphasize conscious assessment of student understanding and altering the pace of instruction according to this information. The focus is on independent performance. Instruction is criterion-based rather than time-based. A stage is mastered before moving onto the next stage.

Clearly, however, there are differences in focus. As stated in the introduction, strategy interventions focus on routines and planful action and/or general principles of handling information, whereas direct instruction focuses on isolated skill acquisition to support higher-order processing. Nevertheless, much of the teaching in both approaches is explicit, relying on oral presentation by the teacher and oral responses by the students.

Thus, although direct instruction has been associated with the behavioral paradigms, cognitive paradigms use some of the same procedures. This point is illustrated by Swanson (1988), who suggests that, in practice, both cognitive and behavioral models use many of the same procedures (e.g., feedback, monitoring, repetition).

In summary, the results show that not all treatments win a prize. Which treatment wins the prize is based upon the level of analysis. At a general level, it appears that a combined direct and strategy instruction model is critical, whereas at the component level it appears that components that load on the explicit strategy and small-group factor are the most important in predicting outcomes.

Keeping these findings in mind, we think there is potential for making significant advances in devising programs for LD students if these components are included in the remediation program. We also think we will have a better chance of determining more robust treatments for LD students if both control and treatment conditions include these components. In this way, the unique aspects of the novel treatment program can be assessed more adequately. There are, of course, qualifications to the present findings. We will conclude with two of these shortcomings.

SOME SHORTCOMINGS

One qualification is that, although studies in this synthesis were selected on rigorous criteria, these studies varied tremendously on a number of methodological variables. The results clearly showed that the methodology composite scores moderated that magnitude of effect sizes. Specifically, five of the eight models based on the factor analysis contributed no significant variance to treatment outcome when the methodological composite score was entered into the analysis. These instructional models were related to models that emphasized monitoring of new information, individualized remedial instruction, ancillary teacher models (peer instruction, homework), attribution instruction, and those emphasizing media or technology.

Further, the age of students with LD did not play an important role in predicting the influence of the instructional variables. Thus, the results show that, for participants with LD across diverse samples, classroom settings, ages, and types of measures (e.g., reading, math, writing) only three factors or models moderate the magnitude of effect size.

The second qualification is related to the coding of instructional components. Although the coding of instructional activities was based on reviews of instructional literature, no attempt was made to code the treatment by *what* aspect of instruction was addressed (e.g., phonological awareness, inferential comprehension), but instead the present synthesis focused on *how* it was taught. Emphasis was placed on "how" the treatments were delivered because one cannot adequately assess the "what" of instruction unless the "how" is clearly identified. As shown by a previous synthesis (Swanson & Hoskyn, 1998), there are tremendous differences in instructional activities, as well as a host of other methodological variables, that improve treatment outcomes. Unless instructional activities are identified and their influence on outcomes is clearly delineated, testing the subtle aspects of content becomes a moot point.

In conclusion, the results of this synthesis show that only a few instructional components significantly improve treatment outcomes for students with LD. The synthesis indicates that explicit strategy instruction and small-group instruction provide a valid model for improving outcomes for students with LD across a broad array of samples, settings, and dependent measures. Our hope is that these components will be a part of all intervention programs in the future.

REFERENCES

Begg, C. B. (1994). Publication bias. In H. Cooper & L. V. Hedges (Eds.), *The handbook of research synthesis* (pp. 400–422). New York: Russell Sage Foundation.

Borkowski, J. G., Estrada, M. T., Milstead, M., & Hale, C. A. (1989). General problem-solving skills: Relations between metacognition and strategic processing. *Learning Disability Quarterly, 12*, 57–70.

Borkowski, J. G., & Turner, L. A. (1990). Transsituational characteristics of metacognition. In W. Schneider & F. E. Weinert (Eds.), *Interactions among aptitudes, strategies, and knowledge in cognitive performance* (pp. 159–176). New York: Springer-Verlag.

Borkowski, J. G., Weyhing, R. S., & Carr, M. (1988). Effects of attributional retraining on strategy-based reading comprehension in learning-disabled students. *Journal of Educational Psychology, 80*, 46–53.

Brophy, J., & Good, T. (1986). Teacher-effects results. In M. C. Wittrock (Ed.), *Handbook of research on teaching* (3d ed.). New York: Macmillan.

Carroll, L. (1962). *Alice's adventure in wonderland.* Harmondsworth, Middlesex, England: Penguin Books. (Original work published 1865)

Cohen, J. (1988). *Statistical power analysis for the behavioral sciences,* (2d ed.) New York: Academic Press.

Cooper, H. & Hedges, L. (1994). (Eds.) *The handbook of research synthesis.* New York: Sage.

Engelmann, S., & Carnine, D. W. (1982). *Theory of instruction: Principles and applications.* New York: Irvington.

Graham, S., & Harris, K. R. (1989). A components analysis of cognitive strategy instruction: Effects on learning disabled students' compositions and self-efficacy. *Journal of Educational Psychology, 81,* 353–361.

Graham, S., & Harris, K. R. (1996). Self-regulation and strategy instruction for students who find writing and learning challenging. In C. M. Levy & S. Ransdell (Eds.), *The science of writing: Theories, methods, individual differences, and applications* (pp. 347–360). Mahwah, NJ: Lawrence Erlbaum Associates.

Hedges, L. V. (1994). Fixed effects models. In H. Cooper & L. V. Hedges (Eds.), *The handbook of research synthesis* (pp. 285–299). New York: Russell Sage Foundation.

Kameenui, E. J., Jitendra, A. K., & Darch, C. B. (1995). Direct instruction reading as contronym and eonomine. *Reading & Writing Quarterly: Overcoming Learning Difficulties, 11,* 3–17.

Kavale, K. A., & Forness, S. R. (2000). Policy decisions in special education: The role of meta-analysis. In R. Gersten, E. P. Schiller, & S. Vaughn (Eds.), *Contemporary special education research* (pp. 281–326). Mahwah, NJ: Erlbaum.

Leinhardt, G., & Greeno, J. G. (1986). The cognitive skill of teaching. *Journal of Educational Psychology, 78*(2), 75–95.

Levin, J. R. (1986). Four cognitive principles of learning strategy instruction. *Educational psychologist, 21,* 3–17.

Lovett, M. W., Borden, S. L., DeLuca, T., Lacerenza, L., Benson, N. J., & Brackstone, D. (1994). Treating the core deficits of developmental dyslexia: Evidence of transfer of learning after phonologically and strategy-based reading training programs. *Developmental Psychology, 30,* 805–822.

Luborsky, L., Singer, B., & Luborsky, L. (1975). Comparative studies of psychotherapies: Is it true that " everyone has won and all must have prizes"? *Archives of General Psychiatry, 32,* 995–1008.

Mastropieri, M. A., Scruggs, T. E., Bakken, J. P., & Whedon, C. (1996). Reading comprehension: A synthesis of research in learning disabilities. In T. E. Scruggs & M. A. Mastropieri (Eds.). *Advances in learning and behavioral disabilities* (Vol. 10, pp. 277–303). Greenwich, CT: JAI.

Meichenbaum, D. (1977). *Cognitive behavior modification.* New York: Plenum.

Miller, P. H., & Seier, W. L. (1994). Strategy utilization deficiencies in children: When, where and why. In H. W. Reese (Ed.), *Advances in Child Development and Behavior* (vol. 25, pp. 107–156). New York: Academic Press.

Palincsar, A. S. (1986). The role of dialogue in providing scaffolded instruction. *Educational Psychologist, 21*(1 & 2), 73–98.

Palincsar, A. S., & Brown, A. L. (1984). Reciprocal teaching of comprehension—fostering and comprehension monitoring activities. *Cognition & Instruction, 1,* 117–175.

Pressley, M., Brown, R., El-Dinary, P. B., & Allferbach, P. (1995). The comprehension instruction that students need: Instruction fostering constructively responsive reading. *Learning Disabilities Research & Practice, 10*(4), 215–224.

Pressley, M., & Ghatala, E. S. (1990). Self-regulated learning: Monitoring learning from text. *Educational Psychologist, 25,* 19–34.

Pressley, M., & Harris, K. R. (1994). Increasing the quality of educational intervention research. *Educational Psychology Review, 6,* 191–208.

Rosenshine, B. (1995). Advances in research on instruction. *Journal of Educational Research, 88*(5), 262–268.

Rosenshine, B., & Stevens, R. (1986). Teaching functions. In M. C. Wittrock (Ed.), *Handbook of research on teaching* (3d ed.). New York: Macmillan.

Shuell, T. (1996). Teaching and learning in a classroom context. In D. Berliner & R. C. Calfee (Eds.), *Handbook of educational psychology* (pp. 726–764). New York: Simon & Schuster/Macmillan.

Slavin, R. E., Karweit, N. L., & Madden, N. A. (1989). *Effective programs for students at risk.* Needham Heights, MA: Allyn & Bacon.

Slavin, R. E., Stevens, R. J., & Madden, N. A. (1988). Accommodating student diversity in reading and writing instruction: A cooperative learning approach. Special Issue: The challenge of reading with understanding in the intermediate grades: *RASE: Remedial & Special Education, 9(1),* 60–66.

Sternberg, R. (1998). Principles of teaching successful intelligence. *Educational Psychologist, 33,* 65–72.

Swanson, H. L. (1988). Toward a metatheory of learning disabilities. *Journal of Learning Disabilities, 21,* 196–209.

Swanson, H. L. (1993). Principles and procedures in strategy use. In L. Meltzer (Ed.), *Strategy assessment and instruction for students with learning disabilities: From theory to practice* (pp. 61–92). Austin: Pro-Ed.

Swanson, H. L. (1999). Instructional components that predict treatment outcomes for students with learning disabilities: Support for a combined strategy and direct instruction model. *Learning Disabilities Research & Practice, 14,* 129–140.

Swanson, H. L. (in press). In search of the best strategy instruction model. *Educational Psychology.*

Swanson, H. L., Carson, C., & Sachse-Lee, C. M. (1996). A selective synthesis of intervention research for students with learning disabilities. *School Psychology Review, 25,* 370–391.

Swanson, H.L., & Hoskyn, M. (1998). A synthesis of experimental intervention literature for students with learning disabilities: A meta-analysis of treatment outcomes. *Review of Educational Research, 68,* 277–322.

Swanson, H. L. & Sachse-Lee, C. M. (2000). A meta-analysis of single-subject-design intervention research for students with LD. *Journal of Learning Disabilities, 33,* 114–136.

Swanson, H. L., Hoskyn, M., & Lee, C. M. (1999). *Interventions for Students with Learning Disabilities.* New York: Guilford.

Vellutino, F., & Scanlon, D. M. (1991). The effects of instructional bias on word identification. In I. L. Rieben & C. A. Perfetti (Eds.), *Learning to read: Basic research and its implications* (pp. 189–204). Hillsdale, NJ: Lawrence Erlbaum Associates.

APPENDIX

Intervention activities were coded based on key words and phrases (descriptions are abbreviated here). (* reflects strategy instruction activities, ** reflects direct instruction activities)

_____ Breaking down task by skills**

_____ Children are asked to look over material prior to instruction

_____ Children are directed to focus on material presented

_____ Conduct probes of learning (intermittent test)**

_____ Diagram or pictorial presentation**

_____ Elaborate explanations*

_____ Fading of prompts or cues

_____ Homework

_____ Independent practice (e.g., complete worksheet on own)

_____ Individually paced**

_____ Information is provided before student discussion

_____ Instruction is broken down into steps**

_____ Instruction individually**

_____ Instruction small group (2 to 5)**

_____ Instruction large group (>5)

_____ Level of difficulty applied to each student

_____ Mastery criteria

_____ Modeling—from peers

_____ Modeling of skill—from teachers**

_____ New curriculum

_____ Parent provides instruction

_____ Peer provides daily feedback on student performance

_____ Provide distributed practice (pacing), and review (weekly and monthly reviews)**

_____ Redundant text or materials

_____ Reminders to use certain strategies or procedures*

_____ Repeated practice (e.g., drill and repetition)

_____ Review of material on each session

_____ Reward and reinforcers

_____ Short activities sequenced by teacher

_____ Simplified demonstration

_____ Specialized film or videotape/audiotape

_____ Step-by-step prompts or process, multi-step-process directions*

_____ Student asks questions

_____ Task analysis

_____ Teacher and student talk back and forth (e.g., Socratic dialogue)*

_____ Teacher asks process-related questions*

_____ Teacher demonstrates

_____ Teacher (or experimenter) presents new material**

_____ Teacher (or experimenter) provides daily feedback on student performance**

_____ Teacher (or experimenter) states learning objectives

_____ Teacher presents benefits of instruction

_____ Teacher provides only necessary assistance*

_____ Think-aloud models (modeling aloud by teacher)*

_____ Using media (e.g., computer) for elaboration or repetition

_____ Weekly review

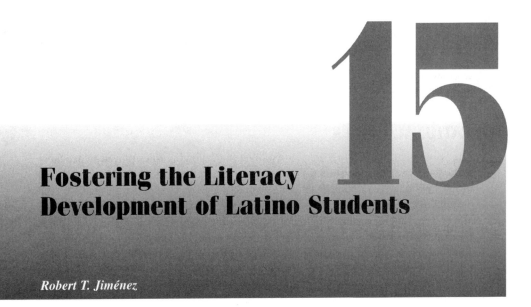

Fostering the Literacy Development of Latino Students

Robert T. Jiménez

The literacy achievement gap between White and Latino students has remained relatively static, as has progress in literacy for Latino students (NCES, 1998a). Valencia (1991) has written about what he calls the persistent, pervasive, and disproportionate academic failure of Chicano students. Valencia's assessment could reasonably be extended to other groups of Latino students, particularly those of Puerto Rican descent and also, possibly, students from Central American backgrounds.

Latino students have attracted the attention of educators, legislators, and the public in general because Latinos now constitute the largest group of minority students in U.S. schools, calculated at 13.5 percent of the total (NCES, 1998b). Latinos experienced a 59 percent growth rate during the 1990s (Pace, 2001).

Invariably, many students who are English language learners and who also are having difficulties with literacy will have contact with professionals in special education (Allington, 1989; Gersten, Brengelman, & Jiménez, 1994). This is partly because of the high rate of growth of limited English proficient (LEP) students in regions and cities that have not previously served this population.

Of concern is that the professional development necessary to effectively address the needs of students from culturally and linguistically diverse backgrounds is not widely available. Because special education teachers often are called upon when students fail to "learn on schedule" or at what is considered an appropriate pace considering their age, they need information and support if they are to serve as student advocates. Cummins (1986) argues persuasively that students from language minority backgrounds are either empowered or disabled to the extent that "professionals involved in assessment become advocates for minority students rather than legitimizing the location of the problem in the student" (p. 21). Advocacy, of course, requires more than simply good intentions. Professionals who are effective in working with second language learning students are familiar with the unique learning needs of this population.

EDUCATIONAL ISSUES

The issues dealt with in this chapter examine the following roles played by teachers and educators, students, students' communities, and the larger societal context: (a) the professional development of educators, both preservice and inservice; (b) the optimal mix of language-sensitive instructional practices for Latino students; (c) the alternative or "contrasting" literacies used within the Latino community and their relationship to school-based literacy; (d) the potential of transfer to facilitate Latino students' literacy learning; (e) the prevailing sociopolitical environment with respect to Latino students and education; and (f) the questions raised by minority researchers and writers concerning the academic performance of Latino students.

The Need for Informed Educators

How can we provide preservice and inservice teachers with the necessary professional development to provide optimal literacy instruction to Latino students? As my colleague, Rosalinda Barrera, and I stated in a recent paper (Jiménez & Barrera, 2000), teacher and administrator education programs seldom place the teaching of linguistically and culturally diverse students at the center of their programs. Instead, diversity is positioned as problematic and marginal to the main task of education. Schooling, in contrast, is considered beneficial for all students, everywhere, all the time (Nieto, 1992). The notion that diversity itself might be beneficial and that schooling might be in need of critique has been a difficult concept for many educators—not to mention the general public and policy makers—to accept.

In addition, teachers at all levels learn and teach a view of literacy that is mainstream and antagonistic to the needs and abilities of a diverse populace (Moll, 1988; NCES, 1997). At the very least, the linguistic and cultural knowledge that Latino students bring into U.S. classrooms is unknown to many educators, unexplored by mainstream researchers, and unacknowledged in prevailing instructional methods and curriculum materials. Inclusive instruction "must begin with the explicit premise that each learner brings a valid language and culture to the instructional context" (Reyes, 1992, p. 427).

What my colleagues and I have argued is that an additional shift in perspective is needed—one that treats diversity as the norm and also sees the possibilities created by diversity. We believe that these possibilities have the potential to benefit all students, including those from mainstream, monolingual, middle-class backgrounds. For example, mainstream students need to learn appropriate ways to interact in diverse settings, and they also can benefit from exposure to non-English languages. At the least, this shift in perspective would have us recognize these students and their families as sources of knowledge and as consumers and producers of multiple literacies (Guerra, 1998; Luke, 1995–1996).

The advantage of a multiple versus a single literacy approach is that it provides teachers and students with access to a broader set of activities, materials, and purposes for literacy than that encompassed within what is typically thought of as "school-based literacy." Attempts to teach this latter type of literacy have not been particularly effective with members of many culturally and linguistically diverse groups within the United States (Macedo, 1994).

The New London Group (1996) outlined some of the critical features that a multiple literacies approach would entail:

> To be relevant, learning processes need to recruit, rather than attempt to ignore and erase, the different subjectivities—interests, intentions, commitments, and purposes—students bring to learning. Curriculum now needs to mesh with different subjectivities, and with their attendant languages, discourses, and registers, and use these as a resource for learning. (p. 72)

In a sense, members of The New London Group are reminding educators to think more deeply about instructional design and choice of materials. The goal is to acknowledge and respect students as capable and potentially successful, to recognize the linguistic and cultural knowledge that learners bring into the classroom. Perhaps what is new about their recommendation is that, while they advocate recognition, understanding, and respect for both the language and culture of diverse groups—a perennial concern of multicultural educators—they also promote specific and visible inclusion of this information in the school curriculum for all students.

In addition, their stance recognizes the curriculum of the school and mainstream ways of thinking, learning, reading, and writing as powerful discourses to which all students need access but which also require critical analysis. The following items are offered as a first step toward fleshing out the vision just proposed and discussed.

- Educators and schools that are effective with Latino students are familiar with programs in which Latino students achieve success. They also are familiar with program evaluation research on effective schools for language minority students. Researchers such as Eugene García (1994), William Tikunoff (1985), Thomas Carter (1986), Tamara Lucas, Rosemary Henze, and Ruben Donato (1990) have described some of these programs in their articles and books. All of the programs they describe actively recognize and promote students' first-language strengths, accept and celebrate their cultures, and implement visible efforts to combat racism and social injustice.
- Teachers and administrators who are effective with Latino students obtain relevant professional development. This development typically involves completion of coursework, as well as relevant professional experience in second language acquisition, English as a second language, multicultural education, and bilingual education.
- Educators who are effective with Latino students recognize the long-term nature of second language acquisition, particularly literacy development. Monolingual individuals typically underestimate the amount of

time necessary to become fluent in a second language, particularly with respect to literacy. Research (Collier, 1987; Thomas & Collier, 1996) suggests that students may attain full grade level proficiency within as few as 2 years but also might require as many as 8 years, depending on factors such as age on arrival to the United States and previous academic achievement in their country of origin. Overall, however, the attainment of age-appropriate, grade level achievement in a second language is typically a 4- to 5-year process.

■ Students' cultural and linguistic backgrounds are viewed as sources of strength, not deficits to be overcome. Students' backgrounds are not viewed as barriers but, rather, as foundations for future learning. In practical terms, students are described as speakers, readers, or writers of Spanish rather than simply as non-English speakers.

Distinctive Nature of Instruction for Latino Students

What is the optimal amount of language-sensitive literacy instruction to foster and successfully establish literacy for Latino students? What combination of sheltered English, English as a second language, and native language literacy instruction is necessary to accomplish this goal?

This question gets to the heart of what is most troublesome to many mainstream educators: Why don't Latino students and many other English language learners follow the same patterns of learning as mainstream students? Collier (1987) projected that a time span of anywhere between 2 to 8 years is necessary for immigrant students from a variety of national and language backgrounds arriving in the United States between the ages of 5 to 15 years old to attain grade-level norms in academic achievement. This projection was made for students from middle class and upwardly mobile families who were recent immigrants with successful students in the countries of origin.

The students in Collier's research received all of their instruction in English with language arts instruction, algebra, biology, and some other classes on an as-necessary basis provided by ESL teachers. Note that the 2 to 8 years probably covers the vast majority of students who must, in addition to learning all that is required at each grade level, also learn a new language. Note also that there is a great deal of variation in terms of time necessary to reach this level of achievement.

Perhaps the most interesting finding from Collier's research is that the amount of time necessary depends on factors such as age on arrival to the United States, which functions as a proxy for the number of years of prior schooling. Students who begin schooling in the United States after age 8 often have completed at least 2 to 3 years of schooling in their home country. This cognitive and academic background can be helpful to students as they learn a new language.

We know from later research (Thomas & Collier, 1996) that *English language learning immigrant students make continuous progress in learning English and in academic achievement for as long as they receive well designed, linguistically sensitive instruction.* That is, students in dual language immersion programs demonstrated the highest ultimate levels of academic achievement by grade 12 as compared to students in transitional bilingual education programs, both early and late exit varieties, and in comparison to structured English-immersion programs.

Submersion models, or all-English instruction in the general education classroom, both with and without an ESL component, fared the worst, with student means falling between the 20th and 40th percentile of National Center for Education Statistics. The provision of services and the quality of those services, then, seem to be two of the most critical features of instruction for English language learners, particularly immigrant students. One of the advantages of dual language immersion and late exit bilingual instruction is that the former is designed to continue providing services through grade 12, whereas the latter is intended to provide services through grade 6. These programs differ considerably from early exit bilingual instruction and sheltered English instruction because services in these models typically are terminated by or before grade 3. Only program models that include substantial native language instruction go beyond 2 or 3 years of support for English language learners.

The intermediate grades (4 and 5) and middle school years (6, 7, and 8) are especially important because student performance during this period influences high school completion rates. Grade 4 is a critical juncture for all students, mainstream and Latino, because of the increase in curriculum demands at that level. These are also the years when Latino students who are learning English have been found to lose ground on language and literacy assessments. Further, this is the time when many language minority students have completed their transition from bilingual and ESL programs to the general education classroom, where all instruction is provided in English. Too many Latino students lag at this point and may be referred for special education services.

In consequence, many of these students begin to view schooling as a painful and humiliating ordeal, possibly unnecessary. Unique in comparison to their mainstream counterparts, Latino students may encounter a curriculum that requires high levels of English literacy *for the first time* as they move into the intermediate and middle school levels. This last fact alone is a strong argument for carefully considering the design of their instructional programs and the services offered to them.

Special language support for English language learners is least likely to be found at the middle school and high school levels. Latino students who first enter the United States during these years face a challenging and densely packed curriculum, as well as the possibility of not receiving either ESL or native language instruction. Of even further concern is that many Latino students are from working class or rural backgrounds, which often means that their access to schooling prior to arriving in the United States may have been limited or even unavailable. In addition, the schools they attend in the United States are often poorly funded and are located in urban settings. All of these factors can have a negative cumulative impact on the academic changes facing Latino students and have to be taken into account when considering group achievement.

Alternative Literacies

Which literacies are most readily recognizable to Latino students? Which literacies have the most potential to help Latino students accomplish their goals? What is the relationship between these literacies and literate practices commonly found in schools?

The possibilities and the promise of alternative literacies for reconceptualizing schooling for Latino students is probably one of the most exciting developments in education today. My research (Jiménez, 2000) found that preadolescent and young adolescent Latino students view particular forms of literacy, or non-school literacies, as highly necessary and desirable. Their parents often depend on them for help to negotiate the demands of English language literacy. The students serve as language brokers to their parents, translating documents such as rental/lease agreements, income tax forms, and other commercial transactions such as telephone and power bills. Many Latino students take these responsibilities seriously and view the help they provide to their parents and other family members as their contribution to the overall well being of the family.

In addition, parents and other adult family members sometimes depend on their children for oral translation in stressful, high-paced interactions such as purchasing a vehicle or returning merchandise to a retail establishment. All of these activities may be viewed as alternative forms of literacy with respect to school-based literacy.

Research on Multiple Literacies

Gregory and Williams (2000) have expanded the notion of multiple literacies by highlighting the distinctive natures of specific literate practices among members of culturally and linguistically diverse communities living in London. Through careful examination of succeeding waves of immigrants living in the Spitalfields borough, they proposed the notion of "contrasting literacies."

One of the communities they examined, Bengali–Sylheti speakers, brought Q'uranic and Bangladeshi literate practices with them into the British school system. Analysis revealed that at first these contrasting literacies created points of tension for students and teachers. With time, though, the students and their families and communities created "syncretic literacies." These latter practices fused elements of school-based English literacy with those the students brought into the schools. The researchers concluded their study by referring to students' out-of-school literacies as "treasure troves" of experiences and information with attending benefits for students and teachers alike.

Of particular interest is that certain instructional practices employed by the British teachers fostered and supported their students' learning whereas others discouraged it. For example, students found that choral reading was compatible with their previous learning. On the other hand, the students found some instructional techniques difficult to reconcile with their out-of-school experiences. For example, teachers repeated students' oral reading as a backdrop for asking questions and to stimulate reflection on the text. The Bengali-British children, accustomed to "echo reading", instinctively repeated what the teacher said to them, just as they did in the Q'uranic and Bengali reading classes. For the most part, however, teachers seemed to be unfamiliar with students' out-of-school literacies and did not consciously connect their instruction to practices that were familiar to the students.

Out-of-School Literacies

For Latino students living in the United States, a growing body of research is beginning to identify language practices and literate behaviors that parallel those of the Bengali-British children examined by Gregory and Williams. I propose that these practices, as they become better documented and understood by researchers, could serve as a bridge for improved and more effective literacy instruction within schools (Barrera & Jiménez, 2000, 2001; Moll, 1988; Reyes, 1992).

Students also may observe or participate in other forms of literacy such as letter-writing activities that involve distant relations in foreign countries. Guerra (1998) described the distinctiveness of this form of literacy as it is used by Mexican immigrants, and he demonstrated in his analysis how it differs from mainstream forms employed in schools. For example, the Mexican immigrants use specific formulaic phrases and their purposes for writing are highly concrete. Kalmar (2001) documented an intriguing case of adult Latino immigrants who created their own writing system for the purpose of transcribing oral English.

An important question for teachers and researchers has to do with how we can build upon these out-of-school literacies so that Latino students receive the benefits associated with their practice. We know that mainstream, middle class forms of literacy such as storybook reading and certain types of written expression dovetail nicely with reading and writing instruction in the beginning grades (Heath, 1983; Sulzby & Teale, 1991, Wells, 1986). I propose that the literacies that many Latino students bring into the schools are at least as complex and demanding as those possessed by their middle class, European American counterparts. Why can't curriculum and instruction be designed to build on and acknowledge these non-school literacies that are familiar and perhaps even more practical to Latino students?

In the following example, Gil discusses the intricacies of "language brokering." Compare this activity, so familiar to Gil and many other Latino students, with your own understanding of the ways in which mainstream students make use of literacy.

> Gil: . . . tienen algo que esta en el libro y si, este, no sé leer, pues, como le voy a entender.. y cuando te dan como así . . . algo que tienes que pagar . . . y no tienen numeros y solamente así como en letras . . . y no vas a saber que vas a pagar. (. . . they have something that is in the book and if, uh, I don't know how to read, well, how am I going to understand it . . . and when they give you something like that . . . *something that you have to pay* . . . and it doesn't have numbers and it only has it like that in letters . . . and you are not going to know what you are going to pay.)

Notice that Gil understands and appreciates the power of literacy, not only for its own sake but also because of the real world consequences of paying or not paying bills. These consequences might mean the difference between having or not having a place to live or phone service. In the following examples and suggestions for instructional practice, I have considered what students such as Gil taught me about the alternative literacies with which they are familiar, and I have attempted to make recommendations accordingly.

- Language brokering, both oral and literate, should be formally recognized as a legitimate and commendable activity. Students can be provided with instruction that helps them to complete these tasks successfully. Teachers may want to investigate how many of their students are involved in these activities, their feelings about the activities, and what they think would help them to accomplish these tasks more effectively. Instructional activities could be designed accordingly.
- Bilingual oral and literate abilities ought to be promoted and encouraged because students need these skills to manage their lives effectively. Business people from the local area could be invited into the school to discuss the ways in which they use both English and Spanish in their work. Alternatively, students could visit local businesses and note how written Spanish and English are used in restaurants, travel agencies, beauty salons, and grocery stores.
- Other literate activities that are uniquely of interest to Latino students and can be encouraged and included in the curriculum include ideas that students can use to facilitate younger siblings and older family members' literacy, letter writing to relatives who live abroad or in another state, and other activities as yet unknown in general but perhaps recognized at the local school level. Just as many schools recognize and reward out-of-school story book reading, the same practice could be extended to reading with younger siblings, participating in letter writing to family members abroad or in another state. Teachers might also want to investigate whether students are aware of other ways that literacy is employed in their homes and communities.

The Potential of Transfer

The question of the most optimal ways to facilitate students' ability to transfer information from first language and life experience to school-based tasks deals with a classic concern in bilingual education. For example, the issue of linguistic transfer is a major component in Cummins' (1979) linguistic interdependence hypothesis. In essence, he proposes that students who receive effective instruction in their native language will transfer what they know if they have adequate exposure to the second language and adequate levels of motivation to learn the second language.

In previous research, my colleagues and I documented that successful bilingual readers consciously transferred information across their two languages (Jiménez, García, & Pearson, 1995). If they were reading a text in English that dealt with the solar system, they would consciously and specifically recall having read Spanish-language text covering the same or a similar topic. In contrast, low- and average-performing bilingual students have much more difficulty knowing when and how to make connections between their two languages; in fact, they appear to view their two languages as mutually disparate and even antagonistic systems (Jiménez, García, & Pearson, 1996).

These stances towards biliteracy may have been instructionally induced by an educational system that does not understand, value, or incorporate the advantages of bilingualism into the curriculum. Prevailing deficit views of Latino students, which consider them to be defective versions of their mainstream counterparts, fail to recognize their linguistic resources and how these might be used to facilitate learning.

Taking the findings of my earlier research, which documented and catalogued the cognitive and metacognitive strategies of competent and less competent bilingual Latino students, I taught some of this information to much lower-performing Latino students, students in bilingual special educational settings, and what their school called a bilingual at-risk classroom. A finding from that research was that these middle school students, who were all performing at least three grade levels behind their expected level, responded quite favorably to instruction that emphasized a bilingual approach to processing text (Jiménez, 1997). They were more than willing to try out a searching-for-cognate-vocabulary strategy, a translating strategy, and strategies designed to facilitate the integration of their prior knowledge and experience with information found in text.

The following example shows how a successful bilingual Latina reader actively used her knowledge of Spanish to improve her comprehension when reading in English:

> Pamela: Like "carnivorous," "carnívoro." OK, some [words] like I know what it is in Spanish. Some words I go, what does that mean in Spanish?

I argued that these strategies were desirable to these students because they were derived from their community, from other bilingual Latino students. I speculated that they were able to intuitively understand and appreciate the benefits that accrued from establishing linkages between their two languages. I also concluded that this approach affirmed their bilingual, bicultural identity. It is possible that prevailing stereotypes about Latino students, their families, and their communities prevent many educators from seeing the full academic potential of Latino students. One especially pernicious stereotype is that knowledge of any non-English language is harmful and potentially confusing for minority students.

In the following recommendations, I encourage teachers to explicitly acknowledge all of the knowledge and experience their English language learning Latino students bring with them into the classroom. The use of transfer strategies is an attempt to support and scaffold students' learning and help them make maximum use of what they already know.

■ Educators who wish to be inclusive and supportive of their Latino students make special efforts to understand and consider the unique challenges and special talents the bilingual students possess. For example, educators know that successful *bilingual* readers use the following strategies:

— *Approaching unknown vocabulary,* which involves use of contextual clues, looking for cognate relationships, and the approximate pronunciations of words.

— *Asking questions,* which involves overt comprehension monitoring.

— *Making inferences,* which includes the integration of prior knowledge, including bilingual language abilities, with information found in print.

When less successful bilingual students are taught these strategies, they can use them in ways similar to more successful bilingual readers.

■ These same educators obtain and examine their students' prior educational histories for information to guide instructional efforts. Students from rural backgrounds in their country of origin, for example, may need more intensive literacy instruction than students coming from urban experiences in their home countries.

■ Students who are recent immigrants and who have had minimal prior schooling are provided with an appropriate beginning literacy program. This program mixes and matches characteristics of programs used with young children and programs used in adult literacy programs. The guiding principle is to challenge the student with as many age-appropriate materials as possible while making sure that success is possible.

■ Many older Latino students need help with word identification skills and reading fluency even at the intermediate and middle school levels. Although their needs may be similar to those of younger students, age-appropriate materials are necessary. I have found that struggling Latino readers at the middle school level respond well to literacy instruction that is grounded in culturally familiar texts, is linguistically sensitive, and emphasizes choral and repeated reading.

■ Students are encouraged to view their dual language abilities as a strength. One way to do this is to show them how to make connections across and between their two languages by accessing cognate vocabulary, by judicious use of translation, and by transferring information learned via their first language.

■ Students are told explicitly how to overcome comprehension problems associated with second language learning. Typical comprehension problems for second language readers include encountering a disproportionately high number of unknown vocabulary words, use of idiomatic expressions, and lack of necessary background knowledge. Teachers can model the think-aloud procedure for students. This can be accomplished by reading a text silently, line by line, and then talking aloud and describing how comprehension problems are handled. For example: "Isn't it interesting that in this story by Sandra Cisneros, the father is going to Mexico. I remember when that happened in my family. My grandfather, who lived in Mexico, died, and my dad had to get on a plane and go to the funeral." Examples like this help students to see how an expert reader connects information in the text to her or his own life.

■ Students are explicitly helped with reading strategies that have been shown to promote the comprehension of readers in general. These strategies include rereading, monitoring of comprehension, using background knowledge appropriately, drawing inferences, and asking questions and finding answers. An example showing how this researcher taught middle school students to ask questions is:

Sara: Quetzalcoatl wanted very much to help the people that he loved.
Researcher: Okay, what's your question now? What kind of question would you ask yourself? He wants very much to help the people that he loves so you wonder, well . . . .
Sara: Is it gonna happen or not?

The same middle school student commented that although she had until then disliked reading, by the end of 10 lessons emphasizing the approach described in this article, she now "kind of liked it because it makes a little more sense now and I can read better."

Xenophobia and Linguicism

Why are mainstream educators, researchers, policy makers, and the general public so eager to believe negative and damaging reports concerning bilingual/multicultural education? Xenophobia is, of course, an unreasonable fear of foreigners, but the term "linguicism" is not always as readily recognized. My definition would be an unreasonable fear or disdain of languages or dialects other than that of mainstream, standard U.S. English. One can often see and hear this disdain in public places where speakers of non-English languages are present.

In California and Arizona, antibilingual education forces have built upon xenophobic and linguicist attitudes and have portrayed bilingual education as something harmful to Latino students. The Ocean Side school district, for example, has reported miniscule gains on the SAT-9 test as "proof" that native language instruction is ineffective (Steinberg, 2000). Note that the scores being reported fall well within the range described by Thomas and Collier (1996) as typical for submersion programs with ESL components.

What the school district didn't report was that many other districts in the state of California posted similar or even greater gains. These were districts that continued to provide native language instruction and those that had never had native language instruction, as well as those that eliminated native language instruction (Butler, Orr, Bousquet, & Hakuta, 2000). In other words, one has to look elsewhere for the 9 percentage point average increase, now at the 28th percentile, posted by this district. Yet, the mainstream media reported this change as if no further discussion were needed on this topic.

In his 1940 book, *Forgotten People,* George I. Sánchez wrote passionately and convincingly of the need for special teacher training, for inclusion of culturally relevant and linguistically comprehensible instruction. Some of the issues he addressed—and for which the community fought long and hard to achieve—are currently in danger of elimination. In our time, Guadalupe San Miguel (1987), and more recently Ruben Donato (1997) and Lourdes Diaz Soto (1997), have documented the protracted and bitter battle waged by the Latino community for bilingual education.

The amount of research support for the benefits of native language instruction is substantial and has proved convincing when subjected to impartial and scholarly examination (General Accounting Office, 1987; Thomas & Collier, 1997; Willig, 1985). As Macedo (2000) so cogently stated,

> The present assault on bilingual education is fundamentally political. The denial of the political nature of the debate is in itself, a political action. In examining the poor performance of linguistic minority students it is both academically dishonest and misleading to point to the failures of bilingual education without examining the larger context of the general failure of public education in major urban areas, which has created minority student dropout rates ranging from 50% to 65% in the Boston public schools to over 70% in larger metropolitan areas such as New York City. (p. 15)

Promising Instructional Models

Why haven't successful forms of bilingual education received as much attention as more problematic examples? Finding problematic results with bilingual education isn't difficult because, as Macedo pointed out, so many programs are located in impoverished urban school settings. These districts seldom receive necessary levels of funding and they often have many other problems in addition to those found within schools. Carter and Chatfield (1986) pointed out some time ago that finding effective bilingual programs can be difficult because so few are housed within effective schools. Programs are much more likely to be influenced by their placement in an effective school than vice versa. Putting the two components together ought to be the goal of everyone concerned with the academic progress of Latino students.

Positive results, however, have been reported in evaluations of dual language immersion programs (Christian, Howard, & Loeb, 2000; Lindholm-Leary, 2001). Actually, the literacy needs of Latino students might be met best in these programs. Dual language immersion is proving to be the most inclusive in terms of students, languages, and literacies. These programs have tremendous potential for increasing the academic achievement and second language acquisition of mainstream and language minority students alike (Fishman, 1982; Thomas & Collier, 1996).

In these programs, students receive at least half of their instruction in Spanish and the other half in English. These programs have many variations. Some offer mornings in English and afternoons in Spanish. Others alternate days in one language and then the other. Some even alternate semesters. Administrators work to ensure that approximately half of the students enrolled in these programs are native English speakers and the other half native speakers of a non-English language—in this case, Spanish.

Dual language programs that continue into the middle and high school years avoid the problems of many transitional bilingual education programs—i.e., the tragic loss of communicative and literate abilities in the student's native language—and foster more complex literacies including biliteracy (Jiménez & Barrera, 2000).

In sum:

- Depending on the availability of staff, resources, and community input, school districts need to work toward upgrading their programs designed for Latino and other English language learning students. A hierarchy of programs, displaying which programs have been most effective for which types of students, can be found in the work of Thomas and Collier (1996).

- Ongoing professional development opportunities are needed for all staff members who work with Latino students. High quality professionally derived information concerning the academic achievement of Latino students has to be made available to teachers and other professionals working with these students. These opportunities can be created through cooperative agreements with local universities.

- Opportunities to observe effective sheltered English teachers, content-based ESL teachers, bilingual teachers, and general education teachers can make good practice models available to novice teachers and others who wish to improve their practice.

A LATINO PERSPECTIVE

Why haven't we as educators been more willing to carefully consider answers to the questions posed by researchers and theorists such as Donaldo Macedo? At present, the discussion is dominated by politically conservative voices, many of which are grounded in questionable views concerning immigrants (Crawford, 2000). In his most recent article, Macedo (2000, p. 19), asks the following questions:

Does cultural subordination affect academic achievement?

What is the correlation of social segregation and school success?

What role does cultural identity among subordinated students play in linguistic resistance?

Does the devaluation of students' culture and language affect reading achievement?

Is class a factor in bilingual education? Do material conditions that foster human misery adversely affect academic development?

These questions go to the heart of the matter concerning the language and literacy development of Latino students. They move away from deficit views of Latino students and hold our public institutions accountable for bringing about real reform and improvement in how we educate Latino students. They move us away from simplistic and reductionistic approaches to literacy instruction such as the current obsessive concern with teaching English while simultaneously devaluing and eliminating students' Spanish language knowledge. They also move us away from a monomaniacal obsession with teaching sound-symbol correspondences to more substantive matters.

These reductionistic approaches primarily entail means for manipulating young Latino students and do not address how we can then interact honestly and with integrity with them as they enter middle and secondary school. It is at this time when they realize that schooling has been designed primarily to strip them of their linguistic and cultural heritage. At this point, short-sighted approaches to working with Latino students pay devastating dividends. Sadly, many students are so alienated from schooling that they look for alternatives such as dropping out.

At the very least, when politically conservative views are presented, there ought to be the chance to hear or read an alternative perspective. These perspectives and research-based views often are available through the websites of the National Association for Bilingual Education, and state and federal sources.

In conclusion, while my colleague Rosalinda Barrera and I (Jiménez & Barrera, 2000) are literacy researchers and teacher educators who believe strongly in the transformative potential of literacy, we are well aware that political literacy—the kind that gets Latino parents to vote—is what matters most. Within a few years Latinos will constitute the largest minority group in the United States, and by the end of the century, some estimates are that Latinos will make up one third of the entire country's population (NCES, 1998a,c).

Numbers translate into votes and votes into political clout—but not without political literacy, which in turn leads to economic development and more adequate healthcare. These in turn influence literacy development every bit as much or more than traditional concerns that are confined to school literacy. We would like to advocate for such a critical/radical curriculum in contrast to the extremely limited choices offered by politicians and some literacy policy makers (Freire & Macedo, 1987).

Note: This work was supported in part by a grant from the Division of Innovation and Development, Office of Special Education Programs, #HO23N70037-97. The opinions included in this report are those of the author and do not necessarily reflect the position or endorsement of the Division of Innovation and Development, Office of Special Education Programs.

REFERENCES

Allington, R. L. (1989). School response to reading failure: Instruction for Chapter 1 and special education students in grades two, four, and eight. *Elementary School Journal, 89*(5), 529–542.

Barrera, R. B., & Jiménez, (2000). *What bilingual education teachers have to say about their literacy practices for Latino students.* Washington, DC: National Clearinghouse for Bilingual Education. http://www. ncbe.gwu.edu/ncbepubs/reports/literacy/index.htm

Barrera, R. B., & Jiménez, R. T. (2001). Bilingual teachers speak about the literacy instruction of bilingual Latino students. In B. M. Taylor & P. D. Pearson (Eds.), *Teaching reading: Effective schools and accomplished teachers* (pp. 335–360). Mahwah, NJ: Lawrence Erlbaum.

Butler, Y. G., Orr, J. E., Bousquet, M., & Hakuta, K. (2000). What can we learn about the impact of Proposition 227 from SAT–9 scores? *NABE News and Notes, 24*(1), 8–10.

Carter, T. P., & Chatfield, M. L. (1986). Effective bilingual schools: Implications for policy and practice. *American Journal of Education, 95*(1), 200–232.

Christian, D., Howard, E. R., & Loeb, M. I. (2000). Bilingualism for all: Two-way immersion education in the United States. *Theory into practice, 39*(4), 258–256.

Collier, V. P. (1987). Age and aquisition of second language for academic purposes. *Tesol Quarterly, 21*(4), 617–641.

Crawford, J. (2000). *At war with diversity.* Buffalo, NY: Multilingual Matters.

Cummins, J. (1979). Linguistic interdependence and the educational development of bilingual children. *Review of Educational Research, 49*(2), 222–251.

Cummins, J. (1986). Empowering minority students: A framework for intervention. *Harvard Educational Review, 56*(1), 18–36.

Donato, R. (1997). *The other struggle for equal schools: Mexican Americans during the civil rights era.* Albany: State University of New York.

Fishman, J. A. (1982). *Sociolinguistic foundations of bilingual education.* Binghamton, NY: Bilingual Press/Editorial Bilingüe.

Freire, P., & Macedo, D. (1987). *Literacy: Reading the word and the world.* South Hadley, MA: Bergin & Garvey.

García, E. (1994). *Understanding and meeting the challenge of student cultural diversity.* Boston: Houghton Mifflin.

General Accounting Office (1987, March). *Bilingual education: A new look at the evidence.* Washington, DC: GAO. (Rep. GAO/PEMD–87–12BR)

Gersten, R., Brengelman, S., & Jiménez, R. (1994). Effective instruction for culturally and linguistically diverse students: A reconceptualization. *Focus on Exceptional Children, 27*(1), 1–16.

Gregory, E., & Williams, A. (2000). *City literacies: Learning to read across generations and cultures.* New York: Routledge.

Guerra, J. C. (1998). *Close to home: Oral and literate practices in a transnational Mexicano community.* New York: Teachers College Press.

Heath, S. B. (1983). *Ways with words: Language, life, and work in communities and classrooms.* Cambridge, MA: Cambridge University Press.

Jiménez, R. T. (1997). The strategic reading abilities and potential of five low-literacy Latina/o readers in middle school. *Reading Research Quarterly, 32*(3), 224–243.

Jiménez, R. T. (2000). Literacy and the identity development of Latina/o students. *American Educational Research Journal, 37*(4), 971–1000.

Jiménez, R. T. & Barrera, R. B. (2000). How will bilingual/ESL programs in literacy change in the next millennium? *Reading Research Quarterly, 35,* (4), 522–523.

Jiménez, R. T., García, G. E., & Pearson, P. D. (1995). Three children, two languages, and strategic reading: Case studies in bilingual/monolingual reading. *American Educational Research Journal, 32*(1), 31–61.

Jiménez, R. T., García, G. E., & Pearson, P. D. (1996). The reading strategies of Latina/o students who are successful English readers: Opportunities and obstacles. *Reading Research Quarterly, 31*(1), 90–112.

Kalmar, T. M. (2001). *Illegal alphabets and adult biliteracy.* Mahwah, NJ: Erlbaum.

Lindholm-Leary, K. (2001). *Dual language education.* Buffalo, NY: Multilingual Matters.

Lucas, T., Henze, R., & Donato, R. (1990). Promoting the success of Latino language-minority students: An exploratory study of six high schools. *Harvard Educational Review, 60*(3), 315–340.

Luke, A. (1995–1996). Text and discourse in education: An introduction to critical discourse analysis. In M. Apple (Ed.), *Review of research in education* (pp. 3–48). Washington DC: American Educational Research Association.

Macedo, D. (2000). The colonialism of the English only movement. *Educational Researcher, 29*(3), 15–24.

Moll, L. C. (1988). Some key issues in teaching Latino students. *Language Arts, 65*(5), 465–472.

National Center for Education Statistics. (1997). Are limited English proficient (LEP) students being taught by teachers with LEP training? Washington, DC: U.S. Department of Education.

National Center for Education Statistics. (1998a). Mini-digest of education statistics 1997. Washington, DC: U.S. Department of Education.

National Center for Education Statistics. (1998b). National assessment of educational progress (NAEP), 1992, 1994, 1998 reading assessments. Washington, DC: U.S. Department of Education.

National Center for Education Statistics. (1998c). Report in brief. NAEP 1996 trends in academic progress. Washington, DC: U.S. Department of Education.

New London Group. (1996). A pedagogy of multiliteracies: Designing social futures. *Harvard Educational Review, 66*(1), 60–92.

Nieto, S. (1992). *Affirming diversity.* New York: Longman.

Pace, D. (2001). Rapidly growing Hispanic population is slow to vote. *News-Gazette,* p. B–5.

Reyes, M. de la luz. (1992). Challenging venerable assumptions: Literacy instruction for linguistically different students. *Harvard Educational Review, 62*(4), 427–446.

Reyes, M., & Halcón, J. J. (1997). Racism in academia: The old wolf revisited. In A. Darder, R. D. Torres, & H. Gutiérrez (Eds.), *Latinos and Education* (pp. 423–438). New York: Routledge.

Sánchez, G. I. (1940). *Forgotten people: A study of New Mexicans.* Albuquerque, NM: University of New Mexico.

San Miguel, G. (1987). *"Let all of them take heed": Mexican Americans and the campaign for educational equality in Texas, 1910–1981.* Austin: University of Texas Press.

Soto, L. D. (1997). *Language, culture, and power.* Albany: State University of New York.

Steinberg, J. (2000). Bilingual ban yields higher test scores. *Seattle Times,* pp. 1, 21.

Sulzby, E., & Teale, W. (1991). Emergent literacy. In R. Barr, M. L. Kamil, P. Mosenthal, & P. D. Pearson (Eds.), *Handbook of reading research, Vol. 2* (pp. 727–758). New York: Longman.

Thomas, W. P., & Collier, V. (1996). Language-minority student achievement and program effectiveness. *NABE News, 19*(6), 33–35.

Thomas, W., & Collier, V. (1997). *School effectiveness for language minority students.* Washington, DC: National Clearinghouse for Bilingual Education.

Tikunoff, W. J. (1985). *Applying significant bilingual instructional features in the classroom.* Rosslyn, VA: National Clearinghouse for Bilingual Education.

Valencia, R. R. (1991). *Chicano school failure and success: Research and policy agendas for the 1990s.* New York: Falmer Press.

Wells, G. C. (1986). *The meaning makers: Children learning language and using language to learn.* Portsmouth, NH: Heinemann.

Willig, A. C. (1985). A meta-analysis of selected studies on the effectiveness of bilingual education. *Review of Educational Research, 55*(3), 269–317.

16

Post-Secondary Education and Transition Services for Students Ages 18–21 With Significant Disabilities

Debra A. Neubert, M. Sherril Moon, and Meg Grigal

For the past 20 years, students with significant disabilities (SD) who remain in public school programs until age 21 have generally participated in functional or community-based instruction (CBI) during their high school years (Agran, Snow, & Swaner, 1999; Billingsley & Albertson, 1999). In some states these students may earn IEP diplomas or certificates of attendance instead of a diploma upon exiting the school system (National Center on Educational Outcomes, 1999). After leaving the school system, these individuals typically have entered supported employment, independent living services, or adult day programs provided by nonprofit community agencies funded by Medicaid, developmental disabilities, and vocational rehabilitation systems (Neubert & Moon, 1999). Many professionals, advocates, and families, however, are questioning when and how often students with SD should participate in CBI during the high school years (Billingsley & Albertson, 1999; Quirk & Bartlinkski, 2001; Tashie, Malloy, & Lichtenstein, 1998) and what type of educational and transitional experiences will lead to more optimal post-school outcomes in integrated settings (Patton et al., 1996; Smith & Puccini, 1995).

In 1995 the Division on Mental Retardation and Developmental Disabilities (Council for Exceptional Children) recommended that students who require educational services beyond the age of 18 be allowed to graduate with their peers and then continue their education in settings such as colleges and vocational–technical schools (Smith & Puccini, 1995). Others have supported this philosophical shift to provide age-appropriate interactions with same-age peers; attend classes and social activities on college campuses; work in the community; and participate in flexible, community-based instruction during the final school years (Falvey, Gage, & Eshilian, 1995; Fisher & Sax, 1999; Moon & Inge, 2000; Patton et al., 1996; Tashie et al., 1998).

Several reports highlighting transition policy and practices for students with disabilities also have targeted a need for different or specialized transition services for students ages 18-21. The National Council on Disability and Social Security Administration (2000) identified "expanding secondary transition programs for students ages 18–21 to include two- and four-year college campuses" (p. 19) in a list of strategies that may lead to more successful post-school outcomes. Also noted was an "intense need for . . . access to individualized and effective post-secondary education services and supports . . . and meaningful options for choice by individuals in the pursuit of education, career training, and individualized services and supports" (p. 17). In a national survey of parent centers funded by the U.S. Office of Special Education Programs (OSEP), respondents considered students who remain in school through age 21 as having the greatest unmet needs (PACER Center, 2001).

As with other emerging issues in special education, particularly in transition services, there is a need to disseminate information on age-appropriate practices for replication purposes. Most important is the need to conceptualize how older students with SD can be served differently during their final years of public school through a range of options that result in more students with SD participating in post-secondary activities. The purpose of this chapter is to provide an overview of options for enhancing age-appropriate educational and transition experiences for students with SD ages 18–21.

First we discuss the rationale behind differentiating educational and vocational experiences in high school settings for students before and after age 18. We then describe two options for extending experiences after age 18: (a) programs that serve public school students on college campuses and in community settings, and (b) individual support approaches for serving public school students in college and community settings. For each option we highlight key features along with replication and evaluation needs.

We base the discussion here on our work through an OSEP outreach grant, On-Campus Outreach, to identify and disseminate information on practices in post-secondary settings for students with SD (see Appendix B) and from a review of the literature of post-secondary educational practices for individuals with SD (Neubert, Moon, Grigal, & Redd, 2001). This information adds to a limited but growing knowledge base on how to develop strategies for supporting students with SD on college campuses and in the community after age 18. We extend this discussion by identifying how schools may consider a variety of services to meet the needs of all older students with SD.

DIFFERENTIATING EDUCATIONAL AND TRANSITIONAL SERVICES FOR SECONDARY STUDENTS WITH SD

The need for providing age-appropriate experiences for students with SD during their final years of public school (age 18–21) is often discussed within the context of when and how often students with SD should participate in employment training and functional, community-based experiences during the high school years. Secondary experiences for students with SD may differ based upon the philosophy of those who are planning instruction and coordinating services.

In some cases secondary instruction for students with SD has focused on community-based instruction, including job sampling, employment experiences, and accessing community resources. Students with SD may spend their years in high school learning functional skills in the classroom and community but often are separated from their peers without disabilities. The rationale for providing educational and transitional services off the high school campus after age 18 is based on the needs to (a) provide students with SD with different experiences during their final years of school, and (b) access post-secondary environments in which they will be expected to live and work as adults.

In other cases, as students with SD have been included in their neighborhood schools and in general education classes, some have questioned whether these students should participate in CBI during the high school years (ages 14–18). For example, Fisher and Sax (1999) advocate that students with SD be given the same access to academic classes as their peers without disabilities during their high school years, and that the IDEA Amendments of 1997 provide the legal mandate to do so. They maintain that "before students with disabilities had access to the core curriculum in middle school and high school, CBI was a reasonable educational alternative" (p. 303).

Billingsley and Albertson (1999) maintain that special educators should be able to work with general educators to implement functional skill activities within general education classes and extracurricular activities. When CBI is offered to students with SD in high school, it should be offered "during periods that do not interfere with general education classes that would address other educational needs of higher priority" (p. 300). When students with SD participate in employment-related activities before the age of 18, they would do so in the same manner as their same-age peers, such as working or volunteering after school and during the summer.

The rationale for providing different services for these students after age 18 is based on the need for age-appropriate experiences in post-secondary courses (e.g., adult and continuing education and community colleges) and in employment sites in the community (Billingsley & Albertson, 1999; Falvey, Gage, & Eshlilian, 1995; Fisher & Sax, 1999; Quirk & Bartlinski, 2001; Smith & Puccini, 1995; Patton et al., 1996; Tashie et al., 1998). These experiences would be based on a person-centered planning process that takes into account the wishes, needs, interests of the student, his or her family, and significant friends or professionals who support the student (Baird & Everson, 1999; Pearpoint, Forest, & O'Brien, 1996).

Outcomes

Although the impetus for proposing differentiated experiences for students with SD during their final years of public school are not the same, the outcomes of these approaches are similar. Students with SD need the opportunity to receive educational and transitional experiences outside of the high school between the ages of 18–21 with age-appropriate peers. Therefore, educational and transition experiences would differ substantially before and after the age 18 for students with SD.

Logistics

Providing students with SD with different experiences based on their age is just one way for professional and families to rethink how public schools provide educational and transition services. The philosophical discussion concerning when and how much CBI students with SD should receive in their secondary years is, to date, not based on documented post-school outcomes. Agran et al. (1999, p. 58) noted that "much of the published literature on the relative benefits of community-based instruction and inclusion is based on researchers' opinions…and has not been either socially or empirically validated." In a survey of 120 special educators in Utah, they found that middle and high school teachers supported inclusive academic and community-based instructional experiences because both offered opportunities for inclusion with peers, coworkers, and community members.

Issues related to staffing will require careful planning to accommodate flexible schedules for students to participate in the community both before and after age 18 (Billingsley & Albertson, 1999; Hart, Zafft, & Zimbrich, in press; Tashie et al., 1998). The roles and responsibilities of teachers will have to be rethought as these professionals will work as case managers, employment specialists, or college-based educators rather than classroom instructors in the high school.

Despite the lack of documentation on what educational experiences (i.e., inclusion in regular classes, CBI, employment training) are best either before or after age 18, programs and individual supports for older students with SD in post-secondary settings are being implemented across the country. In the remainder of this article, we describe these options for educating students ages 18–21 with SD.

PROGRAMS IN POST-SECONDARY SETTINGS

Programs in post-secondary settings have been implemented in a number of states including California, Louisiana, Kentucky, Maryland, and Oregon (Grigal, Neubert, & Moon, 2001; Hall, Kleinert, & Kearns, 2000; Highhouse, 2001; Hunter, 1999; National Clearinghouse on Post-secondary Education for Individuals with Disabilities, 2000; National Transition Alliance, 2000; Sharpton, 1998). These programs have been developed on college campuses and in the community to serve high school students with severe disabilities who are 18 years or older in their final years of public school. The students who attend these programs typically have been in high school for four or more years and may receive an alternative exit document (e.g., certificate of attendance, IEP diploma) as they exit public school. These programs are not located on high school campuses but, instead, in various post-secondary locations, such as universities, community colleges, community businesses, or adult service agencies.

Through our work with On-Campus Outreach (OCO), we have provided technical assistance to 17 programs in 11 local school systems in Maryland and to programs in other states that are serving students with SD between the ages of 18–21 in post-secondary settings. The information presented here is based upon observations, interviews, and experiences gained through this work. For a more detailed description of Maryland post-secondary programs, the reader should refer to our website in Appendix B or Grigal et al. (2001).

Key Features

Post-secondary programs located on college campuses or in the community typically serve between 8 and 21 students a year and are staffed by a special educator or transition specialist and instructional assistants funded by the school system (Grigal et al., 2001; Hall et al., 2000). Students' activities and schedules differ depending on their goals and needs; however, most programs offer some classroom-based instruction (i.e., functional academics) along with opportunities to enroll in college classes, to work on campus or in the community, and to participate in social and recreational activities with college-age peers. Programs located in post-secondary sites often include best practices in transition (e.g., Hughes et al., 1997; Kohler, 1993, 1998; Rusch & Millar, 1998), such as functional academics, job training and follow-along, assessment activities including person-centered planning, self-determination skills instruction, social and recreational skill development, community mobility training, and collaborating with families and post-secondary providers to ensure future access to adult services and supports.

One of the key features of the programs we are describing is that services are coordinated outside of the high school from a designated location in the community. Choosing a site for the program requires the collaboration of members from the school system and the community. The starting point should be a planning committee, consisting of representatives from the various key organizations including school personnel, the program host (college or business), employers, local adult service providers, rehabilitation personnel, and, of course, parents and students. The planning committee should conduct a needs assessment (see Appendix A) and carefully consider the following options in the community when developing a program.

Programs at Four-Year Institutions

In Maryland, two programs are located at four-year universities. Hall et al. (2000) also provide a description of a program at a four-year liberal arts college. Programs based at four-year colleges provide many opportunities for integrated experiences for students with SD. These institutions generally have departments in education and the social sciences and medical fields such as speech, occupational, and physical therapies. Often, students in these fields of study need experiences, both formal and informal, with students who have disabilities.

Working with the staff in these types of departments, partnerships have been formed that serve the students with SD and the college students as well. Students may work with one another in classes, practical experiences, and student service learning experiences. Four-year institutions are larger than community colleges and often provide housing for college students. This affords the programs based on four-year campuses greater access to a constant student population during the daytime, evenings, and weekends.

Programs at Community Colleges

Community colleges are also attractive locations for programs, as they often have open-door policies that may facilitate access for nontraditional students. In addition, these institutions are more prevalent and closer in proximity than many of the four-year institutions. Community college is the first post-secondary experience for many students exiting high school and provides a natural setting for integrated experiences with students ages 18–21 without disabilities.

Program teachers in Maryland, however, report that students in community colleges are transient. They come to the campus to attend their classes and often leave campus soon after class has ended. This may impact the opportunities to access college students to serve as peer buddies or tutors and may limit social interactions and participation in clubs and organizations on campus. In addition, securing office and classroom space has been a struggle for the teachers in these programs.

Programs in the Community

Three programs in Maryland are located in alternative sites in the community. One is based in a community building owned by the school system, one in a local mall, and the other in the office building of an adult service provider. Although initially these sites might not seem like ideal locations, we urge planning committees not to overlook the benefits of locating a program in a community site other than a college.

Programs based in the community often are not faced with the space or isolation concerns of programs located on college campuses. In addition, locating a program in the community does not preclude students from enrolling in classes or recreational and social activities on college campuses.

This approach benefits students who need jobs close to their homes, and it facilitates students with SD accessing the local community college's activities and classes even when it is not ideal to locate the "program" on the campus. If one of the major goals of the program is to promote integrated employment, partnerships with business and industry could be crucial when developing programs for students after the age of 18.

Another factor related to locating a program on campus or in a business setting has to do with the number of schools sending students with SD to post-secondary sites. For example, one urban school system in Maryland provides four sites, one on a four-year college campus, two on community college campuses, and one in an adult service center, to provide more students with SD access to a post-secondary program.

In a program in Oregon, students with SD receive services in an apartment in the community and at a local college (Highhouse, 2001). In the apartment, students learn to prepare meals, wash clothes, and spend time with others or alone in a natural setting. At the local college, they take classes, use public transportation, and participate in other college social activities.

Both the Maryland and the Oregon community examples demonstrate that the use of college and community settings is not mutually exclusive. Also, by providing educational services in the community, school systems may avoid some of the pitfalls of trying to obtain classroom or office space on a college campus, which can be difficult. Providing services in community locations also may increase access to employment opportunities. If a student's post-secondary goals involve employment and community access rather than college experiences, participating in educational services located in the community can be a good alternative for their final school years.

Opportunities for Inclusion

Age-appropriate inclusion has occurred in programs on college campuses in a variety of ways (Grigal et al., 2001; Hall et al., 2000). Students with SD have enrolled in classes such as piano, ceramics, stagecraft, tai chi, math review, weight lifting, aerobics, swimming, family studies, education technology, ecology, and radio production. Participation in classes depends on various factors including level of course content, student interest, and class schedule. Students who attend college classes continue to receive support from the local school staff in much the same manner as they would in inclusive high school situations. Some of the barriers to attending college courses for students with SD include course prerequisites, placement tests, costs, scheduling conflicts, and attitudinal barriers from college instructors.

Some programs have found innovative ways to involve college students without disabilities as instructors or peer tutors in separate classes for students with SD or in community-based instruction. For example, one program at a four-year college in Maryland had three college interns working in the classroom for 3 hours a week for credit, six college students volunteering 36 hours each semester to satisfy their student learning service requirement, and 10 students working as job coaches to support students with disabilities in their employment training.

Many programs have tapped into college activities, volunteer organizations such as Habitat for Humanity, or sororities and fraternities for integrated social and recreational activities. Best Buddies, a nonprofit organization that provides opportunities for one-on-one friendships, has been used successfully in several programs. Students also have many casual opportunities for social interaction by hanging out at student centers, using the library, and attending athletic, cultural, and other college-sponsored events. One of the main opportunities for age-appropriate inclusion may be through job training or paid employment that many students participate in for several hours each day when attending programs in post-secondary sites. Program staff, however, have not yet documented how much or what type of inclusion occurs on these worksites.

Funding and Interagency Linkages

Local school systems in Maryland generally paid for staff and instructional assistants, materials and curricula, and transportation to and from the program at a post-secondary site (Grigal et al., 2001). The program host (the college or business in which the program is located) may contribute to costs by donating space, materials, or access to facilities. Costs for tuition in college courses are determined individually. Some students paid the costs, some colleges waived the costs, or tuition was waived if the student was a recipient of Supplemental Security Income (SSI).

Teachers from several programs have partnered with local adult agencies and state agencies (e.g., vocational rehabilitation and developmental disabilities) to coordinate services for students with SD. In some programs, the staff from an adult service agency provided job-coaching services to students at the worksite or classroom instruction to students on job-seeking skills. In other programs, the staff had developed stronger links with adult service providers, which enhanced the transition planning process as students exited the program.

Therefore, locating a program off the high school site proved beneficial in terms of adult providers getting to know and observe individuals with SD before they left the school system. Hall et al. (2000) also found that having a program on a college campus was beneficial in terms of special educators increasing their knowledge of community resources and linking families to professionals in the community for individualized support. This increased collaboration is important because the National Council on Disability and Social Security Administration (2000, p. 26) found that "vocational rehabilitation and other community service providers have limited involvement in the transition process on a national scale."

Logistics

As programs in post-secondary sites have evolved, a number of issues have surfaced that can be handled in the planning stages (Moon, Grigal, & Neubert, 2001). Before choosing a location, a planning committee should consider the issues addressed in Appendix A. Other issues that should be taken into consideration when developing post-secondary experiences for students with SD include:

1. Staff flexibility and availability of assistants to conduct employment training and "after school hours" activities
2. Scheduling and calendar differences between colleges and public school systems
3. Transportation to and from campus and for job training in the community
4. Identification and location of administrative and related service personnel
5. Availability of medical staff to supervise administration of medications and procedures
6. Equipment needs such as fax machines, laptop computers and printers, and cell phones.

Finally, program evaluation activities have to be addressed during the early stages of program planning. Grigal et al. (2001) found that only two of 14 programs in post-secondary sites had formal evaluation procedures to document student outcomes and satisfaction.

Replicating and Evaluating Programs

Although programs in post-secondary sites embrace the philosophy of alternative experiences to students after the age of 18, it is important to plan a program that promotes inclusive experiences. In a review of literature on programs for individuals with developmental and other SD between 1970 and 2000, we found numerous examples of programs on community college and four-year college campuses that served individuals who had already exited the school system (Neubert et al., 2001). The philosophy behind these programs was to provide integrated experiences in the community; however, most had separate classes or activities on the campus for the adults with SD. These programs often were started and supported through the efforts of parents and community service providers with funds from adult and continuing education, vocational rehabilitation, and vocational education, not by school systems or colleges.

Those designing programs on college campuses would do well to learn from past experience and to ensure that new programs are collaborative ventures that promote full integration of students with SD. They also should document how and why these programs improve post-school outcomes and quality-of-life experiences for students with SD. Without this information, it will be difficult to justify the expansion or addition of staff, programs, and resources.

Finally, given the small number of students served in programs in post-secondary sites, school system personnel and families will have to consider how to serve greater numbers of students with SD who desire a post-secondary experience. This may mean developing multiple sites in the community. Developing a program in a post-secondary site requires careful consideration of the purposes of the program, how students access the program, how resources and supports will be allocated to the program, and how staffing assignments can be flexible to accommodate atypical "school day" schedules. Most important, careful planning is needed with college and community personnel to ensure that students with SD are an integral part of the setting and have access to existing support services in the environment.

INDIVIDUAL SUPPORTS IN POST-SECONDARY SETTINGS

Another framework that some school systems have used to provide students with SD services outside of the high school after age 18 is based on the provision of individual supports (Bishop, Amate, & Villalobos, 1995; Fisher & Sax, 1999; Tashie et al., 1998; Hart et al., 2001; Weir, 2001). Using individual supports (IS), students receive educational and community supports outside of high school without attending a site-based program. Though limited, some case studies describe how these supports are provided to public school students (Page & Chadsey-Rusch, 1995; Tashie et al.,

1998). Hart et al. (2001) also detail a model, developed from a federally funded OSERS grant, to create access to college for 25 students with SD using an individual support approach. Key features of individual supports are highlighted for those who are interested in providing these services in post-secondary settings.

Key Features

A key feature of individual supports is that they are provided and coordinated for one student at a time. The student receives services in a number of locations (e.g., college, employment site, and community environment), as determined by his or her personal needs and goals, instead of attending a program at a specific site. Using this approach, a student is not limited to existing programs or sites. The student and a support team create and implement an individualized schedule of work, college classes, or age-appropriate social activities after age 18.

Those providing individual supports often use a person-centered planning process to: (a) determine the student's interests, needs, and goals; (b) identify the environments in which these goals can be met; (c) determine the supports needed to access the environment and obtain the goals; (d) set up a system of support; and (e) monitor the coordination of support and progress toward goals. Supports can be provided by a number of individuals from the school system, the college, or agencies such as those involved with vocational rehabilitation. Coordination of services and supports usually remains the responsibility of someone in the school system until the student exits at age 21.

Proponents of this approach maintain that each student requires a unique support system based on individual choice. In addition, students with SD are seen as college students or employees, not as persons with disabilities from a "program." This approach clearly enhances opportunities for inclusion with age-appropriate peers in community settings. The emphasis remains on what support an individual student needs to achieve his or her goals, not on where or how a program is implemented. To illustrate how this process might work, Weir (2001), from the Institute of Disability at the University of New Hampshire, provided this description of one young man who accessed his local college via individual supports.

> Marc, a young man with Down syndrome, had completed four years of high school and wanted to learn more about computers so he could possibly pursue a job in that field. His local school system coordinated with a community-based support agency to support him in attending a community college of his choice and take "Introduction to Computers." He also used the learning center at the college to improve his writing skills, and he eats lunch in the college cafeteria. When he is not at class or doing schoolwork at the college, he holds down a part-time job at an office supply store.

Funding and Interagency Efforts

Providing individual supports to students with SD after the age of 18 requires school personnel, students and their families, and college personnel to rethink how services and supports are delivered on college campuses and in the community. Typically students with disabilities receive their instruction and supports from personnel paid by the school system until the age of 21 or 22. Using the IS approach, support is coordinated through various means, which may include the local school system, a college disability support office, or state agencies such as Vocational Rehabilitation (Hart et al., 2001; Rammler & Wood, 1999; Sharpton, 1998; Tashie et al., 1998).

This approach requires continuing dialogue of "who pays for what" and ongoing collaborative efforts on the part of school systems, colleges, and adult service providers to find creative solutions. To date, we have little documentation of how funding issues are resolved between schools and agencies for students needing supports in college and community settings after age 18.

Logistics

Similar to programs in post-secondary sites, logistical issues have to be considered by school system personnel and families when planning for individual supports. These can include the number of hours per day a student is involved in activities, the times of the day individual supports must be provided (e.g., student attends a community college night class), and the roles for staff, student, and family members (Certo et al., 1997). Hart et al. (2001) summarized how the roles and responsibilities for teachers must be designed when using individualized supports. These include: a move from teaching to service coordination or case management; training and supervising of instructional assistants and job coaches; working a variable, 12-month schedule; and helping students develop self-determination skills in preferred environments.

Although many of these responsibilities are similar to what a transition specialist might provide in public schools (Asselin, Todd-Allen, & deFur, 1998; Council for Exceptional Children, 2000), the IS approach requires staff and administrators to truly reconsider how teachers and specialists who support older students can undertake case-management roles. Teachers and instructional assistants must be allowed to spend their time outside of the confines of the high school, work flexible, nontraditional schedules, and determine how natural supports can be used in post-secondary settings.

School administrators must understand the need for these changing roles and support teachers appropriately in terms of their caseload, the time needed for planning and collaborative efforts, and the resources allocated to the students and staff. Finally, community agency personnel must be involved in supporting students before they exit school. This, too, will require a shift in fiscal resources and staff responsibilities for some personnel.

Replicating and Evaluating Individual Support Approaches

An obvious benefit in the individual support approach is that students are not limited, by their schedule or predetermined instruction, to what is available in a separate "program." Weir (2001) maintains that the use of individual supports may allow individuals with SD to continue their education after they exit the school system, because they are not affiliated with a "program" during their transition years. As with the programs described in the previous section, however, no data are available indicating how the provision of individual supports enhances postschool outcomes for students with SD.

Documentation is needed describing what these students do during their final years of school and how individual supports are provided after the individual leaves the school system to maintain independent living, jobs, and social outlets. It also will be important to elicit the perspectives of students and their families regarding their experiences in accessing and retaining individualized supports.

Also, there has been little discussion about the role of or acceptance of college personnel in implementing this approach. We know, from literature and surveys in the 1980s and 1990s, that efforts to serve individuals with developmental disabilities were often separate from college disability support services and programs (Neubert et al., 2001).

A national survey of disability support coordinators in 2000 found that postsecondary institutions rarely offered assistance with the transfer of supports from educational settings to the workplace (National Center for the Study of Post-secondary Education Supports, 2000). Similar to what has been documented in the past, results of this survey indicated that the most common supports for students with disabilities included testing accommodations, notetakers, personal counseling, and advocacy assistance.

We caution school personnel to be realistic about the types of support generally offered on college campuses to students with SD. In the absence of federal funding, such as OSEP post-secondary model demonstration projects, public school administrators and staff must carefully develop cooperative relationships that facilitate the support of students with SD in college and community settings.

SUMMARY

Providing age-appropriate transition services for students with SD during their final years of school provides a variety of benefits such as increased social interaction with same-age peers, age-appropriate courses and job opportunities, access to new environments, and greater opportunities for support from college and community personnel. Our intent in describing programs and individual supports for students with SD ages 18–21 is not to endorse one over the other but, rather, to provide school personnel, families, and community personnel with information about key features, replication, and evaluation issues. What is apparent in the programs and individual support approaches reported to date is that a small number of students with SD participate in these age-appropriate experiences.

We encourage school personnel, families, and community providers to consider several post-secondary options for students with SD. Having a program on a college campus for some students does not preclude the idea that other students should be provided with individual supports on the college campus and in the community. Still other students may benefit from a more traditional approach of remaining on the high school campus and being included in general classes while also receiving CBI and job training after the age of 18.

Finally, we recommend that planning teams use the resources provided in our References and in the Appendices to learn how other school systems have provided educational and transitional services to students with SD outside of the traditional high school. Though the program and individual support approaches described here may seem very different, the implications for practice are somewhat similar. These include redesigning staff roles, rethinking what students need during their first four years in high school (age 14–18), and engaging school systems and community providers in the development and implementation of services outside of the high school. As students with SD and their families continue to learn about opportunities for age-appropriate services in their final years of school, we expect that school systems will implement a number of approaches that will better serve more students.

REFERENCES

Agran, M., Snow, K., & Swaner, J. (1999). A survey of secondary level teachers' opinions on community-based instruction and inclusive education. *Journal of the Association for Persons with Severe Disabilities, 24*, 58–62.

Asselin, S. B., Todd-Allen, M., & deFur, S. (1998). Transition coordinators: Define yourselves. *Teaching Exceptional Children, 30*(3), 11–15.

Baird, P. A., & Everson, J. M. (1999*). Person-centered planning: A guide for facilitators and participants*. New Orleans: Human Development Center, Louisiana State University Health Sciences Center.

Billingsley, F. F., & Albertson, L.R., (1999). Finding a future for functional skills. *Journal of Association for Persons with Severe Disabilities, 24*, 298–302.

Bishop, K. D., Amate, S. L., & Villalobos, P. J. (1995). Post-secondary considerations. In M. A. Falvey (Ed.), *Inclusive and heterogeneous schooling: Assessment, curriculum, and instruction* (pp. 363–393). Baltimore: Paul H. Brookes.

Certo, N. J., Pumpian, I., Fisher, D., Storey, K., & Smalley, K. (1997). Focusing on the point of transition: A service integration model. *Education and Treatment of Children, 20*, 68–84.

Council for Exceptional Children (2000). *What every special educator must know (4th ed.).* Alexandria, VA: Author.

Falvey, M. S., Gage, S. T., & Eshlilian, L. (1995). Secondary curriculum and instruction. In M. A. Falvey (Ed.), *Inclusive and heterogeneous schooling: Assessment, curriculum, and instruction* (pp. 341–362). Baltimore: Paul H. Brookes.

Fisher, D., & Sax, C. (1999). Noticing differences between secondary and post-secondary education: Extending Agran, Snow, and Swaner's discussion. *Journal of The Association for Persons with Severe Disabilities, 24*, 303–305.

Flannery, K. B., Newton, S., Horner, R., Slovic, R., Blumberg, R., & Ard, W. (2000). The impact of person-centered planning on the content and organization of individual supports. *Career Development for Exceptional Individuals, 23*, 123–137.

Grigal, M., Neubert, D. A., & Moon, M. S. (2001). Public school programs for students with significant disabilities in post-secondary settings. *Education and Training in Mental Retardation and Developmental Disabilities, 36*, 244–254.

Hall, M., Kleinert, H. L., & Kearns, F. J. (2000). Going to college! Post-secondary programs for students with moderate and severe disabilities. *Teaching Exceptional Children, 32*(3), 58–65.

Hart, D., Zafft, C., & Zimbrich, K. (2001). Creating access to college for all students. _Journal for Vocational Special Needs Education, 23_(2), 19–31.

Highhouse, P. (2001, June). Lake Oswego post-high transition programs. Presentation at the Region V CSPD Options in Transition Conference, Missoula, MT.

Hughes, C., Eisenman, L. T., Hwang, B., Kim, J., Killian, D. J., & Scott, S. (1997). Transition from secondary special education to adult life: A review and analysis of empirical measures. _Education and Training in Mental Retardation and Developmental Disabilities, 32,_ 85–104.

Hunter, D. (1999, December). _Lesson in transition partnerships: An innovative school district/university relationship._ Presentation at 1999 TASH Conference, Chicago.

Kohler, P. D. (1993). Best practices in transition: Substantiated or implied? _Career Development for Exceptional Individuals, 16,_ 107–121.

Kohler, P. D. (1998). Implementing a transition perspective of education: A comprehensive approach to planning and delivering secondary education and transition services. In F. R. Rusch, & J. G. Chadsey (Eds.). _Beyond high school: Transition from school to work._ (pp. 179–204). Belmont, CA: Wadsworth.

Moon, M. S., Grigal, M., & Neubert, D. A. (2001). High school and beyond. _Exceptional Parent, 31_(1), 52–57.

Moon, M. S., & Inge, K. V. (2000) Vocational preparation and transition. In M. Snell & F. Brown (Eds.), _Instruction of students with severe disabilities_ (5th ed.) (pp. 591–628). Upper Saddle River, NJ: Merrill.

National Center on Educational Outcomes. (1999). _State graduation requirements for students with and without disabilities._ Minneapolis: Author.

National Center for the Study of Post-secondary Educational Supports (2000). _National survey of educational support provision to students with disabilities in post-secondary education settings._ Honolulu: University of Hawaii at Manoa, National Center for the Study of Post-secondary Educational Supports.

National Clearinghouse on Post-secondary Education for Individuals with Disabilities. (2000, December). _Pathways to employment: Nondegree post-secondary options for individuals with developmental disabilities_ (Part 2). Retrieved December 10, 2001 from http://www.heath.gwu. edu/info-from-heath/dec00.html

National Council on Disability and Social Security Administration (2000). _Transition and post-school outcomes for youth with disabilities: Closing the gaps to post-secondary education and employment._ Washington, DC: Authors.

National Transition Alliance. (2000, June). 1999 Selected model programs/ promising practices. _Alliance Newsletter, 4,_ 3–15.

Neubert, D. A., & Moon, M. S. (1999). Working together to facilitate the transition from school to work. In S. Graham & K. R. Harris (Eds.), _Teachers working together: Enhancing the performance of students with special needs_ (pp. 186–213). Cambridge, MA: Brookline Books.

Neubert, D. A., Moon, M. S., Grigal, M., & Redd, V. (2001). Post-secondary educational practices for individuals with mental retardation and other significant disabilities: A review of the literature. _Journal of Vocational Rehabilitation, 16,_ 155–168.

PACER Center. (2001). _Technical assistance on transition and the Rehabilitation Act._ Minneapolis: Author.

Page, B., & Chadsey-Rusch, J. (1995). The community college experience for students with and without disabilities: A viable transition outcome? _Career Development for Exceptional Individuals, 18,_ 85–95.

Patton, J. R. Smith, T. E. C., Clark, G. M., Polloway, E. A., Edgar, E., & Lee, S. (1996). Individuals with mild mental retardation: Post-secondary outcomes and implications for educational policy. _Education and Training in Mental Retardation and Developmental Disabilities, 31,_ 75–85.

Pearpoint, J., Forest, M., & O'Brien, J. (1996). MAPs, Circle of Friends, and PATH: Powerful tools help build caring communities. In S. Stainback & W. Stainback (Eds.), _Inclusion: A guide for educators._ (pp. 67–86). Baltimore: Paul H. Brookes.

Quirk, C., & Bartlinksi, A. K. (2001, March). *No more community-based instruction*? Paper presented at meeting of Maryland State Department of Education/ Maryland Coalition on Inclusive Education Conference, College Park.

Rammler, L., & Wood, R. (1999). *College lifestyle for all!* Available from Rammler and Wood Consultants, LLC, 6 Way Road, Middlefield, CT 06455.

Rusch, F. R., & Millar, D. M. (1998). Emerging transition best practices. In F. R. Rusch, & J. G. Chadsey (Eds.), *Beyond high school: Transition from school to work.* (pp. 36–59). Belmont, CA: Wadsworth Publishing.

Sharpton, W. R. (1998, December*). Creating post-secondary options: Issues and strategies from the field.* Presentation at 1998 TASH Conference, Seattle.

Smith, T. E. C., & Puccini, I. K.(1995). Position statement: Secondary curricula and policy issues for students with MR. *Education and Training in Mental Retardation and Developmental Disabilities, 30,* 275–282.

Tashie, C., Malloy, J. M., & Lichtenstein, S. J. (1998). Transition or graduation? Supporting all students to plan for the future. In C. J. Jorgensen (Ed.), *Restructuring high schools for all students: Taking students to the next level* (pp. 234–259). Baltimore: Paul H. Brookes.

Weir, C. (2001, May). *Individual supports for college success* (On-Campus Outreach, Fact Sheet #7). Retrieved October 12, 2001 from www.education.umd.edu/oco

Wood, R. (1999, December). *A transformation of services for students 18–21 years old.* Presentation at 1999 TASH Conference, Chicago.

APPENDIX A

Convening a Planning Committee and Conducting a Needs Assessment

Step 1: Create and convene a planning committee.

The newly formed committee should meet regularly to design and conduct a needs assessment, to develop an action plan, to monitor progress, to discuss problems and successes with the staff involved in a program or providing individual supports, and to evaluate and make changes in post-secondary services. Possible committee members include older students with SD, special education administrators, secondary special educators, vocational or transition specialists, school psychologists, secondary school principals, parents, advocates, developmental disabilities and vocational rehabilitation case managers, local community rehabilitation program staff, college administrators, and local business people.

Step 2: Identify students with SD ages 18–21 who may benefit from educational and transition services offered in post-secondary sites.

One of the first jobs of the planning committee involves profiling the number of older students with SD who may need or want alternative services in post-secondary sites. Factors that should be considered are numbers of students between the ages of 18 and 21 who are SSI- or SSDI-eligible; will receive an alternative or nonstandard diploma; have paid jobs, have unpaid job experiences; have received travel training; have been included in general education; and have expressed an interest in postsecondary experiences off the high school campus.

Step 3: Review current services received by the students identified in Step 2.

The planning committee must examine educational and transition services currently being provided to students with SD ages 18 to 21, determine what types of changes are needed in each service delivery area, and list possible actions that could lead to change. Possibly the needed changes do not involve creating alternative programs or supports delivered off-campus. Service delivery areas that might be examined include classroom instruction, inclusive educational and social opportunities, curricula, type of community-based or life-skills instruction, employment training, individual behavior or personal support needs, and interagency collaboration with businesses, colleges, community agencies, and community rehabilitation staffs.

Step 4: Determine the need for alternative services.

Based on the needs assessment of the number of students who might need alternative services, the viability of current services, and the possible actions that should be taken, the planning committee must decide what types of post-secondary programs or individual supports should be developed.

Step 5: Develop an action plan, including a timeline, for how, where, and when postsecondary services will occur.

This is a time-consuming process that usually requires six months to a year of ongoing work by the planning committee. Outcomes of this process must include hiring and training service providers, developing formal agreements with colleges and businesses where services will occur, disseminating referred or application procedures, and developing a written plan for handling logistics such as transportation, delivery of related services, IEP coordination, administrative responsibility, and medical and emergency procedures.

APPENDIX B

On-Campus Outreach
www.education.umd.edu/oco

The website includes a list of post-secondary programs in Maryland, a Needs Assessment Form for Developing Programs in Post-Secondary Settings for Students with SD Ages 18–21, sample letters and forms used by personnel in post-secondary programs in Maryland, links to other resources, and a series of fact sheets including:

Fact Sheet #1: How to Start a Program for Students with SD on a College Campus
Fact Sheet #2: Functional, Community-based Curriculum Guides & Materials
Fact Sheet #3: Transition Assessment Practices for Students with SD
Fact Sheet #4: Self-determination & Students with SD on a College Campus
Fact Sheet #5: Definitions and Descriptions
Fact Sheet #6: Evaluating Programs for Students with SD in Post-secondary Settings
Fact Sheet #7: Individual Supports for College Success

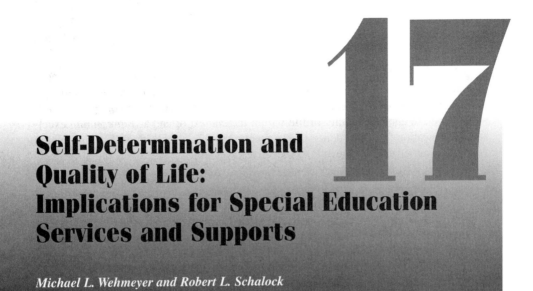

Self-Determination and Quality of Life: Implications for Special Education Services and Supports

Michael L. Wehmeyer and Robert L. Schalock

The United States is engaged in a debate concerning the efficacy of the public school system and about reforms to address the perceived inadequacies of the current system. This is not a new debate or a unique time in the history of education, for such debates ebb and flow as society's understanding of and emphasis on the purposes of education change. We say "purposes" in plural form intentionally, for despite overheated rhetoric to the opposite, the educational system has always had multiple purposes, from learning for the sake of knowledge itself to preparation for employment and citizenship (Pulliam & Van Patten, 1995).

Currently, the debate revolves around the importance of school accountability through, primarily, standards-based reform (Sykes & Plastrik, 1993). Although the intent of this article is not to critique this particular type of reform, there has been concern over the possible conflict between long-held beliefs about the education of students with disabilities and standards-based reform, with special attention to the extent to which testing based on state content and performance standards narrows the curriculum to only core academic content areas and limits the functionality of the curriculum for students with disabilities (Committee on Goals 2000, 1997; Committee on Appropriate Test Use, 1999; Wehmeyer, Lattin, & Agran, in press).

Individualization is a hallmark of the federal legislation mandating the education of students with disabilities and best practice in the field. Consequently, there is considerable concern about the impact of mandates to provide access to the general curriculum on the education of these students.

We begin this chapter, which focuses on self-determination and quality of life in special education services and supports, with reference to these concerns for two reasons. *First,* we recognize that educators working with students with disabilities can no longer consider curricular and instructional content as separate from the general curriculum, whether it is the provision of transition services, the delivery of functional or occupational curriculum, or promoting self-determination to achieve a higher quality of life. *Second,* we want to examine the issue of promoting self-determination to enhance quality of life within the *context* of and as *representing* excellent education for all students. Our contention is that a focus on self-determination provides a means to achieve both objectives.

OVERVIEW OF SELF-DETERMINATION

If teaching students to be self-sufficient citizens is an important outcome for the education system, it seems apparent that too few students with disabilities achieve this objective. Studies show that important adult outcomes, such as employment, independent living and community integration, remain unattainable by many youths with disabilities (Chadsey-Rusch, Rusch, & O'Reilly, 1991).

One of the reasons that students with disabilities have not succeeded once they leave school is that the educational process has not prepared students with special learning needs adequately to become self-determined young people. Martin, Marshall, Maxson, and Jerman (1993) put it this way:

> If students floated in life jackets for 12 years, would they be expected to swim if the jackets were suddenly jerked away? Probably not. The situation is similar for students receiving special education services. All too often these students are not taught how to self-manage their own lives before they are thrust into the cold water of post-school reality.

An educational emphasis on promoting self-determination for students with disabilities emerged through the 1990s as a function of a federal initiative related to the then new federal mandates regarding provision of transition services for adolescents with disabilities (Ward, 1996; Ward & Kohler, 1996; Wehmeyer, 1998) and requiring active student involvement in educational planning and decision making (Morningstar, Kleinhammer-Tramill, & Lattin, 1999; Wehmeyer & Sands, 1998). As a result of this federal focus, numerous instructional and assessment methods, materials, and strategies now are available to enable teachers to promote student self-determination (Field, Martin, Milller, Ward, & Wehmeyer, 1998; Wehmeyer, Agran, & Hughes, 1998). Moreover, research (Agran, Snow, & Swaner, 1999; Wehmeyer, Agran, & Hughes, 2000) indicates that teachers working with students who have disabilities acknowledge the importance of promoting self-determination for students with disabilities, although that acknowledgement does not always translate directly to instructional opportunities for students (Wehmeyer & Schwartz, 1998; Wehmeyer et al., 2000).

Self-Determination as an Educational Outcome

Over the last decade, self-determination has emerged as an important construct in the education of students with disabilities. As a result of federally funded initiatives to define and describe self-determination as an educational outcome (Ward & Kohler, 1996), a number of conceptualizations of self-determination to address educational needs have been formulated (see Field, 1996). Martin and Marshall (1995) summarized the "evolving definition of self-determination in the special education literature" as describing individuals who

> know how to choose—they know what they want and how to get it. From an awareness of personal needs, self-determined individuals choose goals, then doggedly pursue them. This involves asserting an individual's presence, making his or her needs known, evaluating progress toward meeting goals, adjusting performance and creating unique approaches to solve problems. (p. 147)

As illustrated by this description, the *actions* of self-determined people enable them to fulfill roles typically associated with adulthood. We have forwarded a definitional framework in which self-determination refers to "acting as the primary causal agent in one's life and making choices and decisions regarding one's quality of life free from undue external influence or interference" (Wehmeyer, 1996, p. 24). According to the *American Heritage Dictionary of the English Language* an agent is "someone who acts or has the power or authority to act" or a "means by which something is done or caused." A causal agent, then, is someone who makes or causes things to happen in his or her life.

Within this framework, self-determined behavior refers to actions identified by four essential characteristics:

1. The person acted *autonomously.*
2. The action(s) was *self-regulated.*
3. The person initiated and responded to the event(s) in a "psychologically empowered" manner.
4. The person acted in a *self-realizing* manner.

These essential characteristics emerge as children, youth, and adults develop and acquire a set of *component elements* of self-determination. Intervention focuses on the level of component elements.

Essential Characteristics of Self-Determined Behavior

The term *essential characteristic* means that an individual's actions must reflect, to some degree, each of the four characteristics identified. Age, opportunity, capacity, and circumstances can impact the extent to which any of the essential characteristics are present and, as such, the relative self-determination an individual expresses will likely vary, sometimes over time and other times across environments. Nonetheless, these essential elements have to be present. Each characteristic is a necessary but not sufficient element of self-determined behavior.

Behavioral Autonomy

Sigafoos, Feinstein, Damond and Reiss (1988) stated that "human development involves a progression from dependence on others for care and guidance to self-care and self-direction" (p. 432). The outcome of this progression is autonomous functioning or, when describing the actions of individuals achieving this outcome, behavioral autonomy. For the purposes of the definitional framework, a behavior is autonomous if the person acts (a) according to his or her own preferences, interests, and/or abilities, and (b) independently, free from undue external influence or interference.

Autonomous behavior should not be confused with self-centered or selfish behavior. Although humans often act according to personal interests, on some occasions a person must act in ways that do not reflect specific interests. As such, one's preference may be to act in a manner that does not directly reflect a specific interest if that is prudent or useful. Likewise, most people cannot be viewed as strictly acting alone, with no external influences. The field of disability recognizes interdependence as a desirable outcome because all people are influenced daily by others, from family members to strangers. Contextual, cultural, and social variables will define for each person an "acceptable" level of interference and influence.

Self-regulated Behavior

Whitman (1990) defined self-regulation as

> a complex response system that enables individuals to examine their environments and their repertoires of responses for coping with those environments to make decisions about how to act, to act, to evaluate the desirability of the outcomes of the action, and to revise their plans as necessary. (p. 347)

Self-regulated behaviors include self-management strategies (including self-monitoring, self-instruction, self-evaluation, and self-reinforcement), goal-setting and attainment behaviors, problem-solving behaviors, and observational learning strategies. These enable students to become the causal agent in their lives (Agran, 1997).

Acting in a Psychologically Empowered Manner

Psychological empowerment is a term referring to the multiple dimensions of perceived control, including its cognitive (personal efficacy), personality (locus of control) and motivational domains (Zimmerman, 1990). Essentially, people acting in a psychologically empowered manner do so on the basis of beliefs that they (a) have control over circumstances important to them (internal locus of control), (b) possess the skills necessary to achieve desired outcomes (self-efficacy), and (c) expect the identified outcomes to result if they choose to apply those skills (outcome expectations).

Self-realization

Finally, self-determined people are self-realizing in that they use a comprehensive, and reasonably accurate, knowledge of themselves and their strengths and limitations and act to capitalize on this knowledge. This self-knowledge and understanding forms through experience with and interpretation of one's environment and is influenced by evaluations of significant others, reinforcement, and attributions of one's own behavior.

Empirical Validation of the Framework

To test this definitional framework, Wehmeyer, Kelchner, and Richards (1995, 1996) conducted a study of adults with mental retardation to determine their relative self-determination status and the relationship between this status and the hypothesized essential elements (autonomy, self-regulation, perceptions of psychological empowerment, and self-knowledge/realization). Interviews with 408 adults with mental retardation yielded responses to a survey instrument constructed to identify the degree to which individuals acted in a self-determined manner. Respondents were assigned to one of two groups, high self-determination or low self-determination, based on these responses.

This survey instrument (described in Wehmeyer et al., 1995) required that participants respond to a series of questions exploring the individuals' behaviors in six principal domains: (1) home and family living; (2) employment; (3) recreation and leisure; (4) transportation; (5) money management; and (6) personal/leadership. Questions were selected to reflect the amount of choice and control individuals had in each of these areas or the degree to which the individual acted in a manner reflecting self-determination.

Participants also completed a series of assessments designed to determine their autonomy, self-regulation, psychological empowerment and self-realization (see Wehmeyer et al., 1996). Comparisons between groups based on self-determination status found that adults who exhibited more self-determined behaviors were significantly more autonomous (on both measures of autonomy), more effective social problem solvers, more assertive and self-aware, and held more adaptive perceptions of control, self-efficacy, and outcome expectations (Wehmeyer et al., 1996). With the exception of certain domain specific self-concepts, there were significant differences between groups in all areas related to the definitional framework.

Component Elements of Self-Determined Behavior

The *essential characteristics* that define self-determined behavior emerge through the development and acquisition of multiple, interrelated *component elements*, including the following.

- Choice-making skills
- Decision-making skills
- Problem-solving skills
- Goal-setting and attainment skills
- Independence, risk-taking and safety skills

- Self-observation, evaluation and reinforcement skills
- Self-instruction skills
- Self-advocacy and leadership skills
- Internal locus of control
- Positive attributions of efficacy and outcome expectancy
- Self-awareness
- Self-knowledge

Although not intended as an exhaustive list, these component elements are especially important to the emergence of self-determined behavior. Each of these component elements has a unique developmental course or is acquired through specific learning experiences (Doll, Sands, Wehmeyer, & Palmer, 1996). The development and acquisition of these component elements is lifelong and begins early in life. Some elements have more applicability for secondary education instruction and transition, and others focus more on the elementary years. As such, promoting self-determination as an educational outcome will require a purposeful instructional program, one that coordinates learning experiences across the span of a student's educational experience.

In a subsequent section, we describe these component elements and provide suggestions for intervention for each. Prior to addressing instructional issues, however, we want to provide an overview of the quality-of-life construct, and particularly its use in the field of special education.

OVERVIEW OF QUALITY OF LIFE

The concept of quality of life has risen to the fore in the field of special education for a number of reasons (Keith & Schalock, 1994; Schalock, 1995).

1. It is a social construct that is impacting program development and service and supports delivery in special education.
2. It is being used as the criterion for assessing the effectiveness of supports and services for students with disabilities.
3. The pursuit of quality is apparent at three levels in special education services: students and their advocates desiring a life of quality, educators wanting to deliver quality products and see quality outcomes, and evaluators assessing quality outcomes.

Not insignificantly, the standards-based reform movement we discussed earlier is, at its core, a "total quality management" process focused on ensuring high-quality outcomes.

Despite its attractiveness, the quality-of-life concept is neither fully understood nor immune from potential misuse (Hatton, 1998). As the field of special education continues to embrace the concept, it is timely to reflect upon the concept and its application to special education services and supports. As Yogi Berra once stated, "The problem of not knowing where you are going is that you might end up in the wrong place." The primary purpose of this section is to provide an overview of the concept of quality of life. In a subsequent section we will discuss a number of instructional, assessment, and curricular issues in implementing the concept of quality of life for students with disabilities.

Three Uses of the Concept

Over the last two decades, the way we view people with disabilities has changed significantly. This transformed vision of what constitutes the life possibilities of people with disabilities is reflected in terms that are familiar to the reader: self-determination, inclusion, strengths and capabilities, the importance of normalized and typical environments, the provision of individualized support systems, equity, and enhanced adaptive behavior and role status. As a term and concept, quality of life captures this changing vision and currently is used in the fields of disability services and special education as:

- A *sensitizing notion* that gives us a sense of reference and guidance from the individual's perspective, focusing on the individual and his/her environment
- A *social construct* that is an overriding principle to improve and enhance an individual's perceived quality of life
- A *unifying theme* that provides a systematic or organizing framework to focus on the multidimensionality of a life of quality

The Core Quality-of-Life Dimensions

There is increasing agreement that quality of life is a multidimensional concept that precludes reducing it to a single "thing" of which the person may have considerable, some, or none. Current and ongoing research in this area has identified *eight core quality-of-life dimensions* (Schalock, 1996a): emotional well-being, interpersonal relationships, material well-being, personal development, physical well-being, self-determination, social inclusion, and rights. Although the number and configuration of these core dimensions vary slightly among investigators, these eight core dimensions are based on the work of Cummins (1997), Felce (1997), Hughes and Hwang (1996), Paramenter and Donelly (1997), and Renwick and Brown (1996). In reference to these core dimensions, the emerging consensus is that each person values them differently, and the value attached to each varies across one's life.

Quality-of-Life Research

Over the last decade the research and statistical design used to study the quality-of-life concept has changed. Specifically, we have seen a significant shift from a "between" approach to a "multivariate/within" approach. Historically, quality of life was studied from a between-groups (or conditions) perspective; hence, investigators sought to find factors such as socioeconomic status and large demographic population descriptors that could discriminate between persons or countries with a high quality of life and those with a lower quality of life. This "between mentality" spilled over to early work on quality of life in subtle ways, as reflected in the attitude expressed by some that we need to have different measures or quality-of-life indices for those who are higher functioning and those who are either nonverbal or lower functioning.

Shifting to a multivariate research design has a number of advantages:

1. It allows for a focus on the correlates and predictors of a life of quality rather than comparing quality-of-life scores or status. This approach has been used to evaluate the relative contribution to one's assessed quality of life of a number of personal characteristics, objective life conditions, and provider characteristics. Across a number of studies (Schalock, Lemanowicz, Conroy & Feinstein, 1994; Schalock & Faulkner, 1997; Schalock, Bonham, & Marchand, 2000) personal factors (perceived sense of dignity, health status, and adaptive behavior level), environmental variables (perceived social support, current residence, employment, and integrated activities), and provider characteristics (worker stress and job satisfaction) are significant predictors of a person's assessed quality of life.

2. Once these significant predictors are identified, programmatic changes can be made to enhance the person's perceived quality of life through techniques such as personal development and wellness training, quality enhancement techniques, and quality management techniques (Schalock, 1994; Schalock & Faulkner, 1997).

3. Multivariate research designs help us understand better the complexity of the quality-of-life concept and the role of contextual variables in the perception of a quality life.

4. Multivariate research designs shift the focus of our thinking and intervention from personal to environmental factors as major sources of quality-of-life enhancement.

Quality-of-Life Assessment

One of the most significant changes recently has been the shift toward quality-of-life-oriented, outcome-based evaluation rooted in person-referenced outcomes. This emerging focus reflects the subjective and personal nature of one's perceived quality of life, and also the quality revolution, consumer empowerment with the associated expectations that special education programs will result in an improved quality of life for students, the increased need for program outcome data that evaluate the effectiveness and efficiency of special education programs, the supports paradigm based on the premise that providing needed and relevant supports will enhance one's quality of life, and the pragmatic evaluation paradigm that emphasizes the practical, problem-solving orientation to program evaluation (Schalock, in press).

Our approach to quality-of-life assessment is based on four assumptions:

1. Quality of life is composed of the eight core dimensions listed previously.

2. Each of the eight core dimensions can be defined operationally in terms of a number of specific indicators, such as those summarized in Table 1.
3. The focus of quality-of-life assessment should be on person-referenced outcomes.
4. Assessment strategies should use either personal appraisal or functional assessment measures reflecting one or more of the eight core dimensions.

The indicators listed in Table 17.1 can be assessed by using either personal appraisal and/or functional assessment strategies. It should be noted that the *personal*

TABLE 17.1 ■ Quality-of-Life-Referenced Indicators

Dimension	Exemplary Indicators	
Emotional well-being	Safety	Freedom from stress
	Spirituality	Self concept
	Happiness	Contentment
Interpersonal relations	Intimacy	Interactions
	Affection	Friendships
	Family	Supports
Material well-being	Ownership	Employment
	Financial	Possessions
	Security	Social economic status
	Food	Shelter
Personal development	Education	Personal competence
	Skills	Purposeful activity
	Fulfillment	Advancement
Physical well-being	Health	Health care
	Nutrition	Health insurance
	Recreation	Leisure
	Mobility	Activities of daily living
Self-determination	Autonomy	Personal control
	Choices	Self-direction
	Decisions	Personal goals/values
Social inclusion	Acceptance	Community activities
	Status	Work environment
	Supports	Volunteer activities
	Roles	Residential environment
Rights	Privacy	Due process
	Voting	Ownership
	Access	Civic responsibilities

appraisal strategy should be equated to the historical notion of *subjective indicators* and the *functional assessment* strategy to the historical notion of *objective indicators*.

Personal Appraisal

The personal appraisal strategy addresses the subjective nature of quality of life, typically asking the person how satisfied he or she is with the various facets of his or her life. For example, this is the approach we have used in the *Quality of Student Life Questionnaire* (Keith & Schalock, 1995) wherein we asked questions such as, "How satisfied are you with your education situation?" and "How satisfied are you with the skills and experience you have gained or are gaining from your classes?"

Even though the person's responses are subjective, responses have to be measured in psychometrically acceptable ways. Thus, a 3- to 5-point Likert scale can be used to indicate the person's level of expressed satisfaction. The advantages of this approach to measurement are that it encompasses the most common dependent measure (satisfaction) used currently in quality-of-life assessments, it allows one to measure factors that historically have been considered to be major subjective indicators of a life of quality, and it allows one to quantify the level of expressed satisfaction.

Functional Assessment

The most typical formats used in functional assessment are rating scales, participant observation, and questionnaires. Each of these attempts to document a person's functioning across one or more core quality-of-life dimensions and the respective indicator. To accomplish this, most instruments employ some form of an ordinal rating scale to yield a profile of the individual's functioning. For example, one might ask (or observe), "How frequently do you use community recreational facilities?" or, "How many times do you go into the community to shop or eat each week?" The advantages of functional assessment are that this form of assessment is more objective and performance-based, allows for the evaluation of outcomes across groups, and thereby provides important feedback to educators and evaluators as to how they can change or improve their services and supports to enhance the student's perceived quality of life.

An advantage of using the quality-of-life assessment suggested above is that one need not use different indicators for subjective versus objective measurement; rather, the core dimensions remain constant. What varies is whether one uses a personal appraisal or a functional assessment approach to assess the respective indicator. Thus, all assessment is focused clearly on the eight core dimensions of quality of life. It is apparent that some of the domains are more amenable to personal appraisal and others to functional assessment.

For example, personal appraisal might best be used for the core dimensions of emotional well-being, self-determination, rights, and interpersonal relations; whereas functional assessment might better be used for the core dimensions of material well-being, personal development, physical well-being, and social inclusion. Hence, there is a definite need to use both personal and functional assessments to measure one's perceived quality of life.

In summary, we have made significant progress in understanding the concept of quality of life. Specifically, we are closer to understanding that:

■ Quality of life is a multidimensional phenomenon whose core dimensions and their importance vary among persons and within their lifespans.

■ Quality-of-life assessment should be based on core quality-of-life dimensions and their indicators, using measurement strategies that combine personal appraisal and functional assessment.

■ Multivariate research designs allow focus on the contextual nature of a life of quality.

Despite this better understanding, a number of instructional and curricular issues remain. These issues, addressed in the a subsequent section, relate primarily to implementation of quality enhancement techniques, use of positive behavior supports, and persons with disabilities assessing their own quality of life.

HOW ARE QUALITY OF LIFE AND SELF-DETERMINATION RELATED?

The focal points of this article are both self-determination *and* quality of life. These constructs, described separately above, are often mentioned in the same context. Yet, to our knowledge, there has been no systematic treatment or exploration of the relationship between these areas. Nevertheless (and not coincidentally), the theoretical frameworks of both self-determination and quality of life, described previously, rely on or reference each construct as a means of defining the other. In considering the relationship between them and their implications for special education supports and services, we would return to the premise introduced at the beginning of the article. Stated in terms of related theoretical statements, the relationship and importance of these constructs to the education of students with disabilities include the following.

1. It is generally accepted (and, as discussed subsequently, there is empirical evidence) that one factor contributing to positive outcomes in the lives of students with disabilities is enhanced self-determination (Wehmeyer & Schwartz, 1997).

2. People who are self-determined make or cause things to happen in their lives; they are causal agents in their lives. Causal agency, however, implies more than simply making something happen; it implies that the individual who makes or causes that thing to happen does so to accomplish a specific end. Intuitively, and by definition, these ends or changes are designed to improve or enhance the person's quality of life.

3. The extent to which a person is self-determined either influences or is influenced by other core dimensions of quality of life and, in combination with these other core dimensions, influences or impacts global or overall quality-

of-life status.

These statements are important only if some value is placed on quality of life as an outcome relevant to the field of special education. The most visible sense of "outcomes" important to special education are contained in the IDEA's transition services mandates requiring that students with disabilities be provided transition services that are outcomes-oriented. In the early years of special education, this outcomes-orientation focused almost exclusively on one outcome—employment. Within a short time, however, it was generally accepted that these programs and services should prepare students to attain a wide variety of adult outcomes (Halpern, 1985; Sitlington, 1996).

This broader mandate was codified in the 1990 amendments to IDEA and reaffirmed in the 1997 amendments, in which transition services were defined as "a coordinated set of activities for a student, designed within an outcome-oriented process which promotes movement from school to post school activities" [Sec. 602(a)(19)]. Post-school activities were broadly defined to include post-secondary education, vocational training, integrated and supported employment, continuing and adult education, adult services, independent living, and community participation.

Halpern (1993) elaborated upon this broader mandate in the 1990 amendments to IDEA, suggesting that, although the statutory language did not use the term "quality of life," the mandate clearly defined the multidimensional expression and validity of a variety of life goals. He further suggested that the next logical step in defining and evaluating the utility of transition services was to use "quality of life" as a conceptual framework for structuring and examining transition outcomes.

Although this suggestion seemed persuasive from both theoretical and historical perspectives, there has not been an overwhelming surge of effort to make transition programs accountable from a quality-of-life conceptual framework. Instead, special education remains largely reliant on process indicators of quality (e.g., compliance with regulations in the IDEA for what should be in the IEP), and for some basic outcome indicators, such as job and residential placements.

The standards-based school reform movement has introduced a different set of accountability indicators, primarily tests tied to the curriculum, which in turn are tied to state or local educational standards. In some states this testing is high stakes—meaning that the consequences are significant for students, teachers, and/or administrators if students do not show progress on the tests.

Both the process form of accountability inherent in the IDEA (e.g., compliance with regulations pertaining to the IEP) and the accountability system within the standards-based reform movement have an underlying assumption that adherence to the accountability indicators will improve the educational experience and, presumably, improve student outcomes. Indeed, even the "outcomes" listed in the transition services mandates in IDEA are there based on an assumption that, by achieving such outcomes, students will attain a better quality of life.

These assumptions, however, are just that—assumptions. Certainly a good job is one factor contributing to a better quality of life because it provides income for financial well-being, health insurance for physical well-being, opportunities for social relationships, and so forth. Likewise, one can suggest that, by listing what should be in a student's IEP—which, theoretically, should contribute to a better educational program—or by holding students or educators accountable for student progress on tests designed to measure attainment of high standards for educational outcomes, one can improve education and, in turn, improve a student's quality of life as an adult. The problem is that these assumptions may or may not be true. As Halpern (1985) noted, getting a job is not a *prima facia* guarantee of the good life. None of these accountability mechanisms adequately ensures that education leads to a better quality of life, because they simply don't measure that specific outcome.

The difficulty in measuring such outcomes is well documented, but examples in other fields point out instances in which accountability measures were transformed from mainly process indicators to person-centered outcome indicators. For example, in the field of residential services for people with mental retardation, accountability and accreditation traditionally have been based on an agency's compliance with organizational procedures and paperwork regulations.

In 1997, however, the Council on Quality and Leadership in Supports for People with Disabilities, an agency that accredits residential service providers, published a series of personal outcome measures it was using to hold agencies accountable for outcomes that related to quality of life. Some of the "indicators" the Council used to measure quality in service delivery and to accredit high-quality programs included whether people choose personal goals, choose where and with whom they live, are satisfied with their services, choose their daily routine, participate in the life of the community, and exercise their rights.

As the field of special education endorses the importance of promoting self-determination as a valued outcome of a student's educational process, it becomes both an opportunity and an obligation that the field also begin to focus attention more on quality of life. An emphasis on promoting student self-determination is, in essence, a commitment to enable young people to set their own goals to achieve outcomes they value. Those outcomes will vary a great deal according to personal preferences, interests, abilities, and opportunities.

Therefore, it becomes incumbent upon us to move from the complacency of job placement as an outcome for which we are accountable, to enabling young people to move into post-secondary employment circumstances that result in a higher quality of life. In essence, if we are serious about promoting self-determination, we have to become more serious about examining quality of life as an organizing theme to examine personal outcomes. Of course, this call to action is relevant only if promoting self-determination is, indeed, an important educational objective.

ARE SELF-DETERMINATION AND QUALITY OF LIFE IMPORTANT FOR STUDENTS WITH DISABILITIES?

Quality of life is a construct that attempts to conceptualize what "living the good life" means, and, as such, is almost by default a potentially important outcome on which to focus. The question that perhaps is more important is whether promoting self-determination is worth the time and effort involved. The proposition that self-determination is an important educational outcome presumes that self-determination and positive adult outcomes are causally linked.

Although such a link seems intuitively obvious, until recently, limited empirical evidence has examined this assumption. Instead, the link between self-determination and positive adult outcomes for youth with disabilities was established by examining the contributions of the component elements, such as goal-setting and problem solving, to more favorable adult outcomes. In deference to space limitations, we will not overview that literature in detail, but generally the opportunity to make choices, express preferences, set goals, and self-regulate learning and behavior all have been linked to more favorable educational and adult outcomes (see Wehmeyer, Agran, & Hughes, 1998, for overview of this literature).

Research on the component elements of self-determined behavior provides only indirect evidence that youth who are more self-determined achieve more positive adult outcomes. Wehmeyer and Schwartz (1997) measured the self-determination of 80 youth with cognitive disabilities (mild mental retardation or learning disability). One year after these students left high school, they and their families were contacted to determine status in several areas, including student living arrangements, current and past employment situations, post-secondary education status, and community integration outcomes.

This information was analyzed, controlling for level of intelligence and type of disability. The data showed a consistent trend in which self-determined youth were doing better than their peers one year out of school. Members of the high self-determination group were more likely to have expressed a preference to live outside the family home, have a savings or checking account, and be employed for pay. Of the high-self-determination group, 80% worked for pay one year after graduation, whereas only 43% of the low-self-determination group did likewise. Among school-leavers who were employed, youth who were in the self-determined group earned significantly more per hour (Mean = $4.26) than their peers in the low-self-determination group (Mean = $1.93).

If promoting self-determination has positive benefits for students, as the Wehmeyer and Schwartz (1997) study suggests, the next question of merit is whether there is empirical evidence of the link between self-determination and quality of life. We discussed in the previous section the theoretical linkages, but is there evidence to bolster those hypothetical links? Wehmeyer and Schwartz (1998b) empirically examined the link between self-determination and quality of life for 50 adults with mental retardation living in group homes. Controlling for level of intelligence and environmental factors contributing to a higher quality of life, we found that self-determination predicted group membership based on quality of life scores. That is, a person's relative self-determination was a strong predictor of his or her quality of life; people who were highly self-determined had a higher quality of life, and people who lacked self-determination had a less positive quality of life.

More research is needed to examine the impact of self-determination on positive adult outcomes, including quality of life. Nevertheless, the limited direct evidence and the preponderance of evidence from examination of the impact of component elements of self-determined behavior on positive educational, achievement, and adult outcomes suggests that self-determination is, indeed, an important focus for educators.

INSTRUCTIONAL, ASSESSMENT, AND CURRICULAR ISSUES IN SELF-DETERMINATION

Given that self-determination is an important educational outcome, what can educators do to enable students to achieve this outcome? As a result of the federal initiatives of the past decade (Ward & Kohler, 1996), a number of curricular and assessment materials have been designed to promote self-determination for youth with disabilities (see Field et al., 1998; Wehmeyer et al., 1998). In addition, instructional programs are available which enable students with disabilities to become meaningful participants in the educational planning process (see Wehmeyer & Sands, 1998).

The theoretical framework of self-determination described earlier suggests that self-determination emerges as students develop or acquire a set of component elements of self-determined behavior. Efforts to enhance these component elements take three primary tracks:

1. Instruction to promote capacity (skills and knowledge)
2. Opportunities to experience control and choice
3. The design of supports and accommodations.

The primary role of education in this process is in promoting capacity, although this does not mitigate the importance of providing opportunity and identifying supports and accommodations. These capacity-enhancement efforts can be driven by the curricular or other materials discussed earlier, or through instruction on each specific component element. Next we will examine issues related to the latter and offer suggestions for promoting each component. We note at the outset that this involves educational efforts across a student's educational experience, from preschool and elementary grades through secondary and post-secondary education.

Teaching Component Elements of Self-Determination

Choice-Making

Perhaps more emphasis has been placed on the choice-making component as critical to a positive quality of life for people with disabilities than most of the other elements combined. Making a choice is, quite simply, communicating a preference, and instruction in making choices focuses on one or both of these elements—either identifying a preference or communicating that preference. Except in unique circumstances, there usually is no need to "teach" choice-making, per se, although there may be a need to enable or teach children who have problems communicating new, alternative, or even more appropriate ways to indicate their preferences. By and large, educational efforts should be aimed at using choice-making opportunities to provide experiences of control, and to teach students that not all options are available to them and that choice options are constrained for all people.

Shevin and Klein (1984, p. 164) emphasized the importance of integrating choice-making opportunities throughout the school day and listed five keys to maintaining a balance between student choice and professional responsibility:

1. Incorporating student choice as an early step in the instructional process
2. Increasing the number of choices related to a given activity which the student makes
3. Increasing the number of domains in which decisions are made; and raising the significance in terms of risk and long-term consequences of the choices that the student makes
4. Clear communication with the student concerning areas of possible choice, and the limits within which choices can be made.

Similarly, Brown, Appel, Corsi, and Wenig (1993) suggested seven ways to infuse choices into instructional activities:

1. Choosing within an activity
2. Choosing between two or more activities
3. Deciding when to do an activity
4. Selecting the person with whom to participate in an activity
5. Deciding where to do an activity
6. Refusing to participate in a planned activity
7. Choosing to end an activity at a self-selected time.

Problem-Solving

A problem is "a task whose solution is not immediately perceived" (Beyth-Marom, Fischhoff, Jacobs, Quadrel, & Furby, 1991). More specifically, a problem is "a situation or set of situations to which a person must respond to function effectively in his environment" (D'Zurilla & Goldfried, 1971). Problem-solving skills typically have focused on problem resolution in two domains: impersonal problem-solving and interpersonal or social problem-solving. Social problem-solving emphasizes cognitive and behavioral strategies that enable individuals to interact with one another and to cope in an increasingly social world. Much of the focus for intervention in special education has been strictly on social skills training. Although this instruction is important, in the absence of similar emphasis on social problem-solving skills, social skills training alone is not enough to address deficits in social interactions exhibited by youth and adults with disabilities (Chadsey-Rusch, 1986; Park & Gaylord-Ross, 1989; Wehmeyer & Kelchner, 1994).

Instruction in problem solving typically includes three focal points:

1. Problem identification

2. Problem explication and analysis
3. Problem resolution.

Instruction should take place within environments that emphasize the student's capability to solve problems, promote open inquiry and exploration, and encourage generalization. Teachers should serve as role models by verbalizing the problem-solving steps used on a day-to-day basis and should make sure that students are provided adequate support and accommodations.

Decision-Making

Making a decision is a process of selecting or coming to a conclusion about which solution is best given one's circumstances, values, priorities, and needs. Beyth-Marom et al. (1991, p. 21) suggested that most models of decision making incorporate the following steps:

1. Listing relevant action alternatives
2. Identifying consequences of those actions
3. Assessing the probability of each consequence occurring (if the action were undertaken)
4. Establishing the relative importance (value or utility) of each consequence
5. Integrating these values and probabilities to identify the most attractive course of action.

Baron and Brown (1991) proposed that "deficient decision-making is a serious problem throughout society at large and the problem needs addressing in childhood or adolescence." Students need to learn how to define the issue or problem about which a specific decision is to be made, how to collect information about the specific situation, and to use this information to identify options for consideration. Once these options are clarified, students need to learn to be able to identify and evaluate the consequences and outcomes of actions based on the various options. When those consequences have been detailed, choice-making skills can be applied to select a specific alternative. Finally, students must implement this plan of action.

An underlying assumption that many educators and parents hold is that minors do not have the capacity to make informed choices and decisions. This assumption also is made frequently about individuals with disabilities, so the overwhelming assumption about adolescents with disabilities is that they are incapable of participating in the decision-making process. A number of researchers, however, have suggested that minors are competent at making important decisions.

The belief that minors are incapable of making competent decisions results, in part, from the perception that minors and students with disabilities cannot take into account the degree of risk involved with various options. This assumption, however, is not supported by research in developmental psychology. Grisso and Vierling (1978) reviewed the cognitive and behavioral characteristics of minors in relation to the question of competence to consent to treatment. They concluded that "there is no psychological grounds for maintaining the general legal assumption that minors age 15 and above cannot provide competent consent, taking into account risk-related factors." In fact, those authors contended that there are "circumstances that would justify the sanction of *independent* consent" by minors between the ages of 11 and 14.

Similarly, Kaser-Boyd, Adelman, and Taylor (1985) asked students ages 10 to 20, who were identified as having a learning or behavior problem, to list potential risks and benefits of entering psychoeducational therapy. As expected, there was a relationship between age and effectiveness in this task. Even young students, however, were able to identify relevant concerns appropriate to their situation and their developmental needs.

While choice-making should be emphasized early in a student's educational career, decision-making skills probably are better addressed at the secondary level. Beyth-Marom and colleagues (1991) suggest that to achieve generalization, decision making and problem solving should be taught in terms of familiar knowledge domains. By this, they refer to the effectiveness of teaching these skills in the context of a life-skills or functional education curriculum, with decision-making skills learned by applying the process to real world issues.

Be it choice-making or engaging in independent living behaviors, the real barrier for many people with disabilities is that the needs of the caregiver for absolute assurance of safety often tend to lead to the prohibition of activities that have low-level risks. Certainly, behaviors that lead to a certain injury and those that have a moderate probability for harm should be cause for concern. Most behaviors, however, do not involve that level of risk and students with disabilities can be taught to assess the level of risk, and weigh the consequences of action using an effective decision-making process. In addition, students can be taught safety and health-promotion skills that they need to achieve independent living. These skills might include teaching students basic first-aid and job safety skills, nutrition, diet and medication facts, and the prevention of abuse and disease (Agran, Marchand-Martella, & Martella, 1994).

Goal Setting and Attainment

To become the causal agent in his or her life, a person has to learn the skills necessary to plan, set, and achieve goals. Goal-setting theory is built on the underlying assumption that goals are regulators of human action. This is true for educational motivation and achievement. For example, Schunk (1985) found that student involvement in goal setting improved performance on math activities for students with learning disabilities.

Educational efforts to promote goal setting and attainment skills should focus on identifying and enunciating specific goals, developing objectives and tasks to achieve these goals, and taking the actions necessary to achieve a desired outcome. The educational planning and decision-making process revolves around goal setting, implementation, and evaluation. Involving students in this process, across all grades, is a good way to promote goal setting and attainment skills. Teachers and parents can model effective skills such as identifying short- and long-term goals, describing objectives, implementing plans based on these goals and objectives, and reevaluating and refining the plans.

Self-Management Skills

The definitional framework of self-determined behavior identified these actions as self-regulated. Self-regulated behavior includes self-managing one's life, including self-monitoring, self-evaluation, self-instruction, and self-reinforcement. Self-monitoring strategies involve teaching students to assess, observe, and record their own behavior. Self-monitoring strategies are used most frequently to improve work-related activities, such as attention to task, task completion, and task accuracy (Hughes, Korinek, & Gorman, 1991) and, as such, are important to transition-related programs. Self-evaluation activities include the use of systematic strategies to enable students to track and evaluate their progress on educational activities, including goals and objectives. This frequently involves self-recording procedures in which the student graphs, charts, or otherwise documents progress on a goal or objective.

Progress typically is determined through some form of self-observation, during which the student discriminates and records that a given target behavior has occurred, then compares it with a previously determined standard or expected outcome (Agran, 1997). Students can be taught to score worksheets, identify the occurrence of a target behavior, track time intervals for the occurrence or nonoccurrence of a target behavior, and record this information in a graphic or chart format.

A third component of self-regulation is the use of self-reinforcement strategies. Agran (1997) defined self-reinforcement as the self-administration of consequences, either positive or negative, contingent on the occurrence of a target behavior, and suggested that self-reinforcement should have two functions: self-identification of reinforcers and delivery of this reinforcer. Student involvement in the former—identification of reinforcers—can enhance the efficacy of the latter. Self-reinforcement can be more effective than having another person deliver the reinforcer, not the least because self-reinforcement is almost always immediate.

Self-instructional strategies involve teaching students to "provide their own verbal prompts for solving an academic or social problem" (Hughes, Korinke, & Gorman, 1991). This technique has been used successfully to solve job- and work-related problems (Hughes & Rusch, 1989) and to teach social skills that are critical to independence (Hughes & Agran, 1993). In essence, self-instruction strategies move the responsibility for providing verbal prompts and cues from an external source, typically the teacher, to the student.

Self-Advocacy and Leadership Skills

Self-advocacy skills are skills that individuals need to advocate on their own behalf. "To advocate" means to speak up or defend a cause or person. By definition, then, instruction to promote self-advocacy will focus on two common threads— how to advocate and what to advocate. Although elementary-age students can begin to learn basic self-advocacy skills, most instructional emphasis in this area will apply during secondary education. One particularly important area in which students with disabilities should receive instruction involves the education and transition process itself and rights (and responsibilities) within that system. For many students with disabilities, school is a place where they are forced to go to do things that someone else decides for them. It is little wonder that motivation is a problem!

Students who are approaching transition-age can be taught about their rights under the IDEA and, more specifically, about the purpose and process involved in transition decision making. Other topics that could become the "cause" for which students will need to advocate on their own behalf include the adult services system (disability and general), basic civil and legal rights of citizenship, and specific civil and legal protections available to people with disabilities, such as those under the Americans with Disabilities Act. These instructional efforts necessarily will deal with both rights and responsibilities.

Curricular strategies for the "how to advocate" side of self-advocacy include instructional emphasis on being assertive but not aggressive, how to communicate effectively in one-on-one, small-group, and large-group situations, how to negotiate, compromise, and use persuasion, how to be an effective listener, and how to navigate through systems and bureaucracies. Each of these clearly is closely tied to the acquisition and emergence of other self-determination skills. For example, a reliable understanding of one's strengths and weaknesses is an important component if one is to actually use strategies such as negotiation and compromise to achieve an outcome. Likewise, students need to be able to link such advocacy to specific goals and incorporate it into the problem-solving and decision-making process.

Perceptions of Control and Efficacy

The final four essential elements of self-determined behavior focus not on skill development but, rather, on the attitudes that enable individuals to act in a psychologically empowered or self-realizing manner. If people are to act in or upon a given situation, they have to believe that they have control over outcomes that are important to their life. People who hold such beliefs have been described as having an internal locus of control. Rotter (1966) defined *locus of control* as the degree to which a person perceives contingency relationships between his or her actions and outcomes. Internal locus of control has been linked to adaptive outcomes, including positive educational and achievement outcomes and increased time and attention to school-related tasks (Lefcourt, 1976). The locus of control construct for individuals with disabilities has not been extensively explored. The research that does exist suggests that people with disabilities hold perceptions of control that are more external, and thus more maladaptive, than their nondisabled peers.

The role of educators in promoting internal perceptions of control, as well as adaptive efficacy and outcome expectations, positive self-awareness, and realistic self-knowledge, is more complex than just providing adequate instructional experiences. An internal locus of control emerges as children make choices about things they do every day, such as selecting clothing, and as these choices are honored and supported. In addition, an educational program that emphasizes problem solving, choice making, decision making, and goal setting and attainment using student-directed learning activities will provide ample opportunities for students to learn that they have control over reinforcers and outcomes important to them.

Particularly important is to consider the learning environment and to evaluate its effect on student perceptions of control. Teachers who use an overly controlling style, or whose classrooms are rigidly structured, limit their students' development of positive perceptions of control. This does not mean that classrooms must become chaotic; allowing more control is not the same as relinquishing all control and abolishing rules and regulations (Deci & Chandler, 1986). Instead, classrooms can be structured such that students can perform more actions for themselves, such as obtaining their own instructional materials.

Self-efficacy and efficacy expectations are constructs that Bandura (1977) introduced. *Self-efficacy* refers to the "conviction that one can successfully execute a behavior required to produce a given outcome" (Bandura, 1977, pp. 193). Efficacy expectations refer to the individual's belief that if a specific behavior is performed, it will lead to an anticipated outcome.

It should be evident that the two are individually necessary, but not sufficient, for goal-directed and self-determined actions. Simply put, a person has to believe that: (a) he or she can perform a behavior needed to achieve a desired outcome, and (b) if that behavior is performed, it will result in the desired outcome. If a person does not believe that he or she can perform a given behavior (independent of the validity of that belief), he or she consequently will not perform that action. A person may believe, however, that he or she is capable of performing a given behavior, but because of past experience, may not believe that a desired outcome will occur even if that behavior is exhibited and, as such, will not perform the action. For example, a student with a disability may not believe that she has the social skills necessary to initiate a conversation with nondisabled peers and will refrain from initiating such actions. On the other hand, that same student may believe she has the skills, but having been ignored in the past, may believe that she will be ignored again and, therefore, refrain from initiating the action.

Like perceptions of control, perceptions of efficacy and expectancy have been linked to academic achievement and persistence at academic activities (Lent, Bron, & Larken, 1984). Little research has examined the self-efficacy and efficacy expectations of individuals with disabilities. Most of the extant literature in the area of learning disabilities focuses on changing self-efficacy and efficacy expectations through environmental or instructional modifications (Schunk, 1989). Wehmeyer (1994) found that individuals with mental retardation held fewer adaptive attributions of efficacy and expectancy than did their nondisabled peers, and that such attributions became less adaptive as the student got older.

Self-Awareness and Self-Knowledge

For individuals to act in a self-realizing manner, they must have a basic understanding of their strengths, weaknesses, abilities, and limitations, as well as knowledge about how to utilize these unique attributions to beneficially influence their quality of life. Students don't learn what they can or can't do from lectures, role playing, social skills simulations, or any other more traditional teacher-directed instructional activities. They learn, as do all people, through their own interpretation of events and experiences.

This process is not one of pure introspection, however, and does not focus exclusively or even primarily on an understanding of limitations. In many cases, students with disabilities are quite able and more willing to identify what they do poorly than the things they do well. The specter of having a disability, as pictured in disease or deficit models, hovers over any circumstance, and students dwell more on what they are unable to accomplish than what they can achieve. Because special education is essentially remedial in nature, this is not surprising.

INSTRUCTION, ASSESSMENT, AND CURRICULUM ISSUES IN QUALITY OF LIFE

Quality-of-Life-Related Enhancement Techniques

One of the biggest challenges in the field of special education is to implement and evaluate quality enhancement techniques that focus on the impact of services and supports on a student's perceived quality of life. Currently, special education services worldwide are implementing quality enhancement techniques that are environmentally based or program based.

Environmentally based enhancement techniques

Implementation of two concepts related to environmentally based quality enhancement techniques poses challenges and opportunities. One is the belief that an enhanced quality of life is the result of a good match between a person's wants and needs and his or her fulfillment and environments. The importance of these two concepts is supported by data suggesting that reducing the discrepancy between a person and his or her environment increases the person's assessed quality of life (Schalock, Keith, Hoffman, & Karan, 1989).

Two examples illustrate how one might use environmentally based techniques. One technique involves the assessment of environmental characteristics such as: physical or social integration, age-appropriate interpretations and structures, culture-appropriate interpretations and structures, model coherency, developmental growth orientation, and quality of setting (Felce & Perry, 1997). The second involves the design of environments that are user-friendly and meet the following criteria (Ferguson, 1997): opportunity for involvement; easy access to the outdoor environment; modifications to stairs, water taps, door knobs; safety (e.g., handrails, safety glass, nonslip walking surfaces); convenience (e.g., orientation aids such as color coding and universal pictographs); accessibility; sensory stimulation (windows, less formal furniture); prosthetics (personal computers, specialized assistive devices, and high-tech environments); and opportunity for choice and control (e.g., lights, temperature, personal space and territory).

Program-Based Enhancement Techniques

Once the core dimensions of quality of life are identified, it is possible to implement program-based [quality] enhancement techniques that will result in an enhanced perceived quality of life for the student. Examples include:

- Emotional well-being: increased safety, stable and predictable environments, positive feedback
- Interpersonal relations: foster friendships, encourage intimacy, support families
- Material well-being: ownership, possessions, employment
- Personal development: functional, application-oriented education, augmentative technology
- Physical well-being: health care, mobility, wellness, nutrition
- Self-determination: choices, personal control, decisions, personal goals
- Social inclusion: community role, community integration, volunteerism
- Rights: privacy, voting, due process, civic responsibilities

Positive Behavior Supports

Although most closely related to emotional well-being and the program-based enhancement techniques listed above (related to "emotional well-being"), educators are using positive behavior supports increasingly to enhance both positive behavioral change and positive outcomes in students who have problem behaviors. As discussed by Horner (2000), positive behavior support involves focusing on the assessment and reengineering of environments so that students "with problem behaviors experience reductions in their problem behaviors and increased social, personal, and professional quality in their lives" (p. 181).

The technology of positive behavior support applies basic laws of behavior analysis to produce broad changes in the educational environment and options available to students in special education who exhibit problem behaviors. Underlying this technology are three key implementation concepts for students with disabilities who exhibit behavior problems (Horner, 2000, pp. 183–184):

1. Behavior support should reduce problem behaviors and affect how a person lives.
2. Functional assessment is the foundation for understanding patterns of problem behavior.
3. Behavior support should be comprehensive in structure and scope.

Persons With Disabilities Assessing Their Quality of Life

One of the changes over the last two decades is the development of a strong self-advocacy movement in which persons with disabilities are advocating for more opportunities to participate in the mainstream of life. The impact of this change is obvious to most readers who are aware of consumers advocating for increased inclusion and individual supports within regular environments. What might be less obvious is the increasing role that consumers are playing in assessment and evaluation activities. To this end, there is every indication that we will continue to see the emergence and further development of what typically is referred to as "participatory action research," defined as

> an emerging approach to problem solving and social change that is particularly suited to issues of quality of life....[It is] described as the *sine qua non* when studying subjective outcomes. . . . PAR relies on the involvement of stakeholders who can either identify subjective elements of their own lives that warrant change or understand the social contexts in which change occurs. Individuals...can contribute to our collective understanding of how quality of life can be conceptualized, what a life of quality looks like, and ways to improve outcomes. (Whitney-Thomas, 1997, p. 181)

Participatory action research is rapidly becoming the method of choice among quality-of-life researchers. For example, consumers are working jointly with researchers to determine the importance of the core quality-of-life dimensions. Preliminary work suggests that for children and youth, the most important dimensions might be personal development, self-determination, interpersonal relationships, and social inclusion (Schalock, 1996b; Stark & Goldsbury, 1990); for adults, the most important dimensions may well be emotional well-being, material well-being, and interpersonal relations (Elorriaga, Garcia, Martinez, & Unamunzaga, 2000; Verdugo, 2000); and for the elderly, physical well-being, interpersonal relationships, and emotional well-being could be the most important dimensions (Schalock, DeVries, & Lebsack, 1999).

Consumers also are involved in assessing their own quality of life. For example, we (Schalock et al., 2000) have shown that consumers are excellent surveyors and can assess other consumers' quality of life with highly acceptable reliability and validity. By adapting survey techniques and the language used in the survey, 81% of consumers were able to respond for themselves, despite having significant cognitive, physical, and language limitations.

Two significant findings came of these studies. First, among the 50 questions asked in the survey, more than three-fifths of the consumers gave the most positive response to eight questions: have transportation, feel safe in neighborhood, staff help with community integration, get needed services, help with goals, feel part of family, concern with health, and people help you learn. Seven questions received the most negative response by the majority of the respondents: what others expect, have a key to home, dating opportunities, number of groups I belong to, who decides on how I spend my money, housemate choice, and have a job.

Second, a path analysis of the results indicated that two areas of subjective well-being contribute directly to satisfaction with life. The most important of the two is dignity (the more dignity with which consumers feel people treat them, the more satisfied they are with life). The second is their work life (the greater the quality of their work life, the more satisfied they are with life overall).

The path analysis also indicated that the degree of independence consumers feel and their integration into the community do not directly affect measured satisfaction, and that these two variables affect satisfaction only indirectly as they affect dignity and work. Further, the path analysis indicated that consumer abilities, as measured by intelligence tests, have no direct effect on life satisfaction, and characteristics such as age, communication problems, and ambulating difficulties have no effect, either directly or indirectly, on life satisfaction.

CONCLUSIONS

We believe that an emphasis on promoting self-determination and quality of life will provide an entry point for discussions concerning the integration of special education with general education. State and local standards and the curricula derived from these standards emphasize, across elementary, middle, and secondary school ages, instructional experiences pertaining to goal setting, problem solving, decision making and other self-determination-related components. The presence of such standards illustrates the universality of need for instruction in self-determination for all students.

In turn, as the educational programs of all students focus on promoting and enhancing self-determination, it will become more and more important that educational programs, school reform efforts, and accountability systems attend to a student's quality of life as an outcome which is specifically targeted and for which systems become accountable. A focus on self-determination leads inevitably to the need to consider personal and personally valued outcomes for students, and to move beyond accountability systems that rely solely on normative outcomes (via testing) or process indicators (e.g., compliance with IEP mandates in IDEA).

REFERENCES

Agran, M. (1997). *Student-directed learning: Teaching self-determination skills.* Pacific Grove, CA: Brooks/Cole.

Agran, M., Marchand-Martella, N.E., & Martella, R.C. (1994). *Promoting health and safety: Skills for independent living.* Baltimore: Paul H. Brookes.

Agran, M., Snow, K., & Swaner, J. (1999). Teacher perceptions of self-determination: Benefits, characteristics, strategies. *Education & Training in Mental Retardation & Developmental Disabilities, 34,* 293–301.

Bandura, A. B. (1977). Self-efficacy: Toward a unifying theory of behavioral change. *Psychological Review, 84,* 191–215.

Baron, J. & Brown, R.V. (1991). Introduction. In J. Baron & R.V. Brown (Eds.), *Teaching decision making to adolescents.* Hillsdale, NJ: Lawrence Erlbaum Associates.

Beyth-Marom, R., Fischhoff, B., Jacobs Quadrel, M., & Furby, L. (1991). Teaching decision-making to adolescents: A critical review. In J. Baron & R.V. Brown (Eds.), *Teaching decision mak-*

ing to adolescents. Hillsdale, NJ: Lawrence Erlbaum Associates.

Brown, F. Appel, C., Corsi, L. & Wenig, B. (1993). Choice diversity for people with severe disabilities. *Education & Training in Mental Retardation, 28,* 318–326.

Chadsey-Rusch, J. (1986). Identifying and teaching valued social behaviors. In F.R. Rusch (Ed.), *Competitive employment: Service delivery models, methods and issues* (pp. 273–287). Baltimore: Paul H. Brookes.

Chadsey-Rusch, J., Rusch, F., & O'Reilly, M.F. (1991). Transition from school to integrated communities. *Remedial & Special Education, 12,* 23–33.

Committee on Appropriate Test Use. (1999). *High stakes.* Washington, DC: National Research Council.

Committee on Goals 2000 and the Inclusion of Students with Disabilities (1997). *Educating one and all: Students with disabilities and standards-based reform.* Washington, DC: National Academy Press.

Council on Quality and Leadership in Supports for People with Disabilities (1997). *Personal outcome measures.* Towson, MD: Author.

Cummins, R. A. (1997). Assessing quality of life. In R. I. Brown (Ed.), *Quality of life for people with disabilities: Models, research and practice* (pp. 116–150). Cheltenham, UK: Stanley Thornes (Publishers) Ltd.

Deci, E.L. & Chandler, C.L. (1986). The importance of motivation for the future of the LD field. *Journal of Learning Disabilities, 19,* 587–594.

Doll, B., Sands, D.J., Wehmeyer, M.L., & Palmer, S. (1996). Promoting the development and acquisition of self-determined behavior. In D.J. Sands & M.L. Wehmeyer (Eds.), *Self-determination across the life span: Independence and choice for people with disabilities* (pp. 63–88). Baltimore: Paul H. Brookes.

D'Zurilla, T. J.. & Goldfried, M. R. (1971). Problem-solving and behavior modification. *Journal of Abnormal Psychology, 78,* 107–126.

Elorriaga, J., Garcia, L., Martinez, J. & Unamunzaga, E. (2000). Quality of life of persons with mental retardation in Spain. In K.D. Keith & R. L. Schalock (Eds.), *Cross-cultural perspectives on quality of life.* Washington, DC: American Association on Mental Retardation.

Felce, D. (1997). Defining and applying the concept of quality of life. *Journal of Intellectual Disability Research, 41* (2), 126–135.

Felce, D. & Perry, J. (1997). A PASS 3 evaluation of community residences in Wales. *Mental Retardation, 35*(3), 170–176.

Ferguson, R. V. (1997). Environmental design and quality of life. In R. I. Brown (Ed.), *Quality of life for people with disabilities: Models, research and practice* (pp. 56–70). Cheltenham, UK: Stanley Thornes (Publishers) Ltd.

Field, S. (1996). Self-determination instructional strategies for youth with learning disabilities. *Journal of Learning Disabilities, 29,* 40–52.

Field, S., Martin, J.E., Miller, R., Ward, M., & Wehmeyer, M.L. (1998). *A practical guide to teaching self-determination.* Reston, VA: Council for Exceptional Children.

Grisso, T., & Vierling, L. (1978). Minor's consent to treatment: A developmental perspective. *Professional Psychology, 9,* 412–427.

Halpern, A. (1985). Transition: A look at the foundations. *Exceptional Children, 51,* 479–486.

Halpern, A. (1993). Quality of life as a conceptual framework for evaluating transition outcomes. *Exceptional Children, 59,* 486–498.

Hatton, C. (1998). Whose quality of life is it anyway? Some problems with the emerging quality of life consensus. *Mental Retardation, 36*(2), 104–115.

Horner, R. H. (2000). Positive behavior supports. In M. Wehmeyer & J. R. Patton (Eds.), *Mental retardation in the 21st century* (pp. 181–196).

Hughes, C., & Agran, M. (1993). Teaching persons with severe disabilities to use self-instruction in community settings: An analysis of applications. *Journal of the Association for Persons with Severe Handicaps, 18,* 261–274.

Hughes, C. A., Korinek, L., & Gorman, J. (1991). Self-management for students with mental retardation in public school settings: A research review. *Education & Training in Mental Retardation, 26,* 271–291.

Hughes, C., & Hwang, B. (1996). Attempts to conceptualize and measure quality of life. In R. L. Schalock (Ed.), *Quality of life: Vol. 1. Conceptualization and measurement* (pp. 51–62). Washington, DC: American Association on Mental Retardation.

Hughes, C., & Rusch, F.R. (1989). Teaching supported employees with severe mental retardation to solve problems. *Journal of Applied Behavior Analysis, 22,* 365–372.

Kaser-Boyd, N., Adelman, H.S., & Taylor, L. (1985). Minors' ability to identify risks and benefits of therapy. *Professional Psychology: Research & Practice, 16,* 411–417.

Keith, K. D., & Schalock, R. L. (1994). The measurement of quality of life in adolescents: The Quality of Student Life Questionnaire. *American Journal of Family Therapy, 22*(1), 83–87.

Keith, K. D., & Schalock, R. L. (1995). *Quality of student life questionnaire.* Worthington, OH: IDS Publishing.

Lefcourt, H. M. (1976). *Locus of control.* Hillsdale, NJ: Lawrence Erlbaum.

Lent, R. W., Bron, S. D., & Larkin, K. C. (1984). Relationship of self-efficacy expectations to academic achievement and persistence. *Journal of Counseling Psychology, 31,* 356–362.

Martin, J. E., & Marshall, L.H. (1995). ChoiceMaker: A comprehensive self-determination transition program. *Intervention in School & Clinic, 30,* 147–156.

Martin, J. E., Marshall, L. H., Maxson, L., & Jerman, P. (1993). *Self-directed IEP: Teacher's manual.* Colorado Springs: University of Colorado at Colorado Springs, Center for Educational Research.

Morningstar, M. E., Kleinhammer-Tramill, J., & Lattin, D. (1999). Using successful models of student-centered transition planning and services for adolescents with disabilities. *Focus on Exceptional Children, 31*(9), 1–19.

Park, H. S., & Gaylord-Ross, R. (1989). A problem-solving approach to social skills training in employment settings with mentally retarded youth. *Journal of Applied Behavior Analysis, 22,* 373–380.

Parmenter, T. & Donelly, M. (1997). An analysis of the dimensions of quality of life. In R. I. Brown (Ed.), *Quality of life for people with disabilities: Models, research and practice* (pp. 91–114). Cheltenham, UK: Stanley Thornes (Publishers) Ltd.

Pulliam, J. D., & Van Patten, J. (1995). *History of education in America* (6th ed.). Englewood Cliffs, NJ: Merrill-Prentice Hall.

Renwick, R., & Brown, I. (1996). The Centre for Health Promotion's conceptual approach to quality of life. In R. Renwick, I. Brown, & M. Nagler (Eds.), *Quality of life in health promotion and rehabilitation: Conceptual approaches, issues, and applications* (pp. 75–86). Thousand Oaks, CA: Sage Publications.

Rotter, J. B. (1966). Generalized expectancies for internal versus external control of reinforcement. Psychological Monographs, 80, (1, Whole No. 609).

Schalock, R. L. (1994). Quality of life, quality enhancement, and quality assurance: Implications for program planning and evaluation in the field of mental retardation and developmental disabilities. *Evaluation & Program Planning, 17,* 121–131.

Schalock, R. L. (1995). *Outcome-based evaluation:* New York: Plenum Press.

Schalock, R. L. (1996a). Reconsidering the conceptualization and measurement of quality of life. In R. L. Schalock (Ed.), *Quality of life: Vol. 1. Conceptualization and measurement.* Washington, DC: American Association on Mental Retardation.

Schalock, R. L. (1996b). The quality of children's lives. In A. H. Fine & N. M. Fine (Eds.), *Therapeutic recreation for exceptional children: Let me in, I want to play* (2d ed.) (pp. 83–94). Springfield, IL: Charles C. Thomas Publishers, Ltd.

Schalock, R. L. (2000). Three decades of quality of life. In M. Wehmeyer & J. R. Patton (Eds.), *Mental retardation in the 21st century* (pp. 335–358). Austin: Pro-Ed Publishers.

Schalock, R. L. (in press). Outcome-based evaluation, 2d ed. New York: Kluwer Academic/Plenum

Publishers.

Schalock, R. L., Bonham, G., & Marchand, C. (2000). Consumer based quality of life assessment: A path model of perceived satisfaction. *Evaluation & Program Planning, 23,* 77–87.

Schalock, R. L., DeVries, D. & Lebsack, J. (1999). Rights, quality measures, and program changes. In S. S. Herr & G. Weber (Eds.), *Aging, rights and quality of life: Prospects for older persons with developmental disabilities* (pp. 81–92). Baltimore: Paul H. Brookes.

Schalock, R. L. & Faulkner, E. H. (1997). Cross-validation of a contextual model of quality of life. *European Journal on Mental Disability, 4*(1), 18–27.

Schalock, R. L., Keith, K.A., Hoffman, K. & Karan, O.C. (1989). Quality of life: Its measurement and use. *Mental Retardation, 27*(1), 25–31.

Schalock, R. L., Lemanowicz, J. A. Conroy, J. W., & Feinstein, C. S. (1994). A multivariate investigative study of the correlates of quality of life. *Journal on Developmental Disabilities, 3*(2), 59–73.

Schunk, D. H. (1985). Participation in goal setting: Effects on self-efficacy and skills of learning disabled children. *Journal of Special Education, 19,* 307–316.

Schunk, D. H. (1989). Social cognitive theory and self-regulated learning. In B. J. Zimmerman & D. H. Schunk (Eds.), *Self-regulated learning and academic achievement: Theory, research and practice.* New York: Springer-Verlag.

Shevin, M., & Klein, N.K. (1984). The importance of choice-making skills for students with severe disabilities. *Journal of the Association for Persons with Severe Handicaps, 9,* 159–166.

Sigafoos, A. D., Feinstein, C. B., Damond, M., & Reiss, D. (1988). The measurement of behavioral autonomy in adolescence: The Autonomous Functioning Checklist, in C. B. Feinstein, A. Esman, J. Looney, G. Orvin, J. Schimel, A. Schwartzberg, A. Sorsky, & M. Sugar (Eds.), *Adolescent Psychiatry* (Vol. 15, pp. 432–462). Chicago: University of Chicago Press.

Sitlington, P. L. (1996). Transition to living: The neglected component of transition programming for individuals with learning disabilities. *Journal of Learning Disabilities, 29,* 31–39.

Stark, J. A. & Goldsbury, T. (1990). Quality of life from childhood to adulthood. In R. L. Schalock (Ed.), *Quality of life: Perspectives and issues* (pp. 71–84). Washington, DC: American Association on Mental Retardation.

Sykes, G., & Plastrik, P. (1993). *Standards setting as educational reform* (ERIC Clearinghouse on Teacher Education, Trends and Issues Paper, No. 8). Washington, DC: American Association of Colleges for Teacher Education.

Verdugo, M. A. (2000). Quality of life for persons with mental retardation and developmental disabilities in Spain: The present zeitgeist. In K. D. Keith & R. L. Schalock (Eds.), *Cross-cultural perspectives on quality of life.* Washington, DC: American Association on Mental Retardation.

Ward, M. J. (1996). Coming of age in the age of self-determination: A historical and personal perspective. In D. J. Sands & M. L. Wehmeyer (Eds.), *Self-determination across the life span: Independence and choice for people with disabilities* (pp. 1–14). Baltimore: Paul H. Brookes.

Ward, M.J., & Kohler, P.D. (1996). Promoting self-determination for individuals with disabilities: Content and process. In L.E. Powers, G.H.S. Singer, & J. Sowers (Eds.), *On the road to autonomy: Promoting self-competence in children and youth with disabilities* (pp. 275–290). Baltimore: Paul H. Brookes.

Wehmeyer, M. L. (1994). Perceptions of self-determination and psychological empowerment of adolescents with mental retardation. *Education & Training in Mental Retardation & Developmental Disability, 29,* 9–21.

Wehmeyer, M. L. (1996). Self-determination as an educational outcome: Why is it important to children, youth and adults with disabilities? In D. J. Sands & M. L. Wehmeyer (Eds.), *Self-determination across the life span: Independence and choice for people with disabilities* (pp. 15–34). Baltimore: Paul H. Brookes.

Wehmeyer, M. L. (1998). Self-determination and individuals with significant disabilities:

Examining meanings and misinterpretations. *Journal of the Association for Persons with Severe Handicaps, 23,* 5–16.

Wehmeyer, M. L., Agran, M., & Hughes, C. (1998). *Teaching self-determination to students with disabilities: Basic skills for successful transition.* Baltimore: Paul H. Brookes.

Wehmeyer, M. L., Agran, M., & Hughes, C. (2000). A national survey of teacher's promotion of self-determination and student-directed learning. *Journal of Special Education, 34,* 58–68.

Wehmeyer, M. L., & Kelchner, K. (1994). Interpersonal cognitive problem-solving skills of individuals with mental retardation. *Education & Training in Mental Retardation, 29,* 265–278.

Wehmeyer, M. L., Kelchner, K., & Richards, S. (1995). Individual and environmental factors related to the self-determination of adults with mental retardation. *Journal of Vocational Rehabilitation, 5,* 291–305.

Wehmeyer, M. L., Kelchner, K., & Richards. S. (1996). Essential characteristics of self-determined behaviors of adults with mental retardation and developmental disabilities. *American Journal on Mental Retardation, 100,* 632–642.

Wehmeyer, M. L., Lattin, D., & Agran, M. (in press). Achieving access to the general curriculum for students with mental retardation. *Education and training in mental retardation and developmental disabilities.*

Wehmeyer, M. L., & Sands, D. J. (1998). *Making it happen: Student involvement in education planning, decision-making and implementation.* Baltimore: Paul H. Brookes.

Wehmeyer, M. L., & Schwartz, M. (1997). Self-determination and positive adult outcomes: A follow-up study of youth with mental retardation or learning disabilities. *Exceptional Children, 63,* 245–255.

Wehmeyer, M. L., & Schwartz, M. (1998). The self-determination focus of transition goals for students with mental retardation. *Career Development for Exceptional Individuals, 21,* 75–86.

Wehmeyer, M. L. & Schwartz, M. (1998b). The relationship between self-determination, quality of life, and life satisfaction for adults with mental retardation. *Education & Training in Mental Retardation & Developmental Disabilities, 33,* 3–12.

Whitman, T. L. (1990). Self-regulation and mental retardation. *American Journal on Mental Retardation, 94,* 347–362.

Whitney-Thomas, J. (1997). Participatory action research as an approach to enhancing quality of life for individuals with disabilities. In R. L. Schalock (Ed.), *Quality of life: Vol. 2. Application to persons with disabilities* (pp. 181–198). Washington, DC: American Association on Mental Retardation.

Zimmerman, M. A. (1990). Toward a theory of learned hopefulness: A structural model analysis of participation and empowerment. *Journal of Research in Personality, 24,* 71–86.

Supporting Students With Health Needs in Schools

Paris DePaepe, Linda Garrison-Kane, and Jane Doelling

According to the 23rd Annual Report to Congress (U.S. Department of Education, 2001) on the Implementation of Individuals with Disabilities Education Act, 254,110 students were classified as eligible under the *Other Health Impairment* category in 1999–2000. This number represents a 351% increase from the total number of students eligible in that category during 1990–1991. The increase in percentage of students who have health problems that adversely affect their educational performance has been greater than any other eligibility category since 1990. During 1999–2000, 26% of children in early childhood special education (ECSE) received medication and 16% reportedly used medical equipment such as nebulizers and breathing monitors.

Because more children are found eligible for special education services as a result of having an "other health impairment" special education professionals have voiced concern about the inadequate training that preservice teachers receive in this area (Heller, Fredrick, Dykes, Best & Cohen, 1999). This concern is further exacerbated by the increasing trend toward a noncategorical or cross-categorical focus within special education teacher preparation programs in the United States. Teachers who will instruct students with mild to moderate disabilities need a common core of knowledge and skill competencies (Simpson, Whelan, & Zabel, 1993). These students will have mental retardation (MR), learning disabilities (LD), or emotional disturbances (ED) of a mild to moderate nature. Heller (1997) asserted that teachers also need appropriate preservice training to serve students diagnosed with a variety of physical and health impairments and warned that these students are at significant risk when educators are not adequately prepared to meet their specialized health care needs.

The Council for Exceptional Children (CEC) (2000) preservice teacher preparation program standards for beginning special education teachers include specific knowledge and skills critical to teaching students with other health impairments. In part, special educators need to acquire knowledge and skills related to students with health disabilities. Training should emphasize:

- Knowledge regarding health conditions, and their effect on development and student behavior; etiology of and medical aspects of the conditions
- Related psychological and emotional characteristics
- Methods for screening, referral, and placement; implementation of appropriate assistive technology and other accommodations
- Lesson plan adaptation for students with specialized health conditions; use of outside resources for programming
- Collaboration with related services personnel to maximize academic engaged time, as well as identification of specialized service and organizations
- Identification of roles and responsibilities of school medical and related service personnel, as well as professional organizations and networks that may serve as resources.

In addition, CEC noted that beginning special education teachers should have knowledge of infectious diseases and their transmission routes, and must follow confidentiality policies related to both academic and medical records.

Special education and general education teachers must have the background knowledge and skills necessary to plan for and provide appropriate educational services, school-related health services, and accommodations for students diagnosed with a wide variety of health conditions. Heller et al. (1999) assessed the perceived competency of general education and special education teachers, who taught students with physical and health impairments, with respect to their preparation for working effectively with that population. Among special educators who were certified to teach students with physical and health disabilities, 40% reported that they were not well trained in 11 of 23 critical competencies. The authors cautioned that generic cross-categorical special education teacher training programs and certifications will lead to fewer teachers with specialties in physical and health disabilities.

Providing education and related services that include school health care for students with disabilities has brought the field to an educational and medical crossroad (Caldwell & Sirvis, 1991; Johnson, Lubker, & Fowler, 1988; Thies, 1999). This issue is further magnified by the conflicting judicial rulings on what constitutes a related health service or a physician-provided service for students with health impairments (Katsiyannis & Yell, 2000). Currently, individualized education program (IEP) teams must differentiate what service augments and supports this student population versus what constitutes a supplementary aid and service that educates the student in a general education environment (Etscheidt & Bartlett, 1999). School personnel require specialized knowledge about each student's educational and health care needs in order to adequately address them (Caldwell & Sirvis). Johnson et al. asserted that schools are unprepared to accomplish this goal.

The professional literature provides teachers with current and valid information regarding the health conditions of students. With the reauthorization of the Individuals with Disabilities Education Act (1997), attention deficit disorder (ADD) and attention deficit hyperactivity disorder (ADHD) are now specifically included within the Other Health Impairment category; however, readers are directed to Reid (1999) for a comprehensive discussion of educational methods and effective class-room-management techniques for students with ADHD. In addition, in an earlier issue of *Focus on Exceptional Children,* Tyler and Colson (1994) provided a comprehensive review of common pediatric conditions (i.e., Down syndrome, Turner syndrome, fragile X, ADHD, cerebral palsy, leukemia, neurofibromatosis, epilepsy, and traumatic brain injury).

In this chapter we first discuss key components relevant to providing appropriate services for students with health care needs. These include individual health care plans, emergency care, and administration of medication, as well as universal precautions. Following is a review of common health conditions of school-aged children and youth (Cross & Jones, 1996), including food allergies, asthma, cystic fibrosis, diabetes (type 1 and type II), epilepsy, and sickle cell disease. In addition, although less common in children living in the United States than in some countries (e.g., Africa), human immunodeficiency virus (HIV) and acquired immunodeficiency syndrome (AIDS) are included in the discussion. An overview of each condition is provided, including medical management. Finally, we discuss school health care needs and related accommodations that may be made for students with each condition.

WHO ARE STUDENTS WITH HEALTH CARE NEEDS?

Students diagnosed with various health conditions who attend public schools may require some degree of accommodations to allow them equal access to educational services. Some students, with health conditions determined to adversely affect their educational performance, may be found to be eligible for special education and related services under the Individuals with Disabilities Education Act [IDEA] (1997) eligibility category Other Health Impairment. These students have:

> Limited strength, vitality or alertness, including a heightened alertness to environmental stimuli, that results in limited alertness with respect to the educational environment, that—(i) Is due to chronic or acute health problems such as asthma, attention deficit disorder or attention deficit hyperactivity disorder, diabetes, epilepsy, a heart condition, hemophilia, lead poisoning, leukemia, nephritis, rheumatic fever, and sickle cell anemia; and (ii) Adversely affects a child's educational performance (IDEA Final Regulations—34 C.F.R. § 300.7 (b) (9).

The American Academy of Pediatrics [AAP], Committee on Children with Disabilities, and Committee on School Health (1990a), however, noted that children with chronic health conditions often do not require special education but will need specific health services within the school setting. Students with documented health conditions who do not meet eligibility criteria for Other Health Impairment should receive reasonable accommodation provided under Section 504 of the Vocational Rehabilitation Act.

PLANNING APPROPRIATE HEALTH CARE SERVICES AND RELATED ACCOMMODATIONS

The American Academy of Pediatrics (AAP) (1990a) recommends close collaboration among school staff, families, and health care providers to plan the provision of student health care. School nurses play a key role in supporting students with health care needs with the child, parents, school staff, and the child's personnel physician and other health care workers to coordinate appropriate services for the student (Williams & McCarthy, 1995). As two students diagnosed with the same health condition may need very different health care and related accommodations, child-specific information must be obtained from parents or legal guardians and personal physicians. This will facilitate planning appropriate health care services and accommodations for students with chronic health conditions.

School district policies and procedures related to the implementation of first aid, administration of medication, routine health care procedures, and emergency care needed for all students should be in place. Unfortunately, Heller, Fredrick, and Rithmire's study (1997) reported that many schools were without such procedures.

Identifying School Health Services

School health services are identified within the individual health care plan for students eligible under IDEA, and the health care plan is attached to the student's individualized education program (IEP). Rapport (1996) identified medication delivery, skin care, and catheterization, as well as gastronomy and respiratory care, as examples of health-related services and procedures that some students with disabilities may need to benefit from their special education programs. As a result of the seminal related services ruling in *Irving Independent School District v. Tatro* (1984) the U.S. Supreme Court determined that clean intermittent catheterization did constitute a school health service. A service was to be provided as a "school health service" if three criteria were met:

> (a) the child be disabled and so as to require special education; (b) without the necessary service during the school day, the child would be unable to participate in an educational program; and (c) the service could be performed by a nurse or other qualified person, but not by a physician. (Rapport, p. 542)

Such procedures may be consequently determined to be a "school health service" if in part it is a service that can be provided by a school nurse or other qualified person (IDEA Final Regulations—34 C.F.R. § 300.24(b)(12)).

Although federal regulations specify the need for medical service as it relates to diagnostic evaluations, a clear distinction between required educational health care services and medical services has become blurred within the legal system (Janz et al., 1997). For example, Katsiyannis and Yell (2000) noted that several cases since the Tatro ruling, such as *Neely v. Rutherford County School (1995), Granite School District v. Shannon M. (1992), Detsel v. Auburn Enlarged City School District Board of Education (1987)* and *Bevin H. v. Wright (1987)*, did not reflect the previous standard established in the 1984 Tatro decision. In these cases, the judges seemed to rule on several factors that included (but were not limited to) the expense of the health care services, the potential for liability for the districts in implementing the procedures and that "some of the medical services were potentially life-threatening" (p. 321).

Subsequently, the Supreme Court contributed to the debate over what constitutes a school health care service, ruling in favor of the parents in Cedar Rapids Community School District v. Garret F. in 1999. In this case, the student required numerous health services, such as ventilator monitoring and cleaning, tracheotomy supervision, frequent body repositioning, catheterization, and food/liquid intake assistance, while attending school. The court ruled that the student required these services to attend school; therefore, the medical assistance was considered a related educational health care service.

The Garret F. ruling was aligned with the previous (1989) case, *Timothy W. v. Rochester (NH) School District* case, which applied "the zero reject principle established by Congress" (Katsiyannis & Yell, 2000, p. 322).

The comprehensive nature of health care services and plans for students with disabilities has led to school districts and states purchasing liability insurance and developing policy manuals on the administration of these services. For example, "School personnel may be civilly and even criminally liable if they provide services within the scope of nursing practice that have not been properly delegated and supervised by a nurse" (Janz et al., 1997, p. 32). Katsiyannis and Yell (2000), Yell and Shriner (1997) and Yell (1998) provide a comprehensive review of educational court cases and related health care services.

Individual Health Care Plans

Thies (1999) noted that diabetes, cystic fibrosis, and asthma can each impact children to significantly different degrees. Consequently, individual health care plans should be developed by school nurses, teachers, and other school staff (e.g., nutritionist, physical therapist) in close collaboration with parents and health care providers (i.e., physician, specialty nurses) knowledgeable of a child's condition and needs. Components of an individual health care plan are:

- Child's name, picture, and emergency contact information (family and physician)
- Case manager(s) and/or persons responsible for implementation of treatment with qualifications specified (to include primary treatment contact with multiple backup contacts)

- Diagnosis/description of the condition, health history, including specific symptoms and level of severity
- Ongoing daily treatments including health care procedures and medication administration (location of medication, dosage, times for medication delivery, medication delivery route, side effects, expiration date, school personnel responsible for treatment)
- Monitoring responsibilities (specific roles of school personnel, data-keeping responsibilities and data/record forms, symptoms, and characteristics)
- Emergency procedures (if needed, include on first page of health care plan with bold or highlights), including specific symptoms that indicate an emergency, sequenced list of action(s) to be taken (e.g., accessing specific trained school personnel, medication administration, starting CPR, calling emergency medical service), and monitoring responsibilities (e.g., completing injury report)
- Additional accommodations to be provided, including identification of physical access changes (classroom, equipment, other schools environments), changes in instruction and activities (e.g., rest breaks when fatigued, changes in activity type or length), as well as assistive technology.

To reduce potential liability, it is recommended that school officials obtain a *medical release* for treatment that is outlined within the child's health care plan (AAP, 1990a). See Porter, Haynie, Bierle, Caldwell, and Palfrey (1997) for forms (i.e., health care plan checklist, health care plan, health care procedures information sheet, physician order for special health care) useful when planning for students with school health care needs.

A health care plan should identify the individuals responsible for implementing and monitoring school health services. Typically, school nurses' responsibilities include monitoring students' general health, dispensing medications and carrying out nursing procedures, managing emergency situations, and providing supervision to health aides (Williams & McCarthy, 1995). Heller et al. (1997), however, found that in addition to school nurses, teachers, teaching assistants, and parents implemented a range of health care procedures for children within the schools examined. The most common procedures performed were seizure and blood glucose monitoring and medication administration. Those authors noted that training must be provided to those individuals designated to implement such procedures as well as all staff members who are likely to observe potential complications or problems.

Medication Administration

Administration of medication often is included within a student's health care plan (Cross & Jones, 1996). Students' medical needs may require that medication be delivered routinely at school for chronic health conditions (e.g., diabetes, epilepsy, asthma) as well as for acute health problems (e.g., infections associated with cystic fibrosis) (Heller et al., 2000). In these cases, schools have to obtain written parental request to have the medication administered at school, and obtain a signed physician's authorization to have the medication given to the students at school. Additional information related to medication delivery, storage, and common and rare side effects also have to be documented.

School personnel who are routinely responsible for the medication delivery will have to identify and provide appropriate training related to medication delivery, documentation, and monitoring for side effects for each student receiving medication at school. The AAP (1990a) recommended that schools develop policies related to medication administration, storage, and guidelines for student self-administration of medications when appropriate.

The following resources can be used within an initial orientation for school personnel who will be involved with students who receive medication. These people include the staff members directly responsible for delivering medication as well as staff members who will not personally deliver medications but who will be in a position to observe for potential medication side effects.

Assisting Children with Medications at School: A Guide for School Personnel. Denver: University of Colorado Health Sciences Center, School of Nursing, Office of School Health, 1995 (Available from Learner Managed Designs, Lawrence, KS).

> This 35-minute video provides a comprehensive overview of medication delivery for teachers and other school personnel who will be responsible for medication delivery. This video reviews the five rights of medication delivery (i.e., right medication, student, dose, route, and time), medication storage, different medication delivery routes (e.g., oral, inhaled, topical), medication delivery documentation, and demonstrates proper medication administration. This video can provide a basic overview for school personnel to be shown prior to their participating in individualized medication administration training related to specific students.

Medications and Procedures for Administration, by K. Heller, L. Wolff, P. Forney, P. Alberto, M. Schwartzman, and T. Goeckel, in *Meeting Physical and Health Needs of Children with Disabilities,* by K. Heller, P. Forney, P. Alberto, M. Schwartzman, and T. Goeckel (pp. 67–96). Belmont, CA: Wadsworth/Thomson Learning, 2000.

> This book chapter provides a comprehensive discussion of medications and includes content on medication descriptions, administration considerations including receiving medications and medication storage. Standard medication delivery procedures are reviewed in detail. Sample medication authorization and medication delivery documentation forms also are provided.

Emergency Care

The American Academy of Pediatrics (AAP) Committee on School Health (1990b) presented a series of recommendations for emergency care for students in schools. Recognizing that all schools do not hire full-time nurses, the Committee suggested that schools identify specific staff members to be trained and authorized to make urgent care decisions. Schools also should develop and make accessible to school staff *an emergency care manual* and develop procedures for obtaining emergency medical assistance from the community (e.g., fire rescue squads, ambulances). The Committee also recommended that at least two school personnel be trained to manage emergency situations, in accordance with the school emergency manual, until the school nurse, physician, or other emergency personnel can be located.

Training in basic first-aid, identifying and treating anaphylaxis (allergic reactions), and cardiopulmonary resuscitation (CPR) should be provided and be periodically updated. Emergency medical kits, including materials needed to treat severe allergic anaphylactic reactions, should be stored with medications and made accessible to these trained school emergency providers. Finally, procedures for contacting parents, guardians, or other authorized parties must be in place in conjunction with a procedure for completing incident reports related to any school injury or medical incident. See Porter et al. (1997) for sample emergency plans, emergency telephone procedures, and emergency contact information.

Universal Precautions

All school personnel should follow universal precautions, as well as infection control procedures when dealing with blood, bodily fluids, and other body substances (vomit, sputum, etc. when blood is seen within the substances) to protect against the transmission of blood-borne infections (e.g., hepatitis B virus, HIV) to school personnel and students (Giardina & Psota, 1997). Training in the use of universal precautions should be extended to all students, not just those with chronic health conditions.

Protective equipment such as gloves should be used in situations that involve direct exposure (or potential exposure) to blood, skin that has been cut or damaged, mucous membranes, or other bodily substances that may contain blood (Giardina & Psota, 1997). Because some students are allergic to latex and may have a severe allergic reaction after coming in contact with disposable latex gloves, non-latex gloves should be available (Meeropol, 1997).

Universal precautions include appropriate cleaning of contaminated surfaces and proper disposal of all contaminated disposable items (e.g., bandages, gauze, tissues). Nondisposable items should be removed from the area and disinfected while using appropriate protective equipment. A puncture-proof container that can be sealed (called a *sharps container*) should be used in disposing of lancets and needles used by students with diabetes to monitor their blood glucose and administer insulin. Finally, thorough hand washing is recommended especially following removal of gloves (Giardina & Psota, 1997). All schools should develop and follow standard procedures for handling blood and blood-contaminated materials. Future teacher educators should receive specific training in managing blood and other bodily fluids within their teacher training programs (Ballard, White, &

Glascoff, 1990). Resources that provide more indepth reviews of universal precautions are:

Universal Precautions in Schools: Protection from Blood-borne Diseases. Denver: University of Colorado Health Sciences Center, School of Nursing, Office of School Health, 1996 (Available from Learner Managed Designs, Lawrence, KS).

> This 27-minute video provides an overview of universal precautions for school personnel to take to reduce the likelihood of transmission of blood-borne pathogens (e.g., hepatitis B virus, HIV). The video includes a detailed demonstration of proper hand washing to reduce disease transmission to students and school staff and procedures to follow when dealing with student accidents, that introduce blood into the classroom environment.

Universal Precautions and Infection Control in a School Setting, by R. G. Giardina and C. E. Psota, in *Children and Youth Assisted by Medical Technology in Educational Settings—Guidelines for Care* (2d ed., by S. Porter, M. Haynie, T. Bierle, T. H. Caldwell, & J. S. Palfrey, pp. 74–78), Baltimore: Paul H. Brookes, 1997.

> This book chapter reviews universal precautions and infection control procedures designed to prevent transmission of the hepatitis B virus (HBV), human immunodeficiency virus (HIV), and other infections that can be spread through blood.

Clearly, schools have to develop written policies and procedures related to basic first-aid, medication administration, universal precautions, and emergency care for all students. For students with identified health care needs, key staff members must be fully aware of each child's condition, including the cause or etiology, symptoms of and complications of the condition, and an overview of medical treatment of the condition. Of additional importance is to train personnel in specific health care procedures that individual students need.

FOOD ALLERGIES

Educators will have students that have mild to severe food allergies, making knowledge of this condition essential. Food allergies arise because of an immune system overreaction to certain substances in food or drink (Asthma and Allergy Foundation of America [AAFA], 2002). True food allergies occur in 3% to 8% of children (AAFA, 2002; National Institute of Allergy and Infectious Diseases [NIAID], 2001, June 25) and sometimes are confused with conditions such as *food intolerance* and secondary *food sensitivities* (Taylor & Hefle, 2001).

Food intolerance may be described as an abnormal reaction to certain foods or food components and, unlike a true allergy, does not involve the immune system. Lactose (milk) intolerance is offered as a common example. Lactase deficiency affects approximately one in 10 people (NIAID, 2001, June 25). *Secondary food sensitivities* may be an effect of another health condition (such as sensitivity to lactose resulting from a gastrointestinal disorder or medication-induced food sensitivities) (Taylor & Hefle, 2001).

The Asthma and Allergy Foundation of America (2002) reports that "severe, life-threatening reactions are more common with allergies to peanuts, tree nuts, shellfish, fish and eggs" (p. 2) and more severe reactions are noted in individuals with asthma. The latency of the reaction, as well as the severity, depends on the individual's level of sensitivity, amount of food ingested, and how the food is prepared.

Reaction typically occurs within minutes, or up to 1 to 2 hours after the food has been ingested (AAFA, 2002). The eight categories of foods that contribute to more than 90% of allergic reactions are (Taylor & Hefle, 2001, p. 73):

1. Wheat (gluten products)
2. Eggs and egg products
3. Milk and milk products
4. Tree nuts and nut products
5. Shellfish
6. Fish and fish products
7. Peanuts and peanut products
8. Soybeans and soy products

Children frequently outgrow allergies to these foods by age 3; however, peanuts, tree nuts, and shellfish typically cause lifelong reactions (Coutts, 2000; NIAID, 2001, June 25). Symptoms of allergic reactions to food include (Coutts, 2000; Formanek, 2001; NIAID, 2001, June 25):

- Tingling sensation in the mouth
- Difficulty breathing
- Vomiting
- Drop in blood pressure
- Swelling of tongue and throat
- Hives
- Abdominal cramps and/or diarrhea
- Loss of consciousness

Medical Management

Medical management begins with strict avoidance of any food that contributes to an allergic reaction as very small amounts can produce severe symptoms (Coutts, 2000; Formanek, 2001). Because of the severity of the reaction in individuals who are allergic to peanuts, the Department of Transportation ordered airlines to set up *peanut-free zones,* and some schools also followed this recommendation (Hartocollis, 1998). A study by Nowak–Wegrzyn, Conover–Walker, and Wood (2001), however, found that eliminating food allergic reactions in schools is difficult, even in settings where special accommodations have been made for individuals with known food allergies.

Based on the Food and Drug Administration (FDA) guidelines, labeling of food products has become more detailed, with some warnings that indicate when even small traces of peanuts, soy, milk, eggs, or other allergens may be present. Even so, ineffective labeling and identification procedures can contribute to accidental exposures because potential allergens found in peanuts, eggs, and milk may be contained in products not normally associated with those foods (NIAID, 2001, June 25). For additional precautions regarding interpretation of food labels and food preparation, readers are directed to http://www.foodallergy.org/research. html (Food Allergy and Anaphylaxis Network).

Depending on level of severity of an allergic reaction, an oral antihistamine may be prescribed by a child's physician to be administered for reactions that involve mild hives, swelling, or flushing (Hay, Harper, & Coursen, 1994; NIAID, 2001, June 25). Although most children do not have life-threatening allergic attacks, some children do experience a particularly severe allergic reaction known as *anaphylaxis* (Food Allergy and Anaphylaxis Network, 2002, January 2). An anaphylaxis reaction may occur as result of exposure to, or ingestion of, a specific food, medication, or insect sting (Hay et al., 1994). Anaphylactic reactions can be fatal even when they begin with mild symptoms, and immediate treatment with *epinephrine* (adrenaline) followed by medical attention is essential (Dibs & Baker, 1997). If epinephrine has been prescribed for a child at risk for severe allergic reaction to food or other substances, access must be readily available at all times, including recess and school trips.

According to The Food Allergy Initiative (n.d.), the Epi Pen typically is prescribed as a means of injecting needed medication and reversing the symptoms of anaphylaxis. The Initiative recommended that "epinephrine be administered as soon as possible to hold off symptoms, buying time to get to the emergency room for more care" (p. 1). Educators should follow the three R's for treating anaphylaxis:

1. Recognize symptoms.
2. React quickly.
3. Review what happened to prevent it from recurring.

Readers are directed to http://www.foodallergy.org//anaphylaxis.html (Food Allergy and Anaphylaxis Network) and http://foodallergyinitiative.org (Food Allergy Initiative) for detailed information on administration of epinephrine via an Epi Pen; however, personnel designated to administer the Epi Pen, as well as other prescribed medication, must be trained by a medical professional. As a caution, failure to administer epinephrine promptly has been linked to several fatalities and near fatalities (Hay et al., 1994).

School Health Care and Related Accommodations

The physician should provide guidelines for exposure to foods that result in intolerance and sensitivity and should approve any health care plan for a child with food allergies. Even though the child may be well between episodes, the importance of a structured written health care plan, including a plan for emergencies, as a component of the IEP or Section 504 plan is stressed (Hay et al., 1994). In addition to the components already discussed, the individual health care plan for a child with an allergy should include:

- The substance or food the child is allergic to, as well as a detailed plan for food avoidance
- Location(s) of the Epi Pen, instructions for administration, notation regarding expiration date, and directives regarding medical follow-up
- The personnel trained in CPR and administration of the Epi Pen
- A list of foods to be avoided, as well as acceptable foods.

Older children at risk for an anaphylactic reaction may have been trained to self-administer medication and carry a syringe of epinephrine in a purse, fanny pack, or backpack. Because this may conflict with school policy on drugs, this must be addressed by the educational team that includes school personnel, the family, and the child's physician. When the individual does not carry epinephrine directly, the medication should be stored in multiple locations within all school buildings, and the size of the building and time required for access considered.

All educators must be knowledgeable regarding the symptoms of both mild and severe allergic reactions including anaphylaxis. Posting information on symptoms and response procedures in various locations throughout the building is recommended, and this information should be included as standard within district staff development. Wearing a medical alert bracelet or necklace stating the nature of the allergy for any individual at risk for an allergic reaction is also recommended (NIAID, 2001, June 25).

Modifying recipes or menus was a common accommodation reported by more than 50% of school districts (Gandy, Yadrick, Boudreaux, & Smith, 1991). That study indicated that school food service personnel need additional training to serve these students appropriately. The family and physician should guide the school team in developing a *Safe Food and Prohibited Foods List* to be attached to the health care plan. To reduce the possibility of exposure, educators must communicate with families of children within the school and request that foods with the offending allergen *not* be sent to school as treats.

In school settings where foods such as peanuts have been eliminated or contained in zones, caution still is recommended because unknown traces of the allergen may be hidden in foods or a food may have become inadvertently contaminated. Formanek (2001) reports that 25% of 73 varied food samples tested positive for peanuts; however, peanuts were not listed on the labels, so companies had unintentionally introduced allergens into some foods through improper cleaning of utensils and production equipment. Further, one brand of a product may be safe while another is not, and foods previously determined to be safe may have changed ingredients without changing packaging (Formanek, 2001). These findings suggest the need for extreme care in food preparation as well as cleaning routines in the school setting.

ASTHMA

Asthma is a chronic lung condition characterized by inflammation, obstruction, and increased sensitivity of airways (Aronson, 1995). This condition contributes to significant rates of school absenteeism (Getch & Neuharth–Pritchett, 1999; Environmental Protection Agency [EPA] 2001, November 27). In 1981, 3% of children in the United States were diagnosed with asthma, and in 1998 asthma had been diagnosed in 5% of U.S. children (Federal Interagency Forum on Child and Family Statistics, 2001). But Raj, Mishra, Feinsilver, and Fein (2000) and Rana, Jurgens, Mangione, Elia, and Tollerud (2000) caution that asthma may be inadequately diagnosed, resulting in an underestimate of its prevalence, and state the need for diligence in proper identification and treatment. Other sources have indicated that asthma affects as many as 7% to 10% of children (Aronson, 1995; Lung Association, 2002, July 19).

Individuals with this condition have hypersensitive airways, and asthma symptoms may be triggered by food, exercise, weather change, viruses, or environmental substances that irritate the lungs (Celano & Geller, 1993; Simeonsson, Lorimer, Shelley, & Sturtz, 1995). When the person is exposed to a trigger, additional mucus is produced, which subsequently clogs air tubes. The air tubes swell and muscles within the tubes tighten, causing the tubes to narrow or constrict.

Some asthma triggers are:

- Food allergens
- Respiratory infections and viruses
- Exercise (overexertion)
- Cold air
- Environmental allergens (chemicals, gases, cigarette smoke, dust, feathers, mold)

Symptoms and warning signs of asthma include:

- Shortness of breath
- Nasal flaring
- Complaints from child regarding pain, tightness in chest, and/or difficulty breathing
- Wheezing or chronic, persistent cough
- Irritability and/or restlessness
- Blue tint of lips, nails, or change in face color
- Rapid breathing
- Fever and/or headache
- Watery or glassy eyes and sneezing
- Sore throat, itchy throat or chest
- Drop in peak flow reading (Aronson, 1995; Celano & Geller, 1993; Getch & Neuharth-Pritchett, 1999; Schwartz, 1999; Simeonsson et al., 1995)

Increasing hospitalization and mortality rates are being reported among children with this condition (da Costa, Rapoff, Lemanek, & Goldstein, 1997), with symptoms of varying severity. When individuals experience a severe attack, talking and breathing can become difficult (American Lung Association [ALA], 2002a; The Lung Association, n.d.).

Medical Management

Asthma attacks may have to be treated with rest, medications, reductions and restrictions in physical activities, and a trip to a doctor or hospital may be required (Aronson, 1995; Celano & Geller, 1993; Getch & Neuharth-Pritchett, 1999; Simeonsson et al., 1995). A variety of both long-term and short-term control medications are available for individuals with asthma, including inhaled, liquid, and oral medications. Long-term medications, designed to control and prevent asthma symptoms, include cromolyn, inhaled steroids, and nedocromil. Short-term or quick-relief medications are designed to be taken when symptoms such as chest tightening, wheezing, and coughing first appear; these medicines include albuteral, prednisone, and ipratropium bromide. Readers are directed to the brochure "Controlling Your Asthma," published by the National Heart, Lung, and Blood Institute [NHLBI], National Institutes of Health (n.d.), for a listing of common long-term and quick-relief asthma-control medications.

Some asthma medications are inhaled. Possible benefits are smaller medication dosages and medication directed to the needed area without traveling through the stomach and circulatory system (Aronson, 1995). Both metered-dose inhalers and nebulizers may be utilized to deliver inhaled asthma medication. A nebulizer is a machine that creates a mist and delivers medication that is inhaled via a mask or breathing pipe. The medicine is placed in a holding chamber and delivered over a specified period of time.

Individuals with asthma may use metered-dose medication therapies designed to deliver a standard dose of medication to be quickly inhaled. This requires that a child coordinate his or her breathing to inhale at the exact time the medication is delivered, to be able to receive the entire dose of medication. As this can be difficult for some children to accomplish, spacers are available for use with metered-dose medications. Spacers are specially designed chambers or bags into which the medication is first dispensed. The medication then mixes with air within the spacer, allowing the individual to inhale and receive the medication more easily (Cystic Fibrosis Foundation [CFF], 1997a, March).

A peak flow meter, a portable hand-held device used to measure how air flows from the lungs, also may be utilized by individuals with asthma. Peak flow meters identify a drop in the flow of air to allow for a determination of whether medication has to be administered to prevent further symptoms. Readings are compared to acceptable levels established when the child is well to determine when medication is warranted (Aronson, 1995).

School Health Care and Related Accommodations

From an early age, the child with asthma and the caregivers must become familiar with asthma triggers and structure the environment to avoid known allergens and offending substances. School personnel have to be aware of specific asthma triggers that are likely to cause an asthma attack and ways to reduce or eliminate exposure to triggers. Schwartz (1999) recommends that schools conduct cleaning and repairs to reduce and/or eliminate asthma triggers. These efforts may include removing cleaning supplies and plastic furniture and carpeting that may emit toxic fumes, as well as thorough cleaning of the site—in particular, ventilation systems—to reduce exposure to mold, dust, chalk dust, animal dander, cockroaches, and other triggers.

Air quality should be monitored regularly. Sensitivity in scheduling to keep students away from known triggers such as chemicals during cleaning regimens or contained within art supplies may also be beneficial. Preventing exposure to individuals who have respiratory infections is another suggestion (Simeonsson et al., 1995).

Educators also must be sensitive to the needs of students who are susceptible to pet allergens and reduce or eliminate exposure in the school setting. They, too, should be aware of the possibility of exposure via class peers. A study by Almqvist et al. (1999) found an association between the levels of air-borne cat allergens and the number of cat owners in a classroom. This study indicated that allergens may be transferred through direct contact with the pet owner, contact with the pet owner's clothing, or contact with allergen deposits at sites within the classroom.

Other environmental considerations include sensitivity to the effect of cold, dry air, and exercise. Recommendations include encouraging the child to wear a covering over the nose or face in cold weather, ensuring that the child has received the appropriate medication prior to playing outside, and requiring rest after play. In addition, teaching the child to monitor emotional behaviors such as laughing, yelling, or crying may be helpful (Simeonsson et al., 1995).

A management plan based on individual health needs should be developed for each child diagnosed with asthma, for utilization within the school. Information related to peak flow meter use, medication administration, medication delivery devices such as a nebulizer, inhaler, and spacer and other reasonable accommodations (e.g., reducing exposure to triggers, planning for activity restrictions and alternative activities when needed) should be included. The plan should state treatment procedures unique to the individual and be approved by the family and the physician. Specific symptoms that warrant family contact and emergency treatment for a child with asthma should be detailed.

An action plan form that might support the educational team is available by accessing http://www.lung.ca/asthma/ magage/action.html (The Lung Association, n.d.). In addition, the National Heart, Lung, and Blood Institute (n.d.) has developed an asthma action form that can be used to outline routine daily asthma treatment, as well as procedures to follow for mild and more severe asthma symptoms.

For any child receiving medication, teachers must have information on, and monitor for, possible side effects (both common and rare) of all medications the child is taking either at home or while at school. For additional information regarding the use of medication-delivery devices and peak flow meters, medications, and management of asthma, access http://www.lungusa.org/ (American Lung Association). Educators and other school personnel also are directed to "Controlling Your Asthma" (NHLBI, n.d.) for detailed descriptions on correct use of metered-dose inhalers and peak flow meters. A peak flow record chart can facilitate the tracking of peak flow results across days to assist in ongoing treatment planning (see ALA, 2002b).

Celano and Geller (1993) noted the functional relationship between childhood asthma, school absenteeism, and poor academic performance. Diette et al. (2000) found that children with asthma symptoms associated with nocturnal awakenings had both decreased school attendance and academic performance. Given the possible psychosocial effects, as well as the potential for fatigue and missed instruction, a positive behavioral support plan may be warranted for some students with asthma.

In addition, a study by da Costa et al. (1997) indicated the potential for token economy systems to increase adherence to a treatment regimen. Given the prevalence of students with this condition in the school population, as well as the potential severity of the symptoms, educators will have to collaborate with the family and physician, participate in staff-development training, and receive ongoing administrative support to meet the needs of students with asthma.

CYSTIC FIBROSIS

Cystic fibrosis (CF) is an inherited genetic condition that affects the digestive tract as well as the lungs of individuals who have the condition. Those diagnosed with cystic fibrosis have inherited two copies of a defective gene, one from each parent, which causes the condition. Individuals who have only one defective gene are carriers of the condition but are not actively affected by cystic fibrosis (Cystic Fibrosis Foundation [CFF], 2002, March 8). Approximately 30,000 people in the United States have cystic fibrosis (CFF, 2001a, December; Mayo Clinic, 2002, May 14; National Institute of Diabetes & Digestive & Kidney Diseases [NIDDK], 1998, February 12). Estimates are that 1,000 infants are born each year with CF (NIDDK, 1998, February 12) and 1 in 31 individuals in the United States are unaffected carriers of the condition (CFF, 2001a, December).

The condition is seen more often in Caucasians than in African-Americans (CFF, 2002, March 8); CF is found in 1 in 3,000 Caucasian infants (NIDDK, 1998, February 12) and in an estimated 1 in 14,000 African-American live births (cited in FitzSimmons, 1993). Data reported by FitzSimmons (1993) from the National Cystic Fibrosis Patient Registry indicated that, in 1990, 95% of the 17,857 registered patients were Caucasian. Approximately 54% of all registry patients were male, and 61% were 15 years of age or younger. The national registry includes approximately 75% of all diagnosed cases of CF in the United States.

Specifically, CF causes the body to produce "abnormally thick, sticky mucus, due to the faulty transport of sodium and chloride (salt) within the cells lining organs such as the lungs and pancreas, to their outer surfaces. This abnormal mucus clogs the lungs and leads to life-threatening lung infections" (CFF, 2001a, p. 1). These respiratory infections are frequent and at times lead to hospitalizations (NIDDK, 1998, February 12) and possible eventual respiratory failure (Mayo Clinic, 2002, May 14). People with CF have difficulty combating a variety of bacterial infections, most commonly pseudomonas aeruginosa. Individuals diagnosed with cystic fibrosis have a salty taste to their skin (Mayo Clinic).

People with CF also have "insufficient amounts of digestive enzymes for normal digestion. Pancreatic insufficiency causes foul-smelling, bulky bowel movements, malnutrition and slowed growth and development" (NIDDK, 1998, February 12, para. 7). In addition, individuals with CF typically have persistent coughs and wheezing, recurring chest and sinus infections, clubbed (rounding) fingers and toes, and polyps (growths) in the nasal passages (Mayo Clinic, 2002, May 14).

Cystic fibrosis at times affects other parts of the gastrointestinal system (e.g., bile ducts in the liver) as well as the reproductive organs; some women and most men with CF are unable to conceive children (NIDDK, 1998, February 12). Nevertheless, specific symptoms and signs of CF vary based on severity of the disease and age of the person with CF (Mayo Clinic). Cystic fibrosis also is associated with medical complications of obstructions of the intestines, diabetes, and cirrhosis (FitzSimmons, 1993).

Medical Management

Prior to the last decade, cystic fibrosis typically resulted in premature childhood death from respiratory failure (NIDDK, 1998, February 12). Many individuals with cystic fibrosis, however, are now living into their 30s (Mayo Clinic, 2002, May 14), 40s, and 50s (FitzSimmons, 1993). The gene responsible for causing CF was identified in 1989, and research now is being conducted to identify new drugs for treating symptoms (i.e., lung inflammation and infections) (CFF, 2001c, December) and gene therapy targeted at correcting the defective cystic fibrosis cells (CFF, 2001b, December).

Medical management of CF is targeted at fighting infections, decreasing sputum in the lungs, improving lung functioning, and maintaining appropriate calorie intake and overall nutrition. Medications prescribed to treat infections include oral, inhaled, and intravenous (i.e., in the vein) antibiotics (Mayo Clinic, 2002, May 14). Pancreatic enzymes also are prescribed to assist with digestive problems, and increased calorie intake is recommended. DNase, a natural enzyme delivered through an aerosol spray, has been developed to reduce the stickiness of the excessive mucus that persons with CF produce (NIDDK, 1998, February 12).

Individuals with cystic fibrosis need daily manual chest physical therapy (CPT) of the back and chest to help them dislodge and cough up excessive lung secretions (NIDDK, 1998, February 12). Inhaled antibiotics and bronchodilators often are used along with CPT. As an alternative to manual percussioning done during CPT, a device called a "flutter" has been developed for use in loosening mucus (CFF, 1997b).

People with CF whose lung functioning is significantly diminished (i.e., the condition is predicted to lead to death in 2–3 years) may be considered for a lung transplant from a donor who does not have CF. Following the transplant, the new transplanted lungs will not have CF; however, CF will still affect the individual's pancreas, sinuses, reproductive system, and digestive tract. After a transplant, the individual will be placed on immunosuppressive medications to fight organ rejection (CFF, 1999, December).

Henley and Hill (1990) indicated that the child's compliance with prescribed therapy for cystic fibrosis (e.g., CPT, medication) is critical for successful home management of the condition. Those authors recommended that the children and their families be well informed about the condition, including appropriate times for medication delivery, the need for pancreatic enzyme supplements with all meals and snacks, and physical therapy (i.e., CPT).

School Health Care and Related Accommodations

Children with CF may require the delivery of oral and/or inhaled antibiotic medications during the school day to improve their lung function, to fight infections, and in some cases to fight against organ rejection (post lung transplantation) (CFF, 1999). Consequently, this requires identifying at least two individuals to be trained to deliver the student's medication(s), operate and clean devices used for medication delivery, and receive information related to the medication's side effects.

Students with cystic fibrosis may use metered-dose medication delivered through a small inhaler with or without a spacer (CFF, 1997a, March). Inhaled medications also may be delivered via a disposable or reusable nebulizer. Williams–Warren (1998) provides a detailed summary of steps needed to clean and maintain nebulizers. Appropriately cleaning and disinfecting/sterilizing the nebulizers increases their effectiveness and decreases the likelihood of contamination and contracting new infections from bacteria. Because of the potential side effects that can develop from different types of medications mixing when delivered from a common nebulizer, specific medications may have to be dispensed by a nebulizer that is to be used to dispense only *that particular medication* (Williams–Warren).

Along with the delivery of medications, chest physical therapy (CPT) may have to be provided for students with CF during the school day, as prescribed by the student's primary physician. A detailed informational summary of CPT developed by the Cystic Fibrosis Foundation (1997b) overviews the anatomy of the lung, describes CPT techniques (including bronchial drainage, percussioning, vibration, deep breathing, and coughing) and includes instructions for the various bronchial drainage positions that may have to be used with a student who has cystic fibrosis. This summary is available from the Cystic Fibrosis Foundation (see "Additional Sources of Information"). Required chest percussioning can be done by a nurse or a teacher who has received appropriate training. Students also should be encouraged to increase their fluid intake, which assists in loosening mucus (Mayo Clinic, 2002, May 14).

Exercise for individuals with cystic fibrosis helps to alleviate shortness of breath and improves the clearance of mucus (Luder, 1997). Although people with cystic fibrosis can exercise in the heat, they will lose more salt as a result of their exercise than would someone without the condition. Consequently, individuals with CF should increase their liquid intake during exercise.

Cystic fibrosis also can negatively impact learning in that it has been associated with a depressed mood, anxiety, memory and concentration problems, and fatigue (Thies, 1999). After their study of 76 children with CF found 22% of the children to be more than a grade level below in reading and 14% below a grade level in mathematics, Thompson et al. (1992) concluded that some children with CF will require educational evaluation and interventions to promote positive adult outcomes related to employment. Finally, students with CF may have more school absences because of illnesses and hospitalizations related to lung infections and serious respiratory complications.

HIV AND AIDS

Human immunodeficiency virus (HIV) can be transmitted through unprotected sexual contact with individuals who have HIV, or by sharing needles with infected persons, or from contact with infected blood from mucous membranes or broken skin. The virus also can be passed from an infected mother to a child prenatally, during labor and delivery, as well as through breastfeeding (Hale, 1997).

Although in the past HIV also was spread through blood transfusions and other blood products that were *infected* with the virus, improved screening of blood and special heat treatment for blood products has significantly reduced the likelihood of these routes of transmission. Research to date indicates that HIV is not spread through urine, feces, tears, sweat, or saliva. HIV is not transmitted through daily casual contact such as that within schools, given that no bodily fluids or blood are exchanged (NIAID, 2001a, May).

Tests can be done to determine the presence of the HIV tests in an individual's blood. If the virus is identified, that individual is stated as being "HIV-positive." Early symptoms that sometimes appear within the first several months after HIV infection are flulike but may be mild and consequently overlooked (NIAID, 2001a, May).

AIDS is caused by the presence of HIV and may often be identified only after a person has been diagnosed with unusual cancers or infections—called *opportunistic infections*—suggestive of a severe immunodeficiency (NIAID, 2001, May). A common one is pneumocystis carinin pneumonia (PCP) (Hale, 1997). As of December 2000, 4,061 cases of AIDS in adolescents aged 13–19 had been reported to the CDC (NIAID, 2001b, October).

The decreased immune system functioning can cause a variety of neurological complications including nerve, brain, and spinal cord damage, which can lead to encephalitis and meningitis, dementia, strokes, headaches, and behavioral changes. Confusion, low-grade fevers, seizures, vision loss, and memory and cognition deficits also may be seen. Neurological symptoms are mild initially but can increase in severity in the later stages of AIDS. Finally, cancers and opportunistic infections are typical manifestations of persons with AIDS (National Institute of Neurological Disorders and Stroke [NINDS], n.d.).

Medical Management

Currently, AIDS has no cure. Various antiretroviral medications (protease inhibitors) are used to slow the progression of HIV (Brown, Lourie, & Pao, 2000). Other drug-treatment options are available to prevent opportunistic infections and to fight AIDS-related cancers, dementia, and infections (NINDS, n.d.). The health of children with HIV can be seriously compromised by infections and common illnesses of childhood (e.g., rubella, pneumonia, skin infections) and must be treated quickly (Beverly, 1995). The likelihood of children with HIV getting common contagious childhood diseases (e.g., measles, chicken pox) can be reduced by their receiving appropriate immunizations (Task Force on Pediatric AIDS, 1991).

School Health Care and Related Accommodations

Confidentiality policies and practices vary across school districts (Lavin et al., 1994). Hale (1997) noted that parents do not have to disclose that a child enrolled in a public school has HIV. The Task Force on Pediatric AIDS (1991) noted that confidentiality issues will remain critical "as long as HIV and AIDS are stigmatizing" to the families (p. 646). In some cases families may choose to disclose the child's HIV status to only a few key school personnel (e.g., school nurse, primary teacher, principal). In these instances confidentiality of the information provided by the parent must be maintained by those individuals with information about the child's health condition shared only among the specific individuals identified by the parents. The Task Force on Pediatric AIDS (1991) asserted that "it is essential that confidentiality be maintained by limiting disclosures and disclosing information only with the informed consent of the parents or legal guardians and age-appropriate assent of the student" (p. 647).

Given that parents or guardians may not disclose that a child is HIV positive and due to the fact that some individuals within a school environment (i.e., students as well as school staff) may actually be unaware that they have HIV, universal precautions should be used whenever dealing with blood or bodily fluids from *any child or staff member* in a school. These would include wearing a protective barrier (e.g., latex or rubber gloves) when dealing with a bleeding injury. Additionally, the sharing of such items as razors, toothbrushes, or any other item that might be contaminated with blood or bodily fluids should also not be allowed in school settings (Hale, 1997). Lavin et al. (1994) reported that the degree of compliance in schools to universal precautions was variable even though most larger districts had documented procedures and had provided staff training. Barriers to compliance to universal precautions identified included financial constraints, limited access to facilities for hand washing, and unwillingness of school administrators to supply needed gloves and other supplies.

During school hours these students may have to routinely take a variety of medications (Task Force on Pediatric AIDS, 1991), and many of the antiretroviral medication regimens are complex in nature (Brown et al., 2000). These medications absolutely must be taken as directed as missed dosages can lead to viral resistance (Brown et al., 2000). Because students with AIDS may become seriously fatigued arrangements may have to be made for planned breaks and additional opportunities to rest when needed, along with restrictions on specific physical activities.

Students with HIV tend to be absent from school more often than other students, as a result of acute illnesses, doctors' visits, and hospitalizations (Grubman et al., 1995). Care should be taken to limit the exposure of students with AIDS to classmates' common childhood illnesses (Kelker, Hecimovic, & LeRoy, 1994). Some students who are HIV-positive may require special education, but this should be "determined by their learning needs, rather than their HIV status" (Lavin et al., 1994, p. 29). Students who are HIV-positive and those who have AIDS might benefit from counseling.

Kelker et al. (1994) provided a series of suggestions for supports for students with AIDS in schools. For instance, when the parent has allowed information about the child's condition to be shared with classmates, the students might send cards to the child during times of absences because of illness or hospitalizations.

Health education must address bereavement issues related to AIDS (Giardina & Psota, 1997). The school staff should receive initial and updated inservice training on HIV, with a focus on universal precautions and confidentiality issues (Lavin, 1994). HIV/AIDS education programs should be implemented in all schools to further the knowledge of students and school staff regarding methods of transmission and methods of prevention (American Academy of Pediatrics, Committee on Pediatric AIDS, 1998). Such training may facilitate the acceptance of students with HIV within schools (Lavin et al., 1994).

DIABETES

Diabetes is a chronic disorder affecting approximately 125,000 children in the United States (Preboth, 2000). Type 1 diabetes, often referred to as insulin-dependent diabetes or juvenile diabetes, is a disease in which the body fails to produce insulin, a hormone needed for the body to process sugar (glucose) obtained from ingested foods. Type 1 diabetes typically is diagnosed in childhood or adolescence and often is caused by an autoimmune condition that destroys cells in the pancreas that produce insulin. Without the needed insulin, the body cannot process glucose effectively and the level of blood sugar can become dangerously high.

Every year 13,000 children within the United States are diagnosed with type 1 diabetes (National Diabetes Education Program [NDEP], 2002, February). Type 1 diabetes is associated with increased school absences, health care contacts, and reduction in daily activities (Levetan, 2001).

A second form of diabetes, non-insulin-dependent diabetes or type 2 diabetes has been viewed as affecting primarily adults and often is referred to as adult-onset diabetes. Increasing numbers of children, however, are being diagnosed with this type of diabetes (Vargas et al., 1999). At increased risk for type 2 diabetes are children who are obese (i.e., who weigh more than 20% above ideal weight), have close relatives with type 2 diabetes, are African–American, Hispanic, Pacific–Islander, or American Indian, and have acanthosis nigricans (dark, thickened skin on the neck) (Touchette, 2000).

Type 2 diabetes occurs due to the body's resistance to insulin (Hansen, Fulop, & Hunter, 2000) in that the body cannot adequately use its insulin. The American Diabetes Association (ADA) has recommended that the terms type 1 diabetes and type 2 diabetes be used to differentiate the two main types of the disease (National Institute of Diabetes and Digestive and Kidney Diseases [NIDDK], 2000b, April).

Individuals with diabetes can have either hypoglycemia (low blood sugar) or hyperglycemia (high blood sugar). Hyperglycemia (high blood sugar) develops slowly and is characterized by "malaise, fatigue, warm and dry skin, deep breathing, sweet or fruity odor to breath, drowsiness, excessive thirst, and coma" (Yousef, 1995, p. 49). It can be caused by insufficient insulin, illness, or stress (ADA, n.d., b). In contrast, hypoglycemia (low blood sugar)—also called an insulin reaction—develops rapidly, with symptoms that might include "headaches, sudden changes in behavior, nausea and vomiting, blurred vision, restlessness, pallor, profuse sweating, excessive hunger, cold hands and feet, convulsions, and comas" (Yousef, 1995, p. 49). Hypoglycemia can be caused by excessive insulin, strenuous energy output, and insufficient food or failing to eat after taking insulin (ADA, n.d., c; Yousef, 1995).

Individuals with diabetes can develop diabetic ketoacidosis, a condition in which blood glucose is highly elevated, which results in the build-up of keytones (waste products produced when the body burns fat instead of glucose for energy) in the person's blood. Keytones are eliminated in the urine (ADA, n.d., b). Ketoacidosis can lead to severe dehydration, loss of consciousness, coma, and even death (Touchette, 2000).

Individuals with diabetes can have a range of serious complications when their blood sugar is not kept within normal levels across time. These include heart disease, kidney failure, eye damage (which can lead to blindness), nerve damage, limb amputations, as well as premature death (American Diabetes Foundation [ADA], 2002, February 6; NDEP, 2002, February; Touchette, 2000).

Medical Management

Individuals with diabetes will require daily blood glucose monitoring, management of food intake and exercise, and in some instances oral medication or daily insulin administration. Type 1 diabetes is generally managed by balancing insulin (NDEP, 2002, February), food intake, and exercise. Individuals with type 2 diabetes often can manage to keep their blood glucose controlled (within normal levels) through exercise and diet; increased exercise and reduced fat and sugar intake are recommended (Hansen et al., 2000; Touchette, 2000), but, if needed, oral medications such as metaformin (glucophage) or sulfonylureas may be prescribed. When oral medications are ineffective, insulin is prescribed for some individuals with type 2 diabetes (Hansen et al.).

All children with diabetes must have their blood glucose levels monitored frequently. Blood glucose monitoring is done by a finger stick test, typically prior to and after eating each meal, before and after exercising, and as additional circumstances dictate. Blood glucose monitoring is done using a glucose monitor, a lancet, and glucose test strips. To conduct a blood glucose test, a lancet is used to pierce the skin, often from a fingertip, to obtain a small sample of blood that is dropped onto a test strip. The test strip is read by a glucose meter, which displays a reading of blood glucose levels (ADA, n.d., a).

Target blood glucose levels before breakfast and meals are typically 80–120 mg/dl; 2 hours or less after a meal, 180 mg/dl or less; and immediately prior to bedtime, 100–140 mg/dl (NIDDK, 2000c, February); however, physicians identify individual glucose targets for each patient. Many glucose meters now have the capability to store a large number of test results (e.g., 180, 450) within the meter memory and to average blood glucose levels across various time periods (e.g., 1, 2, 3, or 4 weeks, 2 weeks, or 30 days) (ADA, 2002).

If individuals require insulin as part of their daily diabetes management program, syringes as well as insulin injectors, insulin pens, external pumps, and skin patches may be used to administer insulin (see NIDDK, 2000a, February). Insulin can be administered using syringes, injectors, and pens under the skin at various body locations (e.g., thighs, abdomen, arm).

Six different types of insulin are available:

1. Rapid-acting insulin (insulin lispro, Humalog and insulin aspart, Novolog)
2. Short-acting insulin (Regular [R] insulin)
3. Intermediate-acting insulin (NPH [N] or Lente [L] insulin)
4. Long-acting insulin (Ultralente [U] insulin)
5. Very long-acting insulin (insulin glarine, Lantus)
6. Premixed (contains a mixture of NPH insulin and Regular insulin).

The types of insulin vary in terms of how quickly they will start to work, the time taken to lower blood sugar, and the length of time for the insulin to finish working (NIDDK, n.d.). The physician determines the specific types of insulin, amounts to be administered based on specific food intake, frequency and times of routine administration, and amount of insulin to be administered to treat episodes of hyperglycemia. In addition, the physician makes recommendations concerning times to test for keytones.

The physician also determines a specific protocol to be followed when the child's blood sugar is below the normal range. Cases of hypoglycemia may require different treatment protocols depending upon how low the child's blood sugar is. The physician might direct that the child be given a source of sugar such as orange juice, candy, other food items with high sugar content, or chewable glucose tablets. In other instances, a physician might prescribe a glucagon injection. Glucagon is available by prescription only and comes in a kit with a syringe and needle, glucose, and directions for preparing and injecting the glucose. Glucagon kits have expiration dates and should be appropriately discarded after they have expired.

School Health Care and Related Accommodations

The American Diabetes Association (ADA) report that many school personnel do not have adequate knowledge of diabetes and suggest that the child's parents, health care providers, and school personnel develop an individualized diabetes care plan (Preboth, 2000). The recommended components are:

- Procedures for blood glucose monitoring (including scheduled times and frequency, and situations that call for additional testing)
- Food intake while at school (including types and amounts of foods for meals and snacks, times for meals and snacks)
- Insulin administration (including storage requirements, prescribed dosages for specific blood glucose levels, injection sites and times)
- Symptoms of hyperglycemia (high blood sugar) and hypoglycemia (low blood sugar)
- Treatment protocols to be followed for hyperglycemia and hypoglycemia
- Keytone testing and treatment for high keytone levels.

Identified key personnel (e.g., nurse if available, classroom teacher) will have to receive training in related diabetes health care procedures including blood glucose testing, medication administration (including giving oral medications or insulin shots, programming an insulin pump), and ketone testing. In addition, these staff members should receive training in recognizing and treating hypoglycemia and hyperglycemia as specifically prescribed by the child's physician.

Many students are comfortable with having the glucose testing done in the presence of classmates, but others want to have this done in private. Privacy is the norm, particularly when insulin is administered on the thigh, abdomen, or other body area that normally is covered by clothing.

Because the types of insulin vary in the rapidity and duration of their effects, diabetes management information and training must be specific to each student. Furthermore, one student might use syringes for insulin injection, another an insulin injector, and a third an insulin pump that must be programmed to release insulin.

Some students are taught to self-manage their condition (e.g., how to test blood glucose, administer insulin). The diabetes management plan should describe the extent of their involvement in managing their diabetes care while at school. For example, students who plan to exercise may need to eat a snack after exercising or even during exercise to prevent low blood sugar.

Children with type 1 diabetes usually need a higher level of insulin to manage their condition when they go through puberty (Rosenbloom, 2001). Therefore, school personnel should inform the parents of increased episodes of hyperglycemia. As hyperglycemia also occurs when children become ill, appropriate hand washing and use of universal precautions may help to decrease the spread of contagious conditions (such as the common cold).

For field trips, all materials needed for blood glucose monitoring and insulin administration must accompany the child. Many students who use insulin have a small bag with a refreezable ice packet to keep the insulin cool. In addition, a sharps container for appropriate disposal of lancets and insulin needles will be needed.

Teachers of children with type 2 diabetes should encourage their physical activity and healthy foods and snacks. Physical educators who have students with type 1 diabetes must be knowledgeable about the condition and the effect of exercise on the student (Rickabaugh & Saltarelli, 1999). Counseling may be helpful to increase compliance with daily diabetes management activities of students (Weissberg–Benchell & Pichert, 1999).

Students who are diabetic sometimes show fatigue and confusion, have problems with reading and visual scanning, and have slower response times and difficulty attending (Thies, 1999, p. 5). Increased school absences can have adverse effects on educational progress and social development (Thies, 1999) with early onset diabetes associated with cognitive impairments (Wolters, Yu, Kail, & Hagen, 1996). Emotional difficulties may also result from a chronic illness such as diabetes (Thies, 1999).

Recent advances in diabetes care necessitate a comprehensive education program for staff members who provide daily care to students with diabetes in schools. Implementation of a "5 Cs of diabetes care" (cause, classification, complications, care, and cure) education training program to school personnel, described by Siminerio and Koerbel (1999), was associated with statistically significant increases in knowledge of diabetes.

EPILEPSY

Epilepsy, a chronic neurological condition, occurs when clusters of nerve cells or neurons in the brain abnormally signal. For a person to receive a medical diagnosis of epilepsy, the seizure activity must occur more than twice and be considered chronic in nature (Black & Hynd, 1995; Coulter, 1993). During seizure activity, "neurons fire over 500 times a second whereas within normal brain activity neurons fire approximately 80 times a second." In some individuals with seizure disorders, the misfiring of neurons can occur up to hundreds of times a day (National Institute of Neurological Disorders and Stroke [NINDS], 2001, July 1, p. 2). These misfirings may result in convulsions, muscle spasms, and loss of consciousness.

Of the approximately 2,500,000 individuals with some type of seizure disorder, 30% are children. An estimated 125,000 more individuals are diagnosed with some form of epilepsy each year (Epilepsy Foundation [EF], n.d.). Although the age of onset varies, 50% are diagnosed with epilepsy before 25 years of age and 20% before a child enters school. In 70% of the cases the etiology of the epilepsy is unknown. The remaining 30% of cases are associated with head trauma, brain tumors, poisoning, infections, and prenatal injuries. More recent research, however, suggests that epilepsy may be traced to specific gene abnormalities, which increases the probability of reoccurrence of the condition within a family (EF, n.d.).

As the classification of epilepsy types is complex (Coulter, 1993) and beyond the scope of this overview, readers are referred to Black and Hynd (1995) for a comprehensive review of epilepsy and epileptic syndromes. Seizures are classified into two major categories—partial seizures and generalized seizures—with more than 300 types of recognized seizure activity. Partial seizure may cause an individual to experience unusual feelings or sensations, ranging from joy to nausea. When having a partial seizure "the person may lose consciousness and engage in repetitive, perseverative behaviors such as blinking, mouth twitching, or walking in circles" (National Institute of Neurological Disorders and Stroke [NINDS], 2002, July 1, p. 5). Generalized seizures result from abnormal activity in many parts of the brain, which can cause "loss of consciousness, falling or massive muscle spasms." Absence seizures, tonic seizures, myoclonic seizures, and tonic–clonic seizures are different types of generalized seizures (NINDS, 2001, July 1, p. 6).

Most epilepsy cases include generalized seizure activity of various types (absence seizures, clonic seizures, tonic seizures, myoclonic seizures, atonic seizures, and tonic–clonic seizures) with family history noted as a commonality (Black & Hynd, 1995). The most common type of epilepsy involves partial seizures, which typically begin in childhood.

Epilepsy is frequently associated with mental retardation and learning disabilities. Estimates of prevalence rates of epilepsy and mental retardation range from 5% to 50% for individuals with cognitive dysfunction (Eriksson, Erilä, Kivimäki, & Koivikko, 1998). The more significant the cognitive deficit, the greater is the probability for generalized seizure activity to occur (Black & Hynd, 1995). Students who are co-morbid with mental retardation and cerebral palsy were noted to be at higher risk for unsuccessful treatment of seizure activity. Eriksson et al. noted that the more "associated" or co-conditions an individual has with epilepsy, the greater is the risk for poor seizure management and treatment (p. 470).

Medical Management

Typically, epilepsy is diagnosed and monitored using a variety of medical tests. An electroencephalogram (EEG), which records patterns of brainwaves, typically is administered while the individual is awake and asleep to assess the differences in brain activity during seizure activity and nonseizure activity. Other medical tests common to the assessment of epilepsy include brain scans such as computed tomography (CT), positron emission tomography (PET), and magnetic resonance imaging (MRI) scans. These brain scans assist in measuring the structure of the brain and recording the brain activity. All of these tests are conducted in conjunction with blood tests and a comprehensive medical history.

A variety of anti-epileptic drugs (AEDs) are used to treat epilepsy. These include lorazepam (Ativan), phenobarbital (Phenobarbital), clonazepam (Klonopin), and phenytoin (Dilantin) (see EF, 1998, for list of AED medications, typical adult dosages, and a partial listing of side effects). Historically, more than one AED medication often has been prescribed to treat epilepsy, and this sometimes resulted in adverse side effects such as fatigue, loss of appetite, memory problems, and attention lapses. Currently, monotherapy of AEDs (utilization of only one AED) seems to be the pharmological treatment of choice for epilepsy, as it reduces the probability of numerous side effects (Austin, Huberty, Huster, & Dunn, 1999).

When pharmacological interventions are unsuccessful in controlling seizure activity or when the type of seizure activity is spreading within the brain, resulting in additional brain damage, surgery may be the treatment of choice. The types of surgery are as follows.

1. A *lobectomy* consists of removing the exact lesion or origin of the seizure activity with the intent of decreasing the misfiring of the neurons across the lobes of the brain.
2. For individuals with severe generalized seizure activity, *corpus callosotomy* surgery is performed to "sever the network of neural connections between the left and right hemisphere." It is performed to decrease the seizure activity and to protect the brain from continuous damage and spreading of the seizure activity throughout the brain (NINDS, 2001, July 1, p. 14).
3. A newer medical treatment for decreasing seizure activity is implantation of a *vagus nerve stimulator (VNS),* which was approved in 1997. This battery-operated device is surgically placed under the skin, attached and wrapped around the vagus nerve on the lower neck. The VNS provides the brain with electrical stimulation throughout the day and is activated by the surgeon during surgery. The VNS also can be activated for more electrical impulses by placing a special magnet across the device. Because this surgery is relatively new, longitudinal data supporting effectiveness of this treatment are limited. Approximately one-third of the 10,000 individuals who have received this surgery are under 18 years of age (EF, 2002b; NINDS, 2001).

School Health Care and Related Accommodations

Many children with epilepsy require daily administration of the medication within the school day. Therefore, school personnel need training in AED administration, recording, and monitoring for potential side effects. Staff members should administer the AED medications only with water, because of the possible negative effect that fruit juices, citrus juices in particular, may produce with the medication (NINDS, 2001). Common side effects of AEDs vary by specific medication and may include irritability, difficulty concentrating, hyperactivity, clumsiness (Phenobarbital);

difficulty thinking or talking, sleepiness (Topax); and rashes, gum overgrowth, hairiness, clumsiness (Dilantin) (EF, 1998).

Commonly prescribed AEDs are listed on the Epilepsy Foundation website, www.epilepsyfoundation.com, with generic names, side effects, and dosage levels. AED side effects can affect both academic performance and social adaptation within school environments (Austin et al., 1999). Although typically mild in nature, these side effects have to be recorded because they also are indicative of the potential toxicity level of the medication.

Teachers have to be aware of seizure activity the student is likely to have. Students who have absence or partial seizures in the classroom will need more frequent academic reviews because they potentially miss academic content during the seizure activity. In simple partial seizures, students may experience sensations or feelings that are not real and need reassurance from their teachers once the seizure has dissipated. In contrast, in complex partial seizures, a student may become confused during the seizure activity and remain confused after the seizure has ended. Subsequently, the teacher must ensure the student's safety until his or her confusion dissipates. Similarly, teachers need to ensure the safety of students who engage in generalized tonic–clonic (formerly referred to as grand mal) seizures because of the massive body convulsions and potential for falling (EF, 2002b).

The Epilepsy Foundation (2002b) identified the following to be indicators for contacting emergency personnel:

> If a child hits his head with force, either during the seizure or just before it began, one or more of the following signs also call for immediate medical attention:
>
> - Difficulty in rousing after twenty minutes
> - Vomiting
> - Complaints of difficulty with vision
> - Persistent headache after a short rest period
> - Unconsciousness with failure to respond
> - Dilation of the pupils of the eye, or if the pupils are unequal in size. (EF, 2002b, para. 2)

Although generalized tonic seizures are associated with students who have more severe cognitive disabilities, students without disabilities might also need immediate medical attention after falling with force during a seizure.

Teachers who have a student with a VNS will need specific training on how to correctly use the magnet. The magnets have to be refrigerated when not in use. Also, the magnets should not come in "contact with computer, televisions, microwave ovens or other magnets" (EF, 2002b, July 5, p. 1). Further, students with VNS should not have any type of deep-heat treatments. This type of treatment, known as diathermy, can damage the tissue and nerves attached to the stimulator (EF, 2002b).

Individual school health care plans should list types of seizures the student has, prescribed AEDs, responses for seizure activity, and documentation requirements on medication administration and seizure activity. For resources for medication documentation and observed seizure activity within the school environment, see

Coulter (1993). Some students with epilepsy have physician-recommended school activity restrictions and modifications (e.g., cannot swim alone, alternative gym activities to replace gymnastics) that should be documented in the health care plan. In addition, as students approach the age at which drivers education classes are offered, school personnel should become familiar with state guidelines and restrictions related to driving for individuals diagnosed with epilepsy and include relevant information in the health care plan. The health care plan should be attached to the student's individualized educational program, reviewed frequently, and revised when data indicate this is necessary (Janz et al., 1997; Katsiyannis & Yell, 2000).

Students with epilepsy are considered at risk; difficulties in self-esteem, lethargy, and frequent school absences are the most commonly reported school difficulties (Schouten, Oostrom, Jennekens-Schinkel, & Peters, 2001). Students who have high-severity seizures (i.e., generalized tonic– clonic seizures) are considered at higher risk for academic failure specifically in the areas of reading and math (Huberty, Austin, Huster, & Dunn, 2000). Because these students also are frequently absent from school, additional research is needed to determine what component of the condition (i.e., the actual seizures or the associated school absences) primarily affects school performance (Black & Hynd, 1995).

Elementary-aged students with disabilities displayed more complex seizure activity and were treated less successfully both medically and educationally (Tidman, 1999). Similarly, Austin et al. (1999) reported that children with epilepsy were observed to have academic difficulties, and male students performed more poorly than female students. More than 40% of the students had repeated at least one academic grade and had more difficulty with mathematics than same-age peers who did not have epilepsy. It seems that the longer the duration of the seizure activity (in number of years) the greater is the probability of the child's having academic difficulties. Continued research is needed to examine the potential negative effects of epilepsy and academic achievement as it relates to school absences, academic acquisition, and friendship formation within elementary and secondary grades (Coulter, 1993; Huberty et al., 2000).

Teachers of students with various health conditions should inform the student's classmates about the health conditions (Getch & Neuharth–Prichett, 1999; Rosenthal-Malek & Greenspan, 1999), but it can be done only after the student's parent or legal guardian grants permission. The Epilepsy Foundation has produced several publications suitable for use in teaching younger and older elementary students alike about epilepsy and seizures. These include *Seizure Man: In the Classroom*, (targeted for students 5–10 years old) and *Seizure Man: First Aid for Seizures* (for ages 3–8). The following videos provide introductory information regarding epilepsy, seizures, and seizure first-aid.

Understanding Seizure Disorders (available from the Epilepsy Foundation, Catalog Sales, 4351 Garden City Drive, Landover, MD, 20785)

> This 11-minute video provides a basic overview of seizures, testing, and medications, and includes video clips of various types of seizures (generalized

tonic clonic, simple partial, and complex partial seizures). This video is available in both English and Spanish.

Seizure First Aid (Available from the Epilepsy Foundation)

> This 10-minute video includes footage of actual seizures and provides demonstrations of first-aid that should be provided to individuals who have different types of seizures (e.g., generalized tonic– clonic, complex partial). It gives general guidelines on what conditions would constitute a medical emergency related to seizures. This video is available in both English and Spanish.

SICKLE CELL DISEASE

Sickle cell disease (SCD) is an inherited blood disorder affecting more than 50,000 people in the United States (McCarthy, 1993).

> Sickle cell disease (commonly called sickle cell anemia) is an inherited disease in which defective, sickle-shaped red blood cells fail to carry adequate oxygen to tissues in the body. The cells also tend to block and damage the smallest blood vessels in the body, thus damaging the organs that those blood vessels serve. (Key, DeNoon, & Boyles, 1999, p. 16)

Sickle cell anemia and sickle-hemoglobin C disease are common forms of sickle cell disease (Sickle Cell Disease Association of America [SCDAA], n.d.). Children who inherit two sickle genes (one from each parent) will have SCD, and individuals who inherit only one sickle gene will be carriers of the sickle cell trait but will not have the disorder (Georgia Comprehensive Sickle Cell Center [GCSCC] 2002a, April 6). Approximately one in every 375 African-American children is affected with the condition (McCarthy, 1993), and individuals of Arab, Latin American, Greek, Italian, East Indian, and Caucasian ancestry also can inherit sickle cell disease (GCSCC, 2002a, April 6).

SCD causes inadequate oxygen delivery to miscellaneous organs including the brain; however, the lifespan of individuals with this condition has increased from "less than 20 years to more than 50 years of age" (Key et al., 1999, p. 16). Individuals with sickle cell disease are prone to having strokes—a loss of blood flow and oxygen that damages the brain. Of children with SCD, 10% will have a stroke before they become adults. Some children with sickle cell disease have silent strokes—strokes with no observable neurological signs but evidence of brain injury (as indicated by brain lesions identified through the use of magnetic resonance imaging (MRI) exams (Schatz, Brown, Pascual, Hsu, & DeBaun, 2001). The overwhelming majority of these children had cognitive impairments and were more likely than children diagnosed with SCD without silent strokes to have academic difficulties. When silent strokes involve the frontal lobe, deficits in attention and executive functions often are observed.

When the sickle cells block blood flow and break apart, a variety of medical complications can arise. These complications include episodes of pain (sometimes called "pain crises"), strokes, bone damage, leg ulcers, infections, and gallstones, as well as blockages in the lungs, spleen, and liver. Other complications are anemia (low red blood count), eye and kidney damage, jaundice, priapism (painful erections of long duration), and delayed growth. Individuals with SCD also may have delayed puberty and be of short stature (GCSCC, 2002a, April 6). The primary cause of death of individuals with sickle cell disease is acute chest syndrome (ACS), which can stem from infections and other causes (Vichinsky et al., 2000).

Medical Management

McCarthy (1993) recommended the need for "comprehensive health-care services, education about the disease and its complications, and genetic counseling" (p. 1209). Also, infants diagnosed with the condition should be given oral prophylactic penicillin (or another antibiotic) twice a day. This medication has been shown to reduce bacterial infections that lead to recurring illness and death of children with sickle cell disease. Prophylactic penicillin should be given until children are at least 5 to 6 years of age (GCSCC, 2002a, April 6).

Blood transfusions, which may be given every 3 to 6 weeks, have been documented to reduce stroke risk. These transfusions, however, carry risks including possible infections, allergic reactions, and iron overload, which occurs from excessive iron build-up (Key et al., 1999). Some people with SCD who present with acute chest syndrome can be treated successfully with a combination of blood transfusions, oxygen therapy, pain medications (e.g., antibiotics, bronchodilators, and increased fluids, both oral and intravenous) (Vichinsky et al., 2000). The neurological and neurodevelopmental status of children with sickle cell anemia should be monitored across time and should include examinations to identify strokes (Chua-Lim, Moore, McCleary, Shah, & Mankad, 1993).

School Health Care and Related Accommodations

"Those with sickle cell should be treated as normal as possible, with an awareness that they may have intermittent episodes of pain, infection, or fatigue" (GCSCC, 2002b, February 1, p. 1). Teachers should assist students with sickle cell disease to avoid very hot or cold temperatures and overexertion, as well as encouraging them to drink an appropriate amount of fluids to prevent pain episodes. Further, teachers should allow the child to take extra breaks to obtain water or allow the child to keep a filled water bottle at his or her desk. Additional bathroom breaks will have to be provided because of the increased fluid intake and because the kidneys of individuals with SCD have difficulty retaining water. Teachers also should provide breaks to the student when he or she is tired or is having an episode, and should monitor the student to prevent overexertion (GCSCC, 2002b, February 1). Pain medications may have to be administered at school for episodes of pain that can be managed within the school setting.

Teachers should become familiar with, and encourage students to use, various coping strategies during pain episodes. Gil et al. (2001) reported that children and youth with SCD who were trained to use coping skills (relaxation with deep breathing, calming self-talk, and pleasant imagery) to deal with pain episodes were more likely to take an active approach to pain management than were children with SCD who did not receive this training. Those authors indicated that on days that children with SCD had increased pain, they were more likely to take medication, have health care contacts, reduce their activity level, and practice their coping skills. Children who practiced their coping skills on higher-pain days were more likely to maintain their typical activity level at home and school and less likely to have a major medical care contact (i.e., hospital admission, clinic or emergency room visit). The authors recommended more comprehensive skills training for children with SCD to include the coping skills strategies as well as "behavioral strategies such as activity pacing or scheduling pleasant activities during pain episodes" (p. 171).

Warning signs that may indicate that a child with SCD may need to immediately see his or her physician or go to the emergency room include fever of 101°F. or above, sudden change in vision, weakness or loss of feeling, shortness of breath, swelling in the hands, joints, or feet, as well as pain in the head, chest, joints, or penis (GCSCC, 2002a, February 1; Sickle Cell Advisory Committee [SCAC], 1999, September). Vichinsky et al. (2000) documented that children with SCD who were 9 years of age and younger and diagnosed with ACS had initial symptoms including fever, wheezing, and coughing. Teachers should watch for these warning signs and take a child's temperature as needed if a fever is suspected. Warning signs that an individual student is most likely to display must be determined from the child's parents and written into the student's health care plan, along with specific urgent care responses that the school staff should heed immediately when indicated.

Preschool children with sickle cell anemia, compared to children without the condition, were more frequently noted to have deficits in school-readiness skills (Chua-Lim et al., 1993). In addition, students with sickle cell disease may have more absences because of severe pain crises that may require them to stay home, and at times, be hospitalized. Consequently, school personnel will have to arrange for the child to make up the work missed during any absence (GCSCC, 2002b, February 1).

SUMMARY AND RECOMMENDATIONS

Because of the overwhelming increase of students identified in the category of Other Health Impairment, educators must be more responsive to the needs of students diagnosed with a wide range of chronic health conditions. Etscheidt and Barlett (1999) recommend that educational teams take a four-step approach when determining related services and health care needs for children with other health impairments:

1. Review the child's IEP.
2. Discuss the need for supplemental aids and services.
3. Document the decision-making process and product.
4. Determine the data-collection procedures for using these supplemental aids and services.

Schools utilizing this approach should have the necessary documentation and data to assist them in providing appropriate educational services for all the students in their districts.

The need for a comprehensive preservice education program focusing on health care services is essential. In part, the ability to plan for and respond appropriately to the student's educational needs and health needs is contingent on the training received at the preservice level for future special and general educators. State Departments of Education must reexamine teacher-certification requirements to assure that those leaving teacher-preparation programs acquire the knowledge and skills necessary to teach students with physical and health disabilities (Heller et al., 1999).

Furthermore, comprehensive, updated inservice training for school personnel, including practicing teachers and nurses, has to occur to enable students with health conditions to receive an appropriate and safe education in their least restrictive environment. AAP (1990a) called for increased education of school personnel about chronic health conditions and related health care management in part to combat anxiety and fears that teachers may have regarding such conditions. All staff members involved in implementing school health procedures should be given child-specific initial training as well as follow-up training (Heller et al., 1997).

The advent of the Internet has made available a seemingly endless supply of valuable information on chronic health conditions of children, for use by parents, teachers, school nurses, and other school personnel. With this newer and ever-changing means of obtaining information, however, comes the caveat, "Consumers beware." When accessing Internet sources to obtain information, readers must carefully assess the credibility of organizations and authors of websites from which they seek and obtain information. Too, web addresses and uniform resource locators (URLs) change frequently. On occasion, an individual or organization with no connection to the original website utilizes the original web address of an organization or individual. Each of the web site addresses for all text content from the electronic Internet sources included within this article were current immediately prior to publication.

REFERENCES

Almqvist, C., Larsson, P. H., Egmar, A. C., Hedren, M., Malmberg, P., & Wickman, M. (1999). School as a risk environment for children allergic to cats and a site for transfer of cat allergen to homes. *Journal of Allergy and Clinical Immunology, 103*(2), 1012–1017.

American Academy of Pediatrics, Committee on Pediatric AIDS. (1998). Human immunodeficiency virus/acquired immunodeficiency syndrome education in schools. *Pediatrics, 101*(5), 933–935.

American Academy of Pediatrics, Committee on Children with Disabilities and Committee on School Health. (1990a). Children with health impairments in schools. *Pediatrics, 86*, 636–638.

American Academy of Pediatrics, Committee on School Health. (1990b). Guidelines for urgent care in schools. *Pediatrics, 86*(6), 999–1000.

American Academy of Pediatrics, Task Force on Pediatric AIDS. (1988). Pediatric guidelines for infection control of human immunodeficiency virus (acquired immunodeficiency virus in hospitals, medical offices, schools, and other settings). *Pediatrics, 82*, 801–807.

American Diabetes Association. (2001). Care of children with diabetes in the school and day care setting. *Diabetes Care, 24*, S108–S112.

American Diabetes Association. (2002). New diabetes products. *Diabetes Forecast, 55*(1), 1–4. Retrieved on February 11, 2002, from http://www.diabetes.org/main/community/forecast/jan_2002_new_diabetes_products.jsp

American Diabetes Association. (n.d, a). *Complications.* Retrieved on February 11, 2002, from http://www.diabetes.org/maintype2/complications/ complications.jsp

American Diabetes Association. (n.d, b). *Hyperglycemia.* Retrieved on July 1, 2002, from http://www.diabetes.org/main/application/commercewf? orgin=*.jsp&event=link(C4_6)

American Diabetes Association. (n.d, c). *Hypoglycemia.* Retrieved on July 1, 2002, from http://www.diabetes.org/main/application/commercewf? orgin=*.jsp&event=link(C4_5)

American Lung Association. (2002a). Asthma attacks. Retrieved on June 10, 2002, from http://www.lungusa.org/asthma/astasthmatk.html

American Lung Association. (2002b). Peak flow chart. Retrieved on June 10, 2002, from http://www.lungusa.org/asthma/astpeakchrt.html

Aronson, S. S. (1995). Meeting the health needs of children with asthma. *Child Care Information Exchange, 101,* 59–60.

Asthma and Allergy Foundation of America. (2002). "Answers" fact sheets: Food allergies. Retrieved July 10, 2002, from http://www.aafa.org/ templ/display.cfm?id=193&sub=223

Austin, J. K., Huberty, T. J., Huster, G. A., & Dunn, D. W. (1999). Does academic achievement in children with epilepsy change over time? *Developmental Medicine and Child Neurology, 41*(7), 473–479.

Ballard, D. J., White, D. M., & Glascoff, M. A. (1990). AIDS/HIV education for preservice elementary teachers. *Journal of School Health, 60*(6), 262–265.

Beverly, C. L. (1995). Providing a safe environment for children infected with the human immunodeficiency virus. *Topics in Early Childhood Special Education, 15*(1), 100–109.

Black, K. C., & Hynd, G. W. (1995). Epilepsy in the school aged child: Cognitive–behavioral characteristics and effects on academic performance. *School Psychology Quarterly, 10*(4), 345–358.

Brown, L. K., Lourie, K. J., & Pao, M. (2000). Children and adolescents living with HIV and AIDS: A review. *Journal of Child Psychiatry and Allied Disciplines, 41*(1), 81–96.

Caldwell, T. H., & Sirvis, B. (1991). Students with special health care conditions—An emerging population presents new challenges. *Preventing School Failure, 35*(3), 13–18.

Celano, M. P., & Geller, R. J. (1993). Learning, school performance, and children with asthma: How much at risk? *Journal of Learning Disabilities, 26*(1), 23–32.

Chua-Lim, C., Moore, R. B., McCleary, G., Shah, A., & Mankad, V. N. (1993). Deficiencies in school readiness skills of children with sickle cell anemia: A preliminary report. *Southern Medical Journal, 86*(4), 397–402.

Coulter, D. L. (1993). Epilepsy and mental retardation: An overview. *American Journal on Mental Retardation, 98,* 1–11.

Council for Exceptional Children. (2000). *What every special educator should know—The standards for the preparation and licensure of special educators* (4th ed.). Reston, VA: CEC.

Coutts, C. (2000). Food reactions: Allergic or intolerant? *Parenting, 14*(9), 240.

Cross, G., & Jones, M. J. (1996). Addressing medical and emergency procedures in inclusive settings. In D. L. Ryndak, & S. Alper (Eds.), *Curriculum content for students with moderate and severe disabilities in inclusive settings* (pp. 269–288). Boston: Allyn & Bacon.

Cystic Fibrosis Foundation. (1997a, March). Caring for your nebulizer—What you should know. *Homeline*, pp. 4–6. Retrieved on May 16, 2002, from http://www.cff.org/home%20line/home-line199703.htm

Cystic Fibrosis Foundation. (1997b). *Consumer fact sheet—An introduction to chest physical therapy.* Bethesda, MD: CFF.

Cystic Fibrosis Foundation. (1999, December). *Lung transplantation.* Bethesda, MD: CFF.

Cystic Fibrosis Foundation. (2001a, December). *Facts about cystic fibrosis.* Bethesda, MD: CFF.

Cystic Fibrosis Foundation. (2001b, December). *Gene therapy and cystic fibrosis.* Bethesda, MD: CFF.

Cystic Fibrosis Foundation. (2001c, December). *Progress in CF research.* Bethesda, MD: CFF.

Cystic Fibrosis Foundation. (2002, March 8). *Facts about cystic fibrosis.* Retrieved on May 16, 2002, from http://www.cff.org/facts.htm

da Costa, I. G., Rapoff, M. A., Lemanek, K., & Goldstein, G. L. (1997). Improving adherence to medication regimen for children with asthma and its effect on clinical outcome. *Journal of Applied Behavior Analysis, 30*(4), 687–691.

Dibs, S. D., & Baker, M. D. (1997). Anaphylaxis in children: A 5-year experience. *Pediatrics, 99*(1), e 7. Retrieved on May 23, 2002, from http://www.pediatrics.org/cgi/content/full/99/1/e7

Diette, G. B., Markson, L., Skinner, E. A., Nguyen, T. T. H., Algatt-Bergstrom, P., & Wu, A. W. (2000). Nocturnal asthma in children affects school attendance, school performance, and parents' work attendance. *Archives of Pediatric and Adolescent Medicine, 154,* 923–928.

Environmental Protection Agency. (2001, November 27). *IAQ tools for schools: Managing asthma in the school environment—The asthma epidemic.* Retrieved on January 24, 2002, from http://www.epa.gov/ iaq/schools/asthma/asthma_epidemic.htm

Epilepsy Foundation. (1998). Medicines for epilepsy. [Brochure]. Landover, MD: Author.

Epilepsy Foundation. (2002a). *Answerplace-Vagus nerve stimulation.* Retrieved on July 5, 2002, from http://www.efa.org/answerplace/vns

Epilepsy Foundation. (2002b). *Making our schools seizure smart.* Retrieved on July 5, 2002, from http://www.efa.org/answerplace/teach ers/html

Epilepsy Foundation. (n.d.). *Information and education.* Retrieved on December 8, 1998, from http://www.efa.org/education/facts.html

Eriksson, K., Erilä, T., Kivimäki, T., & Koivikko, M. (1998). Evolution of epilepsy in children with mental retardation: Five-year experience in 78 cases. *American Journal on Mental Retardation, 102*(5), 464–472.

Etscheidt, S. K., & Bartlett, L. (1999). The IDEA amendments: A four-step approach for determining supplementary aids and services. *Exceptional Children, 65*(2), 163–174.

Federal Interagency Forum on Child and Family Statistics. (2001). *America's children: Key national indicators of well-being, 2001.* Federal Interagency Forum on Child and Family Statistics, Washington, DC. Retrieved May 20, 2002, from http://childstats.gov

FitzSimmons, S. C. (1993). The changing epidemiology of cystic fibrosis. *Journal of Pediatrics, 122*(1), 1–9.

Food Allergy and Anaphylaxis Network. (2002, January 2). Information about anaphylaxis. Retrieved July 10, 2002, from http://www.food allergy.org/anaphylaxis.html

Food Allergy Initiative. (n.d.). Living with food allergies. Retrieved July 11, 2002, from http://foodallergyinitiative.org

Formanek, R. (2001). When food becomes the enemy. *FDA Consumer,* 35, 10–16.

Gandy, L. T., Yadrick, M. K., Boudreaux, L. J., & Smith, E. R. (1991). Serving children with special heath care needs: Nutrition services and employee training needs in the school lunch program. *Journal of the American Dietetic Association, 91*(12), 1585–1586.

Georgia Comprehensive Sickle Cell Center (2002a, April 6). *Sickle cell anemia.* Retrieved on April 15, 2002, from http://www.scinfo.org/ sicklept.htm

Georgia Comprehensive Sickle Cell Center (2002b, February 1). *Sickle cell information for teachers, students, and employers.* Retrieved on April 15, 2002, from http://www.scinfo.org/ teacher.htm

Getch, Y. Q., & Neuharth-Pritchett, S. (1999). Children with asthma: Strategies for educators. *Teaching Exceptional Children, 31*(3), 30–36.

Giardina, R. G., & Psota, C. E. (1997). Universal precautions and infection control in a school setting. In S. Porter, M. Haynie, T. Bierle, T. H. Caldwell, & J. S. Palfrey (Eds.), *Children and youth assisted by medical technology in educational settings—Guidelines for care* (2nd ed.) (pp. 74–78). Baltimore: Paul H. Brookes.

Gil, K. M., Anthony, K. K., Carson, J. W., Redding–Lallinger, R., Daeschner, C. W., & Ware, R. E. (2001). Daily coping practice predicts treatment effects in children with sickle cell disease. *Journal of Pediatric Psychology, 26*(3), 163–173.

Grubman, S., Gross, E., Lerner–Weiss, N., Hernandez, M., McSherry, G. D., Hoyt, L. G., et al. (1995). Older children and adolescents living with perinatally acquired human immunodeficiency virus infection. *Pediatrics, 95*(5), 657–663.

Hale, A. R. (1997). Human immunodeficiency virus and acquired immunodeficiency syndrome. In S. Porter, M. Haynie, T. Bierle, T. H. Caldwell, & J. S. Palfrey (Eds.), *Children and youth assisted by medical technology in educational settings—Guidelines for care* (2d ed.) (pp. 83–93). Baltimore: Paul H. Brookes.

Hansen, J. R., Fulop, M. J., & Hunter, M. K. (2000). Type 2 diabetes mellitus in youth: A growing challenge. *Clinical Diabetes, 18*(2), 52–56.

Hartocollis, A. (1998, September 23). Nothing's safe: Some schools ban peanut butter as allergy threat. *New York Times, 148*(51289) pp. A1, B11.

Hay, G. H., Harper, T. B. III, & Courson, F. H. (1994). Preparing school personnel to assist students with life-threatening food allergies. *Journal of School Health, 64*(3), 119–121.

Heller, K. W. (1997). The critical need for physical/health disability certification. *Physical Disabilities: Education and Related Services, 16*(1), 1–5.

Heller, K. W., Fredrick, L. D., Dykes, M. K., Best, S., & Cohen, E. T. (1999). A national perspective of competencies for teachers of individuals with physical and health disabilities. *Exceptional Children, 65*(2), 219–234.

Heller, K. W., Fredrick, L., & Rithmire, N. M. (1997). Special health care procedures in the schools. *Physical Disabilities: Education and Related Services, 15*(2), 5–22.

Heller, K. W., Wolff, L., Forney, P., Alberto, P., Schwartzman, M., & Goeckel, T. (2000). Medications and procedures for administration. In K. W. Heller, P. E. Forney, P. A. Alberto, M. N. Schwartzman, & T. M. Goeckel, *Meeting physical and health needs of children with disabilities* (pp. 67–96). Belmont, CA: Wadsworth/Thomson Learning.

Henley, L. D., & Hill, I. D. (1990). Errors, gaps, and misconceptions in the disease-related knowledge of cystic fibrosis patients and their families. *Pediatrics, 85,* 1008–1014.

Huberty, T. J., Austin, J. K., Huster, G. A., & Dunn, D. W. (2000). Relations of change in condition severity and school self-concept to change in achievement-related behavior in children with asthma or epilepsy. *Journal of School Psychology, 38*(3), 259–276.

Individuals with Disabilities Education Act—Final Regulations (1999). 34 CFR § 300.7 (b) (9).

Individuals with Disabilities Education Act—Final Regulations (1999). 34 C.F.R. § 300.24 (b) (12).

Janz, J., Beyer, H., Schwab, N., Anderson, B., Caldwell, T., & Harrison, J. (1997). Legal issues in the education of students with special health care needs. In S. Porter, M. Haynie, T. Bierle, T. Calwell, & J. Palfrey (Eds), *Children and youth assisted by medical technology in educational settings—Guidelines for care* (2nd ed.). (pp. 19–39). Baltimore: Paul H. Brookes.

Johnson, M. P., Lubker, B. B., & Fowler, M. G. (1988). Teacher needs assessment for the educational management of children with chronic illnesses. *Journal of School Health, 58*(6), 232–235.

Katsiyannis, A., & Yell, M. (2000). The Supreme Court and school health services: Cedar Rapids v. Garret F. *Exceptional Children, 66*(3), 317–326.

Kelker, K., Hecimovic, A., & LeRoy, C. H. (1994). Designing a classroom and school environment for students with AIDS: A checklist for teachers. *Teaching Exceptional Children, 26*(4), 52–55.

Key, S. W., DeNoon, D. J., & Boyles, S. (1999). Sickle cell effects on brain found in very young children. *World Disease Weekly Plus,* 16–17.

Lavin, A. T., Porter, S. M., Shaw, D. M., Weill, K. S., Crocker, A. C., & Palfrey, J. S. (1994). School health services in the age of AIDS. *Journal of School Health, 64*(1), 27–31.

Levetan, C. (2001). Into the mouths of babes: The diabetes epidemic in children. *Clinical Diabetes, 19*(3), 102–104.

Luder, D. (1997). Exercise—The facts. *Homeline,* 1–4. Retrieved on May 16, 2002, from http://www.cff.org/home%20line/homeline199703.htm

The Lung Association (2002, July 19). Asthma. Retrieved on June 10, 2002, from http://www.lung.ca/asthma/asthma1.html

The Lung Association (n.d.). *Asthma management.* Retrieved on June 10, 2002, from http://www. lung.ca/asthma/manage/action.html

Mayo Clinic. (2002, May 14). *What is cystic fibrosis?* Retrieved on May 16, 2002, from http:// www.mayoclinic.com

McCarthy, M. (1993). USA recommends universal sickle-cell screening. *Lancet, 341*(8854), 1209.

Meeropol, E. (1997). Alert: Latex allergy. In S. Porter, M. Haynie, T. Bierle, T. H. Caldwell, & J. S. Palfrey (Eds.), *Children and youth assisted by medical technology in educational settings— Guidelines for care* (2d ed.) (pp. 79–82). Baltimore: Paul H. Brookes.

National Diabetes Education Program, National Institute of Diabetes & Digestive & Kidney Diseases, National Institutes of Health (2002, February). *Diabetes in children and adolescents.* Retrieved on May 16, 2002, from http://ndep.nih.gov/get-info/childrensfacts.htm

National Heart, Lung, and Blood Institute, National Institutes of Health. (n.d.). *Controlling your asthma.* Retrieved on May 16, 2002, from http://www.nhlbi.nih.gov/health/public/lung/ asthma/asth_fs.pdf

National Institute of Allergy and Infectious Diseases, National Institutes of Health. (2001a, May). *HIV infection and AIDS: An overview.* Retrieved on May 16, 2002, from http://www.niaid. nih.gov/factsheets/hivinf.htm

National Institute of Allergy and Infectious Diseases, National Institutes of Health. (2001b, October). *HIV infection in adolescents.* Retrieved on May 16, 2002, from http://www. niaid.nih.gov/factsheets/hivadoles cent.htm

National Institute of Allergy and Infectious Diseases, National Institutes of Health. (2001, June 25). *Fact sheet-Food allergy and intolerances.* Retrieved on May 16, 2002, from http://www.niaid. nih.gov/factsheets/food.htm

National Institute of Allergy and Infectious Diseases, National Institutes of Health. (n.d.). *Backgrounder—HIV infection in infants and children.* Retrieved on May 16, 2002, from http://www.niaid.nih.gov/news room/simple/background.htm

National Institute of Diabetes & Digestive & Kidney Diseases, National Institutes of Health. (1998, February 12).*Cystic fibrosis—Research directions.* Bethesda, MD: Retrieved on May 16, 2002, from http:www.niddk.nih.gov/health/endo/endo/pubs/cystic/cystic.htm

National Institute of Diabetes & Digestive & Kidney Diseases, National Institutes of Health (2000a, February). *Devices for taking insulin.* Bethesda, MD: Retrieved on May 16, 2002 from http://www.niddk. nih.gov/health/diabetes/summary/altins.altins.htm

National Institute of Diabetes & Digestive & Kidney Diseases, National Institutes of Health (2000b, April). *Diabetes diagnosis.* Bethesda, MD: Retrieved on May 16, 2002, from http://www. niddk.nih.gov/health/diabetes/pubs/diagnosis/diagnosis.htm

National Institute of Diabetes & Digestive & Kidney Diseases, National Institutes of Health (2000c, August). *Prevent diabetes problems—Keep your diabetes under control.* Bethesda, MD: Retrieved on May 16, 2002, from http://www.niddk.nih.gov/health/diabetes/pubs/complica tions/control/control.htm

National Institute of Diabetes & Digestive & Kidney Diseases, National Institutes of Health (n.d.). *Medicines for people with diabetes—Specific medicines.* Retrieved on May 16, 2002, from http://www. niddk.nih.gov/health/diabetes/pubs/med/specific.htm

National Institute of Neurological Disorders and Stroke, National Institutes of Health (2001, July 1). *Seizures and epilepsy: Hope through research.* Retrieved on May 16, 2002, from http://www.ninds.nih.gov/ health and medical/pubs/seizures_and_epilepsy

Nowak-Wegrzyn, A., Conover–Walker, M. K., & Wood, R. A. (2001). Food-allergic reactions in schools and preschools. *Archives of Pediatrics and Adolescent Medicine, 155*(7), 790–795.

Porter, S., Haynie, M., Bierle, T., Caldwell, T. H., & Palfrey, J. S. (1997). *Children and youth assisted by medical technology in educational settings: Guidelines for care* (2nd ed.). Baltimore: Paul H. Brookes.

Preboth, M. (2000). Diabetes in the school and day care setting. *American Family Physician, 62*(5), 1189.

Raj, A., Mishra, A., Feinsilver, S. H., & Fein, A. M. (2000). An estimate of the prevalence and impact of asthma and related symptoms in a New York City middle school [Abstract]. *Chest, 118*(4), 84S.

Rana, U. A., Jurgens, S. M., Mangione, S., Elia, J., & Tollerud, D. J. (2000). Asthma prevalence among high absentees of two Philadelphia middle schools [Abstract]. *Chest, 118*(4), 79S.

Rapport, M. J. K. (1996). Legal guidelines for the delivery of special health care services in schools. *Exceptional Children, 62*(6), 537–549.

Reid, R. (1999). Attention deficit hyperactivity disorder: Effective methods for the classroom. *Focus on Exceptional Children, 32*(4), 1–20.

Rickabaugh, T. E., & Saltarelli, W. (1999). Knowledge and attitudes related to diabetes and exercise guidelines among selected diabetic children, their parents, and physical education teachers. *Research Quarterly for Exercise and Sport, 70*(4), 389–394.

Rosenbloom, A. (2001). Not "adults-only" anymore. *Diabetes Forecast, 54*(3), 82.

Rosenthal–Malek, A., & Greenspan, J. (1999). A student with diabetes is in my class. *Teaching Exceptional Children, 31*(3), 38–43.

Schatz, J., Brown, R. T., Pascual, J. M., Hsu, L., & DeBaun, M. R. (2001). Poor school and cognitive functioning with silent cerebral infarcts and sickle cell disease. *Neurology, 56,* 1109–1111.

Schwartz, W. (1999). Supporting students with asthma. *ERIC/CUE Digest, 151.* (ERIC Document Reproduction Service No. ED438339)

Schouten, A., Oostrom, K., Jennekens–Schinkel, A., & Peters, A. C. B. (2001). School career of children is a risk before diagnosis of epilepsy only. *Developmental Medicine and Child Neurology, 43*(8), 575–576.

Sickle Cell Advisory Committee. (1999, September). *Sickle cell disease: Information for school personnel.* Trenton, NJ: Special Child, Adult and Early Intervention Services, New Jersey Department of Health and Senior Services. Retrieved on June 23, 2002, from http://www.state.nj. us/health/fhs/sicklecell/index.org/whatistext2.htm

Sickle Cell Disease Association of America, Inc. (n.d.). *What is sickle cell disease?* Retrieved on June 15, 2002, from http://www.sicklecelldisease.org/whatistext2.htm

Simeonsson, N., Lorimer, M., Shelley, B., & Sturtz, J. (1995). Asthma: New information for the early interventionist. *Topics in Early Childhood Special Education, 15*(1), 32–43.

Siminerio, L., & Koerbel, G. (1999). Evaluating the effectiveness of a diabetes education program for school personnel [Abstract]. *Diabetes, 49*(5), A158–A159.

Simpson, R. L., Whelan, R. J., & Zabel, R. H. (1993). Special education personnel preparation in the 21st century: Issues and strategies. *Remedial & Special Education, 14*(2), 7–22.

Task Force on Pediatric AIDS. (1991). Education of children with human immunodeficiency virus infection. *Pediatrics, 88*(3), 645–648.

Taylor, S. L., & Hefle, S. L. (2001). Food allergies and other food sensitivities. *Food Technology, 55*(9), 68–83.

Thies, K. M. (1999). Identifying the educational implications of chronic illness in children. *Journal of School Health, 69*(10), 392–397.

Thompson, R. J., Gustafson, K. E, Meghdadpour, S., Harell, E. S, Johndrow, D. A., & Spock, A. (1992). The role of biomedical and psychosocial processes in the intellectual and academic functioning of children and adolescents with cystic fibrosis. *Journal of Clinical Psychology, 48*(1), 3–10.

Tidman, L. (1999). Epilepsy in children attending primary school. *Archives of Disease in Childhood, 80,* G127.

Touchette, N. (2000). Kids and type 2. *Diabetes Forecast, 53*(11), 79–84.

Tyler, J. T., & Colson, S. (1994). Common pediatric disabilities: Medical aspects and educational implications. *Focus on Exceptional Children, 27*(4), 1–16.

U.S. Department of Education. (2001). *Twenty-third annual report to Congress on implementation of the Individuals with Disabilities Education Act.* Washington, DC: Author. Retrieved on July 8, 2002, from http://www.ed.gov/offices/OSERS/OSEP/Products/OSEP2001AnlRpt/index. html

Vargas, I., Schachner, H. C., Solowiejczyk, J., Almeida, K. L., Leibel, R. L., & Goland, R. S. (1999). Clinical characteristics in an ethnically diverse group of children with type 2 diabetes [Abstract]. *Diabetes, 48*(5), A84.

Vichinsky, E. P., Neumayr, L. D., Earles, A. N., Williams, R., Lennette, E. T., Dean, D., et al. (2000). Causes and outcomes of the acute chest syndrome in sickle cell disease. *New England Journal of Medicine, 342*(5), 1855–1865.

Weissberg-Benchell, J., & Pichert, J. (1999). Counseling techniques for clinicians and educators. *Diabetes Spectrum, 12*(1), 103–107.

Williams, J. K., & McCarthy, A. M. (1995). School nurses' experience with children with chronic conditions. *Journal of School Health, 65*(6), 234–236.

Williams-Warren, J. (1998). Caring for and cleaning your nebulizer and compressor. *Homeline,* 1–7. Retrieved on May 16, 2002, from http://www.cff.org/home%20line/homeline199802.htm

Wolters, C. A., Yu, S. L., Kail, R., & Hagen, J. W. (1996). Short-term memory and strategy use in children with insulin-dependent diabetes mellitus. *Journal of Consulting and Clinical Psychology, 64*(6), 1397–1405.

Yell, M. (1998). *The law and special education.* Upper Saddle River, NJ: Merrill, Prentice Hall.

Yell, M. L., & Shriner, J. G. (1997). The IDEA Amendments of 1997: Implications for special and general education teachers, administrators, and teacher trainers. *Focus on Exceptional Children, 30*(1), 1–19.

Yousef, J. M. S. (1995). Insulin-dependent diabetes mellitus: Educational implications. *Physical Disabilities: Education and Related Services, 13*(2), 43–53.

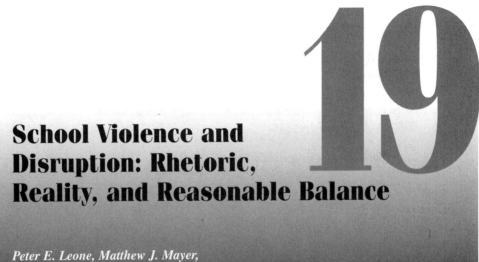

School Violence and Disruption: Rhetoric, Reality, and Reasonable Balance

Peter E. Leone, Matthew J. Mayer,
Kimber Malmgren, and Sheri M. Meisel

During the past few years the specter of school violence has caused many parents, teachers, and administrators to rethink their basic assumptions about the safety of schools. Tragic and senseless shootings of students by students in public schools in the United States have left us stunned and distraught. Images of school shootings and the demand that schools become safe for all children have shaped responses by politicians, parents, and school administrators (Sheley, 2000).

Recent and widely publicized school shootings raise a number of questions: Are public schools less safe than they were 10 years ago? Twenty years ago? Can teachers teach and children learn in an atmosphere where concerns about safety interfere with instruction and management? In addition to these questions, parents and others want to know who has been involved in these school shootings and whether schools have taken steps to ensure that these incidents don't happen in their schools.

Most parents and members of communities believe that schools should be places where children develop intellectually and socially. The idea that school violence, in whatever form, interferes with the orderly operation and safety of schools is anathema to the public. Beyond concerns about physical injury to children, disruption of the school environment interferes with others' learning and can create a climate of fear in which children avoid school or engage in behaviors to protect themselves (Chandler et al., 1998). There is also the concern that minor problems, if ignored, will escalate into major events.

The most current data on school violence and youth victimization in the United States indicate that violence has been declining since 1993. Data reported by the Federal Bureau of Investigation as part of the Uniform Crime Reports (Rand, 1998), as well as students' self-report of victimization that are part of the National Crime Victimization Surveys (Brener et al., 1999), indicate that violence perpetrated by and against youth continues to fall. In spite of this, many segments of the public believe that school violence is increasing (Brooks, Schiraldi, & Ziedenberg, 2000). Some of this misperception may be associated with the widely publicized school shootings at Columbine High School in Colorado and similar incidents in Kentucky, Oregon, and Michigan in the past few years.

Nevertheless, Uniform Crime Reports and data from other sources indicate that schools are the safest places for children to be. Fewer homicides and violent crimes are committed against children at school than in their homes or on the streets (Kaufman et al., 1998; Kaufman et al, 1999; Snyder & Sickmund, 1999). Students are greater than 100 times more likely to be the victim of a homicide away from school than at school (Kaufman et al., 1998).

Another issue that occasionally surfaces when the discussion turns to school violence is the role played by students with mental health problems or other disabling conditions. Some critics believe that special education rules and regulations have tied school principals' hands with regard to discipline and students with disabilities (Hymowitz, 2000). The most recent reauthorization of IDEA (Individuals with Disabilities Education Act) in 1997, however, gave schools a great deal of latitude in responding to disciplinary problems exhibited by students with disabilities. Principals can unilaterally remove special education students involved in weapons or drug offenses and those at risk of harming themselves or others and place them in interim alternative programs (Bear, 1999).

In this chapter we examine issues related to school violence and disruption. We begin by examining the sociocultural context within which school violence occurs, using a nested ecological schema. The first section presents a review of major changes in the status of children and their families, a discussion of availability and consequences of easy access to firearms, and the increase in prevalence of violence in popular media. We also examine media coverage of recent, widely publicized school shootings and the effect that media coverage has on parents' and students' perceptions of school safety. In the second section of the article, we examine prevalence and trends in school violence, with particular attention to the use of firearms on school property. This discussion explores some of the difficulty associated with defining and measuring school violence.

We then discuss the challenge of balancing the right to education with the importance of maintaining safe and orderly schools. In particular, we look at available data on the role of students with disabilities in school suspensions and discuss possible interpretations of these data. Finally, we examine how local schools and school districts have addressed violence and disruption in their buildings and communities. We describe violence-prevention initiatives and present guidelines for parents, teachers, and administrators to assist in ensuring that their schools are safe places that promote academic achievement and healthy behavior among all children and adolescents.

THE CONTEXTS OF SCHOOL VIOLENCE

School violence is a multifaceted phenomenon. Preventing school violence and responding to violent acts that occur within schools require an understanding of the larger community and society. Human behavior is shaped by social-ecological contexts that include individuals with whom we interact daily as well as broad societal contexts that deliver messages about appropriate behavior and relationships among people (Bronfenbrenner, 1979). A widely accepted model (Tolan & Guerra, 1994) of youth and family violence depicts a nested ecological system (see Figure 19.1) of individual factors, close interpersonal relations (e.g., peers and family), proximal social contexts (e.g., school and neighborhood), and societal macrosystems (e.g., media

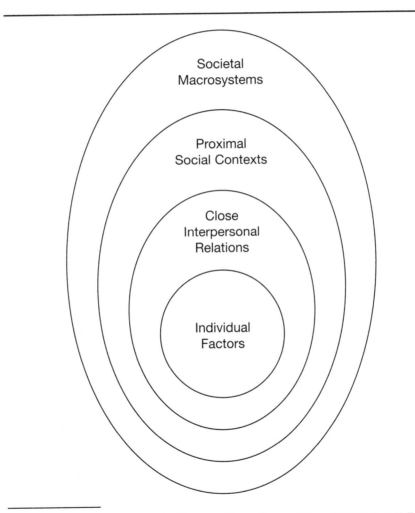

Source: Adapted from "Prevention of Delinquency: Current Status and Issues," (1994), by P. H. Tolan & N. G. Guerra, *Applied & Preventive Psychology, 3,* 254.

FIGURE 19.1 ■ A Nested Ecological System of Influences on Youth Behavior

and laws governing gun use). Schools have created prevention activities and developed school-wide management plans that have reduced disciplinary referrals and suspensions, addressing risk factors and needs at multiple levels (Taylor-Green et al., 1997; Sugai, Sprague, Horner, & Walker, 2000). These efforts and similar community-based initiatives have the potential to make schools more safe and orderly places for children. In this article, we will address aspects of the outer three levels of this nested system that surround the individual, looking at several school, family, and larger societal level factors.

The problem of school violence is linked to changes within our culture and society. Significant changes in family structure and changes in the status of children contribute to the problems that educators see in schools. Violence in the entertainment and news media has increased dramatically in recent years (Lichter, Lichter, & Amundson, 1999) and contributes to a sense that youth are being negatively influenced by the movies they see, the television they watch, the popular music they hear, and the video games they play.

Many youths have easy access to guns (Ward, 1999). At the same time, print and broadcast news media regularly report on a wide range of violent crime committed not just in our own communities but in any hamlet served by an affiliate or a subsidiary of a large media conglomerate (Goldstein, 1994). It is difficult to establish causal relationships between school violence and changes in family structure, violent themes in popular entertainment, the availability of guns, and the reporting of violence by the news media. In each of these areas, however, there have been significant changes in recent years.

Family Structure and Poverty

Changes in family structure and changes in the relative distribution of income within society in recent decades have affected children. In 1950, fewer than 20% of all children in the United States lived in households that were dual-earner nonfarm families and one-parent families. At present, nearly two thirds of all children live in dual-earner nonfarm and one-parent families (Hernandez, 1995). The effect of this drastic change in living arrangements is that fewer adults are at home and available to support students during the non-school hours. Although some of this change may have been offset by an increase in number of parents who work at home, evidence suggests that less time is available for parents to assist and monitor their children. Survey-based estimates suggest that from 4% to 23% of children regularly care for themselves, and several major surveys found that about 12% of children ages 5–12 were in self-care at least once a week (Kerrebrock & Lewit, 1999; U.S. Department of Education, 1999b).

Another major change since 1980 that affects children has been a shift in the distribution of family income. While the mean income of families in the United States has risen, there has been an increasing gap between children in families living at the lowest income levels and those at the highest levels. From 1968 to 1994, income inequality in the United States increased 22.4% (Weinberg, 1996). While the percentage of children living in luxury approaches 20%, an even larger percentage of children live in relative poverty or near-poor frugality (Hernandez, 1995; U. S. Bureau of the Census, 1998; Weinberg, 1996).

More recent data from the U.S. Bureau of the Census, based on the *Gini Index* and quintile shares of aggregate household income (widely used measures of income inequality), show for the most part, from 1993 to 1998, no significant change in income distribution (A. Jones, personal communication, July 17, 2000). Poverty and the availability of parents to supervise their children do not directly create or cause school violence and or disruption. Nevertheless, poverty is one of a number of factors that place youth at risk for school failure, dropout, and delinquent behavior (Walker & Sprague, 1999), and inadequate monitoring and supervision of children is associated with the development of antisocial behavior and delinquency (Patterson, 1982; Farrington, 1995; Hawkins et al, 2000).

Violence in the entertainment industry

A study by the Center for Media and Public Affairs documented the frequency with which violent images are featured in popular entertainment (Lichter et al., 1999). They examined made-for-television movies, television series, music videos, and movies, to determine the prevalence with which violent content was featured. They found that across all forms of entertainment, serious violent images or scenes were featured on the average of 14 times per hour of viewing. When just high violence shows were examined, they found an average of 54 violent acts per hour. Although causal effects between viewing violent images and engaging in violent or disruptive behavior in school are difficult to establish, evidence suggests that exposure to television violence does have an effect on violent behavior (American Psychological Association, 1993; Felson, 1996; Reiss & Roth, 1993).

Media Coverage of School Violence

During the past few years, news media have ratcheted up their coverage of violence in communities and across the country. The evening news and the daily paper chronicle violent acts, both local and across the country, involving juveniles and adults. In the wake of the tragic events and the massive media blitz at Columbine High School in April, 1999, a *USA Today* poll found that 68% of Americans surveyed thought that it was likely or very likely that a school shooting could occur in their town. Other polls of parents' perceptions of school safety taken in the past year revealed similar results (Brooks, Schiraldi, & Ziedenberg, 2000).

Consolidation within the media industry has placed control of radio, television, and newspapers in the hands of fewer and fewer companies (Howard, 1995). As corporate giants compete for audience share or circulation, reporting of violence has become a marketing tool to increase market share (Felson, 1996). Local events in one part of the country become national events as affiliate television and radio stations and newspapers carry reports throughout the country. Although juvenile crime rates fell in the 1990s, the public, informed by media coverage of violence, largely believed that juvenile crime was up and that schools were unsafe (Brooks et al., 2000).

Access to Guns

Handguns and other firearms are more widely available in the United States than in any other industrialized nation in the world, reflecting a permissive policy approach. A 1997 National Institute of Justice report estimated that approximately one third of all households in the United States have guns, with two thirds of gun owners possessing more than one gun (Cook & Ludwig, 1997). At the time of a recent survey 20% of gun owners reported having unlocked, loaded guns in their houses (Cook & Ludwig, 1997). In 1997, more than 4,200 children ages 0–19 were killed by firearms in the United States. More than 2,500 of these killings were homicides and another 1,200 were suicides (Ward, 1999).

Proportionately, young black males are more likely than white youths to be the victims of gun violence. Though federal law restricts sales of guns to minors by licensed gun dealers, in some states children as young as 12 can legally possess semi-automatic weapons and other firearms (Ward, 1999). Yet, unmistakably, the horrific killing of students by students in schools in recent years could not have happened without easy access to firearms by children.

Accountability, Achievement, and Zero Tolerance at the School Level

Our public schools also have changed dramatically during the past decade. Among other things, there has been an increased focus on accountability, information technology, and achievement. At the same time, there has been a decrease in tolerance of deviant behavior. Accountability and an emphasis on literacy for the Information Age have created a greater sense of urgency among educators. Teachers, principals, and superintendents are being asked to measure and demonstrate tangible academic gains in their students' performance. In this climate, disruptive students, particularly those who score poorly on tests that measure the performance of the classroom, school, or school district, are at-risk for being excluded from the education community.

Under the mantle of zero tolerance, schools and school boards have instituted policies that suspend students from school for a wide range of rule infractions that range from threats of violence to possession of weapons to use or possession of drugs on school property. Zero tolerance has created situations in which principals have no latitude or discretion in administering disciplinary sanctions. Thus, students have been suspended for sharing Midol tablets, for bringing a plastic knife to spread peanut butter at lunch, for sharing cough drops, for displaying a manicure kit with a 1-inch knife, and for sharing a prescription inhaler with a student experiencing anaphylactic shock (Tebo, 2000; Skiba & Peterson, 1999).

In sum, changes in the family and the status of children, increases in violent images in popular entertainment, changes in media coverage of violent events, increased availability of guns, and increased accountability at school all set the stage for understanding the current state of school violence and disruption. In the next section, we examine authoritative reports concerning school violence and discuss the difficulty of measuring school violence.

UNDERSTANDING SCHOOL VIOLENCE

Interest in school violence is a relatively recent phenomenon. How we conceptualize and define school violence shapes how schools think about and respond to the problem (Furlong & Morrison, 2000). Depending upon one's definition of the term, acts of school violence can range from threats of physical violence, to bullying, physical assaults, and homicide.

Data on School Violence

Schools are safer than individual homes and neighborhoods. Children are more likely to encounter serious violent crime away from school than at school. Multiple sources suggest that students are approximately three times safer in school than away from school (Elliott, Hamburg, and Williams, 1998; Kaufman et al., 1999; Snyder & Sickmund, 1999). There is less than a one in a million chance of a student experiencing a school-related violent death. Furthermore, the vast majority of school-related injuries are not violence-related and the majority of school crime is non-violent theft (U.S. Department of Education, 1999a).

The picture of school violence that has emerged over the past decade provides reason for concern, yet optimism for the future. The findings are mixed. In 1997, there were 202,000 serious violent crimes (rape, sexual assault, robbery, and aggravated assault) against students ages 12–18 in school and 2.7 million total school crimes (Kaufman et al., 1999). Centers for Disease Control (CDC) data collected in 1999 from the Youth Risk Behavior Surveillance (YRBS) (Kann et al., 2000) found:

— 6.9% carried weapons at school nationally during 30 days prior to the survey, with males (11.0%) reporting much higher rates of weapon-carrying than females (2.8%)
— 7.7% of students nationally reported having been threatened or injured with a weapon on school property during the past 12 months
— 14.2% of students had been in a physical fight at school during the prior 12 months.

Some longer-term data show that certain measures of violence in schools have remained fairly constant over the past 20 years while other measures of violence have shown a clear pattern of decrease during the 1990s. For example, YRBS data (Centers for Disease Control and Prevention, 2000) show a steady, dramatic decline in students reporting having carried a weapon on school property during the 30 days prior to the survey, from 11.8% in 1993 to 6.9% in 1999 (see Figure 19.2).

The same YRBS data show a similarly impressive decline in students reporting having carried a gun during the 30 days prior to the survey, from 7.9% in 1993 to 4.9% in 1999. Also, from 1993 to 1999, the percentage of students who reported having been in a physical fight at school during the 30 days prior to the survey dropped from 16.2% to 14.2%. The *Annual Report on School Safety* (U.S. Department of Education, 1999a) also reports a decline in several measures of school violence during the 1990s.

Several indicators of school violence have remained fairly constant over the past 20 years. For example, from 1976 to 1997, approximately 5% of high school seniors report having been injured with a weapon at school during the previous 12 months, according to data from the ongoing *Monitoring the Future* study (University of Michigan). During the same period, approximately 12% of seniors report having been injured without a weapon and about 12% report having been threatened with a

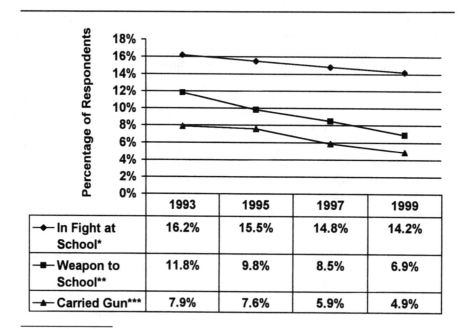

	1993	1995	1997	1999
◆ In Fight at School*	16.2%	15.5%	14.8%	14.2%
■ Weapon to School**	11.8%	9.8%	8.5%	6.9%
▲ Carried Gun***	7.9%	7.6%	5.9%	4.9%

Source: Centers for Disease Control and Prevention. (2000). *Fact Sheet: Youth Risk Behavior Trends*

* Involved in a fight *on school property* at least one time during the 12 months preceding the survey
** Carried a weapon *on school property* at least one time during the 30 days preceding the survey
*** Carried a gun at least one time during the 30 days preceding the survey

FIGURE 19.2 ■ Self-Report of Risk Related Behaviors: 1993–1999 Trends

weapon at school during the previous 12 months (U.S. Department of Education, 1999b; Institute for Social Research, 1997). Other data sources, such as the so-called Principals' and Disciplinarians' Report (U.S. Department of Education, 1998a), show relatively less crime in the schools. That report was based on incidents in which the school called the police. Understandably, administrators may be reluctant to call police or to submit reports suggesting that their school environment is out of control.

This discussion demonstrates that reported measures of school violence differ somewhat depending on the source. A reasonable question to ask is: Why do we see clear signs of decline in some measures, yet relative stability in other measures? Also, how do we decide whether, and to what extent, school violence and disruption is a serious problem? To begin to answer these questions, we need to consider a number of issues surrounding school violence, as well as community-based violence data collection and reporting.

Making Sense of the Numbers

National data on school violence come from several sources. Some sources focus on criminal acts per se, others focus on injury from a health agency perspective, and some privately commissioned surveys (e.g., Metropolitan Life Survey of the American Teacher) focus on various aspects of school violence. The FBI Uniform Crime Reporting (UCR) Program gathers reports from local law enforcement agencies directly or through respective state agencies (Cook & Laub, 1998). As illustrated by Cook and Laub, the UCR data can seriously underestimate true levels of violent crime and provide no information on age of victim or assailant.

Furthermore, some data on juvenile crime are presented in terms of arrests, whereas other data represent convictions. These two categories are quite different, as arrest figures can include innocent individuals (Loeber, Farrington, & Waschbusch, 1998, p. 21). Arrests records do not offer a viable sample of actual crime perpetrators (Cook & Laub, 1998). In addition, law enforcement agencies vary considerably in their reporting of data to the UCR system, thus making year-to-year and other comparisons risky.

A separate source of national level data on violence comes from the National Crime Victimization Survey (NCVS), using household interviews conducted every 6 months (since 1973), and from the School Crime Supplement (SCS) to the NCVS, which is conducted every 4 or 5 years. The NCVS provides information on victimization of youths age 12 and older. Like other forms of self-report, however, this one is subject to errors from a variety of sources, including sampling frame problems, instrument problems, and respondent errors such as inaccurate recall, comprehension problems, omissions, and telescoping effects (Biemer et al., 1991).

Data gathering methods to assess school violence vary considerably, and perceived violence is consistently reported at higher levels than self-reports of violent incidents (Furlong and Morrison, 1994). Methodologically, studies on school violence usually take a [confirmatory] hypothesis verification approach. That is, school violence is assumed to exist and survey questions elicit responses that confirm its existence. A Congressional Research Service report (U.S. Library of Congress, 1994) found problems in data collection efforts regarding school violence in terms of inconsistent definitions and wording of indicators, varying time frames among studies, and underreporting of criminal acts.

Reiss and Roth (1993) offer a detailed analysis of data collection issues pertaining to violence. They cite differences between UCR, NCVS, and National Center for Health Statistics (NCHS) data in terms of: "(a) domain of events, (b) unit of count, (c) timing of counting, and (d) sources of discretion and error in recording and counting events."

Furthermore, events that are measured are social constructs that depend on society's view of crime—something that changes over time. Reiss and Roth also note that crime incidents can be described differently as a function of the location and circumstance, whether they are defined in terms of the perpetrator (arrest) or victim (injury), and whether multiple offenders or offenses are involved. All of these issues can contribute to varying depictions of violent activity in the community as well as in schools.

Agencies responsible for data collection, analysis, and reporting have attempted to ameliorate the situation throughout the 1980s and 1990s. The CDC has supported many efforts to standardize definitions and reporting of injury-related data (CDC, 1997; Mercy, Ikeda, & Powell, 1998). The National Education Statistics Agenda Committee (U.S. Department of Education, 1996) assessed the current status of data collection and reporting among the states regarding criminal and violent behaviors in schools. The committee issued a report describing the existing state of affairs, providing model definitions for data collection and a description of a model data system that states could choose to implement.

Reconciling the differences between CDC data showing a clear decline in school violence and *Monitoring the Future* data that shows stability over two decades is a challenge. The participants, time frames, and wording of questions differ between these surveys. For example, several of the CDC-YRBS survey questions pertain to frequency of weapon-carrying and involvement in a fight. Several of the questions from the *Monitoring the Future* survey pertain to being threatened or injured with a weapon, and having property damaged or stolen.

Although we may choose to think of these questions as proxy variables for school violence and disruption, just because they fall under a common umbrella concept does not necessarily mean that they measure the same behaviors. They each need to be evaluated within the context of the specific survey effort. Unfortunately, no existing procedure allows clear reconciliation of these data differences. The best one can do is to conclude that some serious problems remain with school violence, but that there are several clear signals of an improving situation and that, generally speaking, schools are safe.

BALANCING EDUCATIONAL RIGHTS
WITH AN ORDERLY SCHOOL ENVIRONMENT

Public schools are charged with providing all children with educational opportunities. School administrators and teachers have a vested interest in creating environments in which their students can best learn. Given the diversity and the numbers of children who walk through the public school doors, this is no small feat. School systems and personnel must constantly balance the need for orderliness and efficiency in schools with the rights and entitlements of individual students. Although the needs and desires of school systems often are aligned with the needs and desires of the students they serve, at times the two are at odds.

In the following sections we will discuss some of the entitlements due students in general, and how these entitlements have affected schools' abilities to provide appropriate educational environments. We also will discuss the impact of those additional entitlements afforded students with disabilities, including some of the pitfalls and misperceptions associated with these entitlements.

Educational Entitlements

Compulsory school-attendance laws give children the right, as well as the responsibility, to attend school. Schools must serve all the children in their communities—even children who prefer not to attend. The public schools cannot pick and choose whom they serve, even if picking and choosing would result in more efficiency, higher achievement scores for the school as a whole, or less disruption.

Over time, compulsory school-attendance laws have created problems for schools in jurisdictions where schools and school districts have not adapted to their changing school clientele. Problems have included truancy, disruptive or disrespectful behavior, drug use, threats of violence, and acts of violence. As problems have cropped up, individual schools, school districts, and governmental agencies have crafted ways for schools to deal with those problems. Responses have included (and continue to include) the use of behavioral modification strategies, timeouts, and corporal punishment. For serious violations of the school code, schools have expelled students and placed them into alternative education settings (Yell, 1990; Yell, Cline, and Bradley, 1995; Yell, 1998, ch. 15). Sometimes these responses have been effective in restoring order to the school environment. Other times these responses have gone too far and threatened the rights of the students to whom they are applied.

The U.S. Supreme Court has examined the issue of school discipline on several occasions. In 1977, the Court examined the constitutionality of corporal punishment (*Ingraham v. Wright,* 1977). Although the Court eventually decided that corporal punishment did not constitute "cruel and unusual punishment" and that students were not entitled to a hearing prior to the administration of corporal punishment (under the due process clause of the 14th Amendment), the justices did reiterate that individual teachers or administrators could be held liable or subject to criminal penalties if the corporal punishment administered was later found to be excessive.

Even though the *Ingraham v. Wright* decision did not change the legal status of corporal punishment, the very fact that the Supreme Court heard this case influenced state legislatures to pass additional laws governing the use of corporal punishment (Yell, 1990; Yell, 1998, ch. 15). Corporal punishment remains an option for schools in some states, but its use is limited by requirements such as approval by the principal, presence of an adult witness, and prior parental approval. These limitations protect individual students from capricious and overzealous use of corporal punishment by frustrated school personnel.

Another disciplinary action that has been called into question is suspension from school. In 1975, the U.S. Supreme Court heard *Goss v. Lopez,* in which nine high school students alleged that their constitutional right to due process (under the 14th Amendment) had been violated when they were each suspended for up to 10 days without a formal hearing. In this case, the Court sided with the students, declaring that schools must provide evidence of a student's misconduct at a hearing prior to (or immediately following) the suspension. The Court ruled that students' rights to attend school supersede schools' rights to unilaterally exclude students for misconduct. Although school suspensions for disciplinary purposes are allowable, the process must include oral or written notice of the offense and the right to be heard (Yell, 1998, ch. 15).

In *Honig v. Doe* (1988), the Supreme Court set the stage for revised procedures in dealing with aggressive and violent students. This contributed to a change in attitudes among educators, politicians, and the public with regard to the behavior of students with disabilities. Bill Honig, Superintendent of Instruction for California schools, argued that a dangerousness exclusion to the "stay-put provision" of disability law existed, whereby schools could exclude students who threatened the safety of others. The Court denied his argument and made it clear that the stay-put provision held, and that schools could not unilaterally remove students considered dangerous while their change of placement was being appealed.

The Court's ruling also supported the position that a suspension of more than 10 days is a change of placement. The court affirmed that normal procedures, including temporary suspensions of up to 10 days, timeout, study carrels, and detention could be used with dangerous students (Sorenson, 1993; Tucker, Goldstein, and Sorenson, 1993; Yell, 1998).

In the last 5 to 10 years, particularly in the aftermath of the Honig decision, a number of state and local education agencies have revised school disciplinary codes to reflect the tenor of recent Safe and Drug-Free Schools legislation (Skiba & Peterson, 1999, 2000). This legislation was aimed at eliminating weapons and controlled substances on school grounds. This type of disciplinary approach—popularly referred to as zero tolerance—has serious flaws in its implementation. Some administrators have overlooked small infractions by otherwise well-behaved students (e.g., an honor student who forgets to remove a miniature Swiss army knife from his keychain), and others have enforced the letter of the law to such an unyielding extent that they attract national media attention (e.g., the second-grader who brought his grandfather's watch to show and tell; a 1-inch mini-pocketknife was attached; the student was suspended and sent to an alternative school for 1 month).

The real problem with a zero-tolerance posture is that serious punishments, such as suspensions from school, have been handed out in an arbitrary and inconsistent manner (Harvard University Civil Rights Project, 2000; Skiba & Peterson, 1999; Tebo, 2000). Students with disabilities who have behavioral problems and who typically have few advocates in the schools, as well as African-American students, are particularly vulnerable to harsh disciplinary tactics (Harvard University Civil Rights Project, 2000; Townsend, 2000).

Entitlements of Students with Disabilities

Although basic educational entitlements apply to all students, those with disabilities are afforded separate, additional protections under the IDEA, most recently amended and reauthorized in 1997. Provisions of IDEA pertaining to discipline are frequently a source of contention. For example, if a student engages in aggressive or disruptive behavior as a consequence of his or her disability, a school is not at liberty to unilaterally suspend that child from school for that very behavior. This is not to say, however, that schools have no recourse whatsoever when a student with a disability misbehaves.

A wide-range of commonly used discipline tactics are still available to use with students with disabilities. These include behavior management strategies, restrictions on privileges, and in-school suspension. Even suspension from school is still an option as long as that suspension does not last 10 days or become part of a pattern of suspensions that accumulate up to 10 days in length.

The stay-put provision of IDEA (IDEA Regulations, 34 C.F.R. § 300.514) is a common concern for teachers and administrators. When a student with a disability engages in serious acts of misconduct that could result in that student's removal from his or her current placement, school administrators and the student's parents often concur on a plan of action. When parents and school administrators disagree and parents request a due-process hearing, the stay-put provision comes into play. Under the stay-put clause, schools are not allowed to remove a student from his or her current placement while the disciplinary action is under review.

The stay-put provision often is misinterpreted to mean that children with disabilities can engage in dangerous conduct without fear of ever being removed to a more restrictive setting. To the contrary, if a student with a disability brings a weapon or controlled substance to school, that student is subject to the same disciplinary actions that apply to a student without a disability. The student then can be referred to an Interim Alternative Education Placement (IAEP).

Regardless of the disciplinary outcome, the school system must provide special education services to any student with a disability who ends up being suspended from school for more than 10 cumulative days in a school year. In addition, if a child with a disability engages in behavior that school administrators believe is likely to result in injury to self or others in the school community, the child with a disability can be removed to an IAEP for up to 45 days (Bear, 1999). The critical element is that the child with a disability not lose access to his or her educational services. The educational services provided to children with disabilities—including services designed to address their behavioral and social-skill deficits—are critical to their eventual success.

Occasionally schools use homebound instruction as an IAEP. These cases seem to violate both the spirit and intent of IDEA discipline provisions. Homebound instruction typically is limited to about 6 hours per week. In such circumstances, it is virtually impossible to provide appropriate academic instruction, and this level of service precludes meaningful implementation of a student's IEP.

Behaviors of Students With Disabilities

How often are students with disabilities involved in school violence and disruption? Apart from anecdotal accounts, it is difficult to find authoritative analyses, as data sources are limited. Several sources from recent years, however, present a partial picture and enable us to draw some tentative conclusions. We will examine two reports on implementation of the Gun-Free Schools Act, an analysis of suspensions and expulsions in Kansas, an analysis from Kentucky schools, a look at recent data from Maryland, and data regarding suspensions in Delaware and Minnesota. We also examine a national-level study of suspensions and expulsions by the Research Triangle Institute, a survey of state and local practices from state directors of special education services, and findings in the 21st Annual Report to Congress on IDEA.

Gun-Free Schools Reports

Subsequent to passage of the Gun-Free Schools Act of 1994, Congress mandated that annual reports be issued concerning implementation of the Act, including data on involvement of students with disabilities. The Act required each state receiving federal funds under the Elementary and Secondary Education Act (ESEA) to have a state law in effect mandating a minimum 1-year expulsion of students who brought a firearm to school, allowing chief administering officers the right to modify expulsion terms on a case-by-case basis.

During the 1996–97 school year, 6,093 students were expelled from school under the Act. Of the 43 states reporting on shortened expulsions, 39 states reported on the disability status of these students. Of the 699 students reported, 37% had disabilities under IDEA (U.S. Department of Education, 1998b). During the 1997–98 school year, 3,930 students were expelled from school under the Act. Of the 49 states reporting on shortened expulsions, 48 states reported on the disability status of these students. Of the 1,459 students reported, 38% had disabilities under IDEA (U.S. Department of Education, 1999c).

Suspensions and Expulsions in Kansas

Cooley (1995) examined suspension/expulsion data in Kansas, using survey data from 441 secondary school principals. This study found that students with disabilities had more than double the likelihood of suspension/expulsion than students without disabilities. Students with learning disabilities and behavior disorders were disproportionately represented among the students with disabilities who were suspended/expelled, compared to their proportions among students with disabilities in Kansas.

According to the researchers, however, students receiving special education services were no more likely than nondisabled students to engage in injury-causing behaviors. Furthermore, the acts committed by the suspended students with disabilities were found to be no different than those committed by nondisabled students. The report concluded that the students with disabilities were not receiving IEP-related services appropriate to their needs.

Analysis of Records in Kentucky

An analysis of records of 465 students in an Eastern Kentucky school district (Fasko, Grubb, and Osborne, 1995) found that about 20% of the suspended students were disabled, although students with disabilities composed about 14% of students included in the study. Approximately 83% of the suspensions were given to male students, and 17% to females. Males and females made up 53% and 47% of the student population, respectively.

Maryland Data

Data from Maryland (Maryland State Department of Education, 2000) showed that statewide, 64,103 students were suspended during the 1998–99 school year. Of those students, 15,669 (24.4%) were students with disabilities. Students with disabilities made up 13.1% of the statewide enrollment that year. Prior Maryland data for the 1997–98 school year (Maryland State Department of Education, 1999) provided an inconclusive picture of suspensions of students with disabilities because duplicated and unduplicated counts were mixed, using both incident- and person-specific data. This made comparisons to statewide percent of students with disabilities impossible, because, depending on relative rates of multiple offenses among disabled and nondisabled populations, different conclusions could be drawn.

Suspensions in Delaware

Along a similar vein, data from a study of suspensions in Delaware (cited in Sinclair and others, 1996) found that 23% of the incidents resulting in out-of-school suspensions during the 1994–95 school year involved special education students. These data were based on *incident* counts, not *person* counts. Therefore, we cannot conclude that 23% of the suspended students were special education students. Interestingly, the 1997–98 Maryland data (also not conclusive for similar reasons) found that 23.5% of short-term suspension incidents were associated with students with disabilities.

Suspensions in Minnesota

A University of Minnesota policy research brief (Sinclair et al., 1996) reported that in Minnesota, the overwhelming percentage of suspensions of students with disabilities involved students with learning disabilities and behavior disorders. The study found that, based on data from several other state studies, about 25% of suspension incidents were associated with students with disabilities.

Research Triangle Institute Report

Fiore and Reynolds (1996) conducted an exhaustive study gathering data on discipline issues in special education. The researchers found that for aggregated data from responding states and districts, approximately 20% of suspended students were students with disabilities, a percentage much larger than their proportion of the student population. Approximately 80% of the misconduct by students with disabilities was considered less serious, with about 20% of the misconduct falling into more serious categories. Also, the vast majority of students with disabilities who were suspended were males. Students with emotional disabilities were overrepresented among students with disabilities who were suspended.

The authors noted the paucity of available data on suspension/expulsion of students with disabilities. Only six states and 16 districts provided data on suspensions that included information on students with disabilities. The report demonstrated a tremendous variability among the states with regard to data systems on suspensions and on students with disabilities. The authors urged caution in interpreting the results, as many jurisdictions either had no such data-recording system or failed to provide the requested data. In turn, the available data cannot be construed as a nationally representative sample for students with disabilities.

21st Annual Report to Congress

The 21st Annual Report to Congress on IDEA (U.S. Department of Education, 2000) addressed school discipline and students with disabilities and reviewed some of the research cited above. Citing a 1994 Office of Civil Rights (OCR) report that found no overrepresentation of students with disabilities among suspended students, the Department of Education report discussed discrepant findings concerning discipline and students with disabilities.

Survey of State Departments of Education

A survey of state departments of special education (Morgan, Loosli, & Striefel, 1997) found improvements in maintaining and disseminating behavior standards compared to a similar survey done 5 years earlier. Of the 41 state respondents, 14 states reported that they had no such standards on behavioral procedures. The researchers found considerable variability among the states with regard to maintaining an information dissemination, monitoring, and training system for behavioral procedures for students with disabilities.

CONCLUSIONS DRAWN FROM STUDIES

Although the data discussed above do not constitute a nationally representative sample of students with disabilities, we can still draw several tentative conclusions from these studies.

1. Mounting evidence suggests that a disproportionately high percentage (possibly close to 20%) of suspended students are students with disabilities, compared to a national proportion of about 11% of students ages 6–21 receiving services under IDEA. One OCR study (cited in the 21st Annual Report to Congress) contradicts this conclusion. Several studies demonstrate that students with learning disabilities and emotional disturbance are over-represented among suspended students with disabilities.
2. Several studies have found that the majority of suspension-related behaviors seem to be nonviolent and generally do not result in injuries to others.
3. The nature of the suspension-related behaviors of students with disabilities may not be substantively different than the behaviors of the students' nondisabled peers.
4. Some evidence suggests that procedures to guarantee a system of consistent behavioral procedures for students with disabilities vary tremendously among the states and that students in some states may not be receiving appropriate services. Rather, suspension may be the procedure of choice in lieu of more proactive, supportive approaches.

Research by Mayer and Leone (1999), as well as publications by the Justice Policy Institute and the American Policy Forum (Brooks, Schiraldi, & Zeidenberg, 2000; Mendel, 2000) suggest that punitive, controlling approaches do little to solve continuing problems of school violence and disruption or juvenile crime in the community.

More data regarding specific school experiences with violence, individual school practices, and the role of students with disabilities will be gathered with the new School Survey on Crime and Safety (SSOCS), sponsored by the U.S. Department of Education, National Center for Education Statistics (NCES). NCES plans to conduct the SSOCS every 2 years, and the first SSOCS report is due in December 2000.

Gun-Free Schools Act suspension data revealed 37%– 38% representation by students with disabilities among cases shortened to less than one year for states reporting disability-related data. While it is logical that a relatively high percentage of cases meriting chief administering officer review would involve examination of disability-related factors, these data raise several concerns. *First,* the data (U.S. Department of Education, 1998b, 1999c), is a small and possibly unrepresentative subset of the complete dataset, precluding thorough analysis of the situation. The data must be interpreted with caution.

Second, there is reason to believe that often, students with disabilities get caught more often than nondisabled peers, because of problems with social communication, poor judgment, poor planning skills, and attributional biases that can lead to more confrontation with authority figures. These students may be more easily identified by the system for their infractions. That is not to lessen the egregiousness or unacceptability of such behaviors. Rather, it may simply point to a state of affairs in which students with disabilities are represented disproportionately in such cases, in part, because their nondisabled peers are more adept at eluding detection.

Third, the 37%–38% data could be fairly accurate, in which case schools need to develop new understandings and find more effective interventions to reduce weapon-carrying, particularly by students with disabilities. Additional research may shed more light on the exact nature of this phenomenon.

Schools clearly face many challenges in maintaining a safe and orderly environment. The next section presents several approaches to school- and community-based programming.

HOW SCHOOLS HAVE RESPONDED TO PROBLEMS OF SCHOOL VIOLENCE

Understanding and Shaping School Environments

School-based violence prevention initiatives are considered a best-practice approach to foster positive youth development (Dwyer & Osher, 2000; Mendel, 2000; Walker & Horner, 1996). Federal and state policy makers increasingly are viewing schools as excellent sites for prevention activities, although federal expenditures for these efforts are relatively modest (Gottfredson, 1997). Schools provide consistent access to youth in the early developmental years, and they employ staff members who are focused on ensuring successful academic and behavioral outcomes for students. Another critical advantage is that many risk factors (see Figure 19.3) associated with youth violence are school-related and therefore may be modified within school settings.

Schools should consider three fundamental principles when planning violence prevention initiatives. *First,* evidence strongly supports the effectiveness of *school-wide violence prevention* initiatives based conceptually on a public health model. This model organizes prevention efforts so that schools can systematically address the needs of all students, including those with severe academic, emotional, or behavioral problems.

Second, approaches that emphasize punishment, control, and containment have been demonstrated to be ineffective in preventing or intervening in disruption and violence; punitive orientations may actually exacerbate school disorder (Mayer & Leone, 1999).

Third, effective school-wide prevention initiatives are comprehensive, have several components, and involve a broad range of services and supports provided over a sufficient period. Because the antecedents of youth violence are highly correlated (Dryfoos, 1990; Hawkins et al., 2000), prevention programs that address a range of interrelated risk and protective factors have greater potential than single-focus programs.

The public health approach underlying school-wide violence prevention initiatives was defined by the Institute of Medicine (1994) as a three-tiered ecological perspective incorporating a continuum of strategies at graduated levels of intensity. This model promotes the use of a comprehensive framework of *universal, selective,* and *indicated* prevention strategies (Tolan, Guerra, & Kendall, 1995).

FOCUS ON SCHOOLS: CALVERTON MIDDLE SCHOOL

Calverton Middle School in Baltimore serves nearly 1,200 students in grades 6 through 8. The school has had a history of low achievement test scores, high rates of student and teacher absenteeism, and discipline problems. Seventy percent of the students at Calverton are eligible for free or reduced-price lunches. During the 1999–2000 school year, 56 of the 85 teachers at the school held provisional or probationary certification. Seven teachers were on long-term leave.

Performance at Calverton was among the lowest for middle schools in the state of Maryland. Daily attendance by students for the 1998–1999 school year averaged 69%, and during the Fall of 1999, more than 300 students were tardy to school each day. The school was chaotic and experienced frequent interruptions resulting from pulled fire alarms, fights, and classroom disruptions.

Scores on the statewide Maryland School Performance Assessment Program (MSPAP) from 1993–99 indicated that fewer than 6% of eighth grade students scored excellent or satisfactory in reading and fewer than 5% of eighth graders scored excellent or satisfactory in mathematics. On the Maryland State Department of Education's Middle School Performance Index (SPI), Calverton scored from 22.57 to 28.24 each year from 1993 to 1999. The SPI is the weighted average of a school's relative distance from the satisfactory standards, where a score of 100 is considered satisfactory. Several years ago,

Calverton was placed on a list of schools eligible for reconstitution or takeover by the Maryland State Department of Education.

In February, 2000, a new principal, Karl Perry, assumed administrative responsibility for Calverton. To begin the process of turning Calverton into an effective and caring school, Perry, with the support of staff, instituted a series of measures designed to refocus the attention of staff and students on academic excellence. Following consultation with other administrative staff, the Five Ps—be Present, Punctual, Prepared, Polite, and Positive—were introduced. Perry's primary objectives in assuming the principalship were to gain control of the school and improve the school climate. Principal Perry also introduced the *Drop Everything And Read* (DEAR) program, a regular part of the school day at Calverton. He met with parents, local business owners, and members of the community to develop shared strategies to combat truancy and tardiness.

As a result of using an appropriately tailored combination of universal and selective level interventions, Calverton Middle School has showed early signs of improvement. For example, student attendance has risen from about 69% to over 76%. Tardy arrivals have dropped from about 300 per day during the Fall to about 150 during the Spring semester. Office referrals dropped from more than 2,600 during the Fall semester of 1999 to under 2,200 during the following semester.

<table>
<tr><td>

INDIVIDUAL RISK FACTORS

- Poor academic skills
- Impulsivity
- Substance use
- Poor social problem-solving skills
- Inability to understand the perspective of others
- Poor conflict-resolution skills
- Difficulties in understanding the moral consequences of actions

</td><td>

PEER RISK FACTORS

- Low social status
- Rejection by peers
- Gang involvement
- Shared deviant peer norms
- Association with delinquent peer groups

</td></tr>
<tr><td>

FAMILY RISK FACTORS

- Inconsistent discipline
- Reliance on coercion
- Harsh or abusive discipline
- Poor monitoring of activities
- Insecure attachments
- Defensive communication
- Deviant shared values
- A high percentage of negative interactions
- Low levels of emotional closeness
- Inefficient use of family resources

</td><td>

SCHOOL/COMMUNITY RISK FACTORS

- Lack of student/parent involvement
- Low academic achievement
- Lack of social organization and social support
- Few opportunities for recreation
- Unemployment and economic disparities
- High levels of community crime
- Availability of firearms

</td></tr>
</table>

Source: *A Program Planning Guide for Youth Violence Prevention* (1996, p. 15), by N. G. Guerra and K. R. Williams (Boulder, CO: Center for the Study and prevention of Violence). Copyright © 1996 by the Institute of Behavioral Science, Regents of the University of Colorado. Reprinted by permission.

FIGURE 19.3 ■ Risk factors for youth violence

■ Universal strategies are the foundation of school-wide prevention efforts because they apply a primary prevention approach to the entire school population. Consistent use of these strategies provides sufficient support for a majority (80%–90%) of students in each school, thereby avoiding most instances of new problem behavior. Examples of universal prevention strategies include unambiguous behavioral expectations, proactive classroom management strategies, teacher expectations that support positive student outcomes, opportunities for positive attachment to school, consistent use of incentives and consequences, and school-wide literacy programs.

■ Selective strategies provide increased support for a smaller number of students (10%–15%) in each school. Secondary prevention strategies such as small-group instruction, social-skills training, behavioral contracting, and mentoring are designed to avoid the escalation of emerging academic and behavioral problems.

■ Indicated strategies support a relatively small number of students in each school (1%–5%) who demonstrate significant academic or behavioral problems requiring the most intensive level of support. Prevention strategies for these youth are individualized and often involve long-term involvement of education, mental health, social service, and juvenile justice agencies. Wraparound planning (Burns & Goldman, 1999) and school-based mental health services (Weist & Warner, 1997; Woodruff et al., 1999) are widely regarded as important advances in violence prevention for high-risk youth.

The variety of strategies incorporated in school-based violence prevention plans can be organized as individual or as environmental approaches. Prevention plans may focus on individual risk factors including alienation from school, truancy, poor academic performance, low levels of social competency, and antisocial behavior in the early grades. More broadly, prevention plans may focus on risk factors in the school and community, such as availability of drugs and weapons, negative peer experiences, and inadequate academic or behavioral support. Although examples of prevention strategies at the individual and environmental level are presented separately below, the interdependence of risk factors calls for integrated approaches that incorporate more than a single type of support.

Strategies frequently included in school-wide prevention plans that target individual risk factors include:

1. Instructional programs (identified as the most common prevention strategy used in schools) (Womer, 1997; Larson, 1994). These curriculum-based approaches focus on a range of social competency and academic skills with the goals of preventing or remediating academic failure, heightening awareness and knowledge of social influences on violent behavior, and teaching appropriate responses to these influences.
2. Behavior-management techniques designed to change antisocial behaviors and promote positive behavioral skills. These strategies will be most effective when based on systematic screening to identify students at risk for antisocial behavior (Sprague & Walker, 2000).
3. Peer strategies including peer coaching, mediation, and counseling.
4. Counseling and mentoring strategies.

Examples of environmental strategies are a strong academic mission, defining norms for appropriate behavior, promoting student attachment to school, and modifying organizational and structural conditions in the school by decreasing class size and providing a consistent climate of emotional support (Leone, 1997). In this context, prevention strategies should become a normative part of the school routine. For example, programs that teach nonviolent problem-solving strategies have a greater chance for success when the school climate regularly supports and models that approach to conflict (Gottfredson, 1997). School-wide prevention plans should be a high priority for the school and school system, a commitment reflected by strong administrative leadership at the school and district level and the provision of sufficient fiscal resources.

Efficacy of These Approaches

Although prevention science strongly supports the efficacy of school-wide approaches that incorporate multiple interventions and link schools and their environmental contexts, research on the impacts of these approaches is lacking (University of Vermont, 1999). As a result, numerous prevention initiatives have been implemented but reliable data of their effectiveness are not widely available. Despite the limited availability of rigorous evaluation studies in the 1990s, efforts to document the effectiveness of youth violence prevention programs are increasing. Schools using prevention plans report positive outcomes including improved academic performance and staff morale (Dwyer and Osher, 2000), as well as reduced behavior problems, reflected by fewer disciplinary referrals and suspensions (Sugai, Sprague, et al., 2000).

In an exhaustive study of school-based crime prevention efforts, Gottfredson (1997) found positive effects for programs that clarify behavioral norms, offer comprehensive instruction in a range of social-competency skills over a long period, provide behavior modification, and restructure schools to create smaller and more supportive units of instruction. Evidence also points to approaches that are *not* effective, including insight-oriented individual counseling and peer counseling (Gottfredson, 1997; Tolan & Guerra, 1998).

Our discussion of the advantages and strategies associated with school-wide prevention approaches is extended in the next section. We also present examples of research-based, school-wide prevention programs that show promise in reducing school disorder and promoting successful academic and social outcomes.

Promising Approaches

Numerous programs across the United States have shown positive results. Although it is beyond the scope of this article to review specific programs, we highlight three promising approaches to provide a perspective of the wider prevention and early intervention landscape. The listing of resources and websites (at the end of the article) leads to many other excellent program approaches and models.

Positive Behavioral Interventions and Supports: PBIS

Positive behavioral interventions and supports (PBIS) is a systems approach to creating and sustaining school environments that foster academic and behavioral competence for all students. As compared with traditional school-based approaches that target problem behavior demonstrated by individual students, PBIS focuses broadly on identifying policies and practices of the school itself that support or impede successful outcomes.

FOCUS ON SCHOOLS: RICHARD MONTGOMERY HIGH SCHOOL

Richard Montgomery High School (RMHS) in Rockville, Maryland, serves approximately 1,650 students in grades 9–12 in a suburban Washington, DC, school district. The school serves a diverse student body that is 12% African-American, 15% Asian, 16% Latino, and 55% non-Latino Caucasian students. Nearly 9% of students receive services because of limited English proficiency, 7% of the students receive special education services, and 10% of the students receive free and reduced-price meals. The mobility rate at RMHS is 6%. Students at RMHS perform well academically; approximately 500 students in the school are enrolled in the International Baccalaureate program—a rigorous college preparatory program—and 69% of students attend 2- or 4-year colleges after graduation.

In spite of average daily attendance above 90% and a strong academic program, the school has had an unacceptably high number of serious disciplinary incidents in recent years. In the 1997–98 school year, there were 35 serious disciplinary incidents at the school, including racial incidents, major vandalism, fights, and drug incidents. Mark Kelsch, a new principal appointed at the beginning of the 1998–99 school year, set out to reduce serious disciplinary incidents and improve academic performance of the school through greater participation and involvement of students and teachers in all aspects of the school. Kelsch's approach—a form of universal or primary prevention—combines a strong emphasis on relationships between adults and students and among students with rules that count and are fairly enforced.

The changes Kelsch has brought to RMHS include a daily 10-minute televised program produced by students and broadcast throughout the school. The program includes information from the principal, student groups, teaching staff, and others. Other changes include a focus on student achievement and recognition, reorganization of the school schedule so that all teachers in an academic area have common planning time, and consistent enforcement of attendance and tardy policies. These changes appear promising. During the 1999–2000 school year, 12 serious disciplinary incidents occurred—a reduction of nearly two thirds from just 2 years ago. The number of students losing course credit because of unexcused absences and being tardy to class dropped by 50% from the previous year. This past year Richard Montgomery High School received the Blue Ribbon Award for excellence from the U.S. Department of Education. For more information about the school, visit the web site: http://www.mcps.k12.md.us/schools/rmhs/

In this approach, classroom management and instructional practices are viewed as parallel processes; effective teaching of both academic and social skills involve strategies such as direct instruction, positive reinforcement, modeling, and precorrection (Sugai, Kameenui, et al., 2000). The PBIS framework emphasizes data-based assessment of the school climate and individual student progress through measures such as disciplinary referrals, attendance rates, and suspension rates. Functional behavior assessments are used in response to more intense problem behaviors.

Skill-Building: Violence Prevention Curricula

Violence prevention curricula based on social learning theory are used widely in school settings to improve students' problem-solving and anger-management skills, and to increase their knowledge of nonviolent responses to interpersonal conflict (Kenney & Watson, 1999). Conflict resolution and social skills are taught directly as a distinct curriculum or through integration in other coursework.

Numerous models for violence prevention through problem solving are available. For example, an interpersonal cognitive problem-solving approach with demonstrated effectiveness focuses on primary prevention in the elementary grades (Shure, 1999). In this approach, parents and teachers are trained to instruct children directly in using specific thinking and communication skills designed to prevent conflict in school and at home. *Second Step* is a violence prevention curriculum designed for use in preschool through ninth grade (Frey, et al., 2000). The curriculum emphasizes building protective social and emotional competencies and reducing aggressive and antisocial behaviors.

The Violence Prevention Curriculum for Adolescents (Prothrow-Stith, 1987) is designed to teach alternatives to aggressive behavior and to create supportive classroom environments in urban schools. Evidence suggests that the program is effective in reducing aggressive conflicts among students.

Mental Health and Social Services in Schools: Linkages to Learning

Linkages to Learning is a primary prevention model for the delivery of mental health, health, and social services for at-risk children and their families at 11 elementary and middle schools in Montgomery County, Maryland. The program was established in 1992 as a joint effort among public and private nonprofit agencies to respond to the increased needs of low- income children and their families. Parents are viewed as partners in this effort, taking an active role in developing solutions to individual, family, and community challenges. The overall goal of the program is to address social, emotional, and somatic health problems that undermine children's ability to succeed in school.

Participating children and families receive mental health assessment and counseling; assistance in obtaining shelter, food, housing, and employment; medical/dental care; assistance with immigration, translation, and transportation; and educational support including academic tutoring, mentoring, and adult education classes. Researchers at the University of Maryland completed a comprehensive longitudinal impact evaluation of children in a participating school and a control school (Fox et al., 1999). The evaluation found positive outcomes for children and parents, including improved academic achievement and behavioral functioning at home and school, increased consistency in parenting practices and overall family cohesion.

DEVELOPING A PLAN TO PREVENT SCHOOL VIOLENCE

In this section we present an overview of the major steps involved in establishing an effective school-wide violence prevention plan.

1.   Assessing school needs.

Even though fundamental principles for organizing effective prevention plans can be identified and consistently applied, schools cannot follow "one size fits all" formulas or blueprints. The first step in developing a violence prevention plan that incorporates promising practices and responds to the local school context is to conduct a needs assessment.

A systematic needs assessment enables the staff to understand the structural, economic, cultural, linguistic, and developmental variations that influence the functioning of specific schools. The unique features of schools that would be addressed in needs assessment include differences in size and physical structure; personal and cultural attributes of students, staff, and the community; prior experiences with prevention strategies; and current perceptions of the level of order and disorder. Using information gathered in needs assessment helps to shape a school-wide prevention plan that incorporates specific performance goals tailored to the strengths and priorities of each school and community (Walker & Horner, 1996).

2.   Developing parent and community support.

Because schools operate within environmental contexts, prevention initiatives that incorporate strong parent and community partnerships can mediate positive outcomes for youth. Kellam (2000) underscores the promise or perils associated with school/community partnerships when he emphasizes that "how prevention program leaders relate to community concerns will dictate the fate of their efforts (p. 2)."

Effective school-wide prevention plans operate best when they involve individual parents and parent organizations in meaningful ways. Parent/school collaboration enhances opportunities for schools to work successfully with troubled youth, extending prevention initiatives beyond schools and into local communities.

Links between the school and the larger community may take many forms, including collaboration among child-serving agencies, local business, law enforcement, and advocacy organizations. An important consideration in developing community support is to ensure that violence prevention initiatives are culturally competent. This is especially critical given the differential application of school disciplinary practices that result in the disproportionate suspension of African American youth (Townsend, 2000).

3. Developing a leadership team.

School-wide prevention plans that are actively supported by school- and district-level personnel, students, and families will likely produce the most effective and durable results. Team-based decision making can enhance ownership and acceptance of school violence prevention plans. Such a leadership team would be composed of staff members representing the various disciplines and roles within the school (e.g., general and special education teachers, counselors and school psychologists, administrators, paraprofessionals), and may include students, parents, and community members. Given the many risk factors associated with youth violence, the leadership team also could function as the organizational mechanism for systematic collaboration with mental health, social service, law enforcement, and other community agencies.

The leadership team conducts and analyzes the needs assessment, formulates short- and longer-term goals, identifies potential prevention strategies, monitors progress, and evaluates results (Dwyer & Osher, 2000). Teams can be formed specifically to address school-wide prevention efforts, or they can be built from and coordinated with other school-based management teams that exist in many schools.

4. Providing staff development.

As is the case in all school reform efforts, staff training is essential to ensure understanding, support, and consistent use of the school-wide violence prevention plan. Carefully designed and implemented training, available for *all* school staff, operationalizes the concept of a school-wide violence prevention agenda. This training involves teachers, counselors, bus drivers, cafeteria workers, clerical staff, and others working in the school. An important focus of training is skill development that supports achievement of instructional and behavioral competence for all students.

The content of training is also tailored for staff with specialized responsibilities, such as members of the leadership team. Further, given the complex nature of youth violence, staff development should reflect sustained rather than isolated training activities. Inservice training that follows this approach supports the reliable and consistent application of prevention strategies throughout the school.

5. Evaluating the plan.

Evaluation is the systematic collection and analysis of relevant data to inform decision making (Muraskin, 1993). Despite growing evidence supporting the use of school-wide violence prevention plans, specific prevention programs and practices have not typically been evaluated through rigorous research. Without benefit of evaluation, school staff and policy makers may respond to troubling behavior based more on political expediency than empirically validated practice.

Evaluation begins with needs assessment and can extend to process, outcome, and cost-benefit research (Flannery, 1998). When examining school-wide prevention programs one or more of the major types of evaluation may be appropriate to use.

■ *Process evaluations* address the qualities that make school-wide prevention programs work or not work.

■ *Outcome evaluations* focus on determining the impact of school-wide prevention programs on the school climate and for individual students.

■ *Cost-benefit evaluations* identify whether specific programs are cost-effective.

Evaluation design has been constrained by difficulties in identifying and measuring outcomes related to prevention of violence in schools (discussed in previous section). Further, the impact of violence prevention programs has not been measured reliably because most evaluations have focused on immediate results in a limited number of sites rather than on longer-term results and replication in different types of schools and communities.

CHALLENGES AHEAD: NEXT STEPS

Many reports have shown that school and community-based adolescent violence has been declining in recent years and that schools are considerably safer than surrounding neighborhoods. At the same time, addressing school violence remains an appropriate concern for educators, parents, political leaders, and other members of the community. We've learned from program evaluations, as well as a vast body of research in the fields of education, mental health, social services, and juvenile justice, that school violence must be addressed on the individual, family, school, neighborhood, and larger societal levels. Multifaceted interventions must target specific risk factors, be developmentally appropriate, and be culturally sensitive. In addition, interventions should involve parents and members of the community, promote interagency collaboration, address multiple levels of the child's life (e.g., school, family, neighborhood), and involve an evaluation component.

Schools will continue to face challenges while working with students with disabilities. State and local school systems must develop, disseminate, and monitor the interventions used in addressing behaviors of students with disabilities, using research-based best practices. Schools need to explore alternatives to school suspension, keeping students engaged in their school responsibilities and promoting their academic success. Responsive and flexible approaches require, and real progress demands, long-term investment and commitment. There are no quick fixes. Schools should examine their climate and programming to ensure that they are addressing their students' needs. Successful school programs require a buy-in by <u>all</u> school staff—teachers, support staff, and school administration—not just by a particular program's leadership team.

Data collection and analysis of prevention efforts should be ongoing, using rigorous methodology, as exemplified by the PBIS approach (Sugai, Kameenui, et al., 2000). School- and community-based programs have to maintain ongoing data collection and record keeping and should evaluate student and family needs and progress. At present, the role of students with disabilities in school violence and disruption is not well understood. Meaningful prevention and intervention efforts require thorough understanding of the challenges facing school administrators in serving students with disabilities, particularly those with behavioral problems.

In the face of pressure to offer politically expedient responses to media accounts of school violence and disruption, all members of the community must cultivate a balanced approach to the problem. Parents, educators, administrators, local officials, and other community members should gather accurate information relevant to their community circumstances and needs. A wide range of resources and supports now available from federal agencies, public interest advocacy groups, and private foundations are listed below.

A FINAL NOTE

Professionals sometimes are affected by the pressures and circumstances of their daily working environment and may react to problems by seeking the most expedient solution. In addressing the complex needs of students with behavioral difficulties, we must force ourselves to take stock of the situation and proceed thoughtfully, in a reasonable and balanced manner. Teamwork and collaboration among all stakeholders, careful study and thorough planning, and a commitment to reflection and self-evaluation all hold the promise of ultimate success.

REFERENCES

American Psychological Association. (1993). *Violence and youth: Psychology's response.* Washington, DC: Author.

Bear, G. G. (1999). *Interim alternative educational settings: Related research and program considerations.* Alexandria, VA: National Association of State Directors of Special Education, Project Forum.

Biemer, P. P., Groves, R. M., Lyberg, L. E., Mathiowetz, N. A., & Sudman, S. (1991). *Measurement Errors in Surveys.* New York: Wiley.

Brener, N. D., Simon, T. R., Krug, E. G., & Lowry, R. (1999). Recent trends in violence-related behaviors among high school students in the United States. *Journal of the American Medical Association, 282*(5), 440–446.

Bronfenbrenner, U. (1979). *The ecology of human development: Experiments by nature and design.* Cambridge, MA: Harvard University Press.

Brooks, K., Schiraldi, V., & Ziedenberg, J. (2000). *School house hype: Two years later.* Washington, DC: Justice Policy Institute.

Burns, B. J., & Goldman, S. K. (Eds.) (1999). Promising practices in wraparound for children with serious emotional disturbance and their families. *Systems of care: Promising practices in children's mental health, 1998 series, Vol. IV.* Washington, DC: Center for Effective Collaboration and Practice, American Institutes for Research.

Centers for Disease Control and Prevention. (1997). *Recommended framework for presenting injury mortality data.* Morbidity & Mortality Weekly Report, 1997; 46 (No. RR-14): 4–5.

Centers for Disease Control and Prevention. (2000). *Fact sheet: Youth risk behavior trends.* [online], http://www.cdc.gov/nccdphp/dash/yrbs/ trend.htm

Chandler, K. A., Chapman, C. D., Rand, M. R., & Taylor, B. M. (1998). *Students' reports of school crime: 1989 and 1995.* Washington, DC: U.S. Departments of Education and Justice. (NCES 98-241/NCJ-169607)

Cook, P. J., & Laub, J. H. (1998). The epidemic in youth violence. In M. Tonry, & M. H. Moore (Eds.), *Youth Violence* (pp. 27–64). Chicago: University of Chicago Press.

Cook, P. J. & Ludwig, J. (1997, May). Guns in America: National survey on private ownership and use of firearms. *Research Brief* (NIJ Rep. No. NCJ-165476). Washington, DC: U.S. Department of Justice, National Institute of Justice.

Cooley, S. (1995). *Suspension/expulsion of regular and special education students in Kansas: A report to the Kansas State Board of Education* (ERIC Document Reproduction Service No. ED 395 403). Topeka: Kansas State Board of Education.

Dryfoos, J. (1990). *Adolescents at risk.* New York: Oxford University Press.

Dwyer, K. & Osher, D. (2000). *Safeguarding our children: An action guide.* Washington, DC: U. S. Departments of Education and Justice, American Institutes for Research.

Elliott, D., Hamburg, B., & Williams, K. (Eds.). (1998). *Violence in American schools.* New York: Cambridge.

Farrington, D. P. (1995). The challenge of teenage antisocial behavior. In M. Rutter (Ed.), *Psychological disturbances in young people: Challenges for prevention* (pp. 83–130). New York: Oxford University Press.

Fasko, D., Grubb, D. J., & Osborne, J. S. (1995, November). *An analysis of disciplinary suspensions.* Paper presented at annual meeting of Mid-South Educational Research Association, Biloxi, MS. (ERIC Document Reproduction Service No. ED 393 169)

Felson, R. B. (1996). Mass media effects on violent behavior. *Annual Review of Sociology, 22,* 103–128.

Fiore, T. A., & Reynolds, K. S. (1996). *Analysis of discipline issues in special education.* Research Triangle Park, NC: Research Triangle Institute. (ERIC Document Reproduction Service No. ED 425 607)

Flannery, D. J. (1998). *Improving school violence prevention programs through meaningful evaluation.* New York: ERIC Clearinghouse on Urban Education. (ERIC Document Reproduction Service No. ED 417 244)

Fox, N., Leone, P., Rubin, K., Oppenheim, J., & Friedman, K. (1999). *Final report on the linkages to learning program and evaluation at broad acres elementary school.* Unpublished manuscript, University of Maryland at College Park.

Frey, K. S., Hirschstein, M. K., & Guzzo, B. A. (2000). Second step: Preventing aggression by promoting social competence. *Journal of Emotional & Behavioral Disorders, 8*(2), 102–112.

Furlong, M. & Morrison, G. (1994). Introduction to miniseries: School violence and safety in perspective. *School Psychology Review, 23*(2), 139–150.

Furlong, M., & Morrison, G. (2000). The *school* in school violence: Definitions and facts. *Journal of Emotional & Behavioral Disorders, 8*(2), 71–82.

Goldstein, S. Z. (1994). Corporate communication: A futurist vision. *Communication World, 11*(1), 26–28.

Goss v. Lopez, 419 U.S. 565 (1975).

Gottfredson, D. C. (1997). School-based crime prevention. In L. W. Sherman, D. C. Gottfredson, D. L. MacKenzie, J. Eck, P. Reuter, & S. D. Bushway. *Preventing crime: What works, what doesn't, what's promising: A report to the United States Congress.* [online] http://www.preventingcrime.com/report/index.htm

Gun-Free Schools Act, 20 U.S.C. § 1415 (e) (3).

Harvard University Civil Rights Project. (2000). *Opportunities suspended: The devastating consequences of zero tolerance and school discipline policies.* [online] http://www.law.harvard.edu/groups/civilrights/conferences/zero/zt_report2.html

Hawkins, J. D., Herrenkohl, T. I., Farrington, D. P., Brewer, D., Catalano, R. F., Harachi, T. W., & Cothern, L. (2000, April). Predictors of youth violence. *Juvenile Justice Bulletin.* Washington, DC: U.S. Department of Justice, Office of Juvenile Justice and Delinquency Prevention.

Hernandez, D. J. (1995). Changing demographics: Past and future demands for early childhood programs. *The Future of Children, 5*(3), 145–160.

Honig v. Doe, 479 U.S. 1084 (1988).

Howard, H. H. (1995). TV station group and cross-media ownership: A 1995 update. *Journalism & Mass Communication Quarterly, 72*(2), 390–401.

Hymowitz, K. S. (2000). Who killed school discipline? *City Journal, 10*(2), 34–43.

Ingraham v. Wright, 430 U.S. 651 (1977).

Institute of Medicine (1994). *Reducing risks for mental disorders.* Washington, DC: National Academy Press.

Institute for Social Research. (1997). *Monitoring the future study.* Ann Arbor: University of Michigan.

Kann, L., Kinchen, S. A., Williams, B. I., Ross, J. G., Lowry, R., Grunbaum, J. A., & Kolbe, L. J. (2000). Youth risk behavior surveillance—United States, 1999. *Morbidity & Mortality Weekly Report, 49* (SS–5).

Kaufman, P., Chen, X., Choy, S. P., Chandler, K. A., Chapman, C. D., Rand, M. R., & Ringel, C. (1998). *Indicators of school crime and safety, 1998.* Washington, DC: U.S. Departments of Education and Justice. (NCES 1998-251/NCJ-172215).

Kaufman, P., Chen, X., Choy, S. P., Ruddy, S. A., Miller, A. K., Chandler, K. A., Chapman, C. D., Rand, M. R., & Klaus, P. (1999). *Indicators of school crime and safety, 1999.* Washington, DC: U.S. Departments of Education and Justice. (NCES 1999-057/NCJ-178906)

Kellam, S. G. (2000). Community and institutional partnerships for school violence prevention. In S. G. Kellam, R. Prinz, & J. F. Sheley, *Preventing school violence: Plenary papers of the 1999 Conference on Criminal Justice Research and Evaluation—Enhancing Policy and Practice Through Research* (Vol. 2, pp. 1–21). Washington, DC: U.S. Department of Justice, National Institute of Justice.

Kenney, D. J., & Watson, S. (1999, July). Crime in the schools: Reducing conflict with student problem solving *Research brief* (NIJ Rep. No. NCJ-177618). Washington, DC: U.S. Department of Justice, National Institute of Justice.

Kerrebrock, N., & Lewit, E. M. (1999). Children in self-care. *The Future of Children, 9*(2), 151–160.

Larson, J. (1994). Violence prevention in the schools: A review of selected programs and procedures. *School Psychology Review, 23,* 151–164.

Leone, P. E. (1997). The school as a caring community: Proactive discipline and exceptional children. In J. Paul, M. Churton, W. Morse, A. Duchnowski, B. Epanchin, P. Osnes, & L. Smith (Eds.), *Special education practice: Applying the knowledge, affirming the values, and creating the future.* (pp. 91–103). Pacific Grove, CA: Brooks-Cole.

Lichter, S. R., Lichter, L. S., & Amundson, D. (1999). *Merchandizing mayhem: Violence in popular culture.* Washington, DC: Center for Media and Public Affairs.

Loeber, R., Farrington, D. P., & Waschbusch, D. A. (1998). Serious and violent juvenile offenders. In R. Loeber & D. P. Farrington (Eds.), *Serious and violent juvenile offenders* (pp. 13–29). Thousand Oaks, CA: Sage.

Maryland State Department of Education (1999, January). *Suspensions from Maryland public schools (1997–98).* Baltimore: MSDE Results Branch.

Maryland State Department of Education (2000, January). *Suspensions from Maryland public schools (1998–99).* Baltimore: MSDE/PRIM-Information Management Branch.

Mayer, M. J., & Leone, P. E. (1999). A structural analysis of school violence and disruption: Implications for creating safer schools. *Education & Treatment of Children, 22,* 333–358.

Mendel, R. (2000). *Less hype, more help.* Washington, DC: American Youth Policy Forum.

Mercy, J. A., Ikeda, R., & Powell, K. E. (1998). Firearm-related injury surveillance: An overview of progress and challenges ahead. *American Journal of Preventive Medicine, 15*(38), 6–16.

Metropolitan Life Insurance Company. (1999). *Metropolitan Life survey of the American teacher, 1999: Violence in America's Public Schools.* New York: Author.

Morgan, R. L., Loosli, T. S., & Striefel, S. (1997). Regulating the use of behavioral procedures in schools: A five year follow-up survey of state department standards. *Journal of Special Education, 30*(4), 456–470.

Muraskin, L. D. (1993). *Understanding evaluation: The way to better prevention programs* [online], http://ed.gov.offices/OUS/eval/primer1. html

Patterson, G. R. (1982). *Coercive family process.* Eugene, OR: Castalia.

Prothrow-Stith, D. (1987). *Violence prevention curricula for adolescents.* Newton, MA: Education Development Center.

Rand, M. (1998). *Criminal victimizations 1997: Changes 1996–97 with trends 1993–97.* Washington, DC: US Department of Justice, Bureau of Justice Statistics.

Reiss, A. J. & Roth, J. A. (Eds.). (1993). *Understanding and preventing violence.* Washington, DC: National Academy Press.

Sheley, J. F. (2000). Controlling violence: What schools are doing. In S. G. Kellam, R. Prinz, & J. F. Sheley, *Preventing school violence: Plenary papers of the 1999 Conference on Criminal Justice Research and Evaluation—Enhancing Policy and Practice Through Research* Vol. 2, pp. 37–57). Washington, DC: US Department of Justice, National Institute of Justice.

Shure, M. B. (1999, April). Preventing violence the problem-solving way. *Juvenile Justice Bulletin.* Washington, DC: U.S. Department of Justice, Office of Juvenile Justice & Delinquency Prevention.

Sinclair, M. F., et al. (1996, December). On a collision course? Standards, discipline, and students with disabilities, *Policy Research Brief, 8*(4). Minneapolis: Institute on Community Integration, University of Minnesota. (ERIC Document Reproduction Service No. ED 404 793)

Skiba, R. J., & Peterson, R. L. (1999). The dark side of zero tolerance: Can punishment lead to safe schools? *Phi Delta Kappan, 80*(5), 372–378.

Skiba, R. J., & Peterson, R. L. (2000). School discipline at a crossroads: From zero tolerance to early response. *Exceptional Children, 66*(3), 335–347.

Snyder, H. N., & Sickmund, M. (1999). *Juvenile offenders and victims: 1999 national report.* Washington, DC: Office of Juvenile Justice and Delinquency Prevention.

Sorenson, G. (1993). Update on legal issues in special education discipline. *Education Law Reporter, 81,* 399–411.

Sprague, J. & Walker, H. (2000). Early identification and intervention for youth with violent behavior. *Exceptional Children, 66*(3), 367–379.

Sugai, G. M., Kameenui, E. J., Horner, R. H., & Simmons, D. C. (2000). *Effective instructional and behavioral support systems: A school-wide approach to discipline and early literacy.* [online], http://ericec.org/ osep/eff-syst.htm

Sugai, G. M., Sprague, J. R., Horner, R., & Walker, H. M. (2000). Preventing school violence: The use of office discipline referrals to assess and monitor school-wide discipline interventions. *Journal of Emotional & Behavioral Disorders, 8*(2), 94–102.

Taylor-Greene, S., Brown, D., Nelson, L., Longton, J., Gassman, T., Cohen, J., Swartz, J., Horner, R. H., Sugai, G., & Hall, S. (1997). School-wide behavioral support: Starting the year off right. *Journal of Behavioral Education, 7,* 99–112.

Tebo, M. G. (2000). Zero tolerance, zero sense. *ABA Journal, 86,* 40–45.

Tolan, P. H. & Guerra, N. G. (1994). Prevention of delinquency: Current status and issues. *Applied & Preventive Psychology, 3,* 251–273.

Tolan, P. H., & Guerra, N. G. (1998). *What works in reducing adolescent violence: An empirical review of the field.* Boulder, CO: Center for the Study and Prevention of Violence, University of Colorado.

Tolan, P. H., Guerra, N. G, & Kendall, P. C. (1995). Introduction to special section: Prediction and prevention of antisocial behavior in children and adolescents. *Journal of Consulting & Clinical Psychology, 63*(4), 515–517.

Townsend, B. L. (2000). The disproportionate discipline of African American learners: Reducing school suspensions and expulsions. *Exceptional Children, 66*(3), 381–391.

Tucker, B. P., Goldstein, B. A., & Sorenson, G. (1993). *The educational rights of children with disabilities: Analysis, decisions and commentary.* Horsham, PA: LRP.

U.S. Bureau of the Census, Current Population Reports (1998). *Measuring 50 years of economic change using the March current population survey* (Rep. No. P60-203). Washington, DC: U.S. Government Printing Office.

U.S. Department of Education, National Center for Education Statistics. *Recommendations of the crime, violence, and discipline reporting task force* (Rep. No. NCES 97-581). 1996. Washington, DC: National Education Statistics Agenda Committee.

U.S. Department of Education, National Center for Education Statistics (1998a). *Violence and discipline problems in U.S. public schools: 1996–1997* (Rep. No. NCES 98-030). Washington, DC: Author, 1998.

U.S. Department of Education, Office of Elementary and Secondary Education and Planning and Evaluation Service. (1998b). *Report on state implementation of the gun-free schools act—School Year 1996–97.* (Contract N0. EA94052001). Prepared by Westat, Rockville, MD.

U.S. Department of Education (1999a). *Annual report on school safety.* Washington, DC: Author.

U.S. Department of Education, (1999b). *The Condition of Education 1999.* Washington, DC: National Center for Education Statistics. (ERIC Document Reproduction Service No. ED 430 324)

U.S. Department of Education, Office of Elementary and Secondary Education and Planning and Evaluation Service. (1999c). *Report on state implementation of the Gun-Free Schools Act—school year 1997–98.* (Contract No. EA94052001). Prepared by Westat, Rockville, MD.

U.S. Department of Education (2000). *Twenty-first annual report to Congress on the implementation of the Individuals with Disabilities Education Act.* Washington, DC: Government Printing Office. Author.

U.S. Library of Congress, Congressional Research Service. *Violence in schools: An overview* (CRS Report for Congress No. 94-141 EPW). Washington, DC: Author.

University of Vermont. (1999). Prevention strategies that work: What administrators can do to promote positive student behavior. Burlington, VT: Department of Education, School Research Office.

Walker, H. M., & Horner, R. H. (1996). Integrated approaches to preventing antisocial behavior patterns among school-age children and youth. *Journal of Emotional or Behavioral Disorders, 4*(4), 194–220.

Walker, H. M. & Sprague, J. R. (1999). The path to school failure, delinquency, and violence: Causal factors and some potential solutions. *Intervention in School and Clinic, 35*(2), 67–73.

Ward, J. M. (1999). *Children and guns.* Washington, DC: Children's Defense Fund.

Weinberg, D. H. (1996). *A brief look at postwar U.S. income inequality* (Rep. No. P60-191). Washington, DC: U.S. Bureau of the Census.

Weist, M. D., & Warner, B. S. (1997). Intervening against violence in the schools. *Annals of Adolescent Psychiatry, 21,* 235–251.

Womer, S. C. (1997). *What kinds of school-based prevention programs are publicized?* Ellicott City, MD: Gottfredson Associates.

Woodruff, D. W., Osher, D., Hoffman, C. C., Gruner, A., King, M. A., Snow, S. T., & McIntire, J. C. (1999). The role of education in a system of care: Effectively serving children with emotional or behavioral disorders. *Systems of care: Promising practices in children's mental health, 1998 Series* (Vol. 3). Washington, DC: Center for Effective Collaboration and Practice, American Institutes for Research.

Yell, M. L. (1990). The use of corporal punishment, suspension, expulsion, and timeout with behaviorally disordered students in public schools: Legal considerations. *Behavior Disorders, 15,* 100–109.

Yell, M. L., Cline, D., & Bradley, R. (1995). Disciplining students with emotional and behavioral disorders: A legal update. *Education & Treatment of Children, 18,* 299–308.

Yell, M. L. (1998). *The law and special education.* Upper Saddle River, NJ: Prentice-Hall.

PART THREE

Risk, School, and Society

Thomas M. Skrtic

The chapters in Part Three address the book's fourth theme: the emergence of broader reforms in schools and communities to address new risks and needs for children and families created by social, economic, and demographic changes in society. The chapters to this point have been concerned largely with the opportunities, challenges, and advances associated with the policy shift to standards-based accountability and the renewed emphasis on effective instruction and academic outcomes. As significant as these are for special education practice, in a broader sense they are limited in that they are concerned almost exclusively with formal education and, thus, with one of several institutions that affect the lives of students with disabilities and their families.

Part Three has a much broader focus, more oriented to human needs and opportunities that could and should shape special education practice in the immediate future. The chapters in this Part take us beyond education by considering individual and environmental conditions that contribute to the development and educational achievement of children, as well as the various institutions and professions that traditionally have been responsible for addressing them, directly or indirectly, on behalf of children and families. The main point of these chapters is that we have reached a point in society and the human services professions where we no longer can consider these conditions, or the institutions and professions that study and address them, in isolation from one another. Given the complexity and interdependence of human needs and achievement, and of today's social conditions and problems, we must address the welfare of children and families more contextually and interdependently, working across social contexts, institutions, and professions.

In Chapter 20, "Risk, Families, and Schools," Barbara Keogh introduces the concept of "risk," reviews risk research on children, families, and schools, and recommends the risk perspective as a framework for studying and serving children at-risk for developmental and educational problems. After defining risk broadly as "negative or potentially negative conditions that impede or threaten normal development," (p. 510) the author notes that it is a useful perspective because "it does not necessarily imply the actual presence of a deficit or a disability" (p. 510). Rather, risk is a probability statement in which "early individual and environmental conditions" (p. 510) are used to predict future outcomes.

Fortunately, the path from early conditions to future outcomes is nonlinear and uncertain because of the presence of what risk researchers call "protective" or "promoting" factors. These protective influences can be in-child factors such as dispositional attributes or biological predispositions, or environmental context variables such as a stable family or safe neighborhood, or any number of positive events such as gaining access to needed child or family services. According to the author, positive factors such as these are protective or promoting influences because they can minimize or mitigate the impact of in-child and environmental risk conditions.

Drawing on her own and others' risk research, the author operationalizes and integrates the variables that have been shown to contribute to risk for development and achievement problems with those that have been defined as protective influences. In this regard, she notes that, unless they are extreme, single in-child risk indicators are not always associated with subsequent problems. Rather, for predictive purposes she recommends a "multi-risk" or additive model in which "the more risk signs in the early years, the more likely is a negative outcome" (p. 513). The author also stresses the necessity of considering child conditions and family circumstances alike in risk assessments, noting for example that the impact of in-child risk conditions increases when the child lives in poverty.

Expanding on this latter point, she identifies and integrates the risk and protective variables commonly associated with family, social, and economic conditions, untangling, among other things, the complicated nonlinear relationship among race, poverty, and educational achievement and social adjustment. Key to understanding this relationship, and to operationalizing and integrating family risk and protective factors generally, is the author's methodological convention regarding the necessity of looking beyond family demographic variables in making risk assessments. Although in-child risk factors must be considered within the context of family conditions, her point is that, in doing so, one must look beyond the distal aspects of family and home demographics to more proximal levels of information derived from understanding how families actually function.

The author applies this methodological insight to school risk and protective factors. She identifies a number of largely demographic risk and protective variables commonly associated with schools and schooling. Then she considers three functional aspects of schools in greater depth, arguing that "risk status is, in part at least, a function of 'goodness of fit' between child attributes and schooling demands" (p. 519). With regard to the first functional aspect of schools, *instructional programs*, she suggests that too often failure to learn is attributed to limitations of children and families when the problem actually may be the result of a poor fit between child and program. She notes that limited understanding of the interactions between instructional methods and child characteristics is particularly evident in the ongoing "reading wars" between advocates of phonologically based and whole-language approaches to reading instruction, as well as in the overuse of whole-class instruction aimed at the "modal" student. Regarding the second functional aspect of schools, *curriculum*, the author criticizes the common practice of determining curriculum content by grade level rather than by students' attainment of requisite skills. Under these conditions, students who have the potential for learning but lack the skills required by the curriculum face constant failure in the classroom and, as a result, become increasingly passive and discouraged or begin to act out, placing them increasingly at risk by the conditions of schooling.

The third functional aspect of schools reviewed in this chapter is *teacher perceptions and expectations*. Here, Keogh considers differences in teachers' personal attributes, attitudes, beliefs, and expectations for children's behavior and achievement, noting that these differences can act as either protective or risk influences in the classroom, either buffering or exacerbating children's existing individual and environmental problems. In her own observational studies, she and her colleagues have shown that the nature and frequency of interactions between teachers and students are mutually shaped by teachers' beliefs about children's potential for achievement and students' personal attributes. The most important protective student attributes identified in the author's risk research, and that of others, are an easy-going temperament, and especially the capacity for "resilience," an important attribute to which she devotes an entire section of the chapter.

Author Keogh summarizes her arguments about the importance of the functional environment of schooling under the heading "The Ecology of Classrooms and Schools," with two important concluding points. Her first point is both an implicit critique of the standards-based reform framework of NCLB and IDEA 97, and a restatement of the methodological significance of the ecology of schooling. It is "easy to hold teachers and schools responsible for children's learning problems, and to assume that the effectiveness of schools may be measured with standardized achievement tests" (p. 521). But, she notes, it is critically important to recognize that, as complex social systems, schools, like children, may themselves be at risk. From the risk perspective, understanding the effects of schooling on children at-risk requires "going beyond the usual quantitative, summarizing descriptors . . . to get a more complete picture of what actually happens in school classrooms" (p. 521–522).

The author's second point in this regard is that, although questions of risk and protective factors in schools require further research, other aspects of schools "require immediate action, not research" (p. 522). These other functional aspects of schools—unsafe buildings, overcrowded classrooms, ill-prepared teachers, inappropriate instructional materials, and inadequate resources—are risk conditions that do not require further research. These risks can be modified and improved directly and immediately "through commitment of resources and energy" (p. 522).

Chapter 21, "Integrating Services, Collaborating, and Developing Connections with Schools," by Hal Lawson and Wayne Sailor, is a natural follow-up to Chapter 20. Its primary topic is the service integration reform movement, which is motivated by the reality that increasing numbers of children and families face the very types of environmental risk factors delineated in the previous chapter. Moreover, the concept of integrated services is premised on minimizing these risk factors and, in Keogh's terms, maximizing protective environmental factors. For Lawson and Sailor, this is to be achieved by integrating human service systems, promoting interprofessional collaboration within and across systems, and ultimately connecting these systems and their professionals with schools and the children, families, and communities they serve.

The authors introduce the chapter by noting the confusion surrounding the integrated services concept, caused by a proliferation of associated reforms and companion concepts and terms. These include, among others, interprofessional collaboration, interdisciplinary case management, interagency coordination, interprofessional education and training, full-service schools, and comprehensive systems of care. Given the scope and complexity of their topic, the authors limit the aim of their chapter to providing an action-oriented planning framework for achieving integrated services. Their goals in this regard are to foster shared meaning and understanding of the integrated services concept, promote improved service integration policies and practices, enable self-directed learning, and ultimately to contribute to the improved well-being of children, youth, and families and the work lives of the professionals who serve them.

The authors set the stage for their planning framework by tracing the history of the service integration movement across five waves of reform initiatives. Each of these initiatives and the broader movement itself seeks to transform the existing system of discrete, self-contained professions (e.g., educators, social workers), service organizations (e.g., schools, social welfare agencies), and categorical government policy sectors (e.g., education, social welfare). The contemporary service integration movement began in the 1970s, when the head of the now-defunct U.S. Department of Health, Education and Welfare, characterized the problem as "a hardening of the categories" and proposed to cure this bureaucratic "disease" by "de-categorizing and blending funding, while integrating programs and services" (p. 529). In more practical terms, the system of professions that is reinforced by categorical services and institutions was (and is) characterized as "uncoordinated, fragmented, duplicative, and inefficient" (p. 529). Children and families with multiple needs and problems, the authors note, can have as many as 14 different professionals in their lives. Moreover, because the professionals often are unaware of each other and have different disciplinary languages and conceptions of needs, problems, and interventions, they often work at cross-purposes. As a result, the authors claim, "the system of professions and its correlates are the problem (disease) . . . . [and] service integration and its companions (e.g., collaboration) are the solution (cure)" (p. 529).

The first wave of service integration began in the 1970s and early 1980s and continues today in some states and Canadian provinces. According to the authors, this wave is characterized by top-down mandates for integration in which separate governmental departments or ministries are integrated into a single agency. The idea behind this "first-wave thinking" is that structural and policy changes at the top will "trickle down" through agency managers and supervisors to change and improve front-line practice. The second wave is bottom-up, in part, because it emerged in the 1990s during federal efforts to "reinvent government" and devolve authority and responsibility to localities, and also because it is a response to the failure of first-wave reforms to trickle down to front-line professionals.

Whereas first-wave reform initiatives suffered from insufficient practitioner information and assistance and, thus, lack of understanding and acceptance of the concept, the second-wave reforms were impeded by ineffective communication channels. Second-wave initiatives included schools, but this occurred on a limited, experimental basis to test whether linking services to schools improved access and facilitated early intervention and prevention.

Although the nature and limited effects of first- and second-wave reforms are generally recognized, the authors identify three additional waves. The third or "school-linked services" wave, in which integrated services must be linked to schools, is well under way in several states. Because its primary concern is the worsening environmental conditions of children and families, and especially the effects of these conditions on children's readiness to learn, school-linked services (SLS) initiatives are designed to promote learning readiness by addressing these environmental barriers to learning and development.

The authors' emerging fourth wave is concerned with linking the service integration concept with educational reform, with "incorporating SLS as a vital element in school improvement (p. 531)". They describe the nascent fifth wave of reform as a movement to develop "comprehensive, neighborhood- and community-based systems of care (p. 531)." The "systems of care" framework focuses anew on poverty and its correlates by incorporating SLS and community-based integrated services, as well as interprofessional and lay–professional collaboration. In addition to benefiting children, families, and schools, this wave seeks to revitalize neighborhood communities, revive civic engagement, and ultimately promote strong democracy.

The chapter further delineates the disagreements and confusion surrounding the service integration concept. This includes disagreements about its purposes (e.g., improving services versus maximizing efficient use of limited resources), vision (better professional–client relations versus continued professional power), scope (systems change versus cross-systems change), and strategy (single-sector versus multi-sector initiatives). Confusion also surrounds the meaning and indicators of collaboration and interprofessional collaboration, as well as whether service integration and interprofessional collaboration are distinct or interdependent concepts and practices.

To alleviate some of the confusion, the authors provide their own multifaceted definitions of service integration and interprofessional collaboration and present a planning framework for complex change—that is, for integrating services, promoting collaboration, and developing connections with schools and the children, families, and communities they serve. Consistent with Keogh's point about schools being at-risk themselves, they expand on the idea of "connecting with schools, children, and families" by criticizing third-wave SLS reforms for ignoring the fact that "schools have to be readied for the learning and healthy development of children, youth, and families" (p. 552). Moreover, they implicitly comment on the importance of conditions of professional practice—one of the themes of this book—by noting that, even under the best conceived SLS initiatives, poorly designed schools that fail to provide optimal environments for children's learning and "for professionals' work" will not improve student achievement.

In the end, the authors reject third-wave thinking because most SLS initiatives simply add services to schools without changing the deep structure of schooling. Instead, they favor fourth- and fifth-wave thinking. Of the two, fourth-wave thinking is preferable, they assert, because it goes beyond mere "services reform" to "reinvent American schooling, especially for its most vulnerable populations challenged by poverty and its companions" (p. 552). Further, consistent with Keogh's position in Chapter 20 on the importance of social ecology, fourth-wave thinking "takes a social and ecological view of schools, families, and their surrounding community context" (p. 553). "School improvement and renewal processes are destined to fall short," the authors contend, "[unless] the family and community contexts for children's learning and development are addressed simultaneously" (p. 553). Although SLS and interprofessional collaboration are important in the authors' planning framework, their more comprehensive approach also includes "family-centered collaboration, inter-organizational collaboration, and broad-based community collaboration" (p. 553), which moves them from fourth- to fifth-wave thinking.

In a concluding discussion of poverty, social exclusion, and the future of American democracy, the authors expand upon the social and political advantages of nascent fifth-wave efforts to develop comprehensive, neighborhood- and community-based systems of care. The combined negative effects of globalization and a retreat in the "war on poverty" have increased the gap between rich and poor and, thus, the extent to which Americans live separately in "fortress communities" of "concentrated advantage" or "concentrated disadvantage" (p. 559). Democracy is threatened by both of these related trends, and because families, schools, and community associations are the chief institutions for promoting and sustaining democracy, forms of service integration and interprofessional collaboration that revitalize neighborhood communities by supporting collective citizen engagement and norms of reciprocity also safeguard and strengthen democracy.

Risk, Families, and Schools

Barbara K. Keogh

For a number of years, my associates and I have been involved in the study of children at-risk for developmental and educational problems. I will not document the specific triumphs and vicissitudes of this journey, except to say that, like travel in a foreign land, we have learned to cope with problems in communication and understanding, we have experienced frustrations and fatigue, and, occasionally, even boredom. Our research travels have taken us on some wayward paths and into a number of blind alleys. Ours has been an interesting, if somewhat circuitous, journey.

WHY STUDY RISK?

Understanding risk has implications for clinical/educational decisions and for policy. What kind of educational programs should at-risk children receive? Where should we put our often limited resources? Insights from risk research also throw light on the workings of developmental processes in normally developing individuals, as well as those with problems. It should not surprise us that research has been accelerating that relates early risk to a range of problem conditions, and that many different kinds of risk have been identified. Preterm babies with very low birthweights are considered "at-risk." Children living in extreme poverty are viewed as "at-risk."

Rather than focusing exclusively on one kind of risk, current research efforts approach the study of risk from an interactional or transactional perspective, considering the child in context (Sameroff & Chandler, 1975). This approach takes into account conditions both in the child and in the nature of the environments in which he or she lives. As an example, the recent volume *Risk, Families and Competence*

(Lewis & Feiring, 1998) includes chapters on divergent families, immigrant families, home environments, family-peer relationships, family typologies, children with developmental delays, and gifted children.

Clearly, children's characteristics and the environments in which they live are both important contributors to risk. Further, from a transactional view, they do not function independently but, rather, affect and change each other. Family conditions may intensify or ameliorate children's developmental or behavioral problems. Similarly, family experiences, peers, and teachers will influence children's learning problems.

Recognizing that context is a powerful contributor to risk does not negate the importance of in-child conditions but does make our understanding of risk more complex. Because the terms "risk" and "at-risk" are so broad, major issues in understanding have to do with definition and the specification of outcomes. Consider first how risk is defined.

DEFINING RISK

Broadly defined, risk identifies "negative or potentially negative conditions that impede or threaten normal development (Keogh & Weisner, 1993, p. 4). Werner and Smith (1992) described risk factors as "biological or psychosocial hazards that increase the likelihood of a negative developmental outcome in a group of people" (p.3). Ramey, Trohanis, and Hostler (1982) defined risk as "a comparative and relative term used to express the likelihood of a current or future development or handicap that, at present, is uncertain" (p. 8).

Central to these definitions is the recognition that risk is a probability statement. That is, early individual and environmental conditions are used to predict future outcomes. *Risk* is a useful term in that it does not necessarily imply the actual presence of a deficit or a disability. Rather, it suggests the possibility of subsequent problems. Thus, it is important to specify what constitutes early risk. Does the individual have a genetic or biological condition, such as chromosomal anomalies or perinatal organic insults? Or is risk present in the environment or the context in which the individual lives, such as poverty, disrupted families, or abusive parents? Many risk conditions likely are confounded or associated. For example, the possibility of peri- and neonatal problems may be greater if the mother does not receive proper prenatal medical care because she lives in poverty and services are not available. Identifying the risk conditions is only half of the equation, however.

To understand the significance of early risk, the antecedent conditions and their possible consequences both must be considered. Clearly stressful and negative early life conditions may have many possible consequences or outcomes, but certain risk indicators may be associated with problems at particular developmental periods and may be gender-related. Elderly individuals might be at-risk for Alzheimer's disease, adolescent boys for delinquency, women for breast cancer, young adults for drug and alcohol abuse. Important questions, then, have to do with at risk for what and when? School failure? Developmental delay? Delinquency? Alcoholism? Mental health problems? Thus, risk is understood best within a developmental framework, as the nature of problems may differ at different ages.

PREDICTING OUTCOMES

The path between early conditions and outcomes is not a single one, nor is it linear, and prediction from early conditions to specific outcomes is limited. Many experiences and opportunities affect a given individual's developmental path. These have to do with biological status, with environmental conditions, with opportunities and stresses, with traumatic events.

To illustrate: In current work at UCLA (Keogh, Bernheimer, & Weisner, 2000) we have followed a group of children identified at age 3 as having developmental delays of unknown etiology. They are now 23 years old. Findings based on detailed follow-up of 30 individuals indicated that, for the group as a whole, there were continuing problems: 10 are in group placements, 15 are still living at home, fewer than 9 are employed. Yet, examination of individuals within the group documents a wide range of outcomes: 15 have basic or adequate reading skills, four are attending 2- or 4-year colleges, two have married, and one has started a family.

Thus, an important caution for making clinical decisions is that predictions from early risk signs are often valid for groups but are much less powerful for individuals within groups. Think of high-achieving people who spent their childhood years in poverty and in educationally disadvantaged circumstances. Think of children from high economic, "advantaged" situations who became involved in illegal or personally destructive behaviors. How can we explain these differences in outcomes? The question leads to consideration of protective factors in children's lives and to the concept of resilience.

PROTECTIVE FACTORS

Werner (1986) emphasized the importance of "environmental context variables that mediate the expression of potentially harmful biological and psychosocial events over time" (p. 18). Garmezy, Masten, and Tellegen (1984) considered protective factors as "dispositional attributes, environmental conditions, biological predispositions, and positive events that can act to contain the expression of deviance or pathology" (p. 109). Rutter (1979, 1987) proposed that protective factors have modulating or buffering effects on stressful events. Protective influences may have to do with the characteristics of the individual (e.g., positive temperament) or with the environment (e.g., stable family). And like risk factors, protective factors may differ across developmental periods and may be related to gender.

It should be noted that some uncertainty surrounds the issue of how to define protective factors and how they operate *vis a vis* risk factors. That is, are they best defined as the "flip side" of risk factors and, thus, effective only in response to risk? Or do they make independent contributions to child status regardless of risk conditions? Sameroff et al. (1998) argued that a better term for protective factors is *promoting factors*, identifying conditions that aid or contribute positively to a child's development.

Examples of promoting factors are a mother's good mental health and a positive family climate. Work by this research group has documented that "the more risk factors, the worse the outcomes; the more promotive factors, the better the outcomes" (p. 172). Thus, they underscore the importance of identifying protective influences as well as documenting risk conditions as proposed by Garmezy (1985).

When we think of risk as a probability statement, many factors, both positive and negative, clearly contribute to the development and achievement of individuals, whatever their group status. Some of these positive factors serve as protective or promotive influences, minimizing or mitigating the impact of risk conditions, thereby affecting predictions. Based on their review of risk research, Keogh and Weisner (1993) proposed four generalizations about prediction from early indicators:

> Prediction is more accurate for groups than for individuals within groups; the power of specific risk indicators varies relative to ecological and cultural context; risk conditions may be mediated by the presence of protective factors; outcome status varies according to the time and content of assessment. (p. 3)

OPERATIONALIZING RISK AND PROTECTIVE FACTORS

A number of conditions have been identified as contributing to risk for development and achievement. Similarly, protective influences have been defined. Real issues involve how to operationalize these variables and how to integrate them. In this chapter I consider briefly three aspects of risk and protective factors: early in-child signs, families, and schools.

In-Child Risk Factors

Clinicians and researchers alike have provided clear evidence that the probabilities of negative outcomes are increased when risk factors are present, and a number of conditions associated with negative outcomes at a later time have been identified. A good deal of research has focused on in-child risk conditions in the neonatal and perinatal periods.

Keogh and Bernheimer (1995) for example, found that 28 of 69 children with developmental delays at age 3 had histories of problems or distress perinatally or within 28 days after birth. These included preterm birth, low birthweight, anoxia, seizures, and medical conditions that required prolonged hospital stays. These findings are consistent with a large literature base that suggests that children with serious peri- and neonatal stresses may be at risk for subsequent developmental problems. Common early in-child conditions associated with risk are summarized in Table 20.1.

It is important to underscore that very early conditions may be, but are not always, associated with subsequent problems. Unless they are extreme, single risk

TABLE 20.1 ■ In-Child Early Risk Signs

Preterm birth (37 weeks gestation or less)
Low birthweight (2500 grams or less)
One-minute Apgar scores (4 or less)
Asphyxia
Metabolic disorders
Infection
Intracranial hemorrhage
Delayed development at age 1
Head circumference at age 1
Difficult Temperament

Source : From *Minimal Brain Dysfunction* by P. L. Nichols & T-C Chen (Hillsdale, NJ: Lawrence Erlbaum & Associates,1981); Risk and Protective Factors in the Lives of Children with High-incidence Disabilities, by E. E. Werner, in *Developmental Perspectives on Children with High-incidence Disabilities* (Mahwah, NJ: Lawrence Erlbaum Assoc., 1999). Pp. 15–22.

indicators have limited prognostic or predictive power. Rather, prediction is more powerful when a multi-risk or an additive model is used (Sameroff, Seifer, Baldwin, & Baldwin, 1993). That is, the more risk signs in the early years, the more likely is a negative outcome. Further, the impact of in-child biological risk conditions increases when the child is in a socioeconomic (SES) disadvantaged environment (Werner, 1993, 1999). This, of course, necessitates taking into account both child conditions and family circumstances.

Family Risk and Protective Factors

The impact of family, social, and economic conditions on negative outcomes has been well established. Compared to more economically advantaged children, those from poor families are less likely to succeed educationally, have poorer jobs as adults, and have more personal adjustment problems. Their early life conditions put them at-risk for later accomplishments.

A number of researchers have documented characteristics or variables that describe such families and the conditions surrounding them. For example, Sameroff and his colleagues described environmental variables that were correlated with SES but were not equivalents (Sameroff et al., 1998). These included:

1. Maternal mental illness
2. Parental perspectives
3. Unskilled occupation
4. Disadvantaged minority status
5. Large family size.

The researchers then compared subgroups of high- and low-risk children identified on these variables. The low-risk group had higher (better) cognitive and mental health outcomes on each of the variables than did the high-risk group. Group differences, however, were relatively moderate, "certainly not enough to detect which specific individuals with the risk factor would have an adverse outcome" (p. 165). Commonly identified risk signs are shown in Table 20.2. Note that many describe demographic variables.

Findings from the Nichols and Chen (1981) follow-up of over 38,000 children who were part of the National Collaborative Perinatal Project (NCPP) are instructive in this regard. Their findings are notable because of the large and geographically representative sample. Learning difficulties were strongly associated with demographic variables such as large family size, low SES, and frequent changes in residence.

In the Nicols and Chen work, demographic variables also were associated with hyperactive/impulsive (HI) behavior and evidence of minimal brain dysfunction (MBD). Race was not a significant discriminator when SES and demographic variables were controlled.

It should be noted, however, that in the United States, more minority than nonminority children live in poverty, leading to a higher incidence of risk in minority groups. The Nichols and Chen findings of the relatively high frequency of academic and behavior problems of children from lower SES homes have been supported by the work of other investigators (e.g. Grizenko, & Pawluk, 1994; Ramey & Campbell, 1992).

As discussed earlier, prediction from risk factors alone is not sufficient as protective or promoting factors also influence outcomes. Commonly identified protective factors are shown in Table 20.3. Most of these factors describe conditions that

---

TABLE 20.2 ■ Family Risk Variables

Low SES—poverty
Unsafe neighborhood
Low parent education
Large family size
Children closely spaced
Overcrowded home
Frequent changes in residence
Frequent parent absence
Mother's mental health
Parent criminality
Parent substance abuse

Source : From *Minimal Brain Dysfunction* by P. L. Nichols & T-C Chen (Hillsdale, NJ: Lawrence Erlbaum & Associates,1981); Risk and Protective Factors in the Lives of Children with High-incidence Disabilities, by E. E. Werner, in *Developmental Perspectives on Children with High-incidence Disabilities* (Mahwah, NJ: Lawrence Erlbaum Assoc., 1999). Pp. 15–22.

TABLE 20.3 ■ Family Protective Variables

Safe neighborhood
Stable residence
Adequate income
Fewer than four children
Spacing between children
Parents present
Good mental and physical health (parents)
Kin and alternative caregivers available
Services available

Source : From Protective Factors in Children's Responses to Stress and Disadvantage by M. Rutter, in M. W. Kent and J. E. Rolf (Eds.) *Primary Prevention of Psychopathology* (Hanover, VT: University Press of New England, 1979). Pp. 49–72. No Concept of Risk from a Developmental Perspective by E. E. Werner, in B. K. Keogh (Ed.) *Advances in Special Education Vol. 5: Developmental Problems in Infancy and the Preschool Years* (Greenwich, CT: JAI Press, 1986). Pp. 1–23.

are associated with SES, and many are the opposite of the risk factors found in Table 20.2 (e.g., safe or unsafe neighborhood, stable residence/frequent changes in residence).

Given the well established findings of significant associations between SES and subsequent educational achievement, it is tempting to view SES as a causal condition. But it is important to emphasize that many children in low-SES homes grow up in positive environments, have close and stable families, and have good role models and mentors. Although limited economically, these homes provide protective influences that enhance children's development and well-being. Three points are to be emphasized:

1. SES is not an explanatory concept but, rather, captures a cluster of conditions.
2. Outcomes within groups classified on SES criteria vary widely.
3. Problems in development and achievement are evident across the full SES range.

Clearly, conditions captured by demographic indicators are powerful contributors to risk, as evidenced for groups of individuals, but they do not explain differences in outcomes for individuals within groups. Predicting outcomes for individual children in SES-identified groups is "iffy"at best.

Note that most of the risk and protective factors shown in Tables 20.2 and 20.3 describe distal aspects of families and homes. Although these are important characteristics, they do not provide insights about how families function. To understand what happens in families, it is necessary to get to more proximal levels of information. How families function differs greatly among families identified on demographic characteristics, and these differences are not necessarily related to SES.

Almost 30 years ago, Baumrind (1971) described three types of parenting styles that subsequently were found to be associated with children's achievement:

1. Authoritative
2. Permissive or laissez-faire
3. Authoritarian.

Hechtman (1991) suggested that homes characterized by "warmth and support....where emotional expressions, open communication and independence are encouraged" (p. 418) were likely environments for the development of resilient children. In their seminal longitudinal study, Werner and Smith (1992) found a number of characteristics of children and their families to be associated with positive outcomes for the individuals more than 30 years later.

The affective climate of the home and the nature of caregiver practices are important, as these make up the ongoing content of family life. Like the risk and protective variables shown in Tables 20.2 and 20.3, however, family climates are summarizing terms and do not necessarily capture the functional interactions within families. Rende and Plomin (1993) stressed the importance of understanding the "proximal variables that reflect environmental processes that reflect the risk factors for individuals" (p. 531). The daily interactions between children and parents over time likely are the basis for these process variables.

Consistent with this kind of thinking, in longitudinal research at UCLA, we have studied children identified as "at-risk" in the preschool years and their families over a 20-year period, documenting the ways in which families organize their lives. We have found that the functional and ongoing interactions of children and their families are captured in the family daily routine. By "daily routine," we mean the everyday, mundane, common "stuff" of family life, the "things that are done and the things that are not done" (Bernheimer & Keogh, 1995). Everyday activities comprise the content of family life and are the basis for parent-child interactions and, thus, for children's learning and self-views.

Rutter (1984) suggested, for example, that children learn problem-solving skills by watching how their parents deal with everyday matters. Masten, Best, and Garmezey (1991) proposed that a child's mastery motivations and self-esteem develop within a family context, as parents provide opportunities for learning and serve as behavioral models. Sigel (1998) argued that prerequisites for schooling are acquired through parents as socializing agents, and specifically through verbal interactions between parents and children.

Based on their studies of "at-risk" families, Ramey, Ramey and Lanzi (1998) identified six "psychosocial mechanisms" or "priming mechanisms" related to intellectual and social changes in children and adults in poverty circumstances:

1. Opportunities to explore and gather information
2. Being mentored in new skills
3. Celebration of developmental achievements
4. Review and rehearsal of new skills and knowledge

5. Avoidance of inappropriate punishment and ridicule
6. Language as a mechanism for learning.

These researchers concluded that

> there are systematic and practically important differences among poverty
> families with respect to their children's levels of academic and social risk.
> This finding is a necessary prelude to the more intriguing question: What
> kind of interventions work best for whom?" (p. 203)

In summary, a number of risk and protective conditions in families have been
shown to affect children's development and achievement. Yet, families are only part
of the context of children's lives. School is a second major component of context, a
context that most children experience for a good many years. Despite many common
aspects, their experiences in school vary widely and the contributions of schooling
to their intellectual progress and their social adjustment differ. For some, school is a
safe haven; for others, it is an ongoing nightmare. Like child-family interactions,
schooling brings together characteristics of children and characteristics of the environment. Some fit well together, and others are discordant. It is important, therefore,
to consider risk and protective influences in schools.

School Risk and Protective Influences

The current emphasis on improving educational outcomes has illuminated major differences among schools, and research on schools and schooling is receiving
increased attention and support. Research on and in schools is slow work, and a
number of methodological problems have to be addressed (see Maughan, 1988, for
discussion).

First, what should be assessed and how should schooling be measured?
Children's characteristics and their educational outcomes have been limited, for the
most part, to narrow, normative measures, such as standardized aptitude and achievement tests. Test scores allow the designation of students as failing or successful, as
risk or non-risk, but do not necessarily provide insight into the mechanisms or
processes that account for these outcomes.

Second, when schools are taken into account, they often are treated as if they
represent a single main effect when in fact they vary greatly within and across school
districts. Thus, we cannot assume homogeneity of effects.

Third and finally, most studies have used cross-sectional or short-term longitudinal designs, and the nature of the interactions and transactions over time is not
known. Despite such problems, a number of characteristics of effective and less
effective schools have been identified. Examples of risk conditions are shown in
Table 20.4.

Analogous to understanding risk within families, it is important to emphasize
that not all children in high-risk schools have poor achievement and adjustment, and

TABLE 20.4 ■ School Risk Variables

High crime area
Physically unsafe
Overcrowded classrooms
Inadequate materials and supplies
Frequent changes in staff
High rate staff absenteeism
Frequent moves by pupils
High-rate pupil absenteeism
Few resources or special programs
Many low-ability/achieving peers

Source : From Risk and Protective Factors and Achievement of Children at Risk by D. V. Krasner (Doctoral Dissertation: Graduate School of Education, UCLA, 1992). Pp. 1–124. *Fifteen Thousand Hours: Secondary Schools and their Effects on Children* (London: Open Books, 1979).

that many schools within risk areas function well. As in families, certain protective factors characterize schools. Commonly identified protective factors are summarized in Table 20.5.

The characteristics shown in Tables 20.4 and 20.5 have potentially powerful influences on children's academic and personal development. Even though these risk and protective factors are well known, like many descriptors of families, they tend to identify structural, demographic aspects of schools. Further, until recently only limited research has been done on the functional aspects of how risk and protective influences work.

Many of the risk and protective aspects of schools shown in Tables 20.4 and 20.5 are well known and require little discussion. Clearly, safety is important; quality

TABLE 20.5 ■ School Protective Variables

Physically safe
Low-crime area
Not overcrowded
Adequate materials and supplies
Stable staff
Low absenteeism (staff and pupils)
Special resources and programs available
Adequate/high-ability peers

Source : From Risk and Protective Factors and Achievement of Children at Risk by D. V. Krasner (Doctoral Dissertation: Graduate School of Education, UCLA, 1992). Pp. 1–124. *Fifteen Thousand Hours: Secondary Schools and their Effects on Children* (London: Open Books, 1979).

programs require adequate and appropriate materials. Yet, in some schools, especially schools in low-income communities, children are at-risk educationally because buildings are rundown, physical safety is questionable, and students do not have needed instructional materials. These conditions compound the developmental and educational status of at-risk children. The importance of safe and adequate school environments is not a scientific question that requires more research. Rather, it tests our social/political commitment to children and education.

FUNCTIONAL ASPECTS OF SCHOOLS

Like families, schools may be categorized according to demographic indicators. Also like families, as noted earlier, schools vary greatly when defined demographically. This, of course, underscores the importance of understanding how individual schools function. Important domains of schools have been specified in a number of major studies (National Education Longitudinal Study, 1988). These include instructional programs, administrative practices, and school environments and climates—domains that are consistent with the findings from research on schooling effects on at-risk students (Rutter & Madge, 1976).

In this chapter I focus on the impact of three functional aspects of classroom environments on children's school experiences, arguing that risk status is, in part at least, a function of "goodness of fit" between child attributes and schooling demands (Keogh, 1982, 1986). Marginal or risk pupils in the early years likely are especially vulnerable to schooling effects, including instructional and curricular demands and teachers' perceptions and expectations.

Instructional Programs

Children bring different aptitudes, motivations, and personal competencies and problems to school. These personal characteristics interact with the programs provided—in some cases leading to successful learning and in others resulting in failure to learn. This perspective on risk clearly broadens the conceptualization of risk and has implications for assessment and instruction. Too often, failure to learn is attributed to limitations of children and families (e.g., "He's not learning because he lacks ability," "She's unmotivated," or "His parents don't value education"). Alternatively, the problem may be based in the fit between child and program or viewed as "instructional failures."

This issue is well illustrated by the ongoing "reading wars" that pit whole-word methods against phonologically based methods. Advocates of each argue that their method is better, implying that a certain method is effective for all children. Common sense, as well as accumulating evidence, suggests that both approaches have merit with some, but not all, children.

Major research programs under the auspices of the National Institute of Child Health and Human Development (NICHD) provide compelling evidence of the effectiveness of phonologically based instruction for most beginning readers and many children with reading problems (see Lyon, 1995; Lyon, Alexander, & Yaffe, 1997, for reviews). Less is known about instruction directed at reading comprehension and fluency, or about the development of literacy (see Pressley et al., 2000). Further, almost all programs report that a small percent of children are nonresponders resistant to treatment. They do not learn to read even when effective interventions are implemented.

To date, there is limited understanding of the interactions between instructional methods and the characteristics of the children so instructed. Some children enter school with good phonemic awareness skills, having already mastered the alphabetic code. Others are woefully behind in these skills and need intense and specific instruction. The point to be emphasized is that both child characteristics and instructional methods must be included in the learning equation. This point is particularly relevant for children who enter school at-risk, as they may not have had the opportunities and experiences provided their more advantaged peers, and, thus, may be especially sensitive to the instructional program.

Effects on students' learning also are seen in the ways in which the content of instruction is delivered. Some children receive more teacher attention than others, as teacher time is not spread equitably across all students in a classroom. Some programs are individualized, but most rely on whole class instruction.

Zigmond and her colleagues have used both qualitative and quantitative methods to study classrooms (see Zigmond, 1996, for a review of this work). A study of 12 general education classrooms revealed that there was little if any differentiated instruction and that teachers "were more committed to routine than to addressing individual differences, and that they were more responsive to district mandates than to evidence from their students that the curriculum or pacing needed to be adapted" (p. 165). In further studies, these researchers also found that most instruction was targeted at the modal student, suggesting that the level of instruction might be inappropriate for students at the upper and lower ends of the achievement distribution.

I emphasize that teachers are not solely responsible for students' academic progress, as they struggle with many constraints on their opportunity to teach. Rather, problems for at-risk children reflect systemwide conditions.

Curriculum

Despite the call for individualization of instruction, many school districts determine curriculum content according to grade level—that is, according to what students *ought* to learn at given ages. Teachers are obligated to cover the materials so defined. Yet the demands of the curriculum may not be consistent with at-risk students' skills. I illustrate with two children who live in a homeless shelter in a major city. Both are of ethnic-minority backgrounds, both attend public elementary schools, and both have normal ability as evidenced in everyday competencies.

The 6-year old boy is being promoted to second grade, but his reading is limited to a half dozen simple words (e.g., cat, dog). The reading curriculum in the last months of his first grade consisted of work on endings (ings and eds)—content that clearly was beyond his reading level. The 12-year old girl is an adequate reader, but her arithmetic skills are limited to basic addition and subtraction. She cannot do long division or multiply two-digit numbers. The arithmetic curriculum in her class focused on decimals and fractions.

Both of these children have potential for learning but are in situations where their skills are so discrepant from the content of the curriculum that they face daily failure. The girl's reaction to the discrepancy between her arithmetic skills and the demands of the curriculum was to become increasingly passive and to give up. The boy has started to act out already. Both children have potential but are slipping behind in programs that are discrepant from their functional levels in specific content areas. They are increasingly at risk.

Teachers' Perceptions and Expectations

Other influences on how classrooms function have to do with teachers' goals and expectations for students' performance. Teachers differ in their knowledge of subject matter, in their instructional practices, and in the ways they organize classrooms. They also differ in their personal attributes, attitudes, and beliefs, as well as in the expectations they have for children's behavior and achievement. These differences may serve as protective or risk influences, as some teachers are able to buffer children's problems and others may enhance or exacerbate problem conditions.

In classroom observational studies, UCLA researchers have shown that both the frequency of interactions and the nature of the interactions between teachers and students are related to teachers' beliefs about children's potential for achievement and students' personal attributes, including temperament (Keogh, 1982; Keogh & Burstein, 1988). For some children the interactions with teachers are positive and social, and for others the teacher-child interactions are limited primarily to management. Children may be at increased risk because teachers have low expectations for performance related to ethnic or cultural factors, or because of the children's personal characteristics and behavioral styles. Students with easy temperaments are more likely to have positive interactions with teachers than are children with difficult temperaments (Keogh, 1986).

THE ECOLOGY OF CLASSROOMS AND SCHOOLS

The importance of classroom and school environments for at-risk students is well documented in current research and has led to increased interest in the ecology of schools (see Speece & Keogh, 1996). Schools and children alike may be at-risk. In the name of accountability, it is easy to hold teachers and schools responsible for children's learning problems, and to assume that the effectiveness of schools may be measured with standardized achievement tests. It is important to emphasize, however, that schools are complex social systems, and to understand the long-term outcomes for children at-risk, we must take into account the functional nature of schools. This means going beyond the usual quantitative, summarizing descriptors (e.g. size, SES) to get a more complete picture of what actually happens in school classrooms.

A number of questions about risk and protective factors in schools require further research. These include issues related to programmatic modifications and the long-term consequences of given risk conditions. Other aspects of schools, however, require immediate action, not research. These have to do with issues of safety, the school environment, and the need for well trained teachers and adequate instructional materials. Overcrowded classrooms, in which children are in close physical proximity, and inadequate materials and supplies are risk conditions that may contribute to children's educational and social/behavioral problems. These are risks that we can modify and improve through commitment of resources and energy.

RESILIENCE

Any discussion of risk would not be complete without considering the notion of resilience. Resilient children are those who develop well even in conditions that for most lead to negative outcomes. Masten, Best, and Garmezy (1991) defined resilience as "the process of, capacity for, or outcome of successful adaptation despite challenging or threatening circumstances." (p. 426). They noted that protective factors may moderate the negative impact of personal or environmental conditions.

Smith and Prior (1995) considered resilience to be the "capacity to maintain healthy functioning in an unhealthy setting, or the maintenance of mastery under stress" (p 168). They stated further that "resilience presumes a capacity of the individual child to recover, bounce back, or remain buoyant in the face of adversity, life stresses, illness, misfortune, and the like."

Richmond and Beardslee (1988) noted that resilience is "successful coping or adaptation or mastery" (p. 157). Egeland, Carlson, and Sroufe (1993) viewed resilience as process and emphasized the interactions and transactions that lead to developmental outcomes. Rutter (1989) concurred, noting that resistance to stress is relative, not absolute, and that the degree of resistance varies over time and according to life circumstances.

Certainly there are many examples of children who have managed well despite stressful and negative conditions that resulted in damaging outcomes for their peers. Werner and Smith (1989) found about one in 10 of their sample to be resilient. An interesting question is: What accounts for their good outcomes? A number of personal and environmental conditions characterized the resilient children in the Werner and Smith research. Early on, they were active and socially responsive, had strong attachment to their mothers, good self-help skills as toddlers, and effective problem-solving and communication skills in the middle years. Compared to peers, they experienced fewer life stresses and had networks of friends, both peers and adults. Their caregiving conditions were generally positive, including cohesiveness of the family.

In their longitudinal Australian study, Smith and Prior (1995) found that resilient and nonresilient children differed on personal characteristics, including temperament, although all were in stressed or "risk" environments. Similar to the Werner and Smith (1989) findings, resilient Australian children were socially responsive, attractive to other people, easy-going, even-tempered, and not easily distressed. Smith and Prior emphasized that temperamental characteristics influenced both positive (social competencies) and negative (behavioral adjustment) outcomes.

Clearly, resilience is not a single, unitary concept but, rather, involves a number of personal capacities and conditions (Masten et al., 1991). Resilient children are described as having easy and positive temperaments, as "engaging,"—characteristics that likely smooth the nature of their interactions with others. Because they are good problem-solvers and good learners, they are able to deal effectively with difficult situations. They are competent in areas that others value, which provides positive feedback and reinforces their sense of competence. But children live in families and go to school, so the context of their lives also must be considered. We should expect that changes related to development, age, and gender, and therefore predictions about long-term outcomes for resilient young children, like those about children at risk, must be made cautiously.

The focus on resilience provides a needed and important direction to research on risk, as it moves us away from the traditional emphasis on pathology and negative outcomes (Garmezy, 1985). Rather, interest in resilience forces us to consider a broad array of influences which lead to healthy development and adjustment. Many of the processes accounting for resilience have not been specified, nor is the nature of their interactions known. There is, however, a clear move toward identifying the factors which lead to positive outcomes for at risk individuals. These include contextual conditions such as families and schools, as well as personal characteristics.

In a recent publication (Keogh, in press) I cite the comments of Norman Garmezy, who wrote the Foreword to Werner and Smith's book, *Vulnerable But Invincible* (1989): "Were we to study the forces that move children to survival and to adaptation, the long-range benefits to our society might be far more significant than are the many efforts to construct models of primary prevention to curtail the incidence of vulnerability" (p. xix). His wise words provide direction to the work to be done to improve our understanding of risk in children's lives.

REFERENCES

Baumrind, D. (1971). Current patterns of parental authority. *Developmental psychology monographs, 4* (1, Part 2).

Bernheimer, L.P. & Keogh, B.K. (1995). Weaving interventions into the fabric of everyday life: An approach to family assessment. *Topics in Early Childhood Special Education, 15,* 415–433.

Egeland, B., Carlson, E. & Sroufe, L.A. (1993). Resilience as process. *Development & Psychopathology, 5,* 517–528.

Garmezy, N. (1985). Stress-resistant children: The search for protective factors. In J. E. Stevenson (Ed.), *Recent research in developmental psychopathology. Journal of Child Psychology & Psychiatry Book* (Supplement No. 4), 213–233.

Garmezy, N. (1989). Foreword. In E.E. Werner, *Vulnerable but invincible* (pp. xiii–xix). New York: Adams, Bannister, Cox.

Garmezy, N., Masten A., & Tellegen. A. (1984). The study of stress and competence in children: A building block for developmental psychopathology. *Child Development, 55,* 97–11.

Grizenko, N. & Pawliuk, N. (1994). Risk and protective factors for disruptive behavior disorders in children. *American Journal of Orthopsychiatry, 64,* 534–544.

Hechtman, L. (1991). Resilience and vulnerability in long term outcome of attention deficit hyperactive disorder. *Canadian Journal of Psychiatry, 36,* 415–421.

Keogh, B. K. (1982). Children's temperament and teachers' decisions. In R. Porter & G. Collins (Eds.), *Temperamental differences in infants and young children,* (pp. 269–279). London: Ciba Foundation/Pitman.

Keogh, B. K. (1986). Temperament and schooling: What is the meaning of goodness of fit? In J. V. Lerner & R. M. Lerner (Eds.), *Temperament and social interaction during infancy and childhood: New directions for child development, No. 31* (pp. 89–108). San Francisco: Jossey-Bass.

Keogh, B.K. (In press). Understanding risk for learning and development. *Learning Disabilities: A Multidisciplinary Journal.*

Keogh, B.K. & Bernheimer, L.P. (1995). Etiologic conditions as predictors of children's problems and competencies in elementary school. *Journal of Child Neurology, 10* (Supplement Number 1), 100–105.

Keogh, B.K., Bernheimer, L. P., & Weisner, T. (2000). UCLA research in progress.

Keogh, B.K. & Burstein, N.D. (1988). Relationship of temperament to preschool children's interactions with peers and teachers. *Exceptional Children, 54*(5), 456–461.

Keogh, B. K. & Weisner, T. (1993). An ecocultural perspective on risk and protective factors in children's development: Implications for learning disabilities. *Learning Disabilities Research & Practice, 8,* 3–10.

Krasner, D. V. (1992). *Risk and Protective Factors and Achievement of Children at Risk.* Unpublished Doctoral Dissertation, UCLA.

Lewis, M., & Feiring, C. (1998). *Families, risk, and competence,* Mahwah, NJ: Erlbaum.

Lyon, G.R. (1995). Research initiatives in learning disabilities: Contributions from scientists supported by the National Institute of Child Health and Human Development. *Journal of Child Neurology, 10,* 120–127.

Lyon, G.R., Alexander, D., & Yaffe, S. (1997). Progress and promise in research in learning disabilities. *Learning Disabilities: A Multidisciplinary Journal, 8,* 1–6.

Masten, A.S., Best, K.M., & Garmezy, N. (1991). Resilience and development: Contributions from the study of children who overcome adversity. *Development & Psychopathology, 2,* 425–444.

Maughan, B. (1988). School experiences as risk/protective factors. In M. Rutter (Ed.), *Studies of psychosocial risk: The power of longitudinal data.* Cambridge, MA: Cambridge University Press.

National Educational Longitudinal Study (NELS). (1988). Washington, DC: U.S. Department of Education, National Center for Educational Statistics.

Nichols, P. L., & Chen, Ta-Chuan. (1981). *Minimal brain dysfunction.* Nahwah, NJ: Lawrence Erlbaum Associates.

Pressley, M., Wharton-McDonald, R., Allington, R., Block, C.C., Morrow, L., Tracey, D., Baker, K., Brooks, G., Cronin, J., Nelson, E., & Woo, D. A study of effective first grade literacy instruction. *Scientific Studies in Reading.* In press.

Ramey, C. T., & Campbell, F.A. (1992). Poverty, early childhood education, and academic competence. The Abecedarian experiment. In A. Huston (Ed.), *Children in poverty.* New York: Cambridge University Press, 190–221.

Ramey, C. T., Ramey, S. L., & Lanzi, R. G. (1998). Differentiating developmental risk levels for families in poverty: Creating a family typology. In M. Lewis & C. Feiring (Eds.), *Families, risk, and competence* (pp. 187–206). Mahwah, NJ: Lawrence Erlbaum.

Ramey, C., Trohanis, P.L., & Hostler, C. (1982). An introduction. In C. Ramey & P.L. Trohanis (Eds.), *Risk in infancy and early childhood* (pp. 1–18). Baltimore: University Park Press.

Rende, R., & Plomin. R. (1993). Families at risk for psychopathology: Who becomes affected and why? *Development & Psychopathology, 5,* 529–540.

Richmond, J. B., & Beardslee, W.R. (1988). Resilience: Research and practical implications for pediatricians. *Developmental & Behavioral Pediatrics, 9,* 157–163.

Rutter, M. (1979). Protective factors in children's responses to stress and disadvantage. In M.W. Kent & J.E. Rolf (Eds.), *Primary prevention of psychopathology: Vol 3. Social competence in children* (pp. 49–72). Hanover: VT: University Press of New England.

Rutter, M. (1984). Resilient children. *Psychology Today,* 57–65.

Rutter, M. (1987). Psychosocial resilience and protective mechanisms. *American Journal of Orthopsychiatry, 57,* 316–331.

Rutter, M. (1989). Psychosocial resilience and protective mechanisms. In J. Rolf, A.S. Masten, D. Cicchetti, K. H. Nuechterlein, & S. Weintraub, (Eds.), *Risk and protective factors in the development of psychopathology* (pp. 161–214). New York: Cambridge University Press.

Rutter, M., & Madge, N. (1976). *Cycles of disadvantage: A review of research.* London: Heinemann.

Rutter, M., Madge, N., Mortimore, P., Orston, J., & Smith, A. (1979). *Fifteen Thousand Hours: Secondary Schools and their effects on Children.* London: Open Book.

Sameroff, A.J., Barto, W.T., Baldwin, A., Baldwin, C., and Siefer, R. (1998). Family and child influences on the development of child competence. In M. Lewis & C. Feiring (Eds.), *Families, risk, and competence* (pp. 161–186). Mahwah, NJ: Lawrence Erlbaum.

Sameroff, A., & Chandler, M. (1975). Reproductive risk and the continuum of caretaking casualty. In F.D. Horowitz (Ed.), *Review of child development research* (Vol. 4,187–244). Chicago: University of Chicago Press.

Sameroff, A., Seifer, R., Baldwin, A., & Baldwin. C. (1993). Stability of intelligence from preschool to adolescence: The influence of social and family risk factors. *Child Development, 64,* 80–97.

Sigel, I.E. (1998). Socialization of cognition: A family focus. In M. Lewis & C. Feiring (Eds.), *Families, risk, and competence* (pp. 289–307). Mahwah, NJ: Lawrence Erlbaum.

Smith, J. & Prior, M. (1995). Temperament and stress resilience of school-age children: A within-families study. *Journal of Child Psychology & Psychiatry, 34,* 168–179.

Speece, D. L., & Keogh, B. K. (Eds.). (1996). *Research on classroom ecologies: Implications for inclusion of children with learning disabilities.* Mahwah, NJ: Lawrence Erlbaum.

Werner, E. E. (1986).The concept of risk from a developmental perspective. In B.K. Keogh (Ed.), *Advances on special education: Vol. 5. Developmental problems in infancy and the preschool years* (pp. 1–23). Greenwich, CT: JAI Press.

Werner, E. E. (1993). Risk and resilience in individuals with learning disabilities: Lessons learned from the Kauai longitudinal study. *Learning Disabilities Research and Practice, 8,* 28–34.

Werner, E. E. (1999). Risk and protective factors in the lives of children with high-incidence disabilities. In R. Gallimore, L.P. Bernheimer, D.L. Macmillan, D.L. Speece, & S. Vaughn (Eds.), *Developmental perspectives on children with high-incidence disabilities.* Mahwah, NJ: Lawrence Erlbaum, pp.15–32.

Werner, E. E. & Smith, R. (1989). *Vulnerable but invincible: A longitudinal study of resilient children and youth.* New York: McGraw-Hill.

Werner, E. E., & Smith, R.S. (1992). *Overcoming the odds: High risk children from birth to adulthood.* New York: Cornell University Press.

Zigmond, N. (1996). Organization and management of general education classrooms. In Spece, D. K., & Keogh, B. K. (Eds.), *Research on classroom ecologies: Implications for inclusion of children with learning disabilities* (pp. 163–190). Mahwah, NJ: Lawrence Erlbaum.

Parts of this article were included in a presentation at the Lab School of Washington Conference on "Who Is the Child At-Risk?" Washington, DC, October 13, 2000.

Integrating Services, Collaborating, and Developing Connections with Schools

Hal A. Lawson and Wayne Sailor

When a new cottage industry develops around a bewildering array of buzzwords, something important is happening. When competent people from all walks of life struggle to make sense of these buzzwords, they are identifying important policy needs and problems with practice. When schools are in trouble, and when results for vulnerable children, youth, and families do not improve, the seeds are being sown for self-doubt, cynicism, skepticism, and maltreatment dynamics. When practicing professionals protect themselves from blame by pointing their fingers at others, when they manifest some of the same needs as the most vulnerable families, and when a growing number of them burn out and drop out, systemic problems are being implicated.

When children kill other children, their teachers, and their parents, and when America's schools become their killing fields, something is clearly wrong, and that something needs to be fixed. When no one knows all that's wrong, and when there are competing definitions of what is wrong that needs fixing and what is good and right that needs strengthening, individuals, groups, entire professions, and organizations often work at cross-purposes. As they work at cross-purposes, they are effectively manufacturing diversity and simultaneously adding to the list of buzzwords. Finally, when the American "quick-fix mentality" reigns, even the most promising innovations often are constrained, stalled, or eliminated because of insufficient time, limited resources, inadequate supports, and ill conceived evaluations.

The state of the art and science of integrated services—the topic addressed here—belongs in this context. For example, the concept of integrated services has become a mainstay in the buzzword industry. In fact, integrated services is associated with a long list of companion buzzwords. These include: interprofessional collaboration, interdisciplinary case management, inter-agency coordination; interprofessional education and training, capitated services community schools, full-service schools, charter schools, voucher and choice plans, asset-based youth development, policy decategorization, systems change and cross-systems change, and comprehensive systems of care. The length of this list is sufficiently bewildering. It becomes all the more challenging when human beings use these buzzwords. Often, they have in mind different meanings when they use the same words, and they mean the same things when they use different buzzwords (Lawson & Briar-Lawson, 1997).

Challenges like these are not limited to the United States. Like other American industries, this buzzword industry, including integrated services, has a global reach (e.g., OECD, 1998; van Veen, Day, & Waldren, 1998). International comparisons and examples add to the diversity and complexity. Obviously, the topic of integrated services demands an entire book, and our analysis is unavoidably selective and limited.

Thus, we approach the topic of integrated services with considerable humility and with a clear sense of purpose. Our aim is to provide an action-oriented planning framework. Toward this aim, we have identified four related goals:

1. To foster shared meaning and understanding
2. To promote improved policies and practices;
3. To enable self-directed learning
4. To contribute to improvements in the well-being of children, youth, and families and in the working lives of the professionals who serve them.

Like all action-oriented frameworks, ours is grounded in firm value commitments, implicit in our sensitizing language as well as in the critical and evaluative narrative we provide. Predictably, our value commitments are most evident when we shift from a descriptive-evaluative narrative to a normative-prescriptive one.

As our title suggests, we emphasize three related, but analytically different, processes; integrating services, collaborating, and developing connections with schools. We are convinced that such a process emphasis lends precision to planning, implementation, evaluation, and research; and that precision is needed today. On the other hand, our process emphasis is not an end in itself. We argue that these three processes are becoming best-practice strategies because they promise to improve results. With Gardner (1999), we promote results-oriented accountability, along with learning and improvements systems in support of progress charting, theory development, and barrier busting. Improved results are the aim, then, and integrating services, collaborating, and developing connections with schools are three related processes for achieving this aim.

Some of the most basic, practical questions in life also are the most important ones. What are integrated services? Why are they being developed and promoted? Who is promoting them? Where? How are they being implemented and evaluated? Whose needs and interests do they serve? What difference do they make? Do they improve children's learning and school performance? What are some of the main barriers, lessons learned, and facilitators? Are there areas of selectivity and silence? Is today's approach as good as it gets? If not, what is next? These kinds of questions structure our analysis of integrated services and its companion concepts.

We begin by sketching a context for integrated services. Once we have provided aspects of its history, we focus on the modern service integration initiatives. We suggest that they can be viewed as forming five different (but not mutually exclusive) waves, and that each carries its own meanings, definitions, and functions. After we have identified some of the conflicts and alternatives, we offer our working definition of integrated services and its close companion concept, interprofessional collaboration. Then we connect our analysis to schools. Next we describe the complexity, difficulties, and opportunities associated with school-related integration and collaboration. Here, we rely on three of the five waves to emphasize important choices and developmental processes. We conclude by exploring emergent challenges for American democracy.

SKETCHING A CONTEXT

Our analysis begins with the historical context. Upon closer inspection, service integration has an interesting history (e.g., Halpern, 1999b; Hassett & Austin, 1997; O'Looney, 1996; Tyack, 1992). Although schools have been mentioned in some cases, and they are implicated in others, the fact remains that service integration can be viewed as a unique initiative involving immensely complex changes.

Viewed in this historical context, modern service integration initiatives aim to reform and transform the institution-building efforts of the late 19th century and most of the 20th century. Industrial-age thinking and planning, which relied on the root metaphor of the machine and the assembly line, served as the crucible for an array of specialized helping professions. Reflecting and fueling their efforts, organizations such as schools and social service agencies were instituted to house these professions. Specialized, categorical governmental policy sectors (e.g., education, social welfare) developed in support of these professions and their organizations.

Each profession and its respective organizations claimed that it met a specific human need, or that it addressed a significant social problem. The underlying assumption was (and is) that each need or problem could be isolated and categorized. Once isolated and categorized, it could be assigned to the relevant profession. Each profession (e.g. educators) and its organization (e.g., schools) assumed responsibility for solving special problems and meeting special needs (e.g., children's learning and healthy development). In turn, these professions' and organizations' external accountability systems developed in relation to their self-proclaimed responsibilities. An entire system of professions has evolved in the process (e.g., McKnight, 1995).

Risking exaggeration, for nearly every conceivable part of the human being, there is now a specialized profession (Lawson, 1998). Unfortunately, the professions have competed with each other. This competition is inevitable because the current system has an economic dimension; it is market-driven (Abbott, 1988; Lawson, 2001; McKnight, 1995). Each profession seeks the equivalent of an economic monopoly over practice areas and special categories of people. Simultaneously, it seeks cultural power and authority. As it gains power and authority, it strengthens its abilities to influence policy decisions in support of its respective professional monopoly. This system of discrete, self-contained professions sets the stage for the contemporary service integration movement.

Today's Service Integration Movement

Today's service integration movement began in the early 1970's (Gerry, in press). At that time, the federal government had a separate department of health, education, and welfare. Its secretary, Elliott Richardson, publicized the problems associated with so many categorical funding and program initiatives. Allegedly, he summed up his "diagnosis" of the federal bureaucracy's "disease" by claiming that it suffered from "a hardening of the categories."[1] The cures included de-categorizing and blending funding, while integrating programs and services.

Because the system of professions is reinforced by these hardened categories, it was implicated as part of the problem. It was (and is) characterized as uncoordinated, fragmented, duplicative, and inefficient (e.g., Gardner, 1999; Lawson, 1998). For example, children and families manifesting multiple needs and problems have as many as 14 different professionals in their lives (Briar-Lawson & Drews, 1998; Halpern, 1999b). These professionals often are unaware of each other. They also have different conceptions of needs and problems, and they rely on different language systems and interventions. Consequently, they often work at cross-purposes.

Predictably, children and families are not served effectively, and results often do not improve. Even worse, competing service providers may cause harm. They may force-fit their preferred diagnostic categories and intervention strategies on families instead of tailoring their assessments and interventions. Or their problem-focused, deficit-oriented language may shape the self-definitions of children and families, resulting in learned hopelessness, depression, and despair.

In this line of thinking, the system of professions and its correlates are the problem (disease). If so, service integration and its companions (e.g., collaboration) are the solution (cure).

Five Waves of Service Integration

Waldfogel (1997) analyzed federal and state policies, incentives, and innovations related to service integration. She described "two waves" of service integration.

First Wave

Waldfogel's first wave was formed during the 1970s and the early 1980s by top-down mandates for integration. This wave continues today. For example, the state of Minnesota, like the Canadian Province of British Columbia, has integrated once separate governmental departments (ministries) into one. Other states now regularly

---

[1] For example, Gerry (in press) claims that the 1998 Federal Budget included more than 500 separate, categorically identified programs, and at least 300 of them were intended for children and families.

convene state agency heads in pursuit of better coordination and integration, perhaps leading to significant structural changes. In first-wave thinking, structural changes and new policies at the top "trickle down" through top-level supervisors and middle managers, ultimately changing and improving front-line practice.

Second Wave

The second wave came later. It accompanied the reinvention of government and the devolution of authority and responsibility.[2] Whereas the first wave was top-down, the second wave was bottom-up. Second-wave initiatives developed because of the limitations associated with "trickle-down thinking." Front-line practitioners, whether working alone or in teams structured by top-down mandates, did not receive all of the information and assistance they needed, nor did they always understand and accept what they heard and learned. Moreover, problems related to effective bottom-up communication channels impeded service integration and systems change initiatives, including the Annie E. Casey Foundation's New Futures initiatives (e.g., Annie E. Casey Foundation, 1995; White & Wehlage, 1995). Although this second wave involved some schools, in reality a limited number were involved. When they were, these pilot schools were part of a grand experiment.

The twin questions for this second wave experiment were as follows.

1. When services are located at, and linked to, schools, does access to service increase?
2. Do these services facilitate early intervention and prevention?

Some so-called full-service schools (e.g., Dryfoos, 1994) developed because of these second wave initiatives. Similarly, a resurgent community schools movement received boosters in this second wave policy context (Melaville & Blank, 1998).

Third Wave

We propose three other waves. The third wave already has formed. It began as states developed targeted service integration initiatives. These initiatives were targeted in the sense that they had to be linked to schools. The appealing idea of school-linked services (SLS) is promoted in this wave. (The adjectives "comprehensive" and "integrated" may or may not accompany the descriptions of SLS.) Examples include California (Healthy Start), Missouri (Caring Communities), Utah (Families, Agencies and Communities Together), Kentucky (with school-based youth centers and family resource centers), Indiana (Step Ahead), and New Jersey (the school-based, youth services initiative).

This third wave reflects, and fuels, concerns about the changing conditions of children and families, especially concerns about children's learning readiness. The fullest expression of this concern was stated in the first educational goal for the

---

[2] Then, as now, the principle of subsidiarity was invoked. The core idea is to devolve responsibility and accountability to the lowest levels of government and to invest localities with power and authority.

nation—namely, that all children will enter school ready and able to learn. In response, school-linked services (SLS) were structured to promote learning readiness by addressing barriers to learning and healthy development (Lawson, 1999b). Twin claims were made: (a) that school-linked services were examples of integrated services; and (b) that service providers would collaborate as they integrated services.

Proposed Fourth Wave

The fourth wave is still forming. It is concerned with expanding the boundaries of school improvement, and especially with incorporating SLS as a vital element in school improvement (e.g., Adelman & Taylor, 1998; 2000; Corrigan & Udas, 1996; Franklin & Streeter, 1996; Hatch, 1998; Honig, Kahne, & McLaughlin, in press; Lawson, 1999 b & c; Lawson & Associates, 1999; Sailor & Skrtic, 1996; Wynn, Meyer, & Richards-Schuster, 1999). Similarly, national school reform initiatives include SLS in their structured approaches. Examples include Success for All (e.g., Slavin, Madden, Dolan, & Wasik, 1996), the School Development Program (e.g., Comer, Haynes, et. al., 1996), schools for the 21st century (e.g., Zigler, 1997), and community schools (e.g., Lawson & Briar-Lawson, 1997; Melaville & Blank, 1998).

Proposed Fifth Wave

The fifth wave is so early in its development that it is barely discernable as a "wave." Because of space limitations, we cannot describe and explain it. We are, however, obliged to introduce it. This fifth wave may be described as the movement to develop comprehensive, neighborhood- and community-based systems of care (e.g., Adams & Nelson, 1995; Bruner & Parachini, 1997; Lawson, 2001; McKnight, 1997; O'Looney, 1996). A technical planning framework for service in one sense, in reality it is much more comprehensive. It focuses anew on poverty and its companions, especially in identifiable areas plagued by concentrated disadvantage.

In this system of care framework, SLS and community-based integrated services initiatives, though vital, are not the only important components. Interprofessional collaboration is not the only kind of collaboration needed. For example, natural helpers and professionals learn to collaborate (e.g., People Helping People, 1997). The school is not the only beneficiary.

This fifth wave is focused on revitalizing neighborhood communities, promoting civic engagement, relying on indigenous support and helping systems, and, all in all, promoting strong democracy. In this wave, colleges and universities play pivotal roles in fostering new approaches to teaching and learning, research, and academically based community service and scholarship. Because this wave promotes such broad community engagement, it is associated with the concept of community collaboration and with university-school-community-family partnerships (Benson & Harkavy, 1997; Himmelman, 1996; Lawson & Barkdull, 2001; Lawson, in press a; O'Looney, 1996; Sailor, in press), and with the emerging concept of the "civic professional" (Skrtic, 2000).

Continuing Lack of Agreement on Meanings and Functions

The five waves described are evidence in support of an important claim: Although some basic consensus may be developing, disagreements and confusion surround service integration and its companion concepts (e.g., Hooper-Briar & Lawson, 1994; O'Looney, 1996). As conflicts surface, stress often increases and disenchantment tends to grow.

Gerry (in press) has chronicled some of the differences that pose conflicts. His list of alternative (and perhaps competing) purposes include: (1) improving the service system; (2) maximizing the efficient use of limited resources;[3] (3) maximizing the independence of families by freeing them from long-term dependence on the government; (4) rebuilding and restoring the capacities of families and local communities; (5) expanding economic and social development and increasing parental employment; and, (6) improving outcomes for children and families.

We suggest three additional purposes: (7) contributing to improvements in school performance; (8) improving professionals' working conditions, efficacy, performance, and job satisfaction; and, (9) revitalizing and empowering local neighborhood communities to mobilize effectively for collective action and to facilitate democratic participation. As if these nine alternatives are not enough, one or more of them can be combined to create others.

In brief, service integration continues to evolve, and predictable challenges and needs accompany its five waves. To reiterate, diverse advocates frequently use the same words, but often they are employing various definitions and promoting different functions. Basic problems such as these constrain well intended efforts.

Furthermore, some definitions, which were offered early in the development of integrated services, may have outlived their usefulness. Recent revolutionary policy changes identified toward the end of our analysis reveal the limitations of earlier thinking about service integration. For example, some early advocates for service integration viewed interprofessional collaboration as its synonym. As a result, disproportionate emphasis has been placed on the formation of team and team-related dynamics. A nearly singular focus on teams and issues surrounding who should serve on them and how they should operate may substitute for a focus on the actual services, including what qualifies as a service, the quality of service delivery, and, indeed, spurious assumptions about the people targeted for services.

INTRODUCING INTERPROFESSIONAL COLLABORATION

For many proponents of service integration, the problem is not so much one of specialization per se. The problem is one of restructuring organizations and their

---

[3] The case can be made that cost containment and reduction are the twin driving forces behind many service integration initiatives. In this economic calculus, these initiatives are key strategies for the down-sizing of the welfare state. Here, the welfare state is being transformed into the competition state—"lean and mean" and ready for the demands of the global economy (e.g., Lawson, in press b).

relationships to orchestrate the work performances of specialized professions. Using this logic, it is assumed that when the performances of diverse, specialized professionals are orchestrated, duplication and fragmentation will be eliminated. In turn, access to services, the quality of services, and results will improve.

Reflecting this main assumption about the need to orchestrate the work of diverse, specialized professionals, the concept of interprofessional collaboration usually accompanies service integration (e.g., Hooper-Briar & Lawson, 1994; O'Looney, 1996). Unfortunately, this concept of interprofessional collaboration also has become a buzzword, and, as such, it may not offer any more clarity than service integration. Often one buzzword is used to define the other.

For example, professionals may be led to believe that, merely by collaborating, they are integrating services. If practitioners communicate better, if their offices are moved to the same building, if they have tried to coordinate their efforts, and if they use the language of collaboration, services are being integrated. Similarly, when professionals claim that they are integrating services, they also may assume that they are collaborating. As a case in point, consider service providers' and educators' responses to two basic questions (Lawson & Briar-Lawson, 1997).

Q: What's new and
   different here?

A: We're collaborating
   and integrating services.

Q: How are things
   different and better?

A: We're collaborating
   and integrating services.

Patterns like this one are predictable when the practical, learning, and development-oriented dimensions of *collaborating* and *integrating services* are ignored. Here, everyone assumes that merely by announcing them both, interprofessional collaboration is occurring as services are being integrated. In these instances, it is easy to escape critical self-examination and evaluation, and needs for technical assistance are not identified or addressed.

From this perspective, our process emphasis is a safeguard against such inviting, self-sealing assumptions because it raises key questions:

Are diverse professionals really collaborating?
What does this process mean to them?
How would you know it if you were to see it?
Does it improve their practices and results?
Are providers, in fact, integrating services?
What does this process mean to them?
How are their efforts measured?
What are the indicators of effectiveness?

These questions frame the "acid test of practice."

Unfortunately, this important test is not administered when bold proclamations of service integration and its companion buzzwords encourage the quick acceptance of self-sealing assumptions. Although service integration may be announced at a higher level, something entirely different usually is operating closer to the ground. Familiar orientations and well established routines endure as part of the deep structures of schools and community health and social-service agencies alike.

Grand Visions and Two More Buzzwords

As they promote service integration, some leaders operating at higher organizational and policy levels often have in mind grand visions. At the very least, they envision better inter-system relationships, more personalized attention to each child and family, and better stewarding across professional, organizational, and systemic boundaries. Frequently, these leaders describe inter-system gaps, gulfs, and cracks, which often become permanent homes for "crossover kids" and multi-system families.

At the very least, these cracks have to be filled, and the gaps and gulfs have to be bridged. For them, service integration and its companion concepts serve to fill the cracks and bridge the gulfs and gaps. As cracks are filled and gaps are bridged, inter-system relations improve, and so should efficiency and effectiveness.

Professions' power and authority, however, remain essentially unchallenged in this new system of relations. The core ideas of professional and client remain, along with the power of professionals to define the very needs they address, creating clients in the process (e.g., Cowger, 1998; Lawson, 2001; McKnight, 1995).[4]

At least two cautions follow. If the basic assumptions underlying the service system are flawed, then this approach to systems change; i.e., via interprofessional collaboration and service integration, is not likely to address most of these root problems (e.g., Gardner, 1994; Mitchell & Scott, 1994). This approach to systems change, then, may not yield improved results. Indeed, this is why critics have been quick to point out that, as long as professions exclusively control the service system, assuming that "professionals know best" and effectively ruling out lay knowledge and indigenous solutions, systems change will not occur. So the second caution concerns the selectivity and silences in the interprofessional collaboration and service integration approach.

Certainly some leaders envision something more than building inter-system relations, and they promote changes in the professions' power relations. Consistent with the meanings of the word "integration," for these leaders service integration implies a complex whole that derives from many specialized parts formed by the various professions and their respective, specialized services. In this view, the whole is greater than the sum of the parts. This whole connotes, for some proponents, an entirely new service system. They use the "systems change" buzzword to describe it.

Integration connotes action verbs such as blending, melding, unifying, and joining. The language for practice follows suit. It includes sensitizing and generative

---

[4] For example, most professionals rail at the proposals offered by McKnight (1995) and Gerry (in press). Both propose giving neighborhood community leaders and their associations the funds now designated for the professions, allowing local residents to determine what they want and need, along with who will provide it.

ideas such as *seamless services, wraparound services, comprehensive, coordinated case management,* and *holistic services.* Alternatively, a market orientation guides this work, and when it does, the language reflects the logic of the market and economic exchanges. Service integration means *one-stop shopping,* made possible when providers move their offices to one place (called *co-locating* providers and services). Similarly, emphasis is placed on determining *customers' satisfaction* and *consumers' needs* (e.g., Gardner, 1999). Others emphasize *consumer-guided* services to ensure that they are responsive, tailored, and more effective. In fact, these advocates for a new consumerism also promote *consumer-delivered strategies,* along with new careers for former clients in the social and health services and in schools (e.g., Alameda-Lawson & Lawson, 2000; Briar-Lawson & Drews, 1998).

Systems change is the buzzword used to describe complex changes like these as they occur in any one system such as child welfare or juvenile justice. When all of the professions, their respective organizations, and their governmental sectors are involved, systems change often is accompanied by a sister concept—*cross-systems change.*

Grand visions like this one regarding systems and cross-systems change provide an important reminder for educators, social and health service professionals, and other readers whose interests are focused on schools. These service integration and interprofessional collaboration initiatives are not limited to schools.

To the contrary, the service integration ideal is being promoted in many neighborhood and community settings. In some ways, interprofessional collaboration and service integration are part of a grand, evolving experiment regarding how human needs can be met effectively and efficiently, and how the responsibilities of government can be determined in relation to these needs. In some people's minds, the so-called reinvention of government also includes the reinvention of the service system, including a fresh, perhaps harsher, determination of governments' responsibilities to vulnerable citizens. When competing political ideologies and agendas operate, as they so often do, some of the issues get muddled.

Multi-sector Initiatives

This much is clear. Interprofessional collaboration and service integration are being promoted in a variety of settings and for a variety of reasons. For example, in healthcare settings such as hospitals, community health centers, and medical clinics, physicians, nurses, social workers, pharmacists, and other professionals claim to collaborate to integrate services (e.g., American Academy of Pediatrics, 1994). In child welfare, social workers, domestic violence counselors, lawyers and judges, substance-abuse professionals, and others often are involved with the same family (e.g., Briar-Lawson, Lawson, Petersen, et al., 1999), and neighborhood-based child-welfare teams also engage in early intervention and prevention initiatives (e.g., Van Wagoner, Boyer, Wisen, Ashton, & Lawson, 2001). The language of collaboration and service integration is gaining popularity in child welfare.

Similarly, efforts to promote interprofessional collaboration and service integration have been underway in community mental health systems (e.g., Bickman,

1996; Caplan & Caplan, 2000). They also are evident in juvenile justice systems (e.g., Cocozza & Skowya, 2000), as well as in early childhood education initiatives and prenatal programs (e.g., Kagan, Goffin, Golum, & Pritchard, 1995). Professionals working with populations with developmental disabilities and challenges, including children and youth in special education, also are endeavoring to integrate services and collaborate (Sailor, in press, Sailor, Kleinhammer-Tramill, Skrtic, and Oas, 1996). And with the enactment of Temporary Assistance to Needy Families (TANF), with its work-related and self-sufficiency requirements, interprofessional collaboration among adult educators, vocational counselors, income-support specialists, substance-abuse counselors, disability specialists, and other professionals has become more common in public sector welfare programs (e.g., Sandfort, 1999).

As if these sector-specific initiatives were not enough, there are cross-system initiatives. For example, some involve "crossover kids"—children and youth in mental health, special education, juvenile justice, and child welfare (e.g., Kamradt, 2000), sometimes including kids with important medical needs that are not addressed.

In this broad context, it makes sense, for planning purposes, to separate some facets of this growing movement for service integration and interprofessional collaboration from the work of educators and schools. It also is prudent to make distinctions between service integration and interprofessional collaboration. Although the case can be made that service integration and collaboration are interdependent (e.g., Hooper-Briar & Lawson, 1994; Lawson & Barkdull, 2001; O'Looney, 1996), they often are defined and implemented separately in real-world practice settings.

For example, as desirable as collaboration may be, professionals may not engage in it. They may try to integrate services merely by communicating more effectively. Similarly, professionals can selectively define "collaboration" as involving more effective communication and cooperation (e.g., Quinn & Cumblad, 1994). In this case, they may or may not be integrating services.

Everyone who studies integrated services and interprofessional collaboration, like all of the people charged with implementing them in practice, confronts messy situations like these. It is impossible to avoid them. In fact, when we alert readers to these messy situations and the challenges they pose, we are working toward the achievement of the four goals for our analysis. If there are needs to foster shared meaning and understanding, to enable self-directed learning, to promote improved policies and practices, and, to contribute to improved results, there is no choice.

We must ground our analysis in current practice situations—in what Schön (1983) characterized as the swamplands of practice. Well intentioned professionals will not be able to get out of these swamps unless the constraints of their swamps are clearly identified. Once they see their situations as swamps, they need more concrete, desirable, and effective alternatives. And they must be given change- and learning-related improvement frameworks that enable them to get to where they want, and need, to be in relation to their respective swamplands.

DEFINING SERVICE INTEGRATION AND INTERPROFESSIONAL COLLABORATION

Clearly, in today's context, there are clear and ever-present needs for effective working definitions. Researchers and practitioners alike need precise, concrete answers to three basic, practical questions.

1. How would you know it if you saw it?
2. How would you know if you were doing good work?
3. If you have not achieved the results you need, what do you need to keep doing, stop doing, and start doing?

Although working definitions may not provide all of the answers to these three questions, they mark a good beginning. But a basic problem remains: All definitions are unavoidably selective, and ours are no exception. We begin with service integration.

Service Integration Defined

Gerry (in press) has suggested that service integration initiatives can be described in relation to one or more of four basic features. We have added three more. These seven features are like building blocks for a working definition.

1. Operational definitions of "the problem," including what is wrong that needs fixing, and what is good and right that needs to be maintained and strengthened[5]
2. The populations being served, especially targeted populations
3. The types of services, programs, and supports offered
4. The locus of service coordination
5. The kinds of strategies used to link and coordinate services
6. The nature of governance structures and processes
7. How lead responsibility is assigned and how accountability is determined.

To foreshadow a key part of our analysis, educators, special educators, and student support professionals may have limited views of SLS, service integration, populations in need, and the nature of their needs. The school's accountabilities and educators' responsibilities structure these views. In contrast to these school-oriented views of SLS, the vast majority of service integration initiatives are focused on the needs of children, youth, families, and their local neighborhood communities. Poverty and its correlates often are implicated in the conception of the problem.

Although these service integration initiatives often include special-needs children in the special education system, they are not limited to these children. Nor are these service integration initiatives limited to psychotherapeutic interventions. A growing number of service integration initiatives include job and income supports, along with broader community economic and social development programs.

---

[5] In practice, these definitions often are implicit. Both practice and research will improve as each site's "theory, or theories, of the problem" are made explicit and interventions are planned to fit the problem.

These broader service-integration initiatives also include interorganizational relationships, which may be described as interorganizational collaboration (Lawson & Barkdull, 2001). These new organizational relationships involve the development of tightly coupled organizations in substitution for uncoupled, or loosely coupled, organizations (e.g., O'Looney, 1996, Skrtic & Sailor, 1996). At the same time, these broader service integration initiatives may focus on partnerships among private and public sector organizations. Most also include provisions for changes in government agencies. Our definition of integrated services belongs in this broad context; it incorporates three key phrases from Gerry's (in press) definition.

> Service integration is a set of strategies by which a community seeks to ensure that all of its residents enjoy immediate, uninterrupted access to children's services, adult services, and family services. Both residents and professionals qualify as service providers. Integration demands that all services are personalized and caring. Where co-occurring needs are evident, service providers coordinate their efforts, and they treat individuals and families in need as partners. Working together, service providers tailor their services to fit what children, parents, and families want and need. Where children are concerned, service integration seeks to optimize the cognitive, social, emotional, and physical development of each child, while simultaneously supporting and strengthening families and enhancing the security and safety of their neighborhood community. Service integration includes job training and supports in service of greater economic self-sufficiency for families. It includes blended approaches to community economic and social development. Finally, it promotes empowerment strategies that enable individuals, groups, and entire communities to mobilize effectively for collective action and for democratic participation.

This definition of service integration is new, in some important respects, and it is more comprehensive than other definitions. Although our definition incorporates many of the familiar requirements for effective practice, it also suggests new ones. Unfortunately, we cannot explore with our readers all of the implications of our definition and its practice requirements; however, we can identify two immediate implications.

The first implication involves the contrast between our definition and claims about full-service schools. When service integration (and integrated services) are defined comprehensively, and when this definition includes the requirement that they be personalized and tailored to fit unique needs, the claim that any school provides the full range of services needed by children, adults, families, and neighborhood communities is suspect.

Furthermore, our definition of integrated services raises the normative question: With our definition of service integration as a guide, should schools try to become full-service organizations? Given our definition, this question is a rhetorical one.

The second implication involves inclusion of local residents and family members as service providers. Here we offer two reminders.

1. Families and neighbors already provide the bulk of services, supports, and resources needed, and delivered, in local communities.

2. The service industry provides abundant opportunities for meaningful employment for local residents.

Local residents often are the keys to effective solutions (e.g., Briar-Lawson & Drews, 1998). Providing them meaningful employment, along with career advancement ladders, is an important way to stabilize families, strengthen local neighborhood communities, and contribute to school improvement (e.g., Haveman & Wolfe, 1995; Feikema, Segalavich, & Jeffries, 1997; Keith, 1996).

EXAMPLES OF REQUIREMENTS FOR SERVICE INTEGRATION

- A single point of entry into all public service systems, and with private-service systems that have contracted to work with public-sector children and families.

- Authority of each organization (e.g., community agency, neighborhood organization, school) to determine eligibility for services.

- Shared intake and outreach procedures and criteria by organizations and their professionals.

- A comprehensive, child- and family-friendly initial assessment and case history protocol.

- Services offered without the child or the family demonstrating proof of harm.

- An advocate for each child or family, who convenes other providers for integrated case planning, management, and evaluation.

- Assurances that each child and family will be treated as a unique case, and that services will be personalized and tailored as needed.

- Safeguards against stereotyping by one or more professionals, resulting in a pattern of fitting the child or the family into the preferred intervention.

- Assessment of co-occurring child and family needs, including the child's and the family's self-assessment.

- Opportunities and supports are plentiful for groups of professionals to convene for problem-identification and problem-solving.

- Clear, well understood, and effective procedures for referral and access to services.

- Clear, well understood, and effective communication procedures, channels, and networks.

- Designation of child and family advocates who ensure that children and families do not fall through the cracks because providers assume that referral forms and procedures "speak for themselves."

- General acceptance of the principle of "least intrusive intervention" (of professionals intruding as little as possible into the everyday lives of children and families).

- Clear, well understood, and enforced criteria and procedures for ensuring confidentiality.

- Clear and well understood criteria and procedures for sharing information about a child and a family.

- Clear and well understood criteria and procedures for monitoring progress and evaluating results.

(continued)

EXAMPLES OF REQUIREMENTS FOR SERVICE INTEGRATION *(continued)*

- Clear and well understood criteria and procedures for entering information into public data systems.

- Integrated data and management information systems are harmonized across service sectors (e.g., education, juvenile justice, child welfare).

- Clear, well understood, and routine approaches for examining and addressing pervasive, inequalities based on gender in family systems.

- Clear and well understood procedures for assessing the safety and security of homes, schools, and local neighborhood communities.

- Clear and well understood procedures for helping parents get and maintain jobs and suitable housing.

- Clear, well understood, and developed norms and standards for the care and treatment of children and youth, and for how parents may be helped with their roles with children.

- Clear, well understood, and routine approaches for assessing and improving the well-being of children in the content of their family systems.

- Clear, well understood, and enforced norms and standards regarding parental substance abuse and child abuse and neglect.

- Clear, well understood, and routine approaches for assessing and addressing the special needs of women, including domestic violence, spousal abuse, caregiving roles, income supports, child care, transportation assistance, and occupational development.

- Clear, well understood, and routine approaches for assessing and addressing the racial, ethnic, and cultural particularities of the child, family, and neighborhood community.

- Decategorization (blending) of funding streams and flexible use of funds by frontline professionals.

- Clear, well understood, and routine approaches to assigning individuals, professions, and agencies lead responsibilities for addressing a need or solving a problem.

- Performance-based accountability systems allowing flexibility and discretion replace rigid rule- and compliance-based systems.

- Clear, well understood, and routine procedures by which front-line professionals communicate needs for policy amendments and changes to middle managers and top level supervisors.

Interprofessional Collaboration Defined

For services to be integrated, professionals serving the same people and communities have to stop working at cross-purposes. At the very least, they need to communicate better, coordinate their efforts, and cooperate effectively.[6] From this perspective, the idea of interprofessional collaboration can be introduced simply and clearly.

---

[6] For working definitions of these "c-words" related to collaboration, see Mattessich and Monsey (1992); Winer and Ray (2000); and Lawson and Barkdull (2001).

Every professional working with the same child, adult, and family has to be "on the same page."

But a basic question remains. Why bother? In response to this question, we provide five interrelated sensitizing concepts.

Interdependence

The first concept, interdependence, is manifested in the following ways:

1. Children's well-being depends on their peer relations and networks, families, and community systems.
2. In contrast to the system of profession's categorical assumptions, human needs and problems cannot be neatly isolated. Social-ecological analyses have emphasized that human needs and problems often nest in each other. Find one (e.g., substance abuse), and sooner or later, you may find others (e.g., mental health needs, domestic violence, child abuse and neglect).

These interdependent, co-occurring needs are especially challenging to the system of professions. They make it difficult, if not impossible, to effectively address one need unless the others also are addressed (e.g., Briar-Lawson, Lawson, et. al., 1999; Lawson & Barkdull, 2001).

As a result, the professions depend on each other. That is, any one profession (and its organization) is not likely to achieve its goals and meet its accountability requirements without the assistance and support of the other professions (and their organizations). To put it another way, when humans depend on their peer networks, families, and community systems, and when human needs and problems co-occur and nest in each other, the specialized professions and their work organizations also are interdependent. Each requires the others in order to succeed.

Conditional Equality

The second concept is conditional equality. Power, authority, and expertise are shared, and democratic relationships prevail. Mindful of their interdependence, everyone, including individuals and families in need, knows that they are either part of the problem or part of the solution. All know that they are "in the same boat."

Unity of Purpose

The third concept, unity of purpose, is grounded in an understanding of interdependent relationships, and it is a unique feature of collaboration. It also might be called the "neglected feature." For example, when professionals co-locate in the same place, they are able to communicate better and their working relationships may improve, but they may not develop unity of purpose. They can coordinate their efforts, sharing the same forms and information systems and addressing confidentiality issues, but they need not develop unity of purpose.

Unity of purpose is evident when professionals truly understand their interdependence and engage in holistic planning. Instead of viewing each child or family narrowly, in relation to the specialized need or problem that their own profession addresses, professionals are concerned with the whole child and the entire family system. Each is equally concerned with every aspect of a child's or a family's well-being.[7] These professionals' shared concern does not mean that they deny, or sacrifice, their special expertise. To the contrary, needs and problems are assigned to them based on their special expertise. The most appropriate professional (the one whose specialization corresponds to the need) is assigned lead responsibility for addressing a risk factor, or for meeting a need.

For example, the classroom teacher may identify signs of child abuse and neglect, but she cannot be expected to address this problem. A social worker with expertise about abuse and neglect assumes lead responsibility for addressing it. Yet, the teacher is no less concerned because lead responsibility has been assumed by, or delegated to, the social worker. The teacher knows that she will not be successful and that the child will not be successful in her classroom unless the social worker also is successful in her efforts to ensure the child's safety and security. The teacher thus celebrates the social worker's success, and reciprocally the social worker celebrates when the teacher succeeds. Unity of purpose is expressed in basic, important interactions like these. It is a key, defining feature of collaboration.

Shared Responsibility for Results

When unity of purpose has been achieved, professionals assume shared responsibility for results (e.g., Gardner, 1999; Lawson & Barkdull, 2001). This focus on improving results includes related activities such as progress charting, learning and improvement systems designs, and barrier busting. This results orientation, framed by unity of purpose, also guides data-gathering and the development of data systems, including practitioners' action research methods. Absent a focus on results, data systems are aimless, and the data sets are meaningless.

With unity of purpose and a focus on results, learning and improvement, through data and data systems, are facilitated. Everyone is more likely to know what data are important; why they are important; how, when, where, and why to collect data; and how to use these data in support of strategic improvements, learning, and capacity-building. They know that these activities are in their best interests, as well as in the interests of those they serve.

Enlightened Self-Interest

Accordingly, the fifth sensitizing concept is enlightened self-interest. At first this concept may seem crass because many conversations about collaboration convey the impression that everyone should put aside their specialized needs and interests. In this environment, it may not be safe to ask and answer two basic, important questions:

1. Why should I (and my agency or school) participate in this collaborative work?

---

[7] Alternatively, when risk and protective factors substitute for well-being in the planning framework, each professional is equally concerned with a child's overall risk and protective factor profile.

2. What's in it for me and us?

For a host of reasons, questions like these are viewed as the opposite of collaboration, and people who insist on asking them may be perceived as selfish and unprepared to collaborate (Lawson & Barkdull, 2001). When that environment prevails, and when people are unable to ask and address these questions, collaboration is constrained, limited, and perhaps prevented. Busy people with excessive workloads and job pressures simply cannot be expected to attend meetings and participate genuinely unless they have good reason to believe that their attendance and participation will improve their jobs and lead to improved results. So, when professionals acknowledge their interdependence and agree to collaborate to improve results, they are enlightened because they know that, by joining forces, they gain "the collaborative advantage" (e.g., Lawson & Barkdull, 2001; Sarason & Lorentz, 1998).

Enlightened self-interest also means that every professional has a stake in this collaborative undertaking. Various stakeholders agree to collaborate, and their collaboration is sustained as long as it benefits them. Collaboration of this kind is a voluntary activity, and it requires willing participants. Although meetings can be mandated, true collaboration cannot be forced. Interprofessional collaboration is not done to people, or for them—it is done by them (e.g., Himmelman, 1996).

Reciprocity

The sixth sensitizing concept is reciprocity. When professionals collaborate because they cannot achieve their goals unless they do, and when they do so as a matter of enlightened self-interest, they are more willing to give and share as well as to receive. Reciprocity implies mutuality, and mutuality means developing common grounds for working together.

Reciprocity also suggests an exchange system built on these common grounds. In this sense, interprofessional collaboration is a reciprocal exchange relationship. I help and support you while you help and support me and us. Each successful exchange builds on the others.

Over time, strong social trust networks develop around task-focused work. In the process, former strangers and competitors become acquaintances, colleagues, and even close friends. Reciprocity emphasizes the importance of social and cultural bonding and networking, which derive from successful task completion and joint problem-solving. True collaboratives tend to become vibrant communities of practice (e.g., Wenger, 1999).

> Interprofessional collaboration occurs when two or more professions join forces and develop unity of purpose to improve results. It occurs when (and because) they depend on each other to achieve their goals and meet their accountability standards. When professionals truly collaborate, they do because they understand their interdependence; they view collaboration as part of enlightened self-interest; and they promote and reward reciprocity.

Professionals who collaborate share missions, goals, and objectives. They also share definitions of "the problem(s)," including what's wrong that needs fixing and what's good and right that needs strengthening. They develop shared language, problem-solving protocols, and barrier-busting strategies. They also learn to share resources, supports. They develop shared governance structures. Thus, true interprofessional collaboration is durable; it tends to have sticking power and staying power.

Generativity

Generativity is the seventh concept. True collaboratives generate creative, innovative approaches to the theory of the problem and to intervention and improvement strategies. They also generate learning, development, and systems change in relation to professional and organizational boundaries and boundary relationships. Last, but not least, when collaboratives become communities of practice they generate affective commitments and identity changes. Effective and appropriate collaboration changes people's lives, not just their jobs.

Defined in this way, interprofessional collaboration is grounded in firm ethical-moral imperatives. It is a best-practice strategy, and at times it may be the only way to improve results for people in need—to truly serve them.

The basic requirements for collaboration are:

- Reasonable people who are able to listen, learn, compromise, adjust, and adapt.
- Collaborative, interprofessional leaders and facilitators who are able to cross professional, community, and organizational boundaries and build relationships.
- Norms that prevent blame and maltreatment dynamics and improve the quality of mutual treatment and interaction.
- Special settings (places and environments) that support joint performances, learning, and development.
- Supportive organizational climates and structures.
- Organizational incentives, rewards, supports, and resources for joint work and ventures.
- Special governance structures and processes (e.g., school-community planning teams).
- Communicative and linkage mechanisms for the various professionals and for their organizations.

The complexity increases when the third part of our title is added to the mix: *developing connections* with schools. In short, instead of just two challenges (integrating services and collaborating), there are three. Although developing these connections in a strategic and effective way can be difficult in its own right, maintaining these connections may be even harder. Even when some service providers have established connections with schools, these connections are not necessarily evidence of either service integration or interprofessional collaboration.

Confusing Connections

Presently, some community services may be linked to schools already, but they are not necessarily integrated. Often, community service providers respond only to specialized needs identified by the school. For example, a social worker may respond to calls regarding child abuse and neglect. Or a substance-abuse counselor may respond to a call about an adolescent's drug problem. Especially in large schools, these two professionals may not be aware of each other.

Even if community service providers are made aware of each other, and they are encouraged to collaborate to integrate their services, there is simply too much going on in their professional lives to expect too much, too fast. At the same time, they are trying to figure out *whether* to collaborate and integrate services, they must learn *how* to do them both. And still the third challenge remains. They also must decide whether, and how, to develop strategic, effective connections to schools. And then they must figure out, with educators, how to maintain these connections. None of this work is easy.

The work becomes even more complicated when important people at the school are omitted from planning and policy discussions. Consistent with third-wave thinking, many SLS initiatives involve only social and health service professionals from the community. In short, the growing SLS movement often has ignored a fact obvious to anyone who knows schools: Schools have their own collection of social and health service providers, including school nurses, speech and language therapists, physical and occupational therapists, social workers, counselors, and psychologists. Once this reminder is provided, the work of developing connections gains importance.

Even if services are being integrated in the community, they may not be connected to, or integrated with, the school's pupil support professionals. Nor are some community-oriented SLS initiatives connected with special educators, or with the school's classroom teachers (e.g., Adelman & Taylor, 1998; 2000; Lawson, 1999 b & c). Once this fact is entertained, intra-school challenges related to collaborating, integrating, and making connections also are evident.

Despite an emphasis on school-based collaboration (e.g., Christiansen, Goulet, Krentz, & Maeers, 1997), especially in relation to special education children and youth (Sailor, 1991; in press), each school's pupil support professionals' services, special educators' work and classroom teachers' efforts are not automatically connected or integrated. Nor do these school-based professionals and educators automatically collaborate. For example, in large, highly challenged, low-performing urban schools, staff turnover alone makes mutual awareness and understanding the real challenge. Collaboration, if it ever results, comes later.

PLANNING FOR COMPLEX CHANGE

A complex change initiative is formed when the three process elements are joined: integrating services, collaborating, and developing connections with schools. Complex change and its orchestration pose considerable challenges (e.g., Lawson, 1999a).

Despite these challenges, there are good reasons for proceeding. In our view, collaborating, integrating, and connecting practices are a good thing to do; and they are the right thing to do. Done right, they promise help and supports for children, youth, families, and professionals. Done right, this triumvirate of practices also will improve schools, help children, support families, and strengthen their neighborhood communities.

Given competing definitions of integrated services and its companion concepts, however, questions remain: What does it mean to do it right? Is there just one definition? Who decides? Who decides who decides?

These questions involve basic, important issues regarding purpose, vested interests, power, and authority. Often they serve to divide good people who need to become united. Place matters. That is, these questions are framed by local people, contexts, and cultures (e.g., Armstrong, 1997; Foster-Fishman, Salem, et. al., 1999). And just because they were considered and answered at one point in time, there is no guarantee that they will be addressed in the same way later. With time, fresh awareness, and changing circumstances, they may be addressed differently. There is simply no way to deny and avoid the complexity of the post-modern age (Skrtic & Sailor, 1996).

The Import of Our Process Emphasis

In the post-modern era, one size fits few. Mindful of unprecedented variability, complexity, novelty, and uncertainty, we have provided a process emphasis, along with a tough-minded focus on results. This process emphasis is justified because the work associated with *integrating, collaborating* and *developing connections* is never finished. After all, human needs and societal problems change. New policies often create new needs. Furthermore, this work is never-ending because, over time, people come and go. Veterans, especially leaders, leave, while newcomers join. Our process emphasis gives due recognition to these basic realities.

Furthermore, our process emphasis also may act as a safeguard against self-congratulatory and self-sealing patterns. It forces difficult questions rather than accepting at face value what people and their organizations proclaim about themselves, or have announced in their behalf. And, because it encourages planners and analysts to ask the most basic, practical questions, it helps identify important needs for technical assistance, education, and training, and capacity-building. Identifying these needs is a key benefit.

Despite its advantages, our process orientation is not a panacea. For example, two ever-present dangers loom when people focus on these three processes.

Lost in the Process

The first danger is evident when professionals become so preoccupied with integrating services, collaborating, and developing connections with schools that they forget that these processes are strategies (means), not goals (ends). This is the familiar problem of goal displacement, which is also called an *ends-means inversion.*

When new strategies, or means, become ends or goals in their own right, significant problems result.

In brief, our process emphasis should not be viewed in any of the following ways: It is not a justification for collaboration because it enables professionals to make new friends, for service integration for its own sake, or for making connections with schools as a productive leisure pursuit. Rather, we view integrating services, collaborating, and developing connections as essential best-practice strategies. They are essential means to other ends—improved results.

Linear Change and the Categorization of Each Process Component

A second danger introduces an irony. When people view the change process as linear, and when they take an extreme view of the differences among the three processes of integrating, collaborating, and developing connections, they effectively undermine the basic purposes of the service integration movement. Simply stated, they make each process (e.g., integrating) a hard-and-fast category. Because of their linear view of the change process, they place each process category in a step-wise progression. In other words, these linear, categorical views of change foster a "one at a time" line of thinking. Reflecting this orientation, well intentioned people describe change as occurring in steps.

Step one: The various professions have to learn how to collaborate.
Step two: They have to integrate services.
Step three: They have to make connections with schools.

Here, the lessons of the first three waves of service integration are instructive. This linear, categorical approach takes years. It also overlooks the fact that the work of integrating, collaborating, and developing connections is never finished. More to the point, by the time the third step is anywhere near someone's definition of completion, another generation of children (and their families) has had to endure needs without the help and supports that professionals could have provided. In this linear, categorical approach, professionals from all walks of life themselves do not receive the mutual supports they need and deserve.

With these limitations in mind, our process-oriented approach promotes a non-linear approach to change. Change, in this view, proceeds in interacting phases, not in linear steps (e.g., Lawson, 1999a). In contrast to "one at a time" thinking, the advantage of this approach is that several beneficial processes can be launched simultaneously, effectively reducing the time needed to see progress and improve results. Unfortunately, this non-linear, multi-phasic approach to change is associated more with the fifth wave of service integration than it is to waves three and four.

THIRD-WAVE THINKING: CHILDREN AND YOUTH READY AND ABLE TO LEARN

Third-wave thinking continues to dominate SLS planning and operations. States have supported targeted SLS initiatives for several related reasons. Two are especially relevant. SLS initiatives are one response to America's changing demographic profile, especially the characteristics of its children and families (e.g., Cappella & Larner, 1999). Because more children and families evidence vulnerability and needs, SLS initiatives, in essence, perform double duty. SLS may meet these needs at the same time that they enable children and youth to enter school ready and able to learn. Using this logic, schools are supported and will improve.

A dominant "theory of the problem" can be derived from third wave thinking (Lawson, 1999b & c). The real problem is with the learning readiness and healthy development of children and youth, in turn implicating parental and family needs. Once these needs are addressed, schools will be effective. This thinking thrusts responsibility for meeting these needs onto families and, of course, on school-linked social and health service providers. In this view, SLS is a challenge for service providers, especially community-based social and health service providers. Teachers need not be concerned or directly involved.

In this context, educators have viewed service integration in general, and SLS in particular, as serving them. Educators view SLS, in essence, as a one-way exchange system. The problem is not with them and the school (e.g., Gardner, 1994). A "fix, then teach" approach reigns (e.g., Honig, Kahne, & McLaughlin, in press). Educators thus are inclined to blame service providers and parents when children and youth come to school, not ready and able to learn. When service providers and parents do not do their jobs, educators have trouble with theirs.

Meanwhile, community health and social service providers, some parents, and community leaders take a different view. In their view, the problem is with the schools. Schools have to be readied to enable the learning, academic achievement, and healthy development of all children and youth. And, just as educators expect service providers to personalize and tailor their services, so, too, do service providers expect educators to personalize and tailor their instruction. For example, some educators are unprepared for growing child and family diversity, including the challenges of inclusive education.

Just as service providers may typecast children and families and provide routine, preferred services, so, too, do some teachers typecast children and youth in their classes and use routine, preferred teaching and instructional strategies. When educators do not do their jobs, service providers have trouble with theirs. After all, school problems are associated with, and may even cause, substance abuse, delinquency and crime, family stress, domestic violence, and other personal-social problems. So, while educators may be blaming them, service providers may be blaming educators.

In a nutshell, there are mutual blame and maltreatment dynamics here (Lawson & Briar-Lawson, 1997), and these dynamics are among the most important barriers to mutual understanding and effective collaboration. They help harden the categories. Instruction and teaching belong to teachers, and they occur in classrooms. Service delivery belongs to social and health service providers, and it occurs in their offices.

Teachers may not benefit from having service providers in their classrooms and gaining access to new pedagogical strategies (e.g., Mooney, Kline, & Davoren, 1999), and service providers may not benefit by having classroom teachers serve on their teams. No wonder academic achievement may not improve significantly when SLS initiatives are implemented. The social arrangements work against the most important requirements for collaboration, especially unity of purpose.

Principals' jobs become more complicated with third-wave initiatives. Principals are involved because providers may wish to relocate at their schools, and a host of new challenges arise when office space must be provided. This relocation (also called co-location) often constitutes what some analysts call school-based services and, perhaps, full-service schools and community schools.[8] Moreover, student support professionals and special educators also must be involved, if for no other reason than to protect their jobs and prevent unnecessary competition and conflicts.

Three Focal Points

Although Howard Adelman and Linda Taylor (1998, 2000) are among the leaders of what we call "fourth wave," their work spans third- and fourth-wave thinking. Arguably, their interprofessional frameworks for SLS are the clearest and most precise.

Mindful of the problems and conflicts that result when state- and community-sponsored SLS initiatives are proclaimed without taking into account the schools' student support professionals, Adelman and Taylor make a key distinction between school-owned and community-owned services (and related resources). They correctly assert that planning must focus on the relationship between these two kinds of services. Knowing that in the most vulnerable communities, qualified professionals will remain in short supply, and seeking greater efficiency and effectiveness, Adelman and Taylor have provided clear guidelines and useful assessment inventories. Adelman and Taylor (1998, 2000) also have developed an elaborate planning framework for coordinating, harmonizing, and synchronizing, school-owned services and community-owned services. We commend their work to readers.

The second key point marks a departure from the full-service school. In lieu of expecting just one school to provide all of the services, entire feeder patterns are a more appropriate unit of analysis. Here, too, Adelman and Taylor (1997 a & b) have provided important leadership. The core idea is that services have to be articulated across P-12 in the same way that school subjects are.

The third focal point is related to the first. It entails developing common principles and practices among all of the service providers, whether school-owned and supported or community-owned and supported. Here, SLS initiatives intersect with other, community-based interprofessional collaboration and service integration initiatives (e.g., those in medical clinics and child welfare agencies). The requirements listed earlier may apply directly to the design of SLS. Otherwise, SLS initiatives will be in direct competition with other interprofessional collaboration and service

---

[8] Thanks to the work of a National Coalition for Community Schools, consensus is growing about new kinds of schools that incorporate many different components. Past-present differences, however, can be identified among full-service schools, community schools, and full-service community schools (e.g., Lawson, 1999c). These differences are important because they provide choices.

integration initiatives. In fact, "inter-collaborative competition" is already in evidence in several large communities.

With other service providers, SLS providers must make informed choices. They must choose their practice principles and, presumably, their service-delivery orientations from a growing number of alternatives, that list "best-practice principles." Typically these lists provide a kind of shorthand language for service providers. This shorthand includes descriptors such as child-centered, family-focused, empowerment-oriented, culturally sensitive, integrated, collaborative, strengths (asset)-based, solution-focused, and results-oriented. Often they are structured to present a from-to orientation—that is, the "old" principles are contrasted with the "new" principles.

These choices are especially important. But, they are complicated by at least two major factors.

The Buzzword Factor

The first might be called the "buzzword factor." Because each profession's literature may not provide clarity and precision, and because providers and their agencies have established preferences for service design and delivery, multiple meanings, orientations, and functions accompany these so-called best-practice lists. For example, empowerment has multiple meanings (e.g., Ackerson & Harrison, 2000). Moreover, one list may emphasize family-focused practice while another emphasizes family-centered practice. Although both feature the family, they entail very different strategies.

In family-focused practice, for example, the child is situated in the context of the family as professionals design and try to integrate services. In family-centered practice, family members enjoy equal power and authority; they are joint designers of services (e.g., Briar-Lawson & Drews, 1998). In the same vein, significant differences develop when differences among culturally sensitive, culturally relevant, and culturally responsive practices are unpacked. It is not easy to resolve these differences.

In short, as helpful as lists of best-practice principles are, they do not guarantee harmony, synergy, collaboration, and service integration. Third-wave thinking presents another complicating factor.

The School Factor

The second complicating factor is "the school factor." We explore this one in greater detail after the next section on fourth-wave thinking. For now, suffice it to say that, for many of the school's student support professionals, the shift from student-focused, or child-centered, practices to practices involving families and communities is nothing short of revolutionary. As Tyack (1992) has demonstrated, these school-supported professionals have a long history of working with individual children, at school, to improve their school-related behavior and performances. Providers, then, are at the school in support of the school, its missions, and its accountabilities.

Little wonder, then, that evaluators and policy-makers alike have expected, and looked for, improvements in children's academic achievement as SLS initiatives have been implemented. For a host of reasons, however, these expectations have not been met. Although modest gains have been reported in selected elementary and middle schools—importantly, schools in which teachers often work closely with service providers—SLS alone do not yield impressive, generalizable improvements in children's school achievement (e.g. Wagner, Newman, & Golan, 1996).

Warren's (1999) superb evaluation of New Jersey's school-based youth services program (SBYS) provides especially significant findings. These findings signal some of the limitations of third-wave thinking and, at the same time, they illuminate important choices and fresh opportunities.

SBYS is primarily an after-school initiative that combines programs and services. It uses recreation and personal-social support services as "hooks" or "magnets" for youth. Prior evaluations of SBYS had indicated reductions in personal-social problems such as teen pregnancy and substance abuse. Similarly, Warren's evaluation yielded promising data in support of important progress in youth development.

Arguably, one of her two most important findings concerns academic achievement. Warren learned that SBYS successfully attracts youth—youth who might not otherwise come to school, attend, and stay. Because they do not drop out, however, and their academic performances are included in the school's achievement profiles, overall school performance may not improve. Indeed, it may even decline!

Enter Warren's second important finding. Many youth are challenged by poverty and its close companions, as well as by family issues, and neighborhood-related problems. SBYF simply cannot address all of the needs these youth evidence. Many SLS initiatives in other states face the same kinds of challenges.

Key choices and important opportunities thus derive from third-wave thinking and its SLS experiments. For example, trade-offs are involved. Healthy child and youth development as promoted by SLS, including the prevention of school dropouts, may run counter to expectations about improved performance on academic achievement tests (see also Halpern, 1999a). So is it better to keep children in school, contributing to their learning and healthy development, even if their performance on standardized achievement tests affects the school's overall achievement profile? Opportunities may emanate from trade-offs like this one.

For example, both fourth wave and fifth wave thinking derive from these kinds of trade-offs and related findings about third wave SLS. In fact, the connections among these three waves emerge. Is it possible the third wave thinking is not so much flawed as it is incomplete? In other words, is SLS a necessary, but insufficient, intervention? Furthermore, where are families, family support networks, and indigenous community service, support, and resource systems in third wave approaches to SLS? Where is the private sector, and what importance is placed on jobs and economic development?

Questions like this one are associated with fourth wave and fifth wave thinking. Indeed, our definitions of service integration and interprofessional collaboration indicate our stance in relation to these questions and others.

FOURTH-WAVE THINKING

Without question, children and youth need to come to school ready and able to learn. However, Goals 2000, like third-wave thinking about SLS, ignored another key goal: *Schools have to be readied for the learning and healthy development of all children, youth, and families* (Lawson, 1999b & c). If schools are not optimally designed, and if they do not provide optimal environments for children's learning, or for professionals' work, even the best conceived SLS will not result in improvements in the school's academic achievement profile.

In third-wave thinking, SLS are ratcheted onto schools. Real schools, especially their deep structures, are not changed (Tye, 2000; Tyack & Cuban, 1995).

Fourth-wave thinking proceeds beyond services reform. It is a concerted effort to reinvent American schooling, especially for its most vulnerable populations challenged by poverty and its companions. More than a new approach to schooling and school improvement, this reinvention of the American school is tied to a growing national movement in support of children and their families.

SLS Variations

Significant differences thus accompany fourth-wave thinking. These SLS differences are important because they provide different cognitive maps for the change targets, the key actors, and the change processes. For example, Lawson (1999c) has identified these different versions of SLS.

- Co-locate service providers and link them to schools to address the needs of at-risk students. Here, the assumption is that children need to be "fixed" so schools can work as planned—the problem is with the children, not with schools.
- Co-locate service providers to help families and adult community members, in addition to children and youth.
- Co-locate and link service providers to schools and make them conform to the requirements of a particular model for school reform (e.g., Comer School Development Plan; Accelerated Schools; Success for All).
- Recast the roles of existing school support professionals for child study and assistance, involving interprofessional case management, school-based resource teams, or both.
- Prepare parent paraprofessionals for service delivery, family support, and community development.
- Use SLS initiatives as the catalyst for broad-based community collaboratives, which are home to SLS but are not limited by them.
- Hybrids formed by combinations of the above alternatives.

Each of the above alternatives is based on different assumptions about "the theory of change, " and each stipulates different responsibilities and roles for teachers, principals, other professionals, and families. Whether a school's, or a school district's, SLS configuration qualifies as either "comprehensive services" or "integrated services" depends on the alternative selected.

Joining Schools, Families, and Communities

Fourth-wave thinking derives from understanding patterns of interdependence. It takes a social and ecological view of schools, families, and their surrounding community context. Employing the planning frame provided by "the school community" and focusing on "educational reform and renewal," this new line of thinking escapes the limitations associated with the school as a standalone institution in which educators do it all alone (e.g. Lawson & Briar-Lawson, 1997). SLS is incorporated into a broader, more comprehensive planning framework.

For example, Adelman and Taylor (1998, 2000) focus on addressing barriers to children's learning and healthy development to enable learning and success in school. They call their approach "the enabling component," and they identify six enabling areas meriting school and community collaboration.

Similarly, Lawson and his colleagues (e.g., Lawson, 1999c; Lawson & Briar-Lawson, 1997; Lawson & Associates, 1999; Lawson & Barkdull, 2001) also have promoted multiple forms of collaboration. Interprofessional collaboration and SLS are part of this planning frame, but they are not alone. These two important initiatives are accompanied by family-centered collaboration, inter-organizational collaboration, and broad-based community collaboration.

Different in some important respects, these two approaches, like others that are developing, share a simple, yet compelling logic: *School improvement and renewal processes are destined to fall short of their intended aims until such time as the family and community contexts for children's learning and development are addressed simultaneously.* In other words, start with the factors and forces known to influence and determine children's learning, healthy development, academic achievement, and success in school; and then ask how professionals, parents, and other diverse stakeholders in school communities can work collaboratively to address them. This work entails institutional change involving schools, social and health services and their providers, and their boundary relations.

Interdependence, Enlightened Self-Interest, and Reciprocity

At least in the dominant institutional definition, the American public school is a standalone organization. It is designed for children and youth. Its purpose is to enable their learning and academic achievement. Educators assume responsibility for this learning and academic achievement, and they are held accountable for them. In this institutional definition, educators and their colleagues located at the school are expected to focus on this special category formed by children's learning and academic achievement, and they also are expected to "do it all, alone." In turn, teachers expect to work in classrooms alone, and external constituencies share this expectation.

Little wonder, then, that so many school reform and improvement proposals emphasize a reduction in class size and perhaps more funding. Nor is it surprising that the overwhelming majority of school improvement proposals focus on changes inside the organizational and institutional box of schools (Lawson, 1999c). The main assumption is clear: Educators can control experiences only inside the schoolhouse walls.

The controversies surrounding the so-called full-service school (Dryfoos, 1994), especially the mixed reviews they receive from professionals and laypersons alike, provide an important case in point. Their criticism is revealing, and it goes something like this.

Schools are for children's learning. Principals and teachers should concern themselves only with teaching as it affects learning. Schools should not be community social and health service organizations. When full-service schools are created, and when schools become the primary service providers, resources are deflected from the school's mission. Principals and other educators, already overloaded, are asked to take on additional responsibilities for which they have not been prepared. The problems of service design and delivery belong to the community, not to the school.

This critique could be offered by anyone who has ever gone to school. Its logic may be called "common sense" about schools. It is evidence of a powerful underlying institutional field. And it suggests that even the best reforms and improvements related to integrating services, collaborating, and developing connections with schools will not last, nor will they penetrate the school's deep structures, unless reformers take into account, and address effectively, the forces associated with these institutional fields.

Paradoxically, anyone who spends a few days in schools and sits down for awhile in the teachers' lounge will hear a familiar lament: "If only I had some influence and control over what this child experiences and does outside my classroom, I could really help him or her succeed." Although it remains unspoken, another important lament accompanies the first one: "And if I did enjoy more influence and control, I'd feel more successful, too." These important laments never get beyond the status of a patterned occupational complaint, even though they signal important opportunities.

Here, five "facts" are embedded in schools, and together they structure the school's institutional field. They form a familiar pattern, one that is viewed as inevitable and "natural."

1. Children spend less than 15 percent of their time in schools.
2. An even smaller portion of this time in schools is devoted to academic learning.
3. Some of the most important influences on learning, academic achievement, success in school, and graduation from high school are rooted in peer networks, families, and community systems.
4. Because educators have little or no influence or control over these extra-school factors and forces, their abilities to produce improvements in learning and academic achievement are destined to remain limited.

5. Educators are caught in double-binds because, even though they do not enjoy much influence and control over some of the most important factors that influence and determine learning and academic achievement, they nevertheless are held accountable for them, and they are being judged in relation to their abilities to demonstrate improvements.

This familiar pattern is called a competency trap (e.g., Argyris, 1999). Good people get trapped into believing that their limited success is inevitable and unavoidable, and they are unable to imagine and implement alternatives that get them out of the trap.

Competency traps are dangerous, and they can cause harm. For example, a growing number of teachers and principals are lamenting the gross injustice of being blamed and maltreated when academic achievement and school performance do not improve, when they have little, if any, influence and control over children's lives outside the school. In turn, when feelings of being blamed and unappreciated spread, this affects the retention, morale, and future recruitment of teachers and principals.

Collaboration is needed because no one profession (e.g., educators), or its organization (e.g., the school), can achieve its goals and meet its accountabilities without the supports of other professions (e.g., child welfare professionals, health professionals) and their organizations (e.g., child welfare organizations, community health clinics). Professions and organizations thus collaborate out of practical necessity, reflecting their self-interest. As they develop common grounds, especially unity of purpose, they also develop norms and procedures for reciprocity. For example, the school is served when service providers enable children and youth to come to school ready and able to learn. In turn, service providers are supported and reinforced when children and youth succeed in school. Each system improves and gets stronger because of its new boundary relationships and exchanges.

In fact, the case is being made that the most important school-related, peer-related, family-related, and community-related factors for improved academic achievement, learning, and success in school are the very same factors that predict success in the child welfare, juvenile justice, mental health, health, and employment sectors (Lawson & Associates, 1999). The keys to educational improvement and renewal, then, also are the keys to improvements and renewal in other child and family-serving systems. By addressing school-related needs, other systems' needs also can be addressed. Special education professional practices, for example, have implications for persons with disabilities that extend far beyond the confines of educational settings (Sailor, 1996). This is the core idea behind our comprehensive definition of integrated services, our results-orientation for collaboration, and our insistence on making certain that connections with, and at, schools are strategic ones.

A focus on job training for parents and community economic development will be as new to some service providers as it is to educators, but it is essential. For example, addressing the employment needs and security of a parent lessens family stress and facilitates the work of a child welfare worker. It also helps stabilize families, in turn reducing the school-related transience of children and youth. Furthermore, suitable parental employment is associated with a lower probability of school drop-outs and a higher probability of graduation (e.g., Haveman & Wolfe, 1995). Focusing strategically on one important area—parental employment—benefits every profession and agency working with the same child and family.

So simple and basic in one sense, this work also is incredibly difficult because it requires new job descriptions and orientations along with supportive organizational structures, cultures, and accountability requirements. For example, interprofessional leadership is essential (Lawson, 1999b; Sailor, in press). Unfortunately, few professionals and community leaders have been prepared for this kind of boundary-spanning and -crossing work. Whatever their name—school-family-community coordinators, facilitators, resource coordinators, family advocates, community school coordinators, assistant principals, or more plainly social workers, counselors, and special educators—their functions are much the same. They help orchestrate diverse people, and they help structure school community settings for collaboration. They enable educational reform and renewal because they support principals, teachers, and parents to engage in conjoint problem-solving.

Teachers' roles and responsibilities change, too. For example, they learn to detect risks and needs, work with referral agents and systems, and partner with service providers and parents. The firm dividing line between pedagogy and service integration dissolves, and so do the ethnic and cultural lines that divide a growing number of children and families from teachers, principals, and other professionals.

Principals' roles and responsibilities also change as they and their schools accept new challenges (e.g., Lawson, 1999c). For example:

- *Facilities challenges:* Although some school facilities have been designed and constructed in response to this emergent prototype (e.g., the Children's Aid Society schools in New York City), in most cases principals and other leaders have had to work within the confines of existing school facilities. Principals must find space for service providers. They also must make sure that facilities used in the non-school hours (e.g., adult eduation, after-school programs for students) are returned to normal after their use. This involves coordinating the work of custodians, service providers, program leaders, and teachers.
- *Funding challenges:* These challenges include leveraging and, if needed, reallocating Title 1 funds, Title IV-E and Title XIX funds of the Social Security Act, and IDEA funds. Other funding streams also have to be tapped. There is never enough money.
- *Supervision and evaluation challenges:* As principals' roles are recast, some instructional supervision and evaluation may have to be delegated to mentor teachers and assistant principals.
- *Time challenges:* Principals will have to delegate and give away some responsibilities to find the time needed to help coordinate all of the people at the school. Teachers initially will express frustration because the

principal is not readily available to them. They need to understand why other key people, such as service providers, community leaders, and parents, demand so much time.

■ *People challenges:* People need help in changing their mindsets about themselves and other people, and in changing their "mental models" for schools and school reform. The full-service community school increases people traffic at the school. More people bring more challenges, at least initially. Principals have the lead responsibilities for working out rules, roles, and responsibilities and for promoting positive interactions among people and for ensuring safety and security. Liability issues also have to be ironed out.

■ *Collaborative leadership:* A new style of leadership is required, one that fosters voluntary commitments, develops a sense of empowerment, is results-focused, and relies less on rule enforcement and compliance. Leadership involves new school-community connections and developing cross-school improvement plans with other principals.

■ *Resource generation and effective utilization:* Especially in high-poverty communities, resources are a priority. The principal becomes a key resource-broker. The principal secures new resources and learning supports for the school. In return, the principal offers to community agencies and neighborhood organizations school-related resources that support them.

■ *Advocacy for children and youth:* The principal becomes a tireless, passionate advocate for kids' learning, success in school, and healthy development. This principal is a tone-setter in the school community, helping others set and achieve high performance standards for all children and youth. This advocacy is broad-based and family-centered. In short, the principal is a key leader for the development of Caring School Communities for children and youth.

■ *Family support:* The principal helps other educators and service providers appreciate the need for parents and families to be supported, and they are instrumental in the creation of school-based family resource centers and in the training and employment of parent paraprofessionals.

Benefits to Schools

So is it worth the effort? Based on his research, Hatch (1998) claims that it is. Here are key examples of the benefits he identified.

■ Improvements in the physical conditions and resources that support learning.

■ Increases in the number and kinds of people that support learning and the schools.

■ Improvements in the attitudes and expectations of parents, teachers, and students.

■ Improvements in the depth and quality of the learning experiences in which students, teachers, and parents participate.

Hatch is not alone in documenting these kinds of improvements (e.g., Dryfoos, 1998; Melaville & Blank, 1998; Schorr, 1997), and we would add two others (Lawson & Associates, 1999). A "can do" attitude spreads as the individual and collective efficacy of professionals, children, and parents grows, and, as a result, the well-being of professionals, including their job satisfaction, improves. Clearly, all of these benefits and others waiting to be developed, and documented, justify the effort.

POVERTY, SOCIAL EXCLUSION, AND THE FUTURE OF AMERICAN DEMOCRACY

Children and youth are literally dying for attention. The tragic killing in Littleton, Colorado, like those elsewhere in the nation and in other parts of the world, indicate that children and youth from all walks of life have needs for services, supports, and resources. Where the well-being of the nation's children and youth is concerned, the case can be made for profound governmental and social institutional neglect. Because integrated services, interprofessional collaboration, and new school community connections effectively address this neglect, they are good things to do, and they are the right things to do. Whether they are enough, and whether they are designed to address every important need are separate questions. Service providers and educators alike deserve plaudits for their efforts. They are trying to work together—even to collaborate. Indeed, growing numbers are succeeding.

The fact remains, however, that poverty and its companions remain an important challenge even though "wars on poverty" are apparently out of fashion. Gaps between the very rich and the very poor continue to grow, and the divides between them are separated by place and space dynamics. America's cities and some of its poorer rural areas now have identifiable social geographies. Service integration, interprofessional collaboration, and school-community improvement renewal initiatives also have place-based, or social geographic, dimensions (e.g., Briar-Lawson & Lawson, 1998; Lawson, 1999a).

For example, in an increasing number of cities, urban planners now work closely with service providers. They employ computer-generated geographic information (GIS) surveys, which effectively map personal-social needs. As it turns out, some postal codes are associated with living in a community characterized as one of "concentrated disadvantage." These communities, evidence disproportionately high child abuse and neglect, school problems, crime and delinquency, unemployment and underemployment, substance abuse, and health and mental health needs. As Sen (1999) notes, the life circumstances and expectancies of citizens in some social geographic areas of American cities are now lower than those in so-called developing nations such as Bangladesh.

Economic globalization, especially the loss of industry and low-skilled jobs, is part of the problem. In these communities, it is difficult to recruit and retain highly qualified professionals in schools, medical clinics, and social and health service agencies. Once-generous policies in support of the poor are now gone and others are on the wane. Social welfare advocates characterize these changes as part of "the race to the bottom."

The irony of it all is striking. Even though many special educators and other child advocates promote inclusion of special needs children in general classrooms, social exclusion is occurring in America's cities and rural communities. Meanwhile, almost one third of Americans now live in walled-in communities characterized by concentrated advantage (e.g. Putnam, 2000). Each of these two extremes—concentrated advantage and concentrated disadvantage—has been called "a fortress community." Each has its "enclave institutions." Private schools always have been enclave institutions, and, thanks to new voucher plans, publicly supported enclave institutions are developing. At the same time, many of the nation's full-service schools are enclave institutions in fortress communities plagued by concentrated disadvantage.[9]

In brief, as poverty is normalized and neglected, and as profound social and economic isolation is becoming commonplace, American democracy is threatened. Schools depend on democracy. Along with families and community associations, schools are the chief institutions for promoting and sustaining a strong democracy.

Ultimately, all of this new-century work is about promoting and ensuring the well-being of every American citizen, especially the children. Service integration and interprofessional collaboration have to support collective citizen engagement, promoting collaboration among citizens and supporting norms of reciprocity. Reciprocity means helping others and being helped, all the while upholding constitutional rights and encouraging others to honor their responsibilities. Americans allegedly once knew how to do this new-century work. So some of it involves going "back to the future" (Lawson, 2001). Nevertheless, other facets will have to be invented because the global age presents unprecedented challenges and opportunities.

Thus, when we claim that this important combination of new- and old-century work is part of an emergent, fifth wave of service integration (which we could not address here), we also are inviting readers' engagement in something better than today's well intended, important, but insufficient approaches. We conclude, therefore, by claiming that the work of integrating services, collaborating, and developing connections with schools is ultimately about promoting individual, family, and collective well-being, safeguarding, and strengthening democracy for us, our children, and our children's children.

REFERENCES

Abbott, A. (1988). *The system of professions: An essay on the division of expert labor.* Chicago: University of Chicago Press.

Ackerson, B., & Harrison, D. (2000). Practitioners' perceptions of empowerment. *Families in Society: Journal of Contemporary Human Services, 81,* 238–246.

Adams, P., & Nelson, K. (1995). (Eds.). *Reinventing human services: Community- and family-centered practice.* New York: Aldine de Gruyter.

Adelman, H., & Taylor, L. (1997a). Addressing barriers to learning: Beyond school-linked services and full-service schools. *American Journal of Orthopsychiatry, 6,* 108–421.

Adelman, H., & Taylor, L. (1997b). Toward a scale-up model for replicating new approaches to schooling. *Journal of Educational & Psychological Consultation, 5,* 197–230.

Adelman, H., & Taylor, L. (1998). Reframing mental health in schools and expanding school reform. *Educational Psychologist, 33*(4), 135–152.

Adelman, H. & Taylor, L. (2000). Looking at school health and school reform policy through the lens of addressing barriers to learning. *Children's Services: Social Policy, Research, and Practice, 3,* 117–132.

Alameda-Lawson, T., & Lawson, M. (2000, February). *Consumer-led community collaboratives: Building social cultural capital and promoting cultural democracy.* Paper presented to Council on Social Work Education, New York.

American Academy of Pediatrics. (1994). *Principles to link by integrating education, health and human services for children, youth and families: Systems that are community-based and school-linked.* Washington, DC: Author.

Annie E. Casey Foundation. (1995). *The path of most resistance.* Baltimore: Author.

Argyris, C. (1999). *On organizational learning.* London: Blackwell Business.

Armstrong, K. (1997). Launching a family-centered, neighborhood-based human services system: Lessons from working the hallways and streetcorners. *Administration in Social Work, 21*(3/4), 109–126.

Benson, L., & Harkavy, I. (1997). School and community in the global society: A Neo-Deweyian theory of community problem-solving schools and cosmopolitan neighborly communities and a Neo-Deweyian "manifesto" to dynamically connect school and community. *Universities and Community Schools, 5*(1–2), 11–69.

Bickman, L. (1996). A continuum of care: More is not always better. *American Psychologist, 51,* 689–701.

Briar-Lawson, K., & Drews, J. (1998). School-based service integration: Lessons learned and future challenges. In D. van Veen, C. Day, & G. Walraven (Eds.), *Multi-service schools: Integrated services for children and youth at risk* (pp. 49–64). Leuven/Appeldorn, The Netherlands: Garant Publishers.

Briar-Lawson, K., & Lawson, H. (1998). Collaboration and integrated, community-based strategies on behalf of individuals and families in rural areas. In S. Jones & J. Zlotnik (Eds.), *Preparing helping professionals to meet community needs: Generalizing from the rural experience* (pp. 111–126). Alexandria, VA: Council on Social Work Education.

Briar-Lawson, K., Lawson, H., Petersen, N., Harris, N., Sallee, A., Hoffman, T., & Derezotes, D. (1999, January). *Meeting the co-occurring needs of child welfare families through collaboration.* Paper presented at Society for Social Work and Research, Austin, TX.

Bruner, C., & Parachini, L. (1997). *Building community: Exploring new relationships across service systems reform, community organizing, and community economic development.* Washington, DC: Institute for Educational Leadership & Together We Can.

Calfee, C., Wittmer, F., & Meredith, M. (1998). *Building a full-service school: A step-by-step guide.* San Francisco: Jossey-Bass.

Caplan, G., & Caplan, R. (2000). Principles of community psychiatry. *Community Mental Health Journal, 36*(1) 7– 24.

Cappella, E., & Larner, M. (1999). America's schoolchildren: Past, present, and future. *The Future of Children, 9*(2), 21–29.

Christiansen, H. Goulet, L, Krentz, C., & Maeers, M. (1997). *Recreating relationships: Collaboration and educational reform.* Albany, NY: SUNY Press.

Cocozza, J., & Skowyra, K. (2000). Youth with mental health disorders: Issues and emerging responses. *Juvenile Justice, 7*(1), 3–13.

Comer, J. Haynes, N., Joyner, E., & Ben-Avie, M. (1996*). Rallying the whole village: The Comer process for reforming education.* New York: Teachers College Press.

Corrigan, D., & Udas, K. (1996). Creating collaborative, child- and family-centered education, health and human service systems. In J. Sikula, T. Buttery, & E. Guyton (Eds), *Handbook of research on teacher education* (pp. 893–921). New York: MacMillan.

Crowson, R., Boyd, W., & Mawhinney, H. (1996). (Eds.). *The politics of education and the new institutionalism: Reinventing the American school.* London: Falmer Press.

Cowger, C. (1998). Clientilism and clientification: Impediments to strengths-based social work practice. *Sociology & Social Welfare, 25*(1), 25–38.

Dryfoos, J. (1994). *Full-service schools: A revolution in health and social services for children, youth and families.* San Francisco: Jossey-Bass.

Dryfoos, J. (1998). *Safe passage: Making it through adolescence in a risky society.* New York: Oxford University Press.

Feikema, R., Segalavich, J., & Jeffries, S. (1997). From child development to community development: One agency's journey. *Families in society: Journal of Contemporary Human Services, 78,* 185–195.

Foster-Fishman, P., Salem, D., Allen, N, & Fahrbach, K. (1999). Ecological factors impacting provider attitudes toward human service delivery reform. *American Journal of Community Psychology, 27,* 785–816.

Franklin, C., & Streeter, H. (1996). School reform: Linking public schools with human services. *Social Work, 40,* 773–782.

Gardner, S. (1994). Conclusion. In L. Adler & S. Gardner (Eds.), *The politics of linking schools and social services* (pp. 189–200). Washington, DC & London: Falmer Press.

Gardner, S. (1999). *Beyond collaboration to results: Hard choices in the future of services to children and families.* Fullerton, CA: Center for Collaboration for Children, California State University.

Gerry, M. (in press). Service integration and achieving the goals of school reform. In W. Sailor (Ed.), *Inclusive education and school/community partnerships.* New York: Teachers College Press.

Goodlad, J. (1984). *A place called school.* New York: McGraw Hill.

Halpern, R. (1999a). After-school programs for low income children: Promises and challenges. *The Future of Children, 9*(2), 81–95.

Halpern, R. (1999b). *Fragile families, fragile solutions: A history of supportive services for families in poverty.* New York: Columbia University Press.

Hassett, S., & Austin, M. (1997). Service integration: Something old and something new. *Administration in Social Work, 21*(3/4), 9–29.

Hatch, T. (1998). How community action contributes to achievement. *Educational Leadership, 55*(8), 16–19.

Haveman, R., & Wolfe, B. (1995). *Succeeding generations: On the effects of investments in children.* New York: Russell Sage Foundation.

Himmelman, A. (1996). *Communities working collaboratively for a change.* Minneapolis: Himmelman Consulting.

Honig, M., Kahne, J., & McLaughlin, M. (in press). School-community connections: Strengthening opportunity to learn and opportunity to teach. In V. Richardson (Ed.), *Fourth handbook of research on teaching.* New York: Macmillan.

Hooper-Briar, K., & Lawson, H. (1994). *Serving children, youth and families through interprofessional collaboration and service integration: A framework for action.*

Kagan, S., Goffin, S., Golub, S., & Pritchard, E. (1995). *Toward systemic reform: Service integration for young children and their families.* Des Moines, IA: National Center for Service Integration.

Kamradt, B. (2000). Wraparound Milwaukee. *Juvenile Justice, 7*(1), 14–23.

Keith, N. (1996). Can urban school reform and community development be joined? The potential of community schools. *Education & Urban Society, 28,* 237–268.

Lawson, H. (1998). Collaborative educational leadership for 21st century school communities. In D. van Veen, C. Day, & G. Walraven (Eds.), *Multi-service schools: Integrated services for children and youth at risk* (pp. 173–193). Leuven/Appeldorn, The Netherlands: Garant Publishers.

Lawson, H. (1999a). Journey analysis: A framework for integrating consultation and evaluation in complex change initiatives. *Journal of Educational & Psychological Consultation, 10,* 145–172.

Lawson, H. (1999b). Two frameworks for analyzing relationships among school communities, teacher education, and interprofessional education and training programs. *Teacher Education Quarterly, 28*(5), 9–30.

Lawson, H. (1999c). Two new mental models for schools and their implications for principals' roles, responsibilities, and preparation. *National Association of Secondary School Principals' Bulletin* (in publication).

Lawson, H. (2001). Back to the future: New century professionalism and collaborative leadership for comprehensive, community-based systems of care. In A. Sallee, H. Lawson, & K. Briar-Lawson (Eds.), *Innovative practices with vulnerable children and families.* (pp. 393–419). Dubuque, IA: Eddie Bowers Publishers.

Lawson, H. (in press a). From community involvement and service learning to engaged universities. *Universities and Community Schools.*

Lawson, H. (in press b). Introducing globalization's challenges and opportunities and analyzing economic globalization and liberalization. In K. Briar-Lawson, H. Lawson, C. Hennon, & A. Jones, *Family-centered policies and practices: International implications.* New York: Columbia University Press.

Lawson, H. & Associates. (1999). *Developing caring school communities for children and youth: Unity of purpose for strong families, schools, community agencies and neighborhood organizations.* An interprofessional leadership guide for facilitators, prepared for the Missouri Department of Elementary and Secondary Education, Jefferson City, MO.

Lawson, H., & Briar-Lawson, K. (1997). *Connecting the dots: Integrating school reform, school-linked services, parent involvement and community schools.* Oxford, OH: Danforth Foundation & Institute for Educational Renewal at Miami University.

Lawson, H., & Barkdull, C. (2001). Gaining the collaborative advantage and promoting systems and cross-systems change. In A. Sallee, H. Lawson, & K. Briar-Lawson (Eds.), *Innovative practices with vulnerable children and families.* (pp. 245–270). Dubuque, IA: Eddie Bowers Publishers.

Mattessich, P., & Monsey, B. (1992). *Collaboration: What makes it work* (5th ed.). St. Paul, MN: Amherst H. Wilder Foundation.

McKnight, J. (1995). *The careless society: Community and its counterfeits.* New York: Basic Books.

McKnight, J. (1997). A 21st century map for healthy communities and families. *Families in Society: The Journal of Contemporary Human Services, 78,* 117–127.

Melaville, A., & Blank, M. (1998). *Learning together: The developing field of school-community initiatives.* Flint, MI: Mont Foundation, Institute for Educational Leadership and National Center for Community Education.

Mitchell, D., & Scott, L. (1994). Professional and institutional perspectives on interagency collaboration. In L. Adler & S. Gardner (Eds.), *The politics of linking schools and social services* (pp. 75–92). Washington, DC & London: Falmer Press.

Mooney, J., Kline, P., & Davoren, J. (1999). Collaborative interventions: Promoting psychosocial competence and academic achievement. In R. Tourse & J. Mooney (Eds.), *Collaborative practice: School and human service partnerships* (pp. 105–136). Westport, CT & London: Praeger.

Office of Economic Cooperation and Development. (1998). *Case studies in integrated services for children and youth at risk: A world view.* Paris: Author.

O'Looney, J. (1996). *Redesigning the work of human services.* Westport, CT: Quorum Books.

Putnam, R. (2000). *Bowling alone: The collapse and revival of American community.* New York: Simon & Schuster.

Quinn, K., & Cumblad, C. (1994). Service providers' perceptions of interagency collaboration in their communities. *Journal of Emotional & Behavioral Disorders, 2,* 109–116.

People Helping People (1997, Summer). Walking our talk in the neighborhoods: Building professional/natural helper partnerships, *28*, 54–63.

Sailor, W. (1991). Special education in the restructured school. *Remedial & Special Education, 12*(6), 8–22.

Sailor, W. (1996). New structures and systems change for comprehensive positive behavioral support. In L. K. Koegel, R. L. Koegel, & G. Dunlap (Eds.), *Positive behavioral support: Including people with difficult behavior in the community* (pp. 163–206). Baltimore: Paul H. Brookes.

Sailor, W. (in press). Devolution, school/ community/ family partnerships, and inclusive education. In W. Sailor (Ed.), *Inclusive education and school/community partnerships.* New York: Teachers College Press.

Sailor, W., Kleinhammer-Tramill, J., Skrtic, T., & Oas, B. K. (1996). Family participation in New Community Schools. In G. H. S. Singer, L. E. Powers, & A. L. Olson, *Redefining family support: Innovations in public-private partnerships* (pp. 313–332). Baltimore: Paul H. Brookes.

Sailor, W., & Skrtic, T. (1996). School/community partnerships and educational reform: Introduction to the topical issue. *Remedial & Special Education, 17*, 267–270.

Sandfort, J. (1999). The structural impediments of human service collaboration: Examining welfare reform at the front lines. *Social Service Review, 73*, 314–339.

Sarason, S., & Lorentz, E. (1998). *Crossing boundaries: Collaboration, coordination and the redefinition of resources.* San Francisco: Jossey-Bass.

Schön, D. (1983). *The reflective practitioner: How professionals think in action.* New York: Basic Books.

Schorr, L. (1997). *Common purpose: Strengthening families and neighborhoods to rebuild America.* New York: Anchor Books Doubleday.

Sen, A. (1999). *Development as freedom.* New York: Alfred A. Knopf.

Skrtic, T. (2000) *Civic professionalism and the struggle over needs.* Keynote address: Office of Special Education Programs (OSEP) Leadership Training Conference. July 11–12. Washington, DC.

Skrtic, T., & Sailor, W. (1996). School-linked services integration: Crisis and opportunity in the transition to postmodern society. *Remedial & Special Education, 17*, 271–283.

Slavin, R., Madden, N., Dolan, L., & Wasik, B. (1996). *Every child, every school: Success for all.* Thousand Oaks, CA: Corwin Press.

Tyack, D. (1992). Health and social services in schools: Historical perspectives. *The Future of Children, 2*(1), 19–31.

Tyack, D., & Cuban, L. (1995). *Tinkering toward utopia: A century of public school reform.* Cambridge, MA: Harvard University Press.

Tye, B. (2000). *Hard truths: Uncovering the deep structure of schooling.* New York: Teachers College Press.

van Veen, D., Day, C., & Walraven, G. (1998). (Eds). *Multi-service schools: Integrated services for children at risk.* Leuven/Appeldoorn, The Netherlands: Garant.

Van Wagoner, P., Boyer, R., Wisen, M., Ashton, D., & Lawson, H. (2001). Introducing child welfare neighborhood teams that promote collaboration and community-based systems of care. In A. Sallee, H. Lawson, & K. Briar-Lawson (Eds.), *Innovative practices with vulnerable children and families.* (pp. 323–360). Dubuque, IA: Eddie Bowers Publishers, Inc.

Wagner, M, Newman, L., & Golan, S., (1996). *California's healthy start school-linked services initiative: Results for children and families.* Menlo Park, CA: SRI International.

Waldfogel, J. (1997). The new wave of service integration. *Social Service Review, 71*, 463–484.

Warren, C. (1999, January). *Lessons from the evaluation of New Jersey's school-based youth services program.* Paper presented at National Conference on Improving Results for Children and Families by Connecting Collaborative Services with School Reform Efforts, Laboratory for Student Success at the Temple University Center for Research in Human Development and Education and the Council of Chief State School Officers, Washington, DC.

Wenger, E. (1999). *Communities of practice: Learning, meaning, and identity.* Oxford, UK: Cambridge University Press.

White, J., & Wehlage, G. (1995). Community collaboration: If it is such a good idea, why is it so hard? *Educational Evaluation and Policy Analysis, 17*(1), 23–38.

Winer, M., & Ray, K. (2000). *Collaboration handbook: Creating, sustaining, and enjoying the journey.* Minneapolis: Amherst H. Wilder Foundation.

Wynn, J., Meyer, S., & Richards-Schuster, K. (1999, January). *Furthering education: The relationship of schools and other organizations.* Paper presented at the National Conference on Improving Results for Children and Families by Connecting Collaborative Services with School Reform Efforts, Laboratory for Student Success at The Temple University Center for Research in Human Development and Education and the Council of Chief State School Officers, Washington, DC.

Zigler, E. (1997). Supporting children and families in the schools: The school of the 21st century. *American Journal of Orthopsychiatry, 67,* 396–407.

The authors wish to acknowledge the editorial suggestions and technical assistance provided by Cindy Asmus, Dawn Anderson-Butcher, Michael Lawson, and Carmen Collins.

Name Index

Subject Index